COLLECTED WORKS OF ERASMUS

VOLUME 78

COLLECTED WORKS OF
ERASMUS

CONTROVERSIES

SPONGIA
DETECTIO PRAESTIGIARUM
EPISTOLA CONTRA PSEUDEVANGELICOS
EPISTOLA AD FRATRES
INFERIORIS GERMANIAE
ADMONITIO ADVERSUS MENDACIUM
PURGATIO
ADVERSUS EPISTOLAM LUTHERI

HISTORICAL EDITOR   GENERAL EDITOR
James D. Tracy   Manfred Hoffmann

University of Toronto Press

Toronto / Buffalo / London

The research and publication costs of the
Collected Works of Erasmus are supported by
University of Toronto Press

© University of Toronto Press 2011
Toronto / Buffalo / London
Printed in Canada

ISBN 978-0-8020-9866-5

∞

Printed on acid-free paper

Library and Archives Canada Cataloguing in Publication

Erasmus, Desiderius, d. 1536
[Works]
Collected works of Erasmus

Each vol. has special t.p. ; general title from half title page
Translation of: Spongia, Detectio, Epistola contra pseudevangelicos, and
others. Des. Erasmi Roterodami
Includes bibliographical references and index
Contents: v. 78. Controversies / Historical Editor, James D. Tracy ;
General Editor, Manfred Hoffmann
ISBN-10: 0-8020-2831-4 (set).–ISBN-13: 978-0-8020-9866-5 (v. 78)

1. Erasmus, Desiderius, d. 1536–Collected works. I. Title

PA8500.1974   199'.492   C740-06326x- rev

University of Toronto Press acknowledges the financial assistance to its
publishing program of the Canada Council and the Ontario Arts Council

Canada Council   Conseil des Arts   ONTARIO ARTS COUNCIL
for the Arts   du Canada   CONSEIL DES ARTS DE L'ONTARIO

University of Toronto Press acknowledges the financial support for its
publishing activities of the Government of Canada through the Book Publishing
Industry Development Program (BPIDP).

Collected Works of Erasmus

The aim of the Collected Works of Erasmus
is to make available an accurate, readable English text
of Erasmus' correspondence and his
other principal writings. The edition is planned
and directed by an Editorial Board, an Executive Committee,
and an Advisory Committee.

Contents

Desiderius Erasmus of Rotterdam against a
Most Slanderous Letter of Martin Luther
Purgatio adversus epistolam non sobriam Martini Lutheri
Introduction and annotation by James D. Tracy
Translation by Peter Macardle
395

General Introduction

This volume presents Erasmus' polemical works against critics who called themselves evangelicals, and who would now be called Protestants. Much has been written about Erasmus' standpoint vis-à-vis the Reformation,[1] but for present purposes the essential point is this: In a time of sulphurous theological polemics, and an occasional war,[2] he was conspicuous for maintaining that the main points at issue, at least between Catholics and Lutherans, could and should be resolved by compromise. In the fall of 1520, as *Exsurge Domine* (the papal bull threatening Luther with excommunication) was circulating in Germany and the Low Countries, Erasmus and a Dominican friend, Johannes Faber, published an anonymous tract claiming that the bull was not authentic; their vain hope was to postpone an open breach, long enough for Europe's princes to seize the moment and convene men of good will from either side for a theological discussion.[3] In December 1520, in a letter to Cardinal Lorenzo Campeggi Erasmus indicated how much might be lost by stilling Luther's voice: 'I seemed to detect [in Luther's writings] rare natural gifts and a nature finely adapted to expound the mysteries of Scripture in the classical manner, and to blow the spark of gospel teaching

* * * * *

1 A good place to begin is Cornelis Augustijn *Erasmus, His Life, Works and Influence* tr J.C. Grayson (Toronto and Buffalo 1991).
2 In the first religious war of the Reformation era, Zürich's militia was overwhelmed by the forces of the Swiss Confederation's 'forest' or Catholic cantons, and Huldrych Zwingli himself lay among the dead (Battle of Kappel, 11 October 1531). At the time, some Protestant cantons (Zürich and Bern, but not Basel) were preventing shipments of food to forest cantons in the Alps, prompting Catholics to declare war on Zürich: see Allen Ep 2559:15–20, with Allen's note.
3 For the *Consilium cuiusdam*, or *Minute Composed by a Certain Person Who Seriously Wishes Provisions to be Made for the Reputation of the Roman Pontiff and the Peace of the Church*, see CWE 71 xl–xlvi, 106–12; also Epp 1149–51, 1156.

into flame.'[4] This letter was subsequently published by Erasmus in one of his epistolary collections. In a private letter of March 1523, he ventured to offer advice on ending the schism to Adrian of Utrecht, an acquaintance from his Louvain years who was now Pope Adrian VI. The manuscript of this letter breaks off just as Erasmus launches into his recommendations, but the direction of his thoughts seems clear: 'The first thing will be to investigate the sources from which the evil so often springs up afresh ... The world should be given some hope of changes in certain points where complaints of oppression are not unjustified.'[5] A year later, the March 1524 edition of Erasmus' *Colloquies* included a conversation between a Catholic and a Lutheran in which the latter demonstrated, to the former's satisfaction, that Lutherans did not depart from Catholic belief on any single article of the Apostles' Creed.[6]

Partly because he signalled his approval for some of Luther's ideas, Erasmus became embroiled in controversy. Many Catholic theologians and scholars had no patience with a man who claimed allegiance to the church, and yet had paved the way for Luther's revolt (or so it seemed) by his blistering critique of the 'tyranny' of popes and mendicant friars, and the 'superstition' of Catholic believers.[7] And did he not compound his error by offering, in successive editions of his *New Testament*, new and scandalous interpretations of key scriptural passages, even though he was a mere 'grammarian,' without proper training in scholastic theology? In roughly a dozen volumes published between 1517 and 1533, Erasmus defended the tenor of his earlier writings, his programme for a theology based on the study of biblical languages, and the proposition that one could be a loyal Catholic without subscribing to all the opinions of the theologians, such as the doctrine of papal infallibility. The detail in these works is at times tedious – Erasmus chose to respond point-by-point to the indictments laid against him – but also interesting for the light it sheds on his views of matters he seldom discusses elsewhere, such as liturgy or church music.[8]

* * * * *

4 Ep 1167:136–43; cf Ep 1143:16–19, addressed to Pope Leo x. Both letters were published in the *Epistolae ad diversos* of August 1521. For the eight collections of his selected letters published by Erasmus, see the 'Brief Table of Editions' at the head of each volume of Allen.
5 Ep 1352:193–212
6 For *Inquisitio de Fide*, or 'Investigation concerning Faith,' see CWE 39 419–47.
7 Cf Seidel Menchi *Erasmo in Italia* 50, 87–8: Italian Calvinists had prospective converts read Erasmus, as a preparation for initiation into the true gospel.
8 CWE 71, 72, 84; Rummel *Catholic Critics*

Catholic friends expected him to prove his loyalty by writing against Luther, but Erasmus was loathe to do so, in good part because he did not wish to give aid and comfort to Luther's great enemies, the 'mendicant tyrants'; in his mind their 'ceremonious' piety was a graver threat to true religion than Luther was.[9] Only when it became clear that he would otherwise lose credibility among important Catholic patrons did Erasmus decide to engage the Saxon reformer in debate. His *De libero arbitrio* (September 1524) was followed by Luther's *De servo arbitrio* (December 1525), to which Erasmus responded with a two-part *Hyperaspistes* (February 1526, September 1527).[10] Their stark disagreement on this fundamental issue – Erasmus defending human free will, Luther insisting on absolute or unqualified predestination – seemed then and seems now to mark an unbridgeable chasm. Yet Erasmus, if not Luther, took a more nuanced view. Even as he defended against Luther the proposition that man has the capacity to consent to God's grace, he also insisted that the question of free will versus predestination was not to be counted as a dogma or fundamental teaching of the faith. Luther claimed this exalted status for his doctrine of absolute predestination – just as some Catholic theologians did for the doctrine of papal infallibility – but each of these would-be dogmas was in Erasmus' view nothing more than a theological opinion, not binding on the faithful.[11]

Framing things in this way left open the possibility that the true sources of disagreement between Catholics and Lutherans lay elsewhere, and might be subject to negotiation or compromise.[12] Meanwhile, because of sharp conflicts between Luther's followers and those of Huldrych Zwingli, having principally to do with their disagreement over the real presence of Christ in the Eucharist,[13] some Lutherans began to think of Zürich as more an enemy to true religion than Rome was. At the Diet of Augsburg (8 April– 22 September 1530), Philip Melanchthon presented a formal statement of belief on behalf of the princes and free cities in the Holy Roman Empire that

* * * * *

9 Tracy *Low Countries* 78–85, 90–4, 171–4
10 CWE 76 and 77.
11 Tracy *Low Countries* 143–56.
12 This seems to be the point of Erasmus' suggestions to Pope Adrian VI above n5.
13 For Zwingli and the Reformation in Zürich, see W.P. Stephens *Zwingli. An Introduction to His Thought* (Oxford 1992). For the Eucharistic controversies of this era, including the debate between Luther and Zwingli (and others who held to a symbolic understanding of the sacrament), B.A. Gerrish *Grace and Gratitude: The Eucharistic Theology of John Calvin* (Edinburgh and Minneapolis 1993).

now stood behind Luther. The Augsburg Confession forcefully asserted Luther's teaching, but also stressed areas of agreement with Catholic doctrine, and condemned Zwingli's understanding of the Eucharist as a mere symbol of Christ's body. Thus while the four imperial cities that stood behind Zwingli had to submit their own separate confession of faith,[14] the moderate tone of the Augsburg Confession, and its favourable reception among some Catholics, encouraged theologians on the two sides to begin preliminary discussion on the crucial doctrine of justification by faith.[15]

By now Erasmus was convinced that the sad and worsening division within Christendom was a punishment from God for the sins of his church; one could only beseech the Lord for mercy and forgiveness. This was the theme of a short prayer he composed early in 1532, in response to a request from a German friend.[16] Still – in part because of his ongoing and on the whole friendly correspondence with Melanchthon – he had followed with interest the developments at the Diet of Augsburg, where Catholics and Lutherans (with Zwinglians left on the sideline) were initiating a dialogue.[17] His treatise *On Mending the Peace of the Church* (August 1532) combined his now-usual emphasis on the need for repentance for the sins of the church with specific ideas on what might be done in working towards religious peace.[18] Perhaps in reference to conversations at Augsburg, he suggested a possible common ground on the question of justification:

> Let us grant that it is by faith that the faithful are justified (that is, that their
> hearts are purified), provided we profess also that the works of charity are

* * * * *

14 For the Tetrapolitan Confession, written by Martin Bucer and Wolfgang Capito of Strasbourg, see Kittelson *Wolfgang Capito* 153–7. The four imperial cities in whose name the confession was submitted to the diet were Constance, Lindau, Memmingen, and Strasbourg; Zürich and other Swiss Protestant cities were not included, because the Swiss Confederation was not then a part of or subject to the Holy Roman Empire.

15 For the Augsburg Confession, Wolfgang Forell and James McCue, with Wenzel Lohff, eds *Confessing One Faith. A Joint Commentary on the Augsburg Confession by Lutheran and Catholic Theologians* (Minneapolis 1982); for discussions at Augsburg on the doctrine of justification, see Vinzenz Pfnür *Einig in der Rechtfertigungslehre?* (Wiesbaden 1970).

16 *Precatio pro pace ecclesiae* CWE 69 108–17.

17 For their correspondence during the Diet of Augsburg, Allen Epp 2358, 2363, 2365; cf *Epistola contra pseudevangelicos* below 240 n125. See also Timothy R. Wengert *Human Freedom, Christian Righteousness: Philip Melanchthon's Exegetical Dispute with Erasmus of Rotterdam* (New York and Oxford 1998).

18 *De concordia* LB V 469–506.

necessary for attaining salvation. For true faith cannot be idle, rather it is the wellspring and seedbed of all good works. May we not, then, distinguish between a justice (*iustitia*) that purifies and renders innocent of guilt the abode of our inner self, and a second justice that completes the first with good works?[19]

This work was dedicated to Julius Pflug (1499–1564), a young Catholic theologian who came to Erasmus' notice when, in his capacity as a councillor to Duke George of Saxony, he intercepted and 'sent away angry' a Protestant critic of Erasmus who was seeking access to the duke.[20] As it happened, the strongly Catholic Duke George (1471–1539) had a vital interest in promoting reconciliation with Lutherans.[21] He thus sponsored a theological colloquy in Leipzig (29 April–3 May 1534), in which Pflug participated, as did Melanchthon. This discussion had an important sequel, although Erasmus (who died in 1536) would not live to see it. Emperor Charles v (ruled 1520–55) was determined to resolve, one way or another, the problem of religious disunity in Germany.[22] In 1540 he decided to see if unity could be achieved through discussion, without the expense of going to war.[23] A series of theological colloquies, held in conjunction with imperial diets, climaxed at Regensburg, where three Catholic and three Protestant theologians met between 4 April and 31 May 1541. At one point Regensburg's

* * * * *

19 LB V 500B–F: *Concedamus fide iustificari, hoc est, purificari corda credentium, modo fateamur ad consequendam salutem necessaria caritatis opera. Neque enim vera fides potest esse otiosa, qum sit fons et seminarium omnium bonorum operum. Quin potius distinguamus iustitiam repurgantem mentis nostrae domicilium qum recte dixeris innocentiam, et iustitiam locupletantem eam bonis operibus?* (trans JDT). The word *iustitia* might better be translated as 'righteousness,' but I use the word 'justice' to maintain the parallel (as in the Latin) with the verb *iustificari*.

20 The man in question was Heinrich von Eppendorf, the target of one of the polemical works contained in this volume, the *Admonition against Lying and Slander* (*Admonitio adversus mendacium* below 369–94). For the part played by Pflug, as described in Erasmus' letters, see Allen Epp 2395, 2400, 2406.

21 His brother and heir, Henry of Saxony, was a Lutheran, and George did not want the territory converted to Lutheranism after his death.

22 A divided Germany created the possibility of alliances between German Protestant princes and Charles' great enemy, the king of France. See James D. Tracy *Emperor Charles v, Impresario of War* (Cambridge 2002).

23 He subsequently did go to war. Charles defeated the Protestant Schmalkaldic League in the Schmalkaldic War (1546–47), but a new alliance of Protestant princes forced him to accept the Peace of Augsburg (1555), which recognized Lutheranism (but not Calvinism or Zwinglianism) as having the same legal standing in the empire that Catholicism did.

church bells rang out in celebration: the conferees had agreed on a formulation of the vital doctrine of justification, based in part on the idea that one might properly speak of two different kinds of *iustitia*.[24] Yet hope was short-lived; as discussions continued, there was no agreement on the Eucharist, nor on the authority of the pope and of bishops. This was not the last theological colloquy of the era, but for the rest of the sixteenth century the two sides were never again so close to agreement as they briefly seemed to be at Regensburg.[25]

The dream of a reconciliation between Catholics and Lutherans provides an important element of the background for Erasmus' disagreements with Protestant critics in South Germany and Switzerland. Historians speak of 'Reformed Protestantism' to describe a broad swath of sixteenth-century evangelical theology, including the churches led by Ulrich Zwingli in Zürich, Martin Bucer in Strasbourg, and John Calvin in Geneva.[26] The Reformed churches disavowed Catholic belief and practice much more thoroughly than Luther did. If Luther rejected the doctrine of transubstantiation,[27] Reformed theologians denied altogether that Christ's body and blood were truly present in the sacrament. Luther rejected the veneration of saints, but regarded statues and other religious images as aids to piety; the Reformed banned images of all kinds from their churches.[28] In addition, while

* * * * *

24 For *duplex iustitia* in Erasmus, see A.H.T. Levi 'Erasmus and the Humanist Ideal' *The Heythorp Journal* 19 (1978) 243–55; for *duplex iustitia* at Regensburg, and at the Council of Trent (where a formula based on the Regensburg agreement was proposed, but not accepted), Carl E. Maxcey 'Double Justice, Diego Laynez, and the Council of Trent' *Church History* 48 (1979) 269–78.

25 For a brief, authoritative summary see Vinzenz Pfnür 'Colloquies' in OER 1 375–83. See also Matheson *Cardinal Contarini* (Gasparo Contarini [1483–1542], representing Pope Paul III at the diet, was in constant contact with the three Catholic conferees); Cornelis Augustijn *De godsdienstgesprekken tussen Rooms-katholieken en protestanten van 1538 tot 1541* (Haarlem 1967); and *Die Religionsgespräche der Reformationszeit* ed Gerhard Müller (Gütersloh 1980).

26 Eg Williston Walker *John Calvin, the Organiser of Reformed Protestantism* (1906; repr New York 1969); Andrew Pettegree *Emden and the Dutch Revolt: Exile and the Development of Reformed Protestantism* (Oxford 1992).

27 Meaning that the 'substance' of the bread and wine were transformed into Christ's body and blood, leaving only the 'accidents' of bread and wine. Luther affirmed the real presence of Christ's body and blood in the sacrament, but rejected any attempt to explain the mystery by means of the categories of human philosophy, such as Aristotle's doctrine of substance. See Paul H. Jones *Christ's Eucharistic Presence: A History of the Doctrine* (New York 1994).

28 Carlos M.N. Eire *War Against the Idols. The Reformation of Worship from Erasmus to Calvin* (Cambridge 1986).

Lutherans retained the ancient practice of excommunicating public sinners, the Reformed took church discipline more seriously, establishing procedures whereby each congregation could separate out known sinners, and bar them from the communion table.[29] In the 1520s there was no set terminology for distinguishing the 'evangelicals'[30] who followed Zwingli or Bucer from those who followed Luther. Yet Erasmus made such a distinction, as is clear from his letter to Philip Melanchthon in September 1524:

> As for Zwingli, how subversive his methods are! – to say nothing for the moment of the rest. They do not agree with your lot, nor are they at unity among themselves, and yet they expect us to follow their authority and abandon all the orthodox Fathers and councils. You teach that those who cast out images as something impious are in error. And Zwingli has roused such an uproar over images! You teach that a man's fashion of dress is not relevant. Here several people teach that the habit must be utterly rejected. You teach that bishops and episcopal constitutions must be tolerated unless they lead to impiety. Here they teach that all are impious and unchristian.[31]

To be sure, it seems this letter was accompanied by a copy of the *De libero arbitrio*.[32] Erasmus never entirely agreed with the Lutherans either. Furthermore, after having been the object of Luther's unbridled vehemence in *De servo arbitrio*, he had no more good things to say about Luther himself.[33]

* * * * *

29 There were also important differences among the Reformed, especially between the churches of Zürich and Geneva, both in regard to the Eucharist and in regard to church discipline. For a classic study see Walter Köhler *Zürcher Ehegericht und Genfer Konsistorium* (Leipzig 1932, 1942) 2 vols.

30 As early as 1521 Luther proposed referring to the reform movement as 'evangelical,' meaning it was based on the gospel: *Lexicon für Theologie und Kirche* 11 vols (Freiburg 1957–67) 3 1237. The term 'Protestant,' although originating in a 'protest' by Lutheran estates against the actions of the Catholic majority at the 1529 Diet of Speier, was not used in the modern sense until somewhat later; see David Lotz and Siegfried Bräuer 'Protestantism' in OER 3 351–9.

31 Ep 1496:83–92. Erasmus was writing from Basel, which had adopted a doctrine similar to Zwingli's.

32 Ep 1496 intr: 'The day after receiving this letter, Melanchthon sent it on to [Georgius] Spalatinus (Ep 1497) with a copy of *De libero arbitrio* and a note (CR 1673–4) in which he says: "Erasmus appears to have treated us not at all abusively ..."'

33 Karl Heinz Oelrich *Der späte Erasmus und die Reformation* Reformationsgeschichtliche Studien und Texte 86 (Münster 1961) 40–7. See also the introductory note to the 1534 *Purgatio adversus epistolam Lutheri* below 395–411.

Still, the letter to Melanchthon is not an isolated example of his opinions; those who have studied the matter find that he reserved his sharpest criticisms of the Reformation for the Swiss and South German churches and their leaders. His reasons for doing so are to be sought not just in the theological differences among the evangelical party, but also in his personal experience.[34]

He never met Luther, nor, with the exception of Justus Jonas,[35] who came to see him in Louvain (1519), any of the members of his circle. Moreover, because Luther recognized as early as 1516 that he and Erasmus had fundamental differences of opinion,[36] Erasmus was seen from Wittenberg not as a dissembling friend of the true gospel, but as a potential adversary. On this basis the two humanist scholars – Erasmus and Melanchthon – could acknowledge their differences and still maintain a respectful epistolary friendship.[37] By contrast, several leaders of the Swiss and South German churches – Wolfgang Capito (1578–1541),[38] Caspar Hedio (1494–1552),[39] Johannes Oecolampadius (1482–1531),[40] and Conradus Pellicanus (1478–1556)[41] – had been among the humanists who befriended Erasmus after he first came to Basel in 1514.[42] Others (like Zwingli in Zürich, and Martin Bucer [1491–1551] in Strasbourg) devoured Erasmus' works and admired him from a distance.[43] It was in this period that Erasmus was most forthright in condemning the 'tyranny' of popes and mendicant orders, and the 'superstitious' practices of the Catholic faithful. His friends in this region also knew that he was the author of the anonymously published *Julius exclusus e coelo* (1517), a vicious lampoon of the recently deceased Pope Julius II.[44] In the early 1520s these men understood the doctrines they now preached as based on their study of Scripture in the original languages; they could not imagine that Erasmus, the master of this craft, had not undergone a similar intellectual evolution. Thus if he still professed allegiance

* * * * *

34 Oelrich *Der späte Erasmus* (previous note) 25–40; see also Cornelis Augustijn *Erasmus en de Reformatie* (Amsterdam 1962).
35 CEBR II 244–6
36 Ep 501:49–76; see also the sketch of Luther in CWE 2 360–3.
37 See above n17, and Oelrich *Der späte Erasmus* (above n33) 47–9.
38 CEBR I 261–5
39 CEBR II 169–70
40 CEBR III 24–7
41 CEBR III 65–6
42 Ep 300
43 CEBR III 481–6; CWE 1 209–12. Zwingli and Erasmus met in Basel in 1516.
44 See the introductory note to *Spongia* below 27–9.

to the popish church of Rome, the great man was not just misguided, he was lying.

When he moved to Basel in 1521,[45] Erasmus unwittingly put himself in a milieu where his motives were suspect. The first salvo in a new series of book-battles was fired by a warrior nobleman, Ulrich von Hutten (1488–1523), whose *Expostulatio* of April 1523 presented his old friend Erasmus as a turncoat and a coward, unwilling to lend his name to what he knew was the cause of Christ.[46] By the time *The Sponge of Erasmus against Aspersions of Hutten* had appeared in print (August 1523), Hutten had died in Zürich, where Zwingli had arranged a place of refuge. Otto Brunfels, a friend of Hutten's, took up his defence with a *Pro Ulrico Hutteno vita defuncto ad Erasmi Roterodami spongiam responsio* (Strasbourg 1524).[47] Erasmus did not judge Brunfels' tract worthy of a response, but from now on he regarded Capito as an enemy, because it was 'from his house in Strasbourg that that scabby character [Brunfels] issued forth to print his crazy pamphlet.'[48] Another of Hutten's friends, Heinrich Eppendorf (1496–1551), caused further problems. Erasmus blamed Eppendorf for instigating Hutten to write the *Expostulatio*, and for certain malicious rumours emanating from Strasbourg, where Eppendorf now resided. For his part Eppendorf complained (with some justice) that Erasmus had ruined his good name with an important patron, Duke George of Saxony, and demanded reparation. In a dispute that dragged on for several years, Erasmus had the support of friends at the Saxon court,[49] but he also sought to make sure of the outcome by denouncing Eppendorf in his *Admonitio adversus mendacium et obtrectationem* (early 1531).[50]

Meanwhile, in Basel, sometime in the fall of 1523, Erasmus had a run-in with a man he had never met, Guillaume Farel (1489–1565), a French priest recently converted to the new doctrines. Farel (Erasmus referred to him as 'Phallicus') liked to describe Erasmus as 'Balam, as though I had been hired to curse God's people.'[51] He is also said to have boasted that he

* * * * *

45 For his migration from the Low Countries to Basel (November 1521), see Ep 1242.
46 For the *Expostulatio* and Erasmus' reply, see the introductory note to his *Spongia* below 24–9.
47 Cited where appropriate in the notes below as Brunfels *Responsio*.
48 Erasmus to Melanchthon, Ep 1496:120–2
49 Above n20
50 See the introductory note to the *Admonitio adversus mendacium* below 370–8.
51 Ep 1341A:1201; Balam was a prophet bribed by a Moabite king to curse the Israelites, but compelled by God to bless them instead (Numbers 22–4).

'would rather die a martyr's death daily than fail to damage Erasmus' reputation wherever I can.'[52] Oecolampadius and Pellicanus sought to rein in Farel's denunciations, without success.[53] But Erasmus was soon involved in a more serious controversy with these two old friends. In August or September of 1525, Oecolampadius published a treatise defending Zwingli's interpretation of the Eucharist.[54] It is possible that Erasmus began his own treatise on the Eucharist at this point, and that he suspended work on it in consequence of an agreement with Oecolampadius and Pellicanus. But he soon learned from a trusted friend that Pellicanus had been spreading the rumour that Erasmus' views on the Eucharist agreed with his own and those of Oecolampadius. Erasmus replied with an angry letter to Pellicanus, the contents of which were reported by Oecolampadius to Zwingli, who then published a letter asserting that what Erasmus had said in his letter to Pellicanus was not what he really believed about the Eucharist. A few months later Leo Jud, one of Zwingli's colleagues in Zürich, issued a pseudonymous German-language pamphlet arguing that both Luther and Erasmus agreed with Zwingli's doctrine of the Eucharist. This treatise prompted Erasmus' *Detectio praestigiarum* (*The Uncovering of Deceptions*, May 1526). In the Eucharistic controversy, as in the letter to Melanchthon, Erasmus put Luther's followers in one camp and the Swiss reformers in another; while he condemned the latter for their false doctrine and deceptive tactics, he effectively conflated Luther's teaching on the Eucharist with that of the Catholic church.[55]

Whether Erasmus liked it or not, Oecolampadius and his party steadily gained ground in Basel. In the wake of a public meeting in December 1528 celebration of the mass was limited to three churches in the city; following a second popular assembly in February 1529 the mass was abolished altogether.[56] Within two months Erasmus joined the exodus of those who

* * * * *

52 Ep 1510:19–45, 65–81. For Farel, CEBR II 11–13.
53 Erasmus to Antoine Brugnard (in Montbéliard, whither Farel had gone from Basel), Ep 1510:16–18, 'The Lutherans themselves could not endure his [Farel's] insatiable scurrility. Oecolampadius often protested, even by a letter, and so did Pellicanus, but it did no good; he is too far gone.'
54 *De genuina verborum Dei: 'hoc est corpus meum' etc. expositione*
55 See the letter to Pellicanus, Ep 1637, and the introductory note to *Detectio praestigiarum* below 147–62.
56 Guggisberg *Basel in the Sixteenth Century*. Ardent followers of the new doctrine feared a visitation of God's wrath on any city that permitted the (idolatrous) Catholic mass to continue.

packed up their things and migrated to the nearest Catholic city, Freiburg in the Breisgau.[57] Meanwhile, an old friend from the Netherlands was making another attempt to enlist him in the Protestant cause. Gerard Geldenhouwer of Nijmegen (1482–1542), now in Strasbourg, issued what he titled *Epistola Erasmi* 'A letter from Erasmus' on the subject of capital punishment for heretics, with some commentary of his own.[58] A few months later, still in Strasbourg, he published a more extensive work of the same kind.[59] Erasmus had his response ready by December 1529. Both the original edition and the second authorized edition (1531) carried the title *Epistola apologetica contra quosdam qui se falso jactant Evangelicos* 'A letter in defence against those who falsely claim to be evangelicals' (below 207–54). It came to be known as the *Epistola contra pseudevangelicos*; in a letter of March 1530 Erasmus adopted or possibly coined the word *pseudo-evangelicos* to refer to his enemies.[60] This was his derisive term for the Swiss and South German Reformation.

The immediate aim of the *Epistola contra pseudevangelicos* was to refute Geldenhouwer's claim that the passages from Erasmus' works he cited could properly be read as altogether condemning the death penalty for heretics. But as the title suggests, it also cast broad aspersions on the duplicitous tricks practised by those of Geldenhouwer's party, including Martin Bucer, and on their not-so-evangelical manner of living.[61] Geldenhouwer did not continue the controversy, but Bucer did. Under the collective name of the Strasbourg preachers, he published in May 1530 a vigorous defence of the evangelical movement as a whole. He also defended the tactics of Jud and Pellicanus as well as Geldenhouwer, and endeavoured to show that the true gospel had made people better Christians, not worse.[62] Erasmus then

* * * * *

57 His last letter from Basel and the first from Freiburg are dated 13 and 21 April 1529 respectively: Allen Epp 2149, 2150.

58 It was not a letter but an extract from Erasmus' *Apologia adversus monachos* (1528): see Augustijn 'Geldenhouwer' 69 (1978) 136–50, Beilage 151–5.

59 *D. Erasmi Roterodami annotationes in leges pontificas et caesarias de hereticis. Epistolae aliquot Gerardi Noviomagae.*

60 Allen Ep 2287:7. For a comparable word formation, with comparable intent, see the satiric colloquy *Cyclops, sive evangelophorus* 'Cyclops, or the gospel-bearer' (from the March 1529 edition) CWE 40 863–76. The word *pseudo-evangelici* is not attested in Du Cange *Glossarium Mediae et Infimae Latinitatis* (Graz 1956), nor in J.F. Niermeyer *Mediae Latinitatis Lexicon Minus* (Leiden 1976), nor in A. Konstantinides Μέγα Λέξικον τῆς Ἑλληνικῆς Γλώσσης (Athens 1901–06).

61 See the introductory note to the *Epistola contra pseudevangelicos* below 207–17.

62 *Epistola apologetica ad syncerioris christianismi sectatores per Frisiam orientalem et alias Inferioris Germaniae regiones* in BOL I 59–225.

returned to the arena in his *Epistola ad fratres Inferioris Germaniae* (September 1530). In keeping with Bucer's broad *apologia* for the Reformation Erasmus broadened his attack: one could see, he argued, a decline of morals and of good learning among evangelicals in general, including Lutherans.[63] But he also defended (against Bucer's denial) his assertion that people who once thought Luther was nearly a god were now saying that the Saxon reformer was 'crazy.'[64]

No one is at his best when settling scores. As readers will see, when Erasmus responded to erstwhile friends who had accused him of betraying the gospel, he repaid them in the same coin. Yet in his polemical fervour he never completely lost sight of a larger aim, based on his belief that orthodox Christians – those who stood on the common ground of apostolic and patristic tradition – might still be able to settle their differences. Lutherans fitted this description but the 'pseudo-evangelicals' did not. Thus if Catholics and Lutherans were to have a conversation the 'pseudo-evangelicals' had to be shunted aside. This was one reason why, in the *Spongia*, Erasmus described two very different kinds of 'Lutherans':

> I would like to know of whom Hutten is thinking when he so often says 'we' or 'ours.' Does he mean all who favour or support Luther in any way, and wish evil upon the Roman pontiff? As I see it, this category includes different sorts of men. There are on the one hand learned men, not at all bad in my judgment, who approve most of what Luther says, and would like to see the power of the Roman pontiff curtailed, making him a teacher of the gospel instead of a worldly prince, a father instead of a tyrant ... These men support Luther because he has taken up these issues with vigour. I am not bound to them by any treaty, but with them I continue long-time friendships, based on love of good letters, even if we do not agree on everything. Not one of these men approves of what Hutten has done, not even Luther himself.
>
> On the other hand, the Lutheran camp also includes ignorant men of no discernment. Though of dubious morals themselves, they are fault-finders, obstinate and unmanageable, and devoted to Luther in such a way that they neither understand nor follow what he teaches. They merely talk, while neglecting prayer and worship. They think that being a Lutheran means eating whatever they please and cursing the Roman pontiff.[65]

* * * * *

63 Below 273, 339.
64 Below 346.
65 Below 102–4.

The *Epistola contra pseudevangelicos* sharpens the same distinction:

> They love no one except themselves, and obey neither God nor bishops nor
> princes and magistrates; they are slaves to Mammon, to their gullets, bellies,
> and groins; yet all the while they demand to be considered evangelists and
> assert that Luther is their master ... What do they have to do with Luther,
> when they care not a whit for the very foundation of his teaching? Though in
> fact it does not belong to Luther but to Christ and the apostles.[66]

The last work contained in this volume is Erasmus' response to an attack that was even more harsh than anything fired in his direction by Hutten or Bucer. In March 1534, in a published letter to Nikolaus von Amsdorf,
superintendent of the Lutheran church in Magdeburg, Martin Luther char-
acterized Erasmus as 'the worst enemy of Christ, such as there has not been
for a thousand years.' Erasmus was of course no mean polemicist himself,
and it would not have been surprising for him to respond to a vicious blast
of this kind with a full-scale assault on Luther's party, parallel to his attack on the 'pseudo-evangelicals' a few years previously. Instead, he produced a *Purgatio ad epistolam non sobriam Martini Lutheri* whose 'mildness'
disappointed Catholic friends. Although one cannot discount the possibility
that Erasmus was intimidated by Luther, there is a better explanation for
his having moderated any instinct he had to strike back in kind. The kind
of theological dialogue he had been hoping to see was even now under-
way, here and there across Germany. Thus as he wrote to clear his name,
it was important for him to do so in a way that would not cause moderate
Lutherans to take offence.[67]

In the light of subsequent historical events one might be tempted
to write off as naive the whole idea that sixteenth-century Catholics and
Lutherans could ever compromise their differences. Yet there is such a thing
in history as a noble failure. In the works found in this volume and in others, Erasmus did what he could to promote discussion between the two
sides. By the time political circumstances had made these discussions relevant at the level of the imperial diet, Erasmus was no longer among the living. But he may fairly be remembered as a kind of intellectual progenitor
to the noble failure at Regensburg.

* * * * *

66 Below 235.
67 See the introductory note to the *Purgatio adversus epistolam Lutheri* below 405–7.

ACKNOWLEDGMENTS
The editors of and contributors to this volume have benefited from the work of many colleagues. We cannot thank them all, but we would be remiss not to mention the scholarship of Cornelis Augustijn. He has provided (in ASD IX-1) critical texts for all but one of the works included here, and his excellent introductions and annotations have guided us all. His work represents historical scholarship at its best.

It has been a particular pleasure to work with the copyeditor, Philippa Matheson, who also, with Lynn Browne, typeset the book.

Once more we are indebted to the modern patron of this project, the University of Toronto Press, for its dedication to the fulfilment of its vision of making available the major writings of Erasmus in contemporary English.

JDT and MH

THE SPONGE OF ERASMUS
AGAINST THE ASPERSIONS OF HUTTEN

Spongia adversus aspergines Hutteni

translated by
JAMES D. TRACY and MANFRED HOFFMANN

annotated by
MANFRED HOFFMANN and JAMES D. TRACY

Eighty years ago, it was not uncommon for scholars writing on this controversy to praise Ulrich von Hutten for his passionate convictions while censuring Erasmus for his cowardice.[1] Since then, Erasmus has become a good
deal more accessible to scholars, through modern critical editions and translations of his works.[2] Perhaps more importantly, in the wake of a twentieth
century dominated by wars or threats of war, it has become easier to appreciate the fact that Erasmus, in his efforts to define a middle ground between
Catholics and Lutherans, had the courage of a would-be peacemaker.[3] Conversely, the fiery patriotism that made Hutten an icon for German nation-
alist historians of the early twentieth century makes him less interesting
for an age that is in some measure post-nationalist.[4] Thus while there are
new books on Erasmus every year, and a scholarly journal devoted to him,[5]
scholars writing in English still rely on important works on Hutten published between the two World Wars.[6] Even in Germany only about a dozen
books on Hutten have appeared since 1945, half of which were occasioned
by the fifth centennial of his birth in 1988.[7]

It is thus important, in a volume devoted to Erasmus, that Hutten's
perspective on the quarrel be taken into account. In order to do so, this
essay will focus on what both men had to say about the papacy. While

* * * * *

1 Contrast the favourable assessment of Erasmus in Preserved Smith *Erasmus*
(New York 1932) 332–5 with the view of Johan Huizinga *Erasmus* (New York
1924) 202–3: 'Nowhere does [Erasmus] show himself so undignified and puny
as in that "Sponge against Hutten's mire."'
2 Allen, ASD, CWE. Hutten's works have been available in a critical edition since
1861: Eduardus Böcking *Ulrichi Hutteni Equitis Germani Opera Quae Reperi Possunt Omnia* 5 vols (Leipzig 1859–61), hereafter abbreviated as EB.
3 Erika Rummel *Erasmus* (New York 2004).
4 Frank L. Borchardt *German Antiquity in Renaissance Myth* (New York 1971). Be it
noted, however, that Hutten's defence of the Hebrew scholar, Johann Reuchlin,
implied a defence of Jewish learning. None of his writings were included in
a publication that sought to associate the beginnings of the Reformation with
the beginnings of National Socialism: Arnold E. Berger *Die Sturmtruppen der
Reformation* (Leipzig 1931).
5 *The Erasmus of Rotterdam Society Yearbook* (ERSY).
6 Werner Kaegi 'Hutten und Erasmus. Ihre Freundschaft und ihr Streit' *Historische Vierteljahrschrift* 22 (1924) 200–78, 461–514; Hajo Holborn *Ulrich von
Hutten and the German Reformation* (New Haven, Connecticut 1937).
7 The online library catalogue *WorldCat*, key-word 'Ulrich von Hutten,' items 1–
160, lists seven new books devoted to Hutten between 1945 and 1987, six in
German and one in English: Thomas W. Best *The Humanist Ulrich von Hutten*
(Chapel Hill, NC 1969).

Hutten had little grasp of Luther's theology,[8] he saw the effort to free his native Germany from centuries of domination by the papacy as the battle of his life,[9] and he extolled the Saxon reformer as a leader who could free Germany from Roman tyranny, just as Arminius had done against Varus and his Roman legions in 9 AD.[10] In this epic struggle Hutten thought that the great Erasmus stood at his and Luther's side. The impetuous Hutten did not really understand Erasmus, a man of many styles and many points of view, but he did not entirely misunderstand him either.

HUTTEN'S LIFE AND CAREER TO 1520

Ulrich von Hutten was born (21 April 1488) in Steckelberg, a family castle.[11] He was proud of his heritage as a free imperial knight;[12] as will be seen, he often took up arms himself, as a mercenary soldier in Italy, as a combatant in Germany's feuds, and finally as a kind of noble thug, terrorizing the clergy on public highways. As the eldest son, he might have been expected to inherit the family estates. Instead, his father placed eleven-year-old Ulrich in the nearby Benedictine abbey of Fulda. His escape from the monastery six years later – apparently without having taken vows, but much to his

* * * * *

8 Spitz *Religious Renaissance* 119–25; cf Hutten to Count Hermann von Neuenahr, 3 April 1518, Ep LXXV:11–20 EB I 164–8, here 167: the controversy in Wittenberg is described as just another monkish quarrel.
9 For the context, see Stadtwald *Roman Popes and German Patriots*. As noted by Spitz *Religious Renaissance* 112, 'it was only gradually that Hutten made the papacy his major target.'
10 The annihilation of Varus and his three legions by Arminius, chief of the Cherusci, is described in of the *Annals* of Tacitus (2.22), just published in Rome in 1515; 'Hutten's contribution' was to have 'made Arminius the symbol of German character': Holborn *Ulrich von Hutten* 76–7.
11 For Hutten's early life, see Holborn *Ulrich von Hutten* chapters 1 and 2.
12 In the constitution of the Holy Roman Empire, the 'Estate of Imperial Free Knights' (*Reichsritterstand*) consisted of those noblemen who owed allegiance only to the emperor, without being subject to any of the empire's many principalities. The term 'robber-baron' (*Raubritter*) reflects the fact that impecunious knights, unable to support themselves in proper style from the revenues of postage-stamp territories, sometimes preyed on travellers. See William R. Hitchcock *The Background of the Knights' Revolt, 1522-1523* (Berkeley, CA 1958) chapter II; Cord Ulrichs *Vom Lehnhof zur Reichsritterschaft. Strukturen des Fränkischen Niederadels am Übergang vom späten Mittelalter zur Frühen Neuzeit* (Stuttgart 1997) chapter IX.

father's displeasure – may have been abetted by Johannes Crotus Rubeanus, a humanist schoolmaster who would be Hutten's lifelong friend.[13] Over the next few years, at several north German universities, he showed a knack for getting into quarrels, and a talent for philippics in elegant classical Latin.[14] In Vienna in 1511 he encountered a humanist movement with a patriotic tint. It was here that Conrad Celtis (1459–1508), erstwhile leader of the group, had published his polemics against the popes who claimed to lord it over his patron, Emperor Maximilian I (ruled 1495–1519). Hutten's passionate German patriotism may be dated from his brief visit in Vienna.[15]

Funding from his father permitted Hutten to study law in Italy. Through no fault of his own, he became tangled up in the fighting between forces of France's King Louis XII (ruled 1498–1514) and Swiss troops paid by Pope Julius II (ruled 1504–1513); for a time he supported himself as a mercenary soldier. The fruit of this experience was a book of Latin epigrams addressed to Maximilian, urging the emperor to combat the evil French, the godless Venetians, and the perfidious Julius II.[16] Back in Germany, Hutten followed the lead of Crotus Rubeanus in taking up the cause of Johann Reuchlin, the celebrated Hebrew scholar, whose works were under attack by the theology faculty at the University of Cologne.[17] In terms of support for himself, he cast an eye towards Mainz, where the new prince-archbishop, Albert of Brandenburg (ruled 1514–1545), had a reputation as a patron of letters,[18] and where three of Hutten's kinsmen were members of the cathedral chapter.[19]

* * * * *

13 Cf Crotus to Hutten, 3 February 1511, Ep VII EB 17–21 (Crotus intercedes with Hutten's father on his behalf). On Crotus Rubeanus, CEBR I 362–3.
14 Eg the *Loetze Philippics* (*In Lossios querelarum libri duo*) published in 1510, on which see Holborn *Ulrich von Hutten* 37.
15 Stadtwald *Roman Popes and German Patriots* 72–7, 92–3
16 Bernstein *German Humanism* 118–19
17 For Reuchlin, see *Spongia* below n21; for the controversy, Erika Rummel *The Case against Johann Reuchlin. Religious and Social Controversy in Sixteenth-Century Germany* (Toronto 2002).
18 For Albert of Brandenburg, see *Spongia* below n51; the Holy Roman emperor was elected by seven electors, including the prince-archbishops of Cologne, Mainz, and Trier. At some point Albert gave Hutten two hundred Rhine gulden – a handsome sum – with the comment, 'this the prince gives for your literary works': Hutten to Jacob Fuchs, 13 June 1515, Ep XXVI EB I 40–5, here 43.
19 Holborn *Ulrich von Hutten* 49 mentions Frowin von Hutten and Eitelwolf von Stein; see also Hutten to 'his kinsman,' canon Markward von Hatstein, 7 May 1515, Ep XXV EB I 39–40.

It was in Mainz that Erasmus first met Hutten in August 1514 in the company of Reuchlin and another German humanist, Hermannus Buschius.[20] Erasmus was en route from England to Basel, having chosen Johann Froben's firm to publish the works prepared during his three years at Cambridge: an expanded *Adagiorum chiliades* 'Thousands of Adages,'[21] and the *Hieronymi opera* 'Works of Jerome.'[22] As German humanists turned out to greet him, Erasmus became aware, possibly for the first time, of how famous he was. Reciprocating his warm welcome, he complimented 'our native Germany' for having so many fine scholars.[23] The meeting in Mainz also had a specific purpose. Reuchlin had written to Erasmus in Cambridge, apparently without making an impression.[24] Now Reuchlin provided him with copies of the documents at issue: his *Augenspiegel* 'Eye-Mirror' of 1511, its condemnation by the Cologne theologians, and Reuchlin's *Defence*.[25] Hutten gave Erasmus a manuscript of his lampoon of Reuchlin's enemies, the *Triumphus Capnionis*, making its publication dependent on his approval; Erasmus expressed doubt, and Hutten promised to hold it back, as indeed he did, until 1518.[26] Erasmus got the point. From Basel he sent Reuchlin a laudatory letter, describing his *Defence* as a book that deserved to be 'in the hands of all good scholars.'[27] Too late for inclusion in a collection of endorsements published by Reuchlin in 1514, under the title *Letters of Illustrious Men*, this letter found a place in a similar volume of 1519.[28]

Meanwhile, Crotus Rubeanus and Hutten conceived a brilliant stratagem: the *Letters of Illustrious Men* would be followed by a collection of *Letters of Benighted Men*,[29] in which Cologne theologians complained to one

* * * * *

20 For the meeting in Mainz, see Kaegi 'Hutten und Erasmus' 202–3; for Buschius, *Spongia* below n99.
21 Ep 313 introduction
22 Epp 326, 396
23 Ep 305:30–3, 218–22; cf *Spongia* below n487.
24 Ep 290
25 For excerpts from the two Reuchlin texts, see Rummel *The Case against Reuchlin* (above n17) Documents 3 and 4.
26 See *Spongia* below nn45, 114.
27 Ep 300:19. This letter was the full extent of Erasmus' support for Reuchlin; he had no sympathy for Jews, nor for Jewish learning: see *Spongia* below n21.
28 *Clarorum virorum epistolae Latinae Graecae Hebraicae variis temporibus missae* (Tübingen: Thomas Anshelm 1514); cf Ep 300 introduction – Erasmus' letter was printed in the 1519 *Illustrium virorum epistola* 'published in Alsace at Hagenau by Reuchlin's friend Thomas Anshelm.'
29 *Epistolae obscurorum virorum* is commonly translated *Letters of Obscure Men*, but 'benighted' better captures the sense of the Latin *obscurus*, which points a

another, in barbarous Latin, about their maltreatment by Reuchlin's friends. Crotus wrote almost all of the forty-one letters in the first edition, which seems to have appeared in 1515. The second edition (1516) had an Appendix with seven more letters, mostly from Hutten's hand. Finally, in 1517, Hutten, with some help from Hermannus Buschius, produced a second volume of *Letters of Benighted Men*, distinctly sharper in tone.[30] In April 1515, while travelling from Basel back to England, Erasmus made a detour to visit the celebrated book fair at Frankfurt am Main, where Hutten arranged to meet him, together with Reuchlin and Buschius.[31] It was probably on this occasion that Hutten gave Erasmus a sample of the as-yet-unpublished *Letters*. Erasmus puts things this way in the *Spongia*: 'I came across a manuscript letter, ascribed to Hutten, recounting a banquet among professors – nothing more than a harmless joke.' He liked it so much he 'nearly learned it by heart'; later, once again in Basel, Erasmus recited it for the amusement of dinner companions.[32]

Just now Hutten had a chance to repair troubled relations with his relatives. Duke Ulrich of Württemberg (ruled 1498–1519, 1534–1550)[33] had Hutten's cousin Hans murdered, so as to possess the man's wife. Ulrich at once launched a publicity campaign against the murderer, lasting until the duke was driven from his lands in 1519.[34] In October 1515 Hutten wrote

* * * * *

contrast to the 'illustrious' (literally, 'bright and shining') men who supported Reuchlin.

30 Rummel *The Case against Reuchlin* (above n17) 109–10; Stokes *Epistolae obscurorum virorum*.

31 Hutten to Jacob Fuchs, 13 June 1515, Ep xxvi:40–5 EB I, here 43–4; Hutten's cousin and patron, Eitelwolf von Stein, also came to Frankfurt, but Erasmus had already left by the time he arrived. That Erasmus was indeed in Frankfurt at this time is attested by Ep 326B.

32 See *Spongia* below nn141, 142, with Ep 363:6–7. The reference is apparently to the first letter of the first edition (Stokes 3–8), which is often attributed to Hutten.

33 Duke Ulrich of Württemberg (1487–1550) campaigned with Emperor Maximilian I against the Swiss (1499–1500), and with his father-in-law, Duke Albert IV of Bavaria, in the Bavarian succession war of 1504. Having made enemies during his rule, he found himself facing an army of the Swabian League, led by his brother-in-law, William IV of Bavaria, which in 1519 ousted him from his duchy, which then became a Hapsburg trusteeship. A supporter of Luther, he was reinstated in 1534 by an army led by Landgrave Philip of Hesse.

34 See Hutten's *In Ulrichum Wirtenpergensem orationes quinque*, published between 1515 and 1519 (EB V 1–97), as well as the so-called *Steckelberg Collection*, a collection of Hutten's other writings against Duke Ulrich, published in 1519 (EB IV 45, item XXIIII of the Bibliography); cf Holborn *Ulrich von Hutten* 51–2.

to Erasmus that he had been thinking of joining him, and 'might perhaps have followed you as far as England.'[35] But his kinsmen, hoping the talented young man might yet make something of himself in a conventional way,[36] were sponsoring a second trip to Italy for the study of law.

Hutten recounts his adventures south of the Alps in a letter to Erasmus dated 20 July 1517, just after his return to Germany. In Rome, he greeted Erasmus' friend, Paolo Bombace, showing him and other learned men the 1515 Froben edition of the *Adagia*, the 1514 Strasbourg edition of *The Praise of Folly*, 'and everything of yours that I had brought on purpose.'[37] But Rome soon became unsafe: at nearby Viterbo, Hutten got into a quarrel with five Frenchmen, leaving one of them dead, either because they insulted the emperor (according to Hutten), or because the innkeeper served his French guests first (according to a German eyewitness).[38] At the University of Bologna, he learned enough Roman law to despise 'the Bartolists' and all their train, 'whose works now stick like sponges in the ears of princes, and by whose advice they govern their lands'; if Germany was torn apart by contentions, it was because this pestiferous tribe had 'invaded, armed with all their tomes.'[39] He also found time to compose, and send to Germany for publication, his *Phalarismus*, a dialogue representing Duke Ulrich of Württemberg in the next life, praised for his misdeeds by that renowned tyrant of antiquity, Phalaris of Agrigentum in Sicily (c 570–554 BC), but refused passage across the Styx by Charon.[40] In the end he had to leave Bologna as well; having been elected syndic or spokesman for the university's German 'nation,' Hutten was held responsible for a quarrel that broke out between the Germans and the Lombards at the university.[41]

* * * * *

35 Ep 365:18–19
36 The charge that he had not yet done so provided background for Hutten's *Nemo* (*Nobody*) EB III 110–18; cf Bernstein *German Humanism* 119–20.
37 Ep 611:6–10. Hutten must be referring to the Strasbourg *Praise of Folly*, since the 1511 Paris edition would by that time have become known in Italy.
38 Ep 611:12–18; Holborn *Ulrich von Hutten* 81–2
39 Hutten to Crotus Rubeanus, preface to a 1518 edition of *Nemo*, Ep LXXXIV EB I 175–84, here 177–9. The reference is to the school of Bartolo of Sassoferrato (1313–57). For the reception in Germany of Roman law, as distinct from local customary law, Gerald R. Strauss *Law, Resistance, and the State. The Opposition to Roman Law in Reformation Germany* (Princeton 1986).
40 EB IV 1–25; Holborn *Ulrich von Hutten* 85.
41 Ep 611:20–6; Holborn *Ulrich von Hutten* 84–5. At medieval and early modern universities, students and faculty were organized in 'nations,' more according to region than according to what would now be understood as nationality.

While in Italy Hutten came to see papal domination as the source of Germany's troubles.[42] He also began gathering ammunition for a war of words. In the *Annals* of Tacitus he discovered the heroic figure of Arminius, a model for how Germans must deal with Roman tyranny.[43] Back in Bologna for a time, just before setting out to cross the Alps, he came across a manuscript copy of Lorenzo Valla's *On the Falsely Credited Donation of Constantine*, demonstrating that the text on which the papacy based its claims to temporal power had to be a forgery. Hutten insisted on having a copy made, for publication in Germany.[44]

In the late summer of 1517, Hutten obtained a salaried position in Mainz, at the court of Albert of Brandenburg. Now and then Hutten carried out commissions, as in December 1517, when he was sent to Paris for an exchange of treaties between the prince-archbishop and King Francis I (ruled 1515–1547). In the main, however, Albert allowed Hutten leisure to pursue his various interests. Early in 1518 he published letters in support of Reuchlin, together with the *Triumphus Capnionis*, which he had withheld at Erasmus' recommendation.[45] During the summer Maximilian I convened a diet of the imperial estates in Augsburg. Pope Leo x's legate, the learned Cardinal Cajetan,[46] pleaded for a crusade against the rising menace of Ottoman Turkish power in the east.[47] But Germany's princes and town deputies were in no mood to listen to a papal appeal for money. The growing reputation of Martin Luther, who had been summoned to Augsburg for an interview with Cajetan,[48] no doubt intensified widespread suspicion

* * * * *

42 Bernstein *German Humanism* 122
43 Above n10
44 Cochlaeus to Pirckheimer, 5 July 1517, Ep LVI:142–3 EB I; Hutten's preface to his edition of Valla's *Donation of Constantine*, dated 1 December 1517, Ep LXX:155–61 EB I; Holborn *Ulrich von Hutten* 81 17n, the letter was in fact written in 1519, and not published until 1520. On Lorenzo Valla (d 1455), see *Spongia* below n554.
45 Holborn *Ulrich von Hutten* 90 (the mission to Paris); EB I Bibliography items XIV, XVI
46 Below *Spongia* n325.
47 Sultan Selim I (ruled 1512–20) had bested his principal Muslim rivals by defeating the army of the Safavid shah of Iran (1514), and conquering the Cairo-based Mamluk empire (1517). Christian Europe had a respite for a time, but Sultan Suleyman the Lawgiver (ruled 1520–66) began his reign by subduing the two greatest Christian strongholds in the east, the fortress-city of Belgrade (1521), and the island of Rhodes, home to the Knights Hospitaller of St John (1522).
48 For Luther's meeting with Cajetan at Augsburg, Scott Hendrix *Luther and the Papacy* (Philadelphia 1981) chapter 3

of Rome. So did Ulrich von Hutten, to the best of his ability. A dialogue that appeared at this time, *Aula 'The Court,'* presented Cajetan as a pampered sot.[49] In June 1518 Hutten published an *Oration* addressed to Germany's princes. Like other observers, including Erasmus,[50] he condemned the double-dealing of Leo x, whose real purpose in calling a crusade was, as usual, to trick the Germans into sending money. Unlike the others, Hutten was a military man who understood the real danger of an Ottoman thrust into Europe; hence he urged Germany's fighting men to overlook the pope's hypocrisy and mobilize for war.[51]

Early in 1519 came *Fever*, the first of two dialogues Hutten published under that title, ridiculing the Roman curia. Meanwhile, the enemies of Duke Ulrich had won over the Swabian League to their cause. The League's army, led by Duke William IV of Bavaria, invaded Württemberg in March. During the brief and successful campaign Hutten served under one of Germany's leading mercenary commanders, Franz von Sickingen.[52] Hutten persuaded Sickingen to support the cause of reform, meaning Luther as well as Reuchlin;[53] in Stuttgart (Württemberg's capital) he arranged to spare Reuchlin's vacant house from the depredations of victorious troops.[54] Back in Mainz, he gave the printer a treatise on syphilis, the disease that was to bring his early death four years later, and also a collection of his writings against the now-exiled Duke Ulrich.[55]

In 1520, he brought out his edition of Valla's *On the Falsely Credited Donation of Constantine*, as well as an anti-papal tract dating from the Investiture Controversy of the late eleventh and early twelfth centuries,[56] a manuscript

* * * * *

49 EB IV 29–41, 45–74; Holborn *Ulrich von Hutten* 107–9
50 Ep 775:6–8, 'The pope and the emperor have a new game on foot; they use the war against the Turks as an excuse, though they have something very different in mind.'
51 *Hutteni ad Principes Germanos ut bellum Turcis inferant oratio exhortatoria* EB V 97–134. Cf Cochlaeus to Pirckheimer, 26 June 1517, Ep LV EB I 141: 'Hutten was just in Venice with some of his kinsmen, about to set off for Jerusalem; he would have accompanied them, had not Crotus Rubeanus, the preceptor of the Wolfs, held him back. He arrived back here yesterday.' Anyone about to sail from Venice for Jerusalem in 1517 would have had some sense of the great changes afoot in the eastern Mediterranean (above n47).
52 Below *Spongia* n26.
53 Cf Hutten to Sickingen, 1 March 1519, Ep CVIII EB I 247; Holborn *Ulrich von Hutten* 109–11.
54 Hutten to Erasmus, Ep 986:52–52.
55 EB I Bibliography items XXIII, XXIIII.
56 From 1076 to 1122. The issue was whether the Holy Roman Empire's prince-bishops – secular as well as ecclesiastical rulers – would be 'invested' or

of which he had found in the library of Fulda abbey.[57] He also had plans for a German edition of Tacitus' *Annals*, but the printer would not cooperate, citing a ten-year papal ban on copying the 1515 Roman edition; to Hutten, it seemed clear that Rome did not want Germans reading about Arminius.[58] The crowning achievement of his literary campaign against the papacy was a trio of dialogues entitled *Vadiscus*, or *Trias Romana* (*The Roman Trinity*, April 1520). In a conversation at the Diet of Augsburg, Hutten has his main speaker address Cajetan directly: 'Tell me, are the Turks, who now contend with us for dominion, worse enemies of Christ than you Romanists are, fortifying the churches of the most high God with walls of money?'[59] For papal officials in Germany this was too much. Albert of Brandenburg was instructed to dismiss Hutten from his service, and did so – unless (as Hutten's friends said) he left Mainz first, on his own initiative.[60] In the family castle at Steckelberg, Hutten learned that his printer in Mainz was already under arrest, and that the curia planned to proceed against him, unless he disavowed his anti-papal writings. Hutten would not turn back, but neither would he await passively the papal excommunication and the imperial ban that could now be expected.[61] In the battle that was to come, where would Erasmus stand?

'THE PLAGUE OF CHRISTENDOM'

In important respects, Erasmus held the same opinions about the papacy throughout his life as a scholar. He never doubted the unity of orthodox believers in a communion founded by Christ, but he never accepted the

* * * * *

clothed with the symbols of their office by representatives of the emperor, as had been customary, or by representatives of the pope, as a newly invigorated papacy now insisted. In the end, it was agreed that there should be two distinct investitures, embodying a distinction between secular and spiritual power that would prove to be of great significance for the subsequent history of Latin Christian Europe. At the time, however, neither side was happy with the compromise.

57 Holborn *Ulrich von Hutten* 142–3; Hutten to Archduke Ferdinand, the dedication of his edition of *De unitate ecclesiae conservanda*, Ep CLV EB I 325–34
58 From *Vadiscus* or *Trias Romana* (1520) EB IV 149–261, here 154
59 *Trias Romana* EB IV 163 (trans JDT)
60 Below *Spongia* n51
61 Holborn *Ulrich von Hutten* 142–50. Hutten's name was added to a revised version (3 January 1521) of *Exsurge Domine* (first published 15 June 1520), the papal bull that had threatened Luther with excommunication.

common belief that papal authority was founded on Matthew 16:18, where Jesus says that Peter is the 'rock' on which he will build his church; Erasmus interpreted the Lord's words as referring to faith in him, as expressed by Peter in the Matt 16:16. He saw the pope as having *auctoritas* in the church, for the preservation of unity, but it was the authority of a pastor, not a monarch. If questions of doctrine had to be decided, authority lay with an ecumenical council of the church, not with the pope; for the then rather novel opinion that the pope was infallible in matters of doctrine he had no sympathy.[62] But the critique of papal monarchy that appeared in his writings of around 1514–1517 took on a new resonance after Martin Luther appeared on the scene. Since his works were in the public domain, Erasmus had to explain that his words did not mean what they now seemed to mean.[63]

In early writings, like the *Enchiridion* of 1503,[64] he trained his fire on the 'monastic ceremonies' that he saw as obstructing a spiritual understanding of Christian life. The question of how the church was governed first came to his notice, it seems, during his stay in Italy (1506–1509), especially in November 1506, when Erasmus found himself in a large crowd witnessing Pope Julius ɪɪ, clad in armour, make his triumphal entry into the newly conquered city of Bologna. This spectacle – a shepherd of Christ's flock, vaunting in pagan fashion his victory over fellow Christians – he saw as an utter perversion of the papal office.[65] Modern historians, looking to the long term, are impressed that Julius' victories had the effect of freeing the papacy from dependence on a princely protector. But Erasmus' reading of events was not unusual among humanist contemporaries.[66] Forthright expression of such opinions was a different matter.[67] Erasmus entrusted his thoughts to a satiric epigram that was not published until the twentieth century, comparing the warrior-pope to the pagan emperor whose name

* * * * *

62 Gebhardt *Stellung* 267–77.
63 The best study of this dialogue between Erasmus and his readers is Seidel Menchi *Erasmo in Italia*.
64 LB V 2–66
65 CWE 27 156–67
66 See Ferguson *Opuscula*, introduction to *Dialogus, Iulius exclusus e coelo* 38–54, here 51; Christine Shaw *Julius ɪɪ; the warrior pope* (Cambridge 1993); cf the index to Stadtwald *Roman Popes and German Humanists* under 'Julius ɪɪ.'
67 Cf a suggestion that the gap in Erasmus' extant correspondence between 1509 and 1511 represents a suppression of letters containing comments about Julius ɪɪ: J.K. Sowards 'The Two Lost Years of Erasmus: Summary, Review, and Speculation' *Studies in the Renaissance* 9 (1962) 161–86.

he proudly bore.[68] This theme he subsequently elaborated in *Julius exclusus e coelo* 'Julius Excluded from Heaven,' a dialogue at the gates of heaven between the recently-deceased pope, his guiding 'genius,' and St Peter.[69] The *Julius exclusus* is known to have been composed during Erasmus' stay in Cambridge, because Thomas Lupset, who studied with him there, later had 'notebooks' containing works in Erasmus' hand, 'first drafts only,' according to Thomas More, one of which was *Julii genius* 'The Genius of Julius.' Erasmus, concerned about letting the notebooks get out, had More arrange their delivery to him.[70] But when he left Cambridge in 1514 he took another version or copy of the *Julius* with him, for he is known to have made it available to trusted friends; in Basel, Boniface Amerbach completed his own copy of the text in August 1516.[71]

Once he started up the Rhine towards Basel, Erasmus was less cautious about putting his opinions on paper. While still in Strasbourg he gave a printer there a new edition of his *Praise of Folly* containing long additions to the text of 1511, in which Folly pillories the self-satisfied pedantry of scholastic theologians and the hypocrisy of popes and cardinals. By comparison with the ironic tone of Dame Folly's oration in the original edition, these mini-jeremiads strike a discordant note.[72] But they have much in common with other texts that Erasmus published over the next two years, including the essay-length adages added for the 1515 edition of the *Adagia*, like 'War is a treat for those who have not tried it,' or 'A dung-beetle hunting an eagle,'[73] and the *Paraclesis*, a preface to the 1516 *New Testament* imploring readers to put off all pretence and embrace the simplicity of the

* * * * *

68 Cornelis Reedijk 'Een Schimpdicht van Erasmus op Julius II' *Opstellen door vrienden en collega's aangeboden aan Dr F.K.H. Kossmann* (The Hague 1958) 186–207.

69 Whether or not Erasmus was indeed the author was long debated among scholars, but while there are still doubters the argument was effectively settled by McConica 'Erasmus and the "Julius"' 444–82.

70 Epp 502:10–15 (the words cited), 544:38–40

71 Ferguson *Opuscula* 41; for Boniface Amerbach, Ep 408 introduction. Cf Allen Ep 2615:181–7: according to Martin Bucer, Wilhelm Nesen, who knew Erasmus in Basel (CEBR III 13), said he had seen a copy of the *Julius* in Erasmus' hand. Cf Ep 961:44–6, 'I found copies of it in the hands of several people in Germany, but under various names.' The last phrase sounds like part of Erasmus' cover-story, but the rest may well describe an actual state of affairs.

72 Ep 302 introduction; introductory note to *The Praise of Folly* CWE 27:81–2. In the *Praise of Folly*, Dame Folly praises herself by praising all her devotees.

73 *Adagia* III iv 1i: *Scarabaeus aquilam quaerit* CWE 35 178–213; *Adagia* IV i 1: *Dulce bellum inexpertis* CWE 35 399–439

gospel.[74] Appearing in Strasbourg or Basel, these works represented a kind of conversation with the German friends who welcomed him so warmly. For it was at German universities that relations between proponents of the new humanist curriculum and defenders of the established scholastic curriculum were especially tense,[75] not least because of the ongoing Reuchlin controversy. Germany's humanists had also made themselves spokesmen for the long-standing 'grievances of the German nation' against the papacy and the Roman curia.[76] Yet nothing from Erasmus' pen that appeared in print during these years breathes the passion or the vitriol of *Julius exclusus*, where the late pope is presented as a sodomite and a murderer, proud of having unleashed perpetual war upon Christian nations. St Peter understands the church as 'the Christian people, bound together by the spirit of Christ,' but Julius has what he thinks is a better idea: 'What we call the church is the holy temples, the priests, particularly the Roman curia, and above all myself, the head of the church.'[77] To drive the point home, St Peter on several occasions refers to papal rule over the church as 'the plague of Christendom.'[78] To be sure, this philippic against a warrior-pope was also a *jeu d'esprit*, rife with allusions that only learned readers would appreciate. Erasmus did not want it read by the world at large, including his patrons at the Roman curia.[79] Inevitably, however, the *Julius* appeared in print, probably late in 1517. Little is known concerning the circumstances of publication, but a bit of conjecture may not be amiss here, for the issue could bear on Erasmus' relations with Hutten.

The modern editor, Wallace Ferguson, cannot assign dates to the early editions until the seventh in his sequence, which he places in Louvain in March of 1518.[80] The Paris edition that attributes the *Julius* to 'F.A.F.' –

* * * * *

74 *Desiderius Erasmus Roterodamus Ausgewählte Werke* ed Hajo Holborn (Munich 1933) 39–49
75 Erika Rummel *The Humanist-Scholastic Debate in the Renaissance and Reformation* (Cambridge, MA 1995) chapter 4 'The Debate at the Universities.' As Professor Rummel says, 'The conflict was not confined to German universities' (62), but most of the examples in this chapter come from Germany, and the situation of the humanities at Italian universities in particular was 'rather different' (72).
76 Stadtwald *Roman Popes and German Patriots*, especially chapters I–III; Alfred Schröcker *Die deutsche Nation. Beobachtungen zur politischen Propaganda des ausgehenden 15. Jahrhunderts*. Historische Studien 426 (Lübeck 1974).
77 CWE 27:168–97, here 191
78 Ferguson *Opuscula* 66:43n
79 For approaches to Rome that enabled Erasmus to dedicate his *New Testament* to Julius II's successor, Pope Leo X (Ep 384), see Ep 335 introduction.
80 Ferguson *Opuscula* 55–63

Fausto Andrelini of Forli, an old friend of Erasmus – has sometimes been seen as the earliest edition.[81] Andrelini could not have written the *Julius*, but it has been suggested that he lent his name to the project, so as to divert suspicion from Erasmus.[82] Ferguson makes this edition second in his series, giving priority to an edition that closely follows the text of the Amerbach manuscript, printed on paper that can be traced to the 'section of the country' around Basel, if not to the Froben press.[83] Yet the edition that has the better text need not for that reason have come first. One wonders whether someone from Erasmus' circle in Basel would have been the first to breach the secrecy in which he wished the *Julius* to be kept.

Erasmus' correspondence offers clues about the circulation of *Julius*, both in manuscript and in print. In February 1517 Jean Le Sauvage, the chancellor of Archduke Charles of Burgundy,[84] took pleasure in reading

* * * * *

81 Fausto Andrelini of Forli (c 1462–25 February 1518) studied law in Bologna and humane letters in Rome. He was authorized to teach poetry in Paris (1489), and in subsequent years, after quarrels with two of his compatriots, managed to consolidate his position at the university. During his stay in Paris (1495–99), Erasmus and Andrelini became acquainted through a mutual friend, Robert Gaguin (1423–91), a humanist diplomat who was also a professor of canon law and father-general of the Trinitarian order. Erasmus may have renewed his acquaintance with Andrelini in 1511, when he came to Paris for publication of his *Moriae encomium* (it has been suggested that Erasmus' satiric epigram against Julius II [above n68] may have been influenced by current French propaganda against the pope, in which Andrelini had a hand).
82 Cf EB IV 422, which takes Andrelini as the author and the Paris edition as the first edition of the *Julius*, and prints it among Hutten's pseudonymous works; G. Tournoy-Thoen, 'Deux épîtres inédites de Fausto Andrelini et l'auteur du *Julius Exclusus*' *Humanistica Lovaniensa* 18 (1969) 43–75.
83 Ferguson *Opuscula* 62–3. I am most grateful to Professor Silvana Seidel Menchi for sending me a copy of her forthcoming essay on 'Julius, Erasmus, Hutten. A Dialogue in Three Voices' *Erasmus of Rotterdam and the Renaissance Republic of Letters* ed Stephen Ryle (Brepols: Turnhout, Belgium, forthcoming). With arguments more solid than those presented here, the essay gives priority to the F.A.F. edition of the *Julius*, connects Hutten to this edition, and traces the later quarrel between Hutten and Erasmus to the latter's repudiation (Ep 1342) of the view of the papacy presented in his *Julius*.
84 Archduke Charles would only become Charles V after his election as emperor in 1519. Jean Le Sauvage (1455/5–7 June 1518) studied law at Louvain, and rose through the ranks of the civil hierarchy of the Hapsburg-Burgundian state, as president of the council of Flanders (1497), president of the privy council (1508), and chancellor of the kingdom of Castile (1516). He seems to have met Erasmus through mutual friends in Ghent. Le Sauvage obtained a canonry in Courtrai for Erasmus (Epp 421, 436), and got him appointed an

it, as did a member of his entourage.[85] This will not have been a printed
book; Erasmus' loyal and generous patron would have had the privilege
of reading the *Julius* in manuscript. As for how widely a manuscript might
circulate, Erasmus' letters do not begin to show concern until the late summer of 1517, probably because of changes in his circumstances. His protector, Le Sauvage, went off to Spain in June, to prepare for Archduke
Charles' accession as king of Castile and Aragon. In August Erasmus took
up residence in Louvain, where a *Collegium Trilingue* with professorships in
Latin, Greek, and Hebrew was to be established, funded by a legacy from
one of his friends. This was the opportunity to realize Erasmus' hopes
for a new kind of theology, based on study of the biblical languages.[86]
But conservative members of Louvain's theology faculty, heirs to a discipline that had long monopolized the discussion of Scripture, were deeply
suspicious of this mere grammarian, as they saw Erasmus, who was in-
truding on their domain.[87] What might they have done had it come to
their notice that he was also the author of a scurrilous lampoon of the
late pope?

In September, Thomas Lupset, then in Paris, wrote Erasmus to disclaim
responsibility for 'letting that pamphlet get out'; Erasmus assured Lupset he
was not 'annoyed' with him.[88] He worried more about what might happen
in Cologne. Writing from Louvain, in August, he asked Johannes Caesarius
to 'do all you can to get this impious stuff suppressed before it can be

* * * * *

honorary councillor to Archduke Charles (CWE 4 409); for the first year, he also
paid the salary out of his own pocket (Epp 597, 621). Le Sauvage intimated that
there might be a bishopric for Erasmus; apparently in this connection, Erasmus
between October 1516 and February 1517 lived in or near Brussels, where he
attended on Le Sauvage at court, a routine he later recalled as humiliating
(Allen Ep 2613). See Tracy *Politics of Erasmus* 52–5.

85 Epp 532:26–9, 543:12–13
86 For the *Collegium Trilingue* at Louvain, see Henri De Vocht *History of the Collegium Trilingue Lovaniense* 4 vols (Louvain 1951–55); for Erasmus' understanding of theology, Chantraine *Mystère*.
87 Rummel *Catholic Critics*
88 Epp 664:9, 690:1. Cf McConica 'Erasmus and the "Julius"' 470, and John Archer
Gee *The Life and Works of Thomas Lupset* (New Haven, CN 1928) 53–69, 179–80:
during his stay in Paris (1517–19), Lupset saw a number of works through the
press; at times, he acted in serious matters without warrant from his principals.
There is no indication that Lupset had made his own copy of the *Julius*, and
if the text were published at about this time, one would have to explain why
Erasmus does not seem to have become aware of its being in print until March
1518.

printed.'[89] He likewise asked Count Hermann von Neuenahr, a canon of Cologne, to have the pamphlet about Julius II 'suppressed, or better still, destroyed'; Neuenahr apparently had reservations, because a few months later Erasmus repeated his request that it not be printed.[90] Both men had welcomed Erasmus in Cologne in 1514, as he travelled up the Rhine;[91] they were likely among those he trusted to have access to the *Julius*. Another Cologne humanist Erasmus trusted was Hermannus Buschius, whom he had met in Mainz in 1514, in Frankfurt in 1515, both times in the company of Hutten and Reuchlin, and again in Cologne in 1516.[92] No letter to Buschius is extant for this period, but it may have been around this time that Erasmus got Buschius to moderate the tone of his defence of good letters, the *Vallum Humanitatis* '*Rampart of the Humanities*,' which appeared in 1518.[93]

If Buschius and others in Cologne had access to the *Julius*, the same courtesy would have been extended to Ulrich von Hutten. Like Erasmus, Hutten nurtured a loathing for the warrior-pope, Julius II.[94] If, as seems likely,[95] Hutten gave Erasmus a sample of the as yet unpublished *Letters of Benighted Men* when they met in Frankfurt, it would have been appropriate for Erasmus to let Hutten and his companions see the *Julius*. When Hutten spoke of arriving in Rome in 1515, and giving Erasmus' Roman friends not just the 1514 *Moriae encomium* and the 1515 *Adagia* but also 'everything of yours I had brought on purpose,'[96] he was perhaps alluding to the *Julius*. That Hutten knew the *Julius* (which need not mean that he had a copy) is suggested by his *Phalarismus*, of which he sent Erasmus a copy.[97] Erasmus presumably answered the letter of 20 July 1517, in which Hutten recounted his adventures in Italy,[98] but no reply is extant. That he made of Hutten the same request he made of the Cologne humanists – to keep the *Julius* under wraps – seems plausible. In December Hutten was in Paris, on a diplomatic mission from Albert of Mainz. Might he have supplied a copy of the *Julius*

* * * * *

89 Ep 622:14–27. For Caesarius, see *Spongia* below n150.
90 Epp 636:14–29, 703:28–32. For Neuenahr, see *Spongia* below n96.
91 The suggestion (CEBR III 14) that such a meeting may be surmised from Ep 442 seems reasonable.
92 Above nn20, 31; CEBR I 233; for Buschius, *Spongia* below n99
93 See below 60.
94 Spitz *Religious Renaissance* 115
95 Above n32
96 Above n37
97 Above n40; Ep 923:24 and 923:24n: 'The *Phalarismus* ... was based on a plot reminiscent of the *Julius exclusus*.'
98 Above n37

to Fausto Andrelini, in a joint effort to have the dialogue see the light of day, but without implicating their friend Erasmus?[99]

By 5 March 1518, Erasmus had word from Cologne 'that some pamphlet has lately been printed about a dispute between Pope Julius and Peter at the gate of Paradise.'[100] In that same month Erasmus is known to have visited the shop of his Louvain printer, Thierry Martens, which seems to have been the source for what Ferguson classed as the seventh edition of the *Julius*.[101] There was no longer any reason not to let a favoured publisher share the profit. One might also read his letter to Luther's friend Johann Lang – describing papal monarchy as the plague of Christendom – as a tacit acknowledgment of his authorship of the *Julius*.[102] Despite his sponsorship of the Louvain edition, Erasmus now took the position that whoever had published the *Julius* was more to blame than the author. Indeed, one might argue that it was one thing for learned men to joke among themselves, but quite another to resort to publication and thus pour oil on the fire of public discontent with the papacy. This was the case Erasmus made about a year later to two of his protectors among the cardinals of the church, Lorenzo Campeggi and Thomas Wolsey.[103]

From Hutten's point of view, it was a time for fanning the flames, even in disregard of the privacy normally respected among friends. In October 1519, the theology faculty at Louvain was about to follow the Cologne theologians in issuing a formal condemnation of Luther's writings. Erasmus,

* * * * *

99 Above nn45, 81. If a manuscript of the *Julius* was not brought to Paris by Lupset (above n88), or by Hutten, another possibility would be Henricus Glareanus, whom Erasmus had befriended in Basel, and who subsequently directed a private residential school in Paris from 1517–22 (CEBR II 105 and *Spongia* below n77). The fact that Andrelini died on 25 February 1518, while Erasmus had word from Cologne of a printed edition only a week later (below n100), would seem to invalidate the suggestion (CWE 27 156 and 28 490 n9) that Andrelini's initials were used for this purpose after his death.

100 Ep 785:41–5 and Ep 785:42n, 'This is the earliest specific reference to a printed version of the *Julius exclusus*.' Cf a letter dated 19 October 1518, Ep 877:12–13, 'The *Julius* now enjoys widespread circulation and has often been printed.' A Cologne edition of the *Julius* is mentioned by one contemporary writing in June 1518 (Ep 785:42n); Ferguson, *Opuscula* 62–3, thought the third edition was 'probably' printed in France, but 'perhaps' in Cologne.

101 CWE 28 490 n18

102 The Latin *pestis Christianismi* (Allen Ep 872:17–8), used also in the *Julius*, is in Ep 872:20–1 translated as 'the curse of Christianity.'

103 Ferguson *Opuscula* 44–5; Ep 961:40–55, 967:172–96. As Ferguson notes, 'Campeggi, always favourable to Erasmus, allowed himself to be convinced.'

now a member of the Louvain faculty, had recently made peace with his colleagues. But he feared that Luther's case would give certain ignorant theologians an opportunity 'to tie up the ancient tongues and the humanities and Reuchlin and Luther and even myself in the same parcel.' He put his thoughts in a long letter to Albert of Brandenburg, a patron of letters who was rumoured to favour Luther. If Luther found a ready audience, he said, it was because the Christian world was 'burdened with ordinances made by man,' and with the 'tyranny of the mendicant friars,' those 'servants of the Roman see' who treated the pope (so long as he was on their side) as 'more than God.' Erasmus avowed that he did not support Luther, and would not defend him; he regretted that Luther had ignored his advice to 'publish no sedition, nothing derogatory to the Roman pontiff.' But he also believed that Luther was being persecuted by 'those who have found a trumped-up pretext to make a fanatical attack on the humanities,' and that his teaching seemed 'to house some glowing sparks of gospel teaching.'[104] As Erasmus recounts the story in the *Spongia*, he was not certain this letter suited 'the mind' of the prince-archbishop. He 'sent it in a sealed envelope, addressed to a man Hutten knows better than anyone, with instructions to deliver the letter if he saw fit, or, if not, to destroy it.' Instead of giving his prince the letter, Hutten gave it to a printer. By the time Erasmus published his version in August 1521 there were eight unauthorized editions.[105]

Publication of this letter left Erasmus with some explaining to do, especially after publication of the papal bull threatening Luther with excommunication had opened a chasm between Rome and Wittenberg.[106] What indeed was his opinion of a Roman pontiff whom 'mendicant tyrants' extolled as 'more than God'? Choosing his words, he assured Cardinal Campeggi he would not side with Luther 'against the Roman church, which does not differ, I conceive, from the Catholic church.'[107] He put it the same way to Luigi Marliano, bishop of Tuy in Galicia, his patron at the court of the strongly orthodox Emperor Charles v: 'the church of Rome I recognize, and think

* * * * *

104 Ep 1033:222–7, 131–50, 51–64, 70–1, 76–7
105 Ep 1033 introduction; below 125–6
106 Ep 1141:11n: *Exsurge Domine*, issued by Pope Leo x on 15 June 1520, and published in Germany and the Netherlands in September. For Erasmus' response to the bull, see General Introduction above n3.
107 Ep 1167:467–71; on his letter to Albert of Brandenburg, see Ep 1167:278–94. Cf Ep 1167 introduction: this letter of 6 December 1520 was 'intended for circulation at the curia,' and was published in the *Epistolae ad diversos* of August 1521.

it does not disagree with the Catholic church.'[108] Careful readers will have
noticed that Erasmus was professing allegiance to the Catholic church, and
only indirectly to the Roman church. Consistent with his deep reservations
about papal monarchy, this was as far as Erasmus could go. For now at
least, it was enough for him to retain his credibility with Catholic patrons,
and thus his ability to continue working within the church for the reform
of Christian teaching and Christian life. But as Erasmus kept open a bridge
to Rome, his friend Hutten was thinking about going to war.

'CERTAIN MUTUAL SERVICES'

Hutten had reason to think that he and Erasmus were of like mind. In April
1520, Erasmus sent him copies of the formal condemnations of Luther by
the theology faculties at Cologne and Louvain,[109] no doubt with a choice
comment of his own. In May, at Erasmus' request, Hutten contributed to
a collection of critical letters directed to Edward Lee, a Catholic foe of
Erasmus' New Testament scholarship: 'I advise you to recant what you have
greedily vomited forth, before I come after you, which I promise you will be
soon.'[110] A few weeks later, Hutten called on Erasmus at Louvain, seeking
letters of recommendation to members of Charles v's entourage. Sources
for this third and last meeting between the two friends are scant. Hutten
does not mention it, and Erasmus' few recollections are not consistent in
tone. On the one hand, he evokes a jocular exchange: Hutten announced a
war against the Romanists, and Erasmus, not taking him seriously, 'asked

* * * * *

108 Ep 1195:34–5. For Marliano, see *Spongia* below n329. Le Sauvage, a more sympathetic and more powerful patron in Charles' entourage, had died in Spain
in 1518. For a comparison on this point between letters Erasmus chose to publish (like Epp 1167 and 1995) and those he did not publish (like Ep 872: see
above n102), James Tracy 'Erasmus among the Postmodernists: Dissimulatio,
Bonae Literae, and *Docta Pietas* Revisited' in *Erasmus' Vision of the Church* ed
Hilmar Pabel, Sixteenth Century Essays and Studies 33 (Kirksville, MO 1995)
1–40.
109 Crotus Rubeanus to Luther, Bamberg, 28 April 1520, Ep CLX EB I 337:13–15:
*Incidet in sacra sacrum sentimentum Lovaniensium et Coloniensium, Hutheno mis-
sum ab Erasmo Rotherodamo; ingens sane materia et ad ridendum et ad stomachan-
dum.* 'During Mass arrived the holy judgments of the Louvain and Cologne
theologians sent by Erasmus to Hutten – a great occasion for laughter, and
for indignation.'
110 Ep CLXVI, EB I 348:1–8. For the collection of letters, *Epistolae aliquot virorum* Ep
1083 introduction; for Edward Lee, *Spongia* below n126.

in jest what he planned for the Dominicans. He replied with a smile that they too were Romanists.'[111] On the other hand, he complains that it was 'impolite and dangerous' for Hutten to ask him for letters to men close to the emperor; although Hutten 'had already formed a conspiracy against the emperor,' he wanted the letters 'to exploit the emperor's name in his hunt for a wife.'[112] These two accounts of the meeting can be reconciled if one assumes Erasmus thought at the time that Hutten was joking, and realized only after the fact that he truly did plan to go to war against the clergy.[113] More likely, Erasmus was being disingenuous when he said he had thought Hutten was only joking; from Hutten's past history, he ought to have known better. His ironic questions would thus have been a defensive reaction, a timid man's way of fending off the ugly possibility that religious conflict would turn violent.

On this interpretation, one must ask why Erasmus went ahead with letters of recommendation that it was 'impolite' for Hutten to request, and 'dangerous' for him to write. There may be an answer in the *Spongia*, where Erasmus says that his friendship with Hutten, 'mediated by the Muses some years ago,' had since been 'confirmed by certain mutual services.'[114] But if Erasmus wrote the letters of out a sense of obligation, what did Hutten do, or promise to do, as his part of the bargain? Hutten had recently come to Erasmus' aid against Edward Lee,[115] and Erasmus seems not to have minded the fact that Hutten threatened his enemy with bodily harm;[116] perhaps one letter deserved another. Hutten might also have pointed out, as he would in the *Expostulatio* of 1523, that he had in his possession 'certain private letters' from Erasmus.[117] But nothing in Erasmus' private letters contains language about the papacy that is as harsh as the *Julius*, which had now been in

* * * * *

111 Below 60, 135.
112 Below 126; Ep 1445:58–61. For the two letters of recommendation Epp 1114, 1115.
113 Cf Kaegi 'Hutten und Erasmus' 225–7.
114 Below 45. The word translated as 'services' (*officia*) connotes things done from a sense of duty or respect.
115 Cf his belief that the zeal of Reuchlin's friends in defending him had also spared Erasmus from attack: see below 62.
116 Cf Kaegi 'Hutten und Erasmus' 224, citing Ep 998:71–84.
117 EB's edition of Hutten's *Expostulatio* (II 180–248) has printed below it an anonymous German translation, here abbreviated as K: *Ulrichs von Hutten mit Erasmo von Rotterdam Theologo und priester handlung* (J.L., 1523; see item XLVIII of Böcking's bibliography of Hutten's works EB I 83). Cf *Expostulatio* EB II 195:1–3, K 74 par 69.

print for two or more years.[118] The *Julius* itself might have given Hutten another claim for 'mutual service' from Erasmus. That he cooperated with other German humanists in keeping it under wraps, at least for a while, seems likely. Alternatively, as suggested above, he may have had a role in publishing it under Andrelini's name.

In any case Hutten took away from the meeting in Louvain a sense of his own moral superiority, as is evident in the letter he wrote Erasmus from the family castle in Steckelberg. Erasmus had in the past disappointed his friends, Hutten wrote, because he 'showed more weakness than was worthy of you' in defending Reuchlin, and because he 'slit the throat of the *Epistolae obscurorum virorum*, after having·praised it initially.' Now, he was censuring Luther for rousing 'what is better left unroused,' even though Erasmus had done the same 'in various places' in his books. Did he not see that, no matter what he said, his and Luther's enemies would know 'that your real feelings were quite different?' Since Erasmus could not be trusted to do the right thing, he had best stay out of the fight: 'This is what I want you to do. Hold your fire entirely, write nothing; we need you safe and sound.'[119] One cannot tell if this letter recapitulates what Hutten said to Erasmus in Louvain, or if it is a case of what the French call *esprit d'escalier*, an afterthought about what he should have said. Either way, it suggests that the meeting in Louvain was not free of tension.[120]

Lest he involve his parents in his troubles, Hutten left Steckelberg in September for Sickingen's castle at Ebernburg; from here he warned Erasmus that he too was being targeted by the Romanists, and should betake himself to a place of safety.[121] He also circulated appeals for a war against the clergy, to Emperor Charles v, to Luther's prince, Elector Frederick the

* * * * *

118 Eg Ep 872 (above n102).

119 Ep 1135:18–44

120 Ep 1135 introduction, 'It does not seem that Hutten's frank admonitions were taken amiss by Erasmus (cf Ep 1195:157–61) and Hutten himself did not re-peat them in Ep 1161 ... That Hutten should write so freely is perhaps another indication that his recent meeting with Erasmus was untroubled and conge-nial.' To which it may be said that: 'frank admonition' is an mild description for a letter whose message is that Erasmus requires the guidance of a man of integrity; the passage from Ep 1195, which says that Hutten at least takes re-sponsibility for his own rash publications, does not bear on the Louvain meet-ing; and Ep 1161, bidding Erasmus to take refuge somewhere, continues the presumptuously protective tone of Ep 1135.

121 Ep 1161; cf Ep 1161:4n, Hutten thought (wrongly) that Cardinal Adrian of Utrecht, the future Pope Adrian vi, had written Leo x, asking why he suffered Erasmus to remain unmolested.

Wise of Saxony, and to the German estates, but in each case to no avail. Even his host was not ready for battle, at least not yet. Courted by Charles v, Sickingen signed on as one of the emperor's commanders for an army that was to battle French troops who had invaded the Low Countries. From the Diet of Worms (27 January–25 May 1521), where Luther was to have a hearing before the imperial estates, Sickingen held out a hope that Hutten himself might be included in reconciliation with the emperor. But the Edict of Worms, promulgated by Charles v on 26 May, condemned the reformer's writings, and placed Luther himself beyond the protection of the law.[122] Thus even though Sickingen was marching off to a different war, Hutten embarked on his own campaign against the clergy, interrupted by flare-ups of his illness that forced him to take shelter in Ebernburg. He did manage to extort 2,000 Rhine gulden from the Carthusians of Strasbourg; according to Erasmus, who is the only source for these details, he also cut off the ears of two Dominicans, and robbed three abbots on a public highway.[123] But the man he sent to attack monastic properties in the lands of the Count Palatine of the Rhine was caught and executed as a robber.[124] Sickingen, after campaigning on the emperor's behalf, joined a league of imperial free knights who planned to assault Germany's ecclesiastical princes. Sickingen led his forces against an old enemy, the prince-archbishop of Trier in September 1522; repulsed from the walls of Trier, he was besieged in his castle at Landstuhl, where he was wounded and died. Hutten, too ill to join in the assault on Trier, or in the defence of Sickingen's lands, left Ebernburg and set off for the Rhineland.[125]

Meanwhile, now that Luther stood condemned by the imperial estates as well as by the pope, Erasmus was finding that professions of loyalty to the church were no longer sufficient; in the campaign against heresy, more was expected from a man of his talent and stature. Yet he still did not believe that the Saxon reformer's teachings were heretical; the points Luther contested, like the nature of papal authority, or man's freedom to accept or reject divine grace, were matters of theological opinion, not doctrines binding on all the faithful.[126] Furthermore, he remained convinced

* * * * *

122 Holborn *Ulrich von Hutten* 151–73.
123 Below *Spongia* n130.
124 Holborn *Ulrich von Hutten* 174–83
125 Hitchcock *Background of the Knights' Revolt* (above n12) 45–52; CEBR III 247–9; EB II 151, an excerpt from the *Annales* of Kilian Leib, describing the failed assault on Trier.
126 Above General Introduction n11

that theologians of the traditional school hoped to use the momentum of an assault on Luther to snuff out the beginnings of the new theology, based on the study of Scripture in the original languages.[127] Yet Louvain was close to the Hapsburg court in Brussels, and as Erasmus intimates in the *Spongia*, he would not have been able to resist a personal request to write against Luther from his prince, Charles v. Hence he departed from Louvain on 28 October 1521 and took up residence in Basel, where Froben was in any case his printer of choice.[128] Here too, however, he received reminders of his duty to the church, from his old friend Adrian of Utrecht, now Pope Adrian vi, and from a loyal patron among the German princes, Duke George of Saxony.[129] At the beginning of February 1523 he penned a lengthy justification of his position vis-à-vis Luther, destined for publication, in the form of a letter to Marcus Laurinus, a friend in the Low Countries. Luther will not be indignant, he wrote, 'if anyone differs from him at any point and . . . while abstaining from personal abuse, uses the testimony of Scripture, which he thinks so important, and sound reasoning to pursue the truth.'[130] This was the first indication that Erasmus might be willing to engage Luther in debate.

In these months Hutten too had been in Basel. In Schlettstatt in November 1522, he had in some way intimated to Erasmus' friend Beatus Rhenanus that the great man needed a talking-to.[131] Upon arriving in Basel, he was treated by the city council as an honoured guest, but soon made himself unwelcome by publishing polemical tracts, including one against the Count Palatine of the Rhine, whose officials had executed Hutten's man as a robber. While in Basel Hutten sought a meeting with Erasmus in his house, but Erasmus would not receive him; as discussed in *The Sponge*, one reason he gave was that while Hutten's illness would require a heated room, Erasmus kept a cold house because he was made ill by the room-stoves common in that region.[132] Thus Hutten did not meet with Erasmus before leaving Basel for Mulhouse at the end of January. Through an intermediary, and mutual friend, Heinrich von Eppendorf, the two men exchanged letters that are now lost; in one fragment that has been preserved Hutten ridiculed

* * * * *

127 Cf above n104.
128 Below 123; Ep 1242 introduction
129 Epp 1324, 1324A, 1339, 1298, 1340
130 Ep 1342:910–20
131 Below 49–51
132 The fullest discussion of conflicting accounts in the *Expostulatio* of Hutten and the *Spongia* of Erasmus is Kaegi 'Hutten und Erasmus' 462–75.

Erasmus' 'made-up story' (*fabula*) about room-stoves.[133] In the only letter that survives, Erasmus tells Hutten on 3 April 1523 that he has heard from Eppendorf that Hutten is 'planning to write something fairly bitter.'[134] It seems Hutten began his *Expostulatio* in March, before Erasmus wrote this letter, and before Hutten could have seen his letter to Marcus Laurinus, which was published in April.[135] If Erasmus would not sit still for a talking-to, he would get something he liked even less. The *Expostulatio* was given to a printer in Strasbourg, where it was reported to be in print as of June 18.[136]

Erasmus had finished his *Spongia* by early August, when he addressed the preface for it to Ulrich Zwingli in Zürich, where Hutten was now staying, and where he died on 31 August, while the *Spongia* was still in press.[137] His choice of Zwingli as the addressee for this letter was significant, not because Zwingli gave shelter to Hutten in his last days, but because he, with Martin Luther, was the acknowledged leader of what is now called the Protestant Reformation. Just as Erasmus published letters that were intended to keep open his bridges to Rome, he wrote the *Spongia* in such a way as to keep open his bridges to the evangelical movement.

EXPOSTULATIO AND SPONGIA

That Hutten attacks Erasmus for having betrayed the principles they once shared is well known. What is less commonly noticed is which principles he had in mind. The reason Erasmus would not see him in Basel, Hutten says, was that his 'sworn allegiance to the Roman pontiff might be called into doubt' if he did. Yet it was only recently that 'you put the Roman pontiff in his place along with the rest of us, your righteous pen exposed Rome as the centre of crime and iniquity, you damned bulls and indulgences, you railed against ceremonies, you demanded penalties for the courtiers, you denounced canon law and papal decrees, you censured, with utmost severity, all the hypocrisy of the Roman court, and now, beating a retreat, you follow other goals altogether, and enter into a compact with the enemy.'[138]

* * * * *

133 Allen Ep 1934:275–89. Cf Ep 1356 introduction.
134 Ep 1356:1–4
135 Both the letter to Laurinus and the *Catalogus lucubrationum* (Ep 1341A) with which it was published are mentioned in the *Expostulatio*, but Kaegi, 'Hutten und Erasmus' 479–80, thought the main body of the *Expostulatio* was likely to have been written in March.
136 Epp 1356:9n, 1368:32
137 Ep 1378 introduction
138 EB II 185:1–3, 186:18–187:4 (trans JDT)

How could Erasmus in good conscience now speak of a Roman church 'which does not differ, I conceive, from the Catholic church'?[139] Martin Luther has of course a role in the drama as Hutten understood it,[140] but Rome was the main issue. Luther stood condemned because 'he was, if not the first, the most powerful enemy of Roman tyranny'; he thus attacked 'the same things that I did before him.' It is in this sense that Hutten will 'bear' being called a Lutheran; in this sense, he says to Erasmus, 'one can easily persuade everyone that you too are a Lutheran.'[141] He thus charged Erasmus not with betraying Martin Luther, but with betraying the common cause of freeing Germany from papal tyranny.

This indictment makes sense if one assumes, as Hutten likely did, that the *Julius exclusus* represented a full and sufficient statement of what Erasmus thought about the papacy. But if Hutten was a man of action, whose 'fierceness' put off even his friends,[142] Erasmus was above all else 'circumspect,'[143] unwilling to commit himself to any course of action until he had considered it from all angles. In the *Spongia* he responded to Hutten's charges of inconsistency, but without adding a hair's breadth to what he had hitherto been willing to say in favour of papal authority.[144] When he comes to 'what Hutten considers the main point of the whole case,' he shifts the focus away from the papacy, towards Luther: what Hutten charges, he says, is 'that I had once adhered to Luther's party.' He then quotes the passage, cited above, in which Hutten accused him not of deserting Luther, but of deserting the enemies of Rome.[145] Having put the issue in these

* * * * *

139 EB II 218:20–219:8 (cf above n107).
140 Cf EB II 211:8–11 (trans JDT): 'Not even those implacably opposed to Luther can deny that he was the first to open for all Christians the door to a true understanding of the most hidden senses of Scripture.' This evocation of the traditional four-fold sense of Scripture does not suggest a careful reading of Luther's writings.
141 EB II 220:1–223:21
142 Cochlaeus to Pirckheimer, 5 July 1517, EB I 142, Ep LVI:10–11: 'Amo equidem hominis ingenium, ferociam eius non ita; longe certe facilius absentem quam praesentem (ita tecum loqui libet) amicum servabo.'
143 Tracy *Low Countries* chapter 13, 'Circumspect Reformer'
144 Cf the rather lame comment that 'there is a church in Rome; and a multitude of evil men does not make a church any less a church,' below 100–1; elsewhere he acknowledges having written that the authority of the pope is sacrosanct, but he would 'have no hesitation in saying the same of individual bishops, providing they teach nothing impious, for then they would cease to be bishops,' below 109.
145 Below 87; cf above n138.

terms, Erasmus has little trouble showing that he had never declared for Luther's party. As for the Lutheran side, Erasmus notes that he did not use the word 'heresy' in speaking about Luther in his letter to Marcus Luarinus, and that sensible men of Luther's party do not approve of Hutten, and would not slander their opponents as Hutten has done to Erasmus.[146] One gets the impression, as Werner Kaegi remarked, that the *Spongia* is addressed 'less to Hutten himself than to the entire Lutheran party, whose voice [Erasmus] detected in the *Expostulatio*.'[147] In fact, Erasmus had not given up his dream that reasonable men on both sides might yet be able to find common ground. As of the time he was writing the *Spongia*, he had not yet decided to write against Luther, which would mean giving up a good deal of his independence: 'I have constantly declared, in countless letters, booklets, and personal statements, that I do not want to be involved with either party.'[148] Erasmus devotes a good part of his response to the etiquette of friendship, and how Hutten has violated it, not just by this unprovoked attack but by earlier actions as well, such as the unauthorized publication of his letter to Albert of Brandenburg, which he represents as having caused him more trouble than it may actually have done.[149] There is no doubt that the two men liked each other; their friendship was 'mediated by the Muses,' but not limited to common literary interests.[150] But in order to reverse the charge of betrayal – it is not Erasmus who has betrayed certain principles, but Hutten who has betrayed the laws of friendship – he gives a picture of things that at times strains credibility. For example, when Erasmus avers that their friendship remained serene and untroubled until the unexpected news that Hutten was writing a book against him, he sounds like a man who protests too much.[151] He is on firmer ground when he chides Hutten for having misread his published letters. Hutten was a gifted satirist and polemicist but he was not the wordsmith that Erasmus was. One of the charms of the *Spongia* is that it provides a rare glimpse of how he expected his words to be understood by discerning readers – a class of people that evidently did not include Hutten. For example, in a published letter where

* * * * *

146 Below 99
147 Kaegi 'Hutten und Erasmus' 484
148 Below 88
149 Below 114, 125–6
150 The case is made by Kaegi 'Hutten und Erasmus.'
151 Eg below 50, 'Beatus did not return to Basel until some time after Hutten had left. Greeting me in the presence of several friends, including Ludwig Baer, he asked how I was getting along with Hutten. "Very well," I answered, for at that time I was wholly convinced of this.'

Erasmus referred to Jacob Hoogstraten, the inquisitor of Cologne, as 'an old acquaintance of mine if not a friend,' Hutten quite missed the 'irony' that was intended.[152] Likewise, when Erasmus approved of 'public arguments against Luther' at Cologne and Louvain, Hutten should have grasped that he was referring not to the published condemnations of Luther (concerning which Hutten knew Erasmus' opinion well enough) but to the welcome fact that theologians were at least willing to debate the merits of Luther's theses in the usual scholastic fashion.[153]

When he wrote of having a letter from 'the well-known Sylvester Prierias,' a papal theologian who had attacked Luther, his words were intended not to 'spite Luther,' as Hutten thought, but to show that he would have been well received in Rome had he accepted invitations to go there. In describing a colleague on the Louvain theology faculty as 'never praised enough,' he expected readers in Louvain (if not Hutten) to laugh: as vice-chancellor of the university, this man was 'feted every day in solemn encomia.'[154] Finally, in reference to the letter to Bishop Luigi Marliano, cited above, Hutten ought to have taken Erasmus' circumstances at the time into account: 'This was what needed to be said, for I was then accused of conspiring against the papacy.'[155] One might counter that these were matters of style, not of substance. But what most divided Hutten from Erasmus was the latter's conviction that style was a matter of substance. The *Spongia* characterizes Hutten's attack with metaphors that suggest a force of nature, violent and mindless, crashing down on the barriers of human convention.[156] In his 'malicious zeal for finding fault,' Hutten 'fulminates' against Erasmus on trivial matters, 'flinging charges whether fitting or not'; he represents Erasmus as speaking about the papacy not in his own words, but 'with all the savagery Hutten can put in my mouth.'[157] Does Hutten perhaps speak with the indignation of a prophet? Not for Erasmus; in the Acts of the Apostles, where St Peter invokes the power of God to strike Simon Magus dead, he first offers the sinner an opportunity to repent.[158] Zeal of this kind, without measure, is exactly what Erasmus most objects to about Luther: 'His unrestrained abuse and his seeming arrogance.' Even if he

* * * * *

152 Below 58; on Hoogstraten see *Spongia* n20.
153 Below 71; cf above n109.
154 Below 85–6.
155 Below 109; cf above n108.
156 'That torrent of words,' below 57; 'Hutten's thunderbolts,' below 67
157 Below 69, 72
158 Below 112–13 with n435

accepted all of Luther's teachings, he says, 'I must still vehemently reject the obstinacy with which he asserts his opinions and the harsh abuse he has always at hand.' This was, for Erasmus, a test of gospel truth: he has not been able to persuade himself 'that the Spirit of Christ – than whom no one is more gentle – dwells in a heart from which such bitterness gushes forth. Would that I am deceived in what I suspect.'[159] Thus while Erasmus would not characterize any of the Saxon reformer's doctrines as heretical, Luther's unbounded wrath made him wonder aloud if the man himself were inspired by the devil.

In characterizing his own style, Erasmus made a sharp distinction between speaking and writing. 'At meals or in conversations with friends,' he says, 'I will say in jest whatever comes to mind, often speaking more freely than is wise'; this was his 'besetting fault.'[160] But writing required one to keep in mind the likely effects of one's words. If called upon to defend an innocent man before a powerful tyrant, Hutten, 'brave man and defender of truth that he is,' would no doubt begin by denouncing the tyrant for his crimes. Erasmus for his part has no shame in having used 'honeyed words' to address princes, for 'flattery is pious when it helps another.'[161] Hutten called Erasmus 'elusive' because he said different things in letters to different people. But must one say the same thing to everyone, 'fitting, as it were, the same shoe to every foot?' Indeed, 'amid a controversy of this kind, where people are zealous in different directions, who can avoid saying some things indirectly?'[162] Instead of publishing 'abusive books against the pope or the emperor that only produce the opposite effect,' learned men should 'write privately to the pope and the emperor about measures that would seem to promote the welfare of the Christian people and the glory of Christ.'[163] But this was not the tendency of the times. What Erasmus dreaded was a world in which 'one side employs only riots, quarrels, and insults, while the other relies on papal bulls, articles of condemnation, and book-burning,' not to mention death at the stake.[164]

In sum, despite its character as a defence of his own words and deeds, Erasmus seems to have hoped the *Spongia* would be received as a prologue to a badly needed civil conversation between Catholics and Lutherans.

* * * * *

159 Below 112
160 Below 60
161 Below 117, 132–3
162 Below 97
163 Below 143
164 Below 144

But while Erasmus' Catholic friends liked it,[165] Protestants uniformly condemned it.[166] There would indeed come a time for a conversation of the kind that Erasmus hoped for, but he would not live to see it.[167]

JDT

* * * * *

165 Epp 1394:22–4, 1401:1–10, 1428:86–90
166 Epp 1406, 1445:41–69, 1510:70–5
167 On the Regensburg Colloquy of 1541, see Matheson *Cardinal Contarini*.

ERASMUS OF ROTTERDAM TO THAT EXCELLENT SCHOLAR ULRICH
ZWINGLI, PREACHER IN THE CELEBRATED SWISS CITY OF ZURICH,
GREETING[1]

The poison having been brought from here to your part of the world first,
my most learned Zwingli,[2] it seemed appropriate that the antidote should
set off first in the same direction, not that I fear any damage to my reputation
from Hutten's attack in your mind or in the minds of any intelligent men;
my purpose is to cure other people too, who have a prejudice against me, or
by some defect of nature would rather believe what is to a man's discredit
than the opposite. Is there anyone of any character or intelligence who would
not repudiate the precedent set by Hutten? – I never did him any harm in
word or in deed;[3] I have so often praised him[4] even in my published work
more generously, more freely, and more frequently than I have anyone
else, and so often written him letters of recommendation to persons in high
places;[5] and now suddenly, as though he had been lurking in some sort
of ambush,[6] he has published a book like this, attacking a friend who at
the very moment when he was writing it was still speaking of him most
openly and affectionately, and expecting nothing in the world so little as any
unpleasantness started by Hutten. Could anyone imagine anything more
alien to the courtesy and loyalty one expects of a German,[7] more exactly
what the enemies of good literature enjoy and hope for, more likely to hurt
literature itself and damage the cause of the gospel,[8] or, if you like, of Luther

* * * * *

1 This prefatory letter is Ep 1378 dated at Basel, early August 1523. The trans-
    lation of this letter (CWE 10 54:1–56:43) is by R.A.B. Mynors; the notes by pre-
    vious annotators have been taken into account.
2 Huldrych Zwingli was initially influenced by Erasmus. A personal meeting
    at Basel in the spring of 1516 also made a positive impression on the Swiss
    (Epp 401, 404). But Zwingli's change from Erasmian reformer to the Protestant
    reformer of Zürich caused, from September 1522, a growing alienation (Epp
    1314, 1315, 1327), and Hutten's asylum in Zürich was the last straw (Epp
    1376:18–33, 1384:64–90, 1496:8–17). On Zwingli cf CEBR III 481–6; Allen 12 189.
3 Cf Epp 1356:20–2, 1376:20–5, 1379:6–8.
4 See Ep 1341A:1043–51.
5 Cf Epp 745:18–21 and 72–4, 967:115–29, 968:24–6, 1009:78–83, 1114:13–16, 1115:
    47–9, 1341A:1043–51, 1376:20–3, 1445:57–9.
6 See below 134, and Ep 1341A:1055.
7 Cf Expostulatio EB II 198:1, 239:3–240:2; Spongia below 82. On Germans see eg
    Epp 269:43, 305:45, 307:14, 334:9–10, 968:17–23, 998:72–84, 1155:31–3, 1167:11–
    14, 1187:27–9, 1225:383–7, 1244:41–2, 1258:30–1, 1341A:455–66, 1342:216, 543–5,
    577, and 657–8, 1384:36, 1437:104–6, 1512:29–31.
8 See Ep 1379:15–16, 1384:65–71.

even, of which he boasts himself a supporter?[9] He had declared war on the supporters of Rome;[10] and he attacks a friend who has a most sincere regard for him and was expecting nothing,[11] with no previous complaints,[12] and in a pamphlet so bitter that he has never yet written anything more venomous even against an enemy. And since then, I hear, he has added to the book,[13] as though there were not enough venom in it already; nor does it look as though he would ever stop, now that he has once declared war on the Muses and the Graces.[14] For my part, I do not grudge him his generous reception by the Swiss, who give him a refuge[15] in which he can for the moment be safe from the pursuers who mean to punish him.[16] All the same, steps should be taken to see that he does not abuse Swiss kindness by living in safety under their protection while he fires off pieces like this[17] – personal attacks on anyone who has served the cause of public enlightenment, sparing neither pope nor emperor nor the princes of Germany[18] nor even the most honourable men among the Swiss themselves, in which number I include Ludwig Baer.[19] Since he writes this from a refuge in Switzerland, it is to be feared that one day some unpopularity, some unpleasantness may befall the Swiss themselves,[20] whom we wish to see flourishing in public peace

* * * * *

9 Cf *Expostulatio* EB II 223:4–18.
10 Cf *Spongia* below 101.
11 Cf Epp 1341A:1020–1, 1376:26–7; but see Ep 1356:74.
12 See *Spongia* below 52.
13 Erasmus had it on the authority of Oecolampadius (Ep 1384:83–4), who was in close contact with Hutten (Ep 1376 n21), that Hutten had completed an enlarged version of the *Expostulatio*.
14 See *Spongia* below n108.
15 Cf *Spongia* below 119, and Ep 1376:31–2.
16 See *Spongia* below 40. Since 1520 the Roman authorities had been trying to seize Hutten; he was excommunicated in the beginning of 1521 and subsequently outlawed by imperial ban.
17 Cf Ep 1379:14–15.
18 Cf Ep 1379:11; *Expostulatio* EB II 189:15–17, 209:3–210:8 and 16; 219:18–220:2, 221:19–223:4, 227:10–20, 228:8–11, 229:4–6, 231:14–21.
19 Hutten had called Ludwig Baer, professor of theology at Basel (see *Spongia* below n66), and his colleague Johann Gebwiler (see *Spongia* below n261) 'those two deadly plagues of Basel who are sunk in avarice, blinded by ambition, and of all the flatterers of Rome the most abominable, who alone in that city have for a long time now most obstinately opposed the renascent sciences and the emerging studies of the fine arts' (trans JDT; see *Expostulatio* EB II 201:4–12, 213:8–17).
20 Cf Ep 1379:17–18. On the Swiss see *Adagia* I vi 14: *In Care periculum* CWE 32 12–13; Ep 401:9–10, 404:11–16.

and every other blessing. Nothing is easier than to sow discord, while it is a most difficult task to cure the evil once it has started.[21] Farewell.

* * * * *

21 Cf *Adagia* II i 12: *Difficilia quae pulchra* 'Good things are difficult' CWE 33 22–4.

ERASMUS OF ROTTERDAM TO THE FAIR-MINDED READER,
GREETING[1]

Hutten's death has removed some of the appeal from my *Spongia*,[2] if works
of this kind possess any appeal at all. Had I known of it in time, either I
should not have replied, or my reply would have been different; as it is,
there are some things in it which only Hutten was likely to understand.[3]
I do not suppose he had yet read the *Spongia* through, though certain people
have asserted as much,[4] for Hutten died on 29 August,[5] and Froben[6] ended
work on the *Spongia* just about the same time that he met his end. How
I wish that death, which came to Hutten almost as a blessing – for it relieved the poor man from the pressure of so much misfortune, or removed
him from the threat of more – had been granted him, somewhat sooner!
– before he had so far lost his reason as to write such a venomous book,
productive of so much ill will and so much discredit not only for himself
but for the humanities, and for the cause of the gospel, and for all who
call themselves Germans;[7] for the very lightest sufferer in all this is myself.
Not but what, if men were led entirely by reason and judgment, it would
not be fair for anyone to be prejudiced against the humanities by the appearance of a man who uses them perversely, or against the gospel cause,
which Hutten has attacked so brazenly, seeing that even Luther has turned
against him as an enemy of his party;[8] and it would be far more unfair to
assess the nature of a whole nation by the faults of one individual.[9] Scythia

* * * * *

1 This letter is Ep 1389, dated at Basel, c October 1523. The translation of this
  letter (CWE 10 91:1–95:93) is by R.A.B. Mynors; the notes of previous annotators
  have been taken into account.
2 Cf Ep 1388:13–14.
3 See *Spongia* below 125–7; cf Epp 1033 introduction, 1341A:1084–5, 1445:55–64.
4 Cf Ep 1406:17–24.
5 Cf Ep 1388 n12.
6 On Johann Froben, Erasmus' publisher at Basel, see CEBR II 60–3.
7 See above Ep 1378 30 nn7 and 8.
8 Cf *Spongia* below 89, 114. In a letter to Spalatin in the beginning of 1521, Luther
  had disapproved Hutten's violent plans (WA Br 2 no 368:12–15). But there is
  no direct statement that Luther regarded Hutten as an enemy. Erasmus knew
  from letters of Melanchthon to third persons that Luther considered Hutten's
  pamphlet detrimental to the cause of the gospel (Ep 1341A n299), even though
  Luther remained favourably inclined towards Hutten personally. In a letter of
  August 1523 Luther disapproved of the *Expostulatio*: WA Br 1 no 451:14–17.
9 See Ep 1202:284–6; cf *Adagia* I viii 96: *Virum improbum vel mus mordeat* CWE 32
  177: 'it is unfair to judge all Englishmen from this one worthless specimen';
  cf *Spongia* below 70, 72, 86, 132.

produced its Anacharsis,[10] and Athens gave birth to many silly fools.[11] From falling into this disgrace, overlooking any question of the breaches he has made in our friendship, I would have rescued my friend, had not certain persons I could name deliberately seen to it that we should never meet and talk.[12] As it is, I am thankful for one thing at least, that so far I have been able to preserve my old moderation in replying. For even had Hutten attacked me again, as he would I suppose have done, had he lived, either because he had once and for all lost all sense of decency[13] or because there was no lack of people to give the cart a push downhill, as the saying goes,[14] he would have felt my reply to be really just a sponge and no more. Though, as far as I am concerned, Hutten's spirit shall rest in peace, provided that he does not show his teeth against me even after death in some poisonous pamphlet and no one arises to reopen the whole miserable business.[15] It seems to me that this madness has already gone too far. Now that what's done cannot be undone, it remains to bury the damage as far as one can. And since they give us good advice who tell us to pluck what good one can out of evil,[16] I shall learn this as my first lesson from the hard school I have been through: in the future I shall be slower to make

* * * * *

10 Prince Anacharsis of the barbarian Scythians became a sort of 'noble savage,' gaining a reputation in wisdom and virtue superior to that of the Greeks. Around 592 BC he went to Athens, where he was befriended by Solon and numbered among the Seven Sages. Later he was credited with the invention of the potter's wheel, the bellows, and the anchor. The *Letters of Anacharsis* became a model for Cynic diatribes against a corrupt civilization.

11 Cf *Adagia* II iv 72: *Betizare. Lachanizare* CWE 33 227: '*Bliteus* is a word for stupid people.'

12 Probably Eppendorf (see ASD IX-1 97 n26), but cf Ep 1331:63.

13 Cf *Adagia* I viii 47: *Faciem perfricare. Frontis perfrictae* CWE 32 149–50: 'those people are proverbially said to have wiped off the blushes from forehead or face, who have abandoned all modesty ...'

14 *Adagia* I vi 13 *Bene plaustrum perculit* 'He gave the cart a good shove downhill' CWE 32 11–12: 'used of those who urge a man in a direction to which he was already tending of his own accord'; Plautus *Epidicus* IV ii 22; cf *Purgatio adversus epistolam Lutheri* below 413.

15 Epp 1383:32–6 and 1386:31–2 (cf Epp 1397:8–9, 1406:53–8, 1437:186–8, 1466:29–37, 1496:93–119) suggest that Erasmus had Hermannus Buschius (see *Spongia* below n99) in mind. Also Luther heard in the spring of 1523 that Buschius was about to write against Erasmus (WA Br 3 587:6–10). No such work was published, but Erasmus believed that Erasmus Alber's *Iudicium de Spongia Erasmi Roterodami* came from Buschius' hand.

16 Cf Cicero *De officiis* 3.1, 3.

friends,[17] more cautious in cultivating them, more sparing in singing their praises, more prudent in commending them to others. Why should I not, as Solon's famous saying puts it, learn something every day as I grow old?[18] In fact there is a lesson here for the young, that they should aim to acquire good sense no less than good learning and rein in their mettlesome passions with the bridle of reason; for many are indulgent at first to their faults, they forgive wenching and drunken revels as the marks of youth and suppose gambling and extravagance to be proper to noble blood. All the time, their property is dwindling and their debts are growing, their reputation is at risk, and they lose the favour of the princes to whose generosity they owed their bread. Then poverty invites them to seize what they want, at first their robberies are excused under the pretext of war; and then they find their appetites, like the urn of the Danaids,[19] insatiable and are reduced to desperate designs, so that the words friend and enemy now lose all meaning in their thirst for prey. In the end, like a horse that has thrown its rider, they are carried headlong to perdition.[20] Though in Hutten this does not greatly surprise me; for how ill-judged almost all his designs were is more notorious than I could wish. Where I am compelled to deplore a lack of judgment is in the men who pushed him forward onto the stage to act this crazy play,[21] and even now applaud such a sorry spectacle. They wish to appear

* * * * *

17 See *Spongia* below 125; cf *Adagia* II ii 75: *Amicus magis necessarius quam ignis et aqua* CWE 33 114–15 for the necessity of friendship and Ep 1388:24–5, where the Germans are likened to Sejanus' horse that brings misfortune to its owner (*Adagia* I x 97: *Equum habet Sejanum* CWE 32 279). On Erasmus' view of Germany see especially *Spongia* below 119 and the index CWE 9 483.

18 Cf *Adagia* I viii 60: *Senesco semper multa addiscens* 'Age comes upon me learning all the time' CWE 32 159.

19 Cf *Adagia* I iv 60: *Cribro aquam haurire* 'To draw water in a sieve' CWE 31 360–1. For killing their husbands on the wedding night, the daughters of Danaus were punished in Hades by being compelled forever to pour water into a leaky jar.

20 Cf ASD IX-1 177:251–7n; Epp 1341A:1063–78, 1445:43–51. On German Junkers see *Adagia* I ix 44: *Proterviam fecit* CWE 32 204–5: 'But whenever a man's expenses outstrip his income ...'

21 Erasmus describes the whole controversy surrounding both the new philology and Luther's doctrines in terms of the ancient drama (*fabula*), with its last act (*catastrophe*) being the most important one because of its tragic or happy ending (*Adagia* I ii 35 and 36: *Catastrophe fabulae* 'The denouement of the play' CWE 31:177–8); cf Ep 1601:3–8 n1; see also *Spongia* below 136; Epp 758:18–20, 1155:7–12, 1156:12–20, 1202:210–11 and 271–2, 1225: 341–4, 1232:110–12, 1342:827–8 and 970–6, 1389:67, 1481:14–16, 1522:8–13 and

supporters of the humanities, and no man alive has done the humanities more harm than they. They are passionate devotees of Luther, and could not have done more damage to his cause. They love their Hutten, and his worst enemy did not hurt him more than they did. They hate Luther's enemies, and no one has yet provided those enemies with a spectacle more to their liking. They are Germans through and through, and in three hundred years no one has done more harm to the reputation of Germany.[22]

Not that I fail to see the design behind this play and who has acted in it. Straightforward as I am by nature and in no way suspicious,[23] I am not so devoid of all sense of smell, not such a blockhead, such a mere fungus, that I alone cannot see what all men see.[24] All the same, if I may be allowed at this point to have finished my part in this life-and-death struggle,[25] my desire is to be ignorant of what I know and to forget what I remember. But I fear that certain people who are overfond of this sort of wretched business[26] will not let me off; for though they know well enough how courteously I treated Hutten in the *Spongia*, they are not yet ashamed to put it about that I waited till Hutten was dead before publishing my book, as though I meant to do battle with the dead.[27] I replied to Hutten's *Expostulatio* promptly in July.[28] My manuscript was seen by Johann Froben and several other men besides. He would have printed it, but he had no presses idle at the moment, and I thought it wiser to postpone, for fear that some other attack might come out before the fair,[29] to which I should not be able to reply. And again, as it is known that Hutten died on the day I mentioned in a small island a long

* * * * *

57–8, 1526:12, 1581:706–7. For Erasmus' understanding and use of *fabula* in biblical interpretation, see Hoffmann *Rhetoric and Theology* 250 n96; CWE 49:136 n8.

22 See Ep 1378 above 30 nn7 and 8.

23 Erasmus calls himself *simplex* by natural endowment (cf CWE 46:34 n137); but in the *Spongia* he talks about his *lingua libera* (see *Spongia* below 98–9).

24 Erasmus believes Eppendorf is the 'skilled hand behind this story'; cf Epp 1376:27–9, 1437:28–40.

25 Gladiatorial images (eg *pugna gladiatoria; in arenam descendere*) depict his being drawn into the Lutheran affair, particularly after his open attack on Luther with his *De servo arbitrio*; cf Epp 1448:47–50, 1481:17–18, 1489:66–8, 1493:3–5, 1495:4–6, 1499:35–6, 1522:17–18.

26 *Quod scis nescis* (Ter *Eun.* 722; *Adagia* III v 99 CWE 35 124); cf *Spongia* below 119.

27 Cf *Adagia* I ii 53 and 54: *Cum larvis luctari* 'To wrestle with ghosts' and *Iugulare mortuos* 'To cut a dead man's throat' CWE 31 194–5.

28 See Allen Ep 1378 introduction; Ep 1341A:1019–1128.

29 The yearly autumn book fair at Frankfurt am Main (Epp 326A:16n, 1337:11).

way beyond Zürich,[30] and known that Froben started on the *Spongia* on the thirteenth of August and finished it on 3 September,[31] how is it possible that I could have put out the *Spongia* after Hutten's death? – all the more so since Hutten's death, so they tell me in letters,[32] was sudden. Count up how long it would take for the news to be brought here even by special courier,[33] and consider the date on which I had already sent off my parcel; and you will find I had not four hours to write the *Spongia*. That will give you an idea of the effrontery of those who put this about. If the man whom I suspect[34] makes himself known, he will discover that I did not hate Hutten with my whole heart.[35] Farewell, dear reader, learn wisdom from my misfortunes.

* * * * *

30 The island of Ufenau, in the eastern arm of Lake Zürich, belonged to the abbey of Einsiedeln. From early August 1523 to his death from syphilis at the end of August 1523, Hutten stayed there with the priest-physician Hans Klarer, seeking medical treatment. The exact date of Hutten's death is uncertain (see Epp 1388:13 n12, 1437:64; CEBR II 219, III 226 [sv Konrad Schmid]).
31 Cf Ep 1383:14–15.
32 None of these has survived.
33 On 1 September 1523 Erasmus did not know of Hutten's death; see ASD IX-1 121 n102.
34 Probably not Otto Brunfels (Ep 1405), but Hermannus Buschius (Epp 1383:32–6, 1406:129–32; see ASD IX-1 121:60–1n) or perhaps Eppendorf (see above n24).
35 Cf Ep 1406:129–32.

THE SPONGE OF ERASMUS
AGAINST
THE ASPERSIONS OF HUTTEN[1]

If you have the time, listen now to a Laconian orator responding to the
Asian,[2] not just briefly[3] but also politely, for instead of throwing my antagonist's accusations and reproaches back at him, I will merely wipe off with
a sponge the muck with which he has splattered me. I do so because of
our former friendship, and also because such has been my constant habit.
I know that Hutten's aristocratic spirit cannot bear contempt. But just as
he has in the past provoked many with his caustic writings, without anyone deigning to reply, he will now have the honour of a reply from an old
friend. I ask you, gentle reader, to pay close attention, for I want you to be
not merely a witness to this conflict, but an expert witness, indeed a judge.[4]

This tragedy had its prologue[5] when Hutten arrived in Basel, and I
would not grant him an interview.[6] You cannot imagine the dreadful trouble he is trying to stir up because of this. Hence a simple, plain narration

* * * * *

1 Translation by James D. Tracy. Some phrasing has been taken from R.J. Klaw-
  iter *The Polemics of Erasmus of Rotterdam and Ulrich von Hutten* (Notre Dame
  and London 1977) 145–248. Notes by Manfred Hoffmann.
2 For the contrast between Laconian and Asiatic styles, *Adagia* II x 49: *Laconismus*
  CWE 34 146–7; *Adagia* II i 92: *Battologia. Laconismus* CWE 33 70–1; and *Lingua*
  CWE 29 274–5. Cf Cicero *Brutus* 51, *Orator* 25; Quintilian *Institutio* 12.10.16–9.
3 But Erasmus' *Spongia* is twice as long as Hutten's *Expostulatio*.
4 Erasmus will use the judicial genre of rhetoric to sets the facts straight ('a
  simple, plain narration of the truth,' [see below 39]). He will let the true
  case (*causa*) and the actual affair (*res*) rebut Hutten's accusations; cf below 62,
  67–8.
5 Erasmus recounts the controversy in terms of a *tragoedia*. In classical literary
  theory, tragedy proceeds from *initium* to *medium* and *finis*.
6 Cf Epp 1331:63 n24, 1342:760–6; and (perhaps with a bit more frankness)
  1496:6–13. The fullest account is Kaegi 'Hutten und Erasmus' 461–500; Holborn
  Ulrich von Hutten 188–202.

of the truth – not a word will I fabricate. This is what happened. Heinrich Eppendorf[7] – whose name will be mentioned often, and always with due respect – was the first to inform me that Hutten was in Basel. Delighted by the news, I at once inquired after his health, whether he was safe, whether the magistrates were favourably inclined, and other such things we usually ask about those whom we truly wish well. At the time, I was as sincerely well disposed towards Hutten as anyone. The news was good in other respects, but I was sad to hear from Eppendorf that his health was in a very poor state. Finally I asked Eppendorf to use gentle words with Hutten, so that he would not come to visit if he merely wanted to greet me, for a meeting between us, though of no advantage to him, would increase the ill will towards me, of which there is already more than enough.[8] At the same time, nothing having changed in my long-time affection for him, I would be entirely at his disposal if he needed my assistance in any matter. Eppendorf agreed to deliver the message to Hutten, and, polite as he is, I am sure he did so in terms more appropriate than those I had suggested. In any case he says he conveyed my message as politely as possible.

When he came back after a day or two, I asked how Hutten had received my begging off from a meeting. 'Hutten smiled pleasantly,' he said, 'and took it in good part.' I again assured him of my good will towards Hutten, and offered my services should he need them. Many days later I pressed Eppendorf to tell me in confidence whether Hutten seemed to accept my request in the same spirit in which I had meant it, or whether he gave any indication of being offended. He denied having noticed anything of the kind, but, as he was about to leave, he had a further thought: 'Hutten,' he said, 'would perhaps like to speak with you.' I asked if Hutten had said so himself, and he said no, but there was perhaps a matter about which Hutten was eager to speak with me. 'Although I have a strong desire to avoid ill will,' I replied, 'it is not of such great importance to me that I could not easily disregard it if Hutten had something serious to discuss, or if speaking with me meant so much to him.' I said I would go to him myself were I only able to bear a room-stove; he, being in such poor health, perhaps could not do without a stove.[9] But if he could endure the coldness in

* * * * *

7 On Heinrich Eppendorf (CEBR I 439–41; Epp 1283 n4, 1437:10–103; Allen XII 88) see introductory note to *Admonitio adversus mendacium* below 369–78.
8 Erasmus conveyed the same message in a letter to Hutten: Ep 1356:9–14.
9 Cf Ep 1342:764–6; *Expostulatio* EB II 180:11 / K 59–60; below 51. Erasmus repeatedly complained that the heat and stink of German room-stoves adversely

my lodgings, I would gladly talk with him until he had his fill, and would
have the fireplace burning brightly. To this Eppendorf responded that, in
his afflicted condition, Hutten always kept to stove-heated rooms.

Hutten had meanwhile left for Mulhouse.[10] Eppendorf told me how
he had eluded danger,[11] and I was pleased to hear it. Eppendorf can testify
how worried I was that something untoward might befall Hutten. Thus
when Eppendorf was about to set out for Mulhouse, I commissioned him
to warn Hutten to hold everyone suspect: he should not fall into danger by
thinking himself safe, for people were hunting for him.[12] He had published
a really absurd pamphlet against a physician in Basel.[13] I told Eppendorf of
my surprise that Hutten had had leisure to while away the time with such
things, given his illness and his straitened circumstances. Eppendorf replied
that Hutten relaxed his mind with jests of this kind. I said I would prefer it
if, in times like these, he had chosen a theme that demanded all the energy
of his genius, so as to pass on an honourable name to posterity. Eppendorf
replied that Hutten thought only of perfecting his style.[14] As I pondered
these questions about Hutten, as a true and honest friend would, Eppendorf
returned, reporting that Hutten was violently denouncing me, and was

* * * * *

affected his health, see eg Epp 597:54, 1169:19, 1248:14 (and Allen Ep 1248
n10), 1258:34, 1342:213–17, 228–31, and 576–81; *Adagia* II iii 65: *Herculanea bal-
nea* 'Hercules' baths' CWE 33 170–1.

10 Hutten arrived in Basel towards the end of November 1522, and left on January
18 (*Expostulatio* EB II 181:10, 60; C. Augustijn ASD IX-1 93:1n; cf Ep 1437:43–59).

11 Cf below 124 (Erasmus inquired whether Hutten had been able to travel from
Basel to Mulhouse on the public road).

12 Cf Ep 1378 above 31 n16.

13 Johann Roman Wonecker (cf CEBR III 463), a professor of medicine, was town
physician of Basel from 1493 to 1523. As rector of the university in the winter term 1522/23 he published shortly before Christmas anti-Reformation theses in scholastic Latin (cf Ep 1417:30–1). He was attacked in a pseudonymous
*Commentum seu lectura cuiusdam theologorum minimi super vnam seraphicam in-
timationem doctoris Joannis Romani Vuonneck rectoris Basiliensis* (ed H. Zwicker
Flugschriften aus den ersten Jahren der Reformation I [Halle 1906] 253–312). G.
Bossert (*Theologische Literaturzeitung* 32 (1907) 249 and *Flugschriften aus den
ersten Jahren der Reformation* 4 [Halle 1911] 361ff) thought that Hermannus
Buschius might have been the author. But C. Augustijn (ASD IX-1 125:53–4n)
suggests reasons for thinking that Hutten was the author.

14 Erasmus was uneasy with the uses to which Hutten put his felicitous style. 'If
only Hutten had kept his pen under control! I admire his gifts particularly' (Ep
1119:38–9). Hutten should devote 'that happy vein in both prose and verse' to
'happier subjects' (Ep 1195:157–61). Cf below 45.

preparing some sort of frightful book. This news was neither expected nor deserved, and the surprise unnerved me. I asked what all this was about; Eppendorf said Hutten was furious because he had not been allowed to speak with me. 'But,' I asked, 'did you not say that he accepted my request in good part?' 'True,' Eppendorf replied, 'but after leaving Basel, he began to take offence, and it seems that he cannot be placated.'

As word of this development was already spreading, Beatus Rhenanus came to express his concern. With my permission he summoned Eppendorf, and we three discussed what might be done.[15] I took the position that I could be held accountable for displaying a frame of mind at which no one could rightly take offence – but not for what this or that person suddenly began to think. 'My dear Eppendorf,' I said, 'you know that he has no cause to be angry with me about the interview.' They thought Hutten could be placated by the right sort of letter, before he published his book. I indicated it would be better for me to feign ignorance, for temperaments of his type rage all the more if someone attempts to calm them. Since both of them persisted in their opinion, I did write to Hutten, stating that I was not aware of having committed any evil against him.[16] If anything had been falsely reported to him, or if he were suspicious in any respect, let him expostulate with me privately, in a letter, for I had no doubt that I could satisfy him on every point. He ought also to consider whether what he was stirring up would serve our common studies, or the cause of the gospel, or his own interest, given the present state of his affairs.

My original instinct had been correct, for Eppendorf brought back a stinging response to my letter.[17] Hutten had long since written me off as a

* * * * *

15 There is no other record of this conversation. Beatus Rhenanus (1485–1547) studied with Gebwiler in his native Sélestat. After a few years at the University of Paris, where he became a confidant of Lefèvre d'Étaples, he returned to the Upper Rhine region, where, over two decades, he gained a reputation as an independent humanist scholar, working mainly in Basel. Here he became a collaborator and close friend of Erasmus, who entrusted him with editorial and also personal matters, so much so that Beatus became his *alter ego* (Ep 1207:76). He seems to have been sympathetic to the Reformation. Living during the last two decades of his life in Sélestat, where he produced his major works (on German history), he made no objection to Catholic ceremonies; but three evangelical ministers from Strasbourg attended him on his deathbed.

16 Ep 1356 (3 April 1523); cf Brunfels *Responsio* 327:11–128.

17 Hutten's reply to Erasmus' letter of 3 April is not extant, but Erasmus refers to it in the *Spongia*: see Augustijn ASD IX-1 101:52n.

timid soul, trembling with dread even before an attack. He now specified his charges:[18] I gave preference to Capito over Reuchlin in Hebraic studies;[19] I censured Hutten himself, in a letter to Hoogstraten;[20] I besmirched Reuchlin by accusing him of lying;[21] I flattered the theologians at Louvain and

* * * * *

18 These are the charges detailed in Hutten's *Expostulatio*.
19 On Capito and Reuchlin, cf *Expostulatio* EB II 199:8–200:9 / K 79–80; below 64. Wolfgang Faber Capito (c 1478–1541), from Hagenau in Alsace, a member of the humanist circle in Basel, had studied nominalist theology at the University of Freiburg. As cathedral preacher and professor of theology at the University of Basel (from 1515), he became a close associate of Erasmus, who praised his 'extraordinary skills in the three tongues' (Epp 456:190–1, 541:111–2), and relied on his Hebrew scholarship. Although attracted to Luther's teachings as early as 1518, Capito agreed in 1520 to serve as cathedral preacher and theological adviser for Albert of Brandenburg, cardinal-archbishop of Mainz. His evangelical leanings led him to Strasbourg (1523), where he became provost of the collegiate church of St Thomas, and collaborated with Martin Bucer in reforming the city. Capito's new loyalties taxed his relationship with Erasmus. Though critical of Hutten for having published the *Expostulatio* (Ep 1368:32–9), he too urged Erasmus to declare publicly what Capito thought were his true feelings, in favour of the evangelical party (Ep 1374:69–71). Erasmus was soon accusing Capito of instigating Eppendorf and Brunfels to attack his *Spongia* (Ep 1485:1–3).
20 On Hoogstraten cf *Expostulatio* EB II 192:8–193:1 / K 71–2; below 54–7. A native of Brabant, Jacob of Hoogstraten (d 1527) studied at Louvain, entered the Dominican order, and moved to Cologne, where he became professor of theology at the university. As prior of the Cologne Dominicans, and inquisitor for the archdioceses of Cologne, Mainz, and Trier, he backed Johann Pfefferkorn's attack on Reuchlin (April 1511). In August 1519 Erasmus urged Hoogstraten to moderation in his dealings with Reuchlin, but was also critical of the *Epistolae obscurorum virorum*, naming Hutten as one of the authors (Ep 1006:67–8). Hoogstraten, who was instrumental in having Luther's writings condemned by the Cologne theology faculty, sought to link Erasmus with Luther. Erasmus met with Hoogstraten (early 1520) and achieved a partial reconciliation, which he tried to keep intact by suppressing *Hochstratus ovans*, a scurrilous, anonymous lampoon. Hutten was also offended by Erasmus' reference to Hoogstraten, in a letter published in April 1523, as 'an old acquaintance of mine at least, if not a friend' (Ep 1342:669–71).
21 On Reuchlin cf *Expostulatio* EB II 201:10–202:17 / K 81–2; below 65–8. Johann Reuchlin (1454/5–1522), born in Pforzheim, studied in Freiburg, Basel, and Paris. After law degrees from Orléans, Poitiers, and Tübingen, he entered the service of Count Eberhard the Bearded of Württemberg, residing from 1483 mainly in Stuttgart. He alternated assignments as imperial counsellor and triumvir of the Swabian league with periods of teaching Greek and Hebrew at Tübingen and Ingolstadt. Reuchlin became famous as a champion of Hebrew learning and of the Cabala. His public opposition to Johann Pfefferkorn's

elsewhere;[22] finally, I have suddenly deserted the cause of the gospel and directed all my energy towards overthrowing it.[23] He also promised that his book, sent with a servant, would be here within three days. But this copy, which many here have now seen, went first to Zürich,[24] so that I heard from others what Hutten had written against me.

I replied in writing to each of these charges, reminding him of many things that were no less in his interest than in mine.[25] He answered a little more mildly – Franz von Sickingen was dead by this time.[26] Although the pamphlet had already been sent to the printer, he suggested that if I kept silent we could have peace and friendship between us as before.[27] At last a copy of the pamphlet was delivered, neither paginated nor

* * * * *

campaign to suppress Hebrew literature embroiled him in controversy not just with Pfefferkorn but also with the Cologne Dominicans, including Hoogstraten (Ep 290). Erasmus had some sympathy for Reuchlin's position (Ep 636:31–5), but no sympathy for Jews, nor for the Cabala (see Heiko A. Oberman *The Roots of Antisemitism in the Age of Renaissance and Reformation* [Philadelphia 1984] 38–41). By contrast, Hutten, with Crotus Rubeanus, parodied Reuchlin's scholastic foes in the first edition of *Epistolae obscurorum virorum*. Hutten was probably the author of *Reuchlin's Triumph* (*Triumphus Capnionis*), published in 1518 against Erasmus' advice (Epp 636:29–30n, 923:34–5).

22 Cf *Expostulatio* EB II 206:7–17 / K 86; below 69. See also C. Augustijn's list of favourable references to the two universities in Erasmus' letters, ASD IX-1 147:604–5n.
23 Cf *Expostulatio* EB II 216:7–10 / K 96; below 87.
24 Brunfels questions what Erasmus says on this point: *Responsio* 327:43–328:2.
25 This letter, perhaps the one mentioned in Ep 1934:275–7, is lost. For its contents see below 137.
26 Franz von Sickingen (1481–1523) inherited castle Ebernburg from his father Schwicker, chief steward to the Count Palatine of the Rhine. He used his substantial income to hire mercenaries for his private feuds. Although his activities as a robber knight brought him under the imperial ban, Sickingen was kept on the Hapsburg payroll, to prevent his being hired by the French king; after his service to the Swabian League in a war against Duke Ulrich of Württemberg (1519), Charles V named him an imperial councillor. Under Hutten's influence, Sickingen offered protection to Luther (January 1520). In 1522, he followed Hutten's call for a war against the ecclesiastical princes; by invading the archbishopric of Trier, he hoped to strike a blow for the Reformation, and also to improve the standing of the imperial knights. Defeated, he was soon besieged by foes in another of his castles, where he died on 7 May 1523. Although Sickingen had sheltered Hutten in the Ebernburg (fall 1522), Erasmus claimed that he failed to back Hutten in the end (cf below 47).
27 This letter is lost. For a reference to it, below 137 and Ep 1934:277–83.

bound.[28] Even though it was too late for Hutten to prevent its being printed, I was nonetheless seriously urged to send him (good heavens!) some money, so as to get him not to publish it. I was firm in saying that although it would have been better had a book of this type never been written, since it had left the author's hands and was already being scattered about, it ought to be printed, and the sooner the better. I even offered to provide the funds if Hutten agreed.[29] In the meantime Hutten had moved on to Zürich.[30] From there he suggested that we blame his behaviour on Homer's Ate, for he would henceforth act more prudently.[31] After this we had no further communication. That things happened as I have said, the best witness is Eppendorf, for he knows from my writings and from many intimate conversations that I maintained an honest and friendly affection for Hutten, the last person that I thought likely to begin hostilities. Where, then, is that inhumanity of mine that Hutten harps on?[32] How have I shown contempt for such a great man?[33] When have I shown fear of what he calls a rebuke too furious to be sustained?[34] I did ask, politely, that he not gratuitously burden with odium a friend already burdened more than enough; I did not refuse an interview, if he had something serious to discuss.[35] I offered him my service as a friend, even financial help, so far as my straitened circum-

* * * * *

28 Cf Allen Ep 1934:322–7.
29 Cf Epp 1383:2–13, 1384:74, 1397:6–7, 1437:51–5; Allen Ep 1934:294–338. Ep 1437:45–7 seems to suggest that Eppendorf initiated this attempt at extortion, but Erasmus maintains in Ep 1383:2–8 and Allen Ep 1934:336–8 that Hutten was at least in agreement with the plan (below 141). In his 3 April 1523 letter to Hutten (Ep 1356:55–60), Erasmus suggests that Hutten's intention is to 'plunder' him.
30 Hutten probably arrived in Zürich in mid-June (C. Augustijn ASD IX-1 106:76n), where, as Erasmus knew (Ep 1376:30–3), he had support from Zwingli. Erasmus was still 'constantly exchanging letters' with Hutten (Ep 1437:77–8); for traces of these letters, see the introduction to Ep 1356.
31 This letter is lost; cf Expostulatio EB II 239:1–3 / K 117. Ate, a daughter of Zeus (cf Homer Iliad 9.90–133, 11.502–12), was the personification of infatuation or moral blindness because she failed to distinguish right from wrong (cf Adagia I vii 13: Ira omnium tardissime senescit 'Resentment is the last thing to grow old' CWE 32 72–3).
32 Cf Expostulatio EB II 181:18–9 / K 60.
33 Cf Expostulatio EB II 182:12–16 / K 61.
34 Cf Expostulatio EB 185:4–7 / K 64.
35 For Erasmus' refusal to meet with Hutten, above n6. Public association with Hutten would have compromised Erasmus' standing with Catholic patrons, at a time when he hoped to have some influence with church authorities, including Pope Adrian VI (Ep 1352).

stances might allow.[36] In the end, as a way of calming his spirits, I agreed to an interview, even if he had nothing serious to discuss. For this task a gracious and well-spoken mediator was chosen – a man who, being of noble birth, and a kinsman, would have been able to mitigate any unpleasantness that might have arisen.

There is, then, no room for Hutten's constant complaint, 'you refused a meeting.'[37] Far from being unwilling to meet with him, I would at the time not have considered it a burden to ride as far as Constance, if I felt it really mattered so much to Hutten.[38] For I highly valued our friendship, mediated by the Muses some years ago, and since confirmed by certain mutual services. My writings bear witness to the fact that it was in no ordinary manner that I loved Hutten's genius and talent.[39] His habit of taking liberties I attributed to his youth, hoping it would be corrected over time. In his writings I saw a rich, brilliant, and ready store of words – in a word, the gifts of nature; I hoped that reason, judgment, and good sense would come with age, practice, and study.[40] Anyone who considers the state of my affairs at the time (and now as well), and the state of Hutten's affairs, will think that I was prudent in begging off from a conversation that would have meant little to him, but a lot of trouble for me; it is not the one who begged off who will seem discourteous, but the one who took offence. But Hutten attacks me with my own words: Have I not commended his sincerity, saying it is not his custom to burden anyone with ill will?[41] Indeed I did commend his uprightness, for Hutten, unlike those who were publishing books anonymously or under fictitious names, signed his works, and thus cast no suspicion on anyone besides himself.[42] But how is this relevant? My

* * * * *

36 See above n29.
37 Cf *Expostulatio* EB II 180:11 / K 59, EB II 182:2–3 / K 61, EB II 183:7 / K 62.
38 Erasmus blamed Eppendorf for the fact that no meeting actually took place: Eppendorf had not only failed to inform Hutten about Erasmus' intolerance for room-stoves (cf Allen Ep 1934:275–83), he also did not tell Hutten that Erasmus was subsequently willing to see him anyway (see above 39). But as C. Augustijn notes (ASD IX-1 97:26n), Erasmus himself is the only witness that he and Eppendorf had a subsequent conversation about Hutten's coming to see him after all.
39 For praise of Hutten, a 1516 note on Thess 1:2 (see Holeczek *Novum Instrumentum* 555); Epp 1341A:1050–1, 1356:33–66.
40 Cf Ep 1009:79–83. For Erasmus, writing and speaking effectively required not just natural talent, but also prudence, judgment, and good sense (cf below 132; see also Hoffmann *Rhetoric and Theology* 112, 139–42, 191–200).
41 Cf *Expostulatio* EB II 184:1–3 / K 63, EB II 194:2–3 / K 73.
42 Cf Ep 1195:150–61

praise for his sincerity ought to have reminded Hutten to be true to himself. If someone extols a wine as excellent, will he afterwards be accounted a worthless judge if the wine turns sour?

Would Hutten had proven me a worthless judge only in respect to his sincerity! 'Of my own free will,' he says, 'I would have abstained from the pleasure of having your company, had I seen that it would have burdened you with odium.'[43] Since he was prepared to do this voluntarily – for it was clear that a meeting between us would cause trouble for me - why is he indignant that I courteously requested what he intended to do without even being asked? I do not ask around as to the identity of Hutten's enemies, nor do I fear their ill will towards me. In my case, however, reports of our meeting would have gotten to the pope in Rome, to the emperor in Spain, to Brabant, where my enemies are active, and to England, where there is no lack of those who would make of me a Lutheran against my will.[44] If there is even a grain of truth in a report, these people gladly invent much more. It was the odium of such rumours that I feared, as Hutten could easily see from my letter to Laurinus.[45] 'But,' Hutten asks, 'what aid may one expect in time of need from a friend who even in good times shuns the odium of a meeting?'[46] I say true friends are those who know how to preserve themselves for when they are needed, by avoiding a dangerous occasion from which a friend would derive no advantage. In any case I am not discussing whether times are good for Hutten; I would certainly wish him better luck, if he summons from within himself a spirit worthy of good fortune. He says everyone in Basel wished him well: 'One magistrate after another comes to call, and men of every rank crowd my door, as if vying to see me; only Erasmus keeps his house closed.'[47] But has anyone ever seen me leave my house in wintertime, just to visit someone? Besides, I have no need to praise the kindness of this city's magistrates, for I have experienced it more than once.[48] They were indeed kind to let Hutten in, but kinder still when they let him depart.[49] I will add this to their praise: they prefer their

* * * * *

43 Cf *Expostulatio* EB II 184:5–8 / K 63.
44 See above n35.
45 Cf Ep 1342, published in April 1523; Erasmus may have in mind lines 650–706, or 754–66.
46 Cf *Expostulatio* EB II 184:13–6 / K 63.
47 Cf *Expostulatio* EB II 184:19–185:2 / K 63–4.
48 Cf Ep 1342:247–51.
49 Cf *Aktensammlung zur Geschichte der Basler Reformation* 6 vols (Basel 1921–1950) I 46:33.

services to be kept secret rather than broadcast – such is their modesty. If only Hutten were to conduct himself in such a way as to enjoy always the kindness of good men! But those who welcomed him as a guest warned against the sort of speech that could incite tumults;[50] how much less would they have approved pamphlets of the same ilk!

There are people who do not care if ill will be directed against them; they are often men of no account, or men powerful enough to be disdainful. But what has that to do with me? For having nothing but my innocence to protect me, I can scarcely defend myself against ill will. You will cease to wonder how much I fear even a little bit of ill will (than which no plague is more noxious) when you consider that the cardinal of Mainz some time ago dismissed Hutten from his household[51] for no other reason than his wish not to be burdened with odium on his account. And Franz von Sickingen, did he not send Hutten away for the same reason?[52] And why do Hutten's closest kinsmen prefer that he not live on the family estate, unless they too fear odium?[53] People are hardly in the dark about these things – and yet Erasmus is the only one who fears odium!

* * * * *

50 For a reply to these remarks on Hutten's behalf, see Brunfels *Responsio* 328:18–32.
51 Following Hutten's publication of *Vadiscus siue Trias Romana* (April 1520), Pope Leo x requested that Hutten be dismissed from the court at Mainz, and Archbishop Albert replied that he had done so: EB I Epp CLXXVI, CLXXIX, CLXXX:25, CLXXXI, CLXXXIII; cf Allen Ep 1135:2n. According to Brunfels *Responsio* 328:33–40, Hutten left Mainz on his own initiative.
   Albert of Brandenburg (1490–1545), ordained priest in 1513, was consecrated archbishop of Magdeburg (1514), and archbishop-elector of Mainz (1514). Elevated to the college of cardinals in 1518, he backed Charles v in the imperial election of 1519, and thus gained favour with the Hapsburgs. A generous patron of the arts and letters, he attracted to his court in Mainz humanists like Hutten and Capito. Though Erasmus declined his repeated invitations, he dedicated to Albert his *Ratio* of 1517 (cf Ep 745). In the controversies of the Reformation era, Albert pursued, into the 1530s, a policy of mediation between the Catholic and Lutheran estates of the Holy Roman Empire. From 1538, he was among the Catholic princes who rejected compromise.
52 For a different view, Brunfels *Responsio* 328:41–329:4. When Sickingen invaded the archbishopric of Trier (fall 1521), Hutten, his guest, was too ill to participate in the campaign. When his attack was repulsed, Sickingen had to prepare his castles for defence; Hutten, unfit for combat, had to leave (cf EB II 473:12–17; Holborn *Ulrich von Hutten* 182).
53 Cf Brunfels *Responsio* 329:5–11. For Hutten's complicated relations with various members of his extended family, see the references in Kaegi and Holborn.

To be sure, a man whom kings and princes have admitted to their presence is not to be despised,[54] and the dignity of Hutten's name will not be lessened by anything I do. But avoiding ill will is not the same as being contemptuous – unless perhaps I have been contemptuous in declining an invitation from the king of France,[55] who wants me to come as much as I have wanted to live there for the sake of my health.[56] It was fear of ill will that held me back, for relations between the king and the emperor remain unsettled. When I was in Bruges a short time ago, I declined private conversation with a king who loves me,[57] not from contempt, but rather because I hoped (albeit in vain) to avoid incurring ill will from the Romanists.[58] Would that Hutten had moderated his course in like fashion! Had he done so, he would now be honoured among the great – as he was, for the sake of his prince, when he was received at the French court[59] – and everyone could cultivate his friendship without fear of incurring ill will.

* * * * *

54 Emperor Maximilian I crowned Hutten poet laureate in 1517, about the time that he was admitted to the service of Albert of Mainz.

55 In 1523 Francis I and Charles V were at war; as Erasmus notes in his letter to Laurinus, he was 'bound by oath' to the emperor (Ep 1342:626–37).

56 Francis I, king of France from 1515 until his death in 1547, patronized humanists from early in his reign. In 1530 he endowed five professorships in Paris, two in Greek, two in Hebrew, and one in mathematics; this was the historical nucleus of the modern Collège de France. Erasmus had declined an invitation from the king in 1517 (Epp 522:52–8, 725:3–10), but around this time he advertised an interest in living in France (Epp 1319:17–20, 1342:590–649). These two letters were followed by another invitation from the king, with a postscript in his own hand (Ep 1375), but Erasmus again declined, citing 'the confusion of the age' (Ep 1400:3–9).

57 Cf Epp 1342:84–92, 1263:24, 1228:35–9; Allen Ep 1228:30n.
Christian II (1481–1559) inherited in 1513 the throne of Denmark, which, since the Union of Kalmar (1379), included the realms of Sweden and Norway; in 1515 he married Charles V's sister Isabella. After putting down a rebellion in Sweden, he had nearly eighty of the leaders executed in Stockholm (1520). The Swedes rebelled once more; in 1523, they would choose Gustavus Vasa as their king. In the summer of 1521, Christian travelled to the Netherlands (summer 1521) to ask his brother-in-law for help against the Swedes.

58 Christian II was thought even then to harbour the Lutheran sympathies that subsequently became apparent.

59 In December 1517 (Epp 744:52n, 810:6–8) Hutten was sent by Albert of Mainz to Paris, to offer Francis I his support in the imperial election, in exchange for a French pension. But Albert then changed his mind, and, in return for other favours from the Hapsburgs, voted for Charles V in the 1519 election.

As it is, look at the hateful reason he has contrived for my refusing a conversation! You might say our knight was born not for jousting but for slandering.[60] He claims I knew what he wanted to confront me about, so that if I avoided speaking with him it was because of a guilty conscience.[61] But whence comes such authority to this young man Hutten, that I, at my age, would not be able to hold my own against him? Has he suddenly become Cato the Censor?[62] There was a time when in speaking to me he observed a respectful modesty, more fitting to his years than the impudence of tongue and pen he now displays.[63] And how was I to guess that he had something about which he wanted to confront me?

While Hutten was in Sélestat, his letter to me says, he charged Beatus Rhenanus to tell me that he found something wanting in me.[64] But Beatus Rhenanus did not write me a single word from Sélestat, nor, having returned from there after Hutten had already left Basel, did he ever mention that he had spoken with Hutten. This I found out for the first time from Hutten's letter from Mulhouse. By chance, Eppendorf and Beatus were present as I read it. When I came to this passage, I turned to Beatus: 'you are being made a party to the case,' I said, 'you have need of a lawyer.' Beatus freely admitted he had never said anything, and would explain why. After thinking for a bit, he recounted the matter to us in such a way that I had to acknowledge a lack of German candour in Hutten, for he had cleverly manipulated things so he would able to accuse me of acting in bad faith. He did not actually charge Beatus with anything, not in private nor in earnest, nor did he tell him anything I needed to know. He

* * * * *

60 'Not for jousting but for slandering.' The Latin word translated as 'knight' (*eques*) literally means 'horseman.'

61 Cf *Expostulatio* EB 185:4–7 / K 64:23.

62 Not to be confused with Cato the younger, a Roman senator who took his own life rather than submit to the rule of Julius Caesar, M. Porcius Cato (234–149 BC) made the Roman office of *censor* a byword for the upholding of traditional Roman moral standards. He hated Greek influence on Roman culture, and advocated the utter destruction of Rome's great enemy, Carthage. Erasmus edited the *Distichia Catonis* (CWE 29 xxxviii–xxxix), and included in his *Adagia* Juvenal's 'Cato the Third' (*Adagia* I viii 89: *Tertius Cato* CWE 32 172–3: 'an ironical expression ... used of extremely strait-laced men who were severe critics of the way others live').

63 Cf below 118.

64 Hutten's letter from Mulhouse, in response to Erasmus' letter of April 3, has been lost (cf above n27). On his way to Basel, Hutten had visited Beatus Rhenanus in Sélestat (cf Allen Ep 1331:59n; Ep 1496:14)

had merely declared, to all present, that I was not very favourably disposed towards Luther. He interpreted this as fear and said he would inspire me with courage. These were the kind of things he told Beatus, thinking he was about to return to Basel, but without any threats, nor any indication that he was sharpening his pen against me. Moreover, he spoke to Beatus not in private, but in the uproar of a company, amid laughing and joking. At other times, he spoke of me so respectfully that Beatus could not have suspected the coming tragedy.

Subsequently, as Beatus' affairs kept him longer in his home town, Hutten, as if releasing him from a charge, said that he himself would soon be going to Basel, to fill my timid soul with courage.[65] So it was that Beatus said nothing to me, not suspecting the evil about to arise. Nor did it have to come to this, had Hutten and I chanced to speak, for I could have calmed his anger with ten words. In any event Beatus did not return to Basel until some time after Hutten had left. Greeting me in the presence of several friends, including Ludwig Baer,[66] he asked how I was getting along with Hutten. 'Very well,' I answered, for at the time I was wholly convinced of this.[67] Later, when he came by to visit me a second time, Eppendorf showed me a letter Hutten had written to him, asking him to warn me not to inveigh against Luther: He was very well disposed towards me, Hutten said, but he could not treat me as a friend unless I refrained from attacking Luther. Since at the time I had no intention of attacking Luther in writing, it seemed likely that Hutten and I would remain on peaceful terms. Yet, without anything new happening between us in the meantime, the astonishing news soon arrived that Hutten, fired up for battle, was writing something against Erasmus.[68] I have gone into some detail, to make it clear

* * * * *

65 Cf above 41–2.
66 Ludwig Baer of Basel (1479–1554) studied in Paris, where he was a fellow at the Collège de Sorbonne, and earned his doctorate from the faculty of theology. Returning to Basel in 1513, he taught theology, serving twice as dean of the faculty, and twice as rector of the university. A distinguished academic theologian, he upheld Paris' scholastic traditions, while remaining open to humanist scholarship. When Catholic worship was abolished in Basel (1529), Baer, a foe of the Reformation, moved to Freiburg, in Catholic (and Hapsburg) Breisgau; here he was offered a professorship at the university, but declined. He advised Erasmus on a number of his publications, including the *De libero arbitrio* (Epp 1419, 1420, 1423:47–53). Baer also attempted to mediate between Erasmus and Hutten.
67 Cf below 52; Allen Ep 1934:284–6.
68 Cf above 40–1; Ep 1356:1–5, 1437:43–5.

that I had heard nothing from Beatus, and could not have suspected Hutten's animosity. Once this foundation is removed, the whole structure of false accusations built on it by Hutten comes crashing to the ground.[69] Why did he not give his loyal friend Eppendorf[70] here in Basel the same instructions he says he gave Beatus in Sélestat? Beatus, as I have said, reported that Hutten's disposition towards me was calm and peaceful. For I truly liked Hutten, and had I known that suspicion was eating away at his mind, he would not have had to plead for a meeting; I myself would have nipped the evil in the bud, either in person or in writing. The things he wanted to confront me about were in any case mere trifles, as I will shortly explain.

Hutten says I betrayed a guilty conscience in my letter to Laurinus by using room-stoves as a pretext for not meeting with him, as if to avoid the charge of being inhospitable.[71] My answer is that I gladly take occasion to mention friends in my writings; since this letter was to be published, I chose, among the many reasons I had for declining to meet with him, only the one that had nothing hateful about it – even though Hutten in one of his letters calls it hateful.[72] He says too that he often tried to draw me out for a talk by walking past my house, and that this cannot have escaped my notice.[73] Ridiculous! I do sit at the window in the wintertime, to see if anyone passes by, but why should he have to draw me out? Contrary to the custom in Basel, I almost always keep my door open; he could have come in and asked to speak with me. Even if the door were closed he could have knocked.

'But you begged me not to come visit you,' he says.[74] Now he is suddenly bashful! Is it, then, more respectful to write such a book against an unsuspecting friend than to insist on visiting him against his will? A man who writes as many letters as he does should at least have remonstrated

* * * * *

69 Cf below 88.
70 Here and elsewhere, Erasmus calls Eppendorf Hutten's Achates, referring to the faithful companion of Aeneas, whose name stood for loyalty (Virgil *Aeneid* 1.188 and 312, 6.158, 8.521, 10.332, 12.384). Cf below 90; Ep 1437:92; Allen Ep 1934:127.
71 Ep 1342:764–6; cf *Expostulatio* EB II 180:17–181:9 / K 59, 60.
    Marcus Laurinus (1488–1546) of Bruges was educated at Louvain, and earned a doctorate in civil and canon law at Bologna. Returning to Bruges, where he became dean of St Donatian, he remained for many years a faithful friend and correspondent of Erasmus.
72 This letter is lost; above n25.
73 Cf *Expostulatio* EB II 186:4–6 / K 65.
74 Cf *Expostulatio* EB II 181:2–3 / K 60.

with me by letter before beginning this tragedy.[75] Or does he make a practice of attacking friends without warning, reserving for his enemies the
courtesy of advance notice?[76] He will perhaps say that he gave Eppendorf
an inkling of his intentions in my regard. How was I to guess this, when
Eppendorf firmly stated that he had detected no sign of estrangement in
Hutten? Eppendorf said so frequently, not just to me but also in the presence of others, including Beatus, Glareanus, and Botzheim, and even now
he does not deny that this was his true opinion.[77] You see, then, dear reader,
that I did nothing that was impolite, haughty, unfriendly, or prompted by
a guilty conscience.[78] But suppose that I did somehow violate the laws of
the Graces. Since Hutten admits that I was a friend like almost no other,[79]
and that all of Germany is greatly indebted to my labours,[80] should he not
have confronted me in private before publishing a book like this, the most
virulent he has ever written against anyone? Yet he calls it a mere 'remonstrance'; indeed, in one letter he calls it 'very mild,' in view of the frightful

* * * * *

75 Cf 53; Ep 1356:47–52 and 74.
76 As with Hutten's *Invectiva in Aleandrum, Invectiva in Marinum Caracciolum*, and
    Invectiva in Lutheromastigas sacerdotes, all written in March 1521 (cf EB II 16:19–
    33, 20:24, 21:9).
77 Cf above 49; Allen Ep 1934:284–6. On Beatus see above n15.
    Henricus Glareanus (1488–1563) was born at Mollis, canton Glarus, Switzer-
    land. From 1506 he studied theology at the University of Cologne, but his
    humanist Latin poems won him recognition from Maximilian I as poet lau-
    reate (1512). A supporter of Reuchlin, he left Cologne for Basel (1514), where
    he was welcomed by Erasmus. Glareanus directed private residential schools
    (Basel, Paris, Basel again, Freiburg). He also edited classical texts, and pub-
    lished works in several liberal arts disciplines; he gained particular recogni-
    tion as a musical theorist, and his major geographical work, the *Descriptio Hel-
    vetiae*, makes his beloved Swiss Confederation the centre of Europe. Though
    at first open to Reformation ideas, Glareanus, like Erasmus and Ludwig Baer,
    left for Freiburg when Catholic worship in Basel was abolished (1529).
    Johann von Botzheim (c 1480–1535), from an Alsatian noble family, earned a
    doctorate in canon and civil law from the University of Bologna. From 1510
    he was a canon at the cathedral of Constance, where he made his house 'a real
    home of the Muses' (Ep 1342:375–8). Erasmus, who visited him in September
    1522, remained a lifelong friend, and wrote the *Catalogus lucubrationum* of Jan-
    uary 1523 at his request. Botzheim was summoned to Rome in 1524 to answer
    for his Lutheran leanings, but when the Zwinglian Reformation triumphed in
    Constance (1527), he followed the cathedral chapter into exile in Überlingen.
78 *Expostulatio* EB II 181:13–4, 182:16, 185:4–5 / K 60, 61, 64.
79 Cf below 133; *Expostulatio* EB II 184:3–5, 240:7–8 / K 63, 118.
80 Cf below 133–4; *Expostulatio* EB II 195:13–8 / K 75.

import of the issue.[81] So where are the mutual friends he says are aggrieved that I refused to see him?[82] Eppendorf knows I did not refuse to see him, and he disapproves of what Hutten has done; this Hutten cannot deny, for he himself says as much in a letter to me.[83] But enough about my 'refusal' of a conversation with Hutten.

Now let us take up those misdeeds of mine that so greatly enraged Hutten's spirit, gentle as it is by nature. They must be truly vile, for, as he admits, ours was no ordinary friendship. He acknowledges too I have deserved great praise for my service to the cause of scholarship – indeed, he gives me more credit than I would want to claim. For himself he claims the prize for truthfulness,[84] as befits a German, and for humanity, as befits a man of letters.[85] He says too that, as befits a brave and prudent knight, he has not allowed anyone to incite him against a friend. I am sure he knows as well not to accept as true anything that comes from the lips of scandalmongers, by whom whole kingdoms have been brought down. Nor does it escape him how reluctant one must be to break with or harbour suspicions against a true and proven friend. Finally, since he also prides himself on good manners, he knows the respect a young man owes to a friend who is old and grey, who has been and still is worthy of praise for what he does.[86] For I labour incessantly, and to what end, if not to promote the cause of the gospel?

I must, therefore, have committed some horrible crime. For this paragon of humanity, in violation of all the laws of the Graces,[87] and neglectful of my kindnesses to him, and of the respect he owes a man grown grey in the service of the common good, and without the courtesy of advance notice, as is practised among open enemies,[88] has published against me a book that

* * * * *

81 This letter is lost; see above n31.
82 Cf *Expostulatio* EB II 180:9–11 / K 59.
83 This may be the letter quoted below 137; Ep 1437:79–82; Allen Ep 1934:339–43.
84 See below 57; *Expostulatio* EB II 193:1–194:2 / K 72–3.
85 Cf *Expostulatio* EB II 195:1–2; K 74.
86 Cf below 133–4.
87 Cf Erasmus' description of paintings in the house of Botzheim (above n77), Ep 1342:383–5: 'In another place were the nine sisters of Apollo [the Muses] singing, elsewhere the [three] naked Graces, a symbol of simple good will and friendship without feigning.' Cf *Adagia* II vii 50: *Nudae Gratiae* 'Naked are the Graces' CWE 34 25; *Adagia* I ii 85: *Expertes invidentiae Musarum fores* 'The doors of the Muses are free from envy' CWE 31 217.
88 See n75.

is fraught with acrimonious reproaches, not to mention lies and insults. I
do not gainsay his claim to truthfulness, but the matter itself indicates that
in attacking me he followed the advice of a most worthless counsellor.[89] Let
us now hear the terrible charges laid against me;[90] after disposing of them I
shall come to the worst of all, namely, the charge that having formerly been
a champion of the gospel, I have suddenly changed sides, and now bend all
my efforts to subvert Christ and the gospel.[91] (Be it noted that the arrival
of Hutten's book found me here toiling with all my heart to advance the
cause of the gospel, a labour from which I have never taken a rest, even in
these tumultuous and dangerous times).[92] Here is the first charge.[93] Among
my published letters there is one to Jacob Hoogstraten that begins: 'For
some time now, as I read ...'[94] Anyone who has time to read it will see at
once that what Hutten says about this letter is shame-faced calumny. For I
remonstrate with Hoogstraten – for attacking Reuchlin with a bitterness that
ill becomes a theologian,[95] for the hateful reproaches he directed against the
incomparable Count of Neuenahr,[96] and for attacking me, for no reason, in
the book about the Cabala that he wrote against Reuchlin.[97] In making my

* * * * *

89 A reference to Eppendorf; cf below 84.
90 Cf *Expostulatio* EB II 202:5–7 / K 82.
91 Cf *Expostulatio* EB II 186:14–187:4, 214:17ff / K 65–6, 94ff.
92 From April 1523 Erasmus was at work on the *Paraphrasis in Lucam*, which was
    being printed in June and was published in August; cf Ep 1381.
93 Cf *Expostulatio* EB II 192:8–191:1 / K 71–8.
94 Ep 1006; on Hoogstraten, see above n20.
95 Ep 1006:59–62
96 Ep 1006:163–4. Hoogstraten's *Apologia secunda* (Cologne: sons of H. Quentel,
    1519) was a point-by-point refutation of Neuenahr's *Epistolae trium illustrium
    virorum* (Cologne: E. Cervicornus, May 1518).
    Count Hermann von Neuenahr (c 1492–1530) was already a canon at the cathe-
    dral of Cologne when he matriculated at the university (1504), prior to a pe-
    riod of study in Italy. As provost of the cathedral chapter and thus chancel-
    lor of the university (from 1524) he promoted humanist studies; he defended
    Reuchlin, and sharply attacked Hoogstraten. He was also a close collaborator
    of the reform-minded Archbishop Hermann von Wied, whom he accompa-
    nied in 1530 to Augsburg, where he died of an illness contracted during the
    diet. Erasmus cherished Neuenahr's friendship, sought to mediate between
    him and Hoogstraten (Ep 1078), and sought his advice in his quarrel with
    Eppendorf (Allen Ep 1991:63–4).
97 Ep 1006:164–85. In his *Destructio cabalae seu cabalisticae perfidiae ab Ioanne Reuch-
    lin Capnione iampridem in lucem editae* (Cologne: sons of H. Quentel, April 1519),
    an attack on Reuchlin's *De arte cabalistica* (Hagenau: Th. Anshelm, March 1517),
    Hoogstraten criticized what Erasmus had said about marriage and divorce in

point, I do not think I left out any pertinent argument. But I offended Hutten by addressing Hoogstraten as 'Reverend Father' – as if indeed kings do not honour one another with their customary titles even in the midst of war.[98] Hutten accuses me of flattering Hoogstraten by the title, but no one else has thought so – indeed, some suspected I used the title in derision. Hutten was offended by my criticism of him in this letter, where, in reference to the savage attacks on Hoogstraten in letters penned by Hutten, together with Reuchlin, Hermannus Buschius, and the Count of Neuenahr,[99] I stated the following: 'The bitterness of them all I should have found quite insufferable, had I not previously read the things which seemed to have provoked them to this intemperate rage.'[100] These quotations from my letter are verbatim.

Who is so dense or so perverse as not to see that I was merely stating things from the point of view of Hoogstraten, to whom those letters will surely have seemed quite vicious? In fact, Hoogstraten gave me an opening that I used against him, for I told him that he by his own writings had given cause for acrimonious rejoinders of this kind. I made use of a similar ploy elsewhere, stating that I was ignorant of theology and incapable of making judgments.[101] But Hutten, not grasping (or pretending not to) that here too I was merely repeating what certain others say of me, so as to have a better argument against them, asks how it is that I have suddenly become ignorant of theology.[102] In fact, the best way of arguing is to take a spear hurled by

* * * * *

his annotation on Matt 19:8, but without mentioning his name (cf *Destructio cabalae* II 5–12).

98 Ep 1342:670; cf *Expostulatio* EB II 196:11–3 / K 76; see below 70.

99 The *Epistolae trium virorum* (above n96) included, among other attacks on Hoogstraten, letters to Neuenahr from Reuchlin, Hutten, and Buschius, and a letter from Neuenahr to Reuchlin.

Hermannus Buschius (c 1468–1534), from a Westphalian noble family, studied at Deventer, Heidelberg, Rome, Bologna, and Cologne. He taught rhetoric and poetry in many German cities, including Wittenberg (1502) and Leipzig (1503). At the University of Cologne (from 1507) he became a passionate defender of Reuchlin. As rector of the Latin school at Wesel, he wrote his major work, *Vallum Humanitatis* (Cologne: Nic. Caesar, 1518), a defence of humane letters. His friendship with Erasmus began through a joint meeting with Hutten and Reuchlin at Frankfurt (spring 1515). From 1521 Buschius was an ardent champion of Luther; for a time, Erasmus thought Buschius was the author of a tract against him published in 1523 (Epp 1383:32–6, 1466:29–30, 1523:108–10).

100 Ep 1006:67–73

101 Ep 1342:1090–2

102 *Expostulatio* EB II 221:6–11 / K 100

the foe and throw it back at him.[103] I know, Hutten will at this point call me
a trickster.[104] But in the art of rhetoric this is called 'counsel,' and without
understanding one cannot hope to become eloquent.[105] If Christ and the
apostles used arguments of this kind,[106] surely I may do so as well.

Hutten was angered even more by what I said next in my letter to
Hoogstraten: 'And so my feelings as I read were complex. At one moment
it was they whom I was sorry for, at another it was you, fearing from time
to time that fair-minded men of high standards might think that such bitter invective could not be directed against one who was entirely undeserving of it.'[107] Why should this bother him so? I clearly say that good, fair-
minded men will not think it likely that such letters were written against
a man who was utterly without fault. 'But,' Hutten says, 'you speak indirectly, using a figure of speech.'[108] Indeed so, for it suited the case I was
pleading. Yet Hutten has no grounds for complaint, for the point of my letter was to reproach Hoogstraten, not to blame Hutten for writing in an unrestrained, bombastic fashion. Hutten would perhaps have wanted me to
address Hoogstraten in this fashion: 'You filthy cesspool, how dare you defile men of heroic stature with your muck-filled books?' Such a style might
be fitting for Hutten, but not for Erasmus. If Hoogstraten could be brought
to see reason, then civility was appropriate; if not, the very mildness of my
reproach would do him more harm among good men than foul-mouthed
impudence.

Furthermore, the passage in question takes four men to task. So why
was Reuchlin not offended? (In his case I was upset not about what he wrote
against Hoogstraten, but rather about the fact that this fine old gentleman

* * * * *

103 The technical term for this rhetorical strategem was *abusio*; see *Adagia* I ii 4:
Clavum clavo pellere 'To drive out one nail by another' CWE 31:148–9; I ii 5: *Malo
nodo malus quaerendus cuneus* 'A hard wedge must be sought for a hard knot'
CWE 31:149–50.

104 As applied to the art of rhetoric, the normal sense of *artifex*, not intended here,
refers to a skilful orator (Quintilian *Institutio* 2.14.5).

105 For Quintilian, *consilium* is virtually synonymous with deliberative or persuasive speech (cf *Institutio* 2.4.41; 2.10.12).

106 C. Augustijn ASD IX-1 137:327–8n refers to what Erasmus says in the paraphrase on Matthew 22:21 CWE 45 306–7.

107 Ep 1006:73–8

108 Cf *Expostulatio* EB II 196:3–7 / K 75–6; see Ep 1167:182–93. Hutten sees Erasmus'
oblique speech and his use of hyperbole as evasive; Erasmus presents these
aspects of his style as what is required by a persuasive, deliberative discourse
that takes into account both sides of an argument (cf below 84, 96, 97, 98–9,
108, 110).

should be aroused to such a pitch of passion as his letter displays.)[109] And why was Hermannus Buschius not offended either? As for the Count of Neuenahr, a man of most discerning judgment, he was delighted with my letter and even thanked me for it,[110] something Hoogstraten never did. Finally, since the book containing my letter to Hoogstraten had already been published by the time Hutten came to Brabant, why did he not remonstrate with me about it then?[111] All of this is so clear that, as they say, a blind man could see it.[112] So what is the purpose of that torrent of words Hutten pours forth, about his calm and moderate diction, his marvellous truthfulness (on which he always insists), and my own frivolity and dissembling?[113] It was not at my instance that Hutten became Hoogstraten's enemy, for he wrote his *Triumphus Capnionis* against Hoogstraten before he ever laid eyes on me. What I did advise was that he hold the book back, as he did for two years.[114] Yet in the meantime, he says, I spoke about Hoogstraten with real bitterness[115] – one more example of my artfulness.

Before proceeding, I must warn the reader that the rhetorical structure of Hutten's pamphlet is made up of assumptions, fiction, allegations, and exaggerations. Instead of seasoning, he sprinkles on insults here and there. By assumption I mean a statement like this: 'Erasmus burdens Reuchlin with an accusation of perfidy.'[116] How shameless Hutten is! Equally shameless are the other charges he invents. For his reader might ask: Since Erasmus

* * * * *

109 For Reuchlin's letter to Neuenahr, EB *Addenda ad* 1 477–9.
110 Ep 1078:45–7; Cf Allen Ep 1078:38n.
111 Ep 1006 was included in the *Farrago nova epistolarum* (Basel: J. Froben, October 1519). Hutten came to see Erasmus in Louvain in June 1520; they discussed, among other things, the controversy with Hoogstraten; cf below 60.
112 Cf *Adagia* I viii 93: *Vel caeco appareat* CWE 32 174–5.
113 Cf *Expostulatio* EB II 192:16–1999:1 / K 72 par 59–78 par 83. Hutten had reason to say that Erasmus claimed licence for 'pretending, for the time being' ('*Simulandum,*' inquis, '*est pro tempore*': EB II 193:3 / K 75 par 73). In Erasmus' view, one could see from the Epistles of St Paul and from the words of Christ himself in the Gospels that 'the truth does not always have to be stated,' and that 'it makes a difference how it is stated' (cf below 97, 115–16, 131); see Hoffmann *Rhetoric and Theology* 123–4.
114 *Reuchlin's Triumph* was published in Hagenau in late 1518, under the pseudonym Eleutherius Bizenus (text in EB III 413–47, preface and postscript in EB I 238–8). When they first met (Mainz, August 1514), Erasmus advised Hutten to suppress the poem (cf below 136; Epp 636:29–30, 951:45–6).
115 Cf *Expostulatio* EB 194:19–195:1: *quem non hortatus es, ut in hunc stringeret calamum?* 'Whom have you not urged to sharpen the pen against him?'
116 Cf *Expostulatio* EB II 202:9 / K 82 par 97.

has in the past praised Reuchlin so highly, why has he suddenly changed his mind, so that he now seeks to blacken Reuchlin's reputation by accusing him of something so disgraceful? Here Hutten invents, as the reasons for my behaviour, a lack of human decency, and an envy that could not bear to hear Reuchlin called 'Germany's other eye.'[117] But, my dear Hutten, if you wish to be effective as an orator, what you assume must either be self-evident, or it must be proven with suitable arguments. Further, the case you are making must be one that seems probable, in light of the nature and the habits of the man accused. Hutten, however, often has me saying the kind of things that could be said in this controversy – not the kind of things I actually said. He does this for his own advantage, not for the sake of truth. This tactic might perhaps be allowed to those who write about the ancient past, a biographer of Alexander the Great for example. But one who writes about a recent event, for which there may be many witnesses, does not have the same right. Moreover, when he puts words in my mouth, he does not observe the rule of propriety, for he attributes to me language far more splendid and magnificent than I habitually employ. But then, although language ought to conform to the subject as a garment does to the body, for Hutten no topic is too trifling to be invested with words of tragic proportion. These words of warning will give the reader a better picture of Hutten's text.

Notice how he makes an unwarranted assumption right at the beginning, saying that I praised Hoogstraten. Where is the passage that praises him? In the letter to Hoogstraten that seems fawning to Hutten, I speak freely, and not without a few barbs.[118] Elsewhere, when I refer to Hoogstraten as an 'old acquaintance of mine if not a friend,' who can fail to see the irony?[119] But hear what Hutten alleges: 'This scoundrel, whom you now praise, you used to call by different names: a plague sent down by the wrath of God to make an end of good letters and men of genius; the ruin and destruction, indeed the pitiless destroyer, of sound learning; or the torch that set off the great blaze of our times, threatening to engulf all who are devoted to learning.'[120] Who will not recognize in such words the diction of Hutten, not Erasmus?

He says I used to encourage everyone to 'sharpen the pen' against Hoogstraten. Let him produce one such person and he has won! Surely he

* * * * *

117 Cf *Expostulatio* EB II 200:7–9 / K 82 par 88.
118 Cf *Expostulatio* EB II 194:11–4 / K 74 par 68, referring to Ep 1006.
119 Ep 1342:671
120 *Expostulatio* EB II 194:19–195:3 / K 74 par 69.

plays the rhetorician when he says that he will, out of decency, keep back the letters I wrote him that were full of murderous thoughts.[121] The effect is of course to allow greater scope for suspicion. I am not adverse to having my letters published, so long as all of them are published, for they will prove conclusively that I never made a pact with the Lutherans. As for Hoogstraten, I have long been put off by the arrogance of his disposition, hostile to good letters, born to incite tumult, and avid for the kind of fame one gains by bringing others down.[122] I have never sought the man's friendship, nor have I wanted to engage in a feud with him, lest it take time from my studies.

So much for written words. As for words spoken among friends, or in drinking bouts, surely it is boorish to repeat what neither the speaker nor the listeners can properly remember.[123] A man's true opinion comes out when things are discussed in earnest. I wrote to Reuchlin (even before meeting him) that he and his friends should observe greater moderation in attacking Hoogstraten;[124] this was an expression of good will for Reuchlin, not for Hoogstraten. If Reuchlin made a habit of pouring out his secrets to Hutten, I'm sure he will have shown him these letters. When the count of Neuenahr wrote to ask if I thought he ought to give up his feud with Hoogstraten, who had promised an apology, I advised him to forgive the injury in a Christian spirit.[125] Later, after Edward Lee's bitter attack, Neuenahr gave me the same advice, urging that I deal with Lee as he, at my suggestion, had dealt with Hoogstraten.[126] All of this can be seen from our correspondence.

* * * * *

121 Cf *Expostulatio* EB II 195:1–3 / K 74 par 69.
122 Cf Epp 636:32–5, 856:29–54, 877:18–35, 878:14–16, 889:42–6, 1030:21–4, 1040:2–
    11, 1127A:59–64, 1166:57–64, 1196:595–7, 1299:108–10, 1330:53–60.
123 See below n128.
124 Cf Epp 300:23–9 (before Erasmus and Reuchlin had met), 471:27–31, 713:8–9.
125 Both letters are lost; cf the introduction to Ep 1078. For Hoogstraten's apology,
    Epp 1196:317–24, 1892:256–8, 2045:200–6, 2126:116–28.
126 Cf Ep 1078:45–9. Edward Lee (c 1482–1544), a cleric and student of theology
    at Cambridge, enrolled at Louvain to learn Greek (1516). The fact that Erasmus did not incorporate Lee's notes in the second edition of his New Testament provided the germ for controversy (Ep 765). Erasmus knew of a further set of notes by Lee, which he judged to be of little value (Epp 843, 886). Angered by clear if anonymous references to himself in various polemical tracts, including Erasmus' *Apologia contra Latomi dialogum* (cf Ep 936:34n), Lee made arrangements to publish his *Annotationum libri duo* (Paris: Gilles de Gourmont c 15 February 1520). For the two responses Erasmus published soon thereafter – *Apologia qua respondet invectis Lei* and *Responsio ad annotationes Lei* – see CWE 72. Lee's attacks on Erasmus' *Annotationes in Novum Testamentum* (cf

When Hermannus Buschius was about to publish his *Vallum humanitatis*, I admonished him to temper the harshness of his style; so he did, and the book is now read by scholars without offence.[127] In sum, when asked for my advice in a serious way, I have always counselled moderation.

At meals or in conversations with friends I will say in jest whatever comes to mind, often speaking more freely than is wise:[128] as Terence's Phormio says, 'This is my besetting fault'.[129] But would I not be cast out of all civilized society if, yielding to the provocations of the times, I were to give out what friends had written to me in confidence, or blurted out in my presence, trusting in my discretion – even if the friends in question had since become enemies? When Hutten told us he had declared war on the Romanists, I asked in jest what he planned for the Dominicans. He replied with a smile that they too were Romanists. Just after, as we went in to dinner, I asked him how soon Hoogstraten would hang from the gallows. He replied that he would attend to that shortly. But all this was said in such a way that no one would have failed to see from our facial expressions that we were joking.[130] So what is the point of his claiming that in order to gain one man's favour, I tried to make Hutten hateful in the sight of everyone else?[131] As I see it, my writings added something to Hutten's fame and reputation, and not an iota of ill will.[132] Do people look askance at him because I mentioned those four letters? Why, the authors themselves had already published them!

* * * * *

Ep 1037) provoked a response from Erasmus' friends; Neuenahr's letter (Ep 1078) was the opening piece of the *Epistolae aliquot virorum* (Basel: J Froben, August 1520). Lee subsequently became a court chaplain to Henry VIII, and served as the king's ambassador to the emperor (1525–30) and the pope (1530). As archbishop of York (from 1531) he helped carry out the king's plans for the reformation of the church.

127 Cf Ep 1196:324–8. On Buschius, see above n99.
128 Erasmus often refers to his 'freedom of the tongue' ($\pi\alpha\rho\rho\eta\sigma\iota\alpha$) in conversation: cf below 124, 131; Epp 1164:73–4, 1195:89–92, 1225:23–6.
129 Terence *Hecyra* 112
130 This interchange will likely have occurred in June 1520, when Hutten, on his way to Brussels to seek a position at the imperial court, stopped to visit Erasmus in Louvain (cf Ep 1115:47–8; above 57; below 135). Hutten in fact gave himself permission for acts of violence against the clergy in 1522; according to Erasmus (Ep 1341A:1063–74; Allen Ep 1934:260–70), he extorted money from the Strasbourg Carthusians, maimed two Dominicans, and robbed three abbots on a public highway.
131 Cf *Expostulatio* EB II 195:5–8 / K 74–5 par 70.
132 Cf below 106.

He alleges that I was once fiercely hostile to Hoogstraten, and later reconciled with him – what business is that of his? Did I ever make a treaty with Hutten, as kings do, so that I could not befriend anyone with whom he happened to be at war? Hutten remains free to love those I love not, and to hate those I cherish, but it is only fair for me to claim the same right. For while being Christian means bearing enmity to no man, human decency means conducting one's battles in a civilized manner, so as to have done with them at the first opportunity. In any case, I nowhere flatter Hoogstraten, nor have I sought to mend my friendship with him, or in any way troubled or injured Hutten. Nevertheless, and with a bow to the Muses, he has thought it apt to bring up the adage about not deceiving a friend,[133] as though our friendship were at stake if I treated Hoogstraten diplomatically. Would he, then, censure Zopyrus for not speaking frankly to the Babylonians?[134] Hutten strings together one accusation after another, just as one ties one thread to another.[135] In my recently published letter to Laurinus I mention the rumour that Hoogstraten had burned my books in Brabant, indicating that those who spread this report were hoping to trick me into a public attack on Hoogstraten. Lest I offend Luther's supporters, I add that while I do not know what name to give those responsible, some say they were Lutherans.[136] Now some who take pride in this name are anything but Lutherans – factious, unlearned, stupid, dissolute, slanderous men who have nothing in common with Luther except that they too curse the Roman pontiff.[137] Hutten claims I made up the story so as to shake an angry fist at the Lutherans.[138] What will he say if I produce a hundred witnesses who will testify that this rumour came to Basel? What if I produce letters to this effect written by friends to me as well as to others? If he still has any shame, he will merely put on a bold face. Indeed, what else can he do? In any case, even though I knew full well what Hoogstraten wanted to do, and

* * * * *

133 Cf *Expostulatio* EB II 196:3–8 / K 75 par 73; Cicero *De amicitia* 25.192. The commonplace *De non simulando in amicitia* furnished Hutten with one his main arguments against Erasmus.

134 Cf *Adagia* II x 64: *Zopyri talenta* 'The talents of Zopyrus.' CWE 34 152. Zopyrus was a noble Persian who mutilated himself and, on the pretext of being a victim of Darius' cruelty, deserted to the Babylonians, gained their confidence, and became commander of the army. In this capacity, he betrayed the city of Babylon to the Persian king when he came to lay siege: cf Herodotus 3.153–60.

135 Cf *Adagia* I viii 59: *Linum lino nectis* 'You join thread to thread' CWE 32 158–9.

136 Ep 1342:669–80; cf *Expostulatio* EB II 197:1–16 / K 76–7 par 76–8.

137 Brunfels *Responsio* 329:46–331:26.

138 Cf *Expostulatio* EB II 196:11–198:1 / K 76 par 74–7 par 80.

would have done if he could, I was the only one who did not believe the rumour, since nothing of the kind was reported to me from Brabant. Here Hutten throws in the old tale that seven years ago Hoogstraten threatened to attack me once he had destroyed Reuchlin, and that the only thing that 'gave him pause' was 'diligence in protecting Reuchlin' on the part of some of his friends.[139] Suppose the story is true; how is it relevant here? If Hutten wished to persuade me that Hoogstraten was and still is my enemy he would need a long and well-prepared oration. Or does he maintain that the rumour recently spread abroad is really true? The facts prove it is groundless.

Now the waves of his accusation swell to a tide. 'I at first applauded the *Epistolae obscurorum virorum* but then, overcome by fear, sent a letter to Cologne saying that such books displeased me.'[140] Now, my dear reader, hear what really happened and recognize Hutten's craft for what it is! I came upon a manuscript copy of a letter, ascribed to Hutten, recounting a banquet among professors – nothing more than a harmless joke.[141] It gave me great pleasure, and was read so often among among my friends and me that I nearly learned it by heart.[142] After returning to Basel, having lost my copy, I dictated what I remembered of it to Beatus Rhenanus, and wrote to Hutten's friends, asking for a copy of the original.[143] I freely admit all this. But what was the harm in enjoying a letter that poked fun at professors without injury to any one by name? Somewhat later, when the book was published, it also contained letters that were libellous, obscene, and venomous.[144] When the book was read to the company of scholars staying at Froben's house we laughed once more, but those present will testify that while I approved of poking fun, I condemned saying things that would

* * * * *

139 Cf *Expostulatio* EB II 197:7–11 / K 76–7 par 77; see Hutten's letter to Pirckheimer in May 1517 (EB I 135:1–3).

140 Ep 622:2–12; cf *Expostulatio* EB II 198:4–17 / K 77 par 81–78 par 82; Hutten's letter to Richard Coke, 9 August 1516 (EB I 124:10–12); cf Epp 636:3–13, 808:15–28, 961:34–6, 1135:37–8. The *Epistolae obscurorum virorum* were published in two parts, at Hagenau in 1515 and in Cologne in 1517, but copies or parts of the work circulated privately as early as 1514. Modern editions of the *Epistolae* are by Stokes and A. Bömer (Heidelberg 1924). On Hutten's authorship of some of the letters see Stokes lvi–lxviii; Holborn *Ulrich von Hutten* 60–4.

141 *De convivio magistrorum* (EB IV 3–5; Stokes 3–8, 291–4); cf *Expostulatio* EB II 198:8–10 / K 77–8 par 81.

142 Cf Ep 363:6–7.

143 Erasmus returned to Basel in August 1514 (cf Epp 294, 301). No letter asking for a copy of Hutten's text has survived.

144 Erasmus received a copy of part I of the *Epistolae obscurorum virorum*, containing 41 letters, from Wolfgang Angst on 19 October 1515 (Ep 363).

rebound as attacks on others.[145] I also disapproved of the book in other respects. Reuchlin was labelled a heretic[146] – in jest, to be sure, but I doubt that he was pleased to see himself so described.

Upon my return to Brabant,[147] I found that many were convinced I had written the book.[148] Although I knew who the authors were (there were thought to have been three),[149] when I wrote to Caesarius in Cologne, removing suspicion from myself, I did not cast suspicion on anyone else. This letter was then secretly copied and soon appeared in print.[150] Was it, then, wrong to disclaim authorship of the work – a charge that bothered me a good deal – especially when I did not inculpate anyone else? Then came the second part of *The Letters of Benighted Men*. When it was offered to me as a gift in Louvain, I refused to accept it.[151] I likewise refused similar dialogues published soon thereafter in Cologne,[152] a book I have never deigned to read. The reason I condemned these works was that I could see that they would serve only to drag good letters and Reuchlin's cause into disrepute, provoking our enemies instead of refuting them. How is

* * * * *

145 Cf Epp 622:2–5, 636:3–7, 808:21–6.
146 Cf Stokes 19:56–61, 25:37, 31:16–20; cf 222:69–223:92.
147 Erasmus arrived in Antwerp on 30 May 1516 (cf Ep 410).
148 Cf Epp 808:26–8, 961:34–6.
149 Erasmus does not say whom he had in mind (cf Ep 808:27–8). Modern scholars attribute the first part of *Epistolae obscurorum virorum* to Crotus Rubeanus, and the second part to Hutten, who was also responsible for the first letter and the appendix of part I; their friends, especially Hermannus Buschius, contributed letters to both volumes.
150 See Allen Ep 622 introduction. Ortwin Gratius, one of the targets of the *Epistolae obscurorum virorum*, replied in kind with *Lamentationes obscurorum virorum* (1st ed Cologne: Quentel [c March] 1518), in which he included Ep 622 without authorization from Erasmus. Erasmus acknowledged Ep 622 as his letter, but distanced himself from the *Lamentationes* (cf Ep 830:6–7).
   Johann Caesarius of Jülich (c 1468–1550) studied in Cologne and then in Paris under Lefèvre d'Étaples. After several visits to Italy, he taught Greek and Latin as a private tutor, mainly in Cologne, where he trained humanist scholars like Henricus Glareanus, Petrus Mosellanus, Heinrich Bullinger, and Count Hermann von Neuenahr. A supporter of Reuchlin, he was a lifelong friend of Erasmus.
151 Nothing is known about Erasmus refusing a copy of the second part of *Epistolae obscurorum virorum*, published in spring 1517, but in August he asked Pieter Gilles to send him 'the later series of the *Epistolae obscurorum virorum*' in a sealed envelope, so that his servant 'does not know what he is carrying' (Ep 637:15–7).
152 *Dialogi septem festiue candide ... authore S. Abydeno Corallo* (EB IV 553–66).

this a proof of my being feeble or fickle?[153] Two years ago there appeared a
dialogue that seemed to have been written in support of me, called, I think,
Hochstratus ovans. Did I not publicly condemn it, trying as best I could to
prevent its publication? The author of the work knows I am not making
this up, and so does the man who advised him to go ahead.[154] Now comes
another horrible charge. In one of my published letters I say Capito is more
learned in Hebrew than Reuchlin.[155] Lord, how Hutten reaches here for
tragic tones, as if I had poisoned the man! No one denies that Reuchlin was
the pioneer Hebrew scholar among the Germans.[156] But would it be to his
discredit, were a scholar still more learned to follow him? If six thousand
scholars surpass me in every kind of distinction, even during my lifetime, I
would boast about it. So is Capnio[157] injured if, after placing him under the
triumphal arch, I rank Capito ahead of him, at least in Hebrew scholarship?
But Hutten says I compare a man not at all known to one who is most
distinguished.[158] Yet Capito is hardly unknown, for among the learned he
is honoured for his works.[159] Even if he were relatively unknown, that
would be all the more reason for shining the light on a man worthy of
praise. This was my opinion of Capito, and not without reason. What if
specialists in Hebrew now agree with me?

So, dear reader, you have seen the shameless assumption Hutten
makes. Now listen to the reasons he invents to support his charge. I was
galled by Reuchlin's fame, he says, because some 'put him on a par with
me as a promoter of languages, while others hailed him as Germany's other
eye.'[160] But as one who has worked so hard on behalf of languages and good
letters, could I bear to see another share in the labour, especially a friend?

* * * * *

153 Cf *Expostulatio* EB II 198:17–9; K 78 par 83; Ep 1135:21.
154 *Hochstratus ovans* (EB Supplementum 1 461–88) – an anonymous dialogue that
     attacked Erasmus' foe, Edward Lee – appeared in late 1520 and was sometimes
     attributed to Hutten (cf Allen Epp 1083:23n, 1165:22n). See also Ep 1165:11n, a
     rebuttal of Allen's idea that Erasmus was referring in this letter to *Hochstratus
     ovans*.
155 Ep 413:16–7; cf *Expostulatio* EB II 199:1–202:4, especially 201:10–12 / K 78 par
     81–83 – 80 par 95.
156 Ep 333:115–8
157 *Capnio* (Greek for 'smoky') is a pun on the German *rauchig*, a putative source
     for Reuchlin's name.
158 Cf *Expostulatio* EB II 199:16–7 / K 79 par 86.
159 As professor of Old Testament at Basel Capito published an *Institutiuncula*
     for Hebrew (1516), which he expanded into *Hebraicum institutionum libri duo*,
     published in 1518 (cf Epp 459 introduction, 556:26–7).
160 Cf *Expostulatio* EB II 200:7–9 / K 80 par 88; cf above 56–8.

I had to laugh as I read what Hutten says about 'Germany's other eye.' Was I, then, trying to get rid of Reuchlin and make Germany one-eyed? Who does not know how sincerely and constantly I supported Reuchlin?[161] I ask all those with whom I have lived on intimate terms to come forward – I am sure they will say I suffer less from envy than from any other vice.

Now comes yet another shameless assumption: the reason I attribute so much to Capito is that he praised my edition of the *New Testament*, just as Ludwig Baer did. How he ties together things that have no connection! I did indeed appeal to the judgment of my *New Testament* by Baer and Capito, as theologians, so as to mute the clamour of those theologians who want nothing read unless they have first approved it.[162] If only what theologians approve ought to be read, well, my *New Testament*, although condemned by the theologians at Louvain,[163] has been approved by some very distinguished theologians. See, then, the shamelessness and inappropriateness of Hutten's tirade about my disparaging the merits of others.

Now I come to that crime so dreadful that Hutten, the most merciful of men, can hardly put it into words, and will never forgive me for it: in one of my letters to the bishop of Rochester, I accuse Reuchlin of treachery![164] In the case of such horrible villainy I must quote the exact words of my letter: 'It was not safe for him to live at home. The reason, if we may believe what they say, is this. When there was danger that the duke of Württemberg would recapture Stuttgart, Reuchlin persuaded some of his fellow citizens to move elsewhere, planning to do the same himself. They made their escape; Reuchlin, having changed his mind, stayed behind to look after his possessions. Afterwards, when the duke had been beaten back

* * * * *

161 For positive statements, Epp 300:2–8, 324:5 and 27–9, 333:114–28, 334:188–218, 335:318–22, 457:2–31, 543:5–7, 545:4–6, 1167:82–92. But for qualifications cf Epp 636:31–6, 856:36–9, 967:76–86, 1006:160–2, 1033:40–4 and 210–31, 1143:10–14, 1167:105–12.

162 Ep 413:13–9; cf *Expostulatio* EB II 200:4–6, 201:4–12 / K 79 par 88, 80 par 90, 81 par 93.

163 For Louvain critics of Erasmus' *New Testament* (Dorp, Latomus, Lee, and Baechem) see Rummel *Catholics Critics* I.

164 Ep 1129; cf *Expostulatio* EB II 202:5–205:20 / K 82 par 95–85 par 110. After study at Cambridge, John Fisher of Beverley (1469–1535) was in 1504 appointed chancellor of the university and bishop of Rochester. A humanist and patron of learning, he had great admiration for Erasmus, and took special interest in Reuchlin. He opposed both Luther's theology and Henry VIII's Reformation. On 22 June 1535, he was executed for refusing to take an oath upholding the king's Act of Supremacy, and the legitimate succession to the throne of Anne Boleyn's daughter, Elizabeth; he preceded Thomas More to the scaffold.

again, some of Reuchlin's friends secured that the victorious troops should not pillage his house. But the townspeople whom he had let down made trouble for the old man on their return. So now he has safely removed all his property and is living peacefully in Ingolstadt."[165] This is what I said in my own letter.

Now, dear reader, hear the background. First, my friendship for Reuchlin is attested not only by my writings but also by all those with whom I have lived in close company. Some years ago, while I was living in England, Reuchlin, harassed by his detractors, wrote to ask that I persuade like-minded friends to come to his defence.[166] I did more than he asked, for in addition to bringing many to admire him I also commended his cause to a few cardinals in Rome.[167] Among the Englishmen I won over to Reuchlin, the most eminent was Reverend Father John, bishop of Rochester. He became almost infatuated with Reuchlin, by comparison with whom he now felt I did not know anything. He even sought an occasion for travel to the Continent, so as to speak with this man, as if he were an oracle of all mysteries.[168] Having inspired in the bishop such affection for Reuchlin I nurtured it; far from being offended because someone else had obscured the bishop's high opinion of me, I rejoiced that Reuchlin had a backer of such standing. He also consulted me about honouring Reuchlin with a gift[169] and Bishop Fisher can testify that I was not at all envious on this occasion. Subsequently I often wrote to Reuchlin about the bishop's good will, hoping to lift his spirits with some good news.[170] Conversely, if there was news of Reuchlin's affairs, I took care to apprise the bishop, for I knew it would please him.[171] So, in the letter at which Hutten took offence, my point was that while Reuchlin had been in danger, he was now living in peace and tranquility. I also wanted Bishop Fisher to know where Reuchlin was, should he wish to send him something. The thought of accusing Reuchlin of treachery never crossed my mind. In any case deceit is not necessarily treachery;[172]

* * * * *

165 Erasmus quotes from the *Expostulatio* (EB II 202:10–17 / K 82 par 97), not from his letter to Fisher (Ep 1129:8–18).
166 Ep 290:28–32.
167 Cf Erasmus to Cardinals Raffaele Riario (Ep 333:112–47) and Domenico Grimani (Ep 334:187–218).
168 Ep 300:2–10. Fisher never managed to visit Reuchlin, but cf Epp 324:21–4, 457:2–17, 1155:34–6.
169 Cf Ep 457:17–22.
170 Epp 300:2–10, 324:5–25, 457:2–17, 471:16–7, 713:17–24, 1155:34–6
171 Cf Epp 653:21–5, 824:2–8, 1311:38–40.
172 Cf below 97, 108.

for example, secreting some gold under the pillow of a sick friend is a form of deceit, and so is arriving unexpectedly to visit a friend. Had I wished to accuse Reuchlin of treachery, I would not have added the words: 'having changed his mind.'[173] For necessity often compels us to change our plans, indeed there are times when it would be foolish not to do so; hence changing one's mind is not a matter of treachery.[174] Hutten's thunderbolts are thus of no avail, for what he assumes here is plainly false, even without my refuting it. Has anyone but Hutten ever interpreted that passage in my letter to Fisher in this way? Even supposing I had meant to defame Reuchlin, why would I do so in a letter to one of his great admirers? Besides, when the letter was published Reuchlin was still living. Yes, Hutten says, 'But he was on the verge of death.'[175] Who could predict how long Reuchlin was going to live? Since he enjoyed a vigorous and robust old age, I certainly hoped he would be with us for a long time, and would that he had been! After his death I wrote an *Apotheosis* commending him to the younger generation;[176] would I have branded him, while he yet lived, with the mark of perfidy, with no fear of his reaction?

Here Hutten demands proof, witnesses, warrants for their authority – in short, all the clamour of a court proceeding.[177] Well might he do so, if I were bringing our friend before the bar. But this is a matter of dealings among friends, so simple that it speaks for itself, with no need for mobilizing proofs. Hutten accuses me of inventing things, as though I had not heard the story about Reuchlin from others, but had made it up myself, to cast aspersions on his reputation. Consider, dear reader, how evil and perverse it is to attack a friend for trivial reasons. What I wrote the bishop of Rochester was related to me in Louvain by Dr. Johannes Salius,

* * * * *

173 See above n165.
174 While Quintilian recognizes three parts of deliberative speech – *honestum* 'honour,' *utile* 'expediency,' and *necessarium* 'necessity' – he dismisses the third: 'where there is necessity, there is no room for deliberation (*consilium*)' *Institutio* 3.8.22–5. But Erasmus makes room for *necessitas*, which may require speaking evasively (*oblique*), or even deceiving (*fallere*), in cases where one has to make accommodation to circumstances of person, time, or place (see Hoffmann *Rhetoric and Theology* 198–200, 205–8, 287 n215).
175 Cf *Expostulatio* EB 203:2 / K 82 par 98. Ep 1129 was printed in the *Epistolae ad diversos* (Basel: Froben 31 August 1521). Reuchlin died on 30 June 1522.
176 Cf Ep 1311:38–40. Erasmus composed the *Apotheosis Capnionis* 'The Apotheosis of Reuchlin' CWE 39 244–55 (Erasmus' working title: see introductory note CWE 39 244) for the new edition of his *Colloquia*, published in July or August 1522.
177 Cf *Expostulatio* EB 202:18–205:9 / K 82 par 98–85 par 108.

while Emperor Charles was staying there.[178] I thought the more highly of this man because he showed great affection for Reuchlin, recounting certain services he had once rendered him. When this letter appeared in print, in the collection published in Basel (I was in Brabant at the time), would the passage in question not have been edited out, if it were deemed insulting to Reuchlin? For I had given learned friends may permission to make changes as they saw fit.[179] 'Why did you not change it yourself?' Hutten will ask. Because I saw nothing wrong. 'Why then did you give such a commission to others?' Because, knowing the current mood in Germany better than I, they were in a better position to make decisions. 'Then why did your friends not make the changes?' Because they had not the eyes of a Hutten, hoping to gain recognition by maligning Erasmus in every way possible. 'But why were you tentative in recounting the story?' he says.[180] Because Salius, my source, could have been mistaken. In the end, what does it matter for Reuchlin's reputation whether what I wrote was true or not? Further, because Hutten knew people would wonder why I wished ill to Reuchlin, having praised him as much as I have, he had to invent reasons – meanness and envy on my part. But on this supposition, why did I not envy him when he was a magistrate of the Swabian League and an imperial counsellor, when he was at the height of his fortune and reputation? Why envy him when the fallen magistrate had become a mere professor?[181] How crudely, how implausibly these lies are concocted!

* * * * *

178 Johannes Salzmann of Steyr had been the personal physician of Archduke Ferdinand since 1522. But Erasmus wrote Ep 1129 on 2 August 1520, three weeks before Charles v arrived in Louvain. He is mistaken also about his informant, who is referred to in Ep 1129:1–2 as 'a doctor of civil and canon law who was once a councillor to Emperor Maximilian.' This description rules out Salzmann, but would fit the Augsburg humanist Konrad Peutinger (1467–1545), whom Erasmus met in Bruges while Charles v was staying there (25–29 July 1521: cf Ep 1247:2n).
179 Cf above n175. Erasmus left Louvain for Basel on 28 October 1521. For the editing of Erasmus' published correspondence, see Léon-E. Halkin *Erasmus ex Erasmo: Érasme, éditeur de sa correspondance* (Aubel 1983).
180 Cf *Expostulatio* EB I 202:1–4 / K 83 par 102.
181 Cf Juvenal 7.198. From 1502 to 1512 Reuchlin was a member of the three-man governing board of the federation of towns and princes known as the Swabian League. He fled Stuttgart in 1519, during the war against Duke Ulrich of Württemberg (1487–1550), a foe of the League. He was subsequently a professor of Greek and Hebrew at Ingolstadt (1520/1521) and Tübingen (1521/1522).

Here, gentle reader, I would have you consider how shameless Hutten must be. For the man who waxes so indignant when one friend's reputation is falsely impugned does not scruple to invent all manner of charges against another friend. So, after fulminating against me on this most trivial matter, flinging charges whether fitting or not,[182] this is how he introduces the rest of my crimes: 'I want you to know that I well understand how you have decided to turn everything upside down, showering abuse on the well-deserving, while playing the toady to those you deem most dangerous to yourself.'[183] Once again, as if at his direction, he has me speak about the universities of Louvain and Cologne, in such wise that any reader will recognize the tragic style as coming from Hutten himself.

The gist of his charge is that now, in published letters, I speak respectfully of the two institutions I have roundly condemned in private conversations with my friends.[184] What? Have I ever declared war against a university? Is Louvain not a flourishing centre of study, notwithstanding the few stupid men there who fight against good letters? And are there not many at Cologne who wish me well, and support good letters?[185] Have I ever approved of the enemies of learning? And why should I attack the friends of learning? Yet see the verbiage with which Hutten dresses up this nonsense: 'you have changed sides,' he says, 'now you flatter your enemies, as if giving their universities precedence over the academies of Athens, all the while reproaching those of us who still have the audacity to attack them, these modern-day replicas of Plato and Theophrastus.'[186] Who can fail to see how irrelevant his grandiloquence is? I think what offended Hutten was my letter to the Louvain theologians, defending certain passages in my works that Nicolaas Baechem had denounced as heretical, hatefully, and without cause.[187] In the heading I address them as 'honourable brethren,' while in

* * * * *

182 Cf *Adagia* II i 24: *Joca seriaque* 'Grave and gay' CWE 33 30.
183 Cf *Expostulatio* EB II 206:4–7 / K 86 par 112.
184 In his letters, Erasmus sometimes speaks respectfully of university theology faculties (Ep 950:25–30), but he is also critical of their immediate and vehement denunciations of Luther (Ep 1033:78–130, and Epp 1153 and 1164, both to a professor of theology at Louvain). It is worth noting that while Epp 950, 1153, and 1164 were all published by Erasmus, Ep 1033 – where he is more frank in his criticism – was published without his permission.
185 Eg Buschius, Caesarius, Neuenahr.
186 Cf *Expostulatio* EB II 206:14–17 / K 86 par 114.
187 This letter, Ep 1301, was published with the *Catalogus lucubrationum* of April 1523, along with the letter (Ep 1342, to Laurinus) that provoked Hutten to

another letter to the Louvain theologians I call them 'reverend fathers and most respected gentlemen.'[188] Among these men too there are some who wish Erasmus well, others who disapprove of the conduct of Baechem and Vincentius, and still others who are not past all cure.[189] In the first place, it is silly to make a case out of the customary forms of address which, as we have noted, one enemy concedes to another even in the midst of war.[190] And why is it Hutten's business how I defend my case? Would it not be stupid to hurl abusive epithets at those we strive to win over to our side? Moreover, is it not to lash out at an entire order of society?[191] Even if we suppose the whole order to be hostile, it is both prudent and civil to injure as few as possible, for it may happen that some become friends, or at least less hostile. I freely admit that I want to have peace, if possible, not only with the theologians at Louvain but also with the whole Dominican order. Hutten claims that I first ignited a conflagration against them, and am now trying to humour them, by striking out at one friend after another. I will presently show how false this charge is, but for now I will address the matter at hand.

* * * * *

write his *Expostulatio*. Allen Ep 1301 represents a shorter version of the text, not published until after Erasmus' death.

After obtaining his doctorate in theology from Louvain (1505), Nicholaas Baechem of Egmond joined the Carmelites, whose house of study in Louvain he directed from 1510. That Erasmus was also (from 1517) a member of the theology faculty did not prevent Baechem from becoming an early and virulent critic; he admitted (Erasmus says, Ep 948:145–8) denouncing the New Testament of 1516 without having read it. As assistant inquisitor for the Netherlands, from 1521, Baechem attacked Erasmus from the pulpit as a fomentor of the heresies of Luther (Ep 1162). He was incensed by a barb aimed at the Carmelites in the *Colloquia* of March 1522, contained in 'The Godly Feast' (CWE 39 189; cf 'A Fish Diet' [1526] CWE 40 705); this was the attack against which Erasmus defended himself in Ep 1301.

188 Epp 1301, 1217:3; cf *Expostulatio* EB II 206:18–20 / K 87 par 115.

189 Vincentius Theoderici of Beverwijk (1481–1526) joined the Dominicans at Haarlem, and taught theology at Louvain after receiving his doctorate there in 1517. Erasmus counted him among his worst enemies (cf Ep 1196; below 138) and suspected him of instigating the *Apologia in eum librum quem ab anno Erasmus Roterodamus de confessione edidit*, published under a pseudonym (Antwerp: S. Crocus, March 1525), to which he replied with the unpublished *Manifesta mendacia* (CWE 71 113–31).

190 See above n98.

191 For Erasmus' conception of the 'orders' (*ordines*) of Christian society, see Tracy *Erasmus of the Low Countries* 91–4.

Hear, then, another proof of my inconstancy – so Hutten thinks, though it is rather a proof of his own impudence. He says that while I strongly disapproved of the faculties of Cologne and Louvain when they officially censured a number of propositions from Luther's works, I now endorse what I once condemned, as is evident from a letter to the Louvain theologians where I boast that their 'public arguments against Luther have always had my unwavering support.'[192] Here, dear reader, I beg you to take note of Hutten's malicious zeal for finding fault. I never approved of those propositions nor disapproved of them, for I did not want to oblige certain people by giving them the handle they were looking for.[193] In the presence of the rector of the university, I challenged Baechem to cite a single article in Luther's writings that I had ever defended, even while drinking with friends. As he had nothing to say, he pointed to a passage about confession in a letter I had written to the cardinal of Mainz. There I say Baechem had publicly condemned something he did not understand.[194] This was not to defend Luther, but rather to expose the shamelessness of a man who harangues the populace about matters he does not comprehend. Yet, says Hutten, I now support their public arguments. What does this have to do with their official censures? For in such documents they do not argue, they pronounce; instead of teaching, they condemn. I have always disapproved of potentially seditious ranting before the common folk, in which many lies are broadcast. Instead, I have exhorted theologians to set condemnations aside and refute Luther with arguments, showing him, if he has erred, a better way.[195] Afterwards, when they began to conduct themselves with

* * * * *

192 Cf *Expostulatio* EB II 206:7–207:4 / K 86 par 113–87 par 117. The phrase quoted by Hutten and then Erasmus is not from his letters to the Louvain theologians as a group (Epp 1217, 1301), but from a letter to Godschalk Rosemondt, who was both rector of the university and a member of the theology faculty. Certain of Luther's propositions were publicly condemned first by the theology faculty of Cologne (30 August 1519), then by the theology faculty of Louvain (7 November 1519). The two censures were published as *Condemnatio doctrinalis ... Lutheri* (Louvain: Dirk Martens, February 1520). Erasmus was sharply critical of the condemnations in an unpublished letter to Philip Melanchthon in Wittenberg (Ep 1113:38–41), and dismissive of their value in a published letter to Cardinal Campeggio in Rome (Ep 1167:403–9).

193 See *Adagia* I iv 4: *Ansam quarere* 'To look for a handle' CWE 31:321:3–322:29.

194 Ep 1033:90–105. For Erasmus' meeting with Baechem in the presence of Godschalk Rosemondt (above n192), Epp 1153, 1162:10–249, 1172:29–30, 1173:29–109.

195 Cf Epp 939:46–91, 948:88–98, 1033:78–105, 1153:114–40, 1217, 1345:40–5.

greater moderation, I expressed my support.[196] I neither agreed with nor disagreed with the theses proposed in their public debates. When they gave up their mad ravings in order to dispute and teach, I gave my approval. Hutten interprets my position as if I endorsed whatever they had concluded against Luther in the course of their disputations. In the same way, he had falsely assumed that I had wholeheartedly endorsed whatever the theology faculties had pronounced against Luther in their official censures. Can we now deny that Hutten has a genius for distorting things said with the best of intentions?

He alleges a similar inconstancy in reference to the Dominican order: having once been hostile to them, I now endeavour to persuade everyone I have never wished ill to their brotherhood.[197] In fact, as my words and deeds amply testify, I have never been insane enough to wish ill to a whole order.[198] If it were right to hate the whole Dominican order because of its many bad members, one should hate all orders, for there is not one that does not have many bad members. Indeed, one would have to hate all Christians, for the bad outnumber the good. Thus I cannot fairly be accused of inconstancy, for what I express in word and deed is what I have firmly believed. Is it more humane to hate an entire order because of its bad members, or to favour an order because of its good members? Among the Dominicans there are some who wish Erasmus well, and support good letters and the cause of the gospel.[199] If it is not true that I have always advised my friends not to impugn any order or any nation, then Hutten will have proven that I was hostile to the Dominican order as a whole.

He again reproaches me with inconstancy with respect to the Roman curia, about which I supposedly used to speak with all the savagery Hutten can put in my mouth, but which I now shower with praises. 'Now,' he says, 'you make of it the holy Catholic church, where men outshine the lilies in whiteness, and where the very words of the courtiers, no matter how knavish, are likened to rose petals.'[200] These words prove Hutten's

* * * * *

196 Cf Epp 1164:75–8, 1167:445–8 and 460–6.
197 Cf *Expostulatio* EB II 207:4–7 / K 87 par 117.
198 Cf Ep 1217:33–40; Tracy *Low Countries* 90–2, 136–7.
199 Eg Johannes Faber (Epp 1150:4–16, 1152:14–17), and Antonius Pyrata (Ep 1342: 433–5).
200 Cf *Expostulatio* EB 207:8–208:15 / K 87 par 119–89 par 123. For the distinction Erasmus makes between the *ecclesia Romana* and the *ecclesia Catholica*, with which the former 'does not disagree,' see James Tracy, 'Erasmus among the Postmodernists: *Dissimulatio, Bonae Literae,* and *Docta Pietas* Revisited,' in

incredible impudence, nothing more. Has anyone ever approved of the vices of the Romanists? But as for the church, who condemns it? I dare say that in Rome too there are men devoted to Christ. And does anyone ever think of rose petals in connection with the words of hangers-on at the curia, wicked as they might be?[201] Are these not the words of a man who abuses the pen, giving no thought to what he writes, or against whom? But since Hutten prefers to postpone this charge to what he considers its proper place, we shall do likewise.

I turn now to Aleandro, concerning whom Hutten censures my inconstancy yet again, alleging that after speaking out against him openly in the past, I later make honourable mention of him in my correspondence.[202] I start with one sure thing: I have never spoken with Hutten about Aleandro. For when Hutten visited me in Brabant Aleandro was still in Rome; no one had any idea he would soon be coming north on a mission against Luther.[203] Therefore, whatever Hutten has to say on this point he gets from rumours – anyone with any sense knows how little they can be relied on. Still, I want to clarify things. In Venice, some years ago, Aleandro and I were not just friends but close friends.[204] I admired his erudition and loved

* * * * *

Erasmus' Vision of the Church ed Hilmar M. Pabel, Sixteenth Century Essays and Studies 33 (Kirksville, MO 1995) 1–40.

201 In the *Expostulatio* the word *curtisanus* 'courtier' denotes a member of the Roman curia. But Hutten elsewhere uses the term to mean anyone who receives church income from Rome, and defends the papacy – for him, all such men, including the prelates of the German church, preferred Roman tyranny to German liberty (cf Holborn *Ulrich von Hutten* 126–7, 154).

202 Cf *Expostulatio* EB II 207:11–209:3 / K 87 par 119–89. Girolamo Aleandro of Motta (1480–1542) was an accomplished scholar of Greek and Hebrew and a humanist of encyclopedic learning. When Erasmus visited the Aldine press in Venice in 1508, Aleandro was then working for a time as an editor, and the two men shared a bed. From May 1508 he was a popular professor at the University of Paris, where he was rector in 1513. He then entered the service of the church, first in the diocese of Paris, then in the diocese of Liège; from 1519 he was librarian for the Vatican. Sent in 1520 as an apostolic nuncio to Germany and the Netherlands, to promulgate the papal bull against Luther, he became an ardent opponent of heresy, and a trusted counsellor of successive popes. Meanwhile, the one-time friendship between Erasmus and Aleandro gave way to mutual recriminations: Aleandro suspected Erasmus of abetting Luther's heresy (Ep 1167:133–7), Erasmus suspected Aleandro of trying to poison him (Ep 1188:40–2).

203 Hutten visited Erasmus in June 1520 (cf below 135); Aleandro departed from Rome on July 27.

204 Cf Epp 256:6–7, 269:57, 1195:59–61.

his temperament, the more so as he began to promote Greek letters among the French to such good effect.

Later, after Pope Leo had chosen him to carry on the campaign against Luther in our parts, but before he departed from Rome, he grew angry with me, as I learned from a letter of his to the bishop of Liège.[205] The cause of his anger was my first letter to Luther, written in response to a letter from him.[206] Upon his arrival in the Low Countries, even before he got to Brabant, someone with a pernicious tongue took him aside and completely poisoned his mind[207] – a thing I had never imagined would happen. Thus Aleandro seemed to avoid any contact with me,[208] suspecting God knows what. In time some things he was saying about me made the rounds in Louvain,[209] unfriendly, but not yet harsh. When he went back to the city where he had sucked in the poison – it was from there that the emperor had set out for Cologne – the same viper injected more venom into a mind already fevered. So it was that when in Cologne I heard everywhere how Aleandro was saying evil things about me to the great men of the land, and at high feasts.[210] At first I could not find out where he was lodging; having tracked him down, I sent a servant to his inn with the message that I wanted to speak with him. Gladdened by this report, he at once invited me to lunch. I begged off from lunch,[211] but right after lunch I arrived for a conversation. He received his guest with the utmost courtesy and we talked for several hours, each making his complaints known to the other – for he had too had heard I was saying unfriendly things about him. Indeed, I had been asking

* * * * *

205 Aleandro's letter to Erard de la Marck is lost. For its dating, ASD IX-3 149:691n, Ep 1227A:24n; for what it said, cf Epp 1127A:92–3, 1482:9–10, 1496:21–7. Erard de la Marck (1472–1538) came from a noble family with lands on both sides of the Franco-Burgundian border. Destined for an ecclesiastical career, he accumulated prebends in various dioceses, becoming prince-bishop of Liège in 1505, with support from the French king as well as the pope. In 1518 he changed sides, deserting the French king for Archduke Charles of Burgundy, soon to be Emperor Charles v. This move cost him the bishopric of Chartres, but gained him a cardinalate (1521). His attacks on the Roman curia, while he was attempting to secure a cardinalate, made some think he favoured Luther's cause (cf Epp 738 introduction, 916 introduction).
206 Ep 980, in which Erasmus mentioned Erard as one 'who favours your views'
207 Cf Ep 1263 n3.
208 Cf Ep 1482:13–4.
209 Cf Ep 1157:9–11.
210 Cf Ep 1482:16–20. For Erasmus' stay in Cologne (c 23 October–c 13 November 1520), Ep 1155 intr.
211 Ep 1188:37–42 suggests Erasmus was afraid of being poisoned by Aleandro.

people why the man sent from Rome to oppose Luther was raving on about me, as if the Luther business had anything to do with me. Having heard each other out, we parted with a kiss, in token of our long-time friendship.[212] Some months later, when someone in the emperor's entourage wrote me from the Diet of Worms that Aleandro was contriving evil against me,[213] I sent my secretary to him with a letter frankly expressing my complaints against him. I also wrote to his patron, the bishop of Liège. Aleandro wrote back justifying his conduct.[214] Once the diet was adjourned he came back to Brussels, where I went to see him, and we spoke for nearly five hours.[215] Since he is in the habit of speaking frankly, he cited against me some of the same charges that Hutten now makes:[216] I had told everyone Aleandro was a Jew by birth,[217] I was concocting his ruin, and so forth. Thus did those honest and brave Germans manage to direct all of Aleandro's ill will against me.

To all this I say first that neither my friendship with nor my enmity with Aleandro had anything to do with the cause of Luther. He was a friend before Luther's name was ever heard, nor was it because of Luther that I became his foe; rather, it was because he put the blame on me, for no reason, and thus dragged my name into the whole nasty business. Had it not been for those poisonous tongues, Aleandro and I could still be friends – indeed, the Luther affair might possibly have taken a less hateful turn, without those book-burnings in so many cities, serving only to bring rage into the minds of men.[218] But if I was angry with him for trying to ruin me, why would I not resume our friendship once he changed course and

* * * * *

212 For Erasmus' meeting with Aleandro (9 November 1520), see Epp 1155 intr, 1167:20n.
213 Cf Epp 1195:4–10, 1199:10–12, 1342:55–65.
214 In addition to the letters for Erard de la Marck in Liège and for Aleandro in Worms, Erasmus' secretary carried letters to three important men in Charles v's entourage, Mercurino Gattinara, Matthäus Schiner, and Luigi Marliano; of these letters only the one to Marliano survives (Ep 1195). Of the replies, only those from Gattinara and Marliano survive (Epp 1197, 1198).
215 Cf Ep 1233:28n.
216 Cf *Expostulatio* EB II 207:14–208:3 / K 88 par 120.
217 Cf Epp 1166:94, 1717:38 and n17; Allen Epp 2329:105–106, 2578:31; LB X 1645D.
218 Aleandro held burnings of Luther's books in Louvain (8 October 1520), Liège (17 October), and Cologne (12 November [Ep 1157:3n]). Implausible as it seems, the thinking behind these lines may be that an Aleandro whose mind had not been 'poisoned' against him might have endorsed Erasmus' project for a negotiated settlement of the Luther affair (the *Consilium* of October 1520: cf Ep 1149 intr).

sought to undo the damage? At our meeting in Brussels he swore he would
do so, and when I returned to Germany I learned from those who were our
go-betweens in this matter that it was not an empty promise.

So where is the disgrace if, in my books, Aleandro is lauded as a master
of erudition in the three languages?[219] His merits in this respect I freely
acknowledged, even when our feud was at its worst. Though some people
would give me the prize for Latinity, this praise too I yielded to him, as
one adversary to another. In the letter in which Hutten would see Aleandro
strangled, he praises him even more profusely, saying it grieved him to
see such a man possessed of a quality he could envy.[220] What a tribute for
Aleandro, to have an enemy extol his learning as worthy of envy! Note
that my praise was more modest. Indeed, in one of our meetings Aleandro
boasted about the homage paid him by Hutten.

This is my attitude: that wretch who incited Aleandro against me, [221]
and who deserves the worst from me, even his friendship I would gladly
regain, given the chance, and without demanding anything in return. In
any case, since this has nothing to do with the Luther affair, why does
Hutten complain? As far as I am concerned he can hate Aleandro as much
as he likes. But Hutten continues: 'He loves you as no other in an un-
paralleled manner; you hold him dear as well, you get along famously,
prolonging your learned conversations well into the night, and the two of
you have even agreed to travel to Rome together.'[222] Here he is putting
words in my mouth. I did indeed speak in my letter to Laurinus about
my friendly dealings with Aleandro in Louvain, but my point was to refute those who were spreading the rumour that my departure from Brabant amounted to flight. I wanted to make clear that I had set out on my
journey openly, in the sight of everyone.[223] Let us assume for the sake
of argument that Aleandro and I really were enemies, and that I merely
feigned friendship with him, so that he would not speak out against me
as much, which would allow me to hold in check certain theologians who
would stop at nothing. Will Hutten wax indignant if I made use of this kind
of cunning to protect myself, without harming anyone? In fact, there was
in Louvain a certain mad Dominican who promised at the early morning

* * * * *

219 Cf Ep 1341A:1365; *Adagia* II i 34: *Rana gyrina sapientior* CWE 33 36; LB IX 295D.
220 Cf *Invectiuum in Hieronymum Aleandrum* March 1521 (EB II 16:33–6).
221 Cf above n207.
222 Cf *Expostulatio* EB II 208:6–9 / K 88 par 121.
223 Cf Ep 1342:120–67, describing the circumstances of Erasmus' departure for
    Basel (October 1521).

mass that he would reveal strange things about me in another sermon after lunch. I apprised Aleandro of this, and he sent someone to impose silence on the man, rabble-rouser though he was.[224] Is it not called prudence if one can mobilize one's enemies in one's defence? Indeed, because Aleandro and I were on familiar terms for a few days, certain theologians lost much of their boldness. All the while, I said nothing against Hutten in our conversations; rather, I praised his disposition and genius, to the indignation of Caracciolo[225] as well as Aleandro – and this after the Diet of Worms, when Hutten's situation had worsened considerably.[226] In the end, one must ask which is more in keeping with humane sentiments: to honour one's enemies in one's writings, and thus perhaps mitigate their ill will, or to attack, in the vicious tracts that Hutten writes, a friend who not only was well-disposed, but who deserved (and still hopes to deserve) better treatment?

Still another charge: In my letter to Laurinus, I mention the rumour circulating here in Basel that the Roman pontiff had issued some sort of brief against me. Hutten does not hesitate to assert that I made this up, to cast odium on the Lutherans.[227] Is there no end to the shameless frivolity he imputes to a friend? In fact, there are many good men here who know there was such a rumour. I also have letters from learned friends in Augsburg and Constance reporting it as well known that the pope had publicly condemned my books in Rome. Finally, they have my letters asserting that I refused to credit the rumour.[228] Let everyone see, then, how shameless Hutten is!

* * * * *

224 Most likely Laurens Laurensen: cf Ep 1342:40n.
225 Marino Caracciolo of Naples (1468–1538) was appointed papal nuncio to Emperor Charles v in 1520, but neither he nor Aleandro could prevent Luther from gaining a hearing at the Diet of Worms. Erasmus mentions speaking with Caracciolo as well as Aleandro in Brussels (Ep 1342:78); but elsewhere he speaks of Caracciolo as abetting Aleandro's campaign against him (cf Epp 1188:28–30, 1263:1, 1268:76, 1302:57–9, 1305:26–7).
226 Hutten left his refuge at Sickingen's Ebernburg castle in May or June 1521, but he failed to rally others to his war against the clergy, and his sickness forced him to go into hiding until mid-November (Holborn *Ulrich von Hutten* 157–60, 162–82).
227 Ep 1342:720–6; *Expostulatio* EB 209:14–20 / K 90 par 126.
228 Rumours that Erasmus or his books had been condemned by Pope Adrian vi did circulate in the fall of 1522 (cf Epp 1324 intr, 1331:35–40, 1518:24–42), but letters of this description from Erasmus' friends have not survived.
Adrian Floriszoon of Utrecht (1454–1523) enrolled at the University of Louvain (1476) after schooling by the Brethren of the Common Life, perhaps at Zwolle. In 1491 he received his doctorate in theology and was ordained to the

But, he says, I ventured to praise a pope who had as yet done nothing to merit such praise, and who at one time wished me ill.[229] As to this last point, I cannot say that Hutten was wrong, but no hostility on his part was ever reported to me, nor did I suspect it. During our years at Louvain we were on friendly terms,[230] enjoying, as the pope writes, a fellowship of studies.[231] I was never aware of any unfriendly feeling towards me on his part.

In any case what I say about him is that his age, his constant integrity, and his learning lead us to be of good hope.[232] This is encouragement rather than praise. His past accomplishments I do praise – here I can be refuted if I am wrong – but for the future I make only a good prediction. How inappropriate, then, was Hutten's insipid jest: 'But this, oh Timon, you will do.'[233] (No doubt Hutten fancied himself wonderfully amusing). But in the past, Hutten asks, did I not say that little good was to be expected of him? But I never spoke to Hutten about this pope; how does he dare accuse me, before the whole world, on the basis of something he can only have heard from a drinking companion? I did say that I feared he would unfair to Luther.[234] As for the rest I never said a word, although he did show a disposition to make even the Roman curia bear fruit.

Hutten says further that plans were being made to seize me as a heretic.[235] That certain mad friars talked hopefully of such a thing I have

* * * * *

priesthood. As dean of St Peter's, Louvain (from 1497), he was also chancellor of the university. He became tutor (1507) and then a councillor to young Archduke Charles (the future Charles v), who, upon the death of his maternal grandfather, Ferdinand of Aragon, named Adrian as regent in Castile and Aragon, and also bishop of Tortosa. Charles also secured him a cardinalate in 1517, making possible his unexpected elevation to the papacy on 9 January 1522. As a theologian Adrian remained very much in the scholastic tradition, but he and Erasmus were on friendly terms during their years together in Louvain. Upon his election as pope, Erasmus dedicated to him his edition of Arnobius (Epp 1304, 1310). Pope Adrian expected Erasmus to write against Luther (Ep 1324), and his reaction to Erasmus' reply, proposing ways to settle the controversy (Ep 1352) is not known.

229 Cf *Expostulatio* EB 209:3–210:8 / K 89 par 125–90 par 127.
230 Cf Epp 171:13–19, 1304:12–14, 1311:15–19, 1332:69–70.
231 Cf Ep 1324:115–16.
232 Cf Ep 1304:370–7, 515–26; also Epp 1284:51–3, 1313:113–16, 1330:51, 1331:47–51. See also below 101.
233 Cf *Expostulatio* EB II 210:7 / K 90 par 127. In Lucian's *Timon* (50ff), Demeas praises Timon for deeds he was expected to do but has not done.
234 Cf Ep 1166:114–17 – a letter that Erasmus did not choose to include in the correspondence he had published.
235 Cf *Expostulatio* EB II 209:3–14 / K 89 par 125.

no doubt, but among princes it was never considered. In Spain I had
friends who were close to him who is now pope, and in Rome too, while
Leo was still alive, I had friends very different from Hutten. At the emperor's court are important men who I have had no reason not to think
of as friends. From their letters I knew what was being discussed; as
for Hutten, hiding, he could only know what scandalmongers reported.
I have in my possession certain articles presented to the emperor, with
marginal notes in the hand of Glapion.[236] Here there is no reference to
heresy on my part, nor anything like it. I have as well a letter of Chancellor Gattinara, indicating that while certain pamphlets were suspected
to be from my hand because of their elegant style, they contained nothing heretical, meaning, nothing such as Luther writes.[237] In that letter to
Laurinus I also mention Jean Glapion, neither blaming him nor praising
him. Here Hutten resorts to grandiloquence:[238] 'What, Glapion? Oh, how
you blow his horn too.'[239] Here is the fanfare with which I saluted him:
'then Reverend Father Jean Glapion, the emperor's confessor . . .'[240] What
comes next is even more shameless: 'You, who used to curse the man's

* * * * *

236 These 'articles' have not survived, but Glapion is known to have talked with
    members of the Saxon court at the Diet of Worms: cf Ep 1217:55–60, with n16.
    The Frenchman Jean Glapion (d September 1522), of whose early life little is
    known, was from 1511 warden of the Observant Franciscans outside Bruges; he
    was later provincial of the Observants in Burgundy, and commissary-general
    for all Observant houses outside Italy. Appointed confessor to Charles v in
    1520, he was sent to negotiate with Sickingen, Hutten, and Bucer, in hopes of
    winning them over to the emperor's side. At Worms, having failed to persuade
    Luther to recant, he then advocated his condemnation; not long thereafter, he
    pressed Erasmus to write against Luther (Ep 1228:11n).
237 Cf Ep 1197:19–23.
    Mercurino Arborio di Gattinara (1465–1530), a doctor of laws from the Uni-
    versity of Turin, entered the service of Margaret of Austria during her mar-
    riage to the duke of Savoy. Upon her appointment as Regent of the Nether-
    lands (1506), he moved up through the ranks of officialdom, eventually be-
    come grand chancellor (1518) for young Archduke Charles, soon to be Em-
    peror Charles v. Erasmus probably met Gattinara in July 1520.
238 Literally, δείνωσις. As distinct from the *genus humile* and the *genus medium*, the
    grand style of speech (*genus grande*) uses vehement and exaggerated expres-
    sions to appeal to the reader's more vehement emotions (see eg Quintilian
    Institutio 6.2.24, 8.3.88, 9.2.104; Hoffmann *Rhetoric and Theology* 171–2, 188–91).
239 Cf *Expostulatio* EB II 210:8–9 / K 90 par 128.
240 Erasmus quotes from the *Catalogus lucubrationum* (Ep 1341A:1367), with which
    Ep 1342, the letter to Laurinus was published; Hutten seems to have in mind
    Ep 1342:274–82, where Erasmus says that Glapion gave the emperor 'a most
    fair and friendly report on my work.'

wickedness.'[241] Since I never said a word to Hutten about Glapion, in person or by letter, this lie too he got from a drinking companion – such is the gossip from which he has fabricated his calumny of a friend. Here again he has me speak, about Glapion, in words that would never occur to me, even in my dreams. Once I ran into Glapion and greeted him in a few words; this was in Brussels, after the Diet of Worms. For the rest, any business between us was conducted by letter.

What Glapion contrived or carried out against Luther, I know not; whatever he did it was not at my urging. To be honest, I could never entirely trust him, but neither did I bear him ill will.[242] I do know that in the emperor's entourage he more than once showed himself a strong friend of mine.[243] Is it not ridiculous that after only one conversation,[244] our sharp-eyed friend, a veritable Lynceus, can show us the real Glapion, as if the two of them had 'eaten a peck of salt'[245] together? As far as I could discern his character, from the accounts of prudent men and from his letters to me, Hutten could never have understood Glapion, even if he lived with him for ten years. I had to laugh when reading how Hutten makes him a man of extraordinary cunning, and says that I am just like him.[246] If Glapion had been the kind of man Hutten makes him out to be, I would be no more like him than a camel is like a fox. But of my own character I will speak elsewhere.[247] Hutten is also offended by the passage where I mention receiving a polite and friendly letter from Silvester Prierias. Note that I did not dignify him by any title of honour; I merely say, 'the well-known Silvester Prierias' has written me a very civil letter.[248] Oh, what

* * * * *

241 Cf *Expostulatio* EB II 210:9 / K 90 par 128.
242 Erasmus later admitted that despite Glapion's professions of support for him, he mistrusted the man because of his Franciscan habit: cf Allen Ep 1805:172–4.
243 An allusion to Terence *Phormio* 476. Cf Epp 1269:4–6, 1302:63, 1331:15–6, 1482: 21, 1515:46.
244 For Glapion's meeting with Hutten, Bucer, and Sickingen at the Ebernburg (April 1521), cf *Expostulatio* EB II 210:8–211:19 / K 90 par 128–92 par 133.
245 Cf *Adagia* II i 14: *Nemini fidas, nisi cum quo prius modium salis absumpseris* 'Trust no man, unless you have eaten a peck of salt with him first' CWE 33 24–5. Lynceus, one of the Argonauts, had eyes that could discern treasure hidden under the earth.
246 Cf *Expostulatio* EB II 211:19 / K 92 par 133: Hutten likens Erasmus to Glapion, and Glapion to Vertumnus, the ancient Etruscan god of the changing seasons.
247 Cf below 118
248 Cf Ep 1342:352–3. Prierias' letter is lost.
     Silvestro Mazzolini (1456–1523), from Priero in Piedmont (hence Prierias), held several positions in the Dominican order and was also a professor of

extraordinary flattery! Now Luther is contemptuous of Prierias. Thus, says Hutten, you write this 'to spite Luther.'[249] No, I wrote this to show I had reasons to think about going to Rome. Had I wanted to rouse people against Luther, there were other ways of doing so.

Then, in my *Catalogus* I call Marino Caracciolo 'Reverend Father, apostolic nuncio to the emperor'; I say nothing else about him, save that it was he in particular who urged me to write against Luther. But Hutten calls him 'evil.'[250] Suppose he is – what is that to me? Even if he is evil, how does this concern me? I did not call him a good man, although he was a good and obliging friend until this tragedy destroyed all friendships. Hutten is likewise offended because I mention Eck somewhere, without insult;[251] against

* * * * *

logic (at Bologna) and metaphysics (at Padua) before his appointment in 1514 as professor of Thomistic theology in Rome. His appointment in 1515 as master of the sacred palace gave him authority to speak as Pope Leo x's theologian, and as censor of books in Rome. He was a staunch defender of papal primacy and papal infallibility. His attack on Luther's *Ninety Five Theses* was dismissed by Erasmus as 'ill-judged' (Ep 872:19). To Prierias' 'most kind letter' inviting Erasmus to Rome (Ep 1342:353) Erasmus made a courteous reply (Ep 1337A), but Prierias died in the interim.

249 Cf *Expostulatio* EB II 212:2–4 / K 92 par 134. To Prierias' *In presumptuosas Martini Lutheri conclusiones de potestate papae* (Rome: E. Silber June 1518), Luther responded with *Ad dialogum Silvestri Prieratis de potestate papae responsio* (WA 1 644–86, 9 782–7). Prierias responded with *Replica F. Silvestri Prieratis Sacri Palatii ap. Magister ad F. Martinum Lutherum*, which Luther simply re-published, without deigning to make a reply, save in a few prefatory notes.

250 Ep 1341A:1363–4 (on Caracciolo, see above n225); cf *Expostulatio*, EB II 212:5 / K 92 par 135.

251 In letters that he published, Erasmus speaks neutrally of Eck, or addresses him in a tone of respectful disagreement (Epp 769, 844, 1141:20, 1168:14–15); in letters that he did not publish he disapproves of Eck's attacks on Luther, without using the language Hutten attributes to him (Epp 872:24–7, 1186:26–7; cf *Expostulatio* EB II 212:9–11 / K 92 par 136).
Johann Maier of Eck in Swabia (1486–1543) studied at Heidelberg, Tübingen, and Cologne, where he was won over to the Thomist school. At Freiburg, from 1502, he lectured on Aristotle, and received his doctorate in theology. He spent the rest of his life as professor of theology at Ingolstadt. By drawing Luther into the famous Leipzig disputation (27 June–16 July 1519), he compelled the reformer to recognize that he accepted only Scripture as authoritative, not the councils of the church. Thereafter, Eck remained a vigorous, often vituperative opponent of Luther. In 1518, Eck drew a response from Erasmus by criticizing a number of points made in the notes to his *New Testament* (Epp 769, 844); in 1530 Erasmus apparently recognized as his own some propositions in a list of 404 heretical articles prepared by Eck, and responded accordingly (Allen Ep 2387).

this he invents criticisms I had about Eck in the past, as suits his purposes, but do not convey what I said.

Still more intolerable to Hutten is the praise in my letters for the Dominican, Johannes Faber.[252] What kind of man he is now I know not. But in Louvain he convinced me he was preparing to found in Augsburg a college for the teaching of languages and good letters, for which he showed me a charter from Emperor Maximilian. He also had harsh words for Luther's worst enemies, and for the Roman curia itself. I liked his gentle manner and his erudition in theology. Hence I could not refuse him those letters of recommendation. Then in Cologne, while the emperor was there, he sought my company; he also left – for the cardinal of Mainz and for me – a very fair judgment about Luther, written in his own hand.[253] So what can Hutten reproach me with, except that I showed a simple and trusting spirit? If Faber is now such a man as Hutten claims, he possesses a cunning I would never have expected to find in a German. Certainly I could not be responsible for how he would turn out, any more than I could have prevented Hutten – praised highly by me, and from the heart – from turning out to be the kind of man he reveals himself to be in this pamphlet, of which no decent man approves.

As for Johannes Fabri, the canon of Constance, he and I were friends long before the world ever heard of Luther.[254] If I renounce friendship with

* * * * *

252 Epp 1149–1152, 1156; cf *Expostulatio* EB II 212:12–213:2 / K 92–3 par 137. Johannes Faber (c 1470–1530), possibly born in Augsburg, studied theology in Italy, where he directed a Dominican house of studies in Venice, and received his doctorate from Padua. He became prior of the Dominican house in Augsburg (1505) and from 1511 he was vice-general of the Conventual Dominicans in southern Germany. In 1515 Emperor Maximilian I made him a councillor and court preacher. Erasmus' letters of recommendation for Faber were linked to their collaboration on a proposal for a negotiated settlement of the Lutheran controversy, published in Cologne as *Consilium cuiusdam ex animo cupientis esse consultum et Ro. Pontificis dignitati et Christianae religionis tranquilitati* (Ferguson *Opuscula* 349–61; CWE 71 108–12; cf Epp 1156, 1199:36–43, 1217:41–63; and for Erasmus' part in writing it, Allen Ep 1149 introduction; Ferguson *Opuscula* 338–61; Lowry CWE 71 99–100). After the Diet of Worms, Faber changed his mind and joined with Luther's foes, especially as the new teachings took hold in Augsburg. By 1529, according to Erasmus, Faber was in Rome, defaming, before the Roman curia, the good name of his erstwhile collaborator.

253 Cf the *Judicium* subsequently presented to Elector Frederick the Wise of Saxony: *Reichstagsakten, Jüngere Reihe* 11 484.

254 Cf Epp 392:2, 386:953, 976, 1324:128–33, 1335:39–57, 1341A:301n, 1342:358. Johannes Fabri of Leutkirch (1478–1541) studied theology and law both at

everyone who opposes Luther, I will hardly have anyone left among those
to whom I owe so much. Fabri wrote a book against Luther, yes, but not at
my urging. Now Hutten has me saying 'sometime' that this book 'deserved
to be thoroughly smeared with excrement.'[255] Whoever reported this tidbit
to Hutten is the one who deserves that treatment. Not only did I never say
such a thing, the idea never occurred to me, not even in my dreams. While
visiting in Constance I read only the preface, and praised his restraint.[256] I
did look over one passage in which he refutes Luther's assertion that Rome
has at long last pronounced in favour of the immortality of the soul.[257] This
bit I liked, but I am not so brash as to pronounce on a book I have not read
carefully. Besides, not liking a book written against Luther is not the same
as approving of him.

Ludwig Baer too was a sincere friend and faithful patron of mine well
before Luther became known.[258] His support I count among my blessings.
His many exceptional qualities make him the ornament of this city. He
firmly maintains his theological views, but in such wise that he is favourable
to good letters; he is zealous for peace, but in such wise that he favours
restoration of the gospel – though he by no means approves everything
Luther does.[259] But if Hutten has decided to take offence at everyone who

* * * * *

Tübingen and at Freiburg, where he earned his doctorate of civil and canon
law in 1510 or 1511. He became vicar-general of the diocese of Constance in
1517, and in 1521 suffragan bishop. Fabri was initially sympathetic to Luther's
effort to reform the church, but not after Luther attacked the papacy and canon
law at the Leipzig disputation. He became a councillor to Archduke Ferdinand
in 1523, and in 1530 bishop of Vienna, where he founded the trilingual college
of St Nicholas, and resolutely opposed the Reformation.

255 *Opus adversus nova quaedam et a christiana religione prorsus aliena dogmata Lutheri*
(Rome: M. Silber 1522; Leipzig 1523). After Luther ridiculed the book, Fabri
sharpened his critique in a revised version, *Malleus in haeresim Lutheranam*
(Cologne: J. Soter 1524). Cf *Expostulatio* EB II 213:4–5 / K 93 par 138.

256 For Erasmus' visit to Constance (September 1522), cf Ep 1342:369–418; Allen
Ep 1315 introduction. Cf *Adagia* I iii 62: *Nec per somnium quidem* 'Not even in
a dream' CWE 31 286–7.

257 Cf Dr. Johann Fabri *Malleus in haeresim Lutheranam* ed A. Naegele *Corpus
Catholicorum* 23–6 (Münster 1941–52) II 292:23–296:18; cf Luther *Resolutio Lutheriana super propositione sua decima tertia de potestate papae* (WA 2 226:38–40).

258 On Baer, see above n66. His friendship with Erasmus began when he greeted
the *New Testament* 'with enthusiastic devotion' (Ep 413:13–16).

259 Erasmus appreciated Baer as a theologian (Ep 1422:48–53), and consulted him
in writing his *Epistola de esu carnium* (cf Ep 1620:40–3) as well as the *De libero
arbitrio* (Epp 1419, 1420).

thinks ill of Luther, why attack this one man, when there are so many? In any case the things Luther has said well Baer does not distort, as many do, nor does he indulge in stupid vituperation. And he is surely not a *curtisanus*[260] - the kind of cleric who devotes himself to benefice-hunting. Yet this good man – who has never said a word against Hutten's affairs, his good name, or his friends – Hutten attacks with the kind of filthy, harsh language that would be proper for someone who had murdered his own father. With Baer Hutten associates Johann Gebwiler. Whatever kind of man Gebwiler may be, he is certainly no *curtisanus*.[261] He and I have not been friends: he has not called at my house, I do not even know where his is located, and we never greet each other on the street. Yet Hutten, badly served by his scandalmongering friend, has this to say: 'And these two you welcome in your house for daily conversation, while excluding me!'[262] Gebwiler I do not see, as I have said. Baer, though a friend and a neighbour,[263] sometimes lets two months pass without calling on me. Daily conversations indeed! What will people think who read Hutten's words, and know the story? But I should not impute this nonsense to Hutten – he merely follows the lead of the man who has choreographed this drama.[264] Others whom I have censured in the past – Latomus, Baechem, Jan Briart – I am also supposed to have treated ambiguously in my letters, or indirectly.[265] I admit that when we friends of good letters were in league

* * * * *

260 See above n201.
261 Cf *Expostulatio* EB II 213:8–12 / K 93 par 139.
    Johann Gebwiler of Colmar (documented 1465–1530) studied at Freiburg and at Basel, where he took his doctorate in theology (1507), and was appointed professor of theology and rector of the university. He was a determined foe of the Reformation, both from the pulpit of his parish church in Basel (St Alban's), and at the disputations of Zürich (1523) and Baden (1526). When Catholic worship in Basel was prohibited (1529), he joined other cathedral canons in the Catholic exodus to Freiburg.
262 *Expostulatio* EB II 213:15–6; K 93 par 140.
263 Erasmus' house was called *Zur alten Treu*, now *Nadelberg* 15–19 (cf Epp 1316:41–2, 1342:582–4); Baer, as provost of St Peter's, must have had a house nearby.
264 Eppendorf; see above 54.
265 Cf *Expostulatio* EB II 213:17–214:10; K 93 par 141–94 par 142. For Nicholas Baechem, see above n187.
    Jacobus Latomus (c 1475–1544), also known as Masson, studied in Paris and then at Louvain, under Adrian of Utrecht. He received his doctorate in theology in 1519, and served three times as dean of the theology faculty. Latomus would prove an unrelenting literary opponent of the Reformation. Though at first friendly to Erasmus, he strongly objected to the new *Collegium Trilingue*

together against our enemies, I sometimes complained in letters to friends about the obstinate conspiracy of certain individuals against better studies.[266] Even then, however, I waged war in such a way that I was always prepared for peace, should the occasion arise. So, while I never flattered Baechem,[267] I held back from attacking Latomus, hoping he would leave off.[268] Briart was neither mean-spirited nor adverse to good letters, but certain monks and theologians, taking advantage of his irascibility, got him to stage a hateful drama.[269] Indeed their prodding helped bring on his death, for he was of weak health, unable to bear the strain of anger, and unaccustomed to injury. The fact that the present tragedy became all the more violent after his death[270] shows that he had been a moderating influence. What I wrote about him was that he was 'most highly praised by all' yet never 'praised enough.'[271] This gave the Louvain theologians a laugh, for as vicechancellor of the university Briart was feted every day in solemn encomia. By the lights of his personality he was not unfair to me, for he alone was

* * * * *

at Louvain, considering the teaching of Greek and Hebrew dangerous. His *De trium linguarum et studii theologici ratione* (Antwerp: M. Hillen 1519) prompted a reply from Erasmus, *Apologia contra Latomi dialogum* (Antwerp: J. Thibault [1519]; CWE 71:31–84). In the tense years prior to his departure for Basel, Erasmus considered Latomus his most dangerous foe among the Louvain theologians (Epp 1088, 1113, 1123).

Jan Briart of Ath (1460–1520), also known as Atensis, was ordained a priest while studying theology at Louvain. Having received his doctorate in 1500, he held a number of positions in the theology faculty and the university, frequently substituting for the chancellor, Briart's friend Adrian of Utrecht, whose business often called him away. From 1515 Briart was vice-chancellor of the university. When Erasmus joined the theology faculty in 1517 Briart sought to make him welcome; Erasmus reciprocated the courtesy, showing Briart his *Paraphrasis in Romanos* before publication (Ep 695). In later years Erasmus insisted that Briart had also approved of the second edition of his New Testament before he sent the manuscript off for publication (Epp 1225, 1571, 1581). Thereafter, however, Erasmus had reason to think that Briart was siding with his critics; for a time he suspected that Briart was behind the attack on him by Edward Lee (Ep 843:538n).

266 Eg Epp 943:3–9, 948:22–188, 1064, 1126:210–17
267 Cf Epp 1301, 1341A:928–1013; above n187.
268 For the controversy between Latomus and Erasmus, see Rummel *Catholic Critics* I 63–93.
269 Cf Epp 1028:19–26, 1029:2–10, 1123:21–4.
270 Briart died on 8 January 1520.
271 The point is clearer from a more literal translation of Allen Ep 536:23–4 than is given in Ep 536:26–7.

responsible for arranging a peace between me and the rest of the theology faculty.[272] In learning and discernment he far surpassed the others. Shortly before he died, he assured me of peace and friendship as far as he was concerned.

Hutten fears that in the end I might even be reconciled with Edward Lee.[273] I would not mind doing so – I admit it – if only Lee would show a spirit worthy of friendship. In Calais, where we met by chance, I greeted him and shook his hand[274] – why not, since we had settled our quarrel? In any event, the help I got from Germany was not worth very much.[275] Friends from there wrote that the Germans were prepared to tear Lee to pieces, whether I wanted them to or not. I at first advised against their project, and once it was clear I could not prevent it I urged them to use arguments against Lee, not abuse; they should especially refrain from insulting the English nation as a whole.[276] This was exactly what happened, to my great displeasure.[277] I have again and again condemned the *Dialogus* against Lee.[278] Then came an enormous bundle of letters written against Lee by various learned men; this I suppressed, save that I had copies made for two friends, Dorpius and More.[279] When urged by some to publish it,

* * * * *

272 In September 1519; cf Epp 1022 introduction, 1028:19–21, 1217:135–8, 1225: 145–8.

273 Cf *Expostulatio* EB II 214:13–5 / K 94 par 134. On Edward Lee see above n126.

274 In July 1520; cf Allen Ep 1118 introduction.

275 But see Allen Epp 998:66n, 1083 introduction; Ferguson *Opuscula* 233–4; Rummel *Catholic Critics* I 110–15.

276 Cf Epp 1083:36–9, 1088:5–8, 1132:20; cf *Apologia qua respondet invectivis Lei* CWE 72 28, 65.

277 Cf Epp 998:78–91, 1129:19–26. Yet (as Hutten well knew) Erasmus had mobilized German humanists to write against Lee: cf Epp 999:342–51, 1074 introduction, 1075 introduction, 1083 introduction, 1085:4–12, 1088:2–13.

278 Konrad Nesen *Dialogus bilinguium ac trilinguium* (Paris: J. Bade for C. Resch 1519); Ferguson *Opuscula* 204–24; CWE 73 29–47. On the question of authorship, see Bietenholz CWE 7 330–3.

279 Cf Ep 1139:108–11, 1157:2–5. Erasmus must have shown the letters to More when they met at Calais in June 1520 (Allen Ep 1118 introduction). By then the first and possibly the second edition of *Epistolae aliquot eruditorum*, directed against Edward Lee, had already been published (Antwerp: M. Hillen April–May 1520 and June–July 1520). In these volumes were four letters to Erasmus, two in the first edition (Epp 1083, 1084) and two in an appendix to the second edition (Epp 1095, 1099), that would not have been published without his approval.

Maarten van Dorp of Naaldwijk (1485–1525) received a humanist education at Louvain's college of the Lily, and from 1504 taught classical Latin while

I replied that I had decided to keep silence, if Lee would do the same. So, reader, you have the full list of things that might have wounded Hutten's spirit; as you can see, nothing in all of this ought to have sundered even an ordinary friendship.

Now I come to what Hutten considers the main point of the whole case.[280] In refuting him I have to be careful not to prove too much, lest in fleeing Scylla I am swept into Charybdis.[281] Right at the start he joins two propositions that are obviously false, first that I had once adhered to Luther's party, and second that I now fight with all my powers against the gospel. In fact, I have always opposed that party, and I have never ceased promoting the gospel cause with all my heart. This is what he assumes, in high-sounding words but with no sense of shame: 'Was it not but a short time ago that you were with us in putting the Roman pontiff in his place, your righteous pen indicting Rome itself as a cesspool of crime and depravity? Did you not curse papal bulls and indulgence and condemn ecclesiastical ceremonies? Was it not you who called the curial system to account, denouncing canon law and papal pronouncements? In short, you mercilessly flayed that whole array of hypocrisy – the entire hypocritical

* * * * *

studying scholastic theology, obtaining his doctorate in 1515; in 1517 he became president of the college of the Holy Spirit. In 1514 he made objections to the *Moria*, and to the projected critical edition of the New Testament (Epp 304, 337), but seems to have been impressed by replies from Erasmus (Ep 337) and from their mutual friend, Thomas More (Elizabeth Frances Rogers *The Correspondence of Sir Thomas More* [Princeton 1947] Ep 15). Dorp himself taught a course on the Pauline Epistles in 1516, only to have the theology faculty revoke his licence to teach theology. Dorp still had differences with Erasmus but from 1517 the two men were on friendly terms.

Thomas More (1478–1535) lived as a guest at the London Charterhouse while reading law at Lincoln's Inn. He became a member of the House of Commons in 1504, a councillor to Henry VIII in 1518, and speaker of the house in 1523; he served as lord chancellor from 1529 until his resignation on 16 May 1532, one day after the 'Submission of the Clergy.' Refusing to swear an oath to the king as head of the church, as required by the Act of Succession (1534), he was imprisoned in the Tower, tried for treason, and beheaded on 6 July 1535. From the time of their first meeting in England (1499), More and Erasmus were life-long friends. More's humour helped inspire Erasmus' *Moria* (which he wrote while living in More's house in 1509), and Erasmus was instrumental in the publication of More's *Utopia*.

280 Cf *Expostulatio* EB II 186:14–187:4, 214:17–215:18 / K 65 par 32–66 par 33, 94 par 144 – 95 par 147.

281 Cf *Adagia* I v 4: *Evitata Charybdi in Scyllam incidi* 'Having escaped Charybdis I fell into Scylla' CWE 31 387:1–389:87.

structure of that estate. And now this same Erasmus has pulled back, indeed he goes backward in his tracks, entering into an alliance with the enemy.' And again: 'This man it was who unearthed a piety long buried, who brought the gospel from darkness into light, restoring faith and religion. Now he bends all his effort to trample underfoot, to expel, overthrow, and utterly annihilate everything he had worked for!'[282] Now let us see if this accuser has any sense of shame. The way Hutten argues a case is that he first assumes something, then hammers away with varying forms of words, always exaggerating, as if a charge that is in itself groundless can be made true by constantly and boldly asserting it. To this end he marshals all the resources of his eloquence, forceful and vehement. But where the basis on which an argument is built is empty and frivolous, diction is empty and worthless, and the more you thrash about during your speech the more you waste, as they say, both toil and water.[283] In a serious matter like this, one must not arbitrarily make up the stance of one's opponent – a custom that Quintilian censured even in debate exercises, although it was common.[284] See how Hutten anguishes over the reasons that could have led me to turn from a cause so holy and embrace one so evil! He should have concentrated on showing the truth of what he assumed. Instead, our powerful speaker has only this to say: 'Certain people told me.'[285] How grave and fierce he is in denouncing me for having abandoned and betrayed the gospel cause, deserting to the foe; corrupted by money, I bent all my powers to attack good men, gospel truth, and public liberty. Yet before he came to these tragic polemics, what he assumed should either have been agreed between us, or demonstrated by appropriate arguments.

I have constantly declared, in countless letters, booklets, and personal statements, that I do not want to be involved with either party.[286] I give many reasons for my position, and there are others I have not disclosed. But in this respect my conscience does not accuse me before Christ, my judge. Amid all the upheavals of our day, amid so many dangers to my reputation and even my life, I have kept my counsels moderate, so as not

* * * * *

282 Cf *Expostulatio* EB II 186:19–187:4, 216:7–10 / K 66 par 33 (cf K 213–14), K 96 par 150 (trans JDT).

283 Cf Quintilian *Institutio* 11.3.52; *Adagia* I iv 62: *Oleum et operam perdidi* 'I have wasted both oil and toil' CWE 31 362:1–363:49.

284 Cf Quintilian *Institutio* 12.1.10.

285 Cf *Expostulatio* EB II 185:11 / K 64 par 25.

286 Cf Epp 1202:267–70 and 277–8, 1217:149–51, 1225:168–71.

to be the author of any disturbance, nor to support a cause of which I did not approve, nor in any way to betray the truth of the gospel.

How can Hutten be indignant that I do not join him in giving allegiance to Luther? Three years ago, while in Louvain, I avowed in a preface added to my *Colloquia* that I was and would always remain most adverse to that party.[287] Not only that, I have tried as best I can to persuade as many friends as possible to do likewise;[288] I still do, and will not cease doing so. What I call partisan is the kind of zeal that swears by everything Luther has written, is writing now, or will write in the future[289] – an attitude one often finds even among good men.

I have openly told all my friends that if they cannot love me unless I am a Lutheran, they must like me or not, as they wish.[290] I love my freedom, and neither desire nor am able to serve any party.[291] Hutten says I should have stayed with Luther's party if only for the sake of my friends; he claims there are several who deserve better from me, and who would not be torn away from Luther any more than from truth itself.[292] Which friends he means I know not, but I do know that many who were formerly devoted to Luther now remain silent, while others cannot bear to hear his name, and still others condemn what they at first approved. If any friend of mine had ever meant so much to me that I gave myself over to Luther's party for his sake, then for his sake too I would not withdraw from that party. Likewise, if anyone ever saw me so drunk that I wholly approved of Luther, then I will allow him to call me *rhipsaspis*[293] instead of Erasmus. Little wonder if I refuse the name Lutheran, since here in Basel I find no one who can bear being called a Lutheran. [294] Hutten barely accepts the label – not surprisingly, for Luther himself does not acknowledge him, and did not want his protection.[295] Unless I miss my guess, Luther would rather have

* * * * *

287 Cf Epp 1041:50–51, 1225:163–9, 1526:38–40.
288 Cf Epp 1225:298–9, 1236:79–83, 1275:25–9, 1299:25–7, 1386:5–9.
289 Cf Epp 1219:73–4, 1225:276–7.
290 Cf Ep 1342:1096–7.
291 Cf Epp 1002:37–8, 1153:27–9, 1202:268–74.
292 Cf *Expostulatio* EB II 214:17–215:5 / K 99 par 144.
293 Cf *Adagia* II ii 97: *Abjecit hastam. Rhipsaspis* CWE 33 127–8: 'Greek too has a proverbial expression of contempt, *rhipsaspis*, those who throw away the shield, for the cowardly and the despairing who abandon their place in the line and leave their shield behind them.'
294 Cf Epp 1300:92–3, 1342:738–9.
295 In early 1520 Hutten had offered Luther Sickingen's protection (Holborn *Ulrich von Hutten* 122–3, 140–2).

me as an adversary than Hutten as a defender. Perhaps Hutten's affairs are in such a state that he needs the name Lutheran, for there is now nothing else to protect and support him. I have never condemned, out of hatred for the man himself, anything of Luther's that was well said. Hatred for Luther never prompted me to condemn anything that he spoke rightly, nor will love for him make me approve of anything of Luther's that seems wrong.[296] Suppose I had at one time sworn allegiance to him or his companions: I should be congratulated for having come to my senses.

In fact, as is well known to some who used to be ardent Lutherans (what they are now I know not), the whole controversy was launched despite my advice.[297] My very first letter to Luther makes my fears clear: I saw a lack of modesty and evangelical mildness in his writings, and obstinacy in his assertions.[298] These qualities are all the more evident in the books he produces, each more violent than the other, and directed as they are even against the most powerful princes, who, whatever their deserts, ought not be provoked.[299] Among friends I sometimes said, with sorrow, that I had doubts about Luther's spirit,[300] though I never presumed to make a pronouncement.[301] This is all I have had to say about Luther, and I have said it consistently, in speech and writings, in private and in public. Where then is this extraordinary inconstancy? I suspect that what really troubles them is my constancy.

According to Hutten – he must have heard this from a drinking buddy – I am now so furious about Luther that I neglect everything else.[302] But that Achates of his, Eppendorf,[303] could have told him that I had no leisure for plotting against Luther, for I had then just begun my *Paraphrase on*

* * * * *

296 Cf Epp 1217:165–9, 1218:49–50, 1225:276–8, 1305:27–30, 1369:17–20.
297 Cf Epp 1141:6n, 1167:439–42, 1202:271–2, 1252:10–11, 1300:49–51, 1342:824–8.
298 The reference is to Ep 980, published by a mutual friend; cf Epp 947:41–3, 980:43–58, 1033:56–9, 1113:23–4, 1119:32–4, 1127:18–21, 1127A:68–74, 1143:27–46, 1156:70–2, 1166:99–9 and 107–14, 1167:172–5 and 266–70, 1183:115–7, 1202:41–154, 1219:44–9, 1225:182–4, 1313:11–5, 1342:836–7, 1348:8–11, 1384:17–18.
299 To King Henry VIII's *Assertio septem sacramentorum adversus Martinum Lutherum* (London: Pynson 12 July 1521), Luther responded both in German (*Antwort deutsch auf König Heinrichs von England Buch* WA 10-2 227–62), and in Latin (*Contra Henricum Regem Angliae* WA 10-2 180–222). Cf Epp 1342:870–92, 1348:11–26, 1352:79–82.
300 Cf Epp 1033:64–7, 1183:113–14, 1218:31–2, 1259:6–7, 1342:866–8, 1384:18–19.
301 As Brunfels grasped (*Responsio* 333:9–15), Erasmus raises here the possibility that Luther's wrathful spirit was inspired by the devil. Cf Tracy *Low Countries* 149–50. Cf below 112.
302 Not a direct quote, but cf *Expostulatio* EB II 214:17ff / K 94 par 144ff.
303 See above n70.

Luke[304] and was wholly engaged in this project when Hutten, our defender of the gospel cause, launched his attack. But in my *Catalogus*, he says, I promise three dialogues against Luther. Let him find in my writings the phrase 'against Luther'! I do speak of the Lutheran affair, saying that I have in mind 'a discussion rather than a confrontation,' which I have 'not so much undertaken as planned.'[305] I have not yet decided to complete these works, and if I do they will not be published, save at the behest of those who have urged me to write.[306] So, dear reader, though I have offered to write certain things, do not form a premature conclusion.[307] I did not promise the dialogues in question, or if I did promise them, it was not to the public but to the pope and the emperor, at whose wish they would either be published or suppressed.[308] One thing I do promise is that these works will evince the utmost fairness to Luther. Since there will be a speaker to take Luther's part, how can Hutten know whether my dialogues will damage Luther or support him?[309] Already I can hear people saying: meanwhile you keep us in suspense, for you will not declare what you think of Luther. But I do not have enough time to deal with all the books Luther has written; if I did, it would be beyond my capacity to render judgment on all aspects of the matter.[310] And what should I say? If I condemn Luther root and branch, I would be covering up much that is good, while giving aid and

* * * * *

304 Cf Ep 1381 introduction: Erasmus began work on the *Paraphrase of Luke* by 23 April 1523.

305 Cf *Expostulatio* EB II 231:5–10; K 109 par 204–5; Ep 1341A:1338–1416 (remarks quoted on lines 1339–40 and 1373–4). As of April 1522, Erasmus had 'made a fair start with a short treatise on how to end this business of Luther' (Ep 1275:22–4), and in March 1523 Jan de Fevijn reported that Erasmus had in mind a three-part dialogue (H. de Vocht *Literae virorum eruditorum ad Cran-eveldium 1522–1528* (Louvain 1928), Ep 49:9–13). For the concept of a 'discussion' (*collatio*), Hoffmann *Rhetoric and Theology* 179–82, 260 n84; Boyle *Rhetoric and Reform* 31. The work described was not finished, with the possible exception of the colloquy *Inquisitio de fide*, arguably a shorter version of the second dialogue (Thompson *Fide* 34–8). See also Erasmus' proposals to Pope Adrian VI (Ep 1352).

306 Cf Ep 1341A:1372–8.

307 Cf Ep 1341A:1392–3.

308 In Ep 1341A:1388–92 Erasmus speaks of having 'offered the monarchs' not three dialogues but 'a secret plan of my own.'

309 Cf Ep 1341A:1341–9.

310 Cf Epp 939:70–1 and 135–8, 947:41, 961:37–8, 967:86–114, 980:19–21, 993:54–5, 1033:44–7, 1127:25–6, 1127A:66–8, 1143:14–6, 1153:23–31 and 61–7, 1164:73–5, 1167:138–41, 219–21, 233–54, and 442–3, 1183:114–5, 1192:7, 1995:104–5, 1202: 47–52, 1217:152–6, 1219:75–6, 1225:259–61, 1236:84–8, 1244:33–5, 1313:55–60, 1342:324–8 and 831–7.

comfort to a party I know only too well. But if I approve of Luther top
to bottom, I would be acting presumptuously – pronouncing to be good
things I may not understand – while throwing myself into the arms of a
party that includes many whom I want nothing to do with. Those who hate
Luther will do so even if I keep silence; those who favour him expect from
me just another partisan argument, not a judicious weighing of the case.
Were I to render a split verdict, conceding and denying certain things to
each side, I would expose myself to attack from both, serving only to add
to the uproar. Hence I have thought it better to keep my ideas to myself,
until the day when princes and scholars, setting partisanship and polemics
aside, seek the kind of counsel that may conduce to the truth of the gospel
and the glory of Christ.[311] Hutten at this point tries to be clever, suggesting
that, like Caiphas, I allow a word of truth to escape my lips unawares.[312] He
refers to my saying that suppressing the whole of Luther's teaching would
at the same time bring down a good part of evangelical sincerity and public
liberty. But have I not said this constantly, in many conversations and in
many of my writings?[313] It grieves me to see Luther's followers defend
their cause as if they had no wish to preserve it; yet if Luther teaches some
things truly, the teaching is not his but Christ's.

　　Let him assume that I have already decided to write against Luther. Do
I not have the right, as one who never swore allegiance to Luther, and whose
counsels were ignored as the conflict arose and proceeded? Let him assume
that I favoured Luther from the start; must I then approve of everything
he has written subsequently, just because his early works pleased me?[314]
Suppose Luther writes something contrary to the articles of faith – will
Hutten still forbid me to oppose him? And why does Hutten rage as he
does against those who write against Luther,[315] making no distinction between polemic and debate? For Luther himself calls for debate. If his doctrine is true it will shine even more brilliantly by being contradicted, just
as gold is purified by fire;[316] if it is false, let it be attacked by everyone;

* * * * *

311 Cf Ep 1352 introduction: Erasmus had offered specific suggestions to Adrian
　　VI [March 1523], but the fact that he received no reply led him to fear that he
　　had given offence.
312 Cf *Expostulatio* EB II 235:11–15 / K 114 par 222. The reference is to John 11:49–
　　50.
313 Hutten was likely referring to Ep 1341A:1383–8 or Ep 1342:782–4, both of
　　which had been published; but see also Epp 1313:17–22, 1348:29–30.
314 Contrast Ep 1127A:100–2 with Ep 1203:27–32.
315 Cf *Expostulatio* EB II 213:2–5, 231:4–14 / K 93 par 138, 109 par 204–110 par 205.
316 Cf *Adagia* IV i 58: *Aurum igni probatum* 'Gold tested in the fire' CWE 35 476.

and if there is falsehood mixed with the truth, let it be purified. Will I be overthrowing the whole gospel if I dispute Luther's assertions that every Christian is a priest, and that all the works of the saints are sins?[317] Luther has no fear of me, nor indeed of any foe; he waits with stout heart to see if Erasmus will enter the lists.[318] So, when Hutten makes such a racket, it leads people to suspect that Luther's doctrine will stand up only if no one shakes it.

I say these things to refute Hutten's calumnies, not because I wish to confront Luther, even if I had leisure for doing so. To avoid being dragged into the gladiatorial arena, I have done all I could: I have suffered in silence, and I have taken on different guises, like Vertumnus, or Proteus, or an octopus.[319] To those tugging at me to join a princely court I have made excuses. Inducements to join Luther's party I have avoided, or warded off, or simply ignored.[320] I have withdrawn from the emperor's entourage, and have declined handsome offers of money. I can hardly count those to whom I have made excuses – the kings, the princes, the friends, all calling on me to enter the fray. Now if we credit Hutten, those who incite me against Luther 'are either very powerful or very evil, or both.'[321] All the more reason for him to admire my constancy! For while the powerful can destroy as well as protect, and the evil need no excuse to injure others, those who are both are even more frightful. Yet the Erasmus he thinks weak and feeble, swayed by any breeze,[322] has thus far not yielded to any kind of pressure.

* * * * *

317 Cf below 122, 143; and Epp 1195:74, 1225:358–61, 1384:11–15.
318 Luther's letter to a friend was published in 1523 under the title *Iudicium D. Martini Lutheri de Erasmo Roterodamo* (Strasbourg: Johann Schott 1523); cf. WAB r 2 499:19–16, together with Ep 1341A:1251–2, 1342:897–9, 1496:18n.
319 On Vertumnus see above n246. The sea-god Proteus changed into all manner of shapes; if caught and held in his true form he had to answer questions honestly; cf *Adagia* II ii 74: *Proteo mutabilior* 'As many shapes as Proteus' CWE 33 113–14. The *polypus* 'octopus' was seen as adjusting to its environment; cf *Adagia* I i 93: *Polypi mentem obtine* 'Adopt the outlook of a polyp' CWE 31 133:1– 136:85. The principle of accommodation (cf 1 Cor 9:22) was a major theme in Erasmus' rhetorical theology; see eg *Enchiridion* CWE 66 104; *Ratio* Holborn 211:31.
320 Cf Epp 1144:70–4, 1183:144–5, 1195:138–40, 1202:278–81, 1217:118–25, 1218:27– 9, 1219:71–3, 1225:193–7, 1244:9–11, 1342:793–6.
321 Cf *Expostulatio* EB II 231:8–10 / K 109 par 205.
322 Cf *Expostulatio* EB II 185:4–5 / K 64 par 23; EB II 187:8–10; K 66 par 34; EB II 189:14–18 / K 68–9 par 45; EB II 198:18–9 / K 78 par 83; EB II 228:2–3 / K 106 par 190; EB II 232:18 / K 111 par 211; B233:18–20 / K 112 par 216; EB II 237:16–7 / K 116 par 230; EB II 239:4–7 / K 117 par 236.

Hutten laughs at me for saying the whole world was sharpening its pen against Luther. Lutherans, he warns, will sharpen their pens against me; he also demands to know which 'world' I speak of – as if everyone stood with Luther.[323] So let me mention the many who have written against Luther.[324] Among the Italians there is Silvester Prierias, Thomas Todiscus, Jacobus de Vio,[325] and Catarinus; among the Germans, Eck, a Franciscan of Leipzig whose name I have forgotten, Cochlaeus,[326]

* * * * *

323 Cf *Expostulatio* EB II 220:9–14 / K 99 par 162; Ep 1342:907–8, cf Epp 1153:163–8, 1236:90–1 and 112, 1263:53, 1313:62, 1342:324–5.

324 Among the authors Erasmus now brings up to show how many have written against Luther, some have been mentioned above, and others need not be discussed detail. For Prierias, Eck, Fabri, Hoogstraten, Latomus, Vincentius, and Fisher, see above, nn248, 251, 254, 20, 260, 189, and 164. 'Todiscus' refers to the Dominican friar Tommaso Radini Tedeschi (1488–1527), a professor of theology at the University of Rome. Ambrosius Catharinus was the name taken (in honor of St. Catharine of Siena) by Lancelloto de' Politi (1484–1553), who taught law and philosophy in Siena. The Leipzig Franciscan whose name Erasmus forgets was Augustin Alfeldt (c 1480–1535), who taught theology at the Franciscan cloister in Leipzig. Agostino Giustiani of Genoa (c. 1470–1536), known for an edition of the Psalms in Hebrew, Arabic, and Chaldean, was the first professor of Oriental languages at the University of Paris. Eustachius van der Revieren of Zichem (d. 1538) was a professor of theology at Louvain. And Remaclus Arduenna of Florennes (c 1480–1524), the imperial secretary, aided Aleandro in the burning of Luther's books in Brabant.

325 Jacobus de Vio, Cardinal Cajetanus of Gaeta (1469–1534), took the name Tommaso on entering the Dominican order. After studying theology at Bologna, he took his doctorate and taught for a time at Padua before moving on to Rome, where he published his influential commentaries on the writings of St Thomas Aquinas. As head of the Dominican order, he championed papal authority while advocating church reform. As papal legate to Germany in 1518, he confronted Luther at the Diet of Augsburg. Against Luther, he wrote his *De divina institutione pontificatus Romani pontificis*, published in Rome in 1521, and a *Responsio super quinque Martini Lutheri articulos*. Cf *Acta* CWE 71 105.

326 Johannes Cochlaeus (1479–1552), born of a peasant family, adopted a Latin name based on his village, Wendelstein (*Wendel* = spiral, *cochlea* = snail shell). After studies at Cologne he was for a time rector of a Latin school in Nürnberg. He then studied law in Bologna and theology in Ferrara. After his ordination to the priesthood in Rome, he became dean of St Mary's in Frankfurt am Main; as a humanist, he had friendly ties with Pirckheimer, and also with Hutten. Following the Diet of Worms he became a prolific antagonist of Luther, as in his *De gratia sacramentorum liber unus* (1522), and *Adversus cucullatum minotaurum Wittenbergensem* (1523). His *Septiceps Lutherus* (1528) featured a seven-headed Luther on the frontispiece; cf *Purgatio adversus epistolam Lutheri* below 413.

Johannes Fabri, and Hoogstraten; among the French the whole University of Paris,[327] and Augustinus Iustinianus; in Louvain Latomus, Johannes Turnhout,[328] and two Dominicans, Eustathius and Vincentius; and at the imperial court there is Marlianus, bishop of Tuy,[329] and Remaclus, one of the emperor's secretaries. In England there is the king himself,[330] John, bishop of Rochester, and a certain man who is bitter enough that he would readily give Luther the finger.[331] In Spain there is Stunica,[332] and

* * * * *

327 On 15 April 1521 the theology faculty at Paris condemned 104 propositions from Luther's writings: *Determinatio theologicae facultatis Parisiensis super doctrina Lutheriana* (Paris: J. Bade nd).

328 Jan Driedo of Turnhout (c 1480–1535) studied theology at Louvain; he was ordained a priest and became a professor before 1515, and was in subsequent years often dean of the theology faculty. Unlike Latomus, he saw a need for languages in the study of Scripture, and supported the Trilingual College at Louvain. In 1520 he was preparing a treatise against Luther's *Ninety-Five Theses*, but, to the regret of Erasmus, who appreciated his moderation and fairness, it was never published. Cf Epp 1127A:48–50, 1163:11–21, 1165:16–8, 1167:460–6, 1173:99–101; *Acta* CWE 71 104.

329 Luigi Marliano of Milan (d May 1521), a humanist, physician, and diplomat, was physician to Archduke Philip the Handsome of Burgundy (d 1506), and thereafter physician and councillor to his son, the young Archduke Charles. Upon his wife's death he was ordained a priest, and Charles secured his appointment as bishop of Tuy in Galicia. He supported publication in the Netherlands of *Exsurge Domine*, the papal bull against Luther, and also penned a treatise of his own, *In Martinum Lutherum oratio* (Rome [ie Strasbourg 1519–20?]). He accompanied Charles v to the Diet of Worms, where he died of the plague.

330 For his *Assertio septem sacramentorum* (1521) Henry VIII received the title of *Defensor fidei* from Pope Leo x; cf Ep 1227:7–8.

331 Erasmus refers to Thomas More's pseudonymous *Responsio ad Lutherum*, a defence of Henry VIII's *Assertio* (previous note) against Luther's reply, the *Contra Henricum*, which reached England in November 1522. As published, the *Responsio ad Lutherum* represents a major revision in the latter part of 1523. An early version, printed but not released for publication, was sent by More to certain of his friends, including Erasmus, who received his copy on 4 July 1523. See *The Complete Works of St. Thomas More* ed J.M. Headley (New Haven and London 1969) VI 1 (the text), and V 2 introduction 713–847, especially 727, 791–5, 832–4. For Thomas More, see above n279. For 'giving the finger,' a seemingly timeless gesture of supreme contempt, cf *Adagia* II iv 68: *Medium digitum ostendere* CWE 33 225–6.

332 Diego López Zúñiga or Stunica (d 1531), a scholar of ancient languages and a collaborator on the Complutensian Polyglot Bible, taught theology at the University of Alcalá before leaving for Rome in 1521. His *Annotationes contra Erasmum Roterodamum in defensionem tralationis novi testamenti* (Alcalá: Arnao

Caranza.[333] To all these add the papal bull[334] and the emperor's edict.[335] And there are many who have not yet published their books against Luther, others who are not yet finished, and still others unknown to me. These names I mention things only to show Hutten had no cause to ridicule my hyperbole.

Moreover, the idea of Lutherans writing books against me troubles me so little that I regret that none has appeared during the last three years. At times I even thought of getting a friend to provoke some ardent Lutheran to attack me, for it would have served better than anything to free me from suspicion.[336] Now Hutten is surely a Lutheran, and the woeful dribble he puts on paper has to be called writing. Yet I have never held Lutherans in such low esteem as to suspect any of them of slandering someone in this way, nor do I think Luther hates me so much that he would approve of a book like Hutten's. Still, if he did approve it, I would not be troubled.[337] Meanwhile, he says, I keep silent, like Mettius, looking to the outcome of the war – a treachery for which I ought to be torn to pieces.[338] Does a man deserve such punishment if he applies his labour and his fortune to the benefit of both parties? If so, what does a man deserve when he harms

* * * * *

Guillén de Brocar 1520) defended the Latin Vulgate while charging Erasmus with incompetence, impiety, and collusion with Luther (cf H.J. De Jonge's edition of Erasmus' *Apologia ad annotationes Stunicae* ASD IX-2 13–43). But no work of his against Luther is known.

333 Sancho Carranza de Miranda (d 1531), a professor of theology at Alcalá, published a critique of Erasmus' *New Testament* along the lines of Stunica's, but more moderate and respectful in tone. Erasmus replied in a generally similar vein, the two developed friendly relations (Carranza intervened on Erasmus' behalf at the conference of Valladolid in 1527). He is not known to have published anything against Luther.

334 *Exsurge Domine* (15 June 1520, Mirbt / Aland, no 789, 504–13) threatened Luther with excommunication; cf Epp 1141:11n, 1153:40–3 and 142–8, 1156:93–9, 1167: 20n, 449–54, 1183:124–5, 1192:8n, 1196:13n, 1313:67–8.

335 The Edict of Worms (26 May 1521, *Deutsche Reichstagsakten, Jüngere Reihe* II 92 640–59) placed Luther beyond the protection of law in the Holy Roman Empire; cf Epp 1197 introduction, 1216:19n, 1221:43–52, 1238:105, 1313:68–73.

336 Cf Epp 1268:83–90, 1274:53–7, 1278:28–30.

337 In a letter to Pellicanus in Basel (1 October 1523), Luther was critical of Hutten's *Expostulatio*, but more critical of Erasmus' *Spongia* (WAB r 3 661:7–16); cf Epp 1341A:1095–105, 1397:9–10, 1415:47–8, 1429:12–3, 1437:182–5, 1443:27–32.

338 Cf *Expostulatio* EB II 232:10–16 / K 111 par 210. Mettius Fufetius, dictator of Alba Longa, surrendered to the Romans but awaited an opportunity to betray them. Tullius Hostilius, Rome's third king, had him torn apart by chariots driven in opposite directions (Livy 1.23–8; Virgil *Aeneid* 8.642ff).

both parties by his stupid ranting, stirring one side up beyond control, and
burdening the other with opprobrium? Indeed, does he not injure more
grievously the side he claims to favour, giving aid and comfort to those he
claims to oppose? As for me, while Mettius remained idle, I have not, for
my zeal to advance the gospel has been unflagging. Let the young reach for
their weapons. I prepare myself for the day I will be summoned before the
judgment-seat of Christ[339] – a day that awaits us all, but cannot be far off for
me. I see how difficult it is to maintain a tranquil and Christian spirit amidst
the hatred and insults spawned by this affair. But when I concentrate on
my *Paraphrases*, I feel the agitation of my mind subside, and I become better
than I was. On both sides there are men who thank me, and say they have
found fruit in my labours.[340] Even Hutten acknowledges this, for he bids
me to stick to the things that will do more good than I could do by writing
against Luther.[341] Why then, does he interrupt me with his *Expostulatio*?

He says I am elusive because I say different things in various letters. Must I write the same thing to everyone, fitting, as it were, the same
shoe to every foot, notwithstanding the fact that people are different, not to
speak of changes in time and circumstances?[342] Amid a controversy of this
kind, where people are zealous in different directions, who can avoid saying some things indirectly? In that case, Hutten will say, silence would be
preferable. Would that I could keep silence! But, pressured, pleaded with,
and attacked, I have to dispel suspicions that have been raised. Paul himself
often changes his language – now flattering, now reproving, now imploring, now threatening, meanwhile dissimulating many things.[343] This was
not inconstancy, for his goal was ever the same, however he modulated his
voice or countenance. Show me that I have changed my purpose, and you
may charge me with inconstancy. The facts will show that I continue to pursue the goal with which I began: with all my strength I endeavour to promote good letters, and to restore a purer and simpler theology.[344] This I
shall do so long as I live, whether Luther is friend or foe; for he too is but
a man, who can err and lead others into error. Like the rest of us, Luther

* * * * *

339 Cf below 145.
340 Erasmus was especially hopeful about his *Paraphrases* being fruitful for read-
     ers: see below 110, 123, 145.
341 Cf *Expostulatio* EB 231:3–5 / K 109 par 203–4; EB 238:8–10 / K 116 par 233.
342 Cf *Expostulatio* EB II 208:13–4 / K 89 par 123; *Adagia* IV iv 56: *Eundem calceum
     omni pedi inducere* CWE 36 100; and, for the rhetorical idea of *varietas* in persons,
     times, and circumstances, Hoffmann *Rhetoric and Theology* 162–6, 275 n148.
343 Cf above n319.
344 Cf Epp 967:203–4, 1139:76–81, 1183:38–44, 1341A:1132–44, 1379:2–5.

will pass away; Christ alone remains for all eternity. If Luther be led by the spirit of Christ, I pray Christ to bless his endeavour;[345] if not, I grieve for a great misfortune to the public.

Hutten grandly presumes to pronounce on our inner feelings: Luther, he says, loves me with all his heart, whereas I bear towards him a heart full of bile.[346] Oh, ungrateful me, refusing to return another's affection! I will not discuss Luther's attitude towards me, nor the letters (hardly friendly) that he has written to his friends about me.[347] In a matter of such weight personal feelings do not count; the question is not whether Erasmus agrees with Luther, but whether the state of Christendom agrees with gospel teaching. Were I to consider personal setbacks, I should be angrier at Luther than anyone else: he has heaped abuse on me and my books, because of him most of my friendships are broken, or infected with bitterness, and he has done grave damage both to the good letters I always defend, and to the ancient writers whose authority I seek to restore.[348] As I say, such human considerations matter little when the glory of Christ and the truth of the Catholic faith are at stake. If Luther, or anyone like him, were only to look to these goals, I would gladly sacrifice all my books, all my possessions, and even my life. In any case, how does Hutten know what Luther thinks of me? No doubt from a drinking pal, who had it from someone else, and he in turn from another. So the rumour, passing through twenty sets of ears, reached our author. From such sources Hutten has made his pamphlet.

Concerning what I think of Luther he is hardly better informed. I do now and then speak out against Luther – hardly surprising for me. For, at the same dinner, I will, like Carneades,[349] speak for Luther and then against him – sometimes just for fun, fishing for what this or that person thinks, and at other times because I hope to learn something. But at my house a disputation like this never becomes bitter, for I can listen to both sides with equanimity. I enjoy this freedom of discussion, at dinner or in conversation with friends, and often take it too far, judging the temperament of others by

* * * * *

345 Cf Ep 1445:15–6.
346 Cf *Expostulatio* EB II 230:16 / K 109 par 202.
347 Cf above n318.
348 Cf Epp 1168:30–1, 1185:22–3, 1186:1–2, 1202:212–14, 1203:4–8, 1228:43–5, 1244: 15–6, 1342:742–53.
349 Carneades of Cyrene (214/3–129/8 BC), the founder of the New Academy, was a rhetorician and a philosophical sceptic. While in Rome in 156/5, according to Lactantius (*Divinae Institutiones* 4.14.3ff), he delivered a speech in favour of justice one day, and against it the next.

my own.[350] Lest I claim to be free of vices, I acknowledge this as my besetting fault, so implanted in me by nature that I have difficulty controlling it;
at the same time, I have often found that some people (forgetting the things
they have said too freely) remember something I have said and repeat it to
others, sometimes even using it against me, not without exaggeration and
distortion. Now really, let us grant that whatever is said over drinking cups
is written in wine![351] While at the table, have we not bestowed imperial authority on Pope Julius, and the pontificate on Emperor Maximilian?[352] We
also united in marriage monasteries of monks and convents of nuns. Then
again, we formed from them an army against the Turks, or settled them as
colonies on newly discovered islands. In short, we turned the order of the
universe upside down. But our lofty decrees were inscribed in wine, not
on bronze tablets, so that, the revelry over, no one remembered who said
what.

It is even more boorish to build accusations from what friends freely
joke about in their letters, relying on mutual confidentiality. Some intimate
friends of mine, now become mortal enemies, stop at nothing to contrive
my ruin. Yet I have never had the heart to throw back at them things
they said while we were still friends, either in private conversation or in
their letters. Were I to do so, I ought to be expelled from the dwellings
of men and cast out into the company of wild beasts.[353] Now Hutten calls
my letter to Laurinus a hateful attack.[354] Let him find one hateful word
about Luther! The words 'heresy' and 'heretic' are not there. In referring
to the Lutheran controversy I speak of tragedy, discord, and tumult[355] –
words I could equally well have used in reference to the controversy over
the gospel. There are among the Lutherans those who, lacking judgment,
give way to blind impulse, stirring up tragedies at the slightest unfounded
rumour; in that letter I tried to placate them.

Let us note the motive Hutten invents to support his shameless brief:
I turned against Luther, he says, because I envied him his renown, once

* * * * *

350 Cf above n128.
351 Cf *Adagia* I vii 1: *Odi memorem compotem* 'I hate a pot-companion with a good
     memory' CWE 32:66–8.
352 For a description of Pope Julius II acting like an emperor, cf *Julius exclusus* CWE
     27 155–97. When the pope's death seemed imminent in August 1511, Emperor
     Maximilian I had ideas of becoming pope (CEBR II 412).
353 Cf above 60.
354 Ep 1342; cf *Expostulatio* EB II 186:15–26 / K 65 par 32.
355 Cf Ep 1342:742, 1101, 1103, 1108.

his books were in the hands of even more people than mine were.[356] Well,
I do not envy Luther his fame; rather than having such a reputation, I
would prefer to be of less account than a Carian.[357] If Luther suffers for
the love of Christ, he suffers more than death, and no good man would
be right to envy him; if otherwise, only a madman could envy his lot. As
for me, instead of enjoying a momentary celebrity, I would want my works
to be read everywhere and at all times. But if they do not win the approval of readers for their usefulness, I will not lift a finger in their defence, even if no one reads them. But people say, according to Hutten,
'children learn from the cradle to speak Luther's name.'[358] Would it not
be better for them to learn the name of Jesus? In any case I know not
where these children may be; perhaps Hutten saw them in Sickingen's castle.[359] For my part, I see every day how many powerful, educated, serious,
and good men denounce Luther's name; their learning and character are
such that I can hardly suspect them of erring through passion or lack of
judgment.

Concerning the Holy See too I not have spoken inconsistently.[360] The
things that good men have complained about for a long time – tyranny,
greed, and other vices – I have never approved.[361] While I have not altogether condemned indulgences, I have always denounced the shameless
traffic associated with them.[362] What I think of ceremonies my books make
abundantly clear.[363] But where have I condemned canon law and the decrees
of the popes? Now what Hutten means by 'putting the pope in his place'[364]
I do not quite understand. For he will admit there is a church in Rome;
and a multitude of evil men does not make a church any less a church, else

* * * * *

356 Cf *Expostulatio* EB II 187:11–3 / K 66 par 35.
357 Cf *Adagia* I vi 14: *In Care periculum* CWE 32 12–3: 'Risk it on a Carian [merce-
nary]: make a risky experiment on a person or thing of little value.'
358 Cf *Expostulatio* EB II 230:11 / K 108 par 200.
359 Cf above nn52, 226.
360 Cf *Expostulatio* EB II 186:18–187:4 / K 66 par 33.
361 On this point one may contrast unpublished letters (Epp 872:19–24, 983:13–
16) with the milder tone of letters that Erasmus published (Epp 1270:40–3,
1358:12–14).
362 Cf Epp 785:39n, 916:132–40, 933:22–7, 1299:63–6, 1301:140–5; ASD I-3 156:1009–
158:1053.
363 See esp *Enchiridion* CWE 66 73–83, and four *Colloquies* published for the first
time in the March 1522 edition: 'Rash Vows,' 'Military Affairs,' 'The Whole
Duty of Youth,' 'The Godly Feast' CWE 39 35–43, 53–63, 88–108, 171–243.
364 Cf *Expostulatio* EB II 186:20–1 / K 66 par 33.

we would have no churches. I think that church is orthodox. For even if evil members are mixed in, the church remains in those who are good. He will likewise grant that it has a bishop, with the status of a metropolitan; for while there are archbishops in many regions never visited by the apostles, Rome has Peter and Paul, the two greatest apostles. Finally, among metropolitans, what is so unreasonable about granting the Roman pontiff a primacy of honour? As for the vast power the popes have usurped over the centuries, no one has ever heard me defend it.[365] Hutten will not tolerate a corrupt pope. We all hope for a pope worthy of his apostolic office. But if he is not, must he be deposed? By this line of reasoning all bishops failing to perform their duty would also have to be deposed. Hutten thinks Rome has been the world's plague for many years now, and would that I could disagree with him![366] But now we have a pope who, I believe, endeavours with all his might to clean things up at the Holy See and curia.[367] Hutten has no hope for this, but there are many hopeful signs and, as Paul says: 'Charity hopes all things.'[368] If Hutten's war were against vices, and not against men, he would hasten to Rome to assist the pontiff struggling to achieve what Hutten strives for. In fact, he has declared war against the pope of Rome and all who follow him.[369] Has he declared war on a good pope as well? And what will he do to those who cling to the pope willy-nilly? What about the emperor, who is most firmly allied with the pope?[370] Now war means laying waste to fields, razing cities to the ground, pillaging wealth, and dispossessing people of their property; but Hutten has thus far done nothing but load the pope with imprecations; in Rome itself he has not harmed a fly – unless he thinks his victims have been laid low by his insults. He ought also to consider whether it is a good idea to antagonize those whom one has no power to destroy.[371] In fact, Hutten has been the kind of foe the Romanists would like to have. For if the evils of the Roman curia can only be cured by the tumult of war (something that Hutten cannot bring about), throwing everything into confusion, it would be better to bear τό εὐκείμενον κακόν 'an evil that is well-founded,'[372] instead of 'moving

* * * * *

365 Cf Ep 1300:82–4.
366 Cf *Expostulatio* EB II 227:10–1 / K 106 par 188; Ep 872:19–24.
367 Adrian VI (see above n228): cf Epp 1304:12–4, 1332:69–71; see above 78.
368 1 Cor 13:7.
369 Holborn *Ulrich von Hutten* 172–85.
370 Cf Epp 1304:377–80, 1332:76–8.
371 Cf below 132.
372 Cf *Adagia* I i 62: *Malum bene conditum ne moveris* 'Do not disturb a well-founded evil' CWE 31 106–7; Ep 1202:152–4.

Camarina' to the detriment of the whole world.[373] I would like to know of whom Hutten is thinking when he so often says 'we' or 'ours.'[374] Does he mean all who favour Luther in any way, and wish evil upon the Roman pontiff? As I see it, this category includes different sorts of men. There are on the one hand learned men, not at all bad in my judgment, who approve most of what Luther says, and would like to see the power of the Roman pontiff curtailed, making him a teacher of the gospel instead of a worldly prince, a father instead of a tyrant. They would have the tables of the buyers and sellers in the temple of the Lord overturned,[375] so as to suppress the intolerable shamelessness of the indulgence hawkers, and the papal bureaucrats who take fees for compositions, dispensations, and papal bulls. They would want ceremonies to be greatly cut back, leaving room for a zeal for true piety. They would have the power of the gospel restored, after a long period when it was consigned to decrepitude. In their view man-made dogmas and opinions ought to yield to the authority of Holy Scripture, so that scholastic pronouncements no longer have the force of oracles, and man-made laws are not preferred to the precepts of God. They grieve that Christians are burdened with man-made precepts, telling them what they may eat,[376] or how many feast days to observe, or the degrees of kinship within which they may marry, or banning marriage among those related through godparentage,[377] or reserving certain sins to the hearing of

* * * * *

373 Cf *Adagia* I i 64: *Movere Camarinam* CWE 31 107–8: 'To move Camarina, is to bring trouble upon oneself'; Epp 1167:481–3, 1192A:2–3.

374 Cf *Expostulatio* EB II 186:12 / K 65 par 31; EB II 227:15 / K 106 par 189; EB II 228:1, 18–19 / K 106 par 190, 107 par 94; EB II 229:4–5 / K 107 par 195; EB II 231:17 / K 110 par 206; EB II 232:3 / K 110 par 208; EB II 233:5, 9–11, 15–6 / K 111 par 213. 111–12 par 214–5; EB II 234:17–8 / K 113 par 219; EB II 235:16 / K 114 par 223; EB II 236:19 / K 115 par 227 / EB II 238:1, 4–5, 11, 13–4, 16 / K 116 par 231, 232, 233, 234; EB II 244:21 / K 123 par 258; EB II 245:3 / K 123 par 259; EB II 246:15 / K 125 par 265; EB II 247:1, 3–5, 8–9 / K 125 par 267, 268, 126 par 269; EB II 248:1 / K 126 par 271.

375 Matt 21:12

376 Cf Erasmus' 1522 treatise *De interdicto esu carnium* ('On the forbidden eating of meat' ASD IX-1 1–50).

377 From the eleventh century, church law prohibited marriage within the seventh degree of kinship. Because of the affinity (fictive kinship) created by godparentage, a godparent could not marry a co-godparent, the child baptized, or adult members of the child's family: see James A. Brundage *Law, Sex and Christian Society in Medieval Europe* (Chicago: University of Chicago Press 1987) 88–9, 140–1, 191–3, 355–7.

bishops.[378] They would further like the public good to take precedence over certain human laws, such as the idea that consent alone is enough for two people to be joined in matrimony.[379] They would want our consciences not to be entangled by so many nets of human making. They want sermons that are free and holy; they want bishops to be true bishops, and monks – now given to worldliness – to be real monks. These men support Luther because he has taken up these issues with vigour. I am not bound to them by any treaty, but with them I continue long-time friendships, based on love of good letters, even if we do not agree on everything. Not one of these men approves of what Hutten has done, not even Luther himself.

On the other hand, the Lutheran camp also includes ignorant men of no discernment. Though of dubious morals themselves, they are fault-finders, obstinate and unmanageable, and devoted to Luther in such a way that they neither understand nor follow what he teaches. They merely talk, while neglecting prayer and worship. They think that being a Lutheran means eating whatever they please and cursing the Roman pontiff.[380] Their tumultuous disorder and ill-considered plans must sooner or later be suppressed by princes and town magistrates. We may thus have them to blame if the ills about which everyone rightly complains are not corrected. They often make their commitments to the gospel with drinking cup in hand. Indeed they are stupid enough not to grasp that they are themselves the greatest obstacles to their cause; anyone wishing to help them must proceed by trickery, like the physician who deceives a madman in order to administer medicine. I want nothing to do with people of this ilk. Even Hutten seems to disapprove, for

* * * * *

378 Ordinary confessors could not grant absolution for 'reserved' sins; for example, local church councils might decree that only the bishop could grant absolution for sexual acts between men, or even masturbation: Brundage *Law, Sex and Christian Society* (previous note) 214, 471–3, 535.

379 Church law recognized consent between the parties as the sole requirement for a valid marriage. Like many other sixteenth-century reformers, Erasmus argued that this understanding of the sacrament led to the widespread practice of 'clandestine' marriage, by which young people contracted unions without their parents' knowledge or consent: cf *Annotationes in epistolam ad Corinthios priorem* LB VI 698D–E; *Institutio christiani matrimonii* LB V 630E–F; Brundage *Law, Sex and Christian Society* (above n377) 179–80, 276–7, 361–4, 414–5, 440–3, 496–501.

380 Erasmus seems to have in mind the Swiss and south German 'evangelicals,' including those in Basel, against whom he wrote his 1522 *De interdicto esu carnium* ASD IX-1 19–50. See above General Introduction xiv–xv.

he refers to them as 'villagers.'[381] Still others there are who, I suspect, do not support the gospel at all; rather, they see a chance for plunder under the pretext of the gospel. Luther has no use for such people. Their principles are quite different from his: they think whoever claims noble blood has the right to attack travellers on public highways, to rob them or hold them for ransom. So, when a man has wasted his substance on wine, dice, and whores, drink, prostitutes, and gambling, he can declare war on any convenient victim.[382] These are definitely not Luther's teachings. Yet there may be some who, having squandered everything, feign to be Lutherans so as to find patrons. Would Hutten defend these people too? Whenever I speak of 'certain Lutherans' he becomes irritated.[383] If I complain that some Lutheran stole my purse while I was travelling, why does he think this pertains to him? For he complains that I once directed a biting remark at him personally.[384] Since he neither cites a passage nor mentions an issue, I have no idea whereof he speaks. Whatever I wrote, I was not intending to injure Hutten, whom I favoured, as a friend of good letters if nothing else. Suppose things happened as he says (they did not): would this justify his slanderous abuse? Had he skewered me indirectly ten times in his writings, I would have ignored it.

So, when Hutten summons me to rejoin his party, where does he want me to go? To a place where good men live according to the gospel? There I would gladly go, if someone shows the way. Can Hutten point me to men who, setting aside drinking and whoring and gambling, take pleasure in spiritual authors or holy conversations; who, cheating no one of what he is owed, give freely to the needy what they are not owed; who, instead of cursing those who deserve it not, return a gentle response to abuse heaped upon themselves; who neither use nor threaten force against anyone, but instead repay injury with kindness; who are so far from wanting to cause discord that, mindful of Christ's words, 'Blessed are the peacemakers,' they restore peace and harmony wherever they can; and who, far from boasting of their glorious accomplishments – fishing for praise for what they have done badly, or what others have done – attribute to Christ the glory for what they have done well: if Hutten knows such men, endowed

* * * * *

381 Cf *Expostulatio* EB II 228:12–229:3 / K 107 par 194. Whom Hutten has in mind is not clear, but he would not be referring in these terms to the Basel 'evangelicals.'
382 An allusion to Hutten himself, see above 35 and 60 n130
383 Cf *Expostulatio* EB II 228:3–230:6 / K 106 par 191–108 par 198.
384 Cf *Expostulatio* EB II 186:11–2 / K 65 par 31; EB II 192:1–2; K 71 par 56

with truly evangelical virtues, let him point them out and he will have me as a companion.

In fact, I see Lutherans, but none or very few that I would call 'evangelical.' So, just as I do not refuse friendship to learned men who support Luther with moderation and discernment, in the same way I do not refuse friendship to those on the other side who, from pious zeal, oppose Luther with moderation and discernment.[385] Let us assume the latter are mistaken in their judgment; still, their hearts are pious, for they believe that countless souls will perish through Luther's teachings.[386] As occasion arises, I admonish men on either side when I see a spirit of partisanship. In any case I am not pronouncing a judgment about Luther, I am merely responding to Hutten's calumnies.

How does my maintaining civil ties with friends harm Luther? Maybe it will help him in some quarters. The Reverend Father John, bishop of Rochester, published a huge tome against Luther. For many years this man has been an excellent friend and a loyal patron.[387] Will Hutten require that I now declare him a foe, since he has sharpened his pen against Luther? Before Luther became known I was on friendly terms with almost all men of learning. When many began to favour Luther, I did not for that reason cut off ties with them. Some of them have changed their minds, and no longer think so highly of Luther, but this too has not led me to stop treating them as my friends. Nor do I hold myself in balance, as if ready to fly off to whichever party emerges victorious. What can I hope to obtain from the Lutherans?[388] The other side has much to offer, and does so, but I have steadfastly refused.[389] I look to my own tranquility of mind, and if possible try to keep myself uncompromised, so as to be of service to the public good, should the occasion arise. All the while I hope with all my heart to see the gospel invigorated and the glory of Christ flourishing throughout the world. As for me, the Lord will look after me; from this life I expect no happiness. Still, I will die content if I see that the cause of Christ has clearly triumphed.

* * * * *

385 Cf Ep 1342:748–53.

386 Cf Ep 1324:97–8 (a letter from Pope Adrian vi to Erasmus).

387 *Assertionis Lutheranae confutatio* (Antwerp: M. Hillen 2 January 1523); see above n164. For Erasmus' friendship with Fisher, dating from his stay in Cambridge (1505–6), cf Allen i 590–3 (App vi) and above 65.

388 Erasmus could hardly have expected an invitation from Wittenberg; cf General Introduction nn36, 37.

389 Cf eg Ep 980:43–4.

I go back now to the Roman pontiff, for Hutten accuses me of thinking differently about him now than I formerly did. This pope you praise, he
says, and he in turn praises you.[390] I do in fact praise him, for many indications give me hope that he is truly minded to promote the glory of Christ.
Yet I praise him sparingly.[391] Does Hutten wax indignant because my writings have a few words for such a good pope, a former friend who still
wishes me well? In these same writings I praise Hutten often, with many
words, and magnificently, even in a serious work like my *Annotationes in
Novum Testamentum*:[392] and yet Hutten does not label me as a flatterer on
this account? Besides, the pope sent me two briefs, the second more affectionate than the first.[393] These I welcomed all the more, because a number
of old friends prophesied my doom as soon as this man was elected pope –
an expectation in which they were mightily deceived.[394] In any case, let us
suppose that these pontifical letters bring me no further advantage: must
I therefore despise them? Hutten of course sees here another bit of trickery.[395] But these are the defences Erasmus has. Hutten has, for his protection, moated castles, troops with swords, cannon with smoke and fire, and
all the uses of war. My safety is wholly dependent on the favour of certain good and powerful men. I make use of their patronage, yes, but for
the public good, for if I were to think only of myself I would follow a
different path. Maybe the reason that Hutten is brave is that he no longer
has anything to fear. For my part I admit being fearful for the sake of
my books, from which, as even Hutten admits, many people have derived
much fruit.[396] I do not want this fruitfulness to be lost through any rashness on my part. Thus if I protect myself, it is to be able to do some good.

* * * * *

390 Cf *Expostulatio* EB II 188:12–6 / K 67–8 par 39; EB II 209:20–210:1 / K 90 par 127.
391 Cf above n232.
392 The 1516, 1519, and 1522 editions of Erasmus' *Annotationes* contained (at 1
     Thess 1:2) an encomium of Hutten that was deleted in the 1527 edition (cf
     Reeve *Galatians to the Apocalypse* App A 555–1; EB I 103–4). Cf the dedicatory
     epistle of Erasmus' *Ratio* (Ep 745:18–21 and 72–4); also Epp 778:53–5, 874:6,
     967:15–21, 968:24–6, 1009:78–83, 1114:13–6, 1115:47–9, 1341A:1043–51.
393 Cf Epp 1324, 1338. See also Ep 1342:692–5; *Expostulatio* EB II 188:14–6 / K 67–8
     par 39.
394 C. Augustijn suggests that *amici* ('friends') could be a misprint for *inimici* ('en-
     emies'). But in light of ongoing quarrels at Louvain, it seems not unlikely that
     some of Erasmus' friends would have seen no good for him in the elevation
     to the papacy of Adrian of Utrecht, a staunch defender of scholastic theology.
395 Cf *Expostulatio* EB II 209:20–210:8 / K 90 par 127.
396 Cf *Expostulatio* EB II 195:13–8 / K 75 par 71; EB II 234:17–235:3 / K 113 par
     219–20.

He also reproaches me because the pope and the cardinal of Sion praise me in their letters: he praises you to your face, Hutten says[397] – as if it were a fault to be praised by such men. (In fact, I take their praise as a veiled warning).[398] Should I instead have gone about canvassing for favour, so as to be praised by Hutten? In any event is it anything strange to praise those to whom we write? Does Paul not praise the Romans in his Epistle?[399] 'Erasmus,' Hutten says, 'has surrendered himself to the Roman pontiff.'[400] What? Was I ever at war with the present pope, and thus in need of surrendering? Was I not equally submissive to Leo, a pope of lesser repute?[401] You promise, he says, never to abandon the dignity of the Roman see. Indeed; but these words I wrote to those before whom I was accused of conspiring with Luther against the Roman see.[402] Do I thereby pledge myself to defend tyranny, greed, and the other evils Hutten hurls in the face of the Romanists? No, for I say repeatedly that the dignity of the pope and his see is rooted in apostolic virtues;[403] this is the dignity I promise not to abandon.

As for overthrowing the gospel, as Hutten calls it, I doubt that any pope, least of all this pope, would ask for my help, and if he asked I would not give it. Neither fear nor favour of any prince[404] will ever have such

* * * * *

397 Cf *Expostulatio* EB II 188:13–7 / K 67 par 39–68 par 40; Ep 1342:346–53 and 692–5. Matthäus Schiner of Mühlebach (c 1465–1522), the son of a Valais peasant, was ordained priest in 1489 and succeeded his uncle as bishop of Sion in 1499. A persistent foe of French influence in the region, he became a confidant first of Pope Julius II, who made him cardinal and bishop of Novara (1511), and later of the Hapsburg dynasty. Operating from a base in Zürich, he was initially friendly to Zwingli but soon changed his mind. He vigorously defended Erasmus' orthodoxy, and, after Adrian VI's elevation to the papacy, twice invited him to Rome, to join in the campaign against heresy.

398 That is, Erasmus was expected to write against Luther: cf Ep 1342:695–7.

399 Rom 1:8, 15:14, 16:19.

400 Cf *Expostulatio* EB II 215:12–3 / K 95 par 146.

401 For praise of Leo X in Erasmus' published writings, cf Epp 333:11–4, 334:89–95, 335, 384 (dedicatory epistle for Erasmus' *Novum Instrumentum*), 541:11–6 and 33–42, 542:14–18, 566, 761:29–32, 905:26–7, 939:131–5, 967:217–20, 1066:73–7, 1156:30–5, 1167:26–30, 100–4, and 473–5, 1183:72–3, 1236:71–2. But see also Ep 1039:281–3, and, for an unpublished comment, Ep 872:20n. For Leo X see CEBR II 319–22.

402 Cf *Expostulatio* EB II 218:19 / K 98 par 158; Ep 1217:161–3. Cf Epp 1144:9–10 and 82, 1167:386–7 and 470–5, 1195:47–50, 101–3, and 113–20, 1236:193–6, 1342:981–8.

403 Ep 1342:983–6; cf Epp 1144:83–5, 1195:48–50.

404 Cf *Expostulatio* EB II 189:12–190:6 / K 68 par 45–69 par 47; EB II 231:14–232:8 / K 110 par 206–9.

power over me that I would knowingly oppose the truth of the gospel or
the glory of Christ. It is, I think, prudent to cultivate the favour of princes,
but not in such a way as to abandon gospel truth. Only the outcome of this
conflict will show which one of us has more rightly promoted the gospel.
Meanwhile I deceive people by speaking indirectly; so it is that many believe I claim for the Roman curia the right to tyrannize, plunder, and traffic
in matters sacred and profane. In time of crisis one has a right to resort to
ambiguity[405] – even David feigned madness on one occasion.[406] Still, lest
anyone be deceived, I will clarify. I write that I shall not desert the Roman
see unless it deserts the glory of Christ, that I shall support it to the utmost
of my ability if it endeavours by honest means to promote the gospel.[407]
This I stress in many places, but Hutten pretends not to notice. Instead he
has hunted out passages he can distort – pointed out to him, I suspect, by
my accusers.[408] For I can hardly believe that Hutten, occupied as he is with
domestic and military affairs, has had leisure to read my works.

He finds it still more intolerable that I wrote somewhere that every
pious man supports the Roman pontiff.[409] Here he fails to grasp the meaning
demanded by the structure of the sentence: having appeased the pope, I
focus resentment on certain others who have wielded the pope's name in
a clumsy way. And what I said is not false. Those who really support the
pope want him to flourish in apostolic gifts; one might well despise Leo
and yet support the pope. Those who acquiesce in the evil deeds of popes
are not their supporters.

Again, Hutten objects to my saying that 'all of Christendom has for
many centuries followed the authority of the papal see.'[410] This is indeed the

* * * * *

405 On the conscious resort by Erasmus to *dissimulatio*, or to ambiguity, see, respectively, Tracy *Low Countries* 117–8, 177–8, 182–3, and Hoffmann *Rhetoric
and Theology* 174–6, 191–200, 224–5; cf *Expostulatio* EB II 196:3–7 / K 75–6 par
73.
406 1 Sam 21:13–15
407 Ep 1217:165–9; cf Ep 1144:83–5.
408 Erasmus seems to know about the work of Eppendorf, whose marginal notes
on the *Epistolae ad diversos* (cf Allen IV App XVI 615–19) were used by Hutten (see C. Augustijn's detailed comparison with the *Expostulatio*, ASD IX-1
104:71n).
409 Cf *Expostulatio* EB II 219:14–8 / K 99 par 160; EB II 227:16–7 / K 106 par 189; Ep
1195:47–8 fits the context Erasmus describes here, but cf Epp 1144:9–10 and
55–6, 1167:386–7, 1156:31–2, 1342:981–3.
410 Cf *Expostulatio* EB II 220:2–3, 8–9 / K 99 par 161. C. Augustijn (ASD IX-1 181:359–
60n) points out that Hutten can only be referring to Ep 1342:1092–5, where
Erasmus upholds the authority of 'the ancients' [church Fathers] but says nothing of the papacy. Hutten misread the passage, and Erasmus did not check him.

case, and may it be so forever, provided Rome promotes the cause of Christ! Hutten cries out that this will never happen, but I hope for better things, especially from this pope.[411] Is it, then, more holy to follow the authority of Luther[412] than that of the Roman pontiff? This is exactly the contrast I had in mind in the statement to which Hutten objects, about 'authority being confirmed by the consensus of the whole world for many centuries.' Perhaps a man of little learning, like myself, may be forgiven for following, on controverted points, the authority of the Roman pontiff rather than the authority of this or that individual. For some, the fact that Luther says something is grounds for belief: *ipse dixit*.[413] If Luther claims this he is mad; if not those who think so are mad. As for the Roman pontiff, we know that in recent times even the Greek church has accepted his authority.[414] And when I speak of 'world' I mean the Christian world – though Hutten, a good sophist, may object that the Sciopodes[415] have not yet submitted to the pope. Even if the primacy of the pope were not decreed by Christ, it would still be useful to have one man of pre-eminent authority, albeit far removed from any sort of tyranny. I write somewhere that 'the authority of the Roman pontiff is sacrosanct,'[416] and I have no hesitation in saying the same of individual bishops, provided they teach nothing impious, for then they would cease to be bishops. One can scarcely be too emphatic in saying how dangerous it is for the people to get used to trampling underfoot the commands of their bishops, on the grounds that they are evil men; soon enough, nobody will listen to good bishops either.

Elsewhere he objects to my saying somewhere that I am not to be torn away from the Roman see even by death; this was what needed to be said, for I was then accused of having conspired against the papacy.[417] So

* * * * *

411 Cf *Expostulatio* EB II 227:9–13 / K 106 par 188; cf above 78.
412 The text reads 'of Hutten,' but C. Augustijn (ASD IX-1 181:363n) takes this as a slip of the pen for 'of Luther.'
413 Αὐτὸς ἔφα, 'he himself has spoken'; cf *Adagia* II v 87 CWE 33 279–80.
414 Cf *Expostulatio* EB II 220:8–11 / K 99 par 162. Union between the Greek and Latin churches – a political necessity for a fading Byzantine empire, hardpressed by the Ottoman Turks – was proclaimed at the Council of Florence, in the bull *Laetentur coeli* (16 July 1439). The union was repudiated when delegates returned to Constantinople.
415 In Greek mythology, the Sciopodes ('Shade-feet'), living in Libya, had but one leg but two giant feet, with which, lying on their backs, they shielded themselves from the sun; cf John Block Friedman *The Monstrous Races* (Cambridge, MA 1981).
416 Cf *Expostulatio* EB II 224:12–6 / K 103 par 177; Ep 1167:176–7; cf also Epp 1273:30–1, 1275:32–4.
417 Cf *Expostulatio* EB II 222:10–14 / K 101 par 69; Ep 1195:4–8.

what? Did I thereby condone the tyranny or the vices of the Romanists? Hutten thinks me shameless for having said this, for, he says, I had so often broken ranks with Rome. No, it is he who is shameless for making this up, for my writings declare the opposite. I do not break ranks with the Roman see if I criticize some of its doings. Among the Anti-Lutherans are men who condemn the venality of the Roman curia; have they broken ranks with Rome? Indeed one would have to say that the emperor and the present pope have also broken ranks with the Roman see, for they are discussing ways of eliminating its vices.

He likewise rebukes me for these words: 'Who would not support the dignity of a man who by his evangelical virtues represents Christ among us?'[418] What is there to attack here? I indicate what kind of man a pope ought to be, and how far we ought to support him. But, he will say, you use a figure of speech. So? Are we not living in a time that demands figures of speech? And where do I write that I 'can heal these dissensions'?[419] Would that I could; if so, they would not last another day.

Hutten bids me to 'Cry out without ceasing, and declare to the people their transgressions!' [420] I have cried out, more boldly than befits a man of my station, yet only one who is free from sin should decry the sins of others. If I hold back in chastising the sins of others, it is because I am too well aware of the many sins I have acknowledged. Let Hutten cry out: is he not pure, a man against whom no crime may be alleged? Isaiah was ordered in that passage to cry out to the people, but I am no Isaiah. Hutten bids me to cry out against the princes, yet it is written: 'Thou shalt not speak ill of the prince of thy people.'[421] It matters a great deal whether it is God commanding Isaiah to cry out, or Hutten commanding Erasmus. Besides, crying out is useless if it merely provokes tumult and brings more tyranny. Still, I have until now not ceased to cry out in my writings, as long as there was some hope of betterment. My *Paraphrases* are a form of crying out, for is the light of the gospel not a contradiction of our darkness? Let the impartial man judge which is more useful, Hutten's ranting or my silence. And when have I ever deserted the Christian commonwealth, if I was able to be of service?[422] Beside, princes will not suffer themselves to be lectured to by

* * * * *

418 Cf *Expostulatio* EB II 227:8–13 / K 105–6 par 188; Ep 1342:983–5.
419 Cf *Expostulatio* EB II 226:1–2 / K 104 par 183; Hutten says Erasmus has 'boasted' of this, not that he has 'written' it.
420 Cf *Expostulatio* EB II 226:6–7 / K 105 par 184; cf Isa 58:1.
421 Exod 22:28
422 Cf *Expostulatio* EB II 226:1–2 / K 104 par 183; Ep 1135:23–4.

just anyone; this is the duty of bishops, and better done behind closed doors than in public. And to what end shall I undertake labours that are beyond the capacity of my years and my health?

If I am so eager to restore harmony between the parties, Hutten asks, why do I attack one side so viciously?[423] So: I am a conniving Mettius in one place,[424] but here I am directing all my force against one of the two parties. But where is this battle joined? Not until my letter to Laurinus (directed against certain captious men) do I claim that, should it prove necessary, I have the right to dispute against Luther, using sound arguments and the testimony of Holy Scripture, and no abusive language.[425] Even Hutten complains that Luther's foes use nothing but shouts and insults.[426] Yet see how he carries on against one who promises to avoid shouts and insults in any dispute with Luther, proceeding instead in a spirit of a calm comparison,[427] solely on the basis of Holy Scripture and sound arguments. For this is all I promised, and I framed it so as to indicate that I will not go ahead unless I see reason to think it will do some good.

The things that offend me in Luther's writings – his unrestrained abuse and his seeming arrogance[428] – are offensive as well to his sworn followers. I made no bones about this when I met with Elector Frederick of Saxony in Cologne; Georgius Spalatinus was also present.[429] Note that this

* * * * *

423 Cf *Expostulatio* EB II 238:7–8 / K 116 par 232.
424 Cf above n338.
425 Ep 1342:910–20
426 Cf *Expostulatio* EB II 231:13–4 / K 109–10 par 205.
427 By the time the *Spongia* had appeared in print (early September 1523), Erasmus had decided to write against Luther; cf J.M. Estes in CWE 10 xv–xviii. He called his treatise (see *De libero arbitrio* CWE 76 5–89) a *collatio*, meaning a comparison or discussion; see Boyle *Rhetoric and Reform* 31, 44–6; Ch. Trinkaus introduction to CWE 76 lxv–lxix; and Hoffmann *Rhetoric and Theology* 178–81.
428 Cf Ep 1342:859–63.
429 On 5 November 1520; cf Ep 1155 introduction.
      Frederick III, elector of Saxony (1463–1525), called the Wise, a patron of the arts and of education, founded the University of Wittenberg in 1502. A man of traditional piety, he accumulated a famous collection of relics in the castle-church of Wittenberg. Not believing that Luther had had a fair hearing at the Diet of Worms (1521), where the emperor and the papal legate worked to achieve his condemnation, the elector gave Luther sanctuary in his castle at Wartburg.
      Georgius Spalatinus (1484–1545), the illegitimate son of a tanner from Spalt (near Nürnberg), was influenced by humanists during his studies at Erfurt and Wittenberg. He was first licensed as a notary, then ordained a priest (1508),

was even before the *Babylonian Captivity* had appeared.[430] They told me that in his sermons and lectures Luther was most gentle. I rejoiced at this, adding that while Luther's voice reached only a few people, gentleness would be especially helpful in those books of his that were flying off to the ends of the earth. They promised to do their best with Luther. Hutten admits that Luther lacks modesty and mildness, but he asks why it matters.[431] He should not even ask such a question, for as one who tells all and sundry that Luther's cause is just, holy, and pious, he ought to be very angry about a fault that alienates so many of Luther's readers.

If from the outset Luther had explained his teachings in a candid and gentle way, refraining from the kind of language that is patently offensive, we would not have this tumult.[432] Were he my brother three or four times over, and if I accepted all that he teaches, I must still vehemently reject the obstinacy with which he asserts his opinions and the harsh abuse he has always at hand. Nor have I been able to persuade myself that the Spirit of Christ – than whom no one is more gentle – dwells in a heart from which such bitterness gushes forth. Would that I am deceived in what I suspect![433] Yet the spirit of the gospel can also wax wrathful. Yes, but this is a wrath that never lacks the honey of charity to sweeten the bitterness of reproach. Peter's indignation with Simon Magus comes to mind: 'May your money perish with you!' Did he believe 'the gift of God' could be bought for 'money?'[434] Here the vileness of the crime wrings words of abuse from

* * * * *

and became tutor to the young sons of Elector Frederick in Wittenberg in 1511. Here he became a trusted friend of Luther, and (from 1516) private secretary to his prince. Spalatinus advised the elector on religious matters, and mediated between him and Luther. He also developed friendly ties with Erasmus, whose *Axiomata Erasmi pro causa Lutheri* (penned after his meeting with the elector in Cologne: see CWE 71 106–7) helped in persuading the elector to keep Luther under his protection.

430 Luther's *De captivitate Babylonica ecclesiae praeludium* (WA 6 497–573 / LW 36 11–126), a frontal assault on the Catholic sacramental system, was published c 6 October 1520 (thus before Erasmus' meeting with the elector). When he got hold of the book, early in 1521, Erasmus saw it as a watershed in the growing divide between the two parties: Epp 1186:1–10 and n3, 1203:23–32, 1217:43–5, 1263:5–6, 1342:932–3.

431 Cf *Expostulatio* EB II 221:14–15 / K 100 par 167.

432 Cf Epp 1119:32–46, 1127:20–3, 1127A:68–73.

433 See above nn300, 301.

434 Cf Acts 8:20. For the preceding topos (the wrath of the apostles sweetened by charity), see eg *Epistola ad fratres Inferioris Germaniae* below 349.

the gentlest of the apostles. But now comes the seasoning of Peter's anger: 'Repent therefore and pray to God that, if possible, the intent of your heart may be forgiven you.'[435] As for Luther, his prose is tight and sparing of words when he makes an argument, but in taunts and insults he knows no bounds, often indulging in mockery and sarcasm where there is no call for it. For example, in his treatise against the king of England, what reason was there for him to speak as he does: Come forward, lord Henry, and I shall teach you?[436] For the king had written his book in Latin, and not without learning. And yet there are those who find Luther's taunts marvellously funny. Hutten complains that by holding out hope that I will write against Luther, I have encouraged the princes to join in a new campaign against him.[437] No, it is Luther with his pointed pen who provokes everyone against himself; like the wild Scyrian she-goat in the Greek proverb, he gives a pail of good milk, then kicks it over.[438] Somewhere I said that it is not in the spirit of the gospel to drag people into one's camp by tricks or by force. Hutten gnaws away at this too, noting that the early Christians used to hide those who were in danger.[439] Yes, but they admitted into their fellowship only those who came freely and asked to join. By contrast, certain Lutherans have tried to set clever traps from which I cannot escape. Hutten thinks I make this up, and demands that I name names.[440] Let him then tell me, what was the aim of those who made public my first letter to Luther?[441] What about those who excerpted certain troublesome passages from my books and put them out in a German translation[442] – not to mention other things that have been published with an even greater disregard

* * * * *

435 Cf Acts 8:22.
436 Cf WA 10-2 189:19–20; cf above n299.
437 Cf *Expostulatio* EB II 231:22–232:2 / K 110 par 207.
438 Cf *Adagia* I x 20: *Capra Scyria* CWE 32 242.
439 Ep 1342:793–4 and 814–21; cf *Expostulatio* EB II 228:3–230:6 / K 106–8 par 191–8.
440 Cf *Expostulatio* EB II 228:12–3 / K 107 par 193.
441 Cf Allen Ep 948 introduction; Erasmus' first letter to Luther (Ep 980) was published by Petrus Mosellanus, together with a letter to him from Erasmus (Ep 948), and his oration at the beginning of the Leipzig disputation (*Petri Mosellani oratio de ratione disputandi* [Leipzig: M. Lotter nd; Augsburg: S. Grimm and M. Wirsung 1519]).
442 Cf Ep 1202:237–40; in 1521 passages from Erasmus' *Annotationes in Novum Testamentum* were translated into German and published in various anonymous editions (cf Holeczek *Erasmus Deutsch* 81–108). Erasmus thought Hutten had been responsible for some publications of this kind: cf below 126.

for privacy? What was the intent of those who published a private letter I wrote to the cardinal of Mainz, without even delivering it to him?[443] What did such people have in mind, if not to make me give safeguards against my going over to the other side? I touch only on things that are well known, for there are other stories I could tell if I chose. People who have fallen into the water grab anyone they can and pull them down too, even those coming to the rescue. I notice that those who have given themselves to the Lutheran faction behave in the same way, for they try to draw others into the same danger, even those by whom they might be pulled back from the brink.

Perhaps Hutten can explain what he was thinking when he wrote that 'the books you write now, if indeed you write more books, are not as good' – and then he can tell us that no one is trying to drag me over to their side by force. He says I can do nothing to prevent my feet being planted in the camp of Luther, for the books I have written will stand with them, whatever I may say.[444] We have, then, a man who writes these words, and who also warns me about certain private letters in his possession;[445] I ask you, reader, how can he have the effrontery to demand proof that they are trying to pull me into the Lutheran faction by tricks and compulsion? Can it be said that the man who constantly opposes faction of all sorts, and who was first to warn against this danger,[446] has his feet firmly planted in the camp of Luther? I cannot deny what is in my books but I have thus far defended myself without Hutten's help. If my books taught the same things Luther teaches they would have been honoured in the same way his books are honoured – for I have many fierce enemies. But, Hutten says, the books stand on our side. Yet whence comes the 'our'?[447] No matter how often he uses this word, Hutten is not acknowledged either by Luther or by any Lutheran of good judgment.

Another helping of the same gruel: Hutten threatens that if some evil should befall the Lutheran party, the winning side will not treat me any better than the Lutherans.[448] But I have not declared war on the pope,[449]

* * * * *

443 Not without reason, Erasmus suspected that Hutten (then a member of the cardinal's household) had been the culprit. Cf Epp 1033 introduction, 1202:229–33; below 125.
444 Cf *Expostulatio* EB II 234:17–235:3 / K 113 par 219–20.
445 Cf *Expostulatio* EB II 195:1–2 / K 74 par 69
446 Above n297.
447 Cf above nn294, 295.
448 Cf *Expostulatio* EB II 234:7–16 / K 112–13 par 217–18.
449 Cf above n369.

nor written a commentary on the papal bull,[450] nor have I declared myself a protector of the Lutheran faction,[451] nor opposed the emperor's mandate.[452] And why does he say, if something should befall the Lutheran party? Does not the party opposed to Luther reign triumphant? And am I, an unarmed man, not exposed on all sides? What will come of Erasmus? The emperor has honoured him,[453] and Ferdinand likewise,[454] the pope offers both friendship and fortune.[455] The only ones who rage against me are certain men beyond reason, sworn enemies of good letters; Hutten wanted to please them with his book, and no doubt he has. Those who go after Hutten do not care about such matters; they have in mind other issues, relating to a battle in which, as he acknowledges, we were not companions.[456] His friends are now a greater danger to Hutten than is the pope, against whom he long since issued his declaration of war.

He is especially bitter in censuring me for saying that 'it may some-times be expedient to conceal the truth,' and that the manner in which one brings forth the truth is 'always of the first importance.'[457] 'If those who are charged with making heretics recant or consigning them to the flames did their duty,' he says, 'these sacrilegious words would be flung back in your

* * * * *

450 Cf Hutten's *Leonis x contra Lutherum bulla ... cum Huttenis notis* (EB II V 301–33).

451 Cf *Expostulatio* EB II 223:4–18 / K 102 par 172–4.

452 Erasmus probably has in mind Hutten's letter of 27 March 1521 to Emperor Charles V (EB II 44:14–8), in which case the reference would be to the imperial mandate of March 10 (*Deutsche Reichstagsakten* II no 75 529–33; cf 537 n3).

453 In late 1515 Erasmus was named an honorary councillor of Archduke Charles (Ep 370:16–20), to whom he soon dedicated the first edition of his *Institutio principis christiani*. But his annual pension was seldom paid (cf Epp 565:15–7, 621 introduction, 627:7–10, 1151:15–6, 1166:6, 1205:21–4), and was suspended in October 1521, following his departure from Brabant (cf Epp 1273:50–1, 1275:58–9, 1276:9–10, 1287:27–34, 1303:62, 1306:50–1, 1319:21–2, 1341A:1797–1802, 1342:101 and 286–7, 1380).

454 The second edition of Erasmus' *Institutio principis christiani* (Basel: Froben July 1518) was intended for Archduke Ferdinand, if not actually dedicated to him (Ep 853 introduction). Young Ferdinand was much taken by the book (cf Epp 943:22–7, 970:25–9, 1323:1–4), and in later years Erasmus enjoyed more credit at his court than at that of the emperor (cf Tracy *Low Countries* 194–6).

455 Pope Adrian VI offered 'a piece of preferment of a fairly honourable kind, which I refused without more ado' (Ep 1341A:1678–83; cf Epp 1324:126–33, 1338:47–64, 1345:19–20).

456 Cf *Expostulatio* EB II 183:7–8 / K 62 par 14.

457 Ep 1167:182–93; cf Epp 1195:121–36, 1202:137–40 and 323–6, 1219:109–11, 1331:23–7.

throat – for the seriousness of the issue compels me to speak sharply.'[458] Yet when Christ first sent the apostles out to preach he forbade them to reveal that he was the Christ.[459] If he who is truth itself ordered silence for a time about the truth on which our salvation depends, what is novel about my saying somewhere that the truth should be held back? Did Christ himself not keep silence before that criminous council that met in the house of Annas and Caiphas? 'If I tell you,' he said, 'you will not believe me.'[460] He was ready to speak the truth. Why then did he keep silent? Because he knew it would serve no purpose. Did he not keep silence before Herod as well?[461] Let us assume for the moment that what Christ did matters less than what he taught. "Do not,' he said, 'give that which is sacred to dogs,' nor cast pearls before swine.[462] When he bade the apostles depart from a city that showed itself unworthy to hear the gospel, was he not commanding them to keep the truth silent? Peter in his first sermon speaks of Christ as a man but is silent about his being God as well. Paul did likewise in preaching to the Athenians.[463] Among 'the perfect' Paul taught 'wisdom,' always the truth; but among the weak he kept silent about the truth.[464] The apostles Paul calls 'stewards of the mysteries of God.'[465] But a steward will bring some things forth and hold other things back, depending on the needs of his listeners. Why were all the mysteries of the philosophy of Christ[466] not revealed at once to the catechumens? Because they were not yet capable of understanding everything. As for the passages Hutten has in mind, I was speaking there not about articles of faith, but about Luther's paradoxes[467] and his insults of the pope.

Suppose it were clear to me that the feast of Easter is not being celebrated on the correct day; would it be better to proclaim this truth, at the price of a general uproar, or to keep quiet? Suppose I am defending an innocent man before a powerful tyrant: will I tell everything I know, and

* * * * *

458 Cf *Expostulatio* EB II 225:6–10 / K 104 par 180 (trans JDT).
459 Cf Luke 9:21–2; Ep 1202:73–80.
460 Luke 22:67
461 Cf Luke 23:9; Ep 1219:111.
462 Cf Matt 7:6.
463 Cf Acts 2:22, 17:31; Ep 1202:92–5 and 113–5; see also *Purgatio adversus epistolam Lutheri* below 427–9.
464 Cf 1 Cor 2:6.
465 Cf 1 Cor 4:1.
466 For Erasmus' concept of the *philosophia Christi*, see J.B. Payne 'Philosophy of Christ' in OER III 265–6; J.W. O'Malley CWE 66 xxiv–xxv.
467 Cf Epp 1202:56–8 and n10, 1384:5–7 and 97; below 122–3, 143.

thus betray my client, or will I keep some things back? No doubt Hutten, brave man and defender of the truth that he is, would speak as follows: 'O wretched tyrant! Is your cruelty not slaked by the blood of so many good men among your subjects? Must you also have this innocent man put to death?' In fact, some who promote Luther's cause are just as clumsy, raging as they do against the Roman pontiff in their seditious books. Now if Hutten were asking a wicked pope for benefice for a good priest, he would speak as follows: 'Impious Antichrist! You who stamp out the gospel and suppress public liberty! Lickspittle of princes! Give this good man this benefice, lest all your appointments be evil.'[468] Reader, I hear you laughing. But those people are no more sensible in the way they promote the gospel. Besides, I did not say that truth must be passed over in silence all the time, but only on occasion. Is the fact that the pope is the Antichrist (supposing he is) never to be held back? Before he wrote his book against the Arians, did not Hilary of Poitiers keep silent for a time? So he did, and makes his excuses for it.[469] When Cyprian was about to lay his head upon the block for Christ, the Roman magistrate accused him of plotting treason against the emperor. How did he answer? Did he say, yes, we Christians have conspired against the emperor, and rightly so, for he is a worshipper of devils and an enemy of God, worthy of being consigned to hell? Not at all. He denied that he was an enemy of Caesar, for whose health he prayed every day, for the sake of public peace. This is how it is fitting for a Christian bishop to proclaim the truth. As for Hilary, who addressed his book to the emperor, Constantius, did he not pass over many matters in silence, and speak of others with more gentleness than the emperor deserved? For that matter, how does Paul plead his own case before Felix, Festus, and Agrippa?[470] Does he not hold back the truth, and say what he says in a more obliging way than might have been warranted? So where, in my words, is a sacrilege that must be flung back in my throat, or makes me worthy of the stake? Is Hutten not ashamed to make a tragedy of such trifles?

    As for what he imagines about my going to Rome, to be greeted by the cardinals with festivals and rich gifts,[471] no one will take him seriously – though what he says would be more plausible had I indeed undertaken a journey to Rome. Here my accuser makes himself my adviser, for he bids me

* * * * *

468 Erasmus probably has in mind the letter to Pope Leo x with which Luther
    prefaced his *Babylonian Captivity of the Church*.
469 Cf *Contra Constantium imperatorem* 2–3 (PL 10 579–80).
470 Cf Acts 24:10–21, 26:1–29; Epp 1202:117–9, 1342:1006–7.
471 Cf *Expostulatio* EB II 218:5–10 / K 97 par 155.

beware of false friends.[472] How touching his solicitude for my well-being!
But I have no need of such counsellors, for I know better than Hutten what
is happening in Rome. Now comes a jolly section: despite having proven
nothing of what he says about my going to Rome, his feelings are stirred,
he calls me back, he grieves on my behalf, he takes pity on me, then doubts
whether I am worthy of his pity, thinking all the while that nobody catches
on to his game.[473] How foolish to call me from where I have never been[474]
back to where I am. He calls me back from a country of wicked men –
those who consolidate the tyranny of the Romanists, overturn the truth of
the gospel, and obscure the glory of Christ. But against such men I have
always done battle. He calls me instead to his country – though I cannot say
where Hutten is. Here I must fault him for a want of judgment. Throughout
his declamation he presents me as a foolish man of little account, utterly
lacking in constancy, weak, fussy, and bloodless, a man capable of changing
sides for a crust of bread.[475] What, then, is the point of calling such a man
to the land of the brave, this man who is one's friend only for the day,[476]
and who, even if he were to prove steadfast, has nothing more to offer than,
as the Greeks say, wood from a fig tree?[477] At this point I think I have said
enough about Luther and the pope.

Since the context seems to require it, I will now say a bit about my
character, which Hutten keeps promising to expose.[478] (I fear, however,
that his pamphlet discloses more about his character than mine; he might
have served himself better by endeavouring to cover his faults instead of
uncovering mine). Notice how wrongly he acts in setting himself up as
a judge of my character; for although we met a few times,[479] and I had
him for dinner once or twice, we never kept company. Those who have

* * * * *

472 Cf *Expostulatio* EB II 218:14–6 / K 98 par 157.
473 Cf *Expostulatio* EB II 227:19–20 / K 106 par 189; EB II 236:8–18 / K 114–15 par
     225–6; EB II 240:11–5 / K 118 par 239–40; EB II 243:17–20 / K 122 par 254; EB II
     245:3–9 / K 123 par 259. This translation of the last phrase follows a suggestion
     by C. Augustijn ASD IX- 1 187:558n.
474 Erasmus forgets that he spent time in Rome in the summer of 1509.
475 Cf *Adagia* I iii 77: *Frusto panis* CWE 31 297:1–9: 'used ... by the common people
     to mean something quite insignificant and worthless.'
476 Ἐφήμερον 'of the day'; cf *Adagia* IV ii 87: *Ephemeri vita* 'To live as long as
     Ephemerus' CWE 35 546.
477 Cf *Adagia* I vii 85: *Ficulnus* CWE 32 118–9: 'The wood of the fig tree [is] breakable
     and useless for almost any purpose.'
478 Cf *Expostulatio* EB II 239:17–240:2 / K 118 par 238.
479 Erasmus and Hutten met in Mainz (August 1514), and in Frankfurt (March or
     April 1515). Hutten visited Erasmus in Louvain in June 1520; see below 135–6.

lived with me, on familiar terms and for a long time, are the ones who
ought to pronounce on my character. In any event while Hutten approves
of what I teach[480] he disapproves of my conduct,[481] and warns Germans
against imitating it. Shall we, then, divide things, so that German youth take
instruction from me, but look to Hutten for a model of behaviour? In that
case, what is called Germanic sincerity would mean that one who is unable
to harm his enemies can destroy a friend with a book like this, without
warning, and, what is more barbarous still, fashioning from friendship itself
a spear to hurl against the friend – as the saying goes, making a bridle from
the bull's own hide.[482] For if I had not extended my benevolence to him,
Hutten would not have had the means to do me harm. I am however more
indignant at the man who stood behind Hutten,[483] for he too would not
have had the capacity to do me injury had I not accepted him into my circle
of friends.[484] When he betrays his identity he too will have the public notice
he deserves. For now, as the comic playwright says, 'What I know, I do not
know.'[485] Hutten then banishes me to my native Franco-Germany[486] – even
though he himself has no safe place in Germany, and prefers to live rather
as a clandestine guest of the Swiss than as a German among Germans,
in broad daylight. I will not make an issue of his calling the people of
Brussels Franco-Germans – for that region was clearly part of ancient Gaul
– nor about his exiling me from Germany, as if by living in Basel I were
actually in Germany. Even if Hutten were king of all Germany, and had the
right of banishing whomever he wished, he ought to treat me with more
consideration, for although I was born in the Rhine delta, my native place
is closer to France than to Germany. I have never crossed into Germany,
save when visiting towns near the Rhine, like Frankfurt, or, more recently,
Freiburg,[487] nor do I wish to venture farther into the country. I have never

* * * * *

480 Cf *Expostulatio* EB II 216:7–9 / K 96 par 150; EB II 223:19–224:2 / K 102 par 174–5;
     EB II 234:17–235:3 / K 113 par 219–20; EB II 243:3–13 / K 121 par 252.
481 Cf *Expostulatio* EB II 239:10–17 / K 117–8 par 237.
482 'What people are said to do when for the purpose of injuring somebody they
     use something received from that very person' (*Adagia* I ii 77: *Ex ipso bove lora*
     sumere CWE 31 213:1–214:14).
483 Ie Eppendorf; see above nn29, 38, 89, 264, 408, and ASD IX-1 103:67n.
484 Cf Epp 1437:10–13, 20–2; Allen Ep 1934:409–11.
485 Cf Ep 1389 above 36 n26.
486 Cf *Expostulatio* EB II 239:9–10 / K 117 par 236. On *Gallogermania*, see A. Wessel-
     ing 'Are the Dutch Uncivilized? Erasmus on the Batavians and His National
     Identity' ERSY 13 (1993) 68–102, esp 81–3.
487 Erasmus forgets that when he first travelled up the Rhine in 1514, and was
     lionized by humanists in Strasbourg and elsewhere, he was pleased to think
     of himself as a 'German' among Germans: cf. Tracy 'Erasmus Becomes a

sought anything from Germany, nor have I been a burden to her – unless labouring to further higher learning counts as a burden. My purpose in living here for the time being[488] is not to take what belongs to others, but to promote good letters and the cause of the gospel, and at my own expense. Much as I have welcomed the friendship of Germans, I have, thank heaven, never been in need of anyone's kindness.

I have never boasted of my character, and even as an old man I struggle with my faults every day. But I am glad to be free of the vices Hutten so freely attributes to me, as I can show from the testimony of all those with whom I have lived on an intimate basis. Specifically, Hutten makes me so timid and weak-spirited[489] that I am almost afraid of my own shadow.[490] But he should have remembered that bravery is a far cry from foolhardiness. It is madness, not bravery, to attempt something one has no power to carry out, or to provoke those whom one has no power to command. The bravery that snaps the bowstring is the bravery of gladiators.[491] Horace said this wisely in one of his lyric poems:

> Strength wanting in prudence collapses under its own weight.
> Strength moderated, even the gods raise in higher degree.[492]

Anyone who weighs carefully the liberties I take here and there in my books will more likely censure me for temerity rather than for timidity. See, then, how Hutten is being deliberately unfair. Even in his present condition he wants to be taken for a man who fears no one; me he writes off as timid because I fear the emperor and the pope – though not to the point of betraying the truth of the gospel. When he was in Brussels this same Hutten told me he dared not stay, lest Hoogstraten find him; but Hoogstraten was

* * * * *

German' *Renaissance Quarterly* 21 (1968) 281–8. He made several trips along the Rhine, which was in Roman times the border between *Gallia* and *Germania* (cf Allen's introductions to Epp 216, 301, 332, 337, 410, 843, 867, 1242). He visited Frankfurt in 1515 (Ep 332 introduction), and Freiburg in 1523 (Epp 1252:6–7, 1316:40–1, 1353 introduction).

488 Contrary to what he has just said, Erasmus here presumes that Basel is indeed part of 'Germany.'
489 Cf above 93.
490 Cf *Adagia* I v 65: *Umbram suam metuere* CWE 31 443:1–444:18.
491 Cf *Adagia* II vi 36: *Ne in nervum erumpat* 'For fear it break the string' CWE 33 309: 'the metaphor is taken from archers who, by drawing their bowstring with excessive force, sometimes snap it'); see Terence *Phormio* 325.
492 Horace *Odes* 3.4.65ff.

at the time neither the prior of his convent, nor an inquisitor armed with papal bulls or warrants.[493] Hutten so feared this unarmed lion that he stole away from Brussels;[494] and yet I am being timid if I do not heap foolish insults on all the enemies who wished me ill even before Luther appeared, and who are now furnished with princely edicts and papal bulls, not to mention armed retainers! A prudent man will fear, so as not to be afraid. Had Hutten done as much, instead of having to fear everything, he would now be loved by most, and feared by many. Nothing good ever comes of treating one's enemy with contempt.

Did I not speak freely in my *On the Education of the Christian Prince*, which I delivered into the hands of Emperor Charles v?[495] Hutten thinks himself brave if from one or another hiding-place or he hurls a few choice words at this or that foe and then, as they say, having thrown his spear, makes his getaway.[496] I see nothing to regret in the strength of spirit that has sustained me through sicknesses and labours, and through misfortunes and tragedies. I have been strong enough to despise the insults and injuries of my enemies, and to refuse the wealth and honours offered me by kings. Amid all the confusion and the danger of our times I have never slackened in my zeal to accomplish things for the cause of higher learning. Hutten boasts of wanting to infuse in me a strong spirit.[497] He would do better to

* * * * *

493 Hutten talked with Erasmus (in Louvain, not Brussels) in June 1520 (above n479). Hoogstraten was relieved of his duties as inquisitor and prior of the Cologne Dominicans in May 1520, but was then reinstated by a papal order of 23 June 1520 (N. Paulus *Die deutsche Dominkaner im Kampf gegen Luther (1518–1563)* [Freiburg 1903] 99). Aleandro, carrying the papal bull threatening to excommunicate Luther, reached the Low Countries in late September (Ep 1135 n1).

494 According to Brunfels, Hutten left the Netherlands because the papal legate, Caracciolo, had demanded his capture; meeting Hoogstraten by chance on the highway, Hutten drew his sword and threatened him, causing Hoogstraten to fall on his knees and beg pardon (Brunfels *Responsio* EB III 337:40–338:11). This account of the encounter is confirmed in a December 1520 letter from Crotus Rubeanus to Luther (cf EB I no 207 434:10–13 [WAB r 2 no 358:47–50], and in a contemporary dialogue sometimes attributed to Hutten *Hochstratus ovans* (EB I no 212 441:33–42).

495 *Institutio principis christiani* (ASD IV-1 95–219 / CWE 27 203–88). For Erasmus' *libertas* in this treatise cf Epp 337:95–6, 421:96–7, 1341A:716–9, 1429:259–60.

496 An allusion to the tactics of the Parthians, rulers of Iran in late Roman times (*Adagia* I i 5: *Infixo aculeo fugere* 'To flee after planting the dart' CWE 31 53:1–54:38).

497 Cf above 50.

mitigate his own spirit, and add a bit of judgment. Hutten claims that for the truth of the gospel one should even seek death rather than trying to avoid it.[498] I too would not refuse to go that far if the occasion demanded it.[499] But for Luther and Luther's paradoxes I have as yet no wish to seek a martyr's death.[500] For the issues in dispute do not count as articles of faith:[501] whether the primacy of the Roman pontiff is from Christ;[502] whether the college of cardinals is an essential member of the church body; whether confession was instituted by Christ;[503] whether the laws of bishops can bind under pain of mortal sin;[504] whether free choice contributes anything to salvation;[505] whether faith alone brings salvation; whether any human works can be called good;[506] and whether the mass can in any way be called a sacrifice.[507] All of these are topics for debate exercises in the faculties of theology; for such matters I would not wish to risk my life, nor, if I were a judge, would I dare condemn anyone to death. I would hope to be a martyr for Christ, were he to give me strength, but I will not be a martyr for Luther.

Just as my decision not to go to Rome is based on considered judgment, not fear,[508] the same was true for my decision to leave Brabant. For I knew

* * * * *

498 Cf *Expostulatio* EB II 223:4–6 / K 102 par 172; Ep 1161:57–70.
499 Cf Epp 1225:272–4, 1236:133–4.
500 Cf above n467; Epp 1167:487–8, 1218:35–6, 1384:5–7.
501 The point of the list that follows is to lump together all of the theological opinions that are (in Erasmus' view) falsely claimed to be articles of faith, whether such claims are made by Luther, or by Luther's Catholic opponents.
502 In the Catholic tradition, Matt 16:19 was understood to mean that Christ would build his church on Peter; Erasmus, following some of the church Fathers, interpreted the passage to mean that Christ would build his church not on Peter himself, but on his faith in the Lord, as expressed in verse 16:17: Tracy *Low Countries* 143–5. Cf Ep 1113:23–4; WA 1 567–70, 574–84; 3 397–400.
503 Cf Ep 1301:71–97, where Erasmus defends the language of a 1522 colloquy ('The Whole Duty of Youth' CWE 39 97) in which a pious youth would 'leave it to theologians to decide' whether the Catholic practice of confessing one's sins to a priest was instituted by Christ. In his 1524 treatise on the sacrament of confession, *Exomologesis sive de modo confitendi*, he considered the current practice of the church a sufficient refutation of the argument that it was not necessary to confess one's sins to a priest (LB IX 152E–153A).
504 Cf Ep 1301:106–20.
505 Note that the issue (as in the dispute between Erasmus and Luther) turns on free choice (*liberum arbitrium*), not free will.
506 Cf Ep 1384:12–13, with n4.
507 For a brief digest of this important Reformation controversy, OER II 79–80.
508 Cf Epp 1319:7–16, 1342:353–5.

I could not stay there unless I descended into the arena[509] against Luther.[510] But, Hutten asks, had I not already decided what to do if the emperor commanded me to write against Luther?[511] So let Hutten advise. Let us imagine the emperor speaking to me as follows (as no doubt he would have done): Erasmus, we are persuaded that because of your erudition and your elegant style you have authority and favour among learned men in Germany. Help us, therefore, in our efforts to suppress this pestilential Lutheran heresy, and we will amply reward your service. What should I have said? That I did not have the time, or the powers of mind to accomplish what his Majesty commanded? He would have pressed further: From men of learning we know very well what you are capable of, and it is our desire and our will that you comply with our wish; by doing so you will not only find favour in our eyes but also clear yourself from the false suspicion – brought to our notice more than once – that you are a supporter of Luther's impiety.

So, Hutten, what should I have said? Had promised to comply, I would have been pulled into this tragedy, at the cost of all my other work. I would have had to make myself a mouthpiece for certain monks and theologians whom I know only too well. I would not have had leisure for the *Paraphrases*,[512] or for some other things whose benefit will, I hope, not be confined to this generation alone. Had I flatly refused I would have cast myself into a nest of hornets, bringing my own destruction. Could I have fled somewhere? To Hutten's castle? Or to Wittenberg? In either case I would have lost what little income I have. At my age and with my health I cannot roam about, doing without life's necessities, or living like a fugitive. Hence I steered an intermediate course, so that I would neither abandon the cause of the gospel, nor become enmeshed in a labyrinth from which there is no escape.[513] It is not yet completely clear to me whether the truth of the gospel is with Luther. If things are so clear to Hutten, a man so staunch in the defence of truth that he is ready to die for it, why does he flee and hide? Let him go to Rome or to the Low Countries – there he will obtain the martyr's crown for which he longs.[514] So much for the feebleness of my

* * * * *

509 Cf *Adagia* I ix 83: *In arenam descendere* CWE 32 224: 'to enter on a contest.'
510 Cf Epp 1219:128–37, 1384:32–4; Allen Epp 1805:169–80, 2792:17–23.
511 Cf *Expostulatio* EB II 221:2–4 / K 100 par 164.
512 Cf above n340.
513 Cf *Adagia* ii x 51: *Labyrinthus* CWE 34 147–8: 'any speech or course of action which was excessively complicated and hard to unravel.'
514 On 1 July 1523 two Augustinian friars from Antwerp, Hendrick Vos and Jan van den Esschen, were burned as Lutheran heretics in Brussels – the first martyrs of the Protestant Reformation (cf Ep 1384: n2). Cf *Adagia* I iii 4: *Palmam*

spirit; I would not trade it for ten times the spirit of Hutten, who thinks himself braver than Achilles.

Enough, then, about my constancy. Constancy means keeping always on the same course, not saying always the same things. Now Hutten says cunning is not for Germans.[515] So let him tell me, when he left Basel, did he travel to Mulhouse along the direct, public road? And did he leave Mulhouse in broad daylight?[516] While he writes me off as a braggart and a shameless liar, he claims for himself a truthfulness solid as steel. But this is a point on which I yield to few. From a certain instinct of nature I hated liars even as a small boy, before I knew what a lie was.[517] Now I am so repelled by men of this ilk that my very frame quivers at the sight of them. Those who are close to me or have lived in my house will confirm this. Indeed, those who know me best say that speaking too freely – because I know not how to conceal the truth – is my besetting fault.[518] This was also the main reason I abandoned the life of a courtier;[519] there were too many wicked and unworthy things that, like it or not, had to be discussed only in whispers.

He also says I am impolite and even unfaithful to my friends.[520] What he considers impolite I do not know. For the common duties of civility – like escorting visitors about, or seeing them, or for inviting people or even accepting invitations to dinner – I have neither the health nor, because of my many labours, the time. Still, impolite as I am supposed to be, I spend more than half my time writing letters[521] to answer friends, or greet them, or provide recommendations. I may have refused dinner invitations for reasons of health, but often I have endangered my health by accepting them. Sometimes I have complied even with the foolish wishes of friends, often to my regret. To please importunate yet affectionate friends, I have frequently complied with their wishes – a compliance I have often regretted.

* * * * *

ferre 'To bear the palm' CWE 31 237: 'this tree alone was used for the crown common to all sacred contests.'

515 Cf *Expostulatio* EB II 239:3–18 / K 117–18 par 236–7.
516 Cf above 40; Ep 1437:55–9; Allen Ep 1934:379–80.
517 Cf *Compendium vitae* (CWE 4 409:154–7; ASD I-3 709:281–96); see J. Huizinga *Erasmus and the Age of Reformation* (New York 1957) 127–8.
518 Cf above nn128, 129; *Compendium vitae* CWE 4 409:157–8.
519 From October 1516 to February 1517, Erasmus was part of the entourage of his patron, Jean Le Sauvage (d 1517), Grand Chancellor of Archduke Charles of Burgundy, soon to be Emperor Charles V: Tracy *Politics of Erasmus* 51–5.
520 Cf *Expostulatio* EB II 181:13–19 / K 60 par 6; EB II 199:1–205:20 / K 79 par 83–5 par 110.
521 Cf Ep 1341A:1444–5; Huizinga *Erasmus* (above n517) 97–8.

But if there is any friend to whom I have ever refused loyal advice, or help when help was needed, let him come forward! But, he says, there are those who will swear that I am unfaithful.[522] In fact, not even my enemies accuse me of this, and I would not hesitate to call on my friends to speak out if I have ever failed to keep a secret, or deceived anyone by blabbing about what was meant to be private. I can even assert, and rightly so, that very few are more steadfast in their friendship than I.[523] Would that I had been as fortunate or as cautious in forming friendships[524] as I have been faithful in keeping them! I never quarrel with anyone whom I once loved truly and with all my heart; I am content to break off relations – indeed, I do not even do that except for some flagrant violation of the rules of friendship.

Let me give a few examples of how the rules of friendship can be broken. A few years back I wrote the cardinal of Mainz a letter opposing the clamour against Luther among certain theologians of Louvain.[525] I sent it in a sealed envelope, addressed to a man Hutten knows better than anyone, with instructions to deliver the letter if he saw fit, or, if not, to destroy it.[526] Since this man lived in the cardinal's household, as (I thought) a member of his council, he would be in a position to know his prince's mind. What happened? The letter was printed and circulated,[527] without even being delivered to the cardinal. This caused great ill will for the cardinal in Rome,[528] and for me among my enemies in Louvain,[529] who boasted of now having a good grip on me.[530] The cardinal angrily demanded to see the letter, addressed to him, which by then had already been making the rounds for three months. He finally got it, torn and smudged with printer's ink. He was upset with me, as well he might have been, for he suspected that

* * * * *

522 Cf *Expostulatio* EB II 238:17–20 / K 117 par 235.
523 Cf Ep 1225:2–6; Huizinga *Erasmus* (above n517) 119–20.
524 Cf above 34–5.
525 Ep 1033 (19 October 1519); on Albert of Brandenburg, above n51. Cf Epp 1123:5–6, 1127A:94–5, 1152:5–13, 1153:181–90, 1167:125–32, 1196:235–9, 1202: 229–33, 1217:25–9.
526 The man was Hutten: Ep 1152:8–10.
527 Ep 1033 was printed at least eight times, often without a publisher's name, in Cologne, Wittenberg, Nürnberg, Augsburg, Basel, and Sélestat (Allen Ep 1033 introduction and WAB r 1 620 n8); cf above n443.
528 C. Augustijn finds no evidence for this allegation (ASD IX-1 193:713n).
529 Cf Epp 1153:114–5, 1196:125–8 and 224–8, 1217:16–21.
530 Cf *Adagia* I iv 96: *Medius teneris* CWE 31 381:1–9: 'of someone held in such a way [around the middle] that he cannot possibly extricate himself.'

I was at fault. I am not making anything up; the cardinal wrote a letter remonstrating with me about what had happened.[531] What tragedies Hutten would have aroused if I had done something like that to him! First, he betrayed a commission entrusted to him in confidence by a friend. In addition, by making the letter public he did harm to a cause that might have been served if the letter had been read in private, and he exposed both a friend and a well-deserving patron to ill will. Finally, he turned a great prince, who had been my friend, into an enemy. Still, when I saw him I limited my reproaches to a few words. With a bashful smile, he acknowledged what had happened, but blamed it on the carelessness of a secretary.[532] Thereafter, impolite as I am, I said no more, concealing what I suspected.

This same man subsequently did something far more impolite, and far more dangerous to me.[533] Yet I never complained, having decided to be still a friend, but a more cautious friend. And how friendly was it of Hutten to excerpt certain contentious passages from my books and publish them in German?[534] I did not write these words for the masses, and they were not intended to be taken out of context. On this matter I briefly remonstrated with him in a letter:[535] I hear you were responsible for this, I said; perhaps it was done in a spirit of friendship, but I am glad my enemies do not have as much talent for causing me harm. Having made my point, I allowed our former friendship to continue. I could tell many stories like this. Still, rude and impolite as I am, I have yet to renounce the friendship of anyone. If any man can truly lay to my charge just one such crime against the rules of friendship, then I will acknowledge as true all of Hutten's calumnies. Let him therefore bring forward those friends who on their word of honour accuse me of infidelity and I will easily reduce them to silence. Suppose I allowed myself to be equally suspicious of him: whenever he says, certain

* * * * *

531 This letter is lost, but, as C. Augustijn notes, Erasmus' reply (Ep 1152) does not seem to indicate that the cardinal was very angry.
532 This conversation took place in Louvain in June 1520; cf above n130 and ASD IX-1 203:909–17n.
533 Cf Ep 1445:58–61: 'He put pressure on me to write several letters of recommendation to the imperial court, although he had already formed a conspiracy against the emperor – he only wanted to exploit the emperor's name in his hunt for a wife.' Cf Epp 1114, 1115.
534 Erasmus seems to blame Hutten for the German translation of passages from his *Annotationes in Novum Testamentum*: above n442.
535 This letter is lost.

people say, or, I heard in France,[536] I would suspect him of making it up. He might as well say, I dreamed that ...

He says my thirst for glory and fame is insatiable.[537] If this were so, I would long ago have attached myself to the Roman curia,[538] where a whole harvest of glory was once offered to me, or to the imperial court, to which I have been invited more than once.[539] I would have accepted the riches and honours held out to me. In either case I would have devoted my writing to magnificent and popular subjects. Instead, I have stubbornly rejected the paths that lead to glory, holding fast to my inglorious leisure, so as to devote myself to matters that are not in the least ostentatious. Hutten, no doubt measuring my attitude by his, cannot believe me when I swear that I would gladly give up whatever fame I have, if I could. Had I known what a burden fame can be I would have followed Epicurus' advice: λάθε βιώσας 'live a hidden life.'[540] But, he says, I boast of letters from princes, and the praises that others bestow on my works.[541] On this basis he pronounces me a vain and foolish man, for I suspect that is what he means. In fact, I publish barely a tenth of the letters I have from princes and scholars; if I sometimes call attention to such letters, it is to protect myself against the impudence of my detractors.[542] For against their wickedness I have no other weapons or defences except, as I have said, my own innocence, and the good will of princes and learned men.

I have never boasted that the most distinguished Archduke Ferdinand has repeatedly honoured me with gracious letters,[543] nor of the generous gift he sent without my asking or expecting it.[544] Nor do I brag about the king of France writing in his own hand to invite me,[545] although they say he has hardly written three autograph letters since his coronation, or about the king

* * * * *

536 Cf *Expostulatio* EB II 185:11 / K 64 par 25; EB II 200:10–11 / K 80 par 89; EB II 238:18 / K 117 par 235.
537 Cf *Expostulatio* EB II 187:7 / K 66 par 34.
538 In 1509: cf K. Schätti *Erasmus von Rotterdam und die Römische Kurie* (Basel 1954) 22–5.
539 Cf above n519; in 1519 Erasmus was invited to be the tutor for Archduke Ferdinand (cf Epp 596 introduction, 917, 927).
540 Cf *Adagia* II x 50: *Late vivens* 'Live a hidden life' CWE 34 147.
541 Cf *Expostulatio* EB II 218:11–4 / K 97 par 156.
542 Cf Epp 809:146–56, 1299:41–9, 1300:63–9.
543 Ep 1343 (see above n536); cf Epp 943:21–7, 970:25–30.
544 Cf Epp 1341A:1738–41, 1376:13–17.
545 The postscript of Ep 1375 (reproduced in CWE 10 48) was in the hand of Francis I; cf above n56.

of England inviting me just recently.[546] Thus within a few months I have had letters from four rulers of the earth – the emperor,[547] the kings of France and England, and Archduke Ferdinand.[548] Had Hutten received such letters, imagine how puffed up his cheeks would be! He indeed writes to emperors, cardinals, and papal nuncios, but who among them has answered him?[549] He might as well have written to heaven or hell. To be sure, when I declare how kind and generous princes have been to me, I am not boasting but expressing my gratitude. Now as for praises from scholars, I have boxes full of laudatory epistles, and more arrive every day from all over. Sometimes I do not even read them, for this is the kind of correspondence that pleases me least. Do I ever acknowledge or as it were eat up the praises offered me? Do I not instead protest against the fulsome encomia heaped upon me by some people, indicating rejection with my head, my hands, my feet, indeed my whole body?

Hutten claims I am so envious I cannot bear the fame of illustrious predecessors, nor the rising fame of my juniors.[550] But those who from long familiarity know my habits very well – unlike Hutten, who presumes to judge me after a few conversations[551] – will confirm that I am as far from envy as I am from deceitfulness. Has any scholar, in his books, ever been as full or forthright in praising his colleagues, whether older or younger? This includes not a few whose names the world would not know had I not mentioned them. Now Hutten objects that many of those I praise are unworthy.[552] Does a scholar who errs in this direction deserve to be called envious? Moreover, who has worked as hard as I have to restore the works of ancient authors? Is this to be envious of one's predecessors?

As for those who were seen by the previous generation as masters in the world of letters,[553] has anyone paid greater tribute to Lorenzo

* * * * *

546 Ep 1383:29–30
547 Ep 1270 (1 April 1522)
548 These were the rulers to whom Erasmus dedicated his *Paraphrases*: *Matthew* to Charles v (Ep 1255), *John* to Archduke Ferdinand (Ep 1333), *Luke* to Henry VIII of England (Ep 1381), and *Mark* to Francis I (Ep 1400).
549 Cf Brunfels *Responsio* 340:8–341:5; Hutten's *Conquestiones* (EB I 371–419) and *Invectivae* (EB II 12–34, 37–46, 47–50, 59–62).
550 Cf *Expostulatio* EB II 187:6–8 / K 66 par 34; EB II 200:9–16 / K 80 par 89–90; EB II 201:12–202:4 / K 81 par 94–82 par 96; EB II 230:6–9 / K 108 par 199.
551 Cf above n479.
552 Cf *Expostulatio* EB II 192:8–214:17 / K 71 par 58–94 par 153.
553 Erasmus now mentions humanist scholars whose merits he says he has duly acknowledged. Those of less importance in his own scholarly development can be passed over lightly. Johann Reuchlin has already been mentioned (above nn21, 176). The patrician Ermolao Barbaro (1453/4–1493), who served as an official

Valla,[554] Ermolao Barbaro, and Angelo Poliziano? To Rodolphus Agricola[555] and Alexander Hegius[556] I owe practically nothing, yet I give them full recognition in a work everyone believes will endure. I always give Johann Reuchlin his due, and I speak respectfully of Ulrich Zasius, not to mention Thomas Linacre and William Grocyn. Whom among the scholars of my generation have I not been glad to recognize? Am I stingy in praising the merits of Guillaume Budé?[557] As for Jacques Lefèvre

* * * * *

of his native Venice and later as patriarch of Aquilea, is known for his translations and paraphrases of Aristotelian texts into correct humanist Latin. Angelo Poliziano of Montepulciano (1454–1494), who was tutor to the sons of Lorenzo de' Medici and professor of rhetoric at the Florentine studio, published notable critical studies of Greek and Latin authors. Uldaricus Zasius of Constance (1461–1535) studied and then taught law at the University of Freiburg, where he cultivated close ties with humanists in the Upper Rhineland. Thomas Linacre (c 1460–1524) took a degree in medicine from Padua before returning to England, where he became physician to Henry VIII and founded in 1518 London's College of Physicians. The theologian William Grocyn (c 1446–1519) taught the first course in Greek in Oxford, and later supported the humanist curriculum introduced by Erasmus' great friend, John Colet.

554 Lorenzo Valla (1407–57), son of a lawyer accredited to the Roman curia, was educated by private tutors. Between stints as a professor of rhetoric (Pavia, 1431–33; Rome, from 1450), he served as secretary to King Alfonso v of Naples (1435–48), and as *scriptor apostolicus* for Pope Nicholas v (from 1448). His main works included *Elegantiarum linguae latinae libri tres*, a compilation of classical (as distinct from medieval) Latin usage, of which Erasmus published a *Paraphrasis* in 1531 (cf Ep 182; Allen Ep 2416); *De falso credita et ementita Constantine donatione declamatio*, an exposure of the so-called 'Donation of Constantine' (giving the pope the western half of the Roman empire) as a forgery; and *In latinam Novi Testamenti interpretationem ex collatione graecorum exemplarium adnotationes*, a philological critique of the Vulgate New Testament, which was first published by Erasmus (Paris: J. Bade 1505).

555 Roelof Huusman ('farmer,' or in Latin 'Agricola'), from Baflo near Groningen (1444–85), studied at various universities and sojourned in Italy before returning to Groningen, where he promoted the new learning in the northern Low Countries. Erasmus often spoke of him with respect (*Adagia* I iv 39 CWE 31 348–51; Epp 23:57–61, 480:104–6, 1237:13–18).

556 Alexander Hegius (c 1433–98), from Heek in Westphalia, was from 1483 headmaster of St Lebuin's school in Deventer, and made it a centre for humanistic studies. Erasmus was a pupil here, but did not stay long enough to reach the upper classes taught by Hegius. For his praise of Hegius, see Ep 23:61–6; *Adagia* I iv 39 CWE 31 350:54–64; *Adagia* II ii 81 CWE 33 118; *De contemptu mundi* CWE 66 158; *Compendium vitae* CWE 4 404:42–405:47.

557 Guillaume Budé (1468–1540), a law graduate from a prominent bourgeois family in Paris devoted himself to his favourite pastime, hunting, until, with the suddenness of a religious conversion, c 1491, he threw himself into the

d'Étaples,[558] however that quarrel got started, has anyone been more forthright in praising him? My books are a veritable register of the names of my friends. And have I been envious of Hutten's rising star? My countless praises of him say otherwise,[559] even if that book of his now compels me to retract them. Has anyone proclaimed his name more often, or with greater candour and affection? And did I demand a reward in return? For this is what an envious man would do. I praise some young men because of their promising talents, others just to encourage them. Have I ever made myself better than another, or even started a quarrel about who was more learned? Have I not been willing to yield to others the pre-eminence in the qualities that Hutten attributes to me?[560] And have I ever attacked anyone who has not openly attacked me first? Even my enemies I have thus far treated in such a manner that through my writings they become more famous. My work has contributed something of weight to the revival of Greek letters in our time; but do I not rejoice to see hundreds of young scholars whose learning will surpass mine? What kind of envy is this? If anyone wanted to charge me with envy, Hutten is hardly a proper accuser, since I am virtually alone in having commended him οὕτως ἀφθόνως 'so ungrudgingly.' Now, having had more praise from me than from all his friends, this friend of mine throws more accusations at me than all my enemies have done, or

* * * * *

study of classical Greek and Latin. While serving Francis I as royal librarian and master of requests, he persuaded the king to endow lectureships in Greek, Latin, and Hebrew. His *Annotationes in quattuor et viginti Pandectarum libros* (1508) was a milestone in the history of legal humanism, and his *De asse et partibus eius* (1515) may be said to have inaugurated the serious study of Roman institutions. For his relations with Erasmus, see Laurel Carrington 'The Writer and his Style: The Correspondence of Erasmus and Guillaume Budé' ERSY 10 (1990) 61–84.

558 Jacques Lefèvre d'Étaples (c1460–1536) studied and taught in the arts faculty at Paris, initially according to the traditional curriculum. Three visits to Italy (between 1491 and 1507) led him to refocus his teaching of Aristotle. Under the patronage of Guillaume Briçonnet, he devoted himself to a humanist interpretation of biblical texts (*Quintuplex Psalterium* [1509], *Commentarii in Pauli epistolas* [1517]). Attacks by Paris theologians led him to join Briçonnet, now bishop of Meaux, as his vicar-general. He fled briefly to Strasbourg (1525) before being recalled by Francis I. Erasmus remained on friendly terms with Lefèvre, despite their controversy over Heb 2:7 (cf Reeve *Galatians to the Apocalypse* 706–13; *Apologia ad Fabrum* LB IX 17A–50E / CWE 83 4–107; CWE 44 218 n6).

559 Cf above n392.

560 Cf the preface to Hutten's *Nemo* (EB I no 84 183:3–8), his letter to Lee (EB I no 166 346:10–348:12), and his letters to Erasmus (Epp 365, 611, 923, 986, 1135).

than he has done against any of his enemies. Yet in his letter to me he calls his tract a gentle expostulation, in light of my abominable crimes.[561] What a sweet man!

When someone is striving for a worth-while goal, have I not extended a hand? If I have not helped more, it was for lack of means, and not a lack of good will. Certainly whenever I could help anyone by a word of praise or a letter of recommendation or similar courtesies I have done so, even for some who were ill disposed towards me, provided they were advancing the cause of learning. Were I to cite the letters of those who thank me for my kindness, Hutten would call me the vainest man on earth – and they in turn would call him the most brazen of all false accusers. While I lived in Brabant, from my meagre income I gave more to students in one year than many of those who like to brag about such things received from their family estates.[562] So much for my envy of younger scholars! I will not reveal any names, nor do I begrudge anyone the small service I rendered, for I believe that in giving I was rewarded, so long as it was to a deserving man. But these young men are witnesses to the shamelessness of Hutten's charges. 'You would have no equal in eloquence,' Hutten says.[563] In fact I would not take it ill if a great many were ranked ahead of me, as no doubt many should be.

With similar impudence he makes me a creature that readily sheds its skin, a master of pretence and concealment.[564] How little he knows the real Erasmus, to whom pretence and dissimulation do not come easily. This Erasmus (not Hutten's) is by nature forthright and uncalculating, to the point of foolishness, for his tongue is dangerously free.[565] Indeed, it is not my habit to deceive people by a charming demeanour; if something displeases my language will be sharper than what I feel. 'I will not let your smile deceive me again,' Hutten says.[566] But when have I deceived him with a kind face? Rather it was he who imposed on me in this way, for in my company he was always modest, keeping the wantonness of his tongue in check. Either his demeanour then was all a front, or he has since undergone a strange transformation. I swear I did not believe that in all of

* * * * *

561 Cf above n25.
562 C. Augustijn (ASD IX- 1 199:816–17n) has found no documentation of gifts to students by Erasmus.
563 Cf *Expostulatio* EB II 201:17 / K 81 par 95.
564 Cf *Expostulatio* EB II 196:3–7 / K 75–6 par 73.
565 Cf above nn128, 129.
566 Cf *Expostulatio* EB II 237:17–9 / K 116 par 230.

Germany there was so much brazen impudence, so much harsh rudeness as he has put into this one pamphlet.[567] Still, I shall not let it prejudice me against Germans; one false friend will not turn me against those who are true friends.

Despite the frankness of my writings he is not ashamed to call me a Gnatho.[568] I suppose, then, that anyone reading the passages where I praise Hutten will call me a Gnatho flattering a Thraso.[569] Here too I find Hutten wanting in judgment. On the one hand, he hopes to be seen as the defender of Germany's reputation; on the other hand, by writing me off as a crafty flatterer, not to be taken seriously, does he not detract from the praises of Germans that one finds in my books? None of this was flattery, including my commendation of Hutten,[570] which came from the heart. I admired his talent, and his rich facility of speech, and with study, age, and experience I expected great things from him.[571] If he deceived me, and those to whom I commended him, does that make me a flatterer?

But I do speak in honeyed tones when writing to princes! To be sure, I am παρρησιαζόμενος 'very free of speech' when the occasion demands it.[572] Nevertheless, lions have to be treated gently,[573] and Scripture teaches that we owe reverence to princes.[574] And where, in my flattery of princes, do I betray the truth? Does one who rages madly against princes accomplish more than a flatterer like me? In the past kings and queens read nothing but romantic fables;[575] now they have the gospels in

* * * * *

567 Cf Ep 1376:18–20.
568 Cf *Expostulatio* EB II 222:13–5 / K 101 par 170; cf EB II 237:13–4 / K 116 par 229. Gnatho is the parasite and flatterer of Terence's *Eunuchus* (cf ASD I-1 55:11n).
569 In the same comedy of Terence, Thraso was a swaggering soldier (cf ASD I-1 81:14n). In his *Epistola ad fratres Inferioris Germaniae* Erasmus called Eppendorf a Thraso (below 333); in Ep 1492:12 he called Hutten a *miles gloriosus* 'boastful knight,' probably in reference to a play of that name by Terence.
570 Cf above n392.
571 Cf above n39.
572 On the rhetorical principle of παρρησία 'speaking freely,' cf Quintilian *Institutio* 9.2.27, 9.3.99.
573 Cf *Adagia* II v 11: *Leonem radere* 'To shave a lion' CWE 33 247.
574 Matt 22:21; Rom 13:1–7; 1 Tim 2:1–2; Titus 3:1; 1 Pet 2:13–14. C. Augustijn (ASD IX-1 201 n847–8) notes that while the word *reverentia* is not found in any of these passages, Erasmus uses it in his *Paraphrasis in epistolam Pauli ad Romanos* (LB VII 821C / CWE 42 75).
575 Cf *Education of a Christian Prince* CWE 27 250: 'Today we see a great many people enjoying the stories of Arthur and Lancelot and other legends of that sort, which are not only tyrannical but also utterly illiterate, foolish, and on the level of old wives' tales.'

hand, they read Scripture, and rejoice to learn of the mysteries of the philosophy of Christ.[576] Let Hutten tell us what his abusive language has accomplished. Flattery is pious when it helps another, not oneself. If I were
out to gain something from princes, my flattery would be suspect. As it
is, I seek nothing, or if I do it is for the advancement of common learning rather than for myself. In any case, to praise princes does not in itself make one a flatterer. For while the good deserve to be praised, praising the mediocre (or those who show promise) can encourage progress in
virtue, and praising the bad is a way of reminding them of about their
duties, without giving offence. All of this I explained some years ago in
a letter to Johannes Paludanus.[577] This is the kind of Gnatho Erasmus has
been. I, too, could call the popes Antichrists, the bishops idols, and the
princes tyrants, like some others do, but I do not consider it the part of a
good man to heap abuse of this kind on good men who deserve respect. As
for evil men, it is madness to provoke those who, once aroused, cannot be
restrained.

Following the example of learned men of old, I dedicate some of my
works to personal friends, others to princes. From friends I do not even
accept thanks, much less do I try to pry something from them. I do not beg
from princes either, and no one would believe how few of them have given
me something in return for a dedication. I will not go into detail – at least
not here – lest I offend someone. In any case, one needs something to live
on, and a scholar who hunts a generous prince to reward his honest labour
does better than a borrower who does not repay, or a merchant who does
not settle his debts, or a beggar who employs threats when people fail to
show pity.

What gall on Hutten's part to accuse me of incivility and discourtesy,
when his book declares to the world that he himself has not a spark of
human kindness.[578] The barbarous Scythians treat old age with deference,
just as wild beasts know their obligations, and even bandits and pirates
observe among themselves the rules of friendship. Hutten acknowledges
that we have had a special friendship,[579] and that I have done much for the

* * * * *

576 For the 'philosophy of Christ,' above n466.
577 Ep 180, in connection with the *Panegyricus* with which Erasmus welcomes
    Archduke Philip (Charles v's father) on his return from Spain (cf CWE 27:1–
    76). While in Louvain from 1502 to 1504, Erasmus stayed in the house of
    Jean Desmarez ('Paludanus'), who, as canon of St Peter's and professor of
    eloquence, introduced him to local humanists.
578 Cf *Adagia* III vii 75: *Ne guttam quidem* CWE 35 265.
579 Cf above n79.

public good,[580] and some things for him as well.[581] Nevertheless, having suffered no injury to himself, and trampling on all the laws of the Graces, this young man spews forth strife and insults upon his elder, he boxes my ears, beats me about the mouth, grabs me and spins me around, as if he were dealing not with Erasmus but with a slave bought off the block.[582] He seems to think that somewhere among the races of men there must be people rude enough not to condemn this kind of savagery. Perhaps he imagines that such were the customs of ancient Sparta and Massilia[583] – from which he wants German youth to learn.

There was a time when my feelings towards Hutten were such that I thought that if anyone were coming after me, he if anyone would risk his life to prevent me from coming to harm. I spoke warmly about him to my friends, I did him favours, I deplored his misfortune, and worried about his finding a safe haven. Now this high priest of polite learning has come at a friend with this pamphlet, as if from ambush – a friend he had always treated with respect,[584] whose grey hairs he ought to respect, and whose services to learning (not to mention to himself) he acknowledges. He has published a declaration of war on the Romanists,[585] but in fact he wages war on the Muses and the Graces. If the sword meant for his enemies is bloodless, it is the pen he uses against his friends that has drawn blood.

He charges me with instigating all the tumult of our times, and then, once the world was ablaze, disowning my actions, and trying to curry favour with the enemy.[586] Must I overlook an accusation like this? I expect he will also make me the instigator of all the crimes he plans to commit here or there, if the gods of war look favourably upon him. Yet in that letter he sent most recently he says,[587] No one goads Hutten into action, nor will he allow himself to be goaded by anyone. Now if Hutten's θυμὸς ἀγήνωρ

* * * * *

580 Cf above n80.
581 Cf *Expostulatio* EB II 195:15–6 / K 7 par 71; EB II 240:8–9 / K 118 par 239.
582 Cf *Adagia* III i 67: *De lapide emptus* CWE 34 207–8: 'Bought off the block was applied to a quite worthless and utterly obscure man; for among the different kinds of slaves ... purchased slaves were held to be of the lowest quality.'
583 Cf *Expostulatio* EB II 239:10–19 / K 117 par 237–118 par 238; *Adagia* II iii 98: *Naviges in Massiliam* 'You should take ship for Massilia' CWE 33 188–9. Massilia was a Greek colony on the site of modern Marseilles.
584 Cf *Expostulatio* EB II 182:12–16 / K 61 par 11.
585 Cf above n369.
586 Cf the second part of the *Expostulatio*, beginning with EB II 214:17 / K 94 par 144.
587 Cf above n17.

'proud spirit'[588] will not allow him to be goaded into action by any mortal, and if I am besides a man of no consequence, how can he speak of me as instigating all the tumult we see around us? Let us forget about dinner-table talk, written in wine; and let us also set aside those *Colloquia* of mine, in which friends chatter among themselves. For the rest, whenever there was need for serious advice, I have, as I said, always advocated moderation. I warned Reuchlin against offending the religious orders, and deplored the effervescence of his apology.[589] I believe my letters can still be found among his papers, and they will show that I speak truly. I felt the same way about Luther, and I have already mentioned the advice I gave to the Count of Neuenahr.[590] Concerning Hutten I will not reveal any secrets of friendship. I will repeat only what he himself has published in his books so the whole world will know. While visiting me in Louvain he asked for a private conversation, the only one we ever had.[591] When he spoke of declaring war on the Romanists I thought at first he was joking.[592] I asked him how he could hope to prevail, since the pope is very powerful and has many princes on his side. When he said a bit about this, I noted that this was a violent and dangerous business, and that even if the cause were pious it was foolish to launch a campaign that there was no hope of completing. In any case, I told him, I wanted to hear no more of this, for my focus was on labouring for the benefit of public learning. Whatever others might attempt along these lines, I said, he should stay clear of it.[593] So much for my having goaded Hutten to act as he did.

Previously, when he had published some excessively frank pamphlets, I urged him in a letter to temper his pen, so that his prince would continue to favour him; he replied that he would follow my advice.[594] Had he done so he would be a man one could befriend without risk, honoured among the

* * * * *

588 In the *Purgatio adversus epistolam Lutheri*, Erasmus applied this term (used of Achilles by Homer) to Luther: see below 412.

589 More than a year after Reuchlin published his apology (*Defensio Joannis Reuchlin Phorcensis LL Doctoris contra calumniatores suos Colonienses* [Tübingen: Thomas Anselm March 1513]), Erasmus counselled moderation (Ep 300), but none of his extant letters to Reuchlin warn against attacking the religious orders.

590 Cf above 59.

591 Cf above n130; Ep 1114 introduction.

592 Cf Ep 1129:27–31.

593 Cf Ep 951:31–41, 967:161–3.

594 Both letters seem to be lost. Ep 951:45–54 resembles the advice Erasmus mentions, but the next extant letter from Hutten (cf Ep 986 introduction) does not take up the issue, and seems to be responding to a subsequent (lost) letter.

great, and not a fugitive hiding from his foes. Even before this exchange, when we met in Mainz and had our first conversation,[595] he showed me his elegant poem *Triumphus Capnionis*.[596] I gave him two reasons not to publish it: first, lest he be ridiculed for 'celebrating before the victory,' as the Greeks say;[597] second, lest he embitter all the more those enemies of Reuchlin who still had power to do him great harm. In any case, I said, if he would not take my advice, let him at least take my name out.[598] Some months later we saw each other again in Frankfurt.[599] Right away I asked if he remembered my advice. He said he remembered it well, and was resolved to follow my counsel in all things. Yet soon the poem appeared anyway, with a braggadocious wood-cut showing Reuchlin's triumph;[600] the two together only made Reuchlin still more hateful to enemies who were already rabid as it was. No doubt Reuchlin himself disapproved. I am not discussing what his enemies deserved, but what would have been helpful to his cause. My advice was always of this sort, whenever anything important was at stake. Although Hutten and I never had any kind of compact, we were both bound by the laws of the Muses to resist the enemies of languages and good letters. And I admit that I have not really supported Luther's opponents, and even now do not want to see them gain a total victory, for I could see that with Luther defeated they would be insufferable. When Luther appeared on the stage I did not at first wholly disapprove, but I have always disapproved of how the drama is being played out.[601] Suppose Hutten claims (contrary to fact) that in the beginning I too applauded Luther like everyone else, especially the scholars of Germany, and that I entrusted to Hutten, as an honest friend, the secrets of my heart. Would it not be inhumane to broadcast what I told him in confidence to the whole world, once he had, for his own reasons, become my enemy? The Muses notwithstanding, he even calls his vicious accusations a remonstrance. To remonstrate with someone is to bring one's complaint to him privately as a friend, hoping to

* * * * *

595 In August 1514
596 See above n21.
597 Cf *Adagia* i vii 55: *Ante victoriam encomium canis* 'You sing your song of triumph before you have won the day' CWE 32 100.
598 The text does not mention Erasmus, but his editions of Jerome and of the New Testament are cited in the postscript (EB I 238:4–5).
599 In March or April 1515: see Ep 332 introduction.
600 For a facsimile of the four-part wood-cut showing Reuchlin's triumphal procession, see D.F. Strauss *Ulrich von Hutten* (Leipzig 1914) between pp 144 and 145.
601 Cf Epp 872:22–3, 1202:51–2 and 271–2, 1225:296–8, 1313:9–15.

find satisfaction. But Hutten, without warning, brings me before the bar of the whole world; and he is so brazen as to think he can write such things without breaking our friendship. So let him have what friends or enemies he wants. For my part, I want nothing more to do with the type of person that letter of his reveals him to be.[602] By the time Hutten's *Expostulatio* reached Zürich, after passing through the hands of many in Basel,[603] I had already sent a letter responding to the points that angered him,[604] as recounted in his letter to me.[605] I explained that my reasons for not seeing him privately were other than he suspected; I made excuses for my letter to Hoogstraten; and I indicated I had never even dreamed of making accusations against Reuchlin. I also made clear that while I had not changed my opinion of Luther, and had never been one of his partisans, I was still wholly committed to promoting the cause of the gospel. I said too that I had not yet written against Luther, and that if I were to do so I would use sound arguments and testimony from Scripture, avoiding insults; indeed my moderation and fairness would be such that Luther himself would not be offended. Finally, I pointed out that if Hutten followed through on his plans he would do harm to liberal studies and the cause of the gospel, and even to his own position, as it then was. These and many other things I put in my letter.

His learned friends counselled against publication, even Eppendorf, as Hutten himself admits.[606] Making light of all this advice, he published a book that will be especially pleasing to those who are enemies of Luther, classical languages, and good letters – the very men Hutten most despises, if we may take him at his word. How those men will gloat. I can hear them saying to one another, let Erasmus now have the benefit of the Hutten he has praised so much, and the talent he has so extolled; let him now kiss what has come from that elegant diction he so admires! Others may bruit it about that Hutten was hired to write against Erasmus by Hoogstraten and Baechem and their companions. On the face of things this would not be implausible, especially since Hutten jokes about sniffing the bait the pope

* * * * *

602 See above n17.

603 Cf above 43 n24.

604 See above n25.

605 For this lost letter, cf above 44–5 and C. Augustijn ASD IX-1 101:52n.

606 For possible traces of a lost letter in which Hutten may have said this, above 53. C. Augustijn (ASD IX-1 205:964–5n) suggests that Eppendorf may have urged Hutten to demand money from Erasmus in return for not publishing his *Expostulatio*.

has dangled before me.[607] What I smell here is more like the bait monks and
theologians would put out, for this quarrel is not of recent origin, it is an old
boil that is just now being drained of its pus.[608] Several months ago friends
warned me that an attack of some kind was being prepared.[609] I expected
a minor quarrel over one of Luther's dogmas. But I see that this work,
though spawned in a context of its own, has been enlarged with patches
sewn in,[610] made up of denunciations provided by others. For the style is
not consistent, save in the part he wrote at leisure, which is better worked
out.[611] Which is more honourable: to accept a reward from the emperor and
the pope for disputing with Luther, or to accept payment from monks for
flinging insults at a friend? Let Hutten tell us what little morsel the monks
and theologians tossed out to make him bark at me, and I will confess what
I receive from the emperor and the pope if I write against Luther.

He will perhaps deny the truth of what looks to be true. What cannot be denied is that no one has done the enemies of Luther and of good
letters a greater favour than Hutten does with this pamphlet. By addressing the Louvain theologians as 'Reverend Fathers'[612] I am said to heap coals
on Luther's head; but Luther's enemies have much greater pleasure from
this play acted out by Luther's would-be champion. This book of his em-
boldens their spirits and gives swagger to their steps. In my mind's eye I
see those sworn enemies of good letters and good theology everywhere ex-
ulting, jumping up and down, and congratulating one another – Baechem
and Vincentius at Louvain;[613] in Paris Guillaume Duchesne[614] and old beet-

* * * * *

607 Cf *Expostulatio* EB II 188:12–1899:9 / K 67 par 39–68 par 40; EB II 215:6–7.
608 In the paragraphs that follow Erasmus toys with a conceit (that Hutten was
    suborned by Egmond or Hoogstraten) for which there is no basis, either for
    polemical effect, or because he tended to envision his enemies as conspiring
    together against him.
609 That certain Lutherans would write against Erasmus had been rumoured for
    over a year: cf Epp 1263:26–8, 1267:28–31, 1273:31–3, 1274:53–5, 1275:30–1,
    1276:11–3, 1313:60–1.
610 Horace *Ars poetica* 16; cf *Adagia* II iii 79: *Pannus lacer* 'Shreds and tatters' CWE
    33 177–8.
611 Proud of his ability to identify an author from his style, Erasmus sometimes
    claimed to detect the hands of several different enemies in works written
    against him.
612 Ep 1217:3
613 For Baechem and Vincentius, see above nn187, 189.
614 Guillaume Duchesne (de Quercu, Quernum) of Saint-Sever in Calvados (d
    1525) earned his doctorate in theology in 1496, and taught at the Collège
    de Sorbonne. He served on faculty committees that examined the works of

head;[615] in Cologne Theodoricus of Nijmegen[616] with his shabby crew; and in England, I expect, Lee and Standish.[617] I can see them all preparing a triumphal entry for Hutten, outdoing one another in their applause and acclaim: Bravo, bold knight, βάλλ᾽ οὕτως 'keep going'![618] Do us a favour, do away with that Erasmus who attacks us with strange tongues and new ways of writing, and shakes the foundations of our kingdom. Onward! More books like this will make those so-called good letters distasteful to princes and studious youth, letting them see the virulence within them, and that they are good for nothing but calumniating decent folk and inciting rebellion. Pull back the curtain on those lewd poetic mysteries; into the well-spring of the Muses you must spit, blow snot, piss, and shit, so that no one will ever again want to drink there. Or, if you prefer to defile those waters all at once, take a bath! All you have done in the past to offend us we forgive, if you but continue as you have begun.

* * * * *

Reuchlin (1514), Luther (1520/1521, cf Ep 1181), and Lefèvre d'Étaples (1523). He also collaborated with Noël Bédier (see next note) in examining the works of Erasmus (cf Epp 1664, 2043, 2053).

615 *Betaceus*, a pun on *beta* 'beet' and possibly also on *cetaceus* 'whale-like,' and a reference to Noël Bédier (Natalis Beda; cf the colloquy 'A Fish Diet' cwe 40 680:25–6: 'How wise are people who live on beets? Why, as wise as the beets themselves.'; Allen Ep 1963:23). Noël Bédier of Mont Saint-Michel (1470–1537) was from 1504 to 1535 principal of the Collège de Montaigu at the University of Paris; having earned his doctorate in 1508, he was also a member of the theological faculty. As syndic of the faculty from 1520, he played a decisive role in the proceedings against Luther (1521) and against Erasmus (1523, 1525, 1527).

616 Theodoricus Born (Boern, Huysen, te Huyssen, Noviomagus) (d 1530) rose through the ranks as professor and dean of the faculty of arts at the University of Cologne. Having received his doctorate in 1515, he then taught in the theology faculty until his death. He was also, from 1520, provost of St Stephen's at Nijmegen.

617 On Lee, see above n126.
Henry Standish, a Franciscan from an early age, was ordained a priest in 1489 and earned a doctorate in theology from Oxford. He was provincial of the English Franciscans (1505–18), warden of the Greyfriars' house in London (1515–18), and from 1518 bishop of St Asaph in Wales. Erasmus probably met him in 1515 and disliked him from the outset. As a staunch defender of scholastic theology, and a friend of Erasmus' great enemy, Edward Lee, Standish objected to Erasmus' editions of Jerome and the New Testament, and, in 1520, preached against his interpretation of John 1:1 at St Paul's, London. For Erasmus' views on Standish, cf *Adagia* ii v 98 cwe 33 286–90; Epp 1126, 1127A:25–47, 1162:167–74, 1211:611–13.

618 Cf *Adagia* ii iv 28: *Io Paean* cwe 33 204.

How happy Hutten will be to receive from his new friends congrat-
ulatory letters, tokens of friendship, and magnificent rewards. Whether all
this be true I know not. But it is certainly closer to the truth than what he
fabricates about my going to Rome and the cardinals running to meet me
with open arms.[619] For, although provoked in so many ways, I have thus
far written nothing against Luther, whereas Hutten, without provocation,
has published this malicious book against a friend through whose praise
many who have never met him have yet come to know and love him.

Why else would he write such a malicious piece? I have shown that
the reasons he alleges are of no account, as will on the face of things be
obvious to prudent and unbiased men, even those who support Hutten. So
what was his purpose? Did he write for the fun of it? In that case he might
have chosen a better theme for his humour. Did he merely want to perfect
his style?[620] This he could have done without drawing his sword against
a friend who had been and was still ready to be of service to him. Or, as
someone said, maybe he wanted to bequeath to posterity a perfect example
of his eloquence, a swan song (κύκνειον ᾆσμα),[621] like Cicero's *Philippicae*.[622]
Then he ought to have chosen a subject-matter worthy in its own right and
useful to posterity. As it is, if he cares about his reputation, he has only
done damage to it by choosing this topic.

Was he perhaps trying to deter me from writing against Luther? In
fact, nothing would be more likely to provoke me to do so. But far be it
from me either to do or not do anything in this important matter merely
because of Hutten. Things must be going badly for Luther if his defenders
have to depend on books like this, as if they were thrown back on the last
line of battle,[623] or left with nothing but a sheet-anchor.[624] Or did he want to
cut Erasmus' throat? Is this not what a barbarian would do to someone who
neither suspected nor deserved it? He is said to have bandied about brutal
words, worthy of the Scythians,[625] including this: With this book I shall

* * * * *

619 Cf *Expostulatio* EB II 218:5–10 / K 97 par 155; EB II 239:7–8 / K 117 par 236.
620 See above n14.
621 Cf *Adagia* I ii 55: *Cygnea cantio* 'Swan song' CWE 31 195:1–196:36.
622 *In M. Antonium oratio Philippica*, the 14 speeches Cicero delivered in 44–33BC.
623 The *triarii* ('third-men') made up the last of three ranks in the Roman order
     of battle. Cf *Adagia* I i 23: *Res ad triarios rediit* 'Back to the third line' CWE 31
     69:1–71:72.
624 Cf *Adagia* I 24: *Sacram ancoram solvere* 'To let go the sheet-anchor' CWE 31 72:1–
     17.
625 Cf *Adagia* II iii 35: *Scytharum oratio* 'Scythian language' CWE 33 148–9: 'When
     the [Greeks] wanted to convey that something was boorish or barbarous or

drive Erasmus to his bed! Now that, as it happens, I have been laid low by sunstroke,[626] Hutten is perhaps rejoicing and congratulating himself. But I trust he does not think me such a coward that even fifteen such books would cause me to fall ill. Hutten will soon find out whom he has alienated or won over; in my view the book will make me many new friends. Was it such a great thing to please a few Lutherans who will clap for anything? Even among this group he has but few friends, and if they are wise he will have fewer still.

He brags that while in Basel he was surrounded by a crowd of Lutherans.[627] In fact, in the city for whose hospitality he expresses his gratitude, a city where I have now lived for nearly two years, I have yet to meet anyone who wants to be called a Lutheran. Here it is provided by law that no one may teach anything contrary to the gospel, even if he alleges Luther's authority in support of his views.[628] I also wonder if there is not something to the suspicion of those who tell me that Hutten, having traded the war-saddle for a sedentary life, does books like this for profit, indeed a double profit, for while those who commission a work pay him to write it, those against whom he writes pay to prevent him from publishing.[629] Even if Hutten is now my enemy, I feel sorry for him if he has fallen so low. I hear the printer paid him something too.[630] But enough about Hutten, lest I produce something bigger than a sponge. I wanted him to realize that I too could wield a sharp pen, had I not chosen to observe my habitual restraint instead of imitating his example.[631] Never until now have I quarrelled with anyone whom I once loved from the heart; nor have I allowed my pen to be filled with fury, even against those who attacked me in a hateful way. Were I given to vindictiveness, I would rather have an opponent who had never been my friend, and whose circumstances were more

* * * * *

ferocious, they called it "Scythian."' The ancient Scyths were a people of Iranian tongue living north of the Black Sea.

626 There is no record of this, but in July 1523 Erasmus did suffer severe attacks of kidney stones; cf Epp 1411:3–5, 1422:17–21, 1426:16–9, 1434:38–40.

627 Cf *Expostulatio* EB II 229:22–230:1 / K 108 par 198.

628 Cf *Aktensammlung zur Geschichte der Basler Reformation* 6 vols (Basel 1921–50) I no 151 65–9, especially 67:13–15.

629 See above n29.

630 Ep 1383:7–8. The printer was probably Schott in Strasbourg rather than Froben in Basel, who was a personal friend of Erasmus (cf Allen Ep 1383:7n). Brunfels (*Responsio* 342:33–343:5, 15–16) denies the allegation in such a way that he seems to concede it.

631 Cf above 34, 36; Ep 1341A:1024–6.

fortunate. Quarrelling with a friend is not admirable, and heaping sarcasm on a man overwhelmed by troubles is downright cruel.

Since it is by now obvious that what Hutten has done is revolting, my final task is to exhort all who are devoted to good letters to refrain from intemperance of this sort, lest good letters fall into disrepute. Do we not speak of humane studies? Let us see to it that they do not lose this honourable name through any fault of ours. They will truly be good letters only if through them we become better persons, only if through them the glory of Christ is made more clear. They were revived in the schools not to expel the older disciplines but to enable them to be taught more correctly, and with greater benefit.[632] Instead, there is almost as much tumult in the schools as there is in the churches. For many who favour classical languages and good letters promote them to the exclusion of all other studies. On the other hand, those who cling to the traditional curriculum bend all their efforts to the ruin and destruction of polite letters. Should we not rather be working to support one another with our respective talents, instead of each obstructing the other by foolish contentions?[633] Let those proficient in good letters commend them to others by maintaining a demeanour that is honest, sober, and agreeable; and let them ennoble the studies with which they begin by advancing to the weightier disciplines. As for those who have not had this background, let them learn to add a touch of grace to their studies.

Where mutual concord prevails, no one lacks for anything; where discord prevails, even those who have good things cannot enjoy them. Let us all, from the greatest to the least, labour to patch together peace and concord among Christians.[634] For as things now stand we have neither the peace of this world – given the wars that rage everywhere – nor the peace of God; indeed the clash of religious opinions is like an evil leaven that sours everything, so that true friendship and brotherly love are nowhere to be found. Is anyone happy to live in this age? To me it seems most unhappy.[635] So let those who favour the cause of the gospel do so in a prudent and straightforward way, not putting their trust in secret plots, nor in the kind of abusive books against the pope or the emperor that only produce the opposite effect, and make people think ill of the gospel. And let those who are learned, setting aside all obstinacy and human ambition, confer

* * * * *

632 Cf Epp 1002:11–22, 1062:50–72, 1125:40–51, 1127:9–13, 1167:15–26, 1238:89–96.
633 Cf Epp 950:14–22, 1007:39–43.
634 Cf *Ratio* Holborn 245:23–247:30; Epp 1033:31–5, 1183:12–13, 1202:9–11, 1334: 232, 1342:1101–2.
635 Cf Epp 1199:8–10, 1239:14–5, 1248:25–33, 1249:9, 1268:9, 1365:79–80.

among themselves about what can be done to heal this division that cuts across the whole Christian world; and let them write privately to the pope and the emperor about measures that would seem to promote the welfare of the Christian people and the glory of Christ. Let them indicate these to the pope and the emperor in private correspondence.[636] And let them in their discussions be completely honest, as if in the presence of God. Only in this way can we focus our minds on the truth of the gospel, not on quarrels that have no end. For as long as we keep arguing about whether any work of man can be called good,[637] no one does good works. And as long we keep arguing about whether faith alone brings salvation, without works, we come neither to the fruit of faith nor to the reward for good works. Besides, some of the points in dispute are of such a nature that it would not be useful to fill people's heads with them, no matter how true they might be.[638] For example,[639] whether 'free choice' is nothing but an empty word;[640] whether every Christian is a priest and can forgive sins and consecrate the body of our Lord; whether righteousness is brought about by faith alone and our works contribute nothing. Spreading such paradoxes[641] among the common folk only gives rise to dissension and sedition.

At the same time I would implore the rulers of the church and secular princes to put the public good and the glory of Christ ahead of their personal feelings and private interests. This is the will of Jesus Christ, and if we act in such wise he will protect and bless what we do. Let him to whom the spirit of Jesus imparts the gift of deeper insight share it fully but in a gentle way, with forbearance for those who cannot grasp things immediately, just as our Lord Jesus bore with the weakness of his disciples until they understood him better. Princes and bishops are men, they too can make mistakes and be deceived. Is it not better to guide them courteously to an understanding knowledge of the truth, rather than rousing their anger with insults?[642] Let those in Luther's camp who claim to have found spiritual knowledge

* * * * *

636 Erasmus had proposed such a colloquy among scholars on both sides in the 1520 *Consilium cuiusdam ex animo cupientis esse consultum et Romani pontificis dignitati et christianae tranquilitati* (Ferguson *Opuscula* 338–61; cf Epp 1149 introduction, 1156).

637 Cf above n317.

638 Cf Epp 1167:182–7 and 331–2, 1202:56–140, 1342:1067–8.

639 For a similar list, above 93, 122.

640 The reference is to article 36 of Luther's *Assertio omnium articulorum* of 1520 WA 7 142–9; cf Epp 1342:1022–78, 1384:13–4.

641 Cf above n467.

642 Cf Epp 967A:101–19, 980:41–56, 1167:175–85.

consider that they too are men, vulnerable to the same vices as popes and princes. Neither a crown nor a mitre gives a man gospel wisdom, I admit; but neither does any other kind of headgear. And let those who believe they possess the gifts of the Spirit not despise public authority. Likewise, princes, no matter how great or powerful, must not oppose the truth of Christ, no matter how lowly the man who preaches it – for the apostles themselves were of humble birth. We take remedies for bodily ills offered by a man of no education, or even a woman; should we then reject a cure for the soul because it comes from a person of no account?

Let both parties put aside private passions, and let us together beseech the God of peace, lest the Christian world, already shrunken in size, collapse altogether because of our dissensions,[643] and lest Christians start tearing at one another's flesh, like wild beasts or deadly fish, thus providing a welcome sight for Satan, and for the enemies of the Christian name. On all the articles of faith handed down from the early church we agree.[644] So why is the world being torn asunder by these paradoxes? Note that some are of such a nature that they cannot be fully understood, others can be argued for on either side, and still others contribute little to the improvement of morals. No corner of our Christian life is safe and sound, everywhere the world teems with foolish wars, rebellions, brigandage, feuds, brawling, sworn enmity, fraud, guile, sinful extravagance, and sexual licence. Yet, all these things notwithstanding, we take time to battle among ourselves about whether the primacy of the Roman pontiff was ordained by Christ.[645] Each side must adjust to the other. Just as stubborness begets strife, mutual courtesy brings friendship. To what end will we come if one side employs only riots, quarrels, and insults, while the other relies only on papal bulls, articles of condemnation, and book-burning?[646] And what is so great about consigning to the flames some poor wretch who has to die anyway?[647] To teach and persuade, that is something great. For even a recantation,[648] if it come to that, will not change people's minds; they will merely think that the person in question found it better to be shamed than to be burned

* * * * *

643 Erasmus believed that the Christian world had grown smaller than it was in antiquity, because of dissensions within the church; cf his 1530 *De bello Turcico* LB V 345–68.
644 Cf Ep 1300:82–3.
645 See above 122.
646 Cf Epp 1173:106–8, 1202:287–92, 1225:289–93, 1268:24–8 and 47–9.
647 Cf above n514.
648 Cf *Adagia* I ix 59: *Palinodiam canere* CWE 32 214–55: 'To sing a palinode, is to say the opposite of what you said before.'

alive. Bishops are supposed to teach the gospel philosophy; is it right that, because their secular power exceeds that of the great nobles, they employ in matters of faith nothing but pronouncements, imprisonments, torture, and burning at the stake? Let bishops not be ashamed of deferring to Christian love,[649] as the apostles did; and let scholars not be embarrassed about giving bishops their due respect.

This is the advice I offer to both parties, as one who has pledged his loyalty to neither but wishes well to both. I prepare myself for the day that will summon me before the judgment-seat of Christ.[650] This is why I concentrate on things that compose my spirit and give peace to my conscience, leaving aside those contentious issues one can hardly take up without receiving or giving blows, and thus losing something of the serenity of a Christian spirit. Working on my *Paraphrases* is, I feel, fruitful in my own life.[651] Hence this quarrel grieves me all the more, for I have lost six days reading Hutten's false accusations, and wiping off the muck he threw on me. Farewell, honest reader, whoever you are.

End of the purgation of Hutten's Expostulation by
D. Erasmus of Rotterdam

* * * * *

649 Cf *De esu carnium* ASD IX-1 38:584–40:638.
650 Cf above n339.
651 Cf above n340.

THE UNCOVERING OF DECEPTIONS

Detectio praestigiarum cuiusdam libelli germanice scripti

translated by
GARTH TISSOL

annotated by
JOHN B. PAYNE

The context for the publication of the *Detectio praestigiarum* was the Eucharistic controversy of the mid-1520's. Erasmus himself indicated the spark-plug for the debate in two letters from Basel on 10 December 1524. One of these was to Melanchthon in which he reported: 'Karlstadt was here, but he kept his visit a secret. He has published six pamphlets in German in which he explains that nothing is involved in the Eucharist except the symbols of Christ's body and blood.'[1] In the other, to Heinrich Stromer, he stated Karlstadt's doctrine somewhat differently: 'he teaches that the true body of the Lord is not present in the Eucharist.'[2] Actually, there were seven pamphlets published by Karlstadt in October–early November 1524 at Basel, five of which concerned the Lord's Supper.[3] The central role of Andreas Karlstadt, the radical colleague of Luther at Wittenberg, in the early Eucharistic controversy has been more and more acknowledged in recent scholarship. He is seen as helping in late 1524 and early 1525 to move Zwingli at Zürich and Oecolampadius at Basel and their co-workers, Leo Jud and Konrad Pellicanus, as well as the Strasbourg reformers, Martin Bucer and Wolfgang Capito, towards a spiritualistic, symbolic view of the Lord's Supper which denied the corporeal real presence.[4] With respect to Zwingli in particular, one must also take into account the letter of the Netherlands lawyer, Cornelis Hoen, carried to Switzerland by Hinne Rode, from which the Zürich reformer received the idea that *est* in the words of institution should be interpreted as *significat*. This idea he incorporated into

* * * * *

1 Ep 1523:102–104
2 Ep 1522:63–4
3 Andreas Rudolf Bodenstein von Karlstadt (c 1480–1541) was educated at Erfurt, Cologne, and Wittenberg where he obtained his doctorate in 1510. Having become Luther's associate and defender, Karlstadt stood at Luther's side in the debate with Johann Eck at Leipzig in 1519. His activity during the Wittenberg disturbances alienated him from Luther who attacked him in a series of sermons when he returned to Wittenberg from his exile at the Wartburg. After taking over as pastor at Orlamünde in 1523, Karlstadt was expelled from Saxony at Luther's instigation in September 1524. Passing through Basel, he published a series of pamphlets, five of which concerned the Eucharist. After several more years of wanderings, he settled at Basel where he ended his career as a pastor, professor, and dean of the faculty of theology (1536–41) at the University of Basel. On Karlstadt see CEBR II 253–6; OER I 178–80; R.J. Sider *Andreas Bodenstein von Karlstadt: The Development of His Thought 1517–1525* (Leiden 1974); C.A. Pater *Karlstadt as the Father of the Baptist Movement* (Toronto 1983).
4 See Kaufmann 216, 224–37, 253, 262–3 n890, and passim.

a letter to Matthäus Alber, 16 November 1524, which Zwingli published in 1525.[5]

Erasmus himself reported on the development of what came to be known as the Sacramentarian conception of the Eucharist in several letters of October 1525, stating that Zwingli and Oecolampadius had followed in the footsteps of Karlstadt with the view that 'nothing was involved in the Eucharist but bread and wine.'[6] In one he also mentioned the letter of Hoen.[7] Erasmus threw them all together into one basket with no differentiation, focusing on the negative side of their Eucharistic teaching. He did not recognize variations among them, as, for example, concerning how the words of institution are to be understood. Karlstadt was convinced that the 'this' in the words, 'This is my body,' applied to Jesus' own body, not to the elements. Zwingli understood the 'this' to refer to the elements, but he interpreted the verb, 'is,' as meaning 'signifies.' Oecolampadius likewise came to insist on a figurative understanding of these words. But all three made abundant use of John 6:63 ('It is the spirit that quickeneth; the flesh profiteth nothing') in order to stress only a spiritual, not a corporeal, eating in the Lord's Supper.[8] In these same letters of October 1525 Erasmus acknowledged that he was impressed by the arguments in Oecolampadius' treatise on the Eucharist published in late August or early September in Strasbourg. He found that the book was 'so carefully written and so buttressed with arguments and supporting evidence that even the elect could be led astray';[9] it was also 'so thorough and so full of ingenious arguments that anyone who wishes to answer him will have his work cut out.'[10] At the same time as his positive assessment of this work in these letters came statements about his being drawn into the fray willy-nilly. To Bishop Michel Boudet he wrote: 'I must put aside the lute and take up the

* * * * *

5 On Cornelis Hoen see Ep 1358 n7 and CEBR II 192–3, and on his influence on Zwingli's Eucharistic teaching see Stephens *Theology of Huldrych Zwingli* 227–8. An English translation of the letter is in H.A. Oberman *Forerunners of the Reformation* (NY 1966) 268–76.

6 Epp 1620:33–40

7 Ep 1621:22–5 n12

8 See below n21.

9 Ep 1621:27–9. The title of Oecolampadius' book was *De genuina verborum Domini: 'Hoc est corpus meum' iuxta vetustissimos authores expositione liber*. On this work cf Staehelin *Lebenswerk* 276–84. On Oecolampadius himself see also CEBR III 24–7; OER III 168–71.

10 Ep 1624:38–40

sword or it will appear from my silence that I am casting my vote on their side like some humble back-bencher.'[11] He had previously been implored by the jurist Claudius Cantiuncula to take up his pen in response to Oecolampadius' treatise. Erasmus informed his friend that he had already 'begun something on the Eucharist before your letter arrived.'[12] This work he never completed, perhaps, as Allen conjectures,[13] because of a secret agreement between Erasmus and the Basel evangelicals, Oecolampadius and Pellicanus, that they refrain from writing against each other, but more likely because of a decision not to become involved in another heated controversy that would only lead to tumult[14] and because of his awareness of the difficulty of the task.

But Erasmus was forced to express his views on the subject, nevertheless, first in a conflict with his friend and scholarly collaborator, Conradus Pellicanus, who became a reformer at Basel and then at Zürich.[15] Erasmus learned from Jan Łaski that Pellicanus had suggested to the great humanist's young Polish devotee that Erasmus' views on the Eucharist and those of Pellicanus were identical. According to Erasmus, Pellicanus had apparently been spreading this rumour still more widely, and Erasmus was greatly disturbed.[16] To dispel the rumours, Erasmus in October 1525 wrote Pellicanus a long and angry letter that he later published in one of his epistolary collections. He rejected out of hand Pellicanus' insinuation, arguing that he never even agreed with Pellicanus' earlier position, when according to Erasmus, Pellicanus held that 'one should teach that the body of Christ is indeed present in the mass, but how it is present was an issue best left to God, who knows all things.'[17] Erasmus is here repudiating what had been and would remain very much his own position on the subject.[18] Indeed, not only

* * * * *

11 Ep 1618:13–15
12 Ep 1616:22
13 Allen Ep 1616:17n
14 Allen Epp 1893:77–80, 1977:24–6; cf also Epp 1620:97–102, 1621:31–2, 1624:41–2, and ASD IX-1 215 n21.
15 On Conradus Pellicanus see Ep 1637 introduction and CEBR III 65–6.
16 Epp 1637:7–8. On Łaski see Ep 1593 n18 and CEBR II 297–301 and OER II 396–7.
17 Ep 1637:29–32
18 For Erasmus' understanding of the Eucharist see G. Krodel 'Die Abendmahlslehre des Erasmus von Rotterdam und seine Stellung am Anfang des Abendmahlsstreits der Reformatoren' (unpubl diss, Erlangen 1955) and Payne Sacraments 126–54. For the point here, see 144–5, where it is explained that, though Erasmus remained sceptical concerning the dogma of transubstantiation, he believed that the body and blood of Christ are present in the Eucharist in an 'ineffable manner' before which the believer's attitude should be one of

Karlstadt and the early Pellicanus, but also the early Zwingli and Oecolampadius were influenced in their Eucharistic views by Erasmus,[19] who in his early and recent writings did not deny the objective real presence of Christ in the Eucharist, but stressed not a bodily but a personal and ethical participation in the sacrament. In the *Enchiridion* he had written: 'He [Christ] despised even more the eating of his own flesh and the drinking of his own blood if they were not eaten and drunk spiritually as well. To whom do you think these words were addressed: "The flesh is of no profit: it is the spirit that gives life"?'[20] This text would become a central one for Karlstadt and the Swiss Sacramentarians, who would apply it in a more radical manner than did Erasmus.[21] To eat and drink spiritually, according to Erasmus, is to remember Christ's death with thanksgiving and to respond to God's love, as shown in the Eucharistic representation of Christ's death on the cross, with love towards God and towards one's neighbour. A favourite theme of Erasmus, which was also taken over by the Swiss and South German Reformers, was the *synaxis* conception, the notion of the Lord's Supper

* * * * *

silence and reverence, an opinion which is not far removed from Pellicanus' earlier views as described by Erasmus.

19 On the influence of Erasmus on Karlstadt's teaching on the Lord's Supper, see C. Lindberg 'The Eucharist according to Erasmus and Karlstadt' in *Les dissidents du XVIe siècle entre l'humanisme et le catholicisme* ed M. Lienhard (Baden-Baden 1983) 79–89. On the influence of Erasmus on Zwingli's doctrine of the Lord's Supper see Stephens *Theology of Huldrych Zwingli* 9–17, who, however, recognizes limitations to that influence.

20 John 6:63; CWE 66 70

21 On the radicalizing interpretation of John 6:63 by Karlstadt and the Swiss see C. Lindberg (above n19) 85, 87; Kaufmann 184 and n304. For parallels with Erasmus see C. Lindberg 85ff. For Zwingli see W.P. Stephens 'Zwingli on John 6:63' in *Biblical Interpretation in the Era of the Reformation* ed R.A. Muller and J.L. Thompson (Grand Rapids 1996) 168–80; Stephens *Theology of Huldrych Zwingli* 226, 228, 231–2, 235, 237, 245. For parallels but also differences with Erasmus see Stephens *Theology of Huldrych Zwingli* 14–16 and 'Zwingli on John 6:63' 161. Cf T. Kaufmann 261–2, who thinks, however, that it was Karlstadt's rather than Erasmus' interpretation of this text which prompted Zwingli to make it the cornerstone of his Eucharistic theology. For Oecolampadius' following Zwingli here see Staehelin *Lebenswerk* 280–1. Karlstadt's arguments with their use of John 6:63 as proof text had also persuaded Martin Bucer to give up the bodily real presence in late 1524. See Kaufmann 205 and n487, and 235, 244–5; and for Bucer's exegesis of this text see I. Backus 'Polemic, Exegetical Tradition, and Ontology: Bucer's Interpretation of John 6:52, 53, and 64 Before and After the Wittenberg Concord' in *The Bible in the Sixteenth Century* ed D.C. Steinmetz (Durham NC 1990) 173–80. See *Detectio praestigiarum* below 193–4.

as the communion with Christ and of Christians in love and peace with one another, an idea he derived from the ancient Greek Fathers.[22] And yet Erasmus, while often writing ambiguously as to what he considered to be the symbol or sign, does sometimes take the high view, even in his early writings, referring to the body and blood of Christ 'as a most holy sign and pledge both of his love towards us and of the concord of Christians among themselves' – even if he eschews speculation as to 'how the bread is made to change its substance by the mystic words, and how the same body can exist in so small a form and in different places' and places the emphasis upon the reception of the body and blood 'purely by the pure in heart.'[23]

In the letter to Pellicanus, Erasmus seeks to make it absolutely clear that he vehemently rejects the more radical position now espoused by Pellicanus. He insists further that although he may have spoken freely among friends by way of inquiry, no one had ever heard him express, either seriously or in jest, the idea that there was nothing but bread and wine in the Eucharist. He bases his opinion, in the first place, on Scripture. The Gospels and the Pauline letters clearly affirm that Christ's body and blood, and not just the symbols of body and blood, are present in the Lord's Supper.[24] Alluding to John 6:63, he rejects the view that the presence of Christ's body is a hindrance to the spirit. More clearly than in any previous writing, he affirms the real presence with these words: 'It is indeed flesh, though perceived by none of our senses'[25] – a statement that jars somewhat with his phrasing of the matter in the *Detectio* of the next year: 'are not the body and blood, which are in a certain manner exposed to our senses, symbols of those things which can only be discerned by the eyes of faith?'[26] He points out that even Luther 'was constrained by the evidence of Scripture

* * * * *

22 See *Detectio praestigiarum* below n28. For Karlstadt on the Lord's Supper as a community meal see C. Lindberg (above n19) 86; for Zwingli see Stephens *Theology of Huldrych Zwingli* 218–19, 233 and n46; for Oecolampadius see Staehelin *Lebenswerk* 145, 179, 268; for Bucer see J.M. Kittelson 'Martin Bucer and the Sacramentarian Controversy: The Origins of his Policy of Concord' ARG 64 (1973) 176–83. For the *synaxis* conception among the Greek Fathers see below n28 to text.

23 To John Šlechta (1519) Ep 1039:264–7. Cf *Institutum hominis Christiani* (1514) CWE 85 106 (Latin), 107 (English); paraphrase on Mark 14:22 CWE 49 160; paraphrase on Luke 22:19 CWE 48 189.

24 Ep 1637:36–44

25 Ep 1637:80–2

26 *Detectio praestigiarum* below 169

to profess what the Catholic church professes,'[27] an indication that Erasmus considered Luther's views, in contrast with those of the Swiss, to be orthodox.

In addition, he rests his belief on the authority of the church, an argument which will become an increasingly prominent feature of his writings on the subject in the late 1520s and 1530s. He asks whether those who agree with Pellicanus can show him 'any reason why I should forsake a belief which the Catholic church has taught and practised for so many centuries?' He concludes that his mind 'has been kept firm thus far by the universal agreement of the Catholic church.'[28] At about the same time as this letter, Erasmus wrote a letter to the town council of Basel giving his opinion concerning Oecolampadius' treatise on the Lord's Supper. He had been invited along with the theologian Ludwig Baer and the jurists Bonifacius Amerbach and Claudius Cantiuncula to make an assessment of it.[29] He reported that in his view 'the work is learned, well written, and thorough. I would also judge it pious, if anything could be so described which is at variance with the general opinion of the church, from which I consider it perilous to dissent.'[30] In letters to his friend Willibald Pirckheimer over the next two years, he expresses himself more freely about his favourable view of Oecolampadius' work but he always qualifies it with an assertion of his allegiance to the authority of the church defined as a universal consensus of believers.[31] The Swiss Sacramentarians found themselves in a precarious position. Oecolampadius' book on the Eucharist was banned in Basel. They stood alone against both Roman Catholics and Lutherans on this issue. They were concerned that Erasmus not be enlisted on the Catholic side in the conflict. They sought either to persuade him that his position, at least as he had earlier expressed it in the *Enchiridion* and his *Paraphrases*, was basically the same as theirs in spite of his claim of allegiance to the Catholic church or to frighten him into not taking up the pen against them. Conrad Pellicanus, Ulrich Zwingli and Leo Jud will all engage in this effort.

* * * * *

27 Ep 1637:60–3
28 Ep 1637:103–5 and 127–8; see *Detectio praestigiarum* below n191.
29 Allen Ep 1674:63–5. On Baer see CEBR I 84–6; on Amerbach see CEBR I 42–6; on Cantiuncula see CEBR I 259–61.
30 Ep 1636:3–6
31 Epp 1717:60–8, 1729:27–30, Allen Ep 1893:56–60; cf *Detectio praestigiarum* below n191.

Pellicanus made at least three responses to Erasmus' letter.[32] First there was a letter which has been lost in which Pellicanus admits he sympathizes with Karlstadt's position and that he had told Jan Łaski that he and Erasmus were of the same persuasion. In this letter Pellicanus warns Erasmus not to write against the Swiss teaching on the Eucharist by threatening him that Zwingli would write against him. Furthermore, Pellicanus expresses his regret that Erasmus' letter to him had been made public.[33] Erasmus responds by once again explicitly rejecting the rumour he thinks Pellicanus circulated that the two of them agree on the Eucharist. He angrily attacks Pellicanus' threat of Zwingli's pen if he chooses to write against the Swiss position on the Eucharist and urges him not to send any more verbose letters but rather to come to him, and he will listen to his 'reproaches, threats, and scoldings to your heart's content.'[34] Pellicanus did meet with Erasmus but there was no meeting of their minds except as to what Erasmus' view on the Eucharist was. When Erasmus asked Pellicanus concerning his understanding of Christ's presence in the Eucharist, Pellicanus replied that he believed the power of Christ to be there but not the substance of the body. In later reports of this interview, Erasmus states that, when he asked Pellicanus whether he (Erasmus) had ever taken that point of view, Pellicanus answered truthfully that Erasmus had never expressed such an opinion.[35] On his departure for Zürich in February 1526 Pellicanus published two letters written earlier to Erasmus which partly duplicate but also greatly expand upon the lost letter.[36] In the one letter Pellicanus denies Erasmus' contention that he had betrayed their friendship by divulging what Erasmus had said to him in secret. He also rejects Erasmus' description of his position that 'there is nothing in the Eucharist except bread and wine.' He maintains that he never ascribed such a position to Erasmus whose *Paraphrases* show that was not his view, as Pellicanus well knew, and thus he could not have spread such a damaging story as Erasmus alleged.[37] He reports his

* * * * *

32 I agree with C. Augustijn (ASD IX-1 218 n41) against Allen, who is followed by the editor of CWE 11, that Ep 1640 (CWE 11 364–6) is not Erasmus' answer to the two undated letters of Pellicanus (Epp 1638:115–16).

33 One can assume the content of this part of the letter on the basis of Ep 1640:47–74.

34 Ep 1640:11–22 and 52–4

35 Ep 1674:50–71; *Epistola contra pseudevangelicos* below 236

36 See above n32.

37 Ep 1638:12–20. C. Zürcher points out that Pellicanus, in holding on in this letter to a mysterious spiritual real presence in the Lord's Supper, had not yet moved completely over to the position of Zwingli (C. Zürcher *Konrad Pellikans*

agreement with the position set forth in Erasmus' letter to him that those
who are redeemed by Christ's body and blood 'are nourished in some ineffable way by the same flesh and blood.' On the other hand, he makes it clear
that he did not think that the body and blood are present in a substantial,
corporeal sense – a position which he still thought was that of Erasmus in
spite of Erasmus' words in his letter about the presence of Christ as being
the flesh though not perceived by our senses.[38] Countering Erasmus' position concerning the authority of the church as the basis of his Eucharistic
faith, Pellicanus argues that the doctrine of the corporeal real presence was
unknown in the church for its first one thousand years.[39] In another lengthy
letter he repeats his contention that the realistic view of the Lord's Supper
was not advocated for over a thousand years and expressly rejects the doctrine of transubstantiation set forth at the Fourth Lateran Council in 1215.[40]
He compares Erasmus with Luther and concludes: 'On many points you differ very little from Luther, though you always write less offensively.'[41] He
warns Erasmus again that Zwingli and Oecolampadius will write against
him on the Eucharist if he chooses to attack their views on that subject.[42]
According to Erasmus, before he departed from Basel Pellicanus wrote still
another letter, this one directed to the town council of Basel urging that
Erasmus be forced by 'armed entreaties' to reveal 'my sincere opinion.'[43]
Erasmus referred to these published letters sarcastically as singing praises
to his prudence in an oblique way. These letters and the 'armed entreaties'
were unnecessary, argued Erasmus, for he had already made it clear to
the city council that his views on the Eucharist were those of the Catholic
church.[44] Zwingli entered the dispute on the side of Pellicanus, publishing in late October 1525 an anonymous letter written to Oecolampadius in
which he caustically attacked Erasmus' first letter to Pellicanus, of whose
contents he had been informed by Oecolampadius, who had read a copy.[45]

* * * * *

Wirken in Zürich 1526–1556 [Zürich 1975] 256).
38 Ep 1638:44–51
39 Ep 1638:72–80 and 90–104
40 Ep 1639:30–2 and 88–93
41 Ep 1639:208–9
42 Ep 1639:210–12
43 Epistola contra pseudevangelicos below 237; cf Epistola ad fratres Inferioris Germaniae below 292.
44 Epistola ad fratres Inferioris Germaniae below 237
45 The title of the letter is Franci cuiusdam epistola ad quendam civem Basiliensem
and was dated 28 October 1525 (Zwinglis Briefwechsel II Ep 401 407–13 and n1).
For Oecolampadius' letter see Zwinglis Briefwechsel II Ep 396.

Zwingli writes sarcastically that he can scarcely believe that the letter was truly that of Erasmus for it uses weak arguments, even arguments which are no arguments at all.[46] He criticizes Erasmus' statement, 'We are told to be spiritual, as if the presence of the body were an offence to the spirit' by arguing that when Christ uttered the words, 'The flesh is of no use,' he made it once and for all clear that he did not offer his flesh to be eaten by the teeth. But Zwingli goes further also to ridicule a spiritualizing notion of flesh embodied in Erasmus' words 'it is indeed flesh but perceived by none of our senses' and his reference to being 'nourished in some ineffable way by that same flesh and blood.' That position, he argues, is opposed by both faith and reason – for how can there be flesh which is not seen?[47] Zwingli thinks Erasmus was not setting forth his true convictions in his letter to Pellicanus when he stated that he never agreed even with Pellicanus' earlier opinion that Christ is present in the Eucharist but that the manner of his presence is best left to God, since according to Erasmus Christians should not dissent from the authority of the church. Zwingli comments: 'If they [the authority of the councils and the churches] were not opposed, you would think otherwise; therefore your mind is not there where the judgment of the church is.'[48] Zwingli perceived weaknesses in Erasmus' argument but he also perverted his position because he was certain that Erasmus in his inmost heart really agreed with him and Pellicanus on the presence of Christ in the Eucharist. Erasmus disclosed to Pellicanus and Łaski his suspicion that the author of this anonymous letter was the Strasbourg reformer, Wolfgang Capito.[49]

A third effort to seek to force Erasmus to admit that in his true convictions he really sided with the Swiss evangelicals was made by Leo Jud, a colleague of Zwingli in Zürich.[50] In April 1526 he published a pamphlet under a fictitious name in which he sought to show that Erasmus and Luther essentially agreed with the Swiss in their views on the Eucharist.[51] Understandably, Erasmus at first suspected Pellicanus to be the author of this tract

* * * * *

46 *Zwinglis Briefwechsel* II Ep 401 408:4–7
47 Ibidem 409:1–410:2
48 Ibidem 413:11–12
49 Epp 1792A:7–9, 1674:74–9
50 On Jud see CEBR II 248–50; OER II 356.
51 *Des hochgelerten Erasmi von Roterdam / unnd Doctor Martin Luthers maynung / vom Nachtmal unnsers herren Jhesu Christi* ([Zürich: Froschauer] 1526). This pamphlet was in the form of a letter from 'Lodouicus Leopoldi, Pfarrer zu° Leberaw, dein lieber bruder' to 'Caspar Nogolt burger zu° Noerlingen seinem freund und herzlichen bruder.'

or at least the instigator of it,[52] since Pellicanus had already expressed the same view as the author of the pamphlet, namely, that Erasmus differed little from Luther on many things. This suspicion was confirmed for him by a letter of Capito to Pellicanus.[53] Jud's knowledge of Erasmus' thought was no doubt superior to his knowledge of Luther's since he had translated a number of Erasmus' writings including the *Enchiridion* and the *Paraphrases of the New Testament*,[54] but his interpretation of Erasmus' position on the Lord's Supper was not much more accurate than his presentation of Luther's. In each case his tendentiousness is evident. He tried to show that Erasmus' view of the Eucharist, like that of the Swiss, was symbolic and spiritualistic. He affirmed that Erasmus in many places in his writings had called the bread and wine 'symbols' (although he did not provide the specific passages), that he even used the expression, 'symbolic bread,'[55] and that in the fifth canon of the *Enchiridion* he had referred to John 6 as rejecting a fleshly eating while affirming a spiritual eating in faith. Jud cites other texts – from the *Paraphrases* and *Annotations* to the Gospel and the Pauline accounts of the Lord's Supper – which he thinks demonstrate that Erasmus' position is clearly Zwinglian. According to Jud, Erasmus' view is that 'the sacrament is nothing other than a commemoration of the death of Christ.'[56] He reminds Erasmus of the favourable opinion which he had rendered to the town council of Basel concerning the book of Oecolampadius and asks the humanist whether he had really changed the view that he had expressed as a young man in the *Enchiridion*. He accuses Erasmus of holding back his true belief out of fear of the emperor, the princes, and the pope,[57] and prays that God will give Erasmus the strength of his convictions.

So agitated by this pamphlet was Erasmus that he included a preliminary response to it in a letter of 15 May 1526 to the Swiss Confederacy, declining for health reasons an invitation to take part in the Disputation at Baden which took place 21 May–8 June 1526.[58] At this conference

* * * * *

52 See Ep 1708:16–17 with n1 and introduction where Erasmus does not specifically name Pellicanus but there is no doubt that he has Pellicanus in mind; cf ASD IX-1 224 n103.
53 Ep 1737:6–8 with n1 and introduction
54 See CEBR II 249; I. Bezzel 'Leo Jud (1482–1542) als Erasmusübersetzer' *Deutsche Vierteljahrschrift für Literaturwissenschaft und Geistesgeschichte* 49 (1975) 628–44.
55 Cf *Detectio praestigiarum* below 166, 188.
56 *Detectio praestigiarum* below 171–3
57 *Detectio praestigiarum* below 170, 196
58 Ep 1708. A German version was also prepared which Erasmus signed. It is published along with the Latin one by Allen.

the majority Catholic cantons dominated; their chief spokesmen were Johann Maier of Eck, the opponent of Luther and Karlstadt at the famous Leipzig disputation (1519), and Johannes Fabri, the vicar-general of Constance and adviser to Archduke Ferdinand. The city of Zürich and its reformer, Zwingli, refused to attend. The minority Reformation position was represented by Oecolampadius, the reformer of Basel.[59] Erasmus was no doubt concerned to make clear in advance of this debate his own distance from the Swiss Sacramentarian position. He was uncertain whether to accuse the author of the pamphlet of stupidity or malice in so misrepresenting his writings and his own inner convictions. He denies before God that 'any opinion has lodged in my mind that is in conflict with that which the Catholic church has hitherto defended with general consent,'[60] an utterance which is difficult to accept at face value in light of a letter to Willibald Pirckheimer only three weeks later. There he stated: 'Oecolampadius' opinion would not offend me if it did not run counter to the consensus of the church. For if there is a spiritual grace in the elements, I do not see what need there is for a body that is "imperceptible" and could do no good if it were perceptible. Nevertheless, I cannot depart from the consensus of the church nor have I ever done so.'[61] Before the end of May 1526 the more extended response appeared that Erasmus had promised in his letter to the Swiss Confederacy. The *Detectio praestigiarum* 'The Uncovering of Deceptions' is a purely apologetic piece with the intention of defending both his writings on the Lord's Supper and his personal integrity against the misrepresentations of the anonymous pamphlet. It consists of three sections: preface, main argument, and conclusion. In his preface Erasmus rakes the author of the pamphlet over with scorn and sarcasm. He derides him for publishing under a false name and in German and for linking his name with that of Luther. He vigorously defends himself against the contention of the *Maynung* that he had denounced the papacy and all human institutions in his books and that Luther had followed in his footsteps even if Luther had expressed himself 'more boldly and more

* * * * *

59 Concerning this disputation see Irena Backus *The Disputations of Baden, 1526, and Berne, 1528: Neutralizing the Early Church* Studies in Reformed Theology and History I no 1 (Princeton 1993). On Eck see CEBR I 416–18 and OER II 17–19; on Fabri see CEBR I 5–8.

60 Ep 1708:41–3. On Erasmus' view of the consensus of the church see Ep 1708 introduction and the reference there.

61 Ep 1717:60–5. For a brief analysis of Oecolampadius' treatise and the role played by Erasmus' sense of the authority of the church in his reaction to it, see Payne *Sacraments* 148–54.

openly.'[62] He seeks to make it clear that his approach to reform was greatly different from Luther's. The main argument consists of a spirited defence of most of his previously published statements on the Eucharist from the *Enchiridion* (1503) to the *Paraphrase on the Acts of the Apostles* (1524). At the end of this section Erasmus sticks in the knife: 'The facts themselves state that he is more fit for feeding pigs than writing books.'[63] In his conclusion Erasmus gives his views on matters then under dispute: church dogma and the moral abuses in the church and society. He also gives a brief defence of his recent actions in connection with the publication of Oecolampadius' treatise.

In the central part Erasmus seeks to show that the symbolic, spiritualistic interpretation which the anonymous pamphlet attempted to derive from his writings is patently false, and that he had never referred to the bread by itself as symbolic. On the contrary, he had referred to 'the partaking of the Lord's body and blood' as 'a symbol of the mystical body joined to Christ its head, and of the harmony of its members with one another,'[64] or of 'that sacred cup, which we for remembrance of Christ's death take up with thanksgiving and consecrate.'[65] In other passages he contends that he even named the body and blood themselves symbols. Furthermore, Erasmus asks why it would have been dangerous if he had written of the bread as a symbol, for '... are not the consecrated bread and wine symbols of the Lord's body and blood lying hidden under them? Finally, are not the body and blood, which are in a certain manner exposed to our senses, symbols of those things which can only be discerned by the eyes of faith?'[66] Erasmus gave the most attention in his apology to the *Enchiridion* and its canon 5 whose spiritualistic approach to the Eucharist and other sacraments had endeared it to the Sacramentarians. He rejects out of hand the notion that the true body and blood of Christ are not present. He reminds the reader that he has applied the principle of flesh and spirit to all things, including the sacraments, baptism, Eucharist, penance, unction, and marriage in such a manner that, while the physical elements are not rejected, the spiritual are preferred. Just as 'it is useless to be splashed with water, unless the invisible grace of the Spirit is present,' so 'the partaking of the Lord's body and blood does not benefit us, or rather harms us, unless we take it

* * * * *

62 *Detectio praestigiarum* below 165
63 *Detectio praestigiarum* below 196
64 *Detectio praestigiarum* below 170, 192
65 *Detectio praestigiarum* below 184
66 *Detectio praestigiarum* below 169

spiritually,'[67] but, if the physical is not denied in the first example, neither is it in the second. Erasmus even draws on support from Thomas Aquinas. No one has made the case more strongly than he that 'in the *synaxis*, the substance of the Lord's body and blood are concealed by visible appearances,' and yet he 'teaches the very same things that I do in my rule: the flesh of the sacrament brings no benefit if spiritual grace is lacking.' And indeed in his *Summa Theologiae* Thomas did argue that both a sacramental and a spiritual eating are necessary but that the 'sacramental is subordinate to the spiritual eating which is its fulfilment.'[68] While here in the *Detectio* Erasmus wants to make clear that he did not intend to undercut the physical aspect of the sacrament in the *Enchiridion*, he also does not back down from his preference for the spiritual, its meaning as imaging forth Christ's love for humankind and the response in love for the Redeemer as well as the close bond between Christians. His stress continues to be not upon the objective, the *ex opere operato*, but upon the subjective, the *ex opere operantis*, side of the sacrament.

Thus, in response to the accusation of having changed his mind since the *Enchiridion*, he could write with a fair amount of justification: 'I did not change the opinion that I had when young, except to make the point that, under the force of different arguments, I could waver to either side of the question, were I not strengthened by the authority of the church.'[69] He also wrote here with greater honesty than he did in his letter to the Swiss Confederacy just two weeks earlier in which he denied that 'any opinion has ever lodged in my mind that is in conflict with that which the Catholic church has hitherto defended with general consent.'[70] The *Detectio* of June 1526 nevertheless marked a watershed in Erasmus' thoughts on the Eucharist, one which, however, was anticipated by the letter to Pellicanus in the previous October. In it he emphasized more than previously the true presence of Christ in the Eucharist even if he was not specific as to the nature of this presence and even if, as in letters to Pirckheimer, he revealed his waverings on the subject which required the bolstering of the authority of the church.

As with the letter to the Swiss Confederacy, Erasmus had a German version of the *Detectio* published by Froben at the same time as the Latin text. Who did the translation is not certain although both Allen and C. Augustijn

* * * * *

67 *Detectio praestigiarum* below 176
68 *Detectio praestigiarum* below 176 and n91
69 *Detectio praestigiarum* below 177
70 See above n60.

are inclined to look to Georg Carpentarii, a Carthusian monk of Basel.[71] In late summer Leo Jud responded to this German version.[72] He pleaded modesty as his excuse for having published anonymously. He claimed to be only translating or paraphrasing Erasmus and Luther. In the main part of his reply Jud sought once more to interpret along Zwinglian lines the texts that Erasmus had set forth in the *Detectio*. He showed once again that he either did not understand or did not care to understand Erasmus' position.[73] Erasmus did not respond to this work nor to a letter which Jud sent along with a copy of his response.[74] After the *Detectio* Erasmus no longer played a role in the strife over the Eucharist, but he continued to express himself on the subject in ways which definitely set himself off from the Swiss Sacramentarian view. While rejecting speculation and stressing the ineffable mystery, in two writings of 1530, a preface to Alger of Liège's treatise on the Eucharist and in a commentary on Psalm 22, Erasmus made still clearer than in the *Detectio* his affirmation of 'the true substance of the body and blood of the Lord,' in the Eucharist.[75] In these and other texts of the 1530s, one detects less lingering doubt although he continues to refer to the authority of the church as the basis for this conviction.[76]

* * * * *

71 *Entdeckung Doctor Erasmi von Roterdam der dückischen arglistenn eines Büchlin inn teutsch vnder einen erdichten titel, mit diser vberscrifft, Erasmi vnd Luthers meinung vom nachtmal vnsers herren kurtzlich hievor vff den xviij. tag Aprels vßgangen*; see Allen Ep 1708 introduction and ASD IX-1 228 n144.

72 *Vf entdeckung Doctor Erasmi von Roterdam, der dückishen arglisten, eynes tütschen buechlins, antwurt vnd entschuldigung Leonis Jud.*

73 ASD IX-1 229

74 ASD IX-1 230:159n

75 Allen Ep 2284:81–2; *In psalmum* 22 LB V 329A / CWE 64 161. In his 1530 preface to *Concerning the Truth of the Body and Blood of the Lord in the Eucharist* by Alger of Liège (d 1131), which argued for the reality of the presence of Christ's body in the Sacrament, and not just its figurative representation as supported by Berengarius of Tours (d 1088), Erasmus favoured Alger along with Guitmond of Versa (d c 1095), another opponent of Berengar, as theologians who were gifted in philosophy and rhetoric but without ostentation and sophistry. They exemplified, according to Erasmus, the kind of theology which flourished before the time of such scholastics as Bonaventura, Thomas, Scotus, Albert the Great, and even Peter Lombard, who in boasting of the philosophy of Aristotle, adopted his spiritless style and neglected the affections and the rhetorical ornament of speech; see Allen Ep 2284:32–53. On the medieval debate concerning the Real Presence of Christ with references to Berengar, Alger, and Guitmond, see Pelikan *Christian Tradition* III 187–204. Cf Tracy *Low Countries* 143.

76 *De amabili ecclesiae concordia* (1533) LB V 504C; *De praeparatione ad mortem* (1534) LB V 1315A, 1317B–C / CWE 70 442. 'How can the same body be in different

On the other hand, Erasmus' affirmation of the corporeal real presence of Christ in the Eucharist never did include an acceptance of the dogma of transubstantiation, whether prior to the Eucharistic controversy or afterwards. In a letter to Boniface Amerbach in March 1532 he wrote that on the truth of the body of the Lord there ought to be no doubt, but 'concerning the manner of the presence it is permissible for a layman to have some doubt, who may believe *in genere* what the church believes.'[77]

JBP

* * * * *

places at the same time, and how in the Eucharist can the true body of a man be confined in a very small area?' 'In the way the church believes.' See also CWE 70 448.

77 Allen Ep 2631 3–6; cf *Detectio praestigiarum* below n36.

THE UNCOVERING OF DECEPTIONS

ERASMUS OF ROTTERDAM TO HIS BELOVED BROTHERS IN CHRIST[1]
From earliest times it has been the case, dear friends, that the worst patterns of behaviour have crept into human life under the pretext of virtue. So we observe in these times. Pamphlets, worse than defamatory, are publicly disseminated without their authors' names, or – what is still more criminal – under false ascription, by those who profess freedom of the spirit; and a crime that the laws of the heathens punished with death is treated as a game, a joke, by people who chatter only of the gospel.[2] And so, we see in the present discord that no one has more hindered the advancement of the gospel than those who think themselves the most evangelical; nor has anyone so much injured the pope's cause as have those who most strongly believe that they, like Atlases,[3] have set their shoulders beneath the tottering church.[4]

A few days ago there flew forth from the darkness a certain pamphlet, regarding which one would be hard pressed to declare whether its stupidity or its malice is the greater.[5] At its beginning is the title, *The Opinion of the most learned Erasmus of Rotterdam and Martin Luther concerning Our Lord Jesus Christ's Supper, lately published on the eighteenth day of April*.[6] From the start it smacks not of the simplicity of doves,[7] but of the cunning of

* * * * *

1 *Detectio praestigiarum cuiusdam libelli germanice scripti, ficto autoris titulo, cum hac inscriptione, Erasmi, et Lutheri opiniones de coena domini* (Basel: Froben June 1526). The form of greeting in the 1526 edition was changed in 1529: 'To all who love the truth.'
2 Ep 1708:58–62
3 See *Adagia* I i 67: *Atlas coelum* 'Atlas (supported) the sky' CWE 31 110:1–8: 'said about people who get themselves entangled in great and grievous matters'; Epp 1352:59–62, 1721:42–3.
4 Cf Ep 1523:10–15.
5 Cf Ep 1708:16–18.
6 Concerning this work and its exact title see introductory note above n51.
7 Matt 10:16; cf *Epistola contra pseudevangelicos* below 238.

foxes,[8] in that immediately, on the pamphlet's very title page, [its author] joins my name with Luther's, and sets that label also at the beginning of its individual pages. Then in the pamphlet itself he constantly repeats and emphasizes the yoking of our names, thereby promoting the more ill will against me, as if there were much agreement between us, when in our published books it is abundantly shown how little truck there is between us.[9] Also, he makes a display of my name, with an encomium on my superior learning,[10] so that he may appear a friend of mine – judging me so foolishly vainglorious that I will be delighted by defamatory praises and honorific insult. Still further, they published it written in German, just before the recent Disputation at Baden,[11] in order by such a deceit to impose on the naive and inattentive, using my name as a smokescreen to draw the incautious into a snare; and in order that I, since I am ignorant of the common language,[12] would be for a time unprepared to counteract either my own defamation or other people's dangers.[13] The knowledgeable reader will easily judge to what extent such actions smack of evangelical sincerity. It is plain evidence of a bad conscience that, while writers are accustomed to place the name of the author right at the very threshold of the work, this one did not dare to include anywhere the name of the printer, nor of the place of publication. It may be also that the dedicatee is identified by a fictitious name[14] (though that does not matter, since you are free to dedicate your drivel to anyone you please). In consequence, the author is unrevealed, and the dedicatee not greatly annoyed. At least, whoever crafted this crime did not dare to set his own name anywhere, except that he stealthily stuck on at the end the fictitious label of 'Lodovicus Leopoldi,'[15] but in such a way as to make

* * * * *

8 Cf *Adagia* II v 22: *Vulpus non iterum capitur laqueo* 'No fox is caught twice in a trap' CWE 33 252: 'Cunning is a natural quality of this creature'

9 Erasmus and Luther had recently engaged in sharp debate over the issue of free will in which their differences became manifest. See Erasmus *De libero arbitrio* (1524) CWE 76 5–89; Luther *De servo arbitrio* (1525) WA 18 551–787; Erasmus *Hyperaspistes* 1 and 2 (1526 and 1527) CWE 76 93–297, CWE 77 335–749. For a translation of Luther's *De servo arbitrio* see LW 33 *Career of the Reformer* III.

10 Cf Ep 1708 / CWE 12 201:21–5.

11 The Disputation at Baden was held 21 May–8 June 1526. See introductory note above 157.

12 On Erasmus' knowledge of German see Epp 1313:21 and n2; Allen Epp 1313:85n and 2516:115n; Holeczek *Erasmus Deutsch* 228–9.

13 Cf *Epistola contra pseudevangelicos* below 237.

14 The *Maynung* was dedicated to Caspar Nagolt, citizen of Nördlingen, since 1215 a free imperial city in Bavaria.

15 More specifically, the author referred to himself as 'Lodovicus Leopoldi, pastor at Leberau, your dear brother.' Leberau is a village in Upper Alsace.

you wonder whether it identifies the author or printer. Such a maliciously timid trick ought to give the reader sufficient warning that there is nothing sound or sincere in this pamphlet. And though the typography gives ample evidence of the printer's identity,[16] and one can infer by fairly reliable guesswork who the ψευδώνυμος 'pseudonymous' Leopoldus is, along with his abettor,[17] nevertheless, since they fear the light so much, I, for my part, will for the moment let them lie hidden in their own darkness, until they betray themselves. Meanwhile, I will confront this pamphlet, a work not less infamous than stupid, and will show how, with frivolous and plainly false arguments, it attempts to convince naive, inexperienced people that I agree about the Eucharist with Karlstadt,[18] or with any other defender of his view.

The preface to this misrepresentation makes the claim that I was the first to denounce the papacy, and all human institutions, in my books, as in the *Folly*, the *Enchiridion*, the *Annotations on the New Testament*, the *Adages*, and other places; and that Luther followed me in doing so, but more boldly and more openly.[19] What could be more shameless than this lie? There is no passage in any of my books that condemns all human institutions; otherwise I would be condemning civil laws as well, which neither Christ nor Paul condemns. But I frequently do reproach certain pharisees, who burden the people of Christ with such institutions as lead more to superstition than to true piety,[20] and I also reproach the superstition, or rather perverse

* * * * *

16 The printer was Christoph Froschauer of Zürich who published many works of Zwingli and his successor, Bullinger, as well as the famous Zürich Bible (1524–31).
17 On the issue as to whom Erasmus considered to be the author and whom the instigator, see introductory note above n52 and ASD IX-1 224 n103; cf *Epistola ad fratres* below 293.
18 See introductory note above 148 n3.
19 See *Maynung* A 2 r, where Jud writes that Erasmus had touched in Latin 'but politely on the abuses of the papacy and of all human traditions in all his books, as in the *Praise of Folly*, in the *Enchiridion* and in the *Annotations on the New Testament*, in the *Adages*, and in many other places, Luther attacked the Supper more boldly and more openly in German.' 'Erstlich Erasmus der in latein die missbreüch des Bapsttuᵒmms vnd aller menschlichen Tradition gar hoflich in allen seinen buᵉchern angeruᵉrt, als in der Moria, im Enchirydion, in den Annotationibus über das Neuw Testament, in Adagiis vnd in anderen vil orten, welches Nachtmal der Luther dapfferer ja offenlicher in teütsch angegriffen hat.' Pellicanus was of the same conviction as Jud; see Ep 1639:74–5: 'Luther is a man whom I still respect and admire, but I use discretion when I read his writings.'
20 On the burden of human laws as contrasted with Christ's yoke see *Annotationes in Matthaeum* 11:28–30 (LB VI 63–5); cf Reeve *Gospels* 53–6 and J.B. Payne

judgment, of certain people who on account of men's traditions violate God's precepts. Though ceremonies are merely aids to piety these men make them the goal of piety.[21] These things were both said piously, and needed to be said at that time. What then does Luther do? He takes away from popes and bishops every right of establishing laws, not to mention the rest.[22] And so it is plain that Luther does not have the same teachings as I, but entirely different teachings, diametrically opposed to my own. The lucubrations of both authors testify as much, clearly proving the utterly shameless falsehood of those who scatter such rumours among the unaware, some in order to injure me with hostile suspicion, quite a few in order to fortify their faction by the empty smokescreen of my name. I wrote the *Folly* in tranquil circumstances, when the world slept soundly among the ceremonies and prescriptions of men. I would not have written it, had I known in advance about the storm that would blow up in these times.[23] But take note, friendly reader, of this author's utterly stupid reasoning. If the *Folly* demolishes the papacy[24] just because it touches on certain vices of the popes, the same work demolishes all the ranks of human kind generally, since it leaves not one unreproached. Here you have the preface to this misrepresentation, one worthy of the case itself. Now hear the proofs that accord with this preface.

In many places, so he says, I call bread and wine symbols of the Eucharist, that is signs, and bread symbolic, that is bread that signifies something. Yet he is uncertain whether I said this in the *Adages*, or in the *Complaint of Peace*, or in the *Enchiridion*, or in some other of my books.[25]

* * * * *

'Erasmus' Influence on Zwingli and Bullinger in the Exegesis of Matthew 11:28–30' in *Biblical Interpretation in the Era of the Reformation* ed R.A. Muller and J.L. Thompson (Grand Rapids 1996) 63–70.

21 On ceremonies see *Enchiridion* CWE 66 12, 17; *Moria* CWE 27 131–5; paraphrases on Romans and Galatians CWE 42 4, 9, 25, 30, 58, 115.

22 As pointed out by C. Augustijn (ASD IX-1 237 nn57–8), Erasmus may have in mind texts in Luther's *De servo arbitrio* that express a point of view on papal laws quite in opposition to that of Erasmus; see Luther *De servo arbitrio* WA 18 623:28–624:27, 627:24–38 and n1; *The Bondage of the Will* LW 33 48–9 and n54, 54 and n59.

23 Cf Epp 1007:85–7 and n9, 1329:40–1. Erasmus wrote the *Praise of Folly* in 1509.

24 See *Moria* CWE 27 138–9. On Erasmus' attitude towards the papacy see K. Schätti *Erasmus von Rotterdam und die römische Kurie* (Basel 1954); Gebhardt *Stellung* 267–77; H.J. McSorley 'Erasmus and the Primacy of the Roman Pontiff between Conciliarism and Papalism' ARG 65 (1974) 37–54.

25 Cf *Epistola ad fratres Inferioris Germaniae* below 294; see *Maynung* A 2 r, where the author confesses that he does not remember precisely where Erasmus called the bread and wine 'symbols' (*symbola*), that is, 'signifying bread' (*symbolicum panem*), but then he mentions the above-named writings.

What is more shameless than for him to want to incite a misrepresentation of such consequence, and then confess that he does not remember the passage? Come, tell me, who would endure a witness or plaintiff who maintained a charge of theft in such a fashion: 'I don't remember what he stole, nor when, nor where, nor from whom, yet I think I have detected him in committing some theft.' But in misrepresenting me, he acts no less absurdly. He says that the passage slipped from his mind. No, it's rather the man himself who had taken leave of his mind. I nowhere call the bread symbolic, yet he dreamed up this notion from the poem which is added to Cato's writings.[26] Here, speaking about the sacrament of the Eucharist, I call the food mystical, because under visible appearances is hidden the grace of the invisible spirit. The poem runs as follows:

> That mystical food[27] (the Greeks call it *synaxis*),[28] which under the outward appearance of bread and wine clearly tenders to us Christ himself truly present . . .[29]

* * * * *

26 This poem is the *Institutum hominis Christiani* which was a translation of the *Catechizon* by John Colet. Intended for use in St Paul's School, London, it was first published in 1514 together with some writings of Cato; see CWE 85 92–108.

27 *Mysticus ille cibus*; cf Ep 916:70: 'that mystical bread' (*panis ille mysticus*).

28 A favourite expression of Erasmus for the Eucharist. On the origin and growth of the *synaxis* idea in the early church, see H. Leclercq 'Synaxe' in *Dictionnaire d'archéologie chrétienne et de liturgie* ed F. Cabrol and H. Leclercq (Paris 1953) 15 1834ff and F.W. Norris 'Synaxis' in *Encyclopedia of Early Christianity* ed E. Ferguson 2nd ed (New York 1997) II 1099. *Synaxis* may refer simply to the assembly of the faithful gathered for worship whether it included the Eucharist or not or it may refer to the Eucharist itself as Communion. The idea originates with *Didache* 9 4 and was taken up especially by the Greek but also the Latin Fathers. Chrysostom *Hom 24 in 1 Cor 24* (PG 61 200); *Hom 29 in Act* (PG 60 218); Theodoret *Ep 160* (PG 83 1457B–C); Basil *Hom in Ps 28* (PG 30 73B); *Cyprian 63 13, 69 5* (CSEL 3 2 712, 754); Ambrose *Comm in epist 1 ad Cor 10:16* (PL 17 249B–C); Augustine *Tract in Ioannem 26 17* (PL 35 1614); *Sermo 227* (PL 38 1100). Erasmus' primary emphasis is upon the horizontal rather than the vertical dimension of this Communion, as in *Modus orandi* ASD V-1 125:138–40 / CWE 70 153: '. . . the same act is called *synaxis* by the Greeks, that is, the process of being brought together, because at the same time the bonds of love among all members of the body of Christ are therein represented. Consequently, it is also called *communio* "communion," in Latin.' Cf paraphrase on 1 Corinthians 10:17 LB VII 893A–B / CWE 43 135; *In psalmum* 22 ASD V-2 356:903–9 / CWE 64 162; *De praeparatione ad mortem* ASD V-1 366:654–9 / CWE 70 421.

29 CWE 85:98 (Latin) and 99 (English)

And yet this passage clearly teaches that I do not agree with what Karl-stadt teaches.[30] When I say 'tenders,' do I not with sufficient obviousness profess that Christ is substantially present there? Not content with that, I add 'himself,' ruling out any figure of speech. Not content even with that, I add 'truly.' What is lacking except 'substantially?' But that word is admit-ted neither by the metrical scheme nor by the elegance of Latin diction. In the same poem we read the following:

> But when piety and the proper day call me to the heavenly banquet of conse-crated body and blood ...[31]

And a little later,

> I will receive the venerable body of Christ.[32]

Do you not read here 'the feast <of body>[33] and blood?' Why, when he boasts that he carefully combed through my books, did he not cite these words? Or will he evade the question by claiming that these words and others like them are falsely ascribed to me? He did open that loophole for an escape, saying that much bears the names of Luther and Erasmus which did not originate with them. What may be the case with Luther is not my concern. I, at least, have never allowed – and never will allow, as long as I live – anything to be ascribed to me which was not my own. I always make an exception for corruptions introduced by the printers; their errors cannot be laid at my door. And even if I had written 'symbolic bread' somewhere, what danger was there in that? If we accept the view of recent authorities, are not the species of bread and wine symbols of the Lord's body and blood?[34] Or if not, are not consecrated bread and wine symbols

* * * * *

30 In several letters Erasmus renders Karlstadt's opinion as that 'there is nothing in the Eucharist except bread and wine'; see Epp 1620:33–6.
31 CWE 85 106:121–2 (Latin) and 107 (English)
32 CWE 85 106:131 (Latin) and 107 (English)
33 C. Augustijn (ASD IX-1 237 n96) notes that the unknown German translator of the *Detectio* corrected the false reading of the Latin text, *sanguinis* 'of blood,' to *des lybs* 'of the body.' On this translation which was published by Bonifacius Amerbach 2 June 1526, see ASD IX-1 228 n144.
34 Cf the decree at 4th Lateran Council (Denzinger–Schönmetzer 802): ... *Iesus Christus, cuius corpus et sanguis in sacramento altaris sub speciebus panis et vini veraciter continentur, transsubstantiatis pane in corpus, et vino in sanguinem potes-tate divina* ... 'Jesus Christ whose body and blood are truly contained in the

of the Lord's body and blood lying hidden under them? Finally are not the body and blood, which are in a certain manner[35] exposed to our senses, symbols of things that cannot be perceived except with the eyes of faith?[36] So much for the falsehood of 'symbolic bread.'

In the *Adages*, namely in 'War is sweet to those who have not experienced it,' I deplore the madness of Christians who make war on each other, even though they 'eat the same bread' and 'share the same cup.'[37] In the *Complaint of Peace* these are my words: 'Among the heathen friendship is also sacred, when a shared meal has brought men together. Do the heavenly bread and mystical chalice not unite Christians in friendship which Christ himself held sacred?'[38] And a little farther on, 'Does anyone dare to approach that sacred table, the symbol of friendship, the communion sacrament of peace, if he intends to make war on Christians?'[39] So far I have been reviewing what I wrote. I call the partaking of the Lord's body and

* * * * *

sacrament of the altar under the species of bread and wine after the bread has been transubstantiated into the body and the wine into the blood of Christ by the divine power' (trans JBP).

35 Cf below 174, 176 and Ep 1637:80–3.

36 Cf Thomas Aquinas *Summa Theologiae* 2 q 76 a 7: 'But by the mind of the human being, the pilgrim, it cannot be perceived except by faith'; cf Gabriel Biel (*IV Sent* d 8 q 1 a 1: 'The Eucharist is the species of bread and of wine containing truly and really the body and blood of Christ by the priestly consecration.' Biel accepted the dogma of transubstantiation on the basis of the authority of the church even though other interpretations might have been preferable. According to Oberman, Biel did not however regard the decision of the church as arbitrary but rather as the true one. On the variations of opinion on the dogma of transubstantiation in the late Middle Ages, see Pelikan *Christian Tradition* IV 53–8. On the basis of the authority of the church, Erasmus himself affirmed the real presence under the species of bread and wine, but he was cool to the dogma of transubstantiation set forth by the 4th Lateran Council. He thought that on this matter it was sufficient to believe '*in genere* what the church believes especially for a layman' (Allen Ep 2631:3–6). Cf these texts for Erasmus' wavering on the issue of the mode of Christ's presence in the Lord's Supper: Allen Epp 2263:69–72, 2284:89–102; and the annotation on 1 Cor 7:39 (*Novum Testamentum* (1519) II 327 and LB VI 696c, Reeve-Screech 472. On Erasmus concerning the real presence and the authority of the church, see Payne *Sacraments* 149–54.

37 *Adagia* IV i 1: *Dulce bellum inexpertis* CWE 35 416.

38 *Querela pacis* ASD IV-2 76:372–4 / CWE 27 304 (trans JBP). The CWE translation makes into a negative declarative statement what in the Latin is a negative rhetorical question expecting an affirmative answer.

39 ASD IV-2 76:377–9 / CWE 27 304

blood a symbol of the mystical body joined to Christ as its head, and of the harmony[40] of its members with one other. Now where are those words that rule out the actuality of Christ's body and blood? Also, he cannot invent a motive in payments and fear of princes (though this too is a bold-faced lie, since I do not seek or accept payment on this account from any prince),[41] because I wrote these things when the world was still calm, when nobody suspected that one would arise so audacious that he would dare to revive Wyclif's opinion.[42]

Never mind, for now comes a moment when my detractor has fallen off his donkey: with a sound memory he produces evidence from the Fifth Rule of the *Enchiridion*, through which to show what I am concealing in my heart. There I am eager to teach that one must always progress from visible and carnal to invisible and spiritual things.[43] My words, which the crafty fellow has twisted to suit his own convenience,[44] run as follows:[45]

* * * * *

40 C. Augustijn (ASD IX-1 239 n117) corrects the accusative, *concordiam*, to the genitive, *concordiae*, because it gives the better sense and he points to these parallels: ASD IX-1 252:435–6, 254:505–7.

41 Cf *Epistola ad fratres Inferioris Germaniae* below 294; *Maynung* A 4 v: '... es seye dann das jn menschlicher forcht, das hochbochen des Kaysers vnd der fürsten, das fulmen des Bapsts abschrecke vnd hindersich halte ...' '... unless human fear, the might of the emperor and of the princes, the thunderbolt of the pope frightens him and holds him back ...' (trans JBP).

42 Wyclif's opinion was that the true body and blood are present in the Eucharist along with the substance of bread and wine. He rejected the dogma of transubstantiation that the substance of the bread and the wine in a hidden and mysterious manner changes into the body and blood of Christ, while the accidents of bread and wine remain. To Wyclif such a view went counter to his metaphysics and his biblical understanding. In the Eucharist the substance of bread and wine, not just their accidents, remains along with the body and blood of Christ. Concerning the basis of Wyclif's view cf M. Keen 'Wyclif, the Bible and Transubstantiation' in *Wyclif in His Times* ed A. Kenny (Oxford 1986) 11–16, and G. Leff 'Wyclif and Hus' 117–18 in the same volume. While G. Leff stresses the metaphysical basis of Wyclif's opinion, and M. Keen emphasizes its biblical ground, Erasmus seems to think that Wyclif held a purely symbolic, spiritual view of the Eucharist. C. Augustijn (ASD IX-1 239 n122) appears to have that same understanding of Wyclif's position.

43 *Enchiridion* CWE 66 65

44 Cf *Epistola ad fratres Inferioris Germaniae* below 294.

45 *Enchiridion* CWE 66 69–71. C. Augustijn (ASD IX-1 239 n128–73) lists ten minor variations with the *Enchiridion* text in LB V 30B–31B. Only one of these affects the translation; see below n51. This translation of the quotations from the *Enchiridion* follows for the most part that of CWE 66.

And, as Christ himself said in John's Gospel, 'the flesh is of no profit, it is the spirit that gives life.'[46] I would have had scruples to say 'It is of no profit'; it would have been sufficient to say, 'it is of some profit, but the spirit much more profitable.' But Truth itself said: 'It is of no profit.' Indeed, it is of so little profit that according to Paul it is fatal unless it is referred to the spirit.[47]

In another respect, the flesh is useful in this sense: that it leads our weakness to the spirit by degrees. The body cannot subsist without the spirit; but the spirit has no need of the body. But if, on the authority of Christ, the spirit is so great that it alone gives life, then we must strive that in every written word and in all our actions we regard the spirit, not the flesh. And if anyone will take note, he will find that this is the one thing to which Isaiah,[48] chief among the prophets, and Paul, chief among the apostles, call us. There is hardly a single Epistle in which Paul does not treat of this, does not inculcate in us that we must not put any trust in the flesh, that in the spirit there is life, liberty, light, adoption, and those desirable fruits[49] that he enumerates. Everywhere he despises, condemns, and counsels us against the flesh. Be attentive and you will discover that all through the Gospels our master, Jesus, teaches the same lesson, that is, he expresses contempt for the flesh: When he spoke of lifting an ass from the ditch on the sabbath day,[50] when he gave sight to the blind man on the sabbath day,[51] or rubbed the ears of wheat together,[52] in his remarks about unwashed hands,[53] in his eating with sinners,[54] in his parable about the Pharisee and the publican,[55] in matters of fasting,[56] in his reference to brothers according the flesh,[57] or the Jews' glorying that they were the sons of Abraham,[58] or the offering of gifts before the altar,[59] in his teaching about

* * * * *

46 John 6:63; cf CWE 46 88.
47 Cf Rom 7:5–6, 8:5–6 and 13; 2 Cor 3:6; Gal 6:8; CWE 42 45–7, 128.
48 Later on in the *Enchiridion* (CWE 66 81) Erasmus refers to Isa 1:16–17 and 58:6–7 as illustrating the practice of the spiritual life.
49 Gal 5:22–3; Rom 8:6, 10:13–16; Eph 5:9
50 Luke 14:5
51 John 9:1–42. 'Sabbath day' is not in the LB text of the *Enchiridion* or in the CWE 66 translation.
52 Luke 6:1–4
53 Matt 15:20; Mark 7:5
54 Matt 9:10–13; Luke 5:29–32
55 Luke 18:10–14
56 Matt 9:14–16; Luke 5:33–9
57 Matt 12:46–50; Luke 8:19–21
58 Matt 3:9; John 8:33
59 Matt 5:23

prayer,[60] in his comments about the Pharisees' widening their phylacteries,[61] and in many other similar passages. He also scorns the superstition of those who preferred to be Jews publicly rather than in secret.[62] And likewise when he said to the Samaritan woman, 'Woman, believe me, the hour is coming when neither on this mountain nor in Jerusalem will you worship the Father. But the hour is coming and now is at hand when true worshippers will worship the Father in spirit and in truth, for it is such worshippers that the Father seeks to worship him. God is spirit, and those who worship him must worship him in spirit and truth.'[63] He signified the same thing in an external act when at the wedding he changed the water of the cold and insipid letter into the wine of the spirit[64] which inebriates spiritual souls even to the point of despising life.

And do not think it astonishing that Christ despised those practices that we mentioned above. He despised even more the eating of his own flesh and the drinking of his own blood, if they were not eaten and drunk spiritually as well. To whom do you think these words were addressed: 'The flesh is of no profit; it is the spirit that gives life'?[65] They were certainly not meant for those who think they are safe from evil because they have a gospel or a copper cross hung around the neck,[66] and think this is religious perfection, but for those to whom he revealed the sublime mystery of the eating of his body. If such a great sacrament is nothing, or is even harmful, how can we confide in any carnal thing, if the spirit is not present.

Perhaps you celebrate the sacrifice of the mass daily but you live for yourself and are unaffected by the misfortunes of your neighbours. Then you are still in the 'flesh' of the sacrament. But if in offering sacrifice you are conscious of the meaning of that partaking, namely, that you are one spirit with the spirit of Christ, one body with the body of Christ, a living member of the church;[67] if you love nothing but in Christ, if you consider all your goods to be the common property of all men, if you are affected by

* * * * *

60 Matt 6:5–15
61 Matt 23:5
62 Matt 6:1–6,16–18
63 John 4:21–4
64 John 2:1–11
65 See above n46.
66 For the custom of hanging a portion of a gospel around the neck, see Epp 563:270–1. For the practice of wearing a cross as a protective amulet and for performing miracles, see *Handwörterbuch des deutschen Aberglaubens* ed H. Bachtold-Stäubli (Berlin 1932–3) v 535–52; cf ASD IX-1 241 n155.
67 1 Cor 12:12–13; Eph 4:4

the misfortunes of others as if they were your own, then you celebrate mass with great profit, since you do so spiritually. If you feel that you are some- how transfigured in Christ, and live less and less for yourself, give thanks to the Spirit, who alone gives life. There are many who like to count how many times and on what days they attended mass,[68] and buoyed up by this as if it were a matter of great importance, leave the church as if they owed noth- ing more to Christ and return to their former way of life. I commend them for embracing the 'flesh' of piety, but I do not commend them for not going further.

Let what is represented there to the eyes be enacted within you. The death of the Head is represented.[69] Examine in your inmost heart, as they say, to see how close you are to being dead to the world. If you are still subject to anger, ambition, greed, pleasure, and envy, even if you touch the altar, you are still far from the sacrifice. Christ was slain for you. Offer those animals to him as sacrificial victims. Sacrifice yourself to him who once immolated himself for you to the Father. If you confide in him without reflecting on these things, God will hate your flabby and gross religion.

These are my words in the Fifth Rule, which he repeated in a butch- ered and corrupt form,[70] so they could better serve his false accusation.

At this point I appeal to my sound-minded reader to consider whether he hears, in these remarks, any word that shows me to hold the view that in the Eucharist the true body and blood of Christ are not present. In order to

* * * * *

68 Cf *Confabulatio pia* CWE 39 95:3–13.
69 On the theme of the *repraesentatio* of Christ's death in the mass which Erasmus connects closely with *commemoratio* and *imitatio*, see *Enchiridion* CWE 66 71; *De praeparatione ad mortem* CWE 70 422; *Explanatio symboli* CWE 70 341.
70 Erasmus makes a similar accusation in the *Epistola ad fratres Inferioris Germaniae* below 294 and Allen Ep 1708:26–7. For the modifications which the *Maynung* makes in its translation and interpretation of Erasmus' text, see ASD IX-1 241 n174. The *Maynung* (A 3 r) blurs Erasmus' use of the word *sacrificas* 'sacrifice' (LB V 31A) with 'So you use this Supper,' and 'you go with fruit to this Supper.' The words 'I praise them for embracing the flesh of piety,' he translates 'Dass sy an denen leyblichen dingen also geen wie ayn kind an aynem banck, das schilt ich nit vast . . .' 'that in those bodily things you go therefore like a child to a pew, that I do not scold too much . . .' (trans JBP). Between 'death of the Head is represented' and 'Examine in your inmost heart,' the *Maynung* (A 3 v) adds: 'dann diss Sacrament ist nichts anderes dann ain Widergeda°chtnus des tods Christi,' 'for the Sacrament is nothing other than a commemoration of the death of Christ.' With this last statement the *Maynung* clearly makes Erasmus into a Zwinglian.

summon people from visible ceremonies to spiritual progress, I show that in all things, so to speak, flesh and spirit exist; that is, something visible and something invisible. But the invisible, to which the common run of people pays no attention, is far more excellent than what is seen; just as in a human being the soul is better than the body.[71] I apply this universal concept to all types of things: to the speech of God, in which the shapes of elements touch the eyes without effect, and without effect do words strike the ears, unless the heart is touched and struck by a secret force.[72] Without effect, in the case of fasting, is the body kept from food, if the soul is not restrained from perverse desires.[73] I make the same case in other examples; I demonstrate it also in the sacraments of the New Law, namely baptism,[74] the Eucharist,[75] and unction.[76]

In the Eucharist there are elements that affect the senses of sight, touch, smell, and taste; there are words that strike the ears, and there is the physical act of consumption, which is perceived. But not in these is the hope of salvation, unless the things not seen are added as well. These belong partly to the category of gift, partly to that of congruence, and partly to that of example.[77] To 'gift' belong faith and the other gifts of the spirit, which are infused through the administration of visible elements.[78] To 'congruence' belong those things to which the visible signs of the sacraments correspond; as, for instance, in marriage is represented the ineffable union of the divine nature with the human in Christ Jesus; likewise represented is the indivisible link of the mystical body, which is the church, with Christ its head.[79]

* * * * *

71 On this important Platonic theme in the *Enchiridion* and in Erasmus' theology in general, see A. Auer *Die vollkommene Frömmigkeit des Christen nach dem Enchiridion militis Christiani des Erasmus von Rotterdam* (Düsseldorf 1954) 63–79 and passim, and Payne *Sacraments* 35–8, 44–55, 101–3 and passim.

72 Cf *Enchiridion* CWE 66 67–70. On how Erasmus' rhetorical hermeneutic is shaped by this fundamental metaphysical principle, see Hoffmann *Rhetoric and Theology* .

73 Cf *Enchiridion* CWE 66 82.

74 Cf *Enchiridion* CWE 66 71 and Payne *Sacraments* 163–4.

75 Cf *Enchiridion* CWE 66 70–1 and Payne *Sacraments* 133–6.

76 Cf *Enchiridion* CWE 66 71 and Payne *Sacraments* 217–18.

77 For a similar threefold distinction see *Institutio christiani matrimonii* LB V 620A–B, 623A–4A and Payne *Sacraments* 98–9, 119–21, 133–6.

78 Cf *Institutio christiani matrimonii* LB V 620B, 623A–F, 624A; *Explanatio symboli* ASD V-1 284:325–9, 285:348–50 / CWE 70 341–2.

79 Cf *Institutio christiani matrimonii* LB V 620B–621F, 623D. On the medieval background see G. LeBras 'La doctrine du mariage chez les théologiens et les

To 'example' belongs a case like this: in the Eucharist there is signified the immense love of Christ towards humankind, for whose salvation he surrendered himself to death, so that we respond with mutual love for our Redeemer;[80] also signified is the close link of Christians with each other, either because one loaf is made from many grains and wine flows from many grapes, or because food and drink are a symbol of common friendship and companionship.[81]

In these cases, therefore, does one abolish the truth of the elements if one esteems more greatly what is invisible than the visible elements? In marriage, does one abolish the union of bodies if one more greatly esteems the union of souls?[82] If one esteems the gift of faith, which purifies hearts, more than visible baptism, does one abolish the water, the words, and the ministry of the sacrament?[83] In unction, if one sets more value on faith and the grace of the Holy Spirit than on the oil, does one deny that oil is present there?[84] In penance, if one more greatly esteems the hatred of sins, faith, and the Holy Spirit's grace, which pardons sins, does one deny that words and the laying on of hands are present there? By no means.[85] And lest anyone suspect that I condemn what is visible in the sacraments and exercises of piety, I expressly admonish the reader in these words: 'I commend them for embracing the "flesh" of piety, but I do not commend them for going no further';[86] and again, somewhat later: 'Corporal works are not condemned, but those that are invisible are preferred. Visible worship is not condemned, but God is appeased only by invisible

* * * * *

canonistes depuis l'an mille' in *Dictionnaire de théologie catholique* ed E. Amann et al, 2nd ed (Paris 1927) IX 2199–201.

80 Cf Ep 1039:264–7; *In psalmum 22* ASD V-2 356:903–9 / CWE 64 162; *Querela pacis* ASD IV-2 76:372–80 / CWE 27 304; *De praeparatione ad mortem* ASD V-1 368:677–81 / CWE 70 422.

81 See above n28.

82 On the essence of marriage as a union of souls see *Institutio christianis matrimonii* LB V 618A–D, 620E.

83 See above n74.

84 See above n76.

85 For Erasmus' view on penance see J. Massaut 'La position oecuménique d'Erasme sur la pénitence' in *Réforme et humanisme, actes du IVe colloque Montpelier [tenu par le] Centre d'histoire de la réforme et du protestantisme de l'Université Paul Valery, Montpellier, octobre 1975* ed J. Boisset (Montpellier 1977) 241–281; T. Tentler 'Forgiveness and Consolation in the Religious Thought of Erasmus' *Studies in the Renaissance* 12 (1965) 110–33; Payne *Sacraments* 181–216.

86 *Enchiridion* CWE 66 71

piety.'[87] Although, in the *synaxis*, the body is not exposed to the senses,[88] nevertheless the reality is there which can be perceived; and therefore its presence brings no benefit, unless also present are those things that are by nature invisible.

Now observe with me how inept at reasoning is the author of this pamphlet. If someone denies that water is present in baptism merely by saying that it is useless to be splashed with water, unless the invisible grace of the Spirit is present,[89] then I denied that the true body of Christ is present in the *synaxis*, because I taught that the partaking of the Lord's body and blood does not benefit us, or rather harms us, unless we take it spiritually. Surely, those who gather such conclusions from such arguments are the same who could gather thistles from the grapevine, sorb-apples from the fig tree. No one made the case more strongly than Thomas Aquinas that, in the *synaxis*, the substance of the Lord's body and blood is concealed by the visible species. Nevertheless, that author teaches the very same things that I do in my Rule: the flesh of the sacrament brings no benefit if spiritual grace is lacking.[90] Does Paul not teach the same thing, when he admonishes each person to examine himself, lest, approaching the Lord's table unworthily, he eat and drink his own condemnation?[91] Furthermore, just because Paul expresses scorn for Christ's flesh, saying, 'Even though we knew Christ according to the flesh, we now no longer know him [in this way],'[92] this is not the statement of one who denies that Christ's actual flesh was sacrificed and resurrected on our behalf; it is rather the statement of one who more greatly esteems what is more conducive to our salvation. He who more carefully attends to the health of the soul than of the body does not throw away the body but esteems the soul more highly. We scorn wicked desires; we scorn lead compared with jewels.

* * * * *

87 *Enchiridion* CWE 66 81
88 Cf Ep 1637:80–2; for a slightly different formulation ('in a certain manner exposed to our senses'), above 169.
89 Cf paraphrase on Mark 1:10 CWE 49 19; *In psalmum* 22 ASD V-2 349:640–73 / CWE 64 154.
90 Cf Thomas Aquinas *Summa Theologiae* 3 q 80 a 1 ad 2 (Latin text and English trans and ed Thomas Gilby OP [New York and London 1975] 33). Thomas argues that both a sacramental and a spiritual eating are necessary but that the 'sacramental eating is subordinate to the spiritual eating which is its fulfilment.'
91 1 Cor 11:27–9
92 2 Cor 5:16

Consider with me, reader, how this man has convinced himself that inexperienced people lack all human perception. He does not fear to publish this drivel abroad, just as if he were writing such things for pigs and donkeys, not human beings. The shameless man dares to invite even those endowed with but little ability to the spectacle of his reasoning – no doubt so they can bear witness to the fact that the man who wrote this work perceives nothing himself, and that he has impudently mangled, overturned, and corrupted my words.[93] Yet he claims a special trustworthiness for the *Enchiridion*, because I wrote it many years ago,[94] when the fear of princes had not yet arisen in me. I also wrote my poem on the essential qualities of faith many years ago,[95] when no such dread threatened me. Why put trust in the *Enchiridion* and not in the poem? As an old man I did not change the opinion that I had when young, except to make the point that, under the force of different arguments, I could waver to either side of the question, were I not strengthened by the authority of the church.[96] When I wrote the *Enchiridion*, I had so little doubt about the truth of body and blood, that not even in a dream did a different view ever touch my mind.

He also contrived another trick to deprive me of trustworthiness, indicating that even if I write against his view, I will do so through fear of the emperor's might and the pope's thunderbolt.[97] To make this claim more plausible, he represents me as a fearful person, clearly following the rhetoricians' rules in linking a fault of nature to his case.[98] A pious man, however, does not want the fearful treated with scorn, but cared for, and helped with reverent prayers to collect their strength.[99] That trifler yaps away, producing

* * * * *

93 See above n70.

94 Erasmus wrote the *Enchiridion* in 1501–2 and published it in 1503; see CWE 66 3. The *Maynung* (A 4 r) states: 'Vnd diss buechlin hat er vor vil jaren geschriben, do er noch jung war.' 'And this little book he wrote many years ago when he was still young.'

95 He wrote the poem *Institutum hominis christiani* in 1513–14; cf CWE 85 92 and CWE 86 505.

96 Cf Epp 1636:21–4; and Payne *Sacraments* 148–54.

97 See above n41.

98 Cf Quintilian *Institutio* 3.7.10–25, 5.10.27 and H. Lausberg *Handbuch der literarischen Rhetorik* (München 1960) §§243, 245, 376, pp132, 133–4, 205.

99 Cf *Maynung* A 4 v: 'Es sagen wol etlich er seye plaug und schwach, nur dem sey wie im woᵉlle, so gebe jmm Gott stercke das er die warhait vnd mainung, die er bey im selbs im hertzen halt vnd glaubt, auch dapfferlich vnd vnerschrocken harauss sagte. Man sol die schwachen nit verachten, sunder für sy bitten, vnd sy stercken.' 'There are indeed some who say that he is fearful

such drivel as if he were acting a farce for fools, rather than handling a highly serious matter before the Christian public. Charges of timidity, at least, ought fittingly to be made by someone other than that man, who did not dare to sign his own name to his pamphlet. I, fearful as I am, dared to do so in all my books – books in which I freely make many censures and warnings concerning princes, bishops, and monks. Is it not ridiculous for a soldier sheltering behind the ramparts to hurl accusations of cowardice against those in the battle-line? Or for Teucer to call the Trojans timid, while he hides behind his brother's shield?[100] But timidity is good if it checks wrongdoing. That is how the philosopher answered someone who accused him of timidity: 'As a result,' he said, 'I do not commit misdeeds.'[101] This man has not pondered the difference between recklessness and bravery, between timidity and prudence, or religious scruples. To throw human affairs into confusion with no benefit to piety is recklessness, not bravery. To make open assertions, in the presence of others, on matters of which you are not yet convinced yourself, is stupidity. To profess convictions at the peril of your life, over the objections of conscience, on matters that are not well settled in your own mind, is madness. To attack what has been accepted by agreement of the church for so many centuries, is impiety. Let those who boast of new light, of the Spirit,[102] of revelation, give an account of their conviction to God's church. For me, just an ordinary man, it is enough to follow the church's lead.[103]

Here is another theme of his, similar to those above. 'If,' he says, 'Erasmus had a different opinion, he would write a book against those who deny the truth of body and blood in the Eucharist.'[104] As if there were nothing left for me to write, or as if others were not available to write

* * * * *

and weak. Be it to him as he may will. May God strengthen him that he may set forth boldly and unafraid the truth and the opinion which he holds and believes in his own heart. One must not spurn the weak, but rather pray for them and strengthen them.' (trans JBP); cf Epp 1477B:1–3.

100 Homer *Iliad* 8.266–72 and *Adagia* III viii 37: *Alieno auxilio potentes* CWE 35 295–6; cf *Adagia* III viii 42: *In formidolosum* CWE 35 297.

101 The philosopher is Cleanthes; cf *Apophthegmata* LB IV 345D, 238D.

102 Erasmus writes to Zwingli: 'He [Luther in a letter to Oecolampadius] added that I ought not to carry much weight in the things of the spirit' (Ep 1384:160–3, 1670:47–9).

103 See above n96.

104 *Maynung* A 4 v: '... dann ich ye vermain, wenn er yetz ain andere mainung hette, so schribe er die offenlich ...' 'for I suppose that, if he now had a different opinion, he would write that publicly.' Cf Ep 1708:48–51 and *Epistola ad fratres Inferioris Germaniae* below 294.

books, who are far more suited to this domain than I am! I started one, and was among the first to do so; several people saw the beginning of the work. But a pious and serious reason induced me to leave off – unless perhaps someone is frivolous and impious if he takes thought for public tranquility and avoids disturbance. Good and learned men agree upon my honesty in undertaking the work, and my very just reason for leaving it off,[105] unless maybe they call this timidity as well. Let those people pray for the timid; I will pray for the reckless, that God may take their audacity from them, and give them wisdom worthy of the gospel.

So far, he has not sufficiently betrayed his stupidity, without even more conspicuous evidence by which to expose it. And so, lest the brave and nameless man leave anything un-dared, he brings into public view a secret business transacted between the renowned town council of Basel and some learned men,[106] among whom some have erroneously included me as well. Since I do not know German,[107] I provided my opinion in Latin, which this man reports in a corrupted form, as is his wont.[108] For I made clear its actual nature in the following words: 'Right honourable lords of the council, at the request of your excellencies I have read Johannes Oecolampadius' book *De verbis coenae Domini*. In my opinion the work is learned, well written, and thorough. I would also judge it pious, if anything could be so described which is at variance with the general opinion of the church, from which I consider it perilous to dissent.'[109] This man supposes his case to be wondrously obvious. 'You see here,' he says, 'what the excellent man says, if only you are willing to understand it.'[110] What do I say here, un-excellent man? I approve of three things in that pamphlet: its learning, its skill in

* * * * *

105 Cf Ep 1616:22 and n2; see introductory note above 150 and n13.
106 On 20 October 1525 the town council of Basel decided to obtain the advice of two theologians (Erasmus and Ludwig Baer) and two jurists (Claudius Cantiuncula and Bonifacius Amerbach) as to whether Oecolampadius' book on the Eucharist should be permitted to be sold in the city; cf Epp 1792A:63–66; ASD IX-1 245: 282–84n.
107 See above n12.
108 The version of the *Maynung's* German is actually quite close to Erasmus' Latin; cf *Epistola ad fratres Inferioris Germaniae* 295.
109 See Ep 1636:38–40, 1717:60–5 and Allen Ep 1893:51–9.
110 *Maynung* A 4 v–A 5 r: 'Siehst du hie, das gu°t man gnu°g redt, was es versteen wil. Er wil also reden, das er nit in gefahr kumme: es mag aber ain yetliche wol sehen was mainung er ist.' 'You see here, the good man says enough of what he wants to understand. He wants thus to speak so that he may not come into danger: but everyone may well see what his opinion is' (trans JBP). Cf *Epistola ad fratres Inferioris Germaniae* below 295.

argumentation, and its carefulness. And since there are in it many pious remarks about the taking of the Lord's body and blood, I would gladly have
pronounced it pious, if it did not defend a dogma which the church has
condemned as impious.[111]

Do I have the same opinion as Oecolampadius, just because I moderated my opinion with civility? Such a concession is usually made concerning people of whom there is hope that they will turn to better, more
fruitful ways. I made it also for other special reasons, which there is no
use recounting here. Would my judgment have had more weight, if I had
pronounced the book heretical, impious, pestilential, worthy of numerous
bonfires? I said what I felt, and did so with the greater trustworthiness, because I did it without passion. Those three terms of praise, 'learned,' 'eloquent,' and 'well written,' and 'thorough,' I could as well have attributed
to the books of Porphyry[112] or Arius.[113] If one describes a man's face as devoid of any beauty, is one of the opinion that the man is handsome? Would
one be calling a man rich if one were to say, 'This man would be wealthy,
if he had as much as he wanted?' Or would one be calling a man good if
one were to say, 'I would say that this is a good man, if he heeded reason
rather than his emotions?' Such a logician, I believe, would conclude that
wine is sweet, if somebody said it was bitter.

* * * * *

111 The church had condemned the spiritualistic symbolic view of Berengar of
Tours in 1059 at a council at Rome (Denzinger–Schönmetzer 690) as well as
Wyclif's rejection of transubstantiation at the Council of Constance in 1415
(Denzinger–Schönmetzer 1153). The church had affirmed the dogma of tran-
substantiation at the 4th Lateran Council in 1215 (Denzinger–Schönmetzer
802). Cf above nn36 and 42.

112 Erasmus has in mind the Neoplatonic philosopher (232–c 305 AD), who was
a disciple of Plotinus and his biographer; cf A.H. Armstrong *The Cambridge
History of Later Greek and Early Medieval Philosophy* (Cambridge 1967) 283–97;
R. Beutler 'Porphyrios' in *Paulys Realencylopädie der classischen Altertumswis-
senschaft* ed K. Ziegler (Stuttgart 1953) 23 275–313.

113 Arius of Alexandria (c 250–336) taught that Christ, the Son of God, though
called God, was not truly God. Indeed since Christ had a beginning in time,
he was a creature even if he was a perfect one, superior to the rest of creation.
Arianism was condemned at the Council of Nicea in 325 but remained a
popular doctrine in the Eastern empire for much of the 4th century until the
decisive victory of the Nicene faith at the Council of Constantinople in 381.
See J.N.D. Kelly *Early Christian Doctrine* (New York 1958) 226–31; R. Gregg
and D.E. Groh *Early Arianism: A View of Salvation* (Philadelphia 1981) 1–42
and for a critique of this book see C. Kannengiesser *Arius and Alexander: Two
Alexandrian Theologians* (Brookfield VT 1991) 466–71; Tracy 'Erasmus and the
Arians' 1–10.

He betrayed the council's secret, and now the danger is that this worth-less fellow will betray himself as well. He adds that I, giving certain pri-vate letters to my friends, wrote that my opinion never included a be-lief that there is nothing in the *synaxis* but signs of the Lord's body and blood. I did indeed write, but it was to those who had first dropped this lie secretly into their friends' ears, and soon had transformed it into a ru-mour.[114] In these letters also there is no word not written from the heart – no word, at least, that I can claim as my own. Since some of them, when published, proved as unreliable as this book in citing and mentioning my words, I will take care that they be printed just as they were written by both parties, adding the names as well.[115] From these letters it will be clear that the one who sowed that rumour, and the one who spread abroad this utterly frivolous pamphlet, are on the same side. As for whether the rumour and pamphlet have the same author,[116] let others concern themselves with that; it does not much matter to me. As for those trifles concerning a two-fold interpretation of the words 'the flesh is of no profit,'[117] since they

* * * * *

114 In letters to Conrad Pellicanus, Epp 1637:10–16. On Erasmus and Pellicanus see Epp 1637 introduction, 1737 introduction, and 1792A introduction.

115 The private circulation of the correspondence between Erasmus and Pellicanus led to its publication in 1526 under the titles: *Expostulatio ad quendam amicum ad modum pia et christiana Erasmi Roterodami* and *Epistola D. Erasmi Roter. cum amico quodam expostulans. Amici item epistolae duae Erasmianae expostulationi re-spondentes.* The first contains Ep 1637 only; the second contains Epp 1637, 1638, and 1639. Though they were anonymously printed, Erasmus considered Pel-licanus to be the one responsible; cf Ep 1637 introduction and Allen Ep 1637 introduction and *Epistola ad fratres Inferioris Germaniae* below 292.

116 See introductory note above n52 for Erasmus' judgment at this time concerning the authorship of the *Maynung*.

117 The twofold interpretation mentioned by the *Maynung* (A 5 r) has to do with whether these words (John 6:63) refer to the flesh of Christ itself or to a fleshly understanding. On the former exegesis the meaning would be that Christ's flesh ceased to be of value after he ascended into heaven and sent the Holy Spirit. He cannot therefore be present bodily in the Lord's Supper. The second view is that what the Evangelist has in mind by flesh is not Christ's humanity but rather a weak and sinful human understanding unaided by the Holy Spirit. The first interpretation was that of Zwingli and was shared by Oecolampadius, Pellicanus, and Jud; the second was that of Luther. Luther's view was that of Chrysostom (*Hom in Johannem* 47 PG 59 2651), whereas Zwingli's was that of Augustine (*Tract in Johannem* 27 PL 5 617). For Zwingli's view see *Commentarius de vera et falsa religione* in *Zwinglis Werke* III 785:27–41 and in *The Latin Works of Huldreich Zwingli* ed C.N. Heller 3rd ed (Philadelphia 1929) 212; 'Eine klare Unterrichtung vom Nachtmal Christi' in *Zwinglis Werke* IV 820:20–825:27 and

have nothing to do with the business now at hand, I knowingly pass them over.

Returning to me, he assails me with a host of passages, from which he thinks it obvious that I agree with Wyclif about the Eucharist. The first of these is in the annotations which I wrote on chapter 14 of Mark. There I make only two annotations. One is that 'to bless' (*benedicere*) is not the same thing as is commonly meant today – to represent an image of the cross by a motion of the hand – but rather to speak words of good omen that is, to praise God, to give him glory and honour, or to give him thanks.[118] The other [annotation] pertains to the words with which Christ is said to have consecrated the bread and wine. Mark reports them in such a way that they seem to have been pronounced in consecration of the cup *after* the apostles had drunk. Indeed, in this passage theologians provide their explanation through a figure of speech, inverted order of narration.[119] I will

* * * * *

in *Zwingli and Bullinger* ed G.W. Bromiley, Library of Christian Classics 24 (Philadelphia 1953) 207–11; Stephens *Theology of Huldrych Zwingli* 232–7, 239–41, 245–7. For Luther's view see 'Dass diese Wort Christi "Das ist mein Leib" noch feststehen' WA 23 166:28–205:31 and LW 37 78–101; H. Sasse *This is My Body* (Minneapolis 1959) 178–80.

118 Reeve *Gospels* 143. The final form of this text was reached in 1522, although, except for one minor detail revised in 1522 (*boni ominis* ['of good omen'] instead of *bene ominata* ['auguring well']), the words are the same as the 1516 text.

119 That is, πρωθύστερον, mentioned in text quoted below. *Prothysteron* has to do with understanding a sentence as having an inverted order of meaning without changing the words. In this case, Erasmus seems to imply, without expressly saying so, that one could understand the words of institution as constituting the prayer of consecration even though that is not expressly stated in the text. On this figure see H. Lausberg §891 and on its use by Erasmus and by Karlstadt see G. Krodel 'Prothysteron and the Exegetical Basis of the Lord's Supper' *Lutheran Quarterly* 12 (1960) 152–8. Thomas Aquinas pointed out the variations in the previous tradition on the issue concerning the words that Christ used in consecration of the elements and presents his own position that the words used by the priest in consecrating the Eucharist are a recital of the very same words used by Christ; see Thomas Aquinas *Summa theologiae* 3 q 78 a 1. In his annotation on 1 Cor 11:24 Erasmus referred to Thomas' discussion of the variations among scholastics on this matter; see below n186. Cf *Apologia adversus monachos* LB IX 1065B–C where Erasmus refers to Thomas Aquinas and Gabriel Biel as authors who do not hide the fact that the opinions of theologians have differed concerning the words of consecration. See Gabriel Biel *Canonis expositio Lectio 36 Pars 2* ed H.A. Oberman and W.J. Courtenay (Wiesbaden 1965) 42–4. Biel argues that the view held in common by Alexander, Albert, Thomas, and others, *quod Christus in ultima cena consecravit per eadem verba per*

transcribe my words from the annotation, 'Which shall be poured out on behalf of many.' I point out that for the Greeks ἐκχυνόμενον can be read in the sense of present time, 'that is, "which is poured out on behalf of many." For he was already,' I said, 'representing what would be the case a little later.[120] Those who place special emphasis on the words Christ used in performing the consecration – though that is nowhere to be read in specific terms – would annotate the passage, in which the matter is thus narrated, as if Christ first held out the cup, and then, when they had drunk, finally said, "this is the cup," etc.[121] For that is how the words of the Evangelist have it: "And taking the cup, he gave thanks, he gave it to them, and they all drank from it; and he said to them, this is my blood," etc. Yet I would not wish to be perversely argumentative in this matter, since the passage can be excused through the figure of πρωθύστερον [inverted order].'[122]

Up till now I have been recounting my statements word for word. In them you see, reader, that there is not even a syllable which signifies that the actual body of the Lord is not in the Eucharist. The words I quoted are spoken of the cup; there is no mention of the body. Therefore, I am the more astonished at the negligence of this writer, who blathers whatever comes into his head without even having read the passage. Matthew 26 is a passage treated likewise, and at that place there is no word in the annotations which could engender even the slightest suspicion.[123] Luke 22 likewise: not even here is a single word that you could draw into suspicion.[124]

There is another passage in the paraphrase on chapters 10 and 11 of the First Epistle to the Corinthians, where he declares that I, openly and with many words, express a view that in the Eucharist there is bread and wine, which I call symbols, that is, signs that declare something.[125] At this point I am explaining the Apostle's discourse in the tenth chapter on spiritual food and drink, which the Jews also ate and drank in a spiritual fashion; and I remark, in these words, 'We, as many of us as have been cleansed through

* * * * *

que nos conficimus 'that Christ at the Last Supper consecrated by the same words by which we bring it about,' is the more universal and probable one. Cf also Declarationes ad censuras Lutetiae vulgatas LB IX 851C–D.

120 Reeve Gospels 143. This was the extent of the annotation in 1516.

121 'Those who ... etc' was added in 1519; see Reeve Gospels 143.

122 'For that ... πρωθύστερον' was added in 1522; see Reeve Gospels 143.

123 For the annotations on Matt 26:26–28 see Reeve Gospels 101 and LB VI 133E–F.

124 For the annotations on Luke 22:17–22 see Reeve Gospels 208–9 and LB VI 316E–F.

125 Erasmus' language here approximates Jud's: bedeutliche zaichen 'signifying signs' Maynung A 6 r; cf Epistola ad fratres Inferioris Germaniae below 295.

baptism, feed equally on the food of the most blessed body, and all drink from the mystical cup.'[126] And later, 'Christ was at that time rehearsing among them things that for us he has openly and truly performed.'[127] So far to this point. Is there not here mention of the sacred body? Do I not profess that what was shown to the Jews in figures has been shown to us in the Eucharist truly and openly? Again, somewhat farther along, 'Does not that sacred cup, which we for the remembrance of Christ's death take up with thanksgiving and consecrate, demonstrate a fellowship because we have all equally been redeemed through the blood of Christ? Again, that sacred bread, which by the example and ordinance of Christ we distribute among ourselves, demonstrates a covenant and perfect partnership among ourselves as initiates into the same mysteries of Christ,' etc.[128] What is there here that provokes a sinister suspicion? Is it because what I first referred to as the Lord's sacred body I later call bread? Why should I, writing a paraphrase, not do so, when Paul, whom I am explaining, does the same thing more than once?[129]

In fact, I could be more justly blamed for adding the word 'consecrate' on my own, as when I explain Paul's expression 'which we bless'[130] in two senses. For merely frivolous is the view of a certain author, who chatters that I added the word 'consecrate' unintentionally and out of weariness,[131] although I used two words, as I said before, to indicate a two-fold interpretation. One sense is this: 'which we bless,' that is, 'for which we give thanks.' The other sense: 'which we bless,' that is, 'which we consecrate.' The former interpretation found favour with the ancient writers – Theophylactus, to name one – while the latter was added by more recent ones.[132]

* * * * *

126 Paraphrase on 1 Corinthians 10:3 CWE 43 128
127 Paraphrase on 1 Corinthians 10:3 CWE 43 130
128 Paraphrase on 1 Corinthians 10:16 cwe 43 134–5
129 Cf 1 Cor 10:16–17 and *Epistola ad fratres Inferioris Germaniae* below 295.
130 1 Cor 10:16
131 The author is Zwingli; see his *Responsio ad epistolam Ioannis Bugenhagii* (*Zwinglis Werke* IV 568:10–12), where Zwingli makes this interpretation of Erasmus' paraphrase. Cf *Epistola ad fratres Inferioris Germaniae* below 296 and Allen Ep 1644:34–36. As C. Augustijn indicates (ASD IX-1 249 n365–6), the above Zwingli text is more likely the one that Erasmus has in mind than the one to which Allen and CWE 12 489 n17 make reference: *Subsidium siue coronis de eucharistia* (*Zwinglis Werke* IV 498:39–41). Cf Ep 1792A:25–6, 39–40, nn11, 17, which follow Allen Ep 1644 23n.
132 Cf the annotation on 1 Cor 10:16 (1527) where Erasmus names Chrysostom and Theophylact as favouring the former interpretation. From the ancient commentators, Chrysostom and Theophylactus, for example, it is not clear, thinks

Therefore I put it in second place. Why does the word 'consecrate' present an obstacle to this man? Does a thing, when it is consecrated, at once turn into something else? Do not consecrated candles remain candles, and consecrated walls remain of stone? To what purpose do they gather such childish arguments, when the matter at hand is serious?

Likewise, somewhat farther on: 'You cannot drink at the same time from the hallowed cup of Christ and from the accursed cup of demons. Nor can you partake of the table of the Lord and at the same time of the table of a demon.'[133] I use the same words that Paul uses, except that I explain the same thought with less subtlety on account of my more simple readers. And that is quite enough for the author of a paraphrase. There I am not engaging in disputation about the Lord's Supper, nor even now is the question settled whether Paul is specifically speaking about the consecration of the Lord's body and blood in this passage. For I am of the opinion that the apostles did not always perform the act of consecration whenever they distributed bread or extended the cup in memory of the Lord's death.[134] But

*****

Erasmus, that Paul is treating here the priestly consecration of the body and blood of the Lord; see LB VI 711D–E; Reeve-Screech 486. On Erasmus' use of the commentaries of Theophylactus, Archbishop of Ochrid (d c 1108), see CWE 56 15 n25. Erasmus does not mention Chrysostom here probably because he had not yet obtained the Greek Father's *Homilies on the Pauline Letters* which he would have available for use in his 1527 *Annotations*. By August 1526 he had obtained a manuscript copy of Chrysostom's *Homilies on Romans*, see Ep 1736 / CWE 12 285:28–9. For the reference here see Theophylactus *Expos in Epist 1 ad Cor* 10:16 (PG 124: 684D–6A) and for Chrysostom see *Hom 24 in Epist ad Cor* (PG 61:199–200). For medieval writers who refer to the priestly consecration see Peter Lombard (PL 191 1623C–D); *Glossa ordinaria* (Basel 1506–8) 6 gg v v: *Calix benedictionis non solum a Christo in cena est benedictus, sed cui etiam nos sacerdotes benedicimus* 'the cup of blessing is not only blessed by Christ, but we priests also bless it in his name.' Nicolas of Lyra expressly connects this text with the sacrament of the Eucharist, see Nicolas de Lyra *Postilla super totam Bibliam* 4 vols (Strasbourg 1492; repr Frankfurt 1971) IV EE VI V. In his commentary Thomas Aquinas gives both senses: The phrase 'which we bless' he applies to the believers' exaltation of God by believing and giving thanks as well as to the priestly consecration, see *Explanatio in epistola 1 ad Cor 10 Lectio 4, Thomae Aquinatis expositio in omnes S. Pauli epistolas* in *Sancti Thomae Aquinatis Doctoris Ordinis Praedicatorum Opera Omnia* 11 (Parma 1862) 229.

133 Paraphrase on 1 Corinthians 10:21 CWE 43 136
134 Cf Allen Ep 2175:24–6: '... I find no passage in the divine Scriptures whence it is without question evident that the apostles consecrated the bread and the wine into the body and blood of Christ.' In a letter to Cuthbert Tunstall, bishop of Durham, Erasmus qualified this judgment somewhat: 'Nowhere in

on this matter I have no assertions to make, especially since it has nothing
to do with the business now at hand.

And so, now that it has been made clear that this net of chicanery
caught nothing, we shall come to chapter 11, in which I name sometimes
the bread and cup, sometimes the Lord's body and blood, plainly imitating
Paul, of whom I am writing a paraphrase.[135] I say that this act is done
in commemoration of Christ's death.[136] For so the Lord taught us in the
gospel;[137] so teaches Paul, saying, 'You will declare the Lord's death until
he comes.'[138] I see that so great an Apostle spoke in very scrupulous terms
of so great a mystery; I imitated his scrupulousness, as befitted the author of
a paraphrase, except that I more often name the Lord's body than does Paul
himself. I will cite the passages, lest I appear to be avoiding any difficulty.
The first runs as follows: 'For I myself as an apostle received from the Lord
what I then passed on to you, namely, that our Lord Jesus, on that night in
which he was betrayed through a disciple and taken prisoner, took bread,
and having given thanks to God, broke the bread and said: "Take, eat; this
is my body, which is broken for you and is to be shared by all. This which
you see me do, you also are to do after this for the remembrance of me."'[139]
And later, 'In the same manner after distributing the bread, he took the cup
also into his hands and, the meal now finished, said: "This cup is the new
testament through my blood; as often as you drink from it, do so for the
remembrance of me,"' etc.'[140] And again, later, 'Christ wished this feast to
be a commemoration of his death and a symbol of an everlasting covenant,
yet now it is celebrated among you with self-indulgence and division. It is
mystical bread, and all ought equally to be partakers of it. It is a most holy
cup, which belongs equally to all; in no way was it provided in order to
appease the body's thirst, but to represent a hidden matter so that you may
not forget at what price you have been redeemed from the sins of your

* * * * *

the canonical letters does one discover a place where the apostles assuredly
consecrated the body of the Lord as it is now consecrated on the altar except in
one place, the first letter to the Corinthians 11; and yet in chapter 10 according
to his wording Paul does not seem to be concerned with priestly consecration'
(Allen Ep 2263:77–81). Cf the annotation on Acts 2:46 LB VI 446D (Reeve-Screech
282–3).
135 Paraphrase on 1 Corinthians 11:23–9 CWE 43 146–8
136 Paraphrase on 1 Corinthians 11:23–5 CWE 43 146–7
137 Luke 22:19
138 1 Cor 11:25–6
139 Paraphrase on 1 Corinthians 11:23–4 CWE 43 146–7
140 Paraphrase on 1 Corinthians 11:25 CWE 43 147

former life. As often, therefore, as you come together to eat this bread or to drink of this cup, you do not engage in the business of the stomach, but you are mystically representing the death of the Lord Jesus so that the continual memory of him may keep you faithful in your duty until he comes again in person to judge the world.'[141] In this I do not depart one hair's breadth from Paul's meaning. When Paul says 'this bread,' he shows by the pronoun that this is not ordinary bread. By way of explanation, I say, 'the bread is mystical' and 'the cup is sacred.' I explain Paul's statement, 'You will proclaim the Lord's death,' by saying, 'you represent the death of the Lord Jesus by a mystical rite.' I explain his statement, 'until he comes,'[142] by saying, 'until he comes again himself to judge the world.'

Even those who adhere most closely to the views of Aquinas and Scotus[143] will confess that each of these statements is expressed in a pious manner. For in the Gospel of John the Lord refers to himself as 'the bread which came down from heaven.'[144] There is, consequently, no absurdity in referring to the bread in the Eucharist as the Lord's body. But if anyone forces an argument on the basis of the word 'commemoration,' let him not take up his case with me, but with the Lord himself, and with Paul, who speak in this way.[145] Again, if anyone should try to prove from the words 'until he comes' that Christ will not come to earth until he returns in glory to judge it,[146] I will not belabour the absurdity of such an argument: as if Christ declared the earth off-limits to himself, or as if he speaks about a hidden and spiritual coming, and not rather about an evident one, in which his arrival shall be obvious to impious and pious alike. At any rate, one

* * * * *

141 Paraphrase on 1 Corinthians 11:25–7 CWE 43 147–8
142 The quotations from Paul here are all from 1 Cor 11:26.
143 John Duns Scotus (c 1266–1308), outstanding Franciscan philosopher and theologian, was educated at Oxford and Paris and taught at these two universities and at Cologne. In contrast to Thomas Aquinas, who taught clearly a doctrine of transubstantiation of bread and wine into the body and blood of Christ, Duns did not rule out a doctrine of consubstantiation, namely, the presence of body and blood along with bread and wine. However, he held on to the dogma of transubstantiation on the authority of the church; cf E. Iserloh 'Abendmahl' in TRE 3 2 (Berlin 1977) 94; Richard Cross Duns Scotus (New York 1999) 140–2.
144 John 6:51, 58; cf CWE 46 86–7.
145 Cf Luke 22:19 and 1 Cor 11:24–5.
146 The Maynung (A 5 v, 6 r) argued the Zwinglian view that Christ had ascended visibly and bodily into heaven and will not return until the second advent. Thus, he could not be bodily present in the Eucharist, an opinion which the author thought Erasmus had earlier supported.

cannot take up such matters with me, since I do not depart from the sacred words.

If it troubles anyone that I along with Paul mention bread and the cup, that person ought to be troubled by the fact that I speak of the Lord's body and blood. For there follows this remark in my paraphrase: 'because he has treated the Lord's body and blood in a way other than the Lord himself commanded that they be treated';[147] a little later, 'For although the body and blood of the Lord bring salvation,' etc.[148] Again, soon thereafter, 'how fearfully one ought to receive the Lord's body.'[149] Where now is that pamphlet, which says that I call [them] bread and wine, and that these are symbols, that is, signs of things?[150] For he makes me speak as if I nowhere name the Lord's body and blood, though I so often do so in this very chapter. Then the crafty fellow claims that I, in calling bread and wine symbols, wanted them understood as signs of the Lord's body and blood,[151] though I, plainly expressing my real view, called them a symbol of the eternal covenant. My words run as follows. 'Christ wished this feast to be a commemoration of his death and a symbol of an everlasting covenant.'[152] I do not call the body and blood symbols, but I call the taking itself a symbol of the concord between us and a memorial of the sacred death, by which we were redeemed. You see here, excellent reader, what smoke-screens this utterly foolish pamphlet has set before us. Its claim that I refer to blood as wine is a manifest lie.[153] Along with Paul I mention the chalice or

* * * * *

147 Paraphrase on 1 Corinthians 11:27 CWE 43 148
148 Ibidem
149 Ibidem
150 Cf *Maynung* A 2 v: '... nennet er das brot vnd weyn dess Nachtmals an vil orten Symbola, das ist bedeützaychen, vnd Symbolicum panem, das ist ain bedeütlich brot' '... he [Erasmus] calls the bread and the wine of the Lord's Supper in many places symbols, that is, signs, and symbolic bread, that is, bread that signifies'; and *Maynung* A 6 r: 'Dessgleichen in Paraphrasibus über die Episteln Pauli .1. Corinth .10. vnd .11. da hat er genuᵒg vnd mit vil worten zuᵒverston geben, das da sey brot vnd weyn, die er Symbola nennet, das ist, bedeütliche zaichen.' 'Similarly in the Paraphrases on the Epistles of Paul 1 Cor 10 and 11 he has sufficiently and with many words intimated that bread and wine are there present, which he calls symbols, that is, signifying signs' (trans JBP).
151 As C. Augustijn states, Jud does not make that assertion; see ASD IX-1 251 nn428–9.
152 Paraphrase on 1 Corinthians 11:25 CWE 43 147
153 Cf *Epistola ad fratres Inferioris Germaniae* below 295.

cup,[154] but never wine; not because a sound meaning cannot be accepted in such terms, but because I find that usage neither in the gospels nor in the apostolic Epistles.

There is nothing left to discuss, except that someone who loves to cavil could say, 'While you are here treating the topic of the Eucharist at such length, why do you nowhere openly declare that in it is the substance of the body and blood?' I answer, in short, that I am writing a paraphrase,[155] not a disputation. Furthermore, when I was writing those things, no one called into dispute the topic over which debate now rages; and there is nothing I expected less than that this would happen. And so, abandoning whatever was unsuitable to a paraphrase or was ambiguous to no one, I treated those matters that would be of service for understanding Paul's discourse.

There remains one passage on the Acts of the Apostles, in which he shamelessly claims that I write the very same things, only at great length, which I had written on the Epistle of Paul just cited.[156] I will soon make you to understand, Christian reader, that nothing could be more impudent than this lie. These are Luke's words: 'They persevered, moreover, in the apostles' teaching, sharing in the breaking of bread';[157] in my paraphrase of them, I write as follows: '. . . and in taking the token of an unbreakable covenant – they called this the Communion. The practice, handed down from the Lord, was like this: bread was broken, and a small piece was given to each one; while doing this in memory of the Lord's passion, they gave thanks to the kindness of God who had purged them from their sins by the blood of his only Son,' etc.[158] That is all I say there about the sharing of bread.

* * *·* *

154 In his paraphrase Erasmus consistently uses *poculum* (cup) not *calix* (chalice), whereas the Vulgate has *calix*; cf LB VII 897B–D. His 1516 translation, however, uses *poculum* three times and *calix* once.

155 For Erasmus' understanding of 'paraphrase' see CWE 42 xii–xix; Jacques Chomorat 'Grammar and Rhetoric in the Paraphrases of the Gospels by Erasmus' ERSY 1 (1981) 30–68. Jane E. Phillips 'Sub evangelistae persona: The Speaking Voice in Erasmus' *Paraphrase on Luke*' in *Holy Scripture Speaks: The Production and Reception of Erasmus' Paraphrases on the New Testament* ed Hilmar M. Pabel and Mark Vessey (Toronto 2002) 128–50.

156 Cf *Epistola ad fratres Inferioris Germaniae* below 216 and *Maynung* A 6 r and ASD IX-1 253 nn449–50.

157 Acts 2:42

158 Paraphrase on Acts 2:42 LB VII 674A–B and CWE 50 24. On 'taking the token' (*sumendo symbolo*) see CWE 50 118 n115.

Even without my pointing it out, you easily understand, reader, that I am not writing the same things that I had written on the Epistle to the Corinthians. There I name the Lord's body and blood; here, not daring to depart from Luke's words, I only name bread. If you demand the reason, it is because the commentators differ on whether he is here speaking of Christ's body and blood, or of ordinary bread – for that is how the *Glossa Ordinaria* has it.[159] Consequently, I moderated my mode of expression so that it could be accommodated to either sense. For the Lord did not always consecrate his body and blood whenever he broke bread or offered the cup. When he fed the crowd of people in the wilderness, he took bread into his hands, gave thanks and blessed it, broke it and gave it to his disciples[160] – just ordinary bread, not changed by consecration into his body. Again, at Emmaus he was recognized by the two disciples in the breaking of bread,[161] from which they infer that this behaviour was in all cases customary with the Lord at supper. The apostles evidently imitated it as well, yet they did not always consecrate the Lord's body. For there follows, in this very chapter, 'breaking bread from house to house, they took bread with gladness.'[162] Although this passage also can be taken of consecrated bread, yet the commentators do not presume to affirm this. Chrysostom and Bede in fact ignore the

* * * * *

159 The interlinear gloss permits an interpretation of 'bread' here as 'either common or holy'; cf *Biblie ... cum glosa ordinaria et expositione lyre litteralis et morali necnon additionibus ac replicis* (Basel 1496–8) 5 bb r. The *Glossa Ordinaria* was the standard work of biblical exegesis in the Middle Ages. It consisted of marginal and interlinear glosses (notes) taken from the commentaries of the Fathers and early medieval writers. It was compiled in the early 12th century by several collaborators, the most important of whom was Anselm of Laon. Since the late 15th century the *Glossa* was published in many editions, with the *Postilla* of Nicholas of Lyra and the *Additiones* of Paul of Burgos and Matthias Doring. See B. Smalley *The Study of the Bible in the Middle Ages* (Oxford 1952) 46–66 and, by the same author, '*Glossa Ordinaria*' TRE 13 (Berlin 1984) 452–7. For Erasmus' attitude towards the *Gloss* and his use of it, see CWE 44 263 n29, 320–1 n12 and H.J. de Jonge 'Erasmus und die *Glossa Ordinaria* zum Neuen Testament' NAK 56 (1975) 51–77.
160 Mark 6:41, 8:6; Matt 15:36, 14:19; Luke 9:16; John 6:11. As C. Augustijn points out in his note (ASD IX-1 253 nn465–7), Erasmus' recitation does not exactly follow any of those texts. His language seems to have been unconsciously shaped by the phrasing of the words of institution in the Latin mass. See B. Botte and C. Mohrmann 'Ordinaire de la messe: texte critique, traduction et études' *Études liturgiques* II (Paris 1953) 80; A. Fortescue and J.B. O'Connell *The Ceremonies of the Roman Rite Described* (Westminster 1960) 68.
161 Luke 24:30–1
162 Acts 2:46

passage.[163] Therefore, I limited my paraphrase in such a way that neither sense is excluded, whether you wish to take it of consecrated or of ordinary bread.

My words run as follows: 'Then, after the whole day had been spent in such pursuits, they broke bread house by house and ate meals with each other in turn with incredible joy; and with the most sincere simplicity of heart they praised God, by whose kindness they had gained so great a grace.'[164] Moreover, even in the distribution of bread not consecrated into the Lord's body, there is nothing to rule out some symbol of Christian harmony and a commemoration of Christ's death – just as even today in many regions the priest or minister distributes bread to the people cut into many pieces; and the Greeks do likewise, when the rite has been completed.[165] I am, therefore, amazed at this writer for wanting to invite his reader to a consideration of these passages. In them is found nothing remotely like what he claims will be found in conspicuous abundance.

Because he writes at the end of the pamphlet that there are many other passages in my writings in which I betray the fact that I agree with such people, I will bring up one or two passages from my *Paraphrases* in which this topic is treated, lest there be anything that may have slipped from my memory that could offer the malicious any cause for suspicion. Certainly, if

* * * * *

163 Chrysostom *Hom 7 in Acta apostolorum* (PG 60:64) and Bede *Supra Acta apostolorum espositio* (PL 92:950). Neither Chrysostom nor Bede comments on 'breaking bread.' Erasmus had obtained a Greek manuscript of Chrysostom's *Homilies on the Acts of the Apostles* by October 1525, but he had considerable doubt as to its authenticity; see Allen Ep 1623:9n. He apparently did have available for his 1522 edition of the *New Testament* some notes from these *Homilies*, but it was not until the 1527 *New Testament* edition that he made full use of them. The Venerable Bede (c 672–735) was a most influential exegete during the Middle Ages. His commentaries were excerpted in the *Glossa Ordinaria* and circulated in manuscript form into the 16th century. It is not always clear whether Erasmus drew directly from Bede's commentaries or from the *Gloss*; see CWE 44 263 nn28 and 29, and CWE 50 xv–xvi and 154 n9. On Bede see TRE 5 (Berlin 1980) 397–402; *Dictionary of the Middle Ages* ed J. Strayer 13 vols (New York 1982–1989) II 155–6; on Bede as Biblical scholar, see George Hardin Brown *Bede the Venerable* (Boston 1987) 42–61.

164 Paraphrase on Acts 2:46 CWE 50 25–6

165 On this practice see A. Franz *Die kirchlichen Benediktionen im Mittelalter* 1 (Freiburg 1909) 229–59 and J.A. Jungmann *The Mass of the Roman Rite: Its Origins and Development* trans F.A. Brenner (Westminster 1986) 2 452–3: '... the distribution of blessed bread, the *eulogiae*, ... survives in the oriental liturgies and also in France today. It does not necessarily have anything to do with the Eucharist.'

this writer had not been so unaware, he could have gotten a better hold on me from my paraphrase on chapter 26 of Matthew, where, following Paul, I mention 'bread' – but in the same passage I mention 'body and blood.'[166] When I say, farther along in the passage, that 'there is no other sacrifice to be expected for sins,'[167] I mean nothing other than this: that Christ will not die again; rather, it is enough that he died once for the redemption of the human race. That is exactly what St Thomas declares,[168] who most strongly asserts that the mass is a sacrifice,[169] and that the Lord's body is substantially present in the *synaxis*.[170]

Again, I treat the passage in Mark 14 in an equally scrupulous way. I refer to the taking of body and blood as 'the sacred symbol of the Lord's death and of the perpetual covenant.'[171] I do not surround the subject with verbal smokescreens, and my goal is that no one could possibly suspect that I have an opinion about the Eucharist different from that handed down to us by the church. Likewise, when I treat this passage in the paraphrase on chapter 22 of Luke, I call the taking of the Lord's body and blood a mystic symbol, by which the Lord consecrated the new covenant:[172] the old covenant had been consecrated by the blood of a sheep, and the new by the blood of the immaculate lamb. Also here I do not say that bread is a symbol of the body or that wine is a symbol of blood, but I refer to the very consecration and taking as a symbol.[173] Of what thing? Of the same thing that I have frequently explained in other passages; the Lord's death and our union.[174]

Again, explaining the expression, 'in memory of me,' I write in the following fashion: 'My death shall not be repeated. For a single victim suffices for the sins of all the ages. But you will often renew for yourselves

* * * * *

166 Paraphrase on Matthew 26:26 CWE 45 350–1
167 Paraphrase on Matthew 26:27 CWE 45 351
168 Thomas Aquinas *Summa theologiae* 3 q 22 a 3: 'As for the daily sacrifice in the church, it is not a distinct sacrifice from that offered by Christ himself; it is its commemoration' (Aquinas *Summa theologiae* 50:147). But cf 3 q 22 a 6: '. . . the true sacrifice of Christ is communicated to the faithful under the appearance of bread and wine' (Aquinas *Summa theologiae* 50:157).
169 Thomas Aquinas *Summa theologiae* 3 q 79 a 5 and 3 q 83 a 1 (Aquinas *Summa theologiae* 59:18–19, 133–7).
170 Thomas Aquinas *Summa theologiae* 3 q 75 a 4; q 76 a 1 (Aquinas *Summa theologiae* 58:69–73, 92–7).
171 Paraphrase on Mark 14:22 CWE 49 160
172 Paraphrase on Luke 22:19 CWE 48 189
173 Paraphrase on Luke 22:19–20 CWE 48 189
174 See the paraphrase on Matthew 26:26 CWE 45 350–1; paraphrase on Mark 14:22 CWE 49 160; *Querela pacis* CWE 27 304; Ep 1039:264–7; *Modus orandi* CWE 70 153.

the memory of my love towards you.'[175] And shortly thereafter, I add this remark about our act of taking: 'For this will be the holiest sign of the pact made between us.'[176] Take note of this, reader. I do not say that bread is a sign of the body, as that deceitful writer wants it to appear, but I refer to the very consecration and taking as a sign of the covenant between God and us. If my teaching is the same as that of St Thomas,[177] the strongest proponent of the body's substance in the Eucharist, then where does this dreamer get his inference that I hint at something different – unless it is because he desires beyond measure that such a thing be true? Those who are in love also invent dreams for themselves.[178]

On the supper in John 13 I speak as follows in my paraphrase: 'There-fore, after the preparation for that last mystical meal, in which, by giving the sacred symbol of his own body and blood, he was going to establish the perpetual memory of himself, he would also ratify the bond of friendship that would never in any way perish,'[179] etc. Here I refer to the offered body and blood as the sacred symbol, not the bread and wine, clearly deeming the act of offering itself to be a symbol of the friendship that shall never be broken. That, to be sure, I added from the other evangelists, since John does not treat the consecration and the act of taking. If I had not wanted to make mention of the body and blood, I had the option of omitting it here; and in other places, where there was no such option, I could have used some fabrication to twist the subject-matter into another sense.

Again, in the sixth chapter of John, the Lord, using riddles, commends his heavenly doctrine and, according to some, the taking of his body and blood in a sacrament as well; on this passage though I have the option of

* * * * *

175 Paraphrase on Luke 22:19 CWE 48 187. The expression *in mei memoriam* 'in memory of me' would appear once again to be Erasmus' unconscious citing of the mass text. See Botte and Mohrmann 'Ordinaire de la messe' (above n160) 80; Fortescue and O'Connell *Ceremonies* (above n160 69. The Lucan text in the Vulgate is *hoc facite in meam commemorationem* ('do this in remembrance of me'). Erasmus' 1516 translation was the same as the Vulgate, but he changed it to *in mei recordationem* in 1519, which he interprets as in his paraphrase: 'for the renewing of the memory of me.'

176 Paraphrase on Luke 22:19 CWE 48 189

177 Here Erasmus is referring not to the immediately preceding statement but to his whole argument above. On Thomas see above nn36, 90, 119.

178 *Adagia* II iii 90: *Qui amant ipsi sibi somnia fingunt* CWE 33 183–4: 'Those who desire something passionately take every chance to flatter their own wishes, and seize on anything in reach as a foreshowing of the result for which they long.'

179 Paraphrase on John 13:2 CWE 46 160

following the prior interpretation alone,[180] I nevertheless add the following: 'This flesh that you see is also living bread, which I shall pay and hand over to death to ransom the life of the whole world. Believe, take, and eat.'[181] Then, somewhat later, speaking even more clearly about the union of the body and its Head, I add, 'And I shall leave behind, as a mystical symbol of this union, my flesh and blood; but it will do no good to have received even this unless you receive it according to the spirit.'[182] I refer to the flesh and blood in the Eucharist as the symbol left behind, meaning of course a symbol of the communion that exists between Christ and the church, between members of the mystical body. What orthodox person denies that? And yet this pamphlet spews forth smoke, pretending that with the word 'symbol,' I was stating an opinion that the bread and wine are signs of the body and blood, and that the latter are not in actual fact present. Anyone who by such deceptions tries to impose on the minds of the naive is vastly remote from the simplicity of an evangelical dove[183] – more like a polyp that repeatedly changes its shape.[184]

* * * * *

180 Chrysostom alludes to the 'mysteries,' but his interpretation of John 6:51–8 is figurative. The focus of Jesus' discourse was doctrine, faith in himself, not the mode of life (Chrysostom *Hom in Ioannem* 46 1 PG 59:264). Cyril stresses the importance of faith for the eating of Christ's flesh but then proceeds to give the text a Eucharistic interpretation when he refers to the words of institution from Matthew's Gospel (PG 73:577A). Augustine gives to John 6:51–8 likewise primarily a figurative interpretation. Augustine explains the flesh and blood of John 6:53–5 as referring to the community of Christ's body and members, but then he mentions that the sacrament of this thing, that is, the unity of the body and blood of Christ is prepared and eaten at the Lord's table somewhere daily and elsewhere at intervals (*In Iohannis evangelium tractatus* 26 CCSL 36:266– 7). Theophylactus interprets John 6:51–3 as teaching the transformation of the bread into the body of Christ 'through the mystical blessing and the coming of the Holy Spirit' (PG 123:1307). The *Glossa ordinaria* refers John 6:55 explicitly to the sacrament of the altar (*Biblia cum glosa ordinaria* . . . 5 g 2 v). Nicholas of Lyra gives a Eucharistic reading for all of John 6:51–8 and that in a quite realistic sense. When Jesus says: '"My flesh is true food . . ." (John 6:55), he means that it is truly consumed not just figuratively . . .' (*Postilla super totam bibliam* 4 s iiii r-v).
181 Paraphrase on John 6:52 CWE 46 86 and n69. In the paraphrase the text reads: 'Believe, take and live.' The 1524 and 1534 editions, like LB, read *viuite* instead of *comedite*.
182 Paraphrase on John 6:64 CWE 46 88 where the translation varies slightly from the present one.
183 Matt 10:16; cf *Epistola contra pseudevangelicos* below 238 n116.
184 *Adagia* I i 93: *Polypi mentem obtine* 'Adopt the outlook of a polyp' CWE 31 133–6: '. . . take up for the time being this or that kind of behaviour, this or that kind of face.'

There remains only one passage in the annotations on chapter 11 of 1
Corinthians, which lay exposed to someone's misrepresentation – indeed,
to that of a most stupid fellow,[185] who had slipped up in understanding
the grammatical sense, a problem that I encounter all too often nowadays.
In this passage, however, I only touch upon the question of what words the
Lord used to consecrate his body and blood. And in fact, I cite the view of
St Thomas, who pronounces heretical the opinion of those who deny that the
Lord's true body and blood is present in the Eucharist.[186] His view receives
no contradiction from me.

I have made abundantly evident how this pamphlet utterly lacks intelligence and shame. It proceeds as if no one among mortals ever reads
my writings, which in fact offer instant confutation of the drivel in it. In
his conclusion as well, this serious authority expounds what my opinions
are, as often as I name the Lord's body or as often as I name the mass a

* * * * *

185 Erasmus has in mind Vincentius Theoderici (Vincent Dierckx), a Dominican
theologian at Louvain, who he thought had misunderstood, through an incompetence in Latin, his annotation on 1 Cor 11:24; see Epp 1126:76–86. On
Theoderici see CEBR III 317–18 and *Spongia* above n189; on his relations with
Erasmus see Ep 1196 introduction; Rummel *Catholic Critics* I 132–4.

186 In his 1519 annotation on 1 Cor 11:24 Erasmus wrote: 'Thomas admits that
there have been those who have said that Christ consecrated the bread with
other words before, handing it to his disciples, he said: "this is my body."
Although he refutes that opinion, he does not call it heretical in spite of the
fact that he does call heretical the opinion of those who argued that the body
of Christ was not truly in the sacrament of the *synaxis*, but was there as in a
sign. In everything one ought to assent to the judgment of the church, even
if here the word seems [to refer] to the already consecrated bread which he
handed [to the disciples]. To me in matters of this kind, which cannot be taught
by sure testimonies of Sacred Scripture but depend on human conjectures, it
seems more advisable not to be so bold in asserting that we demand that
our opinion be considered as divine revelation. And perhaps it is safer for
ecclesiastical leaders not to pronounce on any number of things which they
cannot demonstrate, since they are themselves human beings and can err.' In
1522 Erasmus inserted 'rashly' between 'not' and 'pronounce.' In 1527 Erasmus
replaced the text which followed after the words, 'the already consecrated
bread which he handed,' in this manner: 'But unless one acquiesces in the
decree of the church, it would be very difficult to prove by human reasoning
what are the words used by the priest in the act of consecration. For if we
grant that Christ had consecrated with words of this kind, how is it evident
that we, using different words, also consecrate this covenant he entered upon
with us. But here, as Paul says, the human mind should be taken captive in
obedience to faith so that the greater the merit of faith is, the less human reason
comprehends.' (trans JBP) LB VI 716E–F / Reeve-Screech 492. For Thomas' view
see *Summa theologiae* 3 q 75 a 1 resp.

sacrifice; and he wants my opinions to appear to be whatever he himself has dreamed up.[187] I do not know how much concession you, most excellent reader, think should be granted to this writer; the facts themselves state that he is more fit for feeding pigs than writing books. I will add one point: that in my writings there is nothing found that contains error concerning the truth of the Lord's body and blood. Although so many hostile critics of my works have come forth, dragging everything into misrepresentation, nevertheless not one has arisen to give me trouble on this score, except Bucenta [ox-driver] alone, stupider than any Coroebus;[188] and he is now ashamed, I believe, of that drivel of his.

Finally, I would like to ask this writer what purpose induced him to make public these trifles. Was it to force me to a confession, in case I was concealing something up my sleeve which I did not dare to profess on account of the fear of princes?[189] For that is what he pretends to be doing. And yet, in the case of a timid man, no contrivance could more quickly drive him to deny what he conceals in his heart; but as for one of pious mind, none could more quickly force him to defend his opinion strongly, and to attack his adversary, as I am doing, at least in this case. Or did he want to drive me to his own conviction? Let him persuade me first, and then I will profess such a conviction. But let that be as it may, let him imagine that I have been silenced and that he has – falsely – persuaded the ignorant of my tacit agreement with Karlstadt: does the sheer number of people making an error excuse it? Does a thing seem true to everyone, just because Erasmus agrees to it? Does their gospel, and their teaching of purest truth, rest so much on props of this sort, that is, upon deception and trickery?

But – to rid ourselves of this fellow and his foolishness – I hear remarks commonly tossed about that a victory of the gospel is within grasp,

* * * * *

187 Jud contended that whenever Erasmus referred to sacrifice, he did not mean something offered by the priest but 'a commemoration of the great sacrifice accomplished by Christ.' Likewise, whenever Erasmus mentioned eating the flesh of Christ and drinking his blood, Jud thought Erasmus referred to 'nothing else than believing that he gave his flesh for us in death and poured out his blood for us. And thus the body and blood are present and are eaten, yet not corporally, but spiritually . . .' (trans JBP) *Maynung* B 6 r–v.
188 For the identification of Theodorici with Bucenta see Ep 1196 n48; Allen Ep 1196 (variant reading to line 6) and 2045:111; cf ASD IX-1 257 nn558–9 and Rummel *Catholic Critics* I 132–3. On Coroebus see *Adagia* II ix 64: *Stultior Coroebo* CWE 34 114: 'A proverbial exaggeration for stupid people and blockheads.'
189 On fear of princes see above 151, 170 and n41.

if I am willing to confess what I conceal up my sleeve.[190] To these remarks I made a very brief response, that at issue here is a two-fold debate: concerning the judgment of dogma and concerning the character of human beings. There are three kinds of dogmas. The first comprises those things which, beyond dispute, the whole church embraces with a great consensus.[191] Of this kind are such things as are expressly contained in Sacred Scripture and in the Apostles' Creed, and to them I would allow to be added the decrees of councils duly called and completed.[192] The second comprises matters about which the authority of the church has made no clear pronouncement, about which the theologians are still disputing among themselves. The third comprises things that are thrust upon us as oracles of the church, though they are in fact opinions of human beings, often contributing greatly to brawls and dissension, very little or nothing to piety.[193]

* * * * *

190 After Erasmus had circulated his correspondence with Pellicanus, Zwingli wrote to Oecolampadius on 28 October 1525 accusing Erasmus of holding one opinion in his heart but expressing another in his words; see *Zwinglis Briefwechsel* II no 401, 407:11–13, 412:34–13:16. Zwingli stressed the disparity between Erasmus' own inner sentiments on the Eucharist and his expressions of loyalty to the authority of the church. 'If they (the church and the pope) did not stand opposed, you would think otherwise; thus, your mind is not in that place where the judgment of the church is' (trans JBP) 413:11–12.

191 *Magnoque consensu*; cf the annotation on Matt 11:28 (1519) LB VI 65D, Reeve *Gospels* 55; Ep 1729:29–30; Allen Ep 1893 59–60; *Epistola ad fratres Inferioris Germaniae* below 271, 279. On the Erasmian understanding of the universal consensus and its roots in classical and Christian history, see McConica 'Grammar of Consent'; Gebhardt *Stellung* 52–72; Tracy 'Erasmus and the Arians' 1–10; *Spongia* above nn153 and 297.

192 An important summary statement of Erasmus' attitude towards church dogma. For discussions of this position see C.J. de Vogel 'Erasmus and his Attitude towards Church Dogma' *Scrinium Erasmianum* 2 101–32; . Gebhardt *Stellung* 359–76; W. Hentze *Kirche und kirchliche Einheit bei Erasmus von Rotterdam* (Paderborn 1974) 139–90. On his high regard for the Apostles' Creed as presenting a summary of the articles of faith contained in Scripture, see CWE 39 432–4 n16; Thompson *Fide* 39–42; *Explanatio symboli* ASD V-1 210:127–32 / CWE 70 241. On his respect for church councils duly called and confirmed by a universal consensus, see 'A Fish Diet' CWE 40 690:6–19 and 732–4 nn96 and 97; *Explanatio symboli* ASD V-1 276:87–8 / CWE 70 329; *Lingua* CWE 29 334; *Hyperaspistes* 1 LB X 1262A–B / CWE 76 127. On Erasmus and conciliarism see McConica 'Erasmus and the "Julius"' 462–7; McSorley above n24.

193 Cf the annotation on Matt 11:28 where Erasmus complains that the laws and opinions of human beings are being treated as articles of faith and he contrasts their complexity and burdensomeness with the simplicity and purity of the philosophy of Christ and the Apostles' Creed (LB VI 64D–F, Reeve *Gospels* 54;

Within the first category there is not an item which I have not always frankly professed in all my writings.[194] If there is anything from the second category which has definitely convinced me, I frankly profess it; if there is anything questionable, I neither approve nor condemn it. If anything fails to satisfy me, if I see no result from it besides disturbance, I remain silent. If I see a hope of benefit, I share it. As a case of this type I regard the question whether confession – what people call sacramental confession – was instituted by Christ himself, or was derived from Sacred Scripture, or was introduced as a result of the general regulation of the church. On this matter I suspend judgment, but in such a way that I yet observe the sacrament as if Christ had instituted it.[195]

* * * * *

cf also his annotation on 1 Tim 1:6 where at great length he satirizes many scholastic disputes as meaningless talk (LB VI 926D–8E, Reeve *Galatians to the Apocalypse* 662–5.

194 This statement is not exactly true since, though Erasmus subscribed to the real presence of Christ in the Eucharist, he apparently never accepted the dogma of transubstantiation, nor did he agree with the universal consensus concerning the prohibition of divorce. In the case of transubstantiation he apparently did not think there was a universal consensus in spite of the declaration at the 4th Lateran Council (1215). For his views on the definition of the church concerning the mode of Christ's presence in the Eucharist see introductory note 153 and above n36. For his attitude towards divorce see his annotation on 1 Cor 7:39 *Novum Testamentum* (1519) II 325–34, LB VI 692D–703C; Reeve-Screech 467–81. For discussions of Erasmus' views on the real presence see G. Krodel 'Die Abendmahlslehre' (above n18) 87, 91–102, 115–24, 149–54 and Payne *Sacraments* 143–54 and 298 n97. For a treatment of Erasmus' attitude towards divorce see E.V. Telle *Érasme de Rotterdam et le septième sacrament* (Geneva 1954) 205–32, 349–66.

195 Already in his 1516 annotation on Acts 19:18 Erasmus questioned the basis of private confession in Christian antiquity. To be sure, confession existed at that time, but it was public, not private. In 1519 he added that the current auricular confession appears to have emerged from private consultations with the bishops whenever some anxiety burdened the soul (LB VI 507F–8E, Reeve-Screech 315). Attacked by Edward Lee on this score, Erasmus responded at length in an apology against Lee in which he argued that 'this law of confession' was *de iure humano*, not *de iure divino*, but 'If the church issues a firm decree that this confession is divine law, if it believes that it was instituted by Christ himself, if it believes that it cannot be abolished, I do not go against the verdict of the church, but adjust my interpretation to its oracular pronouncement, even if it goes against the grain.' *Responsio ad annotationes Lei* LB IX 262D–E / CWE 72 377. Cf Epp 1153:316–20; *Apologia adversus Stunicae Blasphemiae* LB IX 369C; *Apologia ad Stunicae conclusiones* LB IX 389C–D; *Apologia adversus monachos* LB IX 1062C–F. For discussions of this issue see Payne *Sacraments* 181–91 and J.P.

Concerning the third category I have made many admonitions, publicly exposing, so to speak, the fact that they ought to be scrutinized by the learned. These men, however, are demanding a definite and unquestionable judgment about each particular item. Yet it seems hardly an act of piety to ask from *me* a judgment about matters which have been handed down by clear, legitimate, and public authority, and have been accepted by the church. As for the other matters, on which the church has not yet made a definite pronouncement, it is not my task to make pronouncements about them, since I am neither learned nor endowed with public authority. In fact, even in the third category my lack of expertise gives me sufficient excuse. If I seem to be cleverly disguising this lack more than truly confessing it, against those who support the new doctrines I have a very weighty witness in Martin Luther, who so often in his published books declares that I know nothing of theology;[196] against those who support the pope's cause I have as witnesses very many theologians of the highest reputation.[197] Consequently, I can advise such critics to join me and embrace, beyond contention, the traditions which the church has beyond dispute handed down to us, by the inspiration of the Holy Spirit. I also advise them in doubtful cases either to consult those who are pre-eminent in knowledge and authority, or to join me and, suspending judgment, await the decision of the church. Meanwhile, in such cases, let each person have the use of his own conscience, without causing disturbance or setting stumbling-blocks before the weak: just as Paul taught in Romans 14, 'Let everyone flourish in his own mind.'[198]

But let them imagine that I do know something. What benefit will there be in making pronouncements about the matters now under debate? There are so many factions nowadays. Will all persons at once lay aside

* * * * *

Massaut 'La position "oecuménique" d'Erasme sur la pénitence' (above n85) 243–6.

196 In late 1524 Erasmus had been especially agitated by letters of Luther to Oecolampadius and Pellicanus; cf Epp 1384:42–9:47; WA Br 3 no 626:14–29, no 661:6–37. Already before these letters Luther had expressed criticism of Erasmus' theological acumen; see WA Br 2 no 429:2–6, 499:7–29 (Luther's Epp 499 and 661 were published). In the year previous to the publishing of the *Detectio praestigiarum* Luther had disparaged Erasmus' theological knowledge in his *De servo arbitrio*, the response to Erasmus' *De libero arbitrio* (CWE 76); see eg Luther *De servo arbitrio* WA 18 622:14–5:18, *The Bondage of the Will* LW 33 47–51.

197 Epp 1526:39–54 and nn14 and 16; and Rummel *Catholic Critics* II 110–12.

198 Rom 14:5. Erasmus here quotes the Vulgate, where the word is *abundet*. His own translation was 'Let everyone be content (*satisfaciat*) in his own mind.'

their dispute and vote with their feet for my opinion?[199] Of course not. Instead, I would become joined to this or that faction, and would merely compound the conflagration. But if I divided up my opinion and toned it down, as arbiters are accustomed to do, then I foresee no other result than what that fellow experienced whom we read about in the *Ecclesiastical History*: When he ran between two gladiators who were fighting in the arena, wishing to break up their fight, he was stabbed through by both of them, and perished.[200]

On the topic, moreover, of the corrupt moral standards of the church – which everyone admits have slipped so far that now 'we can endure neither our faults nor their remedies'[201] – what can I, a most insignificant being, do other than admonish? Yet I *have* admonished, more freely than was fitting or advantageous to me.[202] That is of course why there has been such an uproar against me from these people, who restore the Pharisees to us.[203] And the evil is not a simple one. Only the smallest part of the pestilence takes its rise from people who openly exhibit their true character through their luxury, lust, dice-playing, and hunting parties. Far greater injury is caused by those evils that creep in under a pretence of piety.

Among these are corrupt interpretations of the Sacred Scriptures, by which it comes about that a rule, provided in order that all may correct their lives to accord with it, becomes misdirected to the gratification of our desires; and light, brought forth to convict the darkness of human life, is hidden under a bushel.[204] By such means the power of gospel teaching, which calls us to scorn this world, becomes buried; besides that, there is the impiety of many, who, receiving power handed down by Christ for building up the church, not tearing it down,[205] wrench this power to purposes of gain and tyranny; in addition, there are some institutions conceived by human

* * * * *

199 *Adagia* II vii 12: *Pedibus in sententiam discedere* 'To vote with one's feet' CWE 34 8–10: 'any form of approval for someone else's view.'

200 This is a sentiment which Erasmus expressed elsewhere: Epp 1616:213–232.

201 Livy 1 preface 9

202 In he *Hyperaspistes* 1 CWE 76 141, Erasmus' first answer to Luther's *De servo arbitrio* published in the same year as the *Detectio praestigiarum*, Erasmus wrote similarly.

203 Cf Epp 1495:15–16.

204 Matt 5:15

205 2 Cor 13:10; cf *Apologia adversus monachos* LB IX 1067A, where Erasmus, like the conciliarists, applied this text to papal authority. For the conciliarist view see B. Tierney *Foundations of the Conciliar Theory* (Leiden 1998) 153 and Louis B. Pascoe SJ *Jean Gerson: Principles of Church Reform* (Leiden 1973) 72.

beings for the express purpose of gain and domination; and, what is more, there are so many splendid ceremonies invented by human beings, under human inspiration, for the glory of human beings. In such cases, the worst offenders are usually princes, bishops, and theologians. Along with them the common people go astray as well, forming topsy-turvy judgments about most matters, setting the greatest store on things that have the least importance, and likewise neglecting those things that are especially important. Sometimes powerful people misuse the witlessness of the multitude for their own advantage. Likewise, the multitude itself partly holds so tightly to what is familiar to it that, even if wise bishops have brought it to the point of making some changes for the better, it protests loudly, confusing heaven and earth; partly it is so inclined to wickedness that, if you give it any release from Judaism,[206] it gallops willy-nilly into extremes of impiety, like a horse that has thrown off its reins and rider. Called from Judaism to Christianity, it is carried away to paganism.

Now if this plague had taken hold of one or two cities, it could be cured by the counsel of virtuous men; but as it is, the fatal evil has pervaded all Europe, though outbreaks are greater in some places than others. What could the private advice of one person accomplish, given to this or that commonwealth? So weighty a matter demands the sober agreement of princes and cities; not only that, they must meanwhile put aside their private aims, and banish far off all rash and precipitate action. There yet remains a powerful influence in preachers and schoolmasters, who instruct the tender youth; in choosing them we must apply the greatest care.[207]

People will say that most princes and bishops are gazing elsewhere. Then let the public take the lead in pondering this matter on its own, lest God, provoked by our crimes, perhaps implant in princes an intention to punish us, as often happens, as we read in the Sacred Scriptures.[208]

* * * * *

206 On Erasmus' attitude towards the Jews and Judaism see C. Augustijn 'Erasmus und die Juden' NAK 60 (1980) 22–38, S. Markish *Erasmus and the Jews* (Chicago 1986); H.A. Oberman *The Roots of Anti-semitism* (Philadelphia 1984) 38–40, 58–9; Hilmar Pabel 'Erasmus of Rotterdam and Judaism: a Reformation in the Light of Evidence' ARG 87 (1996) 9–37; and the views of Dominic Baker-Smith, CWE 63 xlix–lv.

207 Cf Ep 1690:102–10. On the importance of the choice of good teachers see *De pueris instituendis* CWE 26 298, 299, 313–15, 324–6 and *De recta pronuntiatione* CWE 26 372–4.

208 Cf Ep 1640:45–7 where Erasmus mentions Pharaoh, Nebuchadnezzar, and Cyrus as instruments of God's will; see Exod 1:8–23; 2 Kings 25:1–21; Jer 21:1–10; Ezra 1:1–11; Isa 45:1.

Therefore, let the first remedy be that each recognize his own wickedness and amend his life. Thus, perhaps, the Lord, leaving aside his anger and becoming propitious, may bend the minds of princes to more wholesome counsel. Otherwise, Scripture offers bad omens for our complaints: 'as the priest is, so shall the people be';[209] and, 'I have caused tyrants and hypocrites to reign on account of the sins of the people.'[210] And you should not be so eager to overthrow the existing order that you fail to consider whether what succeeds it will be better. For change, quite apart from the strife that it usually brings with it, often tends towards the worse. Such is the unfortunate condition of human affairs; remedies are sometimes harsher than the very evils we are eager to cure.[211] In fact, at no period has Christendom enjoyed such a happily ordered state that we do not find that there have been numerous serious complaints.[212] How often does blessed Paul complain about false apostles, renegades, and heretics![213] How many complaints does Jerome make about bishops, elders, holy virgins, and monks![214]

It has always been and will always be the case that pious and spiritual people will have things to complain of and endure. And so I urge good sense among those who are eager to change everything: they sin no less seriously than those who doggedly hold onto every received tradition, whether rightly or wrongly.[215] I urge even more circumspection by those who try

* * * * *

209 Hos 4:9 and Isa 24:2
210 Job 34:30 Vulgate: 'who causes a hypocrite to reign on account of the sins of the people.'
211 This is an opinion often expressed by Erasmus concerning the reform movement; see Epp 1523:33–5; and *De libero arbitrio* CWE 76 12.
212 Cf Ep 1523:58–60.
213 See eg 2 Cor 11:13; Col 2:8, 16, 20–3; 1 Tim 1:19–20, 4:1–2, 6:3–4; 2 Tim 4:3–5; Titus 3:9–11.
214 Cf Jerome Ep 52 (letter 2 in Erasmus' edition, trans with Erasmus' summary, annotations, antidote, and postscript in CWE 61 135–54). In his description of the ideal life of a cleric, Jerome is more implicitly than explicitly criticizing the lives of bad clerics. In his *Antidote* against misconstruing Jerome's intention, Erasmus underlines what he had said in letter 1 that Jerome 'has overstated his case and has used hyperbole' when he demands of clerics that they embrace absolute poverty (Ep 61:132). In letter 2 he argues that 'Jerome was excessively forceful here' on account of the decline of true piety among clerics and their growing desire for riches. Jerome's effort to spur clerics to poverty was intended to have them adopt at least a middle way and 'be content with a moderate use of wealth' (CWE 61 152).
215 Cf Ep 1369:57–68.

to accomplish such change all at once, in hot haste; not even monarchs and primates of the church would, I believe, succeed at that. They object that the kingdom of this world has driven its roots through all the ranks of human society, and that this net has been woven with indissoluble knots, in such a way that it cannot be untied, and must be torn apart. I will not discuss here how impious it is to rebel against powers that have been ordained by God,[216] nor how unprofitable it is to undertake what you cannot accomplish – if indeed Johannes Cochlaeus is right about what he claims certain people have conceived,in his book defending free will against Melanchthon;[217] I myself have not yet discovered such a conception.

But let them imagine that their goals are right, and have been accomplished: namely, that the very name of emperor has been extinguished, the pope in Rome reduced to size, the bishops bound to the ministry of the divine word as if to the grinding-wheel, that the priests' and monks' houses have been broken up, human laws annulled, and ceremonies abolished, along with anything else that, according to their protests, obstructs the gospel's force. Will life at once lack evils? On the contrary, the danger is that we will long for what we cast aside, once worse conditions have come in to fill the gap. What good does it do, after raising so great a disturbance, not to escape slavery and tyranny, but only to change tyrants, perhaps for the worse?[218] To change hypocrisies, but not to escape hypocrisy?

At this point we ought to recall the fox, an example from fables, who was unwilling to allow biting-flies, once gorged, to be plucked off, lest thirsty ones take their place.[219] They will say, 'Are we therefore to endure this and that forever?' I answer, known evils are endured with less trouble

* * * * *

216 Cf Rom 13:1–4.
217 Compare what Erasmus writes in the next paragraph with Johannes Cochlaeus *De libero arbitrio hominis adversus locos communes Philippi Melanthonis libri duo* (1525) A 3 r v, cited and quoted in ASD IX-1 261 nn673–80. Cochlaeus assails the Lutherans for what he perceives as their treasonous and revolutionary madness, their rejection of human laws, their following the example of the Bohemians in the plundering of churches and monasteries and the robbing of clergy etc. Johannes Cochlaeus (Dobnek d 1552), trained in scholastic theology and humanism, was a prolific polemicist on behalf of the Roman church against Luther and Melanchthon; cf CEBR I 321–3; OER I 369–70; M. Samuel-Scheyder *Johannes Cochlaeus: Humaniste et adversaire de Luther* (Nancy 1993) and *Spongia* above 94 n326.
218 Cf Epp 1495:167–70.
219 Cf *Adagia* IV vii 43: *Muscae* 'Flies' CWE 36 305–6; also Aristotle (*Rhetoric* 2.20.22) and Plutarch (*Moralia* 790C) both of whom ascribe this fable to Aesop; see ASD II-8 93:434n and ASD IX-1 261:684–5n.

than unknown ones.[220] Furthermore, effort should be directed not so much to the undoing of the existing order as to each individual's private correction of his own character. God will assist those who do so, and will inspire the minds of the princes by his spirit. The outcome of disturbances and revolts has always been unprofitable. What I have been saying about princes and bishops I judge likewise applies to the magistrates of cities, whose sober agreement will suppress revolt and break off the immoderate violence of both parties. Our affairs will meet with a happier outcome if faults are healed in such a way that people receive no injury, especially the innocent; if institutions founded on just principles are not torn to pieces; if things that ought to be changed are not destroyed instead, but rather some are kept for their proper time, and others are put up with; if, finally, wrongs are gradually restored to a better condition, just as they gradually crept into customary usage. What does the surgeon or cauterer accomplish if a fever has spread through all the veins of the body?[221] Little by little the harmful humour must be removed, until a healthful balance returns. If Christ's spirit should see fit to incline the minds of kings, prelates, magistrates, and peoples to a plan of this sort, as is my daily prayer, then I would not be reluctant to contribute my advice, however small a share I have of it. But if magistrates sometimes overthrow institutions that appear to deserve just and equitable correction, then we must take care, with the greatest vigilance, that people are not injured who are capable of being healed. At least we must see to it that the innocent are not entangled in the evils of the guilty, and that everywhere, as much as possible, civil concord is securely preserved. Such are my remarks to people who have been spreading unjust complaints, alleging that I keep back advice by which I could amend the schism.[222] I have poured out whatever I conceal in my heart.[223] I confess; I do conceal there many things of an excellent, and many things of a wretched nature: excellent desires, because I wish well for Christendom, and wretched suffering, because I observe matters daily getting worse

* * * * *

220 Cf *Hyperaspistes* 1 CWE 76 117 where Erasmus states: 'But it is easier to put up with evils to which you are accustomed. Therefore I will put up with this church until I see a better one, and it will have to put up with me until I become better.' See *Adagia* III ix 91: *Malorum assuetudo* CWE 35 352–3.
221 A favourite simile of Erasmus. Cf Epp 1352:26–31; and *De libero arbitrio* CWE 76 47 where Erasmus draws on Origen *On First Principles* 3 1 13; see Origen *On First Principles* tr G.W. Butterworth (New York 1966) 181–2.
222 Cf Ep 1616:11–12).
223 C. Augustijn (ASD IX-1 262:707n) thinks these lines refer to the charge that Erasmus was too fearful to express his true opinion (above nn97–99).

through the immoderation of both parties. I fear this outcome: that after many vast calamities we will begin to want measures which we cannot now even hear mentioned.

Now I must briefly placate those who are upset because, in the letter I wrote to the assembly at Baden,[224] I allegedly rendered Oecolampadius' cause the worse, just as in this pamphlet. In fact, there is no mention of Oecolampadius in the letter; I am only beating off the false charge that that foolish, lying pamphlet brings against me. If others possess any portion of light or inspiration, I am not one to stand in the way of God's Spirit. But I will not allow an opinion to be forced upon me that never found a foothold in my mind, never issued from my lips, never was suggested or expressed in any letter of mine. If such a thing happens on occasion to harm Oecolampadius' business, it ought not be imputed to me but to that unfortunate pamphlet: if it had allowed me to keep quiet in this business, I would gladly have done so. I do not think anyone has so little sense of fairness that he would represent this as a just demand: that I have so much consideration for the disputants, that I must keep silent to please them, in the face of misrepresentation that brings me into manifest hazard of my reputation and life; especially when my conscience protests. Against conscience I would certainly have cast a hard stone, if I had allowed the naive, deceived by my name as a trick, to be drawn into an opinion that I have not presumed to admit, because it has not yet convinced me. I have done my duty; I have given an account of my action to the public. For the rest, I pray that the Lord make us all of one accord in sound teaching and unfeigned charity.[225] Amen.

* * * * *

224 Ep 1708 and introduction
225 Cf 2 Cor 6:6; Titus 2:1.

EPISTLE AGAINST
THE FALSE EVANGELICALS

Epistola contra quosdam qui se falso iactant pseudevangelicos

translated by
GARTH TISSOL

introduced and annotated by
LAUREL CARRINGTON

The *Epistola contra pseudevangelicos*, published in 1529, presents a troubling spectacle for those whose impressions of Erasmus are shaped by his lyrical articulation of the *philosophia Christi* in such works as the *Paraclesis* and the *Enchiridion*. Here we find him attacking a younger colleague, Gerard Geldenhouwer, who for years had been a trusted friend. Moreover, following this initial attack, Erasmus proceeded to denounce the entire Swiss and South German Reformation[1] (as distinct from the Lutheran Reformation) in the most unambiguous terms, not shrinking from sweeping accusations of immorality and licentiousness among its supporters. Finally, the *Epistola contra pseudevangelicos* was the opening salvo in what would become a bitter controversy with the Strasbourg reformer Martin Bucer, who responded in March of 1530 with the *Epistola apologetica*, to which Erasmus subsequently replied, in August of that year, with the *Epistola ad fratres Inferioris Germaniae*.[2] There is an unfortunate irony in the fact that Bucer, as leader of the Reformation in Strasbourg, had fashioned his own approach along lines that were distinctly Erasmian in his rejection of extreme solutions, his attempts at mediation between Luther and Zwingli, and his desire to protect those on all sides from persecution and death.

Erasmus wrote the *Epistola contra pseudevangelicos* at a time of personal disillusionment and instability. He had recently moved to Freiburg from Basel, his home since 1521, following the triumph of the Reformation there in February of 1529.[3] His life for almost a decade had been consumed by the kind of religious controversy he had always most sought to rise above in his advocacy of spiritual renewal through the *philosophia Christi*, aided by the civilizing influences of an education in classical literature. His own calls for reform in the Roman church, combined with his controversial philological examination of the New Testament, left him vulnerable to attacks by conservative Catholics – attacks which became increasingly pointed when Martin Luther's vehemence threatened to shatter the unity of the faith. Thus one of Erasmus' bitterest complaints in the *Epistola contra pseudevangelicos* is that the reckless extremes of the Protestant reformers have so polarized the debate that virtually all criticism of authority has now become impossible.

* * * * *

1 A point made by C. Augustijn in his introduction to the *Epistola contra pseudevangelicos* ASD IX-1 267, 277; in this text, two of the three references to Luther highlight the differences between him and the 'pseudo-evangelicals' whom Erasmus sees as his adversaries (below 216).
2 See *Epistola contra pseudevangelicos* below 239 and n121.
3 See *Epistola contra pseudevangelicos* below 231 n76.

The immediate cause for Erasmus' writing in this case was a pamphlet recently published by Geldenhouwer,[4] reproducing fragmentary comments from Erasmus' *Apologia ad monachos quosdam Hispanos* in support of Geldenhouwer's own views advocating toleration for heretics.[5] It was only one in a series of such incidents for Erasmus, in which leaders of the Swiss and South German Reformation had attempted to enlist him in their cause. Such attempts had continued even after Erasmus had tried to establish in his debate with Luther that he remained an orthodox Catholic. These incidents were all the more painful in that, as in the case of Geldenhouwer, they were typically the occasion for the destruction of what had been a friendship. Yet if various younger adherents of evangelical reform repeatedly tried to draw Erasmus into their cause against his will, it was because they saw his own calls for reform as their inspiration. This was certainly true in the unfortunate case of Conradus Pellicanus, who based his claims of Erasmus' support on readings of Erasmus' earlier works, even though Erasmus believed Pellicanus was deliberately attempting to trick him into supporting heresy. The subsequent publication in 1526 of Leo Jud's treatise added to Erasmus' sense of victimization.[6]

It is in the context of these events that we must understand Erasmus' expressions of anger at Geldenhouwer and his cohorts in the *Epistola contra*

* * * * *

4 For Geldenhouwer *Epistola Erasmi*, or *Epistolae aliquot de re evangelica et de haereticorum poenis*, and his *D. Erasmi annotationes in leges pontificus et Caesareus de haereticis*, both published in 1529, see *Epistola contra pseudevangelicos* below 223–4.nn32, 35. For other pamphlets in support of the Reformation, see n30.

5 See below 223. For Erasmus' debates with Luther, see the *De libero arbitrio* of 1524, and, in response to Luther's *De servo arbitrio* of 1525, *Hyperaspistes* 1 and 2 (CWE 76, 77). With rare exceptions, sixteenth-century defenders of religious liberty were advocates not of toleration in a modern sense, meaning a right of dissent, but of toleration in an older sense, meaning a willingness to put up with dissenters until the truth should be made clear; see István Bejczy 'Tolerantia: A Medieval Concept' *Journal of the History of Ideas* 58 (1997) 365–384; see also Mario Turchetti 'Religious Concord and Political Tolerance in Sixteenth- and Seventeenth-Century France' *Sixteenth Century Journal* 22 1 (1991) 15–25.

6 For Conradus Pellicanus, a Hebrew scholar who taught in Basel and Zürich, see Ep 1637 introduction; for Leo Jud, a colleague of Zwingli's in Zürich, CEBR II 248–50. Jud's pamphlet was entitled *Des hochgelerten Erasmi von Roterdam, und D. M. Luthers maynung von nachtmal*. Erasmus' response was to write the *Detectio praestigiarum*, clarifying his position regarding the Eucharist and defending himself against Jud's interpretation of his writings. For this controversy, see introductory note to the *Detectio praestigiarum* above 150–6.

pseudevangelicos. Geldenhouwer was born in Nijmegen in 1482, and like Erasmus he was educated at Deventer. A member of the order of the Crosier Fathers (Crucigeri),[7] he soon became part of the humanist circle at Louvain. An important turning point in his life occurred when he was appointed secretary to Philip of Burgundy, at the time of his consecration as bishop of Utrecht in 1517. The bishop was also a patron of Erasmus, and until Philip's death in 1524, most of Erasmus' correspondence with the bishop went through Geldenhouwer.[8] Thus Erasmus' opening to the *Epistola contra pseudevangelicos*, in referring to Philip of Burgundy and his brother David, likewise recalls happier days in Erasmus' relationship with Geldenhouwer.[9]

Geldenhouwer's attraction to the Reformation began after the bishop's death, during a visit to Wittenberg in 1525 on behalf of Christian II of Denmark.[10] There he encountered Luther, and was won over. In 1526 he married, and in 1527 he settled in Strasbourg, where he was living at the point of his quarrel with Erasmus. He eventually obtained a teaching position in Augsburg in 1531 and remained there until he died in 1542. His main activity on behalf of the evangelical reform consisted of addressing pamphlets to various governing authorities, and it was in so doing that he fell afoul of Erasmus. Two works in particular included pieces from Erasmus' writing: One to the 1529 Diet of Speier (assembled under the authority of Emperor Charles v's brother, Archduke Ferdinand of Austria), where the Reformation was under attack; and another addressed to the Charles v himself.[11] Erasmus was an honorary councillor to Charles v, and had important friends and supporters in Ferdinand's entourage. For Geldenhouwer in his pamphlets to quote Erasmus as having rejected the death penalty for heretics was tantamount to slander, for it implied that Erasmus wished to deprive his Hapsburg patrons of their power to punish those who would threaten public order.

It is likely that Geldenhouwer, like Pellicanus before him, was not acting out of a desire to harm Erasmus.[12] Rather, he assumed that the author

* * * * *

7 The Crucigeri were an order of canons regular, founded in the Low Countries in the thirteenth century.
8 This included a letter that Erasmus wrote in honour of the bishop's inauguration (Ep 645), which Erasmus addressed to Geldenhouwer, and which Geldenhouwer reissued as part of his own commendation, the *Epistola de triumphali ingressu Philippi de Burgundia*. It is printed in Prinsen *Collectanea* 217–18.
9 See the opening paragraph below 218.
10 See Peremans *Correspondance* 71.
11 See *Epistola contra pseudevengelicos* below 223–4 nn32, 35.
12 Despite the sharpness of Erasmus' attack on him in this treatise, Geldenhouwer continued to speak well of Erasmus in his later writings: *Gerard Geldenhouwer*

of such works as *Scarabeus aquilam quaerit*[13] and the unbridled critique of princes in the *Praise of Folly*[14] would be a good source to cite in a letter call-ing for a softening of royal violence. Erasmus himself had indeed written eloquently in several works in favour of instruction and correction rather than force in response to heresy. Three texts in particular provided Gelden-houwer with material for his argument: *Apologia contra Iacobi Latomi dialogum de tribus linguas (Dialogus II 117)*,[15] *Apologia adversus monachos quosdam His-panos (Titulus IV)*,[16] and *Supputatio calumniarum Natalis Bedae (Propositio 32)*.[17]

The *Apologia contra Latomi dialogum*, written in March of 1519, was Eras-mus' defence against Louvain theologian Jacobus Latomus (Jacques Mas-son), who had published a dialogue attacking the approach to New Tes-tament scholarship promoted by Erasmus, based on language studies and the tools of philology.[18] Latomus included the charge that humanist schol-ars challenged the church's authority to place limits on doctrinal debates, claiming that 'they disapprove of canon law, even of the penalties decreed against heretics and schismatics, and that they say that the church defends its beliefs not by reasoned argument but by terror.'[19] In his answer to this point, Erasmus turned to Augustine, who advocated moderation against the Donatists. He emphasized a theme that would recur throughout his writ-ings on the subject: that heretics should be persuaded rather than coerced into right thinking. Erasmus himself points out that what may seem hereti-cal to one person could seem perfectly acceptable to someone else.

The response to Béda, syndic of the theological faculty at Paris, is considerably longer. Erasmus' *Supputatio*, published in 1527, answers a de-tailed critique of his *Paraphrases*, which Béda had issued in the previous year. Among other points at issue, Béda had focused on Erasmus' para-phrase on Matthew 13 and its implications for the church's authority to respond to heresy. This chapter of Matthew presents two parables relat-ing to sowing. In the second, a householder had sown his field with good seed, only to discover later that an enemy had secretly sown tares among the grain. When his servants asked him whether they should root out the

* * * * *

van Nijmegen (1482–1542), *Historische Werken* ed István Bejczy and Saskia Stege-
    man, with Michiel Verwij (Hilversum 1998) 11.
13 *Adagia* III vii 1: 'A dung-beetle hunting an eagle' CWE 35 178–214
14 *Moria* ASD IV-3 675–169 / CWE 27:135–6
15 LB IX 105A–B / CWE 71:82
16 LB IX 1043B–1060F
17 LB IX 580C–583F
18 See Rummel *Catholic Critics* I 63–94 for an account of this dispute.
19 *Apologia contra Latomi dialogum* CWE 71 82

weeds, the householder replied, no, let them grow together, and then separate them at harvest time.[20] To this Erasmus comments, 'The householder,
that is, God, does not wish the false apostles and leaders of heresies to be
destroyed, but tolerated; if perhaps they repent, then they are turned from
weeds into wheat, and if they do not repent they will be preserved to be
judged by him, to whom one day they will pay the penalty.'[21]

In defending this reading of the parable against Béda, Erasmus makes
several necessary distinctions. First, he acknowledges that heretics may need
to be punished; what he objects to is the extreme punishment of the death
penalty. Second, he distinguishes between the role of church authority
and secular authority. Church authority expresses itself properly through
preaching and exhortation, not through bloodshed. Finally, Erasmus distinguishes between heretics who are simply people living in error from
heretics who combine error with active disturbance of the peace. To the extent that such people infringe on the authority of the prince, they can be
punished, but only on the authority of the prince, not of the church. Citing
Augustine once again, Erasmus will allow that the prince may be moved
by God to punish heretics who disturb the tranquillity of the church, but
he will not have bishops calling for the execution of those 'who are heretics
and nothing more.'[22] These opinions are essentially in keeping with the
canons of the Fourth Lateran Council of 1215, which hold secular authorities responsible for banishing heretics and forbid clerics any role in death
sentences.[23] For Erasmus, the reference point, once again, is Augustine, and
the church of that time: 'But to the bishops of old, the ultimate penalty was
anathema.'[24] Theologians who urge judges to consign people to the flames

* * * * *

20 Matt 13:24–30, 36–43; see *Epistola contra pseudevanglicos* below 225 n50. The
paraphrase is found in LB VII 79C–81B / CWE 45:212–13.
21 *Supputatio* LB IX 580C: *Paterfamilias, id est, Deus non vult Pseudo-Apostolos et
Haeresiarchas extingui, sed tolerari; si forte resipiscant, et ex zizaniis vertantur in
triticum: quod si non resipiscant, serventur suo iudicio (sic) cui poenas dabunt ali-
quando.* Erasmus begins by remarking on the fact that Béda has misquoted
him, substituting *iudicio* for *iudici*.
22 *Supputatio* LB IX 581A: *Nec [Augustine] damnat si Deus concitet animos Principum
ad coercendos eos qui turbant Ecclesiae tranquilitatem. Sed quis unquam audivit or-
thodoxos Episcopos concitasse Reges ad trucidandos haereticos, qui nihil aliud essent
quam haeretici?* 'Nor does he [Augustine] condemn it if God rouse the spirits
of princes to repress those who disturb the peace of the church. But who ever
heard of orthodox bishops rousing kings to kill those heretics and nothing
more?'
23 Canon 3; canon 18.
24 *Supputatio* LB IX 580F

are guilty of bloodshed, ambition, and lust for power, the very opposite of the spirit of Christ.

Erasmus emphasizes that he is speaking to clergy, not to princes. Augustine may have exhorted the emperor to spare the Donatists, Erasmus writes, 'but I neither exhort nor dissuade princes from killing heretics; I am demonstrating the duty of the priest.'[25] Béda's great error is that he cannot tell the difference between secular magistrates and leaders of the apostolic church, between capital punishment and anathema, or between capital punishment and other penalties administered by the secular arm. These distinctions will be of paramount importance for Erasmus in his quarrel with Geldenhouwer, for he emphatically contends in the *Epistola contra pseudevangelicos* that he never intended to deprive the secular arm of the death penalty.[26] It will be for Geldenhouwer to take that step, a step Erasmus refuses to take with him.

The third and final text, from *Apologia adversus monachos quosdam Hispanos*, touches on the distinctive character of the Spanish Inquisition.[27] In Spain, the response to Erasmus throughout this period was highly polarized: while Erasmus suffered from the attacks of conservatives such as Jacobus Lopez Stunica, he also had strongly loyal supporters among humanists and biblical scholars, as well as important prelates. His works, including his *Enchiridion* and his New Testament *Paraphrases*, became the occasion for a conference at Valladolid in the summer of 1527 for the purpose of investigating Erasmus' works in detail.[28] Pope Clement VII instructed Spain's inquisitor-general to determine whether Erasmus' works were sufficiently orthodox to be approved reading, while at the same time stating his personal conviction that Erasmus was a good defender of the faith against Martin Luther. The results of the conference were mixed: some of the assembled theologians were supportive of Erasmus' orthodoxy, but others were critical. Many verdicts included statements of overall support intermixed with specific points of contention. However, the outcome was left uncertain when the conference was interrupted in August by the plague and never resumed. Erasmus' *Apologia adversus monachos quosdam Hispanos*

* * * * *

25 *Supputatio* LB IX 582F
26 See below 224.
27 Unlike the inquisitors in most dioceses of the church, who were appointed by the bishop, Spain's inquisitor-general was appointed by the crown; see Henry Kamen *The Spanish Inquisition: An Historical Revision* (London 1997).
28 For the Valladolid Conference, CWE Ep 1786, Allen Epp 1814, 1847, and the correspondence of Erasmus' Spanish friends in CWE 12 520–35.

is his response to the criticisms that were recorded from the Valladolid meeting.[29]

As in the case of Béda, Erasmus' Spanish critics were suspicious of his interpretation of the parable of the sower, regarding it as an attack on the Inquisition itself. In his reply, Erasmus allows that he supports a judicial process for exposing heresy, but distinguishes between an *inquisitio sancta* and an *inquisitio sycophantica*. The holy Inquisition resembles a father's questioning his son in order to provide for his instruction, or a doctor questioning a patient in order to cure him; in the same way those who have authority in the church can question someone to see whether he is in error, with a view towards correction if possible. If this should be impossible, then the unhealthy member can in extreme cases be cut off, by which Erasmus means excommunicated, not killed.[30]

Erasmus' emphasis throughout his reply is that his view of the proper use of church authority draws on the Fathers and the early church, while his opponents have departed from this tradition; it is they who are the innovators. He emphasizes the support of Augustine for his position, adding the names of Jerome, Chrysostom, and Theophylactus. 'How does it concern this matter what Remigius, Anselm, or Béda think? I present Saint Augustine as the font and parent of all scholastic theology, of which they boast more than anything who provoke these tragedies.'[31] While the heretics of the past attacked major tenets of the faith and were even violent criminals into the bargain, today people are charged with heresy over trifles: 'In these times someone is dragged to the flames who doubts that the Roman pontiff has authority in purgatory.'[32] Erasmus blames the schools themselves for having created such traps in their searching out of fine points.

Throughout these three responses to his Catholic critics, Erasmus shows a marked distrust of the motives of those churchmen whose accusations bring their victims before the courts. He emphasizes that the emperor has power to punish those who are legitimately convicted,[33] but lay authorities at all levels are guilty of allowing the reports of clerical accusers to

* * * * *

29 See Rummel *Catholic Critics* II 81–105; see also Marcel Bataillon *Erasme et l'Espagne* rev ed (Geneva 1991) I 253–99, and Lu Ann Homza 'Erasmus as Hero or Heretic?' *Renaissance Quarterly* 50 (1977) 78–113.
30 *Apologia adversus monachos* LB IX 1054B–C
31 *Apologia adversus monachos* LB IX 1058D–E
32 *Apologia adversus monachos* LB IX 1057D
33 *Apologia adversus monachos* LB IX 1055D

stand unchallenged, and of condemning the accused without even knowing the details of the cases.[34] Thus while Erasmus does not seek to disarm the princes in the conduct of affairs of state, he does exhort civil authorities to act responsibly and, to the greatest possible extent, with clemency: '[My interpretation] teaches the gentleness of the gospel, it does not deprive the prince of the right to use the sword.'[35]

It is not difficult to understand how Geldenhouwer, whose relations with Erasmus had been so friendly, would find in opinions such as these the support he hoped to find from a highly esteemed figure – one enjoying the patronage of virtually all the important princes of Europe. Thus he drew together a selection of statements, condensing a number of opinions from Erasmus' long arguments, into a two-page set of 'annotations.'[36] He stressed Erasmus' distinction between heretics and criminals, and between ordinary heretics and those who teach blasphemy. He likewise highlighted Erasmus' contention that traditionally the utmost punishment that the church could invoke was excommunication. In none of these are Erasmus' views actually falsified. However, unlike Erasmus, who addressed his replies to clergy, Geldenhouwer marshalled his arguments to persuade princes, in particular Emperor Charles v. Furthermore, to these annotations he added words of his own, openly exhorting Charles and the princes to protect those whom the Roman pontiffs had named as heretics.

One of Geldenhouwer's arguments in his letter to Charles is that the label of 'heretic' has been placed on certain people by the bishop of Rome and his entourage. However, to those so judged, it is the pope and his supporters who are the real heretics, and not only heretics, but also slaughterers and blasphemers.[37] Geldenhouwer proceeds to cast the history of the church in terms of a priestly usurpation of the freedom of the gospel. The good shepherd Christ said that his sheep would hear and know his voice, but a select few, the bishops and the priests, began to say that they were the leaders, that they were the ones to be listened to, that only they were the ones to administer the word of Christ.[38] Worse yet, they cleverly enlisted well-meaning emperors into supporting their claims through bloodshed. The emperors themselves never demanded this power; the impetus came from the clergy.

* * * * *

34 *Apologia adversus monachos* LB IX 1055F
35 *Apologia adversus monachos* LB IX 1056D
36 Prinsen *Collectanea* 179–80
37 Prinsen *Collectanea* 182–3
38 Prinsen *Collectanea* 185

Geldenhouwer's implications are clear: The laws that give such power to princes are a fabrication by the clergy to enhance their own tyranny; not only are such laws not a valid exercise of secular authority, but the resulting savagery is a blot on the royal office. This is the step that Erasmus himself would not take, and in his *Epistola contra pseudevangelicos* he emphatically sets out to clarify the difference between his beliefs and Geldenhouwer's. From there he launches his attack on the Reformation as well, particularly on those of the Swiss and South German party who have disassociated themselves from Luther.

Geldenhouwer's *Annotations* were published in Strasbourg, and Erasmus' response hit at the heart of the Strasbourg movement by attacking its acknowledged leader, Martin Bucer.[39] Ultimately, the subject of the treatment of heretics would be overshadowed by Erasmus' quarrel with the Reformation itself. His attack is two-pronged: on the one hand, he denounces the personal morals and the methods of the 'pseudo-evangelicals' – an approach he believes is perfectly fair, since the benefits of the new theology ought to reveal themselves in the lives of those who embrace it, if their reforms have any legitimacy. He also highlights divisions within the Protestant movement by emphasizing the split between Luther and the Swiss and South Germans. Finally, he attacks the latter in respect to their goals for the church, both from the standpoint of what they wish to accomplish and from that of what they have brought about. What they wish to accomplish is the reversal of hundreds of years of church history, which is wrong-headed for at least two reasons: First is the historical argument that there is no way one can reasonably expect to return to a past that is long gone. Erasmus also contends that even if one could, one would see that the customs of the early church were in many cases far less worthy of imitation than those of the present. As for what the reformers have actually accomplished, Erasmus argues that rather than bringing freedom and peace to Christendom, they have brought tumults, warfare, and a devastating retaliation from the Roman church.

Bucer would take up his pen in defence of the evangelical reform, answering Erasmus point for point, and Erasmus' reply (*Epistola ad fratres Inferioris Germaniae*) would be as relentless as the *Epistola contra pseudevangelicos*. Thus while Erasmus may have aimed to inspire thoughtful reflection on moderation, the ensuing exchange reveals the hardening of his position

* * * * *

39 See above 208 and n2. Erasmus seems to have targeted Bucer not merely as the leader of the new church in Strasbourg, but also as a reformer with a reputation for using deceptive means to advance the gospel

in relation to the Reformation – just as positions were hardening all over Europe. Erasmus at times seems to say that he still believes the two sides could come together, as when he writes, 'Let us, moreover, make a special effort to join our prayers and beseech God to give up his wrath, become propitious to us, and win over the hearts of all, inducing us on both sides, in evangelical sincerity, to change our lives for the better.'[40] Yet even here he acknowledges that the schism is beyond reasonable, human solutions. Whatever intentions Erasmus may have had to preserve what was positive in both the Roman church and in the Protestant reform, ultimately he would be forced to take his stand in opposition against those whom he called 'false evangelicals.'

LC

* * * * *

40 See *Epistola contra pseudevangelicos* below 245

EPISTLE AGAINST
THE FALSE EVANGELICALS

ERASMUS OF ROTTERDAM TO VULTURIUS NEOCOMUS, GREETINGS.[1]
A certain bookseller gave me a cap, which once belonged to David, bishop
of Utrecht.[2] Covered with tufts of silk, it was of no use to me, but pleased
me on this account, because it brought back recollections both of the man
himself and of his brother Philip, who succeeded him in office.[3] Under the
first of these I was initiated into sacred offices, while the other I considered
to be a highly zealous supporter of my every advantage. He also wanted me
to have in my possession, as a remembrance, a ring, adorned with a brilliant
sapphire and worn in former times by his brother David.[4] The memory of
both men is sacred to me, first because in their appearance they restored

* * * * *

1 In his greeting, Erasmus renames Gerardus Geldenhouwer (who also went
by the name 'Gerard Noviomagus'), calling him 'Vulturius Neocomus.' The
name 'Vulturius' is a pun on Geldenhouwer's first name, the first syllable of
which resembles the Dutch word for 'vulture,' which is 'Gier.' 'Neocomus' is
possibly an allusion to 'Noviomagus.' See Peremans *Correspondance*; see also
Allen Ep 2441, which was appended to the second authorized edition of the
Epistola contra pseudevangelicos.
2 David of Burgundy (1427–96) was the natural son of Philip the Good (see
below n5). He was bishop of Thérouanne, 1451–57, after which he was trans-
ferred to Utrecht. This is the bishop who ordained Erasmus on 25 April 1492.
See CEBR I 226–7 and *Ecclesiastes* LB V 808B–C.
3 Philip of Burgundy, bishop of Utrecht (1464–1524), was yet another natural
son of Philip the Good. He became bishop in Utrecht in 1517; before this
he had been admiral of the Netherlands (see CEBR I 231). Erasmus dedicated
his *Querela pacis* (CWE 27 289–322) to him (see Ep 603). Philip replied both
to Erasmus directly and through Geldenhouwer, his secretary; see Ep 682 for
Erasmus' expression of appreciation for Philip's patronage and his reliance
on Geldenhouwer as an advocate; he ends the letter with the words, 'Farewell
most learned, most kind-hearted Gerard.' See also Epp 727 and 728.
4 On the subject of the ring, see the introductions to Ep 1141 and Allen I 43.

to us their great and illustrious father Philip, called 'the Good'[5] – and you could not find among the dukes of Brabant anyone more praiseworthy; and second, because they were pre-eminent in their zeal for peace and their love of religion. In this respect also they restored their most praiseworthy father to us. The valour of the one brother was tested by frequent revolts,[6] and was consequently the more renowned; but the valour of the other did not avail him for long, since he was already in his declining years when called to the office of prince-bishop. Then, even more contrary to his heart's inclination, he was embroiled in violent wars by his connection to the Emperor Charles,[7] whereupon he left the earth behind and travelled to a happier abode.

As for what you tell me about your burdensome poverty,[8] I am not so hard up that I could not share some gold pieces with an old friend, nor so niggardly that I would begrudge doing so. But how little help would my generosity provide for relieving your poverty! I have very modest means, and there is not much left over for my necessities. This little body of mine, which was delicate even when it enjoyed youth, requires much expense. Old age requires still more, and ill health a huge amount. These are twin diseases, and both incurable; for just as doctors have no cure for old age, they say too that the stone cannot be cured in old men.[9] I am already paying out a good portion to my servants, both presently and formerly in my employ; to messengers and letter-bearers; to those who by their diligence contribute some relief to my labours, that is, those who hunt up old manuscripts,

* * * * *

5 Philip the Good, duke of Burgundy (1396–1467), the third Valois duke of Burgundy, son of John the Fearless and Margaret of Bavaria. He conquered Brabant in 1430.

6 Bishop David had to flee Utrecht in 1477 because of an insurrection in that city; he was unable to return until 1492.

7 The lands of the prince-bishops of Utrecht lay between the Hapsburg provinces of Holland and Brabant and the territories of Karel van Egmond, duke of Gelderland (CEBR I 422–3), who, as a French client, was often at war with the Hapsburgs. In 1527, Henry of Bavaria, Philip's successor as prince-bishop, ceded his lands to Charles V, whereupon Hapsburg forces expelled the duke's troops from Utrecht and forced his submission.

8 Erasmus is referring to a letter that Geldenhouwer wrote to him, which is now lost. In Allen Ep 2329:89–90 Erasmus claims he had actually helped Geldenhouwer financially. Evidently Geldenhouwer also asked Erasmus' help in finding him a position (see below 222 n27). That Geldenhouwer should make such requests is evidence that he considered his relationship with Erasmus as still friendly.

9 *Adagia* II vi 37: *Ipsa senectus morbus est* 'Old age is sickness of itself' CWE 33 309–10. On Erasmus being attacked by the stone cf Allen Ep 2260:316n.

those who collate and annotate them, those who proofread my writings, and copy them.[10] In addition, you would scarcely believe how much household property I gave up when I left Basel.[11] There I had, among other conveniences, a house kept in repair at the expense of others, and furnished with other people's furniture,[12] while here I have to get everything with my own money. Finally, just as the prices of goods are going up at an inordinate rate, so also my net worth is on the decline. The emperor plays his role in a very action-packed drama,[13] so that now not even his creditors dare to dun him; and as for me – a useless honorary councillor, and a bill-collector not less sluggish than modest – far less do I have a chance to get my pension.[14] The finances of King Ferdinand are in such a state that his generosity does not extend beyond the boundary of good intentions.[15] Payments from England and Flanders nowadays arrive so trimmed and eaten away that sometimes a fourth part is lacking – whether the new coinage in England is to blame, or the altered exchange-rate, or the craftiness of the bankers.[16] In fact, for

* * * * *

10 On the subject of Erasmus' servants and their role in his work, see Bierlaire *Familia*.

11 On 13 April 1529 Erasmus left Basel to move to Freiburg. His life in Basel became impossible when that city went over to the Reformation in February of that year; see Allen Ep 2136.

12 For Erasmus' house on the Nadelberg in Basel, called 'Zur alten Treu,' see Augustijn's note, ASD IX-1 285:30–31.

13 On Erasmus' other uses of *fabula* see Ep 1389 above 35 n21, and *Purgatio adversus epistolam Lutheri* below nn15, 65, 124, 256.

14 Erasmus obtained an honorary appointment in 1516 as councillor to Emperor Charles V, as a result of efforts by Chancellor Jean Le Sauvage. He wrote *Institutio principis christiani* for Charles and was to have received an annual stipend of 200 florins, but as he indicates here, payment was not reliable; in fact, he received at most only two payments. See Epp 370:18n and 393; cf *Spongia* above n453.

15 Ferdinand (1503–64), archduke of Austria and brother of Charles V, was elected king of Bohemia in 1526, king of Hungary in 1527, and king of the Romans in 1531; he succeeded Charles as emperor in 1556, ruling until 1564. Freiburg in the Breisgau was part of Anterior Austria (Vörderösterreich), one of Ferdinand's Austrian territories; see Allen Epp 2005 and 2090.

16 Erasmus indeed had problems over the years with his various sources of income, including ecclesiastical benefices in England and Flanders; see J. Hoyoux 'Les Moyens d'Existence d'Erasme' *Bulletin de l'humanisme et Renaissance, Travaux et Documents* 5 (1944) 26–7, and Ep 1583 and Allen Ep 2332:46–53. But these lines overstate his difficulties at this stage of his life, and are unfair to his personal banker, Erasmus Schetz of Antwerp – one of the great merchant-bankers of the age: see Epp 1541 introduction, 1681, 1682, 1750, 1764, 1772, 1783.

a long time now nothing has been coming in from England or Flanders, while formerly the payment of these accounts was very reliable. I suspect that they are feeding some monster.[17] For this reason I send the trustiest of my servants there at vast expense to myself, and – a matter of closer concern to me – at serious hazard to his own safety.[18]

And yet, my good Vulturius, I am surprised that you find poverty burdensome, once you resolved to profess the evangelical life. After all, blessed Hilarion, when he discovered that he did not have enough for his boat-fare, considered it something to boast about, since without knowing it he had arrived at such perfection in the gospel.[19] Paul also boasts of knowing how to possess abundance and endure poverty, since in having nothing he possesses all things.[20] He also praises certain Hebrews, adherents of the gospel, because they received the seizure of their goods with joy.[21] Nobody, I believe, seized anything from you. You, rather, of your own accord, considered your property, scanty as it was, to be mere rubbish, and in all foresight and willingness dedicated yourself to poverty. If, furthermore, the Jews do not allow anyone among them to be poor,[22] how much more fitting is it that they who boast of the gospel relieve their brothers' need by mutual generosity, especially when evangelical frugality is content with very little. If ordinary bread and water are available, those who live by the Spirit do not long for Attic dainties.[23] They know nothing of luxury, and sustain themselves by fasting. We read that the apostles satisfied hunger by rubbing ears of grain together by hand.[24]

Someone else might perhaps be deterred by a bull of Pope Leo, which, I hear, lays a curse upon all who grant aid, in the form of water, fire, or lodging, to adherents of that doctrine.[25] But I interpret that to mean those

* * * * *

17 See *Adagia* II iv 98: *Monstrum alere* CWE 33 236: 'We speak of feeding a monster . . . to convey that some frightful thing is being concealed and kept dark.'

18 Erasmus' servant, Quirinus Talesius, travelled to England and Flanders in 1528, and from October 1529 until January 1530; see Allen Ep 2222:25n and Bierlaire *Familia* 68–70.

19 Cf Jerome *Vita Hilarii* PL 23 47B–C. Hilarion (AD 291–371?) was a Palestinian hermit.

20 Cf Phil 4:12, 2 Cor 6:10.

21 Heb 10:34

22 Lev 25:35, Deut 15:7–11

23 *Adagia* II iii 100: *Attica bellaria* CWE 33 189–90: 'anything which is beyond measure sweet and delightful.'

24 Luke 6:1

25 A reference to the papal bull that excommunicated Luther, *Decet Romanum Pontificem*, issued in January 1521. In June 1520 Pope Leo had issued the bull

who grant aid because they support the sect. If, in another case, I were to assist a brother who was in desperate need of food, doing so for no other reason than that he was a brother, I do not think that the threats of the bull would apply to me. The same I would judge to be the case, if I were to relieve a human being – even though he were a condemned man – for no other reason than that he was a human being. As long as he breathes, there is hope that he will turn to better and more fruitful courses, for, according to Theocritus, it is only the dead who have no hope.[26] In this you may think that I am merely joking, but others will not think so. You will say, 'I am not asking for financial help; I am only asking your assistance in getting me a professorship in poetry.[27] Indeed, one who has complaints to make makes but modest demands.' But I, dear Vulturius, have an even smaller supply of time than of money, and could not provide the aid you request for this purpose without a great deal of trouble, even if I had the power to provide what you ask. Nobody could be farther from the study of poetry than I am – and have been for many years.

As for what you mention about offending me, I could not be angry with such a friend, even if I wanted to. I admit that I am grieved because you rushed into that labyrinth,[28] and I wish I could get you out. I wish that you had asked my advice at that time, not the advice of certain other people, who now, as you write me, hate the very thing that they formerly encouraged. But it is rather late to complain of such things. The evil could have been remedied, had you not betrayed yourself to the world by publishing pamphlets, and even after you were warned you did not abstain from publishing them. It wasn't enough that you brought out an *Epistle to the Diet of Speier*;[29] after a short interval that ridiculous *Comet* of yours, dedicated to the Emperor Charles, burst upon us.[30] Then I warned you a second time in

* * * * *

Exsurge Domine, demanding Luther's recantation; when Luther refused he was excommunicated by the second bull.

26 Theocritus *Idylls* 4.42
27 Cf C. Augustijn ASD IX-1 273 n75.
28 See *Adagia* II x 51: *Labyrinthus* CWE 34 147–8: 'any speech or course of action which was excessively complicated and hard to unravel'
29 There has to be some confusion on Erasmus' part here. Geldenhouwer's treatise on the comet was published in Antwerp in late 1527 or early 1528, but the Diet of Speier convened from 21 February to 25 April 1529.
30 For the publication date of Geldenhouwer's *De terrifico cometa* see the previous note. The comet of the title refers to the appearance of a comet on 11 October of 1527; Geldenhouwer took the comet to be a warning from God, and in a preface to Charles v he urged the emperor to allow scope for preachers of

writing[31] to abstain from such jokes, which were rousing the anger of princes to the point of savagery, and far from helping the cause on whose success your safety depends, were severely damaging it. You answered agreeably enough, but then – as if I had urged you to undertake a similar plan again – you sent a pamphlet once again to the Diet of Speier, at which King Ferdinand was then presiding. This pamphlet bore at its front the name of Erasmus in rather large letters. Its title was *An Epistle of Erasmus*, though it was in fact a fragment culled from various places in my writings.[32] From it an inattentive reader would judge it to be my opinion that it is wrong to inflict capital punishment upon any heretic – a thing that would bring down on my head the wrath of the emperor, Ferdinand and other princes, and likewise the pope in Rome. After this fragment there followed some other things, under your own name, of a frankly seditious nature, as I hear from everyone; I have not yet had leisure to read them myself. I was greatly astonished at this action of yours – so utterly inconsistent with the very nature of civilized behaviour, and of friendship – and other people were filled with loathing. I would have lodged a protest with you, but the troubles involved in my moving are to blame for preventing me. I swallowed my resentment or rather dissimulated it,[33] but then there burst forth upon the autumn fair[34] a similar pamphlet, singing the same

* * * * *

evangelical doctrine. See Augustijn 'Geldenhouwer' 137 n38. In 1526, Geldenhouwer had published letters on the subject of tolerance addressed to Philip von Hesse and Charles of Gelderland, which were reissued in 1529; see Augustijn 'Geldenhouwer' 136 n36.

31 No letters from Erasmus to Geldenhouwer from this period are preserved, but, as Augustijn notes (ASD IX-1 271:60n), when Geldenhouwer republished the *Epistola contra pseudevangelicos*, he did not deny that Erasmus had written him in this vein.

32 The *Epistola Erasmi*, or *Epistolae aliquot de re evangelica et haereticorum poenis* (Strasbourg: C. Egenolff 1529), is known mostly through the *Epistola contra pseudevangelicos*. It was most likely a fragment from Erasmus' *Apologia adversus monachos* in addition to pieces drawn from other works; see Augustijn 'Geldenhouwer' 148; Peremans *Correspondance* 71. Apart from what Erasmus says here, there is no indication that Geldenhouwer sent copies to the Diet of Speier.

33 On *dissimulatio*, see *Spongia* above 57 n113, 97 n342, 108 n405; cf J. Trapman 'Erasmus on Lying and Simulation' in *On the Edge of Truth and Honesty: Principles and Strategies of Fraud and Deceit in the Early Modern Period* ed T. Van Houdt, Intersections: Yearbook for Early Modern Studies 2 (Leiden and Boston 2002) 33–46.

34 Ie the Frankfurt book fair

song. On its title-page, in huge letters, it declared, *Annotations of Erasmus*.[35]
The rest followed under your own name, aimed more at arousing revolt
than piety. Suppose I did, among my many books, somewhere let slip a
remark that heretics should not be executed. Was it the act of a civilized
being to take something perfectly suited to excite animosity against me,
cut it brutally from its context, and bring it before the eyes and ears of
princes, omitting everything that softened the harshness of the utterance,
or that could explain what I really meant? If a stranger did this to another
stranger, who would not find him lacking in both honesty and civilized
behaviour? But your action now is that of friend against friend – an evangelical friend against a friend who never by word or deed gave you any
handle[36] to undo our friendship.

The case is even more dismaying, because I nowhere taught such a
thing – that capital punishment should not be inflicted upon heretics,[37] nor
did I anywhere take the right of the sword away from princes,[38] since Christ
and the apostles did not take it from them.[39] I only advise, in various passages, that princes not be too hasty in taking severe measures, and that they
not readily offer an ear to indictments made by just any theologians and
monks.[40] There are schoolmen's doctrines which it is not always impious to
doubt, and in which they often do not agree among themselves; and there
is simple error:[41] one is not a heretic just because one has slipped up in
some article of faith. In cases where perversity of mind does not underlie
the error, where there is no obstinacy, the person who slipped up should be
assisted by Christian charity, not killed.[42] And besides, there are monks and

* * * * *

35 In the fall of 1529, Geldenhouwer published a collection including four of his
own letters and notes drawn from Erasmus' *Apologia adversus monachos*, with
the words: *D. Erasmi annotationes in leges pontificias et caesareas de haereticis* featured prominently on the title-page. The text is printed in Prinsen *Collectanea*
177–201; see also Augustijn 'Geldenhouer' 151–5, which discusses in detail
what is known about Geldenhouwer's publications on the subject of toleration
for heretics.
36 Cf *Adagia* I iv 4: *Ansam quaerere* CWE 31 321–2: 'on the watch for an opportunity
to go back on an agreement and invalidate it.'
37 Eg *Supputatio* LB IX 582F
38 For instance, Erasmus refers to the *ius gladii* in *Apologia contra Latomi dialogum*
CWE 71 82; *Supputatio* LB IX 580E–F; *Apologia adversus monachos* LB IX 1056D,
1059D–E.
39 Cf Luke 22:38 and Rom 13:1–7; see introductory note 212 and above 223.
40 Cf *Supputatio* LB IX 580C–D; *Apologia adversus monachos* LB IX 1055F, 1056B.
41 For 'schoolmen's doctrines' see *Ratio* Holborn 205–5 / LB V 90B; for 'simple
error,' see Ep 1000:131 n27; cf Allen Ep 1000:128n.
42 Cf *Apologia adversus monachos* LB IX 1056E.

theologians who, induced by the savagery of their natures, by stupidity, by
the delights of glory or gain, or, indeed, by private animosity, make savage
indictments. Not only do their charges consist of trivialities or matters open
to debate pro and con, they also perversely misrepresent even perfectly correct statements. You know Jacob of Hoogstraten,[43] Nicolaas of Egmond,[44]
and Béda;[45] it is enough to cite these names. I pray that they find in God a
milder judge than they themselves were in judging others. I remind such
people of Christian mildness, that they may be – as is fitting for churchmen – more vigilant to heal than to destroy. Such was Christ, such were the
apostles, such were Ambrose,[46] Cyprian,[47] and Augustine.[48] Their charity
restrained the imperial sword, as much as it could, from killing heretics.
They used their power of speech and their writings to manage the affairs
of the church, and they frequently interceded for those who were to be
killed. A prince 'not without reason bears a sword,'[49] I confess; but surely
it is the task of theologians and bishops to teach, to dispute, and to heal: to
teach those in error, to dispute with the obstinate, to heal those who have
been deceived. In a parable of the Lord's there is an admonition about not
removing tares:[50] this applies either to the church in its original, primitive

* * * * *

43 For Jacob of Hoogstraten (d 1527), see *Spongia* above 54–7 and n20. See also
   Rummel *Catholic Critics* I 135 and CEBR I 200–3.
44 For the Carmelite Nicolaas Baechem of Egmond (d 1526) see *Spongia* above
   n187.
45 See introductory note above 211. For Noël Béda (1470–1537), see *Spongia* n615;
   Rummel *Catholic Critics* II 29–59; CEBR I 116–18.
46 In Ep 916:224–8, Erasmus quotes Ambrose *Liber De Viduis* 49 PL 16 262C–263A:
   'It is not by weapons of this world that the church overcomes hostile powers,
   but by the spiritual weapons which owe their strength to God ... The church's
   weapon is faith; her weapon is prayer, which overcomes the adversary.'
47 Cf LB IX 464C, from the *Prologus supputationis*, a preliminary response to Béda's
   Annotations which Erasmus issued in 1526: 'I see that Cyprian fought heretics
   with arguments and books.'
48 On Augustine's leniency, cf Allen Ep 1983:12–15, 2157:183–218; and Erasmus'
   Apologia LB IX 105B, 464C, 580F–581A, 582D, 583C, 1054E, 1055C–D, et al.
49 Rom 13:4; Erasmus repeats here the Vulgate version: *non sine causa*, whereas
   in his *Novum Instrumentum*, he had translated: *non frustra* (Holeczek *Novum
   Instrumentum, Ad Romanos* 22). Cf paraphrase on Romans 13:4 CWE 42 74–5; in
   his *Annotationes in epistolam ad Romanos* (CWE 56 350) he does not justify his
   translation.
50 Matt 13:24–30, 36–43; cf R. Bainton 'The Parable of the Tares as a Proof Text
   for Religious Toleration to the end of the Sixteenth Century' *Church History*
   1 (1932) 67–89; M. Hoffmann 'Reformation and Toleration' in *Martin Luther
   and the Modern Mind: Freedom, Conscience, Toleration, Rights* ed M. Hoffmann
   (Lewiston, NY 1985) 85–123.

state, or to men of apostolic office, to whom no sword is entrusted other
than the sword of the gospel, 'which is the word of God.'[51] That this is my
opinion could not have escaped your notice, since some years before this
affair I made a response to Latomus,[52] then to Béda,[53] and most recently to
the extremely foolish misrepresentations offered by the Spanish monks.[54]
Once again, heresy is something that contains obvious blasphemy, that, for
example, denies Christ his divine nature or accuses the divine Scriptures
of lying; something that employs malicious contrivances to strive, through
disturbances and revolts, after riches, power, and the ruin of human affairs.
In such cases are we to bind up the prince's sword? Suppose that it not be
permitted to kill heretics, still it is lawful to kill blasphemous and seditious
men, and it is necessary to keep the commonwealth safe. Consequently, just
as those who drag men to the flames only because of some error or other
are wrong to do so, those who suppose that a civil magistrate has no right
to employ capital punishment against heretics are also wrong. But when
people who are considered heretics themselves argue that heretics should
not be killed, it should be clear even to a blind man that such people are
not defending the truth but seeking impunity for evildoers. Would not
bandits and pirates want to make a case that a Christian prince has no
right to put anyone to death? Fear, if it deters people from crime, is a
good thing. If someone does not want to be afraid of magistrates, let him
occupy himself with good pursuits, and public authority will give him no
reason to fear but will honour him, as Saint Paul advises.[55] The severity of
princes – which these people call savagery – is something necessary. And
yet it often happens, thanks to human fault, that princes endowed with a
naturally merciful nature are forced into savagery by the wickedness of
wrongdoers. Such people take advantage of their princes' leniency, first
scorning it, then jeering at it, and they interpret mildness in princes as
the sanction for impiety. This is the sort of teaching that my books offer,
whenever the context requires it, not what your frivolous sport tries to
impute to me. And why? Not because you actually have this opinion of me,
but because you want to impose on the unsophisticated.

I ask you, in the name of friendship, do you think me too little
burdened by hostility, so that your efforts are needed to add more to

* * * * *

51 Eph 6:17
52 *Apologia contra Latomi dialogum* LB IX 105A–B / CWE 71 82 (Dialogus II 117)
53 *Supputatio* LB IX 580C–583F
54 *Apologia adversus monachos* LB IX 1054B–1060F
55 Cf Rom 13:3.

my burden? I barely defend myself against so many vipers, so many crocodiles,[56] so many serpents, with the help of the favour I have with monarchs; and nothing could have greater power to alienate them than an attempt on my part to knock the sword out of their hands, and to defend those sects that they consider hateful and desire to tear out by the roots. And they would do so, were their attention not called elsewhere by the vicissitudes of events. I ask you, my friend, could an enemy do anything more hostile? I do not mean to lay an obligation on you, but for my part I have loved you for a long time now in all sincerity. I was always delighted when some advantages came your way, as if I myself had received them, and I grieved at your setbacks as if they were my own. By what crime, then, did I deserve having my life brought into danger by your contrivances? You know the anger of our rulers, you know what thunderbolts our Jupiters hurl when they are angry. 'The king's wrath,' says Solomon, 'is the messenger of death.'[57] And there is not always a good man at hand to placate his wrath; instead there are frequently malicious people at hand to pour oil on the fire.[58] You are well aware of the fact that princes often have little information, and few things receive their full attention; and no wonder, when they are distracted by so many affairs. It has not escaped your notice that slander is armed with many skills, and sometimes has great power even with the highest rulers. The innocent person is often defeated before he knows he has been indicted. And so it continues to amaze me: What do you have in mind when you publish pamphlets of this kind, one after another? If you do it in order to destroy me, then what has become of your former attitude, that was once so friendly, so pure, so sincere? What has become of the laws of friendship? Or perhaps your motive is to force me to a profession of adherence to that sect. But I would have made such a profession long ago, believe me, if this ongoing drama[59] had met with my approval. No mortal, however, will make me profess what my conscience rejects. As my heart now stands, I would rather face death.

What, by the way, has become of that dogma that faith ought to be advanced by persuasion, not by force, and that in the business of the gospel

* * * * *

56 Cf *Adagia* I x 79: *Caput sine lingua* CWE 32 270: 'The crocodile too has no tongue in his head, but its mouth is well set with teeth; and we see so many men like that ... who have no idea how to speak well, but can give one a deadly bite.'
57 Prov 16:14
58 *Adagia* I ii 9: *Oleum camino addere* CWE 31 151: 'to supply a bad thing with nourishment and support'
59 See above n13.

no sword ought to be employed besides the sword of God's word?[60] But if, as I think, you are acting not out of ill will but out of self-indulgent sport, what, I ask you, could be more cruel than this kind of pleasure? Is this your only way of having fun, to take delight in a friend's ruin? There are some who suspect that either you or the printers are getting some profit out of this affair. Is this bit of gain so valuable to you that you pursue it even when a friend greatly loses thereby? Do you not have ingratiating words of your own, of the kind that can seduce a buyer? Or perhaps you are lending or renting out your efforts to others who want to harm me. In that case, what could be imagined more inconsistent with friendship – but not only that, more foul, more debased? If you were hired for a high price, the greatness of your reward would in some way lessen the foulness of your deed; as it is, if there is a reward, it has to be a very small one. Yet the law of friendship demands that whenever one's life or reputation – which is often dearer than life – is brought into danger, a friend plunges right in on his behalf, even at the risk of his life.

But let us pass over consideration of friendship. If you sincerely approve of the views you profess, if you really are convinced that what you are defending is sacred, pious, and pleasing to God, then you could scarcely find a more potent method to alienate the minds of good people from your enterprise. You dedicated your *Comet* to the emperor, and did not suppress your name.[61] Was he not angry enough with you, that you needed to exasperate him still further by such mockery? Do you consider King Ferdinand not angry enough without inflaming him more and more with such fuel – and not only him, but other princes who agree with him? What good has it done you to pour oil on the fire?[62] Does the power of such rulers seem contemptible to you? Though this was not an impious act, do you think it a safe one? Yet the recent case of the peasants ought to provide you with a compelling example.[63] What bravery could be greater than theirs?

* * * * *

60 Eph 6:17
61 See above n30. At about the same time as his treatise on the comet, Geldenhouwer published an open letter to Charles v in which he rejected common arguments to the effect that heresy must be punished by death. Erasmus seems to think the letter came before the treatise.
62 See above n58.
63 The German Peasants' War began with a protest by peasants of the abbey of Saint Blasien in the Black Forest (30 May 1524) and ended with the defeat of a peasant army in Tyrol (June 1526). For the history and character of this vast and complex movement, covering much of south and central Germany, see Peter Blickle *The Revolution of 1525: The Peasants' War from a New Perspective* tr Thomas

Yet by experience they found to be true what Solomon says, 'Pride goes before contrition, and the spirit will be exalted before a fall.'[64] In this case, nonetheless, the Emperor Charles and King Ferdinand remained inactive.[65] I am not, by the way, adopting a role as judge in the cause for which you plead: it has legitimate judges in the emperor and the pope. Let us suppose for the moment that the cause is pious. What has become of that discretion, that shrewdness of serpents, which the gospel mentions?[66] By this quality Paul took diligent care that he not be a cause of offence for the gospel, but rather made himself all things in order to win all to Christ.[67] What has become of that dove-like simplicity that does not even know how to harm its enemies?[68] Did the apostles defend the gospel by tricks of the sort you use?

Yet you boast that you are restoring to the light the evangelical truth that has lain buried for over a thousand years. If what you say is true, you are performing a more difficult enterprise than the apostles had in their day. It was much easier to abolish Hebrew rites and demolish pagan superstitions than it is to root out everything that the leaders of the church have taught over many centuries, and with much agreement, as the oracles of God - everything that they have cherished and held, and hold still today. For the religion of the pagans contained so much absurdity that any pagan who knew his ABCs, or had more than average intelligence, understood what was reported about the gods to be pure fictions. These fictions were thought up by clever people so that the uneducated multitude, which could not be governed by the reasoned arguments of philosophy, might be kept to some extent in check through fear of the gods.[69] The utterances of prophets had

* * * * *

A. Brady and H.C. Erik Midelfort (Baltimore and London 1977), and Tom Scott and Robert Scribner *The German Peasants' War: A History in Documents* (Atlantic Highlands, NJ 1991). Although Erasmus' residence in Basel put him close to much of the action, comments in his extant correspondence are few: eg 'this bloody crisis ... sent about 100,000 peasants into the world of Orcus' (Ep 1633:20–1); 'the peasant rising is almost settled, but the remedy was cruel. The seriousness of the trouble demanded such measures' (Ep 1686:21–2).

64 Prov 16:18
65 In fact, Ferdinand's officials had to confront rebel peasants in Tyrol, one of the territories he ruled as Archduke of Austria.
66 Matt 10:16; cf *Ratio* Holborn 178:19–180:9, 236:29; *Ecclesiastes* ASD V-4 64:579–84, 76:897–8; paraphrase on Matthew CWE 45 170–1; paraphrase on John CWE 46 34, 226.
67 Cf 1 Cor 9:22.
68 See below n118.
69 This narrow reading of Greco-Roman religion reflects not merely Erasmus' standpoint as a Christian, but also a 'euhemerist' tradition in classical authors,

predicted that someday the pagans would abandon the worship of demons and images and would acknowledge the true God.[70] In the same way, it had been predicted that Hebrew ceremonies would vanish like shadows before the gleaming light of the gospel.[71] But in the beliefs which you are uprooting, what, I ask you, is absurd or ridiculous? What prophet ever predicted that in the future the whole world would become unacquainted with Christ, preached by the apostles, and would worship idols instead of God? That all those who duly succeeded to the apostolic office would, in total blindness, see nothing in the Sacred Scriptures; and then, 1300 years later, some kind of new evangelists would recall the world to a recognition of the truth?[72] Furthermore, the apostles' unbroken consistency on matters of dogma, and their miracles, built up trust in their preaching; while you not only disagree among yourselves, but frequently invent new rites as well as doctrines. As for miracles, you are completely devoid of them.[73]

I think, however, that miracles did not have such an impact on renewing the world as did the character of the evangelists, which was in every way pure and blameless. I am not talking about fasting or garments and similar usages, which hypocrites can simulate. Rather, cheerful readiness in time of affliction, calmness in bearing injury, a heart simple and mild, thinking evil of no one and eager to deserve well of everyone, superior to all human concerns and able to hold life itself in scorn – such things commended their teaching. They called people away from their accustomed ways, but led them to ways far better. You strongly cry out against the luxury of priests, the ambitions of bishops, the tyranny of the pope in Rome, the long-windedness of sophists, against prayers, fast-times, and masses.

* * * * *

rationalizing the history of belief. See Robin Lane Fox *Pagans and Christians* (New York 1987), and Marek Winiarczyk *Euhemeros von Messene. Leben, Werk und Nachwirkung* (Munich 2002).

70 Eg Isa 2:20–1.

71 Cf Col 2:16–17; Heb 10:1; paraphrase on Mark CWE 49 83, 109; paraphrase on John CWE 46 196.

72 Cf *De libero arbitrio* LB IX 1218E, 1220C–D / CWE 76 15, 17–20.

73 See J.K. McConica, 'Grammar of Consent' 84: 'Concord, it is clear, is a distinguishing trait of the community duly (and truly) formed by the action of Christ through the Spirit, and so, as Erasmus remarked, the Church actually implies *unanimitas*' (cf *Querimonia pacis* LB IV 632B–C). See also Erasmus' comment on Ulrich Zwingli and his followers, in a letter of September 1524 to Philip Melanchthon: 'They do not agree with your lot, nor are they at unity among themselves, and yet they expect us to follow their authority and abandon all the orthodox Fathers and councils' (Ep 1496:85–7), and *Hyperaspistes* 1 LB X 1263D / CWE 76 130.

And you do not want these things cleansed, but removed. Nothing at all pleases you among accepted usages. You pluck out the tare along with the wheat,[74] or, to put it better, you pluck of the wheat instead of the tare.

Now what do you offer us that is worthy of the gospel, and better, so that we should give up the things to which we are accustomed? Take a look at the evangelical believers and observe whether there you find less indulgence in luxury, lust, and money than among those whom they hate. Show me just one whom that gospel has changed from gluttonous to sober, rapacious to generous, cursing to blessing, or shameless to modest. I will show you many who have become worse than their former selves.[75] Statues have been driven out of churches, but what does that matter, when the idols of their vices are nonetheless receiving worship in their hearts?[76] I do not see with what purpose they have destroyed some images so zealously, unless to provide a rallying point for their conspiracy.[77]

They are simply using the crime of idolatry as a fright-producing pretext. Is anyone really so stone-like that he thinks there is sensation in pieces of stone and wood? Even if there are such people, it would be but little trouble to teach the public that images were introduced only for the purpose of aiding the memory of the uneducated.[78] Prescribed prayers have been driven out, but now there are many people who do not pray at all, though frequent and sincere prayer is a sacrifice especially characteristic of Christians. The mass has been done away with, but has anything more sacred succeeded it?[79] I am not now comparing rites with rites, introduced rites with those that have been abandoned. I have never entered their churches, but I once saw a group of them returning from a sermon inspired, as it

* * * * *

74 See above n50.

75 Cf letter to Martin Bucer on 11 Nov 1527 (Allen Ep 1901:31–4) and Allen Ep 1887:10–11.

76 In the winter of 1528–29, images were removed from the churches in Basel. Erasmus wrote to Francis Vergara in March of 1529, 'I am forced to fly from the nest that I have gotten accustomed to after so many years, for I'm afraid that at any moment the same punishment the ministry have meted out to the saints will fall on me' (Allen Ep 2125:5–7).

77 *Conspiratio* has a double meaning: in a good sense, 'agreement'; in a bad sense, 'conspiracy' or 'plot.' Erasmus later uses this ambiguity to evade the accusation that he considered the 'evangelicals' as seditious; cf *Epistola ad fratres Inferioris Germaniae* below 319 and the comment of Augustijn (ASD IX-1 376:65–7n).

78 Cf *Explanatio symboli* ASD V-1 304:927–30 / CWE 70 366 on the utility of images for the illiterate.

79 Cf Allen Ep 2133:64–70: 'The mass and the rites of the church have been taken away altogether, save that they have sermons now and then.'

were, by an evil spirit. All their faces showed anger and astonishing ferocity. I was accompanied by some worthy men, and not one among them
showed us the courtesy that we show to anyone, except a single old man.
This, I believe, is how soldiers return from a meeting with their commander, after receiving an exhortation to battle and impetuous valour. Who
ever saw at their sermons anyone who wept, beat his breast, or groaned
because of his sins?[80] In fact, a large part of the meeting is used up in attacking the life of priests, and, if truth be told, in sermons that aim more
at sedition than piety. Confession has been done away with, but, all the
same, many people do not even confess their sins to God. They have rejected the distinction of foods, along with fasting, but, all the same, they
eagerly indulge in drunkenness; and so some have escaped what they call
Judaism only to start becoming Epicureans.[81] They trample on ceremony,
but add nothing to spirituality; in fact, it has been greatly decreased, in my
judgment.

Paul observed certain Jewish ceremonies, so as not to alienate Jews
from the gospel.[82] In this spirit, at least, not all ceremonies were to be
rejected. The apostles knew nothing of prescribed fast-days, but they fasted
every day, willingly and unbidden.[83] They knew nothing of distinctions in
foods, but they voluntarily used only the cheapest foods, and maintained
the greatest frugality in all things. No one was required to eat beans, but
they were willingly content with beans, if the situation required it. No one
was forbidden to drink wine, but Timothy willingly lived in such abstinence
that Paul had to admonish him, and prescribe that he take a little wine to
fortify his body in its weak condition.[84] Paula, the mother of Eustochium,
could not be induced to taste wine, sick as she was, even by the authority of

* * * * *

80 Cf Luke 18:13.
81 Epicureans, followers of the Greek philosopher Epicurus, held that the purpose of life is the pursuit of pleasure; however they ranked intellectual pleasure far above the sensual, and thus Epicurean philosophy is not an invitation to crude self-indulgence, as Erasmus understood very well. In his colloquy *Epicureus* 'The Epicurean' (written in 1533) the character Hedonius remarks that 'there are no people more Epicurean than godly Christians' (CWE
   40 1075). See Craig R. Thompson's introduction in Thompson *Colloquies* 535–
   7; see also the colloquy *Convivium religiosum* 'The Godly Feast' written in 1522
   (CWE 39 171–243). Luther in *De servo arbitrio* WA 18:605 accuses Erasmus of
   following 'Lucian or some other porker from the herd of Epicureans,' all of
   whom (according to Luther) are scornful of God and those who believe in
   God.
82 Cf Acts 21:26.
83 Acts 13:2–3
84 1 Tim 5:23

Jerome, and that of her aged bishop.[85] If we embrace evangelical freedom, let us throw off the yoke of the law in such a fashion that charity does more than the law commanded. They have thrown off the yoke of human regulations, but have they submitted their neck to the sweet yoke of the Lord?[86] All the while, human regulations are being exchanged for other human regulations – yet they are actually inhuman! The title only has been changed; they are now called 'God's word.' But the thing itself is so much harsher that many good people prefer voluntary exile to that liberty, so splendidly heralded.[87] While some of the leaders and front-rank men of this faction have reached wealth and power, though not yet the rank of bishop, nevertheless they have shown such examples of their nature that I would rather put myself under the power of bishops than under theirs, if I had the choice.[88] I would prefer to bear the yoke of the most powerful emperor rather than that of certain evangelical magistrates, however humble my lot may be. This is how people shake off the yoke of men, when they submit their necks to your gospel. I have a greater fear that many will carry, instead of the yoke of men, the heavier yoke of the devil. They have thrown off obedience to bishops, with the further result that they do not even obey civil magistrates. At one time Christians lived quietly under pagan princes, zealously making sure that they gave no opportunity to sedition, showing honour where it was due, paying taxes and tribute where they were due.[89] They urged those who were initiated in Christ to obey even idol-worshipping magistrates, and prayed to God daily for the safety of these magistrates.[90] But this people, so evangelical a people, is said to be hateful even to the Sultan of the Turks: he says they are born for sedition.[91] They repeatedly arouse disturbances; they often rush to arms for trivial reasons; they scarcely obey even their own churchmen, unless their ears have been filled with flattering speeches; they are quick to expel a churchman if he too freely criticizes their lives or disagrees with their opinions. At first, Luther was little short of a god to them, but now they think he is completely crazy, because he will not accept their new doctrine about the Eucharist.[92]

* * * * *

85 Jerome *Epistolae* 108.20 (PL 22 879–98)
86 Matt 11:29; *Annotationes* LB VI 63B–5E
87 Cf Allen Epp 2158:87–9, 2217:29–32, 2615:421–3.
88 Cf Allen Ep 1523:77–80.
89 Cf Matt 22:21; Mark 12:17; Luke 20:25; Rom 13:7.
90 Cf Rom 13:1–5; 1 Tim 2:1–2.
91 Cf *Hyperaspistes* 2 LB X 1483E / CWE 77 635.
92 Cf *Epistola ad fratres Inferioris Germaniae* 346; Epp 1523:8–9; *Hyperaspistes* 1 / CWE 76 98, 222, 235.

This is the new evangelical freedom: that each person can do anything, and hold any opinion, with impunity. Paul commands that anyone who has married his stepmother, contrary to natural shame, should be handed over to Satan,[93] and urges his disciples to withdraw from association with a brother who walks in a disorderly fashion.[94] And he wants them not even to share the same table with people notorious for obvious vices.[95] Now take a look with me at this evangelical band: how many adulterers it has, how many drunkards, dice-players, spendthrifts, how many notorious for other vices! And far from avoiding such people, it regards them as its darlings.[96] The apostles, in order to have more time for the gospel, either abstained from the wives that they were permitted to marry, or else treated their legitimately married wives as sisters.[97] Now the gospel flourishes because priests and monks are taking wives – contrary to the laws, at least human laws, and their own vows.[98] Let us grant this practice, and look to see whether their marriages are more virtuous than those of other people, whom they consider pagans. You are well aware, I believe, what stories I could tell you at this point, if I wanted to. And I need not tell of incidents that are well known, which have been brought to public notice by the magistrates, or by the common people, whether the magistrates approve or not. Monasticism has been overthrown, but one could wish that when these men threw off the cowl they would also have thrown off the vices that are said to be peculiar to monks. What good does it do to have set aside the cowl, if the disease of fault-finding remains, together with envy, impudence, self-love, pretence, deception, laziness, desire for other people's food, greed, lust to go gallivanting about, inquisitiveness into other people's affairs, vengefulness, and a mind quick to rush into anger? It seems to me that a new kind of monk is arising, even more crime-ridden than the other (I am speaking only about bad monks).[99] Well-known evils are not evils, as someone has said.[100] It is foolish, therefore, to exchange one set of evils

* * * * *

93   1 Cor 5:1–5
94   2 Thess 3:6
95   1 Cor 5:11
96   Cf Epp 1496:72–92; 1522:95–100 to Heinrich Stromer, a letter that caused particular offence to the reformers. Cf *Epistola ad fratres Inferioris Germaniae* 342.
97   Cf 1 Cor 7:28–9.
98   See Ep 1653:6–10 and Allen Ep 1887:17–19.
99   Cf *Moria* ASD IV-3 158:524–162:576 / CWE 27:130–3.
100 *Adagia* II ix 85: *Nota res mala optima* CWE 34 123–4: 'the adage discourages us from any rash zeal for change and recommends avoidance of what is perhaps the greatest of faults … a passion for novelty, the companion and virtual

for another, and only a crazy person would exchange evils for worse evils. They love no one except themselves, and obey neither God nor bishops nor princes and magistrates; they are slaves to Mammon, to their gullets, bellies, and groins; yet all the while they demand to be considered evangelists and assert that Luther is their master. Yet how can they have the effrontery to claim Luther as their master, when they pay no attention to every important principle that he teaches and inculcates? Luther everywhere preaches faith: wherever faith is, it cannot be idle; it works through charity, it works for the good alone. Luther everywhere preaches the Spirit, and what are the fruits of the Spirit? 'Charity, joy, peace, patience, kindness, goodness, long-suffering, mildness, faith, modesty, restraint, chastity.'[101] Yet in most of them we see the works of the flesh, and no trace of the Spirit. What do they have to do with Luther, when they care not a whit[102] for the very foundation of his teaching? Though in fact it does not belong to Luther, but to Christ and the apostles.[103] Let it be open to question whether good works engender faith, or faith produces good works, or whether good works justify or not, but this point at least is beyond controversy: that no one has a hope of salvation apart from faith, and that from faith, through charity, good works are born by necessity.[104] Consequently, those who have no zeal for good works, and yet boast of their faith, are shameless; and in vain do

*　*　*　*　*

brother of which is ... the rejection of things we had a passion for a short time ago'; cf *Detectio praestigiarum* above 203–4 and n220. Erasmus' fear of innovation corresponded to his zeal for restoration: 'And it is a mark of greater power to repair what is damaged than to bring forth what has never been born' paraphrase on John 9:6 CWE 46 122–3.

101 Gal 5:22

102 *Adagia* I viii 4: *Pili non facio* 'I count it not worth a hair' CWE 32 130.

103 Erasmus' attitude towards Luther seems uncharacteristically favourable in the aftermath of their bitter exchange over the freedom of the will four and five years earlier. One possible reason is that false claims about both Erasmus and Luther were published by Leo Jud (*Maynung*) in the debate over the Eucharist; thus to his own rebuke to the Swiss reformers Erasmus can add by implication Luther's as well. Similarly, Luther was critical of Bucer for his publication of the *S. Psalmorum libri quinque ad ebraicam veritatem versi, et familiari explanatione elucidate* (see below n122). Contemporary readers of the *Epistola contra pseudevangelicos* remarked on Erasmus' attitude, for in a letter attached to the second authorized edition Erasmus responds to the charge that he is flattering Luther (Allen Ep 2441:78–9).

104 Erasmus here remains true to his contention (*De libero arbitrio* CWE 76 78–9) that the full truth about faith and justification cannot be known, but it is necessary that there be both faith and good works.

they promise themselves salvation who boast in a faith that is destitute of good works. I fear that under the name of freedom many pagans are arising among us, if, the more they are free, the less they believe that heaven and hell exist, and that the soul survives the death of the body. Yet, all the same, they boast that their consciences are freed. Perfect piety has a quiet conscience, but so does the greatest impiety. I would prefer to have an unquiet conscience, which the seed of faith, constantly goading, does not allow to be calm. The ill that is not perceived cannot be healed.

To return to the subject, if they have as much faith in their hearts as they have constantly on their lips, why is it that they have so much recourse to clever stratagems and tricks? (I am not now speaking about the common people, but about their leaders.) At Basel I was friendly with a man[105] who was not yet completely inspired with this evangelical spirit. When he had decided to become entirely evangelical, he spread a rumour that I had the same opinion about the Eucharist that he had, when in fact he knew from our conversations that I had a different opinion; at that time this topic was under frequent discussion. I complained to the man about this trick, so out of keeping with friendship. He denied it at first, then became evasive, and finally confessed that he had said as much to certain people: 'Erasmus has a proper opinion about the Eucharist, no doubt the same as my own.' I asked what was his opinion. 'It is the body of Christ,' he said. 'In this,' I replied, 'I agree with you; but is it your opinion that Christ's body is present in substance?'[106] He denied it with disgust. 'In this I do not agree with you,' I said. 'But what do you profess among your own people? That the body is not present except as a symbol?'[107] He agreed. 'When they hear,' said I,

* * * * *

105 The reference is to Conradus Pellicanus (1478–1556); for Pellicanus and his quarrel with Erasmus, see introductory note to *Detectio* above 150–5 and Ep 1637 introduction.

106 Cf *Detectio praestigiarum* above n36. *Substantialiter* reflects a distinction (which the scholastic theologians borrowed from Aristotle) between the essential, underlying reality of a thing (its *substance*) and the external, changeable features (the *accidents*). Thus, Catholic doctrine maintained that the *accidents* (ie the features which give the appearance) of bread and wine could remain the same, while the *substance* of the bread and wine was transformed into Christ's body and blood. This is the miracle of *transubstantiation*, the exchange of one substance (bread and wine) for another (Christ's body and blood). The priest is endowed with the power to perform this miracle in the ceremony of the mass, in pronouncing the words of institution.

107 Luther rejected transubstantiation and the priest's special authority in the mass, claiming that Christ was really (bodily) present ('real presence') in the Eucharist when the words of institution were spoken, but that there was no transformation of substances. The Swiss reformers and their party, including

'that Erasmus has the same opinion as you, are they not all the while being deceived by a fine trick?' He was silent. Then, just before he left town, he issued two letters, in which he repeatedly praised my good sense, giving little hints to the reader that I did not speak sincerely and was cleverly concealing my true opinion.[108] He also left at his house a letter to the city council of Basel, urging them to use armed entreaties[109] to try to persuade me to reveal my sincere opinion; though I had already given the council an answer in writing.[110] I ask you, are tricks of this sort consistent with evangelical purity of heart?

At the instigation of this same man, I believe, there appeared a pamphlet[111] at the time of the Disputation of Baden,[112] which had been convened to discuss this very question. The pamphlet was written in German, so that I could not readily respond to it, and its crafty author tried to prove, by frivolous arguments, that Luther and Erasmus agreed with Karlstadt[113] on the Eucharist. Karlstadt, after first secretly spreading some utterly witless pamphlets, had recently brought the seeds of this controversy to Basel.[114] What could be more shameless than such an act, especially what he claimed to Luther? He had ejected Karlstadt on account of this very doctrine, and, on his return, forced him to a retraction.[115] Though printed pamphlets and letters bore witness to the facts, nevertheless this charming fellow tried

* * * * *

Zwingli, Karlstadt, Oecolampadius, and Pellicanus, rejected any bodily presence and interpreted the words of institution symbolically. See the introductory note to *Detectio praestigiarum* 149.

108 Epp 1638, 1639.

109 Cf *Epistola ad fratres Inferiores Germaniae* 293; *armata prex* can have a negative or a positive meaning: a 'forceful imprecation' or a 'friendly coaxing.'

110 See Ep 1636; cf introductory note to *Detectio praestigiarum* 153.

111 All of the points touched on here are discussed in Professor Payne's introductory note to *Detectio praestigiarum* above 148–153. The reference here is to Leo Jud's *Maynung vom nachtmahl* (*Detectio praestigiarum* introductory note n50).

112 For the Disputation of Baden (21 May–8 June 1526) see *Detectio praestigiarum* introductory note n59; Ep 1708.

113 For Andreas Rudolf Bodenstein (1480–1541), called Karlstadt after his native city, see the introductory note to *Detectio praestigiarum* n3.

114 See Epp 1522:60–4, 1523:102–8, 1620:94–6, 1621:19–22.

115 For Karlstadt's expulsion from Electoral Saxony in September 1524, see above 148. He returned to Wittenberg by the end of June 1525, shortly after the Peasants' War, and at Luther's insistence wrote the *Erklärung wie Karlstadt seine Lehre von dem hochwürdigen Sakrament und andere achtet und geachtet haben will* (WA 18 446–66). This work was sufficiently ambiguous to give rise to controversy; see Ep 1616:34 (and Allen Ep 1616:27n), and Pellicanus' contradictory account in Ep 1639:212–18; cf Mark U. Edwards *Luther and the False Brethren* (Stanford CA 1975) 73–81.

to persuade the world that Luther agreed with Karlstadt, however much they in fact disagreed. And in order to persuade the world that I agreed as well, the author of this pamphlet collected various passages out of books that I had published many years before this question existed – before I had ever dreamed that anyone would have doubts about the Eucharist, far from having doubts about it myself. Do people like this, who conduct their affairs by such contrivances, appear to have evangelical faith? This was their thinking: 'Before Erasmus can find a translator, before he can pre-pare a response, and before his defence can be printed, this pamphlet of ours will pass through everyone's hands and persuade everyone of what we want. This mistake on the part of the populace will bring us victory at the disputation. If he finally does make some response, few will read the Latin, and the whole affair will be carried by the votes of the popu-lace.' I became aware of the trick, and – it was the only thing I could do at that point, since those invited to the disputation had already set out – I snatched up my pen, and in a letter both declared my own opinion and exposed the deception of that crafty author.[116] I took care that my letter be translated into German, addressed to the Swiss Confederacy, and had copies in both languages sent by my own messenger. I asked that it be read out in public, as was in fact done, and a few days later I issued a pam-phlet in my defence, as I had promised in my letter to the Confederacy.[117] If I wished to embellish this villainy with rhetorical devices, comparing it to the moral character of the apostles, you see what rich material I would have. I find lacking in this case not only dove-like simplicity,[118] but even ordinary human intelligence. It would have been easy to figure out that I would not endure such an insult in silence, and, even if I did suppress a response, the facts themselves would refute such impudent mendacity, es-pecially among the learned, but also among the uneducated, such as were not entirely dull-witted. So what was he trying to gain? A temporary bene-fit from the deception. But falsehood, once exposed, earns interest upon its principal, causing those who do not tell the truth to enjoy no trust there-after. 'The truth of the Lord,' however, 'remains forever';[119] the preach-ing of the gospel is not expressed by yes and no, but in all cases is yes.[120]

* * * * *

116 See Ep 1708, addressed to the Swiss Confederacy, Erasmus' response to an invitation to participate in the Disputation of Baden.
117 *Detectio praestigiarum* (above 163–205) was published at the end of May 1526.
118 Cf Matt 10:16; see above n66.
119 Ps 117:2 (116:2 Vulg)
120 Cf 2 Cor 1:19.

He hunted after simple people's minds, that were easily tricked, just as many nowadays, under the shade of literary pursuits, lay traps for young people and women. It is appalling that such actions, while boasting of an evangelical spirit, have no savour of it. You have an example in two leaders of this doctrine. I do not wish you to be like them.

Recently, I hear, a churchman of that party,[121] not without renown, but writing under an assumed name, dedicated a book to the son of the French king, and scattered throughout it various French words, so that suspicion would not fall upon its German author.[122] He also added other false hints to give the impression that the book had been written at Lyon by a Frenchman, and printed there. You are well aware that what I say is true, and it is obvious who committed this tricky act of duplicity, since he has been caught in the same kind of game on other occasions.[123] Even if he were granted his fun in common and profane matters, it would nevertheless be unworthy of a respectable man. Could anything be less

* * * * *

121 Martin Bucer (1491–1551), who would respond to the *Epistola contra pseudevangelicos* with the *Epistola apologetica*, is the churchman Erasmus has in mind. As a young man Bucer became a Dominican friar, and was formally released from his vows in 1521. He subsequently married and settled in Strasbourg, where he became the foremost leader of the reform. He played a major role in attempting to reach a compromise between the Lutherans and the Zwinglians in the Eucharistic controversy; see Andreas Gäumann *Reich Christi und Obrigkeit: Eine Studie zum reformatorischen Denken und Handeln Martin Bucers* (Bern 2001); Amy Nelson Burnett *The Yoke of Christ: Martin Bucer and Christian Discipline* (Kirksville, MO 1994); and *Martin Bucer: Reforming Church and Community* ed D.F. Wright (Cambridge 1994).

122 The book in question is *S. Psalmorum libri quinque ad ebraicam veritatem versi, et familiari explanatione elucidati*, published in 1529 under the pen name Aretinus Felix. Francis I's son Francis, who was at that time the dauphin, died in 1536 before he was able to become king. See C. Augustijn ASD IX-1 299 nn411–15 and 333 nn80–3.

123 Erasmus is referring to two translations that Bucer published in 1526, the first a translation into German of the *Psalter* of Luther's associate Johannes Bugenhagen, and the other a Latin translation of Luther's *Kirchenpostille*. In both cases he freely inserted his own interpretations into the text to suggest agreement between Luther's party and his own on the Eucharist. Both incidents sparked a bitter dispute between Luther and Bucer, especially as Melanchthon had written an approving introduction to the Bugenhagen *Psalter*, not suspecting Bucer's alterations; likewise Bugenhagen, who had originally authorized the translation, registered a protest when he discovered the liberties Bucer had taken. See *Epistola ad fratres Germaniae Inferioris* below 297, and Allen Ep 2615 449:162–4.

appropriate to one who professed himself to be a preacher of the sacred gospel?

I call upon your conscience, Neocomus: do you really think that so serious, so sacred, and so difficult an enterprise ought to be accomplished by employing jokes of this kind? If you sincerely judge your cause to be pious, you must equally desire to entice all people towards the same goal. Yet you could scarcely have found a better means of alienating all the best people. Or, if you are indeed persuaded that this is God's enterprise, not that of men, and nevertheless, over the protests of conscience, you employ such deceptions in order to keep yourselves safe from the multitude, even if you deceive all men, do you not fear God, whose vengeance no one can escape? If he who does the Lord's work in a careless fashion is called accursed, how much more detestable is he who does it in a fraudulent fashion? Christ did not allow the glory of the cross to be attributed to human wisdom,[124] yet these people want it ascribed to games and illusionistic tricks! But if you think the whole business a laughing matter, and are doing something quite different under the banner of the gospel, what do you expect will be the eventual conclusion of this tragedy? What conclusion, if not a bloody and utterly unhappy one? Whether you are dealing seriously or just playing, you should at least have the sense not to anger princes by such impudence, nor to force me to clear my name. The more effort I spend on doing that, the more I embarrass your cause. You see how much Luther stood in the way of a cause that was at first not altogether bad, because of the animosity and violence of his writing. Now Melanchthon[125] follows in his wake – just as prayers of repentance trail after an outburst of rage[126] –

* * * * *

124 Cf 1 Cor 1:17.
125 Of all the reformers, Philip Melanchthon (1497–1560) was the one who was able to maintain the most consistently positive personal relationship with Erasmus, in spite of his continued support for Luther and poor opinion of Erasmus as a theologian. He taught Greek at the University of Wittenberg, and maintained an active correspondence with Erasmus, even during the period of the debate between Luther and Erasmus on free will; see CEBR II 424–9. He also would on occasion attempt to soften the effects of Luther's harsh words; see Allen Ep 1977:69–70.
126 Cf *Adagia* I vii 13: *Ira omnium tardissime senescit* CWE 32 72–3, where Erasmus quotes Homer *Iliad* 9.502–12, mentioning Ate (blind rage) and Litai (prayers). A daughter of Zeus, Ate personified infatuation or moral blindness. Her inability to distinguish between right and wrong brought about many evils. Thrown out of Olympus, she spread evil on earth by walking lightly over human heads without touching the ground. Behind her came the Litai (prayers), the wrinkled daughters of Zeus, who while trying to make amends brought

diligently trying to set right what he threw into confusion. But the facts show how much quicker is the offence than the cure. And so you must see to it that you do not overthrow the whole enterprise, by behaviour utterly unworthy of the gospel. If the cause is impious, you act rightly, though senselessly. But if it is pious – and it seems far otherwise to many – you act not only sense-lessly but impiously. As to how others may react I conjecture from my own experience. You would scarcely believe how greatly the behaviour of these people has alienated me from the whole enterprise. Even if at some point I had approved of it in part, for this reason alone I would be brought to re-coil from it. You will say, 'Nothing in human affairs is so fortunate that it is not corrupted with some admixture of evil. Direct your attention to the vir-tuous among us!' It may be that bad luck is my portion: in my experience, I have known not one who does not seem to have become worse than his for-mer self.[127] What you profess to be doing is difficult, harder than the apos-tles' enterprise, as I pointed out earlier, and you are not aided by prophe-cies or miracles. But if your lives not only fail to commend your teaching, but instead nullify your trustworthiness, and if, casting aside this source of commendation, you rely instead upon wicked plots, seditious disturbances, arms, deceptions, and tricks, then I have no stomach to relate what I fear for you; still more do I pity the many thousands whom this calamity will engulf.

Many things commended the apostles' teaching to the world: what they taught was both heavenly and convincing. They told what they had seen with their eyes, and heard with their ears.[128] They added nothing that had not been foreshadowed in the past, in many ways and shapes, nothing that had not been predicted by the oracles of the prophets. In addition, there was great consistency in their preaching: they said the same things, because they did so in the same Spirit.[129] The power of miracles was present to assist them, as was that fiery Spirit, which manifested itself in their moral character as well as in their faces and eyes. They accomplished nothing by force, they used only the sword of the Spirit,[130] they drove no one into

* * * * *

new evil to the stubborn. See *Epistola ad Fratres Inferioris Germaniae* 343 where Erasmus again likens Luther to Ate and Melanchthon to the Litai; cf LB IX 1619F.
127 See above n75; cf *Epistola ad fratres Inferioris Germaniae* below 314; Ep 1496:124–30; Allen Epp 1887:10–21, 1901:31–4, 2134:74–5, 2205:132–5, 2615:435–9.
128 1 John 1:1
129 Consistency, like harmony, was to Erasmus a sign of truth and right-mindedness. See above n73 and Allen Ep 1901:35–8.
130 Eph 6:17

exile, they seized no one's property, nor did they even shatter the idols of the pagans unless, perhaps, by prayers poured out to God. Also, they did not say one thing among their own people, and another under torture. The many deaths of martyrs must be added in as well. Nevertheless, even teaching of this sort, commended by so many things, took hold in the world only little by little, only gradually.

You are demanding that within nine years everybody on earth should scorn what they received a thousand years ago from their ancestors, and rush with all their might[131] to embrace your doctrines, though these have none of the commendations that we enumerated. What sort of demands are you making of us? To believe that the church lacked Christ for 1400 years; that the bride worshipped ghosts and idols instead of God, while the Bridegroom snored away; that she was utterly blind in expounding the Sacred Scriptures; that the saints' miracles were nothing other than the illusionistic tricks of demons. I will not now proceed to expand this list. You may put things together for yourself, and judge whether what you demand of us is fair, and whether you have made good provision for your salvation in pursuing such a course. If the vices of Christians offend you, show us an example in your own church, which would have no spot or wrinkle,[132] and we will embrace it. If our crimes deserve the Lord's wrath, he is accustomed to punish his people through Pharaohs,[133] Antiochuses,[134] Cyruses,[135] and Nebuchadnezzars,[136] not through evangelical men, as you want yourselves called. I do not know what future you promise yourselves, but to me, the origin and development of your enterprise, indeed all signs, promise only a disastrous conclusion.[137] And it will be an unhappy ending not only for you: the huge crash will drag many people with it. Judge him to be the best prophet who prophesies aright, runs the proverb; and the best kind of divination may be to infer future events from those of the past and present.[138] Evangelical piety grew from small beginnings, little by

* * * * *

131 *Adagia* II vii 12: *Pedibus in sententiam discere* 'To vote with one's feet' CWE 34
      8—10: '. . . any form of approval for someone else's views'
132 Eph 5:27
133 See Exod 5–14.
134 See 1 Macc 1:10–62.
135 Erasmus is mistaken in describing Cyrus as a persecutor of Israel. See 2 Chron
      36:22–3, Ezra 1:1–4.
136 See 2 Kings 24, 25.
137 On *initium-progressus-consummatio* see *Purgatio adversus epistolam Lutheri* below
      n24.
138 Cf *Adagia* II iii 78: *Qui bene conjicet hunc vatem* 'He who guesses right is the
      prophet' CWE 33 177.

little, into something greater and better, and all the best people joined it; nearly all the least reliable people are embracing your teaching. Only in recent times did the popes at Rome, and other bishops, become infected by a love of wealth, luxury, and the lust for rule.[139] You want to gain power instantly, and become rich instantly. What good does it do to talk about luxury? The orders of monks are a human invention, let us grant that; yet the Franciscan and Dominican orders have given us many outstanding men, whether you consider their learning or their holiness.[140] Aegina at first brought forth virtuous men,[141] the Greeks are accustomed to say. Such is the unhappiness of human affairs that from excellent beginnings the orders of friars have gradually degenerated, becoming worse and worse. I am ashamed to relate what sort of origins your enterprise had, how inauspicious were its beginnings.[142]

Examine with me just how things turn into the opposite of what is intended. They tried to demolish the tyranny of popes, bishops, and monks, which consisted in preventing them from eating what they wanted and dressing as they chose; yet they could easily, and at little cost, have acquired such liberty from the bishops or the pope at Rome. Now that theologians and monks are held in contempt, you have raised them to a greater tyranny, permitting them to rob people they dislike of their property, throw them into chains, and finally burn them – a fate many have experienced, and everyone fears.[143] Formerly, we could toss about various questions concerning the power of the pope, indulgences, compensation, and purgatory.

* * * * *

139 On Erasmus' attitude towards the papacy, see Tracy *Politics of Erasmus* (Toronto 1978) 26–32.
140 Erasmus' attitude towards Franciscans and Dominicans is not always this generous. Cf eg the colloquies *Funus* 'The Funeral,' *Concio sive Merdardus* 'The Sermon,' and *Exequiae seraphicae* 'The Seraphic Funeral' (CWE 40 763–90, 938–62, and 996–1032). Even in these cases, however, Erasmus indicates that he is criticizing those friars who discredit their orders, or those whose overzealousness makes a mockery of the ideals of their founders.
141 *Adagia* II v 61: *Primum Aegina pueros optimos alit* 'Of old, Aegina bears most noble sons' CWE 33 268: 'used of anything which from a promising start gradually deteriorates'
142 Perhaps an allusion to the fact that the indulgence-preaching to which Luther reacted was by a Dominican friar, Johann Tetzel, who was then defended against Luther's critique by other Dominicans; cf Allen Ep 2205:76–84.
143 A reference to the burning, in Antwerp (1 July 1523) of two Augustinian friars, the first Protestant martyrs (see Ep 1384 n2), and also to Louis Berquin, one of Erasmus' supporters in France, who was burned by order of the Parlement of Paris in April of 1529, the year of the *Epistola contra pseudevangelicos*. For Erasmus' response, see Allen Ep 2188.

Now it is not safe to open one's mouth, even concerning things that can be said in all piety and truthfulness. We are forced to believe that a person brings forth from himself works that are sufficiently meritorious to deserve eternal life as a matter of right;[144] that the Blessed Virgin can command the Son, reigning with the Father, to hear the prayers of this or that person; and many other things, at which pious minds shudder.[145] Formerly, a person who ate meat received no harassment from anyone, so long as he did so privately; now he is dragged to prison as a heretic and risks execution if he so much as tastes an egg during Lent, even constrained by ill health.[146] Formerly, one could spit on monks and theologians; now you people have equipped them with so many weapons that it is a capital offence to insult one of them. Formerly, you yourselves could travel abroad where you wanted; now you either lie hidden in fear, or you are confined, as if besieged, for there are few cities that welcome you openly.[147] Formerly, the religious dedication of clerics protected them from the rigours of civil law; now priests, just like tradesmen, are tortured, beaten, hung, beheaded, and burned by the executioner, even without first being stripped of their clerical status. This is how you have escaped the power of the pope. You have driven some bishops, canons, and monks from their places; but in driving away flies that were nearly sated, you have made room for thirsty flies.[148]

* * * * *

144 On the difference between *merita de congruo* and *de condigno*, see *De libero arbitrio* CWE 76 n106; *Hyperaspistes* 2 CWE 77 747; Allen Ep 2178:18–19.

145 Cf Ep 2178:15–18. Erasmus felt that he was harshly criticized by the Carthusian Pierre Cousturier (1475–1537) for his insufficient respect for the Virgin Mary, in Cousturier's *Apologeticum in novos Anticomaritas* (1526). Cousturier had been a critic of Erasmus' *New Testament* as well. See Rummel *Catholic Critics* II 71–2. The 1529 colloquy *Synodis grammaticorum* 'A Meeting of the Philological Society' (CWE 40 831–841) is a lampoon on Cousturier and other Catholic critics; see also Allen Epp 2016 and 2197.

146 Erasmus addressed the issue of fasting at length in the 1522 *De esu carnium* ASD IX-1 19–50; see C. Augustijn *Erasmus: His Life, Works, and Influence* tr J.C. Grayson (Toronto 1991) 148–50.

147 Erasmus in 1522 had moved to Basel in order to escape the imperial court as well as the tensions in his relationship with the theological faculty at Louvain, where he had previously resided since 1517. He was accused of having made the move as a sign of support for the Reformation. In April of 1529, the year of the *Epistola contra pseudevangelicos*, religious disturbances compelled him to move again, this time to Freiburg, in order to escape the Protestant Reformation in Basel. See Allen Ep 2149 introduction.

148 Plutarch *Moralia* 790D; cf *Moria* ASD IV-3 100:536 / CWE 27 101, 28 473; *Detectio praestigiarum* above 203.

These are the splendid beginnings of your reborn gospel. You can guess what troubles are coming.

This quarrel, however, has long since grown wearisome, and it is much easier to censure past wrongs than to correct them. I wish that, through the agency of some who profess your conviction, healing could be sought from former conditions. I wish that this affair, however it started, might be restored to moderation, such that obstacles to piety might be cured by suitable, prudent attention.[149] As for the things that are pious, let us agree about them in a Christian spirit. In things not very conducive to piety, and yet not obstacles to it, let us allow each person to content himself as he sees fit; let each, testing all things, hold to what he supposes good.[150] Difficult matters, and those that seem not yet fully discussed, let us put off until another time, so that, in the meantime, a benevolent harmony may prevail among people disharmonious in their opinions; until God may deign to reveal these things to some one. If any wrong creeps in through human failing, let our action be that of a worthy physician: let the faults in things be removed, not the things themselves. Meanwhile, let us remember that in human affairs nothing ever succeeds so well that there is not much to be pardoned. Let us, moreover, make a special effort to join our prayers and beseech God to give up his wrath, become propitious to us, and win over the hearts of all, inducing us on both sides, in evangelical sincerity, to change our lives for the better. Without doubt, this wretched calamity has been inflicted on the world by God because of our crimes: 'the same hand will cause our wound and its cure.'[151] Yet piety does not forbid us to apply remedies to evils of this sort, evils likely sent upon us either by God's will or with his permission; unless, perhaps, he declares his will by some obvious sign, as we read happened once or twice in the Old Testament.[152] If the plague assails us, it is not wrong to seek help for our woes; if the Turks make a violent attack upon Christians, we are not forbidden to fly to arms; if a debtor refuses to pay what he owes, it is not forbidden to force him to do so; and against a slanderer we have every right to defend our reputation, so long as the thing is done through proper agents and by legitimate methods. In the case of disease we may use a doctor; but it is wrong to have recourse to sorcerers and enchantresses. No law forbids us to take

* * * * *

149 Cf Ep 1267:10–24.
150 Rom 14:5; 1 Thess 5:21
151 Ovid *Remedia Amoris* 44: *Una manus vobis vulnus opemque feret*
152 See eg Nathan's rebuke to David in 2 Sam 12:10–12; Jer 17 and 28; Ezek 4 and 5, 12:1–20.

tree-fungus and scammony;[153] but Christian piety does forbid the use of superstitious treatments and magic spells. It is right to repel an enemy's attack by lawful war, but not to destroy him by witchcraft, magic potions, or other demonic arts. Likewise, it is right to claim your money from a dishonest debtor by recourse to the law, and to vindicate your reputation, when it is in danger from a slanderer; but you must not do so by deception, violence, or other wicked arts. Yet even in these cases it is wrong to trust in human remedies more than in God. God wants us carefully to employ all the resources our diligence can provide, but only so far that we rely totally upon him. If things turn out the way we wanted, let us attribute nothing to ourselves, but ascribe all the praise to God. He accomplished a cure through the doctor, a rescue through arms, a successful claim at law; for so it seemed best to him to do. He could, nevertheless, have provided help quite apart from these agents, and without his help they would have provided none themselves, however diligently employed. So the Lord sometimes allows schisms and heresies in his church, so as to test its endurance and instruct it in its ignorance. Who is unaware that through heresies the church has been greatly strengthened and made illustrious? Therefore it has always been fighting heretics, fiercely, not with arms, poisons, tricks, and chicanery, but with spiritual arms. Thus far it has never lost, not because of its own defences, but because of divine favour. Yet all the same it diligently performed its proper functions, advising, entreating, disputing, refuting, killing by the sword of the Spirit,[154] and finally separating the incurable from Christ's body.

The most helpful remedy for evils of this kind would be for us to cut off the causes, at which God took offence and sent such calamities upon us – not, leaving these things uncorrected, to have recourse to confiscations, prisons, swords, and flames. If the shepherds neglect, exploit, desert, and betray the flock, which is very dear to the Lord, and which they themselves ought to love and nourish three times over,[155] God becomes angry at the shepherds, and lets heretical wolves in upon us.[156] Let it be the first care of shepherds to remember their duty and change their own lives for the better, then let them arm themselves against wolves. God has taken offence at the laziness, luxury, pride, and lust of priests. Instead of pleasures, let them

* * * * *

153 Tree fungus was used as an antidote to snake-bite (cf Pliny *Naturalis historia* 25.103). Scammony is bindweed; the resin from its roots was used as a cathartic (cf Pliny *Naturalis historia* 26.59–61).
154 Eph 6:17
155 Cf John 21:15–17.
156 Cf John 10:12; Acts 20:24.

embrace zeal for the Sacred Scriptures; instead of luxury, sobriety; instead of lust, chastity; instead of pride, penitence. Then let them beg the Lord's protection against the authors of heresy and schism. Sometimes princes of this world, denied the taxes due them, take offence at their people's stubbornness. They look the other way while allowing their people to be attacked by an enemy.[157] At this point the people, learning a lesson even by these methods, come to their senses and acknowledge the amount they owe their prince. If they had run straight off to ask their king's help, they would have accomplished nothing but to raise his anger. What I am saying about priests should, I believe, also be understood of monks, indeed of all clerics. Have you yet seen any one of them learning a lesson from these disasters, and embarking on better and more fruitful courses? Has any sent away his concubine? Has any turned luxury into fasting? Has any taken the money he always used to support horses, dogs, and girlfriends, and used it to aid the poor? Has any said farewell to rowdiness and pleasure-seeking, seeking solace instead in the Sacred Scriptures? Has any, casting aside monkish hypocrisy, embraced true piety with his whole heart? I rather think that the moral character of the people is more corrupt still. But if all together, acknowledging their sins, were to run as suppliants to the mercy of the Lord, he would not be deaf, believe me, nor inaccessible to entreaty. If, however, we persevere in the courses that we know caused God's anger – and not only persevere, but even add worse to our former sins, pouring oil on the fire[158] – in vain shall we, relying on our own plans, promise ourselves an end to our troubles.

Never has the church enjoyed such good fortune that it did not have to endure many bad people, with only a few good ones. How many times does Paul cry out against false apostles,[159] dogs,[160] evil-workers,[161] false brothers,[162] and slaves of the belly![163] Every enterprise is in turmoil when it is first beginning. At that time the church's flock was scattered and weak, yet there were dissensions, factions, and quarrels;[164] there was a man who openly had his stepmother in the place of a wife;[165] there was Demas, who abandoned

* * * * *

157 An instance of what might be called political paranoia on Erasmus' part; see Tracy *Politics of Erasmus* chapter 4.
158 See above n58.
159 2 Cor 11:13
160 Phil 3:2
161 Phil 3:2
162 2 Cor 11:26; Gal 2:4
163 Cf Rom 16:18; Phil 3:19.
164 Eg 1 Cor 1:10–13
165 1 Cor 5:1

the gospel to follow the world;[166] there were men who preached the gospel insincerely;[167] others who lied, cheated, defrauded the brothers,[168] or practised circumcision;[169] there were women who idly made the rounds to other people's houses, garrulous, inquisitive, and laden with sins;[170] and widows, who, gathering lascivious fruits from the church's provisions, abandoned Christ and turned back to Satan;[171] there were some who with flattering talk seduced the hearts of simple folk,[172] and others who falsely claimed that angels had appeared to them.[173] In the church were such things and many others at that time, as is clear from the letters of the apostles. So many evils did the church bear even at that time, still in its infancy, and scattered as it was. Are we surprised if a church, become numerous and widespread, still has traits displeasing to the virtuous? Do we conclude that the entire stage-structure of the church should be toppled? It is desirable that all bishops of the church be as well furnished as possible with sacred learning, zeal for piety, charity, and purity of character. They are the shepherds of sheep, but they themselves are sheep, mere men charged with the care of men. But it is not for just anyone to correct their vices, and besides it is largely up to the people to make them good. If laymen show a teachable disposition, they will, by God's providence, not lack teachers. Let them cry out vehemently to the highest Shepherd, that he may be appeased and take thought for his flock. As long as the church's net is still being dragged through the waters of this world, and has not yet reached the shore, we must endure good mixed with bad.[174] The state of human affairs has always been, and will always be, the same, 'more aloe than honey.'[175] If, however, a person always culls out only the evils, of course no part of life will please him. He will instead approve of Silenus' opinion, that not to be born is best, the next best is to be annihilated as soon as possible.[176] If, in exercising judgment, one shuts one's right eye and uses only one's left, even the most excellent things will appear very bad.

* * * * *

166 2 Tim 4:10
167 Cf Phil 1:17.
168 Acts 5:1–11
169 Acts 15:1; Phil 3:2
170 1 Tim 5:13
171 1 Tim 5:15
172 Rom 16:18
173 Col 2:18
174 See above n50.
175 Juvenal *Satura* VI.180
176 *Adagia* II iii 49: *Optimum non nasci* 'Not to be born is best' CWE 33 160–2

Since the church, like all other affairs of mortals, has its beginning stages, development, and culmination,[177] to call it back now to its origins is no less ridiculous than to drag a grown man back to his cradle and his infancy. Time and conditions of events bring much with them, and change much for the better.[178] At one time, Christians met secretly, in small numbers, in private houses; now they all flock to a public, consecrated temple. Which is more fitting? Surely the latter. At one time, the Eucharist was taken during dinners, at which, as Paul bears witness, one person was hungry, another drunk;[179] now it is taken at a sacred table, by people who are fasting. Which is more devout? At one time, one person had a hymn to offer at church, another a revelation, another a psalm, another spoke in tongues, another prophesied;[180] and meanwhile the women were chattering away;[181] now the tasks have been distributed to definite individuals; the others are silent, calmly listening or praying. Which is more devout? At one time, nightly vigils were the custom, excursions to visit the tombs of the martyrs, attended by boys, girls, men, monks, wives, and sacred virgins – and yet crimes, committed under the shade of piety, made it desirable to abolish this kind of vigil.[182] By night the people went forth with silver candlesticks, singing hymns. Sometimes, when other bands met them, professing a different conviction, the hymn-singing turned into a brawl, the candlesticks serving as weapons.[183] Was not, therefore, this custom rightly abolished? At one time, the body of the Lord was handed out, so that people who received it could consume it at home, when they wished; but since there existed people who treated it unworthily, and made ill use of it for the crafts of magic,[184] the custom was changed for the better. At one time, bishops were created by the votes of the people, and ejected to suit public whim – and sometimes stoned as well. The business was full of turmoil, and sometimes

* * * * *

177 See Allen Ep 1844:30–4; cf *Purgatio adversus epistolam Lutheri* below n24.
178 Cf *Ratio* LB V 87F–88A. On the variety of persons, times, and things, see Hoffmann *Rhetoric and Theology* 162–7, and István Bejczy *Erasmus and the Middle Ages. The Historical Consciousness of a Christian Humanist* (Leiden 2001).
179 1 Cor 11:21
180 1 Cor 14:26
181 1 Cor 14:33b–35
182 Cf *De esu carnium* ASD IX-1 28:232–3.
183 See Cassiodorus *Historia ecclesiae tripartita* X 8 CSEL 71:595.
184 Erasmus had described an incident of this kind many years previously: CWE 2, Ep 143:74–135. For a history of the celebration of the mass see Jungmann *The Mass of the Roman Rite* (above *Detectio praestigiarum* n165).

slaughter.[185] So the facts themselves made it desirable to grant the right of appointing bishops, and removing them, to a few reliable people. At one time, when bishops addressed the people, they were obliged to make a theatrical display, just like actors in a play, who, if they failed to please the people – a less than ideal judge – could be driven from the stage with hisses. Sometimes unseemly shouts were heard; people waved their hands about in an unrestrained fashion, and made other boisterous gestures; there were hisses and mocking laughter, if something did not find favour, and much else besides that the common people brought with them from theatres and circuses into God's church. John Chrysostom[186] often complains about this, and so does Jerome from time to time. Now all listen silently with great reverence to one speaking from a raised position. Which practice, I ask you, is worthier of a temple? At one time, the whole people sang and responded 'amen' to the priest. Noise, not unlike thunder, and a laughable confusion of voices showed, on such occasions, a spectacle unworthy of divine worship. Now those who can sing properly have been assigned this task; the rest sing to the Lord in their hearts. The early church accepted no kind of music, and not without protest was it accepted later, first among the Greeks, then among the Latins; but it was more like modulated recitation than song. We can still see a specimen of it in the Lord's prayer, and there may be other examples of this kind. Now, as is the nature of human affairs, the custom has degenerated to such an extent that in many temples virtually nothing is heard except an immense bellowing, or foolish chattering of voices, which provides quicker inducements to lasciviousness than to any emotion of piety.[187] Yet music should not for this reason be entirely removed from temples; rather, what has crept in amiss should receive skillful correction. For some ages it was considered abominable that any painted or sculpted image be seen in the temples of Christians. Piety, according to the

* * * * *

185 See eg Gregory of Tours' description of such disorders in *History of the Franks* II 1 and 13.
186 For example, Chrysostom in *De Lazaro* 2 3 PG 48:985 claims he prefers silence to applause.
187 Here Erasmus begins a series of comparisons that reverse the progress he has been celebrating, to describe instead a trend of degeneration. However, his argument is not to do away with the offending practice, but to cleanse it. The austerity of the early church is not the model to be emulated. For Erasmus' views on the church music of his time see Ep 1756:100–15 and Allen Ep 2205:93–105; see also *Institutio christiani matrimonii* CWE 69 426–7; cf J.-C. Margolin *Erasme et la musique* (Paris 1965) and his *Recherches Erasmiennes* (Geneva 1969) 85–97.

reasoning of those times, convinced people of this view, partly on account
of the Jews, who in consequence of God's command loathed all images, but
were otherwise prone to idolatry, and partly on account of those who came
to the gospel from paganism: it is likely that traces of their old customs remained ingrained in them for a long time. Now the use of images has developed to such an extent that it not only far exceeds proper moderation,
but has also left decorum far behind. We see in temples things that would
be unsuitable if painted on arcades and cookshops. Yet there is no need to
remove pictures entirely; they offer much pleasure, distinction, and usefulness, but whatever contains an element of fault should be corrected.[188] At
one time the church had no public schools, only those in theology, and the
bishop alone did all the teaching. But the founding of schools has brought
immense good to Christianity, especially among the barbarous nations.[189]
Now profit-making and ambition have done some damage to a good thing,
through trivial questions aimed more at ostentation than piety.[190] Should
schools therefore be abolished? Of course not, but their pursuits should
be summoned back to Christian restraint. Yet some have come forth from
that band of yours, who teach, in public and private, that the studies in
the humanities are nothing other than the snares of demons.[191] They have
so far succeeded that you will see very few men in that crowd who have
given serious effort to letters, whether sacred or profane. There is, to be
sure, plenty of zeal directed to profit-making and pleasure. At one time,
the class of monks lacked restraints; but then their numbers increased; they
became disseminated through the world, setting out from Egypt, their place
of origin; they began to commit many crimes under a pretext of piety, and
fears arose that they would bring about the ruin of the whole church. And
so it became necessary to force them into a stricter kind of life.[192] The
distinctions in their garments, at least, are aimed at making it easier to avoid
any who are bad. At one time, there was no fighting against heretics except

* * * * *

188 Cf *Explanatio symboli* CWE 70 364–7, which provides a more detailed discussion
    of appropriate and inappropriate use of images in worship; see also Allen Ep
    2205:87–92.
189 'Barbarous' in a humanist sense, meaning north of the Alps.
190 Cf eg *Moria* CWE 27 127–31; see E. Rummel '*Et cum theologo bella poeta gerit*:
    The Conflict between Humanists and Scholastics Revisited' *Sixteenth Century
    Journal* 23 (1992) 713–26; and, by the same author, *The Humanistic-Scholastic
    Debate in the Renaissance and Reformation* (Cambridge, MA 1995).
191 Cf eg *Hyperaspistes* 1 LB X 1268F / CWE 76 143.
192 Cf Ep 858:443–598, which gives a different picture of the earliest monks. St
    Benedict mentions two types of corrupt monks in chapter 1 of his *Rule*.

with the sword of the Spirit;[193] but after the obstinacy of zealots reached
such a pitch that the situation seemed likely to result in a bloody disturbance
of the world, the power of emperors was forced to offer assistance, through
laws and weapons, to a critical public need. At one time, the protectors of
the church were supported by what the public voluntarily brought them,
and were not armed with any defences other than teaching, prayer, and
tears; but among the more savage nations sheer necessity made it desirable
to fortify them, by resources, buildings, and attendants, against popular
assault.

There is no need of further examples. If Paul were alive today, he
would not, I believe, condemn the present state of the church; he would cry
out against people's vices. Some people are never pleased with anything
unless they founded it themselves, and even then they are not consistently
satisfied. So vices must be remedied, but short of causing disturbance, and
as we proceed we must make sure that the remedies are not worse than the
disease. But if one party allows nothing at all to be altered, and the other
allows nothing to be left the same, what end will there be of quarrelling?
If the bishops of the church and civil rulers were to put aside worldly motives and make their aim the glory of the Lord through the spiritual advantage of the church, this trouble could be settled without great disturbance.
The favour, therefore, of monarchs and princes must be canvassed by honourable methods; their hearts should not have been alienated. It remains
to pray earnestly that Christ inspire such an intention in all. But on these
subjects I have already said more than I had planned.

For the rest, I would do what I have done before, and would urge
you to restore yourself to us, if I had a hope that I would achieve anything
thereby. May the Lord inspire in your heart ways that will contribute to
your salvation. You will forgive my lack of restraint, dear Vulturius. When I
ponder what you are doing, I find many things lacking in you: most notably,
your former sincerity of heart, and a certain good will, especially towards
me; uncommon good sense, and a sober heart as well; in short, the whole
Vulturius whom I, along with many good and learned men, once knew and
loved. May I secure one request at least from you – if not to please me,
at least for your own sake, and finally out of regard for an enterprise that
you consider pious and sacred, and I do not yet entirely despair of, hoping
that it might possibly be brought back to some degree of moderation. The
request is that you restrain yourself from trifles of this sort. If you have the

* * * * *

193 Eph 6:17

desire and leisure to play, you have enough subject matter for your jokes without hurting a friend. But if you want to help him, you must embark on a much different plan. Consider these things written to you by someone who is truly a friend. May the Lord protect you.

Freiburg im Breisgau, November 4, the year of our Lord 1529.

LETTER TO THE BRETHREN
OF LOWER GERMANY

Responsio ad fratres Inferioris Germaniae ad epistolam apologeticam
incerto autore proditam

translated by
PETER MATHESON

annotated by
LAUREL CARRINGTON

The *Epistola contra pseudevangelicos* predictably created a stir among those against whom it was directed. Its intended recipient, Gerald Geldenhouwer, responded by publishing an unauthorized version of the three Erasmus texts whose meaning was under debate, together with his own annotations, refuting Erasmus' accusations.[1] Erasmus was furious, but a more thorough response was yet to come, this time from Martin Bucer, leader of the new church in Strasbourg. The *Epistola apologetica*, published in May 1530, was addressed to the brethren in Lower Germany and East Frisia.[2] It did not bear Bucer's signature, but was attributed to the ministry at Strasbourg as a whole. Thus, while Bucer may have been the author, he intended his pamphlet to speak with a collective voice.

Bucer had been one of Erasmus' most fervent admirers in his youth, and the Strasbourg Reformation, in which he played a leading role, was renowned for its toleration and devotion to humanistic learning. At the time of this exchange, Bucer was attempting to play a mediating role in the controversy about the Eucharist, which had erupted between followers of Luther and Zwingli over the issue of Christ's bodily presence. Yet despite many apparent affinities, relations between Erasmus and Bucer had been cool for several years.[3] This exchange would mark a complete break between them.

Because in the *Epistola ad fratres Inferioris Germaniae* Erasmus responds specifically and at length to Bucer's arguments, a brief review of Bucer's *Epistola apologetica* is in order. The work constitutes a comprehensive defence of the Protestant cause, including a systematic counter-attack against the Roman church. While it takes Erasmus' *Epistola contra pseudevangelicos* as its starting point, it draws liberally upon attacks Erasmus had made against Protestants in his published letters as well. It is clear that Bucer had taken such criticisms to heart, and may even have welcomed the opportunity to respond to them. As a counterweight to the tone of irony that is the hallmark of Erasmus' critique, Bucer sets a tone of dignity and gravity. Acknowledging his awareness of Erasmus' substantial gifts as a writer, Bucer also makes clear that such gifts, without the right spirit, do not have the power to reflect the truth.

* * * * *

1 For the three Erasmus texts at issue, see the introductory note to *Epistola contra pseudevangelicos* above 211 with nn15–17. See Allen Epp 2238, 2289, and 2293.
2 An edition of this work annotated by C. Augustijn is available in BOL I.
3 For relations between Erasmus and Bucer, see *Epistola contra pseudoevangelicos* introductionory note above 216 and text 219 nn121–3. See also CÉBR I 209–212.

Bucer's *Epistola apologetica* begins with a lengthy introduction in which he evaluates the task at hand. Those who believe in the true gospel are being subjected to lies and slanders, coming from an author who is honoured as an erudite and pious man. Nonetheless, Erasmus' attack must be answered, just as the ancient Christians had to endure the verbal assaults of such learned men as Pliny and Tacitus.

The introduction is followed by the first of two sections of the body of the work, incorporating a defence of the Protestants' beliefs and lives. Here Bucer addresses such questions as the freedom of the will, the role of the Holy Spirit in the history of the church, and the sacraments of baptism and the Eucharist. He then proceeds to critique in blistering terms Catholic spiritual practices, concluding with a portrayal of the sober, honest, and temperate lives of the evangelicals that is a deliberate study in contrasts.

The second section follows more closely the lines of Erasmus' attack, responding specifically to the criticisms of the *Epistola contra pseudevangelicos*. According to Bucer's own breakdown, these charges encompass three major issues: First, there is Erasmus' accusation that the evangelicals use craft in promoting their cause, to which Bucer responds in detail, defending many of the individuals against whom Erasmus had written in the *Epistola contra pseudevangelicos*, including himself.[4] Second, Bucer responds to Erasmus' disparaging treatment of the evangelicals' comparison of themselves and their position with that of the apostles, and to his assertion that what they have in fact done is destroyed what was good in the church for over a thousand years and put something much worse in its place. Third, he refutes Erasmus' claims that the extremism of the evangelical party has had the consequence of merely increasing the tyranny of the monks and theologians over all of Christendom. Bucer ends his defence with a brief epilogue.

Throughout the *Epistola apologetica* Bucer has a complex task to perform, as he attempts to articulate a collective response at a time when reformers continue to be divided over the matter of the Eucharist. He begins his section on doctrine by assuming the role of a bridge-builder. Erasmus in the *Epistola contra pseudevangelicos* had asked: 'What sort of demands are you making of us? To believe that the church lacked Christ for 1400 years; that the bride worshipped ghosts and idols instead of God, while the Bridegroom snored away; that she was utterly blind in expounding the Sacred

* * * * *

4 See *Epistola contra pseudevangelicos* nn121–3.

Scriptures; that the saints' miracles were nothing other than the illusion-istic tricks of demons.' Bucer's response is one of absolute denial that any such formulations have been taught by the reformers at any point. He af-firms that 'to be sure, many people in all ages brought forth excellent fruits of the gospel: unquestionably every kind of denial of self, the love of ser-vice to everyone, and a life of singular honesty and gentleness; who there-fore dares to say that the true gospel was shut away, that Christ has been absent from the church, or – which is most odiously attributed to us – that the Bridegroom was snoring while the bride worshipped figments and idols?'[5] In many respects the church has erred, but it has not been sepa-rated from Christ, nor should all that has been done throughout its history be repudiated.

Against this background, Bucer presents the teachings of the reformers as no more nor less than the true message of the gospel. One God created all things by God's own word and power out of nothing, conserves them, and acts to perfect them; God's own Son in turn abolishes sin among his elect.[6] The Holy Spirit is active in the world, although since the time of the apostles it has not manifested this activity through miracles, but through inspiring those who are truly of Christ. Bucer makes every effort to portray the beliefs and practices of the evangelicals in as inoffensive a light as possible, the upshot of his strategy being to show that the evangelicals are not the wild extremists that Erasmus has claimed them to be. It is a strategy that demands he focus at least in part on what the evangelicals have in common with the traditional church, enabling readers to imagine that the reformers are not so much cutting themselves off from past practices as calmly and reasonably shifting their emphases to something more appropriate.

Bucer lists in his own words the essence of Erasmus' accusations against the reformers: '[that they] have forced images from places of wor-ship, removed what are called the solemn prayers of the church, abrogated the mass, got rid of the rule of secret confession, rescinded rules regarding food and precepts from the popes concerning fasting, and obliterated many ceremonies, refashioned human traditions, permitted marriage to everyone and forced new rites in the churches, and changed many other things.'[7] Ad-dressing these accusations one by one, Bucer insists that in each case no dis-ruptive changes have been instituted. For example, regarding confession he writes: 'We have never repealed confession, which may be made to a

* * * * *

5 See above 242; BOL I 87:26–31.
6 See BOL I 88:25–33.
7 BOL I 85:14–20

person empowered to remind one of one's duty, either to clear one's conscience, or to be encouraged in the good faith of God's favour.'[8] However, he continues, people who are dying of their sins cannot expect to seek a remedy from human beings, and if many now have given up the practice, it is not on account of any prohibition from the reformers; besides, such people would not gain anything from confessing in any case. In this manner Bucer redefines the reform as indeed retaining the wheat as it destroys the tares.

In discussing the sacraments, Bucer must walk a line between overvaluing external things, as he believes the Roman church has done, and undervaluing them, which is the fault of the spiritualists and Anabaptists. God instituted the two sacraments of baptism and the Eucharist, Bucer tells us, so that those receiving the celestial doctrine as one body, with Christ as the head, might share among themselves a common understanding; these symbols are God's accommodation to the ways of human intellect.[9] Baptism is essential as a sign of our regeneration: 'Since by baptism sins are said to be washed away, and we to have died and been buried with Christ, the old man has been stripped off and the new, that is, Christ, has been put on, and at last we go forth as new creatures ...'[10] What Christ gives, however, is not just a cleansing with water, but a new spirit.[11] The physical cleansing with water is thus a valued symbol, instituted by God, for the cleansing with spirit that allows the newly-baptized to put on Christ. Bucer affirms infant baptism, emphasizing that God bestows his spirit on infants, because those whom God has designated for glory since before creation have been sanctified right from their mothers' womb.[12] The Eucharist, like baptism, was instituted of old, offering us the spiritual food of our Lord's body and blood by which we are nourished in the life everlasting.[13] Yet Bucer also must acknowledge the fact that 'there are those who contend that beyond this the bodily presence of Christ is consumed in the flesh and blood, some under the appearance of bread, others under the bread itself.'[14] He treats this matter carefully, describing Christ's words, 'This is my body,' as a demonstration to the intellect, comparable to the angel

* * * * *

8 BOL I 156:8–10
9 See BOL I 92:34–93:1.
10 BOL I 93:17–19
11 See BOL I 93:26–8.
12 See BOL I 94:13–16.
13 See BOL I 94:22–5.
14 BOL I 95:4–5

saying to Ezekiel, 'This is Jerusalem.'[15] Yet Bucer hastens to add that what is in the Eucharist is not just bread and wine, but that it is the bread and wine of God, through which those partaking receive that spirit of Christ that animates them to a true service in piety.[16] He explains that the Fathers of the church described the Eucharist as the body and blood of Christ in the same way that they described baptism as the experience of being entombed with Christ. 'The one thing we do not teach,' Bucer emphasizes, 'is that Christ our God, the bread of heaven, the bread of life to those who are perishing, is at the same time brought into the belly.'[17] Yet for all of Bucer's attempts at subtlety, Erasmus in his response repeatedly summarizes his position by saying: 'In the Eucharist there is nothing but bread and wine.'[18]

The bridge-builder transforms himself into the polemicist as Bucer next addresses Roman Catholic practices. He refers first to the mass as full of abominations and superstitions, destructive of all piety, and the source of evil deeds.[19] He repudiates prayers for the dead, special vows, monasticism, and the ceremonial observance of canonical hours, whereas he defends the reformers' removal of images from the churches. He finds particularly offensive the practice of saying private masses for the dead, a source of blasphemy, imposture, and abuse. The role of the reformers in confronting such practices is in his eyes similar to Christ's driving the money-changers out of the temple.[20] Bucer's description of the reformers' lives is calculated to present as strong a contrast as possible to the venality of Rome. 'We flee at the same time from luxury and from sterile parsimony,'[21] he writes. 'Indeed, the spirit here is to harm no one, to help everyone.'[22] It may be the case that some members of our churches are bad, but such was the case in the time of the apostles as well. Why expect more of us?[23] In response to Erasmus' charges of licentious behaviour among the reformers, Bucer has some mud of his own to fling at the Roman camp. He hints broadly at Ludwig Baer when he relates the story that an illustrious canon was heard to complain that whereas prior to the reform there was an abundance of nice

* * * * *

15 Ezek 5:5
16 See BOL I 96:1–7.
17 BOL I 97:9–10
18 See below 267.
19 See BOL I 108:20–6.
20 See BOL I 113:3–8.
21 BOL I 117:35–6
22 BOL I 117:40–118:1
23 See BOL I 120:5–18.

harlots in Zürich, after the reform there were no more to be found.[24] Bucer does not reveal himself in his best light by repeating such slander, and Erasmus in his rebuttal indignantly denies the truth of the story.[25] Bucer is on his shakiest ground, however, as he attempts to defend himself and others against the charge that the reformers have resorted to trickery in promoting their cause. Bucer himself was particularly vulnerable because he had published his *Commentaries on the Psalms* under a false name, written a dedicatory preface to the dauphin of France, and by stylistic clues in the text suggested that he was a Frenchman. The purpose of the ruse was to attract readers who might have avoided the work had they known the author's true identity. Bucer takes the approach of justifying the means by the end: 'We are persuaded that this matter with which we are engaged is of God.'[26] Thus, behaviour that might ordinarily be best avoided can be accepted in such a cause. Paul himself used a pious ruse when he addressed the Athenians concerning the altar with the inscription: 'To an unknown God.'[27] Erasmus will respond both to the defence and to the analogy with indignant scorn.

It is in this spirit that Bucer claims that the fight in which the reformers are now engaged is analogous to that of the apostles themselves who suffered greatly for the cause of Christ, and that the tumults of the present are all in accordance with the predictions of Scripture. 'Certainly,' he writes, 'as our flesh has a horror of the cross, we would have preferred that all either keep silent about these things or else speak more moderately. But the necessity bore down, of preaching the gospel and preaching to every creature; that is, openly testifying that all is to be sought from one Christ, both justification and salvation, nor can anyone no matter how holy, apostles or bishops, do anything other than plant and water; that is, teach and admonish.'[28] To Erasmus' call for moderation, discussion, and patience, Bucer gives his heart-felt concurrence, but adds: 'Would that it were acknowledged what things are the obstacles to true piety.'[29] What indeed would be more suitable and prudent than to confess these things? Erasmus will note this passage in his reply, remarking that 'he approves of this advice of mine, doubtless on condition that they determine for us which things stand in the way

* * * * *

24 See BOL I 120:26–32.
25 See below 285.
26 BOL I 123:16
27 Acts 17:23; see BOL I 124:6–12.
28 BOL I 206:26–31
29 BOL I 207:18–19

of godliness . . .'[30] In his response to Bucer, Erasmus loses no time in showing that he is aware of Bucer's strategies, and is having none of them. For
example, against Bucer's imputation of unity Erasmus unwaveringly maintains the language of pluralism. Throughout the response he returns many
times to the question: 'Who is this *we* that the writer is claiming he represents? Is it the clergy of Strasbourg? I have never had anything to do with
the clergy of Strasbourg,' thus reminding the reader that Bucer's letter is
from a particular place, the product of a particular group.

Much of Erasmus' letter is taken up with details of interpretation. If in
the *Epistola contra pseudevangelicos* he wrote to Geldenhouwer: 'I will show
you many [evangelicals] who have become worse than their former selves,'[31]
he now chides Bucer for taking offence, as if he had said that all evangelicals
had become worse. Even more than in his first letter, he depends on *ad
hominem* attacks to prove his point that the evangelicals cannot claim to
have improved Christendom with their innovations. He refuses to accept
Bucer's excuses for the evangelicals' use of subterfuges as a worthy tactic
in such a holy cause, scoffing at the comparison to Paul. He likewise treats
in scathing terms Bucer's attempt to draw an analogy between the apostles
in the early church and the 16th century reformers: 'They try to prove that
the Christianity existing up to now was no better than the superstition of
the gentiles, that what they now undertake is what was foretold by the
apostles, and by the prophets, namely, that the gentiles, having left the
worship of demons, would come to acknowledge the true God, while Jewish
ceremonies would vanish at the shining of the gospel light. Whose ears can
tolerate such blasphemy?'[32] To Bucer's comparison of the differences among
reformers with those among the apostles, Erasmus replies that the apostles
never disagreed in the teachings of the faith, as the reformers do on the
matter of the Eucharist.

Erasmus combats Bucer's assumption of a dignified tone directly: 'He
calls it a slanderous lie when I said that according to them the bride of
Christ was blind for so many years while her husband was snoring. He
denies that her Bridegroom ever snored, as though I had not been saying this
ironically.'[33] To the substance of Bucer's argument, the contention that the
evangelicals recognize much that was good and holy in the church's history,
Erasmus only responds: 'They who teach that baptism is not necessary for

* * * * *

30 See below 350.
31 See above 231.
32 See below 303–4.
33 See below 346.

anyone's salvation, who teach that in the Eucharist there is nothing but bread and wine, and many other similar things, who say that the old Doctors of the church wrote sheer nonsense, and that there is a danger that they are all in hell, how do they represent the church if not as blind?'[34] He repeats such blunt summaries of the reformers' views often, thus bypassing entirely the mediating language in which Bucer has attempted to recast the essence of his party's goals.

Overall, both Bucer's *Epistola apologetica* and Erasmus' response are something of a hybrid, combining eloquent statements of principles and beliefs with much that is frustrating in the *ad hominem* quality of the argument. The controversy as a whole presents a seemingly endless chain of accusations exchanged and denied, stories told and repudiated, and widely diverging interpretations of the same events. For every story Erasmus can tell about an adulterous or dishonest member of the reform party, Bucer can match him with complaints against the Catholic clergy, while in the meantime both conduct their defence by declaring that it is inappropriate to damn an entire group on the basis of the bad example set by a few of its members. The controversy becomes bogged down in disagreements about both facts and interpretations, leaving the reader at a loss to know whether the reformers were clearly guilty of instigating violence, or absolutely peaceful in asserting their well-justified beliefs against oppressive abusers of power.

Yet in spite of these drawbacks, all three works (Erasmus' *Epistola contra pseudevangelicos*, Bucer's *Epistola apologetica*, and Erasmus' *Epistola ad fratres Inferioris Germaniae*) let us see in high relief the divergence between the humanist reform promoted by Erasmus and Bucer's evangelical reform. At issue between these two men is not a single, overriding doctrinal concern such as the freedom of the will – which Luther congratulated Erasmus on recognizing as the heart of the difference between the two – but rather a entire spectrum of events, phenomena, and interpretations. For example, Erasmus describes the reform in Basel as violent and coercive, whereas Bucer sees it as a moment of triumph for the people and, ultimately, for God. For readers to be able to observe Erasmus and Bucer struggling with a baffling array of such intractable differences offers valuable insight into the dynamics of religious conflict in the early Reformation.

In other words, in this quarrel two people, known at various points in their lives for their advocacy of dialogue and consensus, become unalterably polarized. Yet in probing the defence each makes of his respective

* * * * *

34 See below 346.

view, we are able to understand to a certain extent the rupture between biblical humanists such as Erasmus and humanistically-inclined reformers such as Bucer. The debate between Erasmus and Luther (Erasmus' *De libero arbitrio* and Luther's *De servo arbitrio*) six years earlier pitted men of distinctly opposing temperaments and commitments against each other. This exchange, in contrast, reveals two men of a background that might have led to a possible agreement, reaching the limits of their abilities not only to agree, but to communicate at all.

LC

LETTER TO THE BRETHREN
OF LOWER GERMANY

DESIDERIUS ERASMUS OF ROTTERDAM TO HIS BELOVED BRETHREN
IN CHRIST OF LOWER GERMANY AND EAST FRISIA, GREETINGS
A certain book has appeared here,[1] addressed to brethren in Lower Germany and East Frisia, which leads many to suspect that a great many people in these parts are committing themselves to these new sects which claim for themselves the title of the gospel. It may appear to be written to you, in fact it is directed against me.

However, my grief is much less for the injury I have suffered personally than for the calamity our fatherland has suffered. So my first concern is to beseech you by the salvation of your souls not to let anything remove you from the company of the Catholic church, not to let yourselves be carried around by every wind of doctrine,[2] not to be swept away from the gospel[3] which has been handed down by the bride of Christ and which you have observed thus far. Do not let your minds be easily swayed by letters or pamphlets with a great pretence of mildness and piety but discern whether the spirits are really of God.[4] For Satan is used to transforming himself into an angel of light,[5] the better to deceive simple and incautious folk. Stand firm on Christ, the rock; keep within the ark, lest you perish in

* * * * *

1 Erasmus is referring to Martin Bucer's *Epistola apologetica*, found in BOL I 75–225. The *Epistola*, which Bucer left unsigned, was written in early May of 1530 on behalf of the reformed church in Strasbourg, as a response to Erasmus' *Epistola contra pseudevangelicos* 218–53 in this volume.
2 Eph 4:14
3 Cf Gal 1:6.
4 1 John 4:1
5 2 Cor 11:14; cf *Hyperaspistes* LB X 1309D / CWE 76:238–9. M.O. Boyle writes about Erasmus' use of this phrase in his discussion of the discernment of spirits; see *Rhetoric and Reform* 134–5 n7.

the flood;[6] remain in Christ's little bark, lest the waves engulf you;[7] stay within the flock of the church,[8] lest you become a prey to the wolves and to Satan who never ceases to go about seeking whom he may devour.[9] At the very least wait for the decree from the most religious emperor, the princes, and others at the diet.[10] For I trust that through them the Lord, who alone can command the ocean to be stilled,[11] will deign to settle these stormy events. For the moment, let us simply arouse with pious deeds the one who appears to be sleeping,[12] awakening him with clear and incessant prayers.

From one sect new ones sprout every day.[13] At least allow them time to agree among themselves before you throw in your lot with one or the other. Sober and diligent inquiry about specific matters is not a characteristic of those in error; fanaticism is dangerous and deceptive and once it has taken hold of the mind takes away integrity of judgment. It leads us no longer to regard something as pious if it is pious in nature and in accordance with Scripture and reason, but rather to regard as pious whatever doctrines the sect has produced. Rush, if you must, into matters which can later be modified on better advice. In this matter, in which the salvation of your souls is at stake, if you cannot be strong at least be slow to move. It may sound pleasing to make pronouncements like: no one is obliged to confess to a priest;[14] papal prescriptions about fasts and the

* * * * *

6 Cf Gen 6:17–18.
7 Cf Matt 8:23–7; Mark 4:35–41; Luke 8:22–5.
8 Cf John 10:1–2.
9 Cf 1 Pet 5:8.
10 Emperor Charles v ruled from 1519 until 1555; here, Erasmus is referring to the 1530 Diet of Augsburg. Many of Erasmus' letters during this period testify to his hope that Charles will be able to stop the religious strife and restore order; see Allen Epp 2328:66–9, 2338:63–6, 2341:5–8.
11 Matt 8:26; Mark 4:39; Luke 8:24
12 A reference to the apostles' waking of Jesus in the boat; cf Matt 8:25; Mark 4:38; and Luke 8:24. Jesus rebuked the apostles for their lack of faith.
13 For Erasmus, disunity is a sign of departure from the will of God. Here he is referring especially to the division between Zwingli, Karlstadt, and others and Luther over the Eucharist. See the introductory note to *Detectio praestigiarum* above 149 n6.
14 In *Epistola apologetica* BOL I 156:8–23 Bucer maintains that confession to God is always encouraged, and that well-intended confession to someone who can admonish and encourage a Christian to maintain faith is by no means forbidden. For Protestant criticisms of the Catholic practice of confession, see A.N. Burnett *The Yoke of Christ: Martin Bucer and Christian Discipline* (Kirksville, MO 1994) 9–25 and S.E. Ozment *The Reformation in the Cities* (New Haven 1975) 49–56.

choice of food should be rejected;[15] there is no reason for anyone to become thin as a rake through works of satisfaction, Christ's ransom is more
than enough for us all, and our good works or bad works have no effect
on our salvation, only believe that he died to redeem you and you will be
saved, whatever your works were like;[16] in the Eucharist there is nothing
but bread and wine;[17] the sanctions of popes and bishops are not binding
on anyone; just as vows need not be taken, so those you took are to be rescinded;[18] no one has authority to inhibit anyone's right to get married.[19]
Sayings of this kind are at first sight pleasing to the ears, but you have
to be constantly on your guard lest the cup which is smeared with honey
may conceal poison.[20] Be as simple as doves, lest you harm or deceive anyone, but likewise be wise as serpents,[21] lest Satan with all his thousand devices deceive you, corrupting your minds from the truth which is in Christ
Jesus.

There will be room elsewhere for exhortation. For the moment I will
touch briefly on the issues they have scattered in the books published in
your area,[22] not in order to clear myself in your eyes (such pamphlets do
me no harm in the eyes of sensible people) but because I think that when
you have read our apologia (which I will keep as brief as I can) you will be
more cautious. I had written a warning to a certain friend of mine,[23] with

* * * * *

15 *Epistola apologetica* BOL I 145:28–146:26
16 Cf *Epistola apologetica* BOL I 88:25–89:16.
17 Bucer writes about the Eucharist in *Epistola apologetica* BOL I 94:22–97:15. While
   he does not reduce the bread and wine to mere physical objects as Erasmus
   suggests, he does claim that the true body and blood of Christ remain in
   heaven, while the bread and wine are 'bread and wine, but not that alone, but
   rather the bread and wine of the Lord, from which we are reminded not only
   of the body and blood of Christ, but at the same time of his very soul,' and
   that those receiving these gifts are nourished and inspired to works of piety,
   '... so that they may bear witness through the deed itself that they have taken
   up far more than just the body and bread.' Nevertheless, Erasmus continued
   to resort to his reductionist formula many times in his accusations against
   the evangelicals; see John Payne's introductory note to *Detectio praestigiarum*
   above 154 n37.
18 *Epistola apologetica* BOL I 109:18–110:19
19 *Epistola apologetica* BOL I 184:27–185:5
20 A reference to Matt 10:16; cf *Lingua* CWE 29 263 / ASD IV-1 240:62.
21 Cf Matt 10:13.
22 Ie the works of Geldenhouwer, and the *Epistola apologetica*.
23 He is speaking here of Gerard Geldenhouwer, to whom he addressed the
   Epistola contra pseudevangelicos.

heartfelt sorrow that he had entangled himself in the sects, maintaining at the same time so much good will towards him that (something which is rare now even among the best of friends) I had been willing to support this needy exile with my money.[24] On this occasion I added a word of warning about our contemporary sects. My sole protest had to do with his having attached my name to his pamphlets in very large lettering, causing me to suffer no little animosity,[25] so that even some of my friends in their concern for me thought I needed to be warned. At first I ignored the matter, but when the same thing happened again I protested by letter,[26] and hoped when it was published that my name had been cleared with everyone. This action greatly offended some in Strasbourg,[27] no doubt prompted by the person to whom I protested.[28] For up to then no minister, especially in Strasbourg, had cast any aspersions on me,[29] nor, unless I am mistaken, had I given them any cause to do so, unless they interpret as an atrocious insult that someone is unwilling to depart from the Catholic church and to lend his name to their gospel.

They call their epistle an 'apology' as if they were the ones attacked by me; nor does its title bear anyone's name; only: 'by the ministers of the word of the Strasbourg church.'[30] But since apart from two ministers[31]

* * * * *

24 Cf *Epistola contra pseudevangelicos* above 219; Allen Ep 2329:89–90.
25 Cf *Epistola contra pseudevangelicos* above 223–4.
26 This is the *Epistola contra pseudevangelicos*, published in late 1529.
27 The writer or writers of the *Epistola apologetica*. Erasmus begins by speaking of two writers, but eventually addresses the writer (Bucer) as one person.
28 Geldenhouwer; Erasmus believed at various times that Geldenhouwer was one of the writers, or that he had put the writer of the *Epistola apologetica* up to the task. See below n34.
29 This is not altogether the case; Erasmus had been alienated from the Strasbourg reformers for years. See below n31.
30 The complete title is *Epistola apologetica ad syncerioris christianismi sectatores per Frisiam orientalem, et alias Inferioris Germaniae regiones, in qua Evangelii christi vere studiosi, non qui se falso Evangelicos iactant, iis defenduntur criminibus, quae in illos Erasmi Roterodami epistola ad Vulturium Neocomum, intendit. Per ministros Evangelii, ecclesiae Argentoratensis.* See C. Augustijn's introduction to the *Epistola apologetica* BOL I 67.
31 Wolfgang Capito (1478–1541), born just north of Strasbourg, was educated and took minor orders in Freiburg. He was called in 1515 by Bishop Christoph von Utenheim to be a cathedral preacher in Basel, where he also taught theology in the university. His friendship with Erasmus developed during this time, as Erasmus drew upon Capito's expertise in Hebrew for his biblical scholarship. However, their friendship cooled after Capito became a proponent of the Reformation. He was immediately attracted by Luther's appeal, eventually

I know no one in Strasbourg, how could it have occurred to me to censure them all? It is not my custom to provoke anyone, still less people unknown to me, not to mention inveighing petulantly against any community, and least of all Strasbourg which, as I am deeply indebted on many accounts, I favour more than the rest.[32] They certainly deserve praise for the fact that nowhere else have matters been dealt with more moderately and with less disturbance.[33] Likewise the epistle came to me in the name of the ministers of the word, although I tend to think that no more than two people were architects of the whole business.[34] Having read its title, I set the pamphlet aside, intending never to read it, for it was prolix to a fault, full of fantasies, littered with insults. Later on, when I had some leisure, I began to dip into it, and finally devoured the whole thing.

I wish a thousandth part of that holiness which the pamphlet frequently professes were in everyone's mind! They could not portray themselves better than they have done in that book, indeed they mix in such remarkable deceit to incite against me all the 'evangelical' churches – for they prefer to be called this rather than herètical – and the princes who seem at all favourable to this business, as well as all the 'evangelical' people. What is surprising is that when these people have promulgated

* * * * *

becoming a co-leader, with Bucer, of the Strasbourg church. See Kittelson *Wolfgang Capito*.

Caspar Hedio (1494–1552) was born in Ettlingen, a town in Baden. He like Capito was educated at Freiburg, and arrived in 1518 at the University of Basel, where he was drawn into humanist circles. He travelled with Capito to Mainz, and then to Strasbourg as a preacher at the cathedral. By 1524 he had joined forces with Bucer, Capito, and fellow reformer Matthäus Zell in Strasbourg. His relationship with Erasmus became strained at this time, especially when he gave his support to the printer Johann Schott, who enraged Erasmus by publishing a pamphlet against him authored by Guillaume Farel. See Epp 1477A and 1477B, with introductions; see also CEBR II 169–70, and Kittelson *Wolfgang Capito*.

32 See Erasmus' exchange with Jakob Wimpfeling, Epp 302:12–15 and 305:23–33, regarding Erasmus' visit to Strasbourg (August 1514), when he was the honoured guest of the literary society of the city.

33 For the Strasbourg Reformation, see T.A. Brady *Ruling Class, Regime and Reformation at Strasbourg 1520–1555* (Leiden 1978) and Chrisman *Strasbourg and the Reform*.

34 In Allen Ep 2321:25–40 Erasmus refers to two authors, one of whom he names 'Scopegius,' the other of whom he assumes to be Geldenhouwer (see also Allen Ep 2324:5–7). Later, in Allen Ep 2365:18–20, Erasmus suggests that the *Epistola apologetica* was written by Bucer with Geldenhouwer's involvement.

new dogma, it is legitimate to use deceits and tricks, although even under the civil law this is only permitted providing no one is injured![35] As
if indeed it follows that when secular laws permit something in a secular matter, it is permissible with regard to the gospel, or as if when in
the same book they cast suspicion on the heir to the French throne as
one who does not reject what they have established, this deceit does not
lead to any one being harmed, and as if when they pretend the work has
been written by a Frenchman, they do not attract hostility to the French
people.[36]

   But it is a mark of their 'evangelical' cleverness that they issued the
book in the name of all the churches, lest anyone be sure against whom I
am drawing my weapon, and so if I reply frankly I will provoke a universal chorus against me.[37] In a similar way they twist whatever is said in
general terms in the whole book[38] to refer to the Strasbourg church.[39] And
if they wanted to refute a general statement, they should not have said: 'We
do not do that here'; but: 'What you object to never happened in any church
of our confession.' Again, although I said explicitly in the epistle that I was
not referring to all the 'evangelicals' but only those of whom I had knowledge, they nevertheless interpret me, whatever I say, as attacking the entire
'evangelical' community. And if anything is said against the behaviour of
some people, they tell us what their own teachings are so that often that
proverb comes to mind: 'I asked for sickles.'[40] If they find anything in my
writings which seems to favour their cause, they quote it and praise me,
all of course quite guilelessly,[41] although elsewhere they write these words:
'If Erasmus, moved by the spirit of Christ, or perhaps inadvertently, has

* * * * *

35 See *Epistola apologetica* BOL I 127:21–2: 'For the imperial laws allow that one
   may change one's name, if only it is done without defrauding anyone'; 128:7:
   'It is a pious fraud that hurts no one and benefits many.'
36 This passage reiterates a complaint Erasmus makes in the *Epistola contra pseude-*
   vangelicos, above 239 n123. The work in question is Bucer's *S. Psalmorum libri*
   quinque ad ebraicam veritatem versi, et familiari explanatione elucidati, dedicated to
   the dauphin Francis, son of Francis I.
37 See *Epistola apologetica* BOL I 85:22–32.
38 The *Epistola contra pseudevangelicos*
39 See *Epistola apologetica* BOL I 139:17–27, 159:6–160:4; however, Bucer refers to
   other cities as well; cf 161:11–19.
40 Cf *Adagia* II ii 49: *Falces postulabam* CWE 33:99–100, in reference to those whose
   replies do not address the question asked.
41 See eg *Epistola apologetica* BOL I 135:5–16, quoting directly from Erasmus' letters; also 165:23–5, 211:4. Bucer likewise refers to those of Erasmus' writings
   that had been directly excerpted by Geldenhouwer; see BOL I 129:9–17.

written anything in our favour' etc.[42] Who could miss the 'evangelical' sting here? I certainly did not reproach all those who are followers of the sects, but only the fanatics, who hold fast indiscriminately and indeed zealously to whatever has been retailed to them.

I could scarcely repress a smile whenever they compare themselves to Christ, the apostles, and the martyrs, as they are constantly doing.[43] For they claim as self-evident that they teach Christ purely and present the evangelical truth sincerely to the world. Everywhere they proclaim Holy Scripture, as if neither Christ, nor the gospel, nor Holy Scripture were known by us. Since they have, after all, been condemned as heretical by the supreme pontiff, and by the emperor, and by the theological faculties,[44] indeed by the consensus of the greatest part of the world - if it may be permitted to state the obvious - at least they might concede us equal rights, so that we might be evenly matched in this case.

They themselves regard the Arians as heretics.[45] On what do they base this if not the judgment of the leaders of the church and the consensus of the whole world? But the Arians strongly denied that they were heretics, insisting that Scripture was quite falsely understood by others. They[46] plead extravagantly that heretics should not be killed, although they themselves impose the death penalty on the Anabaptists,[47] who have been condemned on

* * * * *

42 *Epistola apologetica* BOL I 124:3–4
43 See for example *Epistola apologetica* BOL I 75:20–76:7.
44 There were two papal bulls; *Exsurge Domine* (15 June 1520) warned Luther, and *Decet Romanum Pontificem* (3 January 1521) excommunicated him as a heretic. On 26 May 1521 Emperor Charles V issued the Edict of Worms, placing Luther under the imperial ban. In the *Determinatio* of 15 April 1521 Luther's writings were condemned by the faculty of theology in Paris.
45 In church tradition, Arius, a priest of Alexandria, was believed to have taught that Christ is the firstborn of all creatures, not in any essential sense God; it was in opposition to Arius and his followers that the Council of Nicea (325) adopted a creed proclaiming that God the Son is 'consubstantial' with God the Father. Recent scholarship has nuanced the traditional picture of Arius, largely shaped by the writings of his contemporary opponents; see Maurice Wiles *Archetypical Heresy. Arianism through the Centuries* (Oxford 1996) chapter 1.
46 The 'evangelicals'
47 Luther's original attitude of grudging toleration eventually turned to an advocacy of the death penalty for dissenters such as the Anabaptists; see J. Lecler SJ *Toleration and the Reformation* (London and New York 1960) I 160–1. For a discussion of the evolution of attitudes towards the Anabaptists in Strasbourg, see Chrisman *Strasbourg and the Reform* 177–200.

far fewer points and who are said to have very many within their company who have turned from an abandoned life to a most upright one, for all the craziness of their opinions;[48] nor have they taken over any churches or cities, or banded together in alliances against the might of the princes,[49] nor have they dispossessed anyone of their power and means of support; finally they, too, rely on the testimonies of Scripture, rather more convincing ones than those who declare: 'This is my body' means 'This bread is the sign of my body.'[50] Some of them, indeed, pursue their cause so boldly that they force princes who are inclined to clemency to cruel measures.[51] They display an astonishing eloquence in assailing the lives of the pontiffs, the cardinals, bishops, priests, and monks,[52] speaking as if not one of them lived a life that was anything but utterly vicious and deplorable, although I would suppose that many more of them served Christ in sincerity of spirit than is the case with these people.

They are continually attributing mendacity to me,[53] while the whole of this most holy book of theirs swarms with lies and hypocrisy. By using

* * * * *

48 Erasmus' praise of the Anabaptists is largely rhetorical, although many followers of what modern scholars call the Radical Reformation claimed him as their inspiration. Sebastian Franck is a case in point: at the time that Erasmus engaged in his quarrel with Bucer, Franck was living in Strasbourg, and was in the process of publishing his *Chronica*, in which he spoke admiringly of Erasmus as an unjustly persecuted 'heretic.' Ironically, Erasmus had to ask Bucer to suppress the publication of Franck's *Chronica*. See Williams *Radical Reformation* 18–20, 394–8.

49 One exception, a few years subsequent to this writing, would be the uprising in Münster (1534–35), led by followers of the millenarian version of Anabaptism preached by Melchior Hoffman (1495?–1543) and his Netherlands follower Jan Matthijszoon (c 1534); see OER II 240–3, 32 33–5; see also Williams *Radical Reformation* chapter 13.

50 Erasmus is attacking Zwingli, Bucer, and Karlstadt on the troublesome question of the Eucharist.

51 The context indicates that this sentence refers not to the Anabaptists but to the 'evangelicals.'

52 Bucer uses this sequence often in *Epistola apologetica*; eg BOL I 108:19–20, where he writes, *Quis enim, qui Deum modo credit, non totus contremiscat quoties vel cogitat, quam vixerint iam seculis aliquot pontifices, cardinales, episcopi et ordo ecclesiasticus totus?* 'Who indeed, who at least believes in God, does not tremble all over whenever he reflects on how some of the pontiffs, cardinals, bishops, and the entire order of the church is living in these days?' Note that Bucer uses the term *aliquot*, suggesting that he was careful not to assail the lives of all the clergy.

53 As for example in *Epistola apologetica* BOL I 84:23–30

astonishing deception they exaggerate the sobriety, chastity, innocence of life under the 'gospel,'[54] and the superiority of their faith to what is preached by anyone else. What happens in Strasbourg I cannot say. But I know that in other places there has never been more profligacy, more adultery than among the 'evangelicals,' for that is what they like to be called.[55] Even the 'evangelicals' themselves do not deny this.[56] I wish they would all regain the life of virtue, so that I may seem mistaken here!

Has not Luther been compelled to send out visitors to restrain the people from rushing into every form of licence?[57] And did he not say that he preferred the former reign of the pope and the monks to the kind of people who under the pretext of the 'gospel' race into a life worthy of the Sogdians?[58] And did not Melanchthon make the same complaint in his letters to me?[59] Did not Oecolampadius admit the same in conversation?[60]

* * * * *

54 In *Epistola apologetica* BOL I 86:17–18, Bucer announces 'first, then, I will defend the doctrine that we preach, and then the way of life that we practise.' His defence of the evangelicals' life is found in 117:26–119:2.

55 Here Erasmus employs his strategy of responding to the *Epistola apologetica* as a defence of the Strasbourg Reformation rather than of the evangelical Reformation as a whole; see introductory note above 262.

56 See below n59.

57 In November 1525, at the request of his prince, Elector John of Saxony, Luther endorsed a revival of the ancient disciplinary practice of ecclesiastical visitation. Visitations began in 1526, and were soon organized according to instructions penned by Melanchthon, with a preface from Luther (*Articuli ... per visitatores* 1527, *Unterricht der Visitatoren* 1528). For the wider context, Gerald Strauss *Luther's House of Learning* (Baltimore 1976); *Kirche und Visitation: Beiträge zur Erforschung des frühneuzeitlichen Visitationswesens in Europa* ed Ernst Walter Zeeden and Peter Thaddäus Land (Stuttgart 1984).

58 Sogdiana, lying southeast of the Aral Sea, between the Amu Darya and the Syr Darya, was conquered by Alexander the Great; for the evil reputation of the Sogdians, see Strabo 11.11.3. The citation attributed to Luther cannot be identified.

59 On 6 September 1524 Erasmus sent a letter to Melanchthon enumerating his complaints against Otto Brunfels, Wolfgang Capito, Guillaume Farel, Caspar Hedio, Ulrich Zwingli, Heinrich Eppendorf, and others (Ep 1496). Melanchthon's reply of 30 September 1524 (Ep 1500) begins: 'You are quite right, dear Erasmus, to complain of the behaviour of our modern professors of the gospel' (lines 2–3). In the remainder of the letter, Melanchthon begs Erasmus not to allow such people to colour his impression of Luther or his teachings.

60 Oecolampadius (1481–1531), the main leader of the Reformation in Basel, had earlier worked with Erasmus in his preparation of the Greek New Testament. His relationship with Erasmus became strained as he sided with Zwingli's spiritual interpretation of the Eucharist; see Ep 1618:11–13; Rupp *Patterns of*

In fact, they themselves more than once in this book lament that very many live quite abandoned lives under the label of the gospel; 'but we execrate these,' they say, 'we do not recognize them.'[61] And since I do not wield my pen against any one else but those whom they too condemn, there is no disagreement between us, as we too do not countenance the crimes of wicked bishops or reprobate monks. The difference is this: they damn all of us without exception, while I confess that I cannot speak about those unknown to me.[62] So what arrogance is this to interpret what is directed only against the reprobate in such a way as if it were directed against those who want to be regarded as paragons of virtue?

But 'I object,' so they say, 'to their doctrines.'[63] On the contrary, I make no claims to act as a judge in that matter, since their judge is the emperor. All I complain about is that nothing about the present condition of the church can satisfy them, and that, although they toil so mightily, no improvement follows.[64] I urge both sides to see how the church can be restored to its former tranquillity, showing myself more severe with my own side.[65] To advise what to avoid is to help their sect, not to ridicule it. As a friend I admonish both parties to see how they can come together.[66] What they take to be done with gross hostility could also be the acts of a friend anxious to be of service.

Nevertheless, it must be obvious that I do not approve of everything they do, for if I did I would not have had to leave at my own expense and peril the city to which I had for so many years grown accustomed,[67] but would long ago have been wholly committed to their fellowship. Even when I lived there, I made it quite clear both in word and in writing that I

* * * * *

Reformation 3–46. This is the only reference to his having said what Erasmus claims.
61 Epistola apologetica BOL I 156:19–21
62 Cf Epistola contra pseudevangelicos above 231: 'Show me just one whom that gospel has changed from gluttonous to sober, rapacious to generous, cursing to blessing, or shameless to modest. I will show you many who have become worse than their former selves.'
63 See Bucer's defence of Protestant doctrine, Epistola apologetica BOL I 86:28–87:12.
64 Cf Epistola contra pseudevangelicos above 231–2, which ends: 'They trample on ceremony, but add nothing to spirituality; in fact, it has been greatly decreased, in my judgment.'
65 Cf Epistola contra pseudevangelicos above 246–7.
66 Epistola contra pseudevangelicos above 245–6
67 Erasmus is referring to his departure from Basel in the spring of 1529. See Epistola contra pseudevangelicos above 231 n76.

dissented from their doctrines.[68] But now these religious men are no doubt unwilling to make judgments about my conscience, but leave this to God who alone knows the heart.[69] Yet they insinuate all the while that I am fearful or hopeful as if deep down I really share their view, but fear and hope deter me from professing it. Certainly, hope and fear deter me from fellowship with them. I fear hell if I ignore my conscience and profess what I think is impious; I hope God will be more inclined to be propitious to my sins if, however wounded I may be, I have not abandoned his bride. Let them congratulate themselves as much as they like, I will not congratulate myself for any reason other than that I have never assented to any sect, nor have I given my name to one, nor, with Christ's favour, does it seem to me I ever will do so. But rather I have been happy to persuade everyone not to bind themselves to any sect which the Catholic church does not recognize. Some people read their books with discrimination, but I know many who as soon as they have committed themselves, immediately cast away all humanity.

They pretend that I am fired with an extraordinary hate for the 'evangelicals.'[70] If that had been true, I would have wielded my pen against them quite differently. But at first I refrained out of some kind of religious scruple, which I now regret; then I played the Gamaliel[71] and to some extent still do; lastly, when I saw that many of the church leaders were deaf to all warnings, I suspected that these people had been sent by God so that their wickedness would stir us from lethargy – a hard wedge pushing out a hard knot.[72] I was so far from raging against them that some rulers and scholars reproach me for having played the deserter in this conflict, and that my pen has been wanting when the church is in peril. Some have also raised the suspicion that I was a covert supporter of what these people have established.[73]

* * * * *

68 The period in question encompasses most of the 1520s, beginning when Erasmus moved to Basel from Louvain in the autumn of 1521 and ending with his departure for Freiburg in April of 1529. During that decade he would write his *De libero arbitrio*, the *Spongia*, and the *Detectio praestigiarum*, among other works.

69 See *Epistola apologetica* BOL I 77:32–3; cf Acts 1:24, 15:8.

70 Cf *Epistola apologetica* BOL I 79:5–15.

71 Cf Acts 5:33–8.

72 Cf *Adagia* I ii 5: *Malo nodo malus quaerendus cuneus* CWE 31 149:1–150:11: 'This may be used whenever we blunt the power of something bad by malignity of the same kind.'

73 Many letters of Erasmus complain of such critics; see eg Epp 1415:46–7, 1263:43–50, in which Erasmus speaks of the Louvain theologians and of Zúñiga. See also Ep 1324A, which is Adrian VI's exhortation to Erasmus to write against Luther.

However, a religion of words, nothing but pages, does not move me at all; but the Lord says: 'by their fruits you will know them.'[74] A smokescreen like that leaves me cold, it is the power of the spirit which I look for but miss in these people's writings (and I believe I have something of a nose for such matters). But it is by the deceptiveness of these words that the unwary are imperilled. It was always a characteristic of heretics that they fooled the simple with the counterfeit appearance of religion. Maximinus, the Arian, sounds (one could almost say) more holy and religious than Augustine.[75] The Manichees counterfeited piety not only by their words, but by the prodigious asceticism of their life.[76] When people are moved by the Holy Spirit, this shines through in their eyes and, as the saying goes, on their faces,[77] not only in their actions. These people claim this for themselves with great confidence. But if Zwingli and Bucer are inspired with the Spirit,[78] what is there to prevent our side from having those who are gifted with a like charisma? Of himself Erasmus is nothing more than human and cannot discern the things of the Spirit. As if these people were very gods! But as a man I follow those from whom, we believe, the Spirit of Christ has not been absent. This is more credible than believing that Bucer or someone of his ilk writes and does everything under the inspiration of the Holy Spirit.

But to sum up in a few words the very verbose complaint of this person, whoever he is, I will pass over his brawling, prolix quarrel with Pliny and Tacitus[79] and sample more relevant matters. Although, as I said,

* * * * *

74 Matt 7:20
75 Maximinus: An Arian bishop; cf Augustine *Collatio cum Maximino* PL 42:709–42.
76 Manichees, or Manicheans: followers of the third-century Mesopotamian Gnostic, Mani, who taught a strict dualism, rejecting the physical creation as evil. Augustine became involved with this sect for a good part of his youth; see *Confessions* 3.6.10–11.
77 Cf *Adagia* II iv 4: *Ex fronte perspicere* CWE 33 191: 'We are said to see something on the face of it when we perceive it immediately and, as it were, at the very first moment of contact.'
78 See *Epistola apologetica* BOL 1 79:36–80:8, 90:30–91:4.
79 Cornelius Tacitus, a Roman historian born in about 56 AD, described Christianity as a deadly superstition (*Annals* 15:44). His good friend Pliny the Younger (c 61–112), famous for his nine published volumes of letters, recounts in *Letters* 10.96 that while he could find no criminal activity among the Christians, their superstition was 'depraved and excessive.' In *Epistola apologetica* BOL 1 81:8–84:9 Bucer claims that he and his co-religionists have been victims of the same kind of dismissal from learned critics like Erasmus, who, like

I only speak about what is known and certain to me (and not about all these other matters) and bring no accusation against anyone except in general terms, they still say I have thrown at them almost everything their most bitter enemies have up to now been unleashing both orally and in writing.[80] Whoever reads my epistle will surely see at once that this is a manifest lie! I have not even blurted out what is quite well known through common gossip, and I have taken truly extraordinary care to avoid letting slip anything possibly harmful even to Vulturius' good name.[81] I do not care about the charges commonly brought against them, they are nothing to me.

Yet there are quite a few people who in their published works continually call them heretics, schismatics, enemies of the church, blasphemers. What can be read in my books of that kind? But they themselves, so as to incite hostility against me, have picked up some trifling words from my letters, and from each of these they work up a marvellous tragedy, always making an elephant out of a fly or, if possible, something bigger than an elephant.[82] And if these trifling words have such power as to arouse the world's princes to plan their destruction, it is a good thing they were hidden away in a pile of letters! And if what is so very dangerous is my dislike for the 'evangelicals,' I have openly aired this for years in my published works. What fly ever pestered them more because of me? If I were to recall here what stories others tell, or have written about the preachers, then the vanity of that person[83] would emerge very clearly.

In the epistle to Vulturius I criticize no one by name, nor do I censure anyone whom they themselves do not detest (with one or two exceptions). Nor yet do I reveal any of their secrets, but refer only to the matters they themselves wish to be known to the world through their published works. So if they wanted to clear themselves of the charges against them, there are others to whom they should have responded rather than to me. What is the point of those absolutely foolish statements, so often repeated,

* * * * *

Tacitus and Pliny, do not take the trouble to learn the truth about those they criticize.

80 See *Epistola apologetica* BOL I 77:9–17.

81 Vulturius was the name Erasmus used in the *Epistola contra pseudevangelicos* for Gerard Geldenhouwer.

82 *Adagia* I ix 69: *Elephantum ex musca facis* 'You make an elephant out of a fly' CWE 32 219; cf *De libero arbitrio* CWE 76 6; see also M. Boyle's discussion of this phrase in *Rhetoric and Reform* 1–4.

83 Bucer

that Erasmus has loosed a volley of splendid lies and quite hideous charges against innocent confessors of Christ?[84] He says somewhere: 'Do not spare us, Erasmus, let fly against us whatever you've got!'[85] They will never provoke me to act the callow calumniator and descend to such discourteous behaviour. Let them assign this role to others if they wish! I have written countless *apologiae*. Have I ever proceeded against anyone, however insolent, with accusations? No one's wickedness will ever shift me from this honourable behaviour.

But that other statement of his is just as baseless and seditious, namely, that throughout my epistle to the thrice venerable Vulturius I have complained that they spurn the constitutions of the pontiffs and the bishops, that they deride the dogmas of the scholastics, that they throw out images, that they have abrogated the mass, and much more of the same, whereas the epistle itself makes it clear that my only complaint is that when they have introduced such innovations, there is no consequent improvement.[86] And if I were to condemn most strongly what these people do, what else would I do than what the Catholic church did long ago? Certainly, I have never approved of these things being swept away totally, nor am I about to. But I would wish many things corrected. At this point, indeed, they enumerate for us a long list of churches, all of which my letter is supposed to condemn.[87] Let them enumerate any number, the one Catholic church has

* * * * *

84 Cf *Epistola apologetica* BOL 1 78:8–10.
85 *Epistola apologetica* BOL 1 184:1–2.
86 *Epistola apologetica* BOL 1 85:11–21, referring to *Epistola contra pseudevangelicos* above 230–1.
87 *Epistola apologetica* BOL 1 85:22–32: 'All these things [that Erasmus has condemned] are taught and endorsed by many churches in Saxony, all in Hesse, many in Franconia, the churches of Nuremberg and Augsburg, not a few churches in Silesia and Moravia, and all the churches of Zürich, Bern, Strasbourg, Constance, Basel, St Gall, Chur, Mulhouse, Schaffhausen, Lindau, Ulm, Reutlingen, Worms, Frankfurt, and East Friesland.' This is a list of territories and independent cities that had as of that time adopted the Reformation in one form or another, with Worms and [the County of] East Friesland thrown in for good measure. Zürich, Bern, Basel, St Gall, Chur and Schaffhausen were Swiss towns that may be said to have followed Zwingli. Strasbourg, Constance, and Lindau were imperial cities which (along with Memmingen) would soon be submitting to the Diet of Augsburg the so-called Tetrapolitan Confession, an alternative to the (Lutheran) Augsburg Confession, to which they could not subscribe. The churches of Ulm and Mulhouse, together with the territorial church of the Landgrave of Hesse, may also be described as Reformed, while the issue as between Lutherans and Zwinglians hung in the

more weight with me, nor do I wish to conceal my disapproval of those churches, if they are such as we have in part seen and in part heard of, nor do we greatly fear their hostility.

He attributes to me singular dishonesty for writing that they claimed to have restored to light the evangelical truth buried for more than a thousand years. They deny that such a statement has even been heard from them.[88] From whom? From the ministers at Strasbourg? I never wrote specifically against them but generally against the whole company. Let them read what Luther boasts about his 'gospel,' let them see how he treated the most respected Doctors of the church and then let them accuse me of untruthfulness.[89] I do not know what they say in Strasbourg, but when they teach that it is the height of impiety and idolatry to adore the Eucharistic host[90] (which was done before the time of Augustine and Cyprian and, as is to be believed, was handed down from the apostles themselves),[91] are they not condemning the whole church? Let them take refuge in that church no one knows of, under whose title anyone can do what he likes. If credit is to be given to external judgments, then the consensus of so many Fathers, so many councils, and of the whole Christian world is like an oracle for me, especially when the Scriptures too are on our side.

They 'are bringing back,' so they say, 'the rites of the ancient church';[92] let them bring back, rather, the sanctity of the ancient church. Rites are

* * * * *

balance in Augsburg. Nuremberg and Frankfurt were Lutheran, as were the Protestant churches that had been organized in Saxony, Moravia, Silesia, and Franconia. One of Bucer's aims in this treatise was to blur the sharp distinctions that would soon be evident at the Diet of Augsburg.

88 Cf *Epistola contra pseudevangelicos* above 229. Bucer's complaint occurs in *Epistola apologetica* BOL I 86:28–31; see also 87:19–22.

89 Cf *De libero arbitrio* CWE 76 19–20 and *Hyperaspistes* 1 CWE 76 99 for Erasmus' complaint that Luther 'professes to bring back into the light the gospel, which had been buried under mounds of earth for more than fifteen hundred years.' Luther's discussion of the ancient interpreters occurs in WA 18 649–52.

90 Bucer's discussion of the mass occurs in *Epistola apologetica* BOL I 107:13–109:4, describing in particular masses for the dead, repeated by rote, and 206:16–25, where he denounces the mass as blasphemous and idolatrous. Luther's 1523 treatise *The Adoration of the Sacrament* WA 11 431–56 stresses an inner adoration of Christ as opposed to an elaborate show of respect for the elements.

91 For Augustine, see *Enarratio in Psalmos* 98 9 / CCSL 39:1385–6; for Cyprian, see *Epistula* 63 6 / CSEL 3 2:701–17. For a discussion of the Eucharist in the early church, see W. Elert *Eucharist and Church Fellowship in the First Four Centuries* (St Louis 1966).

92 Cf *Epistola apologetica* BOL I 88:18–21.

indifferent things,[93] making us neither pious nor impious, and more than fifteen hundred years ago Peter wrote: 'Obey those set above you, not only those who suit you, but also those who are difficult.'[94] These external matters can be changed to fit the needs of the times. Paul, too, established many things in the churches after Christ because of the needs of that time. In itself it is of no great moment if someone ministers before the altar in a linen garment or a woollen one,[95] but it is of great moment whether you believe Christ is present on the altar or only bread and wine. But if no one is permitted to institute anything apart from what is contained in Scripture, why did John the Baptist prescribe certain prayers and certain fasts for his disciples?[96] Why did James, the bishop of Jerusalem, make a decree [to abstain] from blood, from what is strangled, or sacrificed to idols, which no Scripture prescribed for the gentiles?[97] After this decree, why did Paul dare to say 'To the pure all things are pure,'[98] and 'Eat whatever is sold in the meat market'?[99] Why did our ancestors dare to decree different things to suit the demands of the time, unless perhaps it is a sacrilege for us to eat a goose that has been strangled or sausages made from blood?[100] Finally, if they propose only what the apostles established, why can those same authors allow men and women to sing in church together, despite the fact that Paul insisted that no woman should speak in the church?[101] Moreover, which apostle ordained that psalms should be sung in metre and rhyme, necessitating many changes in the words? They set out for us a summary of their faith, repeating much about three persons of the same essence, about the Father who redeemed our mortal race through his Son, about the Holy Spirit who worked through the holy

* * * * *

93 Erasmus used the Greek term *adiaphora* 'indifferent things,' which for the ancient Stoics meant conditions that were neither good nor evil in themselves. Luther contended that many elements of church ritual were neither commanded nor forbidden by God, and Melanchthon, in his 1521 *Loci communes*, discussed such matters under the heading of *indifferentia*. See Timothy Wengert 'Adiaphora' OER I 4–7.
94 Cf 1 Pet 1:14–16 and 2 Pet 1:5–11.
95 Lev 6:10, 16:4
96 Cf Luke 5:33.
97 Acts 15:13–20
98 Titus 1:15; cf Rom 14:20.
99 1 Cor 10:25
100 See Lev 7:26–7, 17:14; Acts 15:20.
101 1 Cor 14:34–5

apostles, and much more of the same,[102] as if we condemn their whole doctrine, or as if the Arians[103] did not have more in common with the Catholics than these people with us. But meanwhile they constantly claim the inspiration of Christ's Spirit, and hand over others who dissent from them to Satan. In fact, they cover their condemned doctrines with a plaster of fine words, as for instance, there are only two sacraments,[104] baptism is given to infants not for their salvation but to do them honour (being in any case of value only to the predestined, and necessary for no one);[105] in the Eucharist the true body and blood of the Lord are not present (and so what Christ said: 'This is my body,' is the same as was said by Ezekiel: 'This is Jerusalem.')[106] Note the wondrous argument and how the shaft hits home!

They are always inculcating this point (boasting that they are the authors of this new doctrine): salvation is to be sought from Christ alone.[107] As if we seek salvation from the saints, or from images, or from sacrifices! However, if a sinner who is dissatisfied with himself but not yet able to leave his sins, seeks the prayers of pious men so that through them he may secure a good disposition, surely this is not to seek salvation from another than Christ? Not from another but through another! The same can be said of the saints. Now, when they explain why they have abolished the masses, the divine office, chanting, and other things,[108] they speak as if no one had ever treated or will treat these matters piously, as if certain people's sins mean that things salutary in themselves must be abolished root and branch rather than reformed. If whatever countless people abuse must necessarily be abolished, then their 'gospel' itself should be abolished, for under its shadow so many live with total abandon (as they themselves do not deny); the power of princes and magistrates should be abolished, since so many of them abuse their power for profit, exploitation, and tyranny; in the end what will be left in human affairs?

* * * * *

102 *Epistola apologetica* BOL I 88:25–91:4
103 See above n45.
104 See *Epistola apologetica* BOL I 92:34–93:11.
105 Bucer expresses his views concerning baptism in *Epistola apologetica* BOL I 93:12–94:21. Erasmus' rendition here, like his description of Bucer's views of the Eucharist, is misleading and reductive; cf Payne *Sacraments* and his introductory note to *Detectio praestigiarum* above 154 n37.
106 See *Epistola apologetica* BOL I 95:6–9, citing Ezek 5:5.
107 *Epistola apologetica* BOL I 97:9–15
108 See *Epistola apologetica* BOL I 105:8–109:4.

But they attribute a great deal to magistrates to whom the sword has been given by God 'to be a punishment' to evil-doers, 'but for the praise of the good.'[109] Yet they too bear the sword who condemn and punish as schismatics and heretics those who profess what they teach. Why do they not submit to these magistrates? Why do they not obey the supreme power of the emperor and the kings? But they say: 'It is necessary to obey God rather than men.'[110] Yet the secular magistrate has jurisdiction only in matters clearly prohibited by the laws. Others are judges about the Catholic faith. In keeping with judgments by magistrates, the emperor punishes those who are unwilling to come to their senses. But by whom are the magistrates of these people instructed? By the very culprits, for I will not say: heretics.[111] The power of the pontiffs and of the bishops is also from God; why do they not acknowledge this? 'Popes and bishops have nothing' these people say, 'except the sword of the word.'[112] But it is by this sword that these people have had their throats cut and have been handed over to Satan.[113] 'Unjustly,' they say. On what ground? 'Because it is in contradiction to divine Scriptures that lightning strike the innocent.' But they arrogate to themselves the interpretation of Scripture, although meanwhile they disagree among themselves on so momentous an issue as the Eucharist. The outcome is that no Scripture is valid except according to their interpretation, and no civil authority is to be obeyed unless it agrees with them. 'No authority is to be obeyed,' they say, 'unless it exercises power according to the commands of divine Scripture; but it is our prerogative to interpret Scripture, not that of others.'[114]

They acknowledge political authority in all matters which do not lead to impiety. But what impiety is it on certain days to abstain from dinner for those who can do so without any harm to their body, indeed with benefit to body and soul? What impiety is it to sing God's praises in churches or to say the daily office? 'These prayers are said,' they say, 'only for profit; they are said only with the lips.'[115] But this is not true of all; rather, very

* * * * *

109 1 Pet 2:14; cf *Epistola apologetica* BOL I 97:33–38:4.
110 Acts 5:29; cf Bucer's qualification in *Epistola apologetica* BOL I 98:3–4.
111 Cf *Epistola apologetica* BOL I 98:5–11. On the relationship between secular and church authorities in Bucer's thought, see Martin Greschat 'The Relation between Church and Civil Community in Bucer's Reforming Work' in *Martin Bucer: Reforming Church and Community* (Cambridge 1994) 17–31.
112 *Epistola apologetica* BOL I 98:5–17
113 Cf 1 Cor 5:15.
114 Erasmus is putting words into his adversaries' mouths, in this case extending his paraphrase into the *reductio ad absurdam* that is the climax of his argument.
115 Cf *Epistola apologetica* BOL I 105:9–25.

many chant both with their lips and from the heart.[116] Others are earnestly
urged that, as they chant in the spirit, they should think about what they
chant, they are urged to consider not their own profit but rather the good
of their neighbour. Nevertheless, here too 'the workman is worthy of his
hire';[117] it is only fair that whoever serves the altar in any way should also
live by the altar.[118] 'But the priests,' they say, 'do not live by the altar but
live profligately on the stipends of the church.' Let profligacy, then, be cut
off, not the priestly office.

I would love to ask these people if in their churches everyone thinks
about what they are singing. One hears a very different story from those
who attend their assembly, not Catholics, but people of their own confession,
who confirm that many have long found their little melodies repugnant.
They scream that this is a malicious imputation by me against my host
city.[119] What has it to do with a city's dignity, if the piety of some is flagging?
This misfortune it has in common with all cities; it would be an extremely
fortunate city which would wish to change nothing. They will say, as is
their custom, that this is a 'splendid lie,' relayed to me by hopeless good-
for-nothings.[120] What extraordinary 'evangelical' modesty! He calls them
hopeless good-for-nothings, although he does not know the persons who
are the target of this pronouncement. But if I were to name those who
reported certain matters to me it would cause great embarrassment (if they
have any shame at all) to call such people hopeless good-for-nothings. Now,
people who have subscribed to this sect did report to me this and many
other things. But if the 'evangelical' people do embrace hopeless good-
for-nothings, why are they so indignant at me when I desire behaviour
more worthy of the gospel? The same people reported that many attend
the sermon in a way which makes it obvious that they are not affected by
what is said, but are only present lest they seem not to be supporting their
sect. But if the ministers were to denounce the vices of their own followers

* * * * *

116 1 Cor 14:15
117 Matt 10:10; Luke 19:7; 1 Tim 5:18
118 1 Cor 9:13
119 See Bucer's complaint in the *Epistola apologetica* (BOL I 118:8–9) against Erasmus'
     disparaging comment in a March 1529 letter to Juan Vergara about the singing
     in the Reformed churches in Basel. Erasmus writes that women together with
     boys sing psalms that are in the form of rhymes in German (Allen Ep 2133:67–
     8), while Bucer retorts that not only women and boys but also men of all ranks
     join in singing in a language that is edifying for the entire gathering (BOL I
     118:5–9).
120 No such comment appears in the *Epistola apologetica*.

with as much ferocity as they denounce the vices of the priests, I will be surprised if they retain three followers. 'But all the Strasbourgers sing, and sing frequently.'[121] I wish their songs might so portray God that they turn him from being angry to being gracious to us! But why do they bring this up, when I have not been talking about the Strasbourgers?

When in fact they write that it is the practice of their churches to embrace sobriety in a way that is not at all different from fasting,[122] I know that many even of their colleagues will scarcely forbear to smile when they read this. I am not talking about the Strasbourgers (as has to be said again and again); I have no knowledge of what is done there. I am speaking about those whom it has been my lot to know better. But 'the apostle Paul,' as they say, 'put up in his churches with drunken, contentious, fraudulent, and Judaizing people, etc.'[123] I admit it, but he fiercely attacks them, in season or out, making his point, upbraiding, and beseeching, and he also handed some over to Satan.[124] As to whether they are doing this, let them see to it! Nothing of the like has ever come to my ears. The same Paul forbids taking food with someone who commends himself with the title of brother, that is Christian, but is greedy, or adulterous, or evil-speaking.[125] Are we to think that these people do the same? But, they may say, it is no wonder if those who had recently emerged from a most corrupt life, from idols, and the profound darkness of ignorance cannot overnight be moulded to a perfect Christianity. But these people who come to the gospel, whence, I pray, did they come? From Christianity, some from the priesthood and monasticism. In addition, how can this writer know about the type of behaviour prevalent in all their churches? And if their behaviour is everywhere as they claim, what need had Luther of visitors to recall his followers from paganism?[126]

Finally, they sum up in this way: If Paul and Erasmus do not condemn their own churches, although among them are many whose lives are impure, why does he demand more of us?[127] Rather, why do they refuse to let their churches be condemned because of the wicked among them, while they condemn ours for the same reason? Although others would be quick to reply that the remission of sins is available in the Catholic church (while

* * * * *

121 Cf *Epistola apologetica* BOL I 118:10–13.
122 Cf *Epistola apologetica* BOL I 118:20–2.
123 Cf *Epistola apologetica* BOL I 119:6–24.
124 Cf 1 Cor 5:1–5.
125 Cf 1 Cor 5:11.
126 See above n57.
127 Cf *Epistola apologetica* BOL I 120:26–32.

even those who live well in heresy live badly), it is also false that I condemn their churches totally. They have their own judges. I simply require of those who with such confidence claim for themselves the Spirit of Christ, and are so quick to denounce the behaviour of everyone, that they produce more evidence of sanctity of life than we have seen so far. I do not see why they thought they should mention this.

He says he knows 'a canon of a distinguished church' who said 'there was not one harlot to be found in Zürich,' to provide entertainment for a guest, 'although there was an abundance of nice harlots before this gospel swept in there.'[128] I showed this passage to the canon whom they seem to attack (for they add some words which enable one to detect whom they have in mind).[129] He denied with a laugh that he had ever in his life heard anything of this nature from anyone, far less said it himself. And he is a man who by the testimony of all is both of blameless life and quite trustworthy. With similar candour the author goes on to censure another, a vice-dean (adding some information by which the inquisitive reader can identify whom he is criticizing).[130] He says that he has a bad reputation for regularly seducing the wives of others.[131] I have stayed in this man's house, and never noticed the least trace of immorality in word or deed. Those who know him also realize that his reputation is quite different from what is alleged. But these people are hostile to the canon because he has no high opinion of their sect; and they hate the vice-dean because, after initially appearing to be more inclined towards them, on reflection he turned away.[132] How unfitting it is for these things to be written by people who want nothing said about themselves unless you have seen it with your own eyes, touched it with your own hands.[133] They say: 'they have a bad reputation.'[134] But let

* * * * *

128 *Epistola apologetica* BOL I 120:26–32
129 The canon in question is Ludwig Baer (1479–1554), who had been a professor of theology at the University of Basel, and was friendly with Erasmus. *Epistola apologetica* (BOL I 120:28–30) contains language that reflects almost word for word a letter Erasmus wrote to Baer in March of 1529, as he was anticipating leaving Basel to join him in Freiburg, where Baer had moved earlier that year; cf Allen Ep 2136:3–6.
130 Johann von Botzheim (1480–1535), a canon of Constance and coadjutor to the dean of the diocesan chapter, was a close friend of Erasmus; cf *Epistola apologetica* BOL I 161:26–8, and Erasmus' 13 August 1529 letter to Botzheim, Allen Ep 2205:16–19.
131 *Epistola apologetica* BOL I 161:24–6
132 See Ep 1285 introduction.
133 Cf John 20:24–5.
134 Cf *Epistola apologetica* BOL I 160:26.

us pretend that both rumours are somehow true: have they been cleansed of all faults if it is found that one of their accusations is not false? Or is it reason enough to desert the Catholic church because it has one vice-dean who is stained with adulteries?

As to his assertion that what is taken away from the priests has been turned to assist the poor and the students,[135] whether this is the case in Strasbourg is unknown to me. But I know places where it certainly is not the case.[136] And I fear that this happens in more places than it should. But let them themselves see to it by what right they deal with the priests; for he adds: 'according to their rights.'[137] I have no dispute with the magistrates. It is to the emperor and certainly to God that they will have to be accountable. And if the magistracy should do wrong, the fault lies with those who persuade them, as if by the authority of Scripture, that these things are done piously.

They also denounce my writing that wherever this new 'gospel' rules the pursuit of letters languishes.[138] 'The Nurembergers,' he says, 'have decreed more than generous salaries for their language professors.'[139] I know this, but those who live there write that they have almost no students, and that the professors are as indolent in teaching as the students in learning, so that the pupils need a salary as much as the teachers.[140] What their schools scattered through their towns and the countryside[141] will produce for us, I do not know. Up to now I have not heard of anyone in this sect who learned

* * * * *

135 See *Epistola apologetica* BOL I 121:6–19, in which Bucer denies that churchmen have been mercilessly despoiled of their property, and explains how property that has been taken from the church is utilized.

136 On the disposition of ecclesiastical property in Strasbourg, see Brady *Protestant Politics* 170–4.

137 In *Epistola apologetica* BOL I 121:14–15 Bucer claims that the magistrates have made over income to each of the churchmen according to his own right.

138 See *Epistola apologetica* BOL I 181:22–182:14. Although Erasmus indicates such an opinion in the *Epistola contra pseudevangelicos*, above 251, Bucer seems to have in mind remarks he has made elsewhere; cf the letter to Willibald Pirckheimer, Allen Ep 1977:40–2.

139 This contention is not made in the *Epistola apologetica* in so many words, but Bucer does speak of the efforts of the reformers to establish good schools; see *Epistola apologetica* BOL I 181:28–182:4, in which Bucer lists a number of cities, including Nuremberg, that have fostered education. The reference to Nuremberg is related to a comment in Erasmus' letter of November 1527 to Bucer; cf Allen Ep 1901:19–21.

140 Cf Allen Epp 2006:15–17, 2008:33–4.

141 Cf *Epistola apologetica* BOL I 182:4–7.

letters. They entice the learned with salaries and draw young scholars by their wiles so that through such persons they may receive commendation, with consequent great hostility to literary studies. But it all depends on what is taught in their schools. Doctrines and languages above all![142] But these people's doctrines are not suitable for everyone, nor do languages exhaust scholarship.

But I do not see how it makes sense to make a great stir about the academic disciplines when there is no honourable career to attract people. With the elimination of the priesthood and the rites of the church, without hope of wealth and status (to which previously learning brought one), who is going to bother with the heavy expense of educating children?[143] Moreover, he writes that it is a sign of their charity that they continue to pay their emoluments to those priests and monks who have no other way to sustain themselves.[144] That may perhaps be the case in Strasbourg, but in some places it will not be read without a smile. Something is given to those who are ready to lay aside the sacred vestments and obey their laws, the rest are permitted to go where they want, but not even that is granted with their means of support intact.[145] But who would endure a protector who arbitrarily deprives him of his means of support?

Nor can it be read without a smile when they say they do 'not want to harm anyone,' or 'to force anyone,' that they have a 'deep and abiding abhorrence for sedition,' and that they are content to 'preach the gospel at a minimal salary.'[146] God knows whether they are content; it is notorious that some have been pressing the magistrates hard to increase their salary.[147] But let the magistrate put them to the test and offer each preacher a thousand gold pieces; if they refuse it I will admit that they are content with their salaries. But what does this mean: 'to harm no one'?[148] Is this to harm no one: to expel canons from their chapters, monks from the monasteries, to rob abbots and bishops of their power, to remove citizens from office, to rant away in virulent pamphlets even against kings and princely persons? Is this to have a 'deep and abiding abhorrence for sedition'? 'We kill no

* * * * *

142 In *Epistola apologetica* BOL I 182:3 Bucer refers to *linguas et bonas disciplinas*.
143 See Bernd Moeller *Imperial Cities and the Reformation* (Durham, NC 1982) 62–3.
144 *Epistola apologetica* BOL I 121:17–19
145 See Chrisman *Strasbourg and the Reform* 147, 151–2.
146 Cf *Epistola apologetica* BOL I 140:4–5, 162:14–16.
147 For a brief treatment of the issue of clerical salaries among reformed clergy, see C. Scott Dixon *The Reformation and Rural Society* (Cambridge 1996) 84–92.
148 *Epistola apologetica* BOL I 117:40–118:1, 140:4–5

one,' he says; mercy, of course, is shown to those who surrender, otherwise we would have seen a gory battle. Even pirates kill no one if no one resists. I will leave it to others to decide whether these things never happen. It is a fact that we daily hear horrific complaints by many people. It is not evangelical virtue not to harm anyone who does no harm to you, but it is a gross crime to harm an innocent person. Yet 'repaying evil with good,' is, after all, the real gospel.[149]

'We,' he says, 'allow our enemies to live among us unharmed.'[150] I doubt if this happens everywhere. But whom do they call their enemies? All Catholics? Why is this a great matter? Do not they,[151] too, come daily to other cities, either for pleasure or business purposes? But there is no such safety for clerics. Nor is it safe for our bishops to live among them. Moreover, does he judge that there is no difference between the condemned and the non-condemned? People on our side have not been convicted of heresy. And yet when people who have been convicted are among us we look the other way. And if they 'harm no one,' why do so many leave their cities? Why is the air full of complaints in the emperor's entourage? 'They are allowed,' he says,' to live among us with the rights of citizens.'[152] What a pleasure it must be to live among those whom they[153] regard as heretics, and to submit the neck to their yoke. Because if they[154] abide by the faith which they hold to be the most authentic one, they are only too well aware how they will be regarded by magistrate and people whenever there is some trouble, as happens in human affairs. 'But,' they say, 'we are not heretics.'[155] Even if they are not heretics, weighty authorities say they are; if the latter err they do so with so many universities, with the pontiff, with the emperor.

Is this 'to force no one': unless you hear our readings, nothing will be allocated from the stipend; let no one go out on such-and-such a day for such-and-such a feast; let no one hear the mass or receive the Eucharist in neighbouring villages, if he does, let him be fined a *libra*; unless a person comes at Easter season to the minister's table to consume bread and wine instead of Christ, he will be liable to the judgment of the city council? If

* * * * *

149 Cf 1 Thess 5:15.
150 *Epistola apologetica* BOL I 140:10–14
151 The 'evangelicals'
152 *Epistola apologetica* BOL I 140:5–10
153 The Catholics
154 The Catholics
155 *Epistola apologetica* BOL I 128:25–7.

they deny that these things are done in Strasbourg, I will not make an issue of it; but if they claim that it is not done anywhere, they will only have acquired a reputation for shamelessness.[156] For how indeed can there be sincere love among those who disagree about religion? It is for this reason, after all, that the church has prohibited entering into mixed marriages.[157] Here a broad field of discourse might open up for me, but what is the point of mentioning matters which are common talk? I admit that in no city has there been more moderation than in Strasbourg. For it seems that they will cast down images only when compelled to by a treaty.[158]

Next, as he proceeds to rebut the charges he says I make against them, he prays that if in seeking to clear himself he has departed from the truth or concealed anything or obscured anything by what he said, may Christ proclaim this to the world by an open act of vengeance.[159] Amen! Having made this preface, he at once departs from the truth in this very presentation of the charges.

In the beginning I wrote that they used tricks unworthy of one professing the gospel, as well as damaging to their cause.[160] He recounts this as if I impute this crime to all the ministers,[161] although in my letter I mention only a few. And this is one charge whereby I dealt so many noble churches, stretching as far as East Frisia, an intolerable injury![162] But I am astonished that they call this a crime, since they themselves in their published works declare it legitimate to promote the gospel by deceptions and tricks.[163] There was no need to rebut this charge; rather, I am to be credited with stupidity for alleging a quite honest practice was a crime!

The second charge is that I wrote that they are advancing a cause different from the apostles.[164] This certainly was expressed by him obscurely. I wrote that the way in which the apostles and they conducted their affairs was not the same, but that what the apostles did was more easily accomplished than what they laboured to achieve.[165] Then what they add,

* * * * *

156 See Chrisman *Strasbourg and the Reform* 155–76.
157 2 Cor 6:14
158 See below n356.
159 *Epistola apologetica* BOL I 122:15–19
160 *Epistola contra pseudevangelicos* above 236–7.
161 *Epistola apologetica* BOL I 122:20–2
162 *Epistola apologetica* BOL I 85:22–8
163 See above n35.
164 *Epistola apologetica* BOL I 122:23
165 *Epistola contra pseudevangelicos* above 229, where Erasmus writes: 'Yet you boast that you are restoring to the light the evangelical truth, that has lain buried

'Displaying no purity of life,' is nowhere in my letter; I only say, 'But if your life, too, not only fails to commend your doctrine but rather invalidates it' etc.[166] Where now is Christ the Avenger? They added this too on their own: 'as if we are obsessed with this desire, to bring about the πανολεθρίαν "utter ruin" of everything.'[167] This is nowhere to be found in my writings. I only said I feared a disastrous outcome to this business.[168] Oh that I would prove a poor soothsayer!

When someone takes so much liberty at the very beginning, what can you expect from him once he gets going? I admit I expostulated with the person I wrote to at that time[169] because, when two books had already been published on the front of which he had inscribed my name in large letters, he provoked a hostile reaction to me and did his own cause no good, either. And since this seemed to him such a clever deed, he has now done it a third time.[170] If I had known that he was what he revealed himself to be, I would not have wasted one syllable in expostulating with him. I thought I was writing to a friend and did not suspect such a transformation of the gospel. Even if I were a genuine supporter of their cause, I would warn that producing such books achieves nothing but annoying the princes and hindering what they are doing. They say: 'It is permissible to excerpt whatever you please from books which have been published and so made available to all.'[171] But what did such enormous lettering mean? Why was an introduction like this prefixed to such letters?

They say there was nothing seditious in them.[172] But isn't it seditious to urge the princes to withdraw from priests and monks their means of support and transfer them to the use of the poor?[173] As if it is the practice of princes to do such things! Nor is there any doubt that it is the 'evangelical' poor they have in mind. Why does he only quote from me, when Johannes Brenz devotes an entire book to arguing against the death penalty

* * * * *

for over a thousand years. If what you say is true, you are performing a more difficult enterprise than the apostles had in their day.' See also above 241.

166 *Epistola apologetica* BOL I 122:25; *Epistola contra pseudevangelicos* above 241
167 *Epistola apologetica* BOL I 122:29–31
168 *Epistola contra pseudevangelicos* above 242
169 Geldenhouwer
170 Erasmus is referring to Gerard Geldenhouwer's publications of excerpts from his works; cf *Epistola contra pseudevangelicos* above 222–4.
171 *Epistola apologetica* BOL I 124:9–12
172 *Epistola apologetica* BOL I 128:17–19
173 See Prinsen *Collectanea* 191.

for heretics?[174] I urge theologians and monks to Christian clemency, since we have seen that some of them can at times be all too enamoured of the death penalty, so that if the princes had followed their wishes, we would have seen people slaughtered in huge numbers. In fact, I counsel the same princes against the death penalty, if the evil can be healed in other ways.[175] But those whom I call 'heretics' there, he calls 'innocent.'[176] Nor is it true that it is legitimate to excerpt in any way one pleases from other people's writings. If you report some matters from a disputation in isolation, they will appear in the worst light; if you read them in context, there is no reason to complain. When Zúñiga wanted to burden me with egregious ill will, what did he do but amass various quotations from my writings?[177] But he uses me to play the same game as Vulturius delights in, not harming me at all among men of good sense. But unless he is careful he will crash against his Temessaean[178] spirit. 'Paul,' they say, 'twisted the inscription of an altar in Athens into an argument for the gospel.'[179] First of all, what Paul reports is more than likely true: that there was an altar there with the inscription to the unknown God. But if we concede that Jerome's version is correct,[180] surely in these words: 'and to the other unknown gods,' the true God was also included? So what deception did Paul practise? But it is a pure deception for them to affirm that they have quoted my words straightforwardly and in good faith. The facts tell another story.

* * * * *

174 Johannes Brenz (1499–1570), who undertook the Lutheran reform of Schwä-bisch Hall and assisted in the reformation of the Duchy of Württemberg, published in German in 1528 a treatise on *Whether a Secular Government May, in Conformity with the Laws of God and Reason, Condemn Anabaptists to Death by Fire and Sword.* See James M. Estes *Christian Magistrate and State Church: The Reforming Career of Johannes Brenz* (Toronto 1982) 123–9.

175 For what Erasmus had written, and the controversy it generated, see *Epistola contra pseudevangelicos* introductory note above 211–14.

176 *Epistola apologetica* BOL I 128:25–7

177 Diego López Zúñiga (Stunica), one of the scholars working on the Compluten-sian Polyglot Bible, in 1520 published an extensive critique of Erasmus' New Testament: *Annotationes contra Erasmum Roterodamum, in defensionem tralationis Novi Testamenti,* to which Erasmus responded with the *Apologia ad annotationes Stunicae* (ASD IX-2 59–267). For an account of the dispute see Rummel *Catholic Critics* I 145–77.

178 *Adagia* I i 88: *Aderit Temessaeus genius* 'The Temessaean spirit will be there' CWE 31 128–129: 'the proverb ... was used against those who attack a more powerful person than themselves' 129:36–8.

179 Cf Acts 17:23; *Epistola apologetica* BOL I 124:6–8.

180 Cf *Annotationes in Acta* 18:33 LB VI 501E–F.

Yet what, finally, is this truth which has burst forth without our consent? It must be a miraculous voice spoken through me by the spirit as if by Balaam's ass![181] 'I urged,' he says, 'a spiritual partaking of Christ's body and blood, without which that corporeal eating not only avails nothing but is indeed fatal.'[182] How does this support their impious doctrine? Didn't Paul urge just this on the Corinthians?[183] Didn't Augustine?[184] Doesn't any orthodox theologian urge the same today? Does it follow from this that in the Eucharist there is nothing but bread and wine? Is there no shame about setting such absurdities before the eyes of people in published books?

Now, Pellicanus is nicely excused (although my epistle refrained from naming him) because the author in his courtesy thought this too had to be added to inspire ill will towards me.[185] Pellicanus[186] admitted that he told many people I agreed with him on the Eucharist; he also admitted to me that he had never heard any such thing from me.[187] 'But he suspected', the author says, 'that you agreed.'[188] Why? Because I praised spiritual eating as paramount.[189] What relevance has that? Surely he did not spread a new rumour on this account? Why do they not suspect the same about Paul, and Augustine, and all the theologians in whose writings the same thing is read as in mine? But who is so stupid as not to perceive, in those letters he[190] published when he was about to leave the city, the back-handed way in which he sang praises to [my] prudence?[191] I had once responded to the city council that my views on the Eucharist were those of the Catholic church.[192] In the presence of Pellicanus himself I affirmed that I was thoroughly appalled by the view he then communicated to me for the first time. What need was there for these back-handed letters?

* * * * *

181 Cf Num 22:28–30.
182 *Epistola apologetica* BOL I 124:21–3
183 1 Cor 11:29
184 *Sermons* PL 38 1246–8 272 1.
185 See *Epistola apologetica* BOL I 125:8–126:7 for Bucer's defence of Pellicanus. Erasmus' complaint appears in *Epistola contra pseudevangelicos* above 236–7.
186 See Ep 1674.
187 See *Epistola contra pseudevangelicos* above 236–7; see also Ep 1674.
188 Cf *Epistola apologetica* BOL I 125:10–11.
189 *Epistola apologetica* BOL I 125:11–12
190 Pellicanus
191 Cf *Epistola contra pseudevangelicos* above 237; Epp 1638, 1639.
192 Ep 1636

What need was there for the 'armed entreaties' to which he[193] encouraged the magistrates of Basel?[194] But they did not see that letter.[195] Yet the superior of the remaining Franciscans[196] found it in Pellicanus' bedroom. He who saw it, told me. 'But,' they say 'the word armed did not mean for him violent; for that would be the height of levity.'[197] What then did he mean by 'armed'? Coaxing, I suppose, and friendly! As if some there had not flung about coarse threats that I should be detained and not released until I published a detailed account of my views. I knew what some of them wanted to hear. If what I had said was Catholic, I was going to be a prudent and clever dissimulator; if I had gratified the ears of certain persons, I would have put my body and my soul in peril. As a matter of fact, there is no ambiguity: 'armed entreaties' are nothing other than doing violence to the one who is objecting. Therefore, it is not unfitting that they say of their colleague, this deed was the height of audacity. All I say is that actions of this sort are not in accordance with the gospel. Was this not a good defence of Pellicanus? I am reluctant to lower myself to such matters for while I try to maintain my good manners, sometimes I do harm to my own cause. My only complaint about Pellicanus was that he himself wanted to make himself well known by writing. I am more sorry for an old friend than angry at the man. I never discerned anything similar in him before he decided to be a full-fledged 'evangelical.'

It remains for my adversaries to defend Leo who, they say, 'prepared his book without Pellicanus' knowing.'[198] How do they know this? They believe it. Yet those who come from Zürich tell a different story. 'Leo,' they say, 'did not conceal his name, as Erasmus has lyingly declared.'[199] Who,

* * * * *

193 Pellicanus

194 Cf *Epistola contra pseudevangelicos* above 237. From Zürich, Pellicanus apparently sent another letter threatening to have Erasmus expelled from Basel by the magistrates: see C. Augustijn's introduction to the *Detectio praestigiarum* ASD IX-1 221–2.

195 It is Bucer who says this: *Epistola apologetica* BOL 1 126:1–3

196 Pellicanus had been a Franciscan until he left Basel in February of 1526, at the time of the events Erasmus is recounting here, to join Zwingli in Zürich.

197 Cf *Epistola apologetica* BOL 1 126:6–7. Erasmus reads Bucer's *nam est lenitatis eximiae* 'height of mildness' as *nam id esset levitatis eximiae* 'height of levity.'

198 Cf *Epistola apologetica* BOL 1 126:8–9. Erasmus is referring to Leo Jud's *Des hochgelerten Erasmi von Roterdam, und D. M. Luthers maynung vom nachtmahl.* See *Detectio praesigiarum* introductory note above n51; *Epistola contra pseudevangelicos* above 237–8.

199 Cf *Epistola apologetica* BOL 1 126:9–12.

however, would have understood that Ludovicus Leopoldus[200] stood for Leo Jud, except perhaps his colleagues? What author puts his name at the back of the book in an out-of-the-way place? It was placed there so that it would seem to be the printer's name instead. 'But Leo,' so they say, 'never says that I share Luther's view, he only recounted some views of mine in good faith.' Yet whoever reads his book and my response will understand that he is insinuating that I share their views on the Eucharist, and that Luther shares this view. 'He quotes,' so he says, 'my words.' Even granting that he quotes them, he draws a foolish conclusion. In fact, he does not quote my words at all but frequently and shamelessly twists them and reports them in abridged form.[201]

Straight away at the first quotations, see how great his mendacity is! 'At many points,' so he[202] says, 'I call the bread and wine symbols of the Eucharist, that is, signs, and call the bread symbolic,'[203] although these words are nowhere to be found in my writings. But he heard it from someone, for Leo seems not to have read my works. Nevertheless, he is not sure whether I said this in the *Querela pacis*, or in the *Enchiridion*, or in another of my books. Do you notice the good faith of this person who quotes me? The words he quotes from the *Enchiridion* chapter 5 he quotes incorrectly. Indeed, in that very place I call them the flesh and the blood in these words: Christ 'despised the eating of his own flesh and the drinking of his own blood if they were not eaten and drunk spiritually as well.'[204] And this is the passage which reveals what I conceal in my heart out of fear of the pontiff and the emperor, being, of course, a timorous man (for he had also alleged this earlier).[205] 'If,' says Leo, 'Erasmus had a different opinion, he would write a book against those who deny the truth of the body and blood in the Eucharist.'[206] Is not one who speaks in this way saying that I am of one mind with them?

* * * * *

200 This is the name that Jud affixed to his pamphlet.
201 Cf *Epistola apologetica* BOL I 126:12–17; what Bucer denies is that Jud claimed Erasmus and Luther held the same view of the Eucharist as Karlstadt. See *Epistola contra pseudevangelicos* above 237. For distortions of Erasmus' words by Jud, *Detectio praestigiarum* above nn25, 70.
202 Jud
203 Cf *Maynung* A 2 r; Jud cites the *Adagia, Querela pacis*, and the fifth canon of the *Enchiridion*. See *Detectio praestigiarum* above 166 n25.
204 *Enchiridion* CWE 66:70. Jud writes: 'So gar ist das flaisch nichts nütz / dass auch Christus das essen seynes flayschs verwirfft / es sey dann das mans gaystlich durch den glauben esse' (A 2 r–A 2 v).
· 205 *Maynung* A 4 v; cited in *Detectio praestigiarum* above 170 n41.
206 *Maynung* A 4 v; cf *Detectio praestigiarum* above 178.

In fact, he also reports incorrectly the opinion I presented in writing to the city council of Basel.[207] Although it says quite clearly that I have the same beliefs as the Catholic church and disagree with Oecolampadius, yet here he speaks in this way: 'You see here what that good man says, provided you want to understand.'[208] In the same way he most ineptly quotes the annotation on Mark chapter 14, since there I declare it heretical to deny that the real body and blood is in the Eucharist.[209] He adds the passage from the paraphrase on 1 Corinthians 10 and 11, where he claims that I have openly and at considerable length made it clear that it is bread and wine which are in the Eucharist, since these words of mine are to be found there: We also 'have been cleansed through baptism, feed equally on the food of the most blessed body, and all drink from the mystical cup.'[210] In the same passage I call the body of Christ 'bread.' I call it that, but add: 'holy.' How can that be forbidden me, since Paul, whom I am paraphrasing there, does the same in that very place?[211] But he [Leo] also adds this lie: 'I called the bread and wine symbols of the Lord's body and blood,'[212] as if I believe these elements to be signs of the body and blood of the one who is absent, whereas I explain quite clearly what I believe and call the partaking itself 'a symbol of an ever-lasting covenant.'[213] It is an even more shameless lie that he says I call the blood wine.[214] Nowhere do I call it wine, but call it the 'hallowed cup' or 'most holy

* * * * *

207 See *Detectio praestigiarum* above 179 n109; Ep 1636:343–4. The English translation of the letter in its entirety reads as follows: 'Cordial greetings. Right honourable lords of the council, at the request of your excellencies I have read Johannes Oecolampadius' book *De verbis coenae Domini*. In my opinion the work is learned, well written, and thorough. I would also judge it pious, if anything could be so described which is at variance with the general opinion of the church, from which I consider it perilous to dissent.'
208 *Maynung* A 4 r.
209 *Maynung* A 6 v: 'in seinen Annotationibus uber das Evangelium Marci am .14. cap. ist gnug offenbar wie er dise wort (Das ist meyn leychnam) verstande.' Cf *Detectio praestigiarum* above 182–3.
210 *Maynung* A 4 v; cf *Detectio praestigiarum* above 183–4; paraphrase on 1 Corinthians 10:3 CWE 43 129
211 1 Cor 10:16–17
212 For the passage from *Maynung* A 6 r quoted above, *Detectio praestigiarum* above 188 n150.
213 Paraphrase on 1 Corinthians 11:25 CWE 43 147; cf *Detectio praestigiarum* above 182.
214 Cf *Maynung* A 6 r.

cup.'[215] He adduces a passage in *Acts* where he alleges I have written the same things I wrote in the *Paraphrase on 1 Corinthians,*[216] although the fact of the matter shows that this is quite false.

He adds that there are many places in my writings where I show that I believe as they do.[217] What can be more shameless than this lie? There are many other places which show that I believe with the Catholic church,[218] not a word which offers a suspicion of any different view. Why did Leo conceal them? He hints that they have been falsely attributed to me.[219] What books have been issued in my name which are not mine? Although in a published writing[220] I make absolutely evident with how many lies, with what blatant deceits Leo's book abounds, this person,[221] whoever he was, does not fear to mention him and dares also to defend him, dares to affirm that my words are quoted there in good faith, dares to deny that I am under pressure to appear to agree with them.[222]

Leo began this most deceptive book with an open lie. He says I, like Luther, condemn all human constitutions.[223] Shameless mouth, where does he read this in my writings? But what wonder is it that Leo plays the fool in this way, when Zwingli (whom some regard as a semi-god) spins equally insane speculations from the words in which I expound the text of Paul: 'The cup which we bless.' 'That sacred cup,' I say, 'which we take up with thanksgiving and consecrate.'[224] 'That word consecrate,' he says, 'was added insincerely and perfunctorily.'[225] If I did not add it sincerely, I reject consecration. But what necessity forced me to add it since Paul does not use that word? If I had said: 'we consecrate and we bless,' I would have been sincere. Now because the word comes second it was not sincerely added. Oh weighty arguments, and slanderous ones at that! Are these people not ashamed to defend these manifest inanities of Leo?

* * * * *

215 Paraphrase on 1 Corinthians 10:21, 11:25 CWE 43 136, 148; cf *Detectio praestigiarum* above 189.
216 Cf *Maynung* A 6 r; *Detectio praestigiarum* above 190.
217 Cf *Maynung* B 6 r–v; *Detectio praestigiarum* above 191.
218 Cf *Detectio praestigiarum* above 191–3.
219 Cf *Maynung* A 2 r–v.
220 Erasmus is referring to the *Detectio praestigiarum.*
221 Bucer, the author of the *Epistola apologetica.*
222 Cf *Epistola apologetica* BOL I 127:4–7.
223 Cf *Detectio praestigiarum* above 165.
224 Cf the paraphrase on 1 Corinthians 10:16 CWE 43 134.
225 Cf *Detectio praestigiarum* above 184. The reference is to Zwingli's *Responsio ad epistolam Ioannis Bugenhagii* (*Zwinglis Werke* III 568:10–12).

'I could,' they[226] say, 'have learned about the book in time,'[227] although the book only appeared when the disputants had already set out.[228] And it was written in German, and I was at that time completely absorbed with other things. 'What weight,' he says, 'could a little book like that book have had in such a great matter?'[229] It would have had weight among the uneducated and the crude mob. 'We,' they say, 'gave no grounds for suspicion about us of this kind.'[230] Who are you? The Strasbourg ministers? These things were not written about you. For the public stage had not yet seen the man[231] who was to falsify some things in the books of Luther and Pomeranus[232] (not just turning their doctrine to his teaching but totally overturning it), who would teach that it was right for us to use deceits and tricks in the gospel cause, who would commend his books under fictitious titles.[233] And those who do and teach such things, now write: 'We never gave any grounds for such suspicion.' 'It is,' they say, 'on the Word of God that we rely, let every lie vanish.'[234]

They say I 'call the books of Karlstadt quite absurd,' although I have not read them, for they were written in German.[235] But the scholars who have read them declare them to be so. Even Oecolampadius, who embraced his view, condemned the arguments he used.[236] Further, his books appealed so little to the city council that they censored them, since they abounded with so much abuse.[237] They also say, 'He has not recanted.'[238] Why then

* * * * *

226 Bucer
227 Cf *Epistola apologetica* BOL I 127:11–13.
228 Erasmus is referring to the Disputation of Baden; see introductory note to *Detectio praestigiarum* above 157 n58.
229 Cf *Epistola apologetica* BOL I 126:17–20.
230 *Epistola apologetica* BOL I 127:2–4
231 Bucer
232 See *Epistola contra pseudoevangelicos* above n123. Johann Bugenhagen, of Pomerania (1485–1558) was a friend and colleague of Luther. He studied at the University of Wittenberg and was elected pastor of the city church in 1523. He became a professor of theology in 1535. His written works include numerous biblical commentaries and theological works. See C. Lindberg *The European Reformation* (Blackwell 2002) 122–7.
233 See *Epistola contra pseudevangelicos* above 239 nn122, 123.
234 *Epistola apologetica* BOL I 127:4
235 *Epistola apologetica* BOL I 126:14
236 Cf Staehelin *Briefe und Akten* 1 no 235 336–8.
237 See Rupp *Patterns of Reformation* 23–4; the incident is documented in Staehelin *Briefe und Akten* 1 no 226.
238 *Epistola apologetica* BOL I 127:14–15; see *Epistola contra pseudevangelicos* above 237 n115.

is he said to be reconciled to Luther? 'In the book,' he says, 'he said otherwise,' no doubt because he was then beyond Luther's reach.[239] He[240] at least
was more gentle towards Karlstadt than Zwingli was to Balthasar, whom
the people of Zürich, so they say, detained in prison for six months and
who was not released without a public recantation; in fact, he was not released, he escaped from prison.[241] At least at Basel there was a public report that Karlstadt had recanted. And what harm would there have been
if he repented of such error? Lastly, if someone condemns the assertion of
doctrines which he previously asserted, is that not to recant? But enough of
Leo and Karlstadt.

There remains another minister whom they say is certainly the chief
architect of the book to which we now respond.[242] And for that reason he
conceals his name! Perhaps we can call him Bucephalus. Under a false title
he wrote a book to the heir of the king of France, mixing in some French
words to make it seem as if it were written by a Frenchman to a Frenchman.[243] 'It is a pious ruse,' he says, 'which hurts no one and is advantageous to many.'[244] First, does heresy harm no one? The churchman in question would get this response straight away from someone else, for this is
how his party has been adjudged. Does not such a prince and a most religious nation suffer when it is burdened with ill will? What similar example
could be produced from the apostles or approved Doctors of the church? If
this disguise harms no one, why did Luther take it so ill that his books had
been corrupted by this man? Why did Pomeranus too complain about his
rashness? What is regarded by others and even by the laws themselves as
a most grave crime of forgery is for this fine 'evangelical' a pious ruse.

* * * * *

239 Cf *Epistola apologetica* BOL I 127:16–18.
240 Luther
241 The Anabaptist Balthasar Hubmaier (1481–1528), originally a protégé of Johannes Eck, became a priest in the parish of Waldshut. He came into contact
with the Swiss reformers, introduced the Reformation in his own parish, and
supported the peasants during the Peasants' War. Although he took part in
the Second Zürich Disputation, he fell out of favour with the Zürich lead-
ership because of his rejection of infant baptism. Forced into exile, he tried
to take refuge in late 1525 in Zürich, where he initially recanted, but when
called to make a public proclamation of his recantation he withdrew it, with
the result that he was imprisoned and tortured. He eventually recanted a second time and was allowed to leave the city; see Williams *Radical Reformation*
233–9.
242 See n34 above.
243 See *Epistola contra pseudevangelicos* above 239.
244 *Epistola apologetica* BOL I 128:7

As far as Vulturius[245] is concerned I have already responded, for I have already come to know very well his simplicity, good faith, and sincerity. Let it be taken as a mark of our former friendship that I will write nothing too bitter against him. If the comet of which he wrote was a serious matter, his book was ridiculous – such an inept piece of writing.[246] I have not yet been able to secure his books to which he had prefixed my name. But men of the utmost credibility read them and report that these books encourage German princes to deprive priests and monks of their means of support.[247] The same is maintained in the epistle entitled *Argyrophylax*; but I am not at all sure it was the same epistle.[248] If there was nothing harmful in these books, why did the city council here in Freiburg (whose members are anything but stupid) forbid their distribution, so effectively that no one can find a copy? Moreover, that was done before I knew that some copies were brought here. I did see the second one at Basel, but did not deign to read it.

Nor does Vulturius write the same things I do, as this author now alleges. I would not want heretics who have simply gone astray in their views to be dragged off immediately to the stake; he calls anyone who is dragged off innocent.[249] If they are innocent, the princes who inflict the death penalty on them are wicked; and if they hold to the gospel truth, the emperor who orders them to be killed is worse than a heretic. He attributes to Vulturius a genuine sanctity which I would indeed have hoped was found both in him and in me, and I let him meanwhile enjoy these praises. Nor does it matter to me how much money of his own or of others he has forsaken, although I think more came from others. How religiously he observed the laws of friendship, with how evangelical a faith he married his wife, he himself knows and it is no secret to me either. But let us leave him to his holiness!

I mentioned the example of the peasants lest those who pursue their object by disorder should end up with a similar outcome.[250] Elsewhere he[251] denies that the disorder was due to the gospel but attributes it to

* * * * *

245 Geldenhouwer

246 See *Epistola contra pseudevangelicos* above 222 n30; see also *Epistola apologetica* BOL I 128:11–17.

247 Cf *Epistola contra pseudevangelicos* above 223; *Epistola apologetica* BOL I 128:17–129:6.

248 See Prinsen *Collecteana* 189–92; Geldenhouwer deplores the excess wealth and the immorality of the clergy.

249 See introductory note to *Epistola contra pseudevangelicos* above 215 nn36–8.

250 *Epistola contra pseudevangelicos* above 228

251 Bucer

the harshness of the lords.[252] I can scarcely deny that, but it is hidden from no one that very many who arrogated to themselves the title of the 'gospel' were later involved in that rabble. And I know one of the foremost pillars of the 'gospel' who, when I said I feared a disastrous outcome for the peasants, just laughed, indicating that he hoped for better things. And although the ministers never ceased to rage against the life of the priests, they were virtually speechless when it came to the peasants. The 'evangelical' people, however, had many in their ranks who were so far from disapproving of that drama that the magistracy in Basel, concerned for the security of the community, was more fearful of them than of outsiders; one of the pillars of the 'gospel' was ordered into exile.[253] The guardsmen said they arrested him on the evening of Good Friday, not while adoring the cross (something those people regard as contrary to divine law) but while active in the mysteries of the goddess of Paphos.[254] I doubt if anyone will read this without a smile.

'There is,' he says, 'no one who abhors radical change more than we.'[255] If he is speaking on behalf of his city, I accept that. If he is speaking about the evangelical party as a whole, Luther abhors it even more to some extent, for he did not remove the images from the churches or prohibit anyone (if he wished) from saying mass; he also does not force anyone to his communion table and does not forcibly expel the canons from their churches nor the religious from their monasteries. 'We wish,' this man continues, 'to please the monarchs in every respect.'[256] Why, then, do some of them pillage churches that monarchs have erected? 'But when monarchs command impious things,' he says, 'they should be despised.'[257] Yet it will become clear that impious is defined as what is disadvantageous to them [the

* * * * *

252 *Epistola apologetica* BOL I 169:6–15
253 This was Boniface Wolfhart, a chaplain at St Martin's, the church where Oecolampadius preached. He was banished in May of 1525 because of his complicity in the Peasants' Revolt. For a brief description of the unrest in the town of Basel during the Peasants' War, in which reformers' preaching played a decisive role, see Guggisberg *Basel in the Sixteenth Century* 27–9.
254 Aphrodite, goddess of love, was said to have arisen from the sea foam off the coast of the Isle of Paphos.
255 *Epistola apologetica* BOL I 130:23
256 Cf *Epistola apologetica* BOL I 130:13–15.
257 See *Epistola apologetica* BOL I 131:15–16: *Iam inter haec praecipuum est libera veritatis in loco confessio errantiumque in tempore monitio* 'For especially in such circumstances there is need for frank confession of the truth and a timely warning to those who have gone astray.'

'evangelicals']. Is it not a fact that many Saxons have denied the emperor and King Ferdinand subsidies against the hostile force of the Turks – following Luther's teaching, which he now recants?[258] Have not the 'evangelicals' noised abroad that they would rather fight for the unbaptized Turk than for the baptized Turk (their way of describing the emperor)? Not to mention what was done at Rome, or how 'evangelically' they behaved in Vienna.[259] Who is not appalled by that story?

Nor can anyone read the following without a smile: 'We teach,' they say, 'and take to heart' that to him who strikes the right 'cheek we also turn the left,' and 'give him who steals the tunic the cloak as well,' etc.[260] If the Strasbourg ministers are like that, I can only congratulate that community heartily. Otherwise, it is unfitting for such things to be written by those who destroy what others have erected at their expense, who seize the chapters and monasteries and say: 'let the old inhabitants depart,' who rush armed into the marketplace. What did the ministers say? 'Do not harm anyone unless he has first harmed you, but prepare arms and cannons lest anyone

* * * * *

258 The Türkenhilfe was a subsidy granted to the emperor by the Diet of the Holy Roman Empire in the event of an anticipated Ottoman attack. Under Sultan Suleyman the Lawgiver (1520–66), the Ottomans conquered the key fortress-city of Belgrade (1521) and subsequently destroyed the army of the kingdom of Hungary at Mohács (1526). Like many Christians, Luther saw Turkish victories as a punishment from God for the sins of Christendom. Although initially opposed to resistance to the instrument of divine vengeance, he reluctantly approved of defensive war against the Turks. Meanwhile, the Diet of Speier (1526) voted to relax enforcement of the Edict of Worms, in effect giving local governments authority to establish Lutheran churches. When this provision was rescinded by the Catholic majority at the 1529 Diet of Speier, the evangelical estates lodged the 'protest' that has given the 'Protestant' movement its name. In this context, the evangelical estates voted to grant only a small portion of the large Türkenhilfe sought by Ferdinand. But as it became clear that a huge Ottoman force was marching up the Danube, towards Vienna, Protestants joined in mobilizing an army, some of whose units reached Vienna in time to help withstand the siege: see S.A. Fischer-Galati *Ottoman Imperialism and German Protestantism 1521–55* (Cambridge 1959) chapter II.
259 In May 1527 a runaway imperial army subjected Rome to a brutal sack, in which thousands of civilians were massacred: see E.R. Chamberlin *The Sack of Rome* (London 1979). Notwithstanding the fact that the soldiers included Catholic Spaniards as well as Lutheran Germans, Catholics, including Erasmus, blamed Luther and his followers; see eg Allen Ep 2059. In the case of Vienna Erasmus is referring to the defection of certain Protestant militiamen during the 1529 siege; see Spitz *Religious Renaissance* 194.
260 *Epistola apologetica* BOL I 130:24–8

oppress you.' I know that some were thrown into prison because a word against the ministers escaped them, and one who was even in danger of losing his life.

I pass over what is popularly said about Zwingli's clemency.[261] May the view of Hesiod be false that what popular rumour reports is never forgotten.[262] But if they truly are taking evangelical patience to heart, why do they rage in such biting and slanderous books against this person and that: Zwingli against Emser;[263] Luther against the king of England, and George, the duke of Saxony, and the emperor;[264] Jonas against Faber;[265] Luther, Hutten, and Otto against me?[266] 'We fight for the "gospel,"' they say – another might chime in 'for heresy' – but even if we concede the point, what need is there for such insults and derision? Where all the while is the left cheek offered to the blow? In this man's book how many figurative stings, how many devices to load opprobrium on me, how much zeal to incite the princes, cities, and regions against me, how much poison covered with honeyed words!

But Erasmus too, he says, complains about an age that has produced some who 'virtually preferred the authority of the pontiff' to that of 'Christ, who measured the whole of piety by ceremonies, who greatly tightened the bonds of confession,' so that 'the monks ruled with impunity, even to

* * * * *

261 See above n241.
262 Cf *Adagia* IV viii 34: *Rumor publicus non omnino frustra est* 'General report not always groundless' CWE 36 377–8, citing Hesiod *Works and Days* 763–4.
263 Zwingli's *Adversus Hieronymum Emserum antibolon* (1524, *Zwinglis Werke* III 230–87) was written in response to an attack by Jerome Emser entitled *Canonis missae contra Huldricum Zuinglium defensio* (1524). Emser (1478–1524) studied at Basel and then later at Leipzig, where he trained in theology and canon law.
264 In 1521 Henry VIII wrote the *Assertio septem sacramentorum*, which prompted Luther's 1522 response *Contra Henricum Regem Angliae* (WA 10-2 175–262); see E. Doernberg *Henry VIII and Luther: An Account of their Personal Relations* (Stanford 1961). One of Luther's bitterest antagonists was Duke George of Saxony (1471–1539), against whom Luther aimed his *Von heimlichen und gestohlenen Briefen* (WA 30-2 1–48). With regard to Charles V what Erasmus has in mind is unclear, since Luther did not publish a book against the emperor.
265 In 1522 Johannes Fabri (1478–1541), vicar to the bishop of Constance, published his *Opus adversus dogmata Martini Lutheri*, to which Justus Jonas (1493–1535), an admirer of Erasmus who became an adherent of Luther and Melanchthon, responded in 1523 with the *Adversus Johannem Fabrum Constantiensem vicarium scortationis patronum pro coniugio sacerdotali Justi Jonae defensio*.
266 Erasmus is referring to Luther's *De servo arbitrio*, the response to Erasmus' *De libero arbitrio*; to Hutten's *Expostulatio*, to which Erasmus responded with the *Spongia*; and to Otto Brunfels' *Responsio ad Erasmi spongiam*.

the point of meditating an out-and-out Pharisaism.'[267] 'There is agreement between us and Erasmus,' he says further, 'it is only that what he condemns we want overthrown.'[268] But come now, when did Erasmus ever teach that the mass was an abomination, that altars should be broken down, that the Eucharist is idolatrous, that confession is neither necessary nor useful, that all ceremonies should be abolished, that all pontifical edicts are contrary to the word of God?

If a ceremony is whatever is done through outward signs, then baptism itself would have to be abolished. Nevertheless, he who says 'some' (which was the term I used) does not condemn all, nor do those [evangelical] people want only the faults to be overturned, they want the good swept away with the bad. 'Erasmus,' they say, 'writes that the use of images in the churches "not only far exceeds proper moderation, but has also left decorum far behind."'[269] But nowhere does he write that all of them should be taken away quite indiscriminately and thrown into the fire, excepting those made of gold and silver. Erasmus criticizes that elaborate type of music found in some churches,[270] but does not condemn those who religiously sing the psalms in the churches, or who recite the prayers of the hours in a seemly way. Here is the conclusion this amazing logician draws from my words: If we pluck out things that are absurd, we mean to tear up everything; if some member is defective, the whole body must be removed. Where did he learn this logic?

I pass over that whole section in which (so as to teach that they are equal to the apostles) they try to prove that Christianity existing up to now was no better than the superstition of the gentiles, that what they now undertake is what was foretold by the apostles and by the prophets, namely, that the gentiles, having left the worship of demons, would come to acknowledge the true God, while Jewish ceremonies would vanish at the

* * * * *

267 *Epistola apologetica* BOL I 132:13–16, citing the 1529 revision of Erasmus' letter to Bucer in November 1527; see Allen Ep 1901:72–5. In the original letter Erasmus had used the word *phalarismus* to characterize the monks. For the *Opus epistolarum*, a collection of his letters he published in 1529, Erasmus changed *phalarismus* to *pharisaismus*. Phalaris (c 570/65–554/49 BC), tyrant of Acragas (Agrigentum), was known for his cruelty, particularly the roasting alive of enemies in a hollow brazen bull. See below n645 and Ep 1495:33.
268 *Epistola apologetica* BOL I 132:23–4
269 *Epistola apologetica* BOL I 134:22–4, citing *Epistola contra pseudevangelicos* above 251
270 *Epistola apologetica* BOL I 134:17–20, citing *Epistola contra pseudevangelicos* above 250

shining of the gospel light.[271] Whose ears can tolerate such blasphemy? If they merely note the places from the New Testament against the pseudo-apostles and bad Christians and heretics, and do not quote them, it is a matter of prudence, for these words may forthwith be turned against them. Outstanding predictions indeed, and worthy of comparison with the oracles of ancient prophets![272] But hear now a Chrysippean enthymeme.[273] 'What happened to Erasmus,' they say, 'for although he has so many times attacked ecclesiastical chanting, prayers droned out without thinking, and the subtle sophistications of the theologians, he now asks us what is so absurd about these things we are tearing out?'[274] And yet I did not condemn the things themselves but the conduct of some who made ill use of good things; these people tear out things which are in themselves good. What happened to this man that he slanders what he cannot understand?

They charge me with mendacity because I wrote they had boasted that they had brought back to light the truth of the gospel hidden for more than a thousand years since, they say, the early Doctors of the church had understood nothing of Holy Scripture. 'We never said this,' they say.[275] Who these 'we' are, I do not know. Yet what else do Luther and Zwingli boast in their books? For I spoke in general. If someone says that Jerome, Augustine, Chrysostom, Gregory, and the rest of them were in the flesh – but the flesh knows nothing of the things of God, since Holy Scripture is only understood through the Spirit of Christ (which he denied them to such a degree that he almost consigns them to hell) – is such a man not speaking as I said?[276] Since they take Luther to task only in regard to the Eucharist, it is probable that they agree with him on this point. Further, since these people also characterize as idolatrous, blasphemous, and insulting to Christ and the Holy Scriptures those things that the ancients taught and religiously adhered to for so many centuries gone by, such as fasting (which was known in the time of Origen),[277] chanting in the churches (which was there before Ambrose

* * * * *

271 Cf *Epistola apologetica* BOL I 132:29–34.

272 See *Epistola apologetica* BOL I 135:30–136:13.

273 Chrysippus (280–207 BC), a Stoic philosopher, was noted for the subtlety of his logic. On *enthymema* see CWE 25 122; Quintilian *Institutio* 5.10.1–3, 14.1–4.

274 *Epistola apologetica* BOL I 134:17–135:4

275 *Epistola apologetica* BOL I 135:9–14

276 For Zwingli, see *Apologeticus Archeteles* in *Zwinglis Werke* I 282:16; cf G.W. Locher *Huldrych Zwingli in neuer Sicht* (Zürich and Stuttgart 1969), 94ff. For Luther, *De servo arbitrio* WA 18 641–2, 649–52, 658–65.

277 See Origen *Homilia X in Leuiticum* PG 12 528B.

and Augustine),[278] the sacrifice of the mass, the Eucharist, the invocation of saints, statues in the church (which Gregory did not condemn,[279] while Jerome himself beat his breast before an image of the crucified),[280] free will, monasticism, and a great many other matters: do they not show the greatest respect for the early Doctors of the church?

Let them look again at the books of their authors before they say that 'much is said' by Erasmus 'not in the manner of a theologian.' For, they say, 'Erasmus' manner of speaking is not ours; he is unwilling to call a fig a fig.'[281] They are not content to have made their prophecies equal to those of old; they say theirs are better. I will give one example from many. In *Acts* chapter 20 Paul speaks in this way: 'I know' that after my departure 'fierce wolves' will come in 'among you which will not spare the flock, and from you will emerge men who say perverse things in order to seduce people to follow them.'[282] To which of the two sides are these words more pertinent? To us, who hold by what the church has handed down for fifteen hundred years, or to those who arouse such tumults with their new doctrines? What, then, did Christ foretell in Matthew chapter 24? 'See to it that no one leads you astray. For many will come in my name, saying: I am Christ, and they will lead many astray. And many false prophets will arise and lead many astray.'[283] Is it not obvious that they are παλίμβολα 'feckless'?[284] And what Paul says in Thessalonians chapter 2 seems as if addressed to us: 'We ask you not to let yourself be easily swayed from your view and not to be dismayed.'[285] But who is that 'man of sin and son of

* * * * *

278 Augustine (*Confessiones* 9.7.15) describes the introduction of psalm singing into the church at Milan, during the period of struggle between Ambrose and the Arian empress Justina in 386.

279 Gregory I *Epistula* 9 105 PL 77 1027, 11 13 PL 77 1128

280 Jerome gives an account of his penitential fervour in Ep 22 7; see CWE 61 159.

281 *Epistola apologetica* BOL I 135:13–14, 28–9; according to Bucer, when Erasmus himself disagrees with the church Fathers, he says there are things in Scripture that 'they did not see.' He continues, '"they did not see" is Erasmus' way of speaking, not ours, for he is unwilling to call a fig a fig.' Cf *Adagia* II iii 5: *Ficus ficus, ligonem ligonem vocat* 'He calls figs figs and a spade a spade' CWE 33 132–3: 'It suits a man who speaks the truth in a simple and countrified style, who tells of things as they are, and does not wrap them up in ornamental verbiage.'

282 Acts 20:29–30

283 Matt 24:4–5

284 *Adagia* II vii 35 CWE 34 19

285 2 Thess 2:2

perdition'?[286] The Roman pontiff, in this man's view; yet the pope would give these words a different interpretation!

What does Paul teach in 1 Timothy chapter 4? He predicted that people would arise who prohibited marrying, who commanded abstention from foods.[287] These words fit those who condemn all matrimony without exception as unclean by its very nature. Such men the Catholic church execrates. On the other hand, he who has taken one wife, is he not rightly forbidden to marry again? Did not Paul forbid marriage to a stepmother? Did not John the Baptist condemn Herod's marriage? The church only excludes from marriage those who have renounced marriage. But if they cannot remain chaste, let them deplore their own temerity or weakness, not condemn the church.

Let us hear the prophecy in the first Epistle of John chapter 2: 'My little sons, it is the last hour and just as you have heard that Antichrist is coming, already many antichrists have come to be. They arose from us, but they were not of us,' etc.[288] They see these things can be thrown back at once into their faces. Similarly, what is contained in chapter 4 of the same Epistle surely seems to be said to us: 'Beloved, do not believe every spirit, but test the spirits whether they are of God, for many false prophets have gone out into the world.'[289] What of the second Epistle of Peter chapter 2: 'But false prophets also arose among the people, just as there will be lying teachers among you, who will bring in destructive sects.'[290] Of whom is Peter prophesying? Let common sense judge: those words certainly do not apply to us! And predictions of this kind are clearer than prophecies, because Paul has confirmed them by his authority.

Next they compare their own disagreements with one another with the disagreements of the apostles and the Fathers.[291] The apostles never differed in the teachings of the faith. For as to the statement of some people that Peter erred in faith and was reproached by Paul for that reason, Augustine gave an incorrect account of the matter, and more recent writers have followed without thinking.[292] Nor is there the same basis for the dis-

* * * * *

286 2 Thess 2:3: 'Let no one deceive you in any way; for that day will not come unless the rebellion comes first and the lawless one is revealed, the one destined for destruction.'
287 1 Tim 4:3
288 Cf 1 John 2:18–19.
289 1 John 4:1
290 2 Pet 2:1
291 *Epistola apologetica* BOL I 136:22–32, 80:21–34
292 In Gal 2:11–14 Paul describes his rebuke to Peter at Antioch for refusing to eat with the gentiles in deference to the circumcision faction. Augustine and Jerome engaged in a lengthy exchange arguing their contrasting views of this

agreements of the Fathers and the quarrels of these people. One can excuse Origen and Cyprian for disputing about some scriptural matters which were not properly understood and on which no ecclesiastical authority had yet pronounced. Similarly, one can excuse Chrysostom, and Ambrose, and Jerome, and Augustine in many matters.[293] But whether it is true that these people never disagree about matters necessary for our salvation, let them see to it themselves!

We certainly believe that one's views about the Eucharist pertain to what is necessary for salvation, not to mention many other matters. Nor did I accuse them of introducing new doctrines in the sense that they now bring forth some matters on which they were initially silent;[294] my point was that in their books and sayings they teach contradictory things. If that is false, let them refute those who quote so many places where Luther and Zwingli disagree even with themselves! Their books are available, so that it is not necessary for me to undertake this task, although I can do it and can also mention matters omitted by others. Let them prove that there is no difference between the teaching of Luther and Zwingli! They must find another device to excuse their disagreement. But they also want to be excused for not understanding some things at first, in the same way that Peter had to be urged by the brethren at Antioch to baptize the family of Cornelius,[295] for there were among the Jews those who wanted to impose the burden of the Law on the gentiles, and some wished to combine the whole of the Law with Christ.[296] With such assumptions they defend the discrepancies in their doctrines. But the flock of these brethren is not my concern here.

The apostles (with whom these people compare themselves) never, as I said, disagreed on the teachings of the faith. The ceremonies of the Law were not evil in themselves, nor was dietary observance, nor did God

* * * * *

incident. According to Jerome (PL 26:363–6), who was unwilling to accept the possibility that Paul would criticize Peter, Paul did not actually impute guilt to Peter for his action, but rebuked him as a pretence in order to underscore a point for the edification of others about the replacement of the law by the gospel. Augustine (PL 35 2113–14), however, maintained that the passage must be understood in its literal meaning as reflecting truthfully a fault that Paul found with Peter. Erasmus in his annotation on this passage (LB VI 807D–810C) took Jerome's part; see also Allen Ep 1841 59–76. The 'more recent writers' referred to here are the theologians of the University of Paris.

293 Cf *Epistola apologetica* BOL I 80:31–4.
294 Cf *Epistola apologetica* BOL I 138:3–10.
295 Acts 11:1–3
296 Acts 15:1–5

wish his Law to be suddenly overthrown; rather he allowed it little by little to go out of date, lest it should seem to have been impious, since even those ceremonies which were to be abolished were a type[297] of Christ. On the other hand, since the Lord had ordered the apostles to begin from Jerusalem, the whole of Judaea and Samaria (and then to go to the very ends of the earth),[298] it was possible for Peter to doubt that the time had come when God wished it openly taught that the ceremonies of the Law should be abolished, and so was admonished by Paul that the time had indeed come. Furthermore, the hesitation Peter showed about baptizing Cornelius,[299] and the murmuring of the brethren against Peter, and the rebuke by Paul were nothing other than God's dispensation to ensure that it was clear to all that these changes had their source in God's will, not human inconsistency. But when did any apostle approve of idolatry? And yet at first these people approved of the mass and offered it as a sacrifice, although they now consider it the height of idolatry. Let them excuse this by their rhetoric if they can!

He[300] says they disagree with my writing that at first the apostles kept the divinity of Christ secret.[301] They report me as saying that the apostles, after having received the Holy Spirit, accepted some into the grace of the gospel to whom they did not disclose the divinity of Christ. Far be it from me for such a thought ever to enter my mind! But I do note, following the judgment of orthodox authors, that Peter in his first sermon to the ignorant multitude calls Christ 'a man approved of God,'[302] saying nothing about his divinity, for if he had referred to it then, he would not have kept the attention of his hearers. Likewise Paul, when among the Athenians who could not yet grasp the mystery, calls Christ a man by whom God had determined to help the human race.[303] For who could at that point have tolerated that a man nailed to a cross should be called God? This was appropriate for that time and for those unlearned people. To be sure,

* * * * *

297 Ie a foreshadowing of Christ.
298 Acts 1:8
299 Acts 10:28; Peter does not hesitate, but he points out that his presence among the gentiles is the direct result of God's instructions to him.
300 Bucer
301 *Epistola apologetica* BOL I 138:6–7. Bucer has in mind Erasmus' annotations on Acts 2:22 and 1 Tim 1:17: LB VI 444D and 930C–931C; he defended himself against attacks on this score in *Apologia adversus monachos* LB X 1047C–F.
302 Acts 2:22; see Erasmus' annotation on this passage, added in 1527, in LB VI 444D; cf *Purgatio adversus epistolam Lutheri* below 427–30.
303 Acts 17:31 refers to Christ as 'a man whom [God] has appointed.'

they no doubt disclosed the mystery of the divine nature to their disciples from the beginning. But when they were sent by Christ throughout the cities of Judaea to preach the gospel, they were forbidden to say that Jesus was the Messiah, much less pronounce him to be God.[304] What is it, then, that these people do not recognize? Let them admit, rather, that they have not understood what I wrote! Let them remove their verbal posturing and desist from comparing themselves with the apostles! For the time being I will not enter into discussing the councils of the church, which they treat with such contempt; we do not defend all of their decisions either.

The discussion returns to questions of conduct, and they go on at such length about the clemency and gentleness of their party and especially of the Landgrave of Hesse[305] that, if I had written it, they would be shouting that I was flattering magistrates and princes. But since these matters pertain to princes, I am not inclined to respond, especially since I have scant knowledge of distant events. The views of Hesse's prince are unknown to me, and I pay no attention to popular rumours. What these people declare about those they think favourable to what they have established does not interest me any more than what they force on us about themselves. I could not hold back a smile when they adduce as an argument for 'evangelical' clemency that, although in my letters I had for so long been arousing the minds of the monarchs and all mortals against them by heaping such dire and false accusations on them, yet I had got off scot-free.[306] And where are these 'dire and false accusations'? Why do they not shout out against Eck,[307] the bishop of Rochester,[308] and many others who contend against

* * * * *

304 Luke 9:20–2

305 *Epistola apologetica* BOL I 140:23–141:10. Philip Landgrave of Hesse (1504–67) became a supporter of the Reformation in Strasbourg and a close associate of Bucer. See Brady *Protestant Politics* 55–7.

306 *Epistola apologetica* BOL I 141:21–142:2

307 Johann Maier of Eck (1486–1543), professor of theology at Ingolstadt, is best known for his role as Luther's adversary in the Leipzig disputation of 1519. His relationship with Erasmus first became strained as a result of his disapproval of Erasmus' *Novum Testamentum*. They clashed again when in 1530 Eck published his *Articuli 404*, in which Erasmus believed he found references to his own works; see Epp 769, 844; Allen Epp 2365, 2387, and 2406; cf *Spongia* above 81 n251.

308 John Fisher (1469–1535), bishop of Rochester and chancellor of Cambridge University, was one of Erasmus' friends and patrons throughout his life. In 1527 he published *De veritate corporis et sanguinis Christi in Eucharistia, adversus Johannem Oecolampadium*. He was eventually condemned to death for treason

these sects in earnest? They who declare them heretics and schismatics are hurling all the charges simultaneously. Let them see with what colourful terms Johannes Eck has adorned them in this gathering of princes! I have always dissuaded the princes from ferocity to the best of my ability, and I myself have been so far from ferocious against those people that to many I seem to collude with them. So many barbed pamphlets, full of bitterness and such grievous insults, fly about far and wide that you would not easily find anything analogous among the pagans, and yet they so often boast to us of their wonderful gentleness which offers the left cheek for striking when the right has been struck. 'We,' my opponent will say, 'do not do the things you attribute to us.' Since my way of speaking is in general terms, let him not say: 'We do not do those things,' but 'what you are objecting to never happens.' They want to be able with impunity to pour out all the abuse they like against bishops, kings, and princes. Let anyone who wishes test whether anyone gets away with impunity, if he rages in a similar way against their ministers or magistrates!

Personally, I have had abundant experience of the gentleness of some of them. I knew someone whom for more than ten years I loved like a very son, and in turn he regarded me as a parent, having an inborn inclination, you might have said, to integrity.[309] But as soon as he inhaled the 'evangelical' spirit, contrary to all expectation he began to be a good gamester, burning the night away with cards, and a stylish fornicator, and having laid aside the scholar's robe he began to carry about a long sword and to think of marriage. Finally, wounded by a little word, from being such a friend (or so it seemed) he suddenly turned into a viper eager for vengeance, as if I had slain his mother with a sword.

Why should I recall a second super-'evangelical' person who was never wounded by a word of mine but praised both by my speaking and my writing and who made good use of my assistance? After his visit to Basel (although he had never complained to me) he displayed an exceedingly hostile

* * * * *

because of his refusal to support Henry VIII as supreme head of the church in England; cf CEBR II 36–9.

309 Ludovicus Carinus (Kiel) of Lucerne (c 1496–1569) received his degree from the University of Basel in 1514. Erasmus wrote in glowing terms of him (Epp 1034, 1091); however by July 1528 their relationship seems to have cooled. While Erasmus referred to Carinus as a 'viper,' numerous friends testified that Carinus was speaking ill of Erasmus (Allen Epp 2048, 2063, 2085, 2101). Carinus went to Strasbourg in 1531, where he formed cordial relations with Bucer and Capito.

attitude and never seems to have enough sting in his tongue to threaten me and reads out a book directed against me to his drinking companions.[310] How have I deserved this? Because I was unwilling to play the madman with a madman. Nevertheless, as far as I was concerned he could do what he pleased. I made excuses for him in a very good-natured manner to Bishop Christoph,[311] and when danger threatened him from the magistracy, I warned him privately by a letter.[312] Nor was this an untimely admonition. Ordered to appear before the magistracy he preferred to leave the city. And this is one of the 'evangelical' leaders!

When would they offer the other cheek to someone striking them, since they reward those who have deserved well of them like this? How could Hutten sharpen his pen against someone by whom he had been so beloved, so praised in published writings, and not inconsiderably assisted? Did the 'evangelical' people not praise him as a champion of the 'gospel'? And yet a certain well-known defender of that doctrine in one of his letters calls him a maniac;[313] Luther deplores his having been spattered by the *Spongia*.[314]

What need I say now about the commoners among the evangelicals? I have known so many of them who were most impatient about the least injuries they had received and took ferocious revenge for some frivolous offence. I will touch on one case among many. A certain youth was thrown into prison for a rather serious crime.[315] His friends pressured me to seek pardon for him through the ambassador of the king of England who by chance was present. It was done, he was set free, the fine was waived; so I was compelled to express gratitude in his name to the council as if for a great boon. But this good man, on the very day he was set free, drunk with the wine of those by whom he had been freed, ranted against me in terms speakable and unspeakable, with drawn sword even threatening Erasmus with death. Asked the next day whether he meant what he said,

* * * * *

310 Cf Ep 1496:93–119 and *Spongia* above 55 n99.
311 Christoph von Utenheim (d 1527), bishop of Basel; cf CEBR III 361–2.
312 This letter is not extant.
313 The reference is to Melanchthon: CR I, letter 254, column 627, and letter 255, column 627. C. Augustijn believes that Erasmus saw copies of letters from Melanchthon expressing strong disapproval of the *Spongia*: ASD I-ix 110 n113; Epp 1429:12, 1437:45 and 185.
314 WA Br 3 no 661:7–9: 'I wish that Hutten had not expostulated, and still more that Erasmus had not wiped his expostulation off.'
315 Cf Allen Ep 2874:53–82; the young man is not identified. Allen (58n) assumes that the English ambassador was Richard Pace.

he blamed it on his drunkenness. Truly an 'evangelical' excuse! Then he set off to Constance and pretended to Botzheim[316] (whom he knew to be very closely linked to me) that he had been a servant to Erasmus. With the help of this recommendation he was hospitably treated there for some weeks. From there he betook himself to Wittenberg to complete his 'gospel' mission.

You have your examples of gentleness, now take an example of good faith and truthfulness. I expostulated with a certain passionate 'evangelical'[317] because he had wandered through his fatherland giving schoolteachers and tutors (who teach young people at home) a pamphlet containing some sixteen articles: that confession is superfluous, that pontifical constitutions are not at all binding, and various matters of this kind. Though he denied other things to which I also objected, he spoke quite frankly of this. Despite my advice to the contrary, he returned to his homeland. He had scarcely departed when he was arrested, but he escaped. When he had told me the whole story, I asked what offence he had committed to be pursued with such zeal by the officers of justice. 'You must,' I said, 'have done or said something which made them realize that you were no different from the sects.' He solemnly swore that he had not done or said anything. 'What are you saying, you shameless fellow,' I said, 'did you not admit to me in the presence of so-and-so that you disseminated those articles?' He denied it. The more I pressed him, the more he denied it.

Another individual burst into my house, seeking to talk with me.[318] As I learned from my servants that he was a πλανήτης 'a vagabond,' I instructed them to say that I was not free. On being told to leave for a first and then a second time, he said: 'I put no value on the words of Erasmus, I want his money.' What was to be done? After a whole hour (when I thought he had

*　*　*　*　*

316 Johann von Botzheim (c 1480–1535), who was made a canon at the cathedral in Constance in 1512, was at first favourable to the Reformation, but then turned against it. For many years he extended hospitality to scholars, including Erasmus, until he was forced to leave Constance in 1527 because of the triumph of the Reformation. Erasmus wrote his famous *Catalogus lucubrationum* (Ep 1341A) in the form of a letter to Botzheim in January of 1523.

317 Michael Bentinus, a native of Flanders, (d 1527) worked for Froben in Basel in 1520 as a corrector of Latin texts, including Erasmus' *Adagia*, but Erasmus was displeased with his work (Ep 1437:174–81). He had become an adherent of the Reformation by 1524 (cf Ep 1514:18–26), and became friendly with Eppendorf, Farel, Oecolampadius, and the reformers of Strasbourg; cf CEBR I 123–4.

318 This event also occurred in 1524; the fugitive Franciscan has not been identified. Cf Ep 1536:4–6.

long since gone), just as I left my bedroom, I found him gossiping quite
familiarly with my servants. Now, he was a Franciscan, as he had freely
blabbed out to my servants. While talking he happened to say that he was
just about to go straight to Nuremberg. I wrote to Willibald[319] and gave
the man seven coins. He did not deliver the letter, but when I happened to
send one of the servants to Venice, he found that 'evangelical' man there.

Another person approached me complaining of extreme poverty and
offering his services.[320] I was unwilling to admit into my service someone
unknown to me, but having given him four coins I instructed him to return
to me the next day. He returned, and I gave him a manuscript to transcribe
so that he would learn to write; having contracted to pay him two coins each
day, I added, apart from the four coins I had given him already, fourteen
more I had to hand. This good man having obtained his travelling allowance
proceeded without my knowledge to Zürich and found employment with
someone or other there. When after six days he never put in an appearance,
I had enquiries made; they said he had left. He was said to have left my
book with his host, but this man denied anything had been left with him.
I did not get my book back until the host ordered in his own handwriting
that it be returned. The man returned to Basel but never gave back the
money or acknowledged in writing what he had received, or even thanked
me. Indeed, when going by with some friends he did not greet me even by
removing his hat.

I refrain from mentioning the many others who were suborned to
rush into my house to deliver letters or pamphlets written to mock me. I
found some who even went to those they knew were friendly with me,
offering their service if they wanted something taken to Erasmus; they then
took the letters given them to their brethren in order to learn my secrets.
I can offer a hundred stories of this kind.[321] But if they deny that such
men were 'evangelicals,' they are arguing on my behalf, for that is why

* * * * *

319 Willibald Pirckheimer (1470–1530) of Nuremberg, one of Erasmus' staunch-
    est allies in defence of *bonae litterae*, came from an elite family and received
    a thorough humanist education. He served on the town council in Nürnberg
    for many years, at the same time maintaining his literary pursuits, mostly as
    an editor and translator. Initially sympathetic to Luther, he became a defender
    of the Roman church, writing two treatises against Oecolampadius. He main-
    tained an active correspondence with Erasmus. See CEBR III 90–4; Allen Ep
    2493.
320 According to C. Augustijn the person in question is unknown, and the event
    nowhere else mentioned by Erasmus.
321 Cf eg Ep 1547:5–8.

I have regarded them as pseudo-evangelicals. Still, there is a great heap of human refuse like this, who from the outset have played no small part in this drama and have further alienated many people of good will from this business. Therefore, they should not become angry with me if I am adverse to what they themselves also condemn.

But I return to what I had begun. He[322] adduces also as an example of 'evangelical' gentleness that even those who oppose their sect may live among them in all comfort.[323] I will not deal with how that stands at the moment. Certainly, I hear complaints; I see people going into exile, some of whom have changed their minds after finding out how holy the 'evangelicals' are. It is most shameless and inane for them to claim that while, as they say, 'in Strasbourg, Basel, and Constance so many have turned to a faultless life,' I write about them just the same as if 'none of them had begun to live a better life, rather as if every single one had deteriorated.'[324] Shameless mouth, where does Erasmus say anything of the kind? On the contrary, he asserts that he only knows of a few,[325] and writes solely about the ones he knows; and what I write is most accurate, and I can back it up by many proofs, lest they imagine I am relying on common rumour. Men whom I had known before as pure, frank, and guileless, when they committed themselves to the sect, began to talk about girls, play dice, and abandon prayer; they became obsessed with material things, sensitive to any injury, vindictive, abusive, vain, they behaved like adders, and put off all humanity. I will not bring up the popular rumours about the extravagance of some of them. I have found that in business matters many 'evangelicals' are harder and less reliable than others. If so many have become better, that is a cause for joy, and it may be this has happened without my knowing it.

As to how people live at Rome, or how the canons of collegiate churches live, it is of no import to me nor do I know much about it. For he contents himself with a false hyperbole – 'No one knows better,' he says, when in fact scarcely anyone knows less than I.[326] But let them abstain

* * * * *

322 Bucer
323 *Epistola apologetica* BOL I 140:10–14; see Chrisman *Strasbourg and the Reform* chapter 13.
324 *Epistola apologetica* BOL I 144:3–12
325 *Epistola contra pseudevangelicos* above 241: 'Show me just one whom that gospel has changed from gluttonous to sober, rapacious to generous, cursing to blessing or shameless to modest. I will show you many who have become worse than their former selves'; cf Allen Ep 1901:30–4.
326 *Epistola apologetica* BOL I 143:16–18, where Bucer claims no one knows better than Erasmus about the kind of lives people live in Rome, or in collegiate churches or monasteries.

from comparing their ministers with our bishops for the moment; when they have arrived at honours and wealth, then will be the time for comparison. Now, though the intention may be there, the opportunity is lacking. Unless I am mistaken, all bishops of Rome up to the twenty-first bore the crown of martyrdom.[327] We will see what kind of a person the twentieth successor to Zwingli, or Oecolampadius, or Capito turns out be. However, I have known among our bishops men whose sanctity I would prefer to a thousand 'evangelicals.' Therefore, what they falsely impute to me (that I speak as if none of the 'evangelicals' lives a good life) can quite properly be turned back on those who speak of the priests, monks, and bishops as if they are all the most wicked people and enemies of Christ.

I wrote that they abolish prayers and fasts;[328] they kick up a row about this: 'If this is not slander, then what is?'[329] I will echo their words back to them: 'If this is not slander, then what is?' I said they abolish the fasts set by the church, the prayers of the hours prescribed by the church. Since they themselves admit as much, why are they yelling about slander? What I condemned was not so much the fact that they abolished these things, but that after they were abolished many neither pray nor fast at all any more. 'True prayer,' they say, 'cannot be enjoined by man, since this is not in the power of man.'[330] The church does not arrogate something to itself, it merely prescribes what is conducive and helpful for spiritual prayer, among which the principal things are fasting, alms-giving, the reading of sacred writings, and the vocal recitation of prayers; that which cannot be demanded the church encourages. 'Why,' they say, 'do the pontiffs arrogate to themselves what the apostles did not arrogate to themselves?'[331] Because in those days people prayed and fasted spontaneously; now there is need for a muzzle and goads for our indolence, and it is probable that if the apostles had lived in an age like this, they too would have imposed harsher regulations on our behaviour. And now they[332] even deny that they have abolished the mass.[333] What, then, is the meaning of

* * * * *

327 See J.N.D. Kelly *The Oxford Dictionary of Popes* (Oxford 1986); numerous legends, most without foundation in fact, attributed martyrdom to the earliest bishops of Rome. C. Augustijn (ASD IX-1 373 977–8n) notes that liturgical writings at Erasmus' time portrayed as martyrs all bishops of Rome up to Silvester (314–55).

328 *Epistola contra pseudevangelicos* above 231

329 *Epistola apologetica* BOL I 145:24–8

330 *Epistola apologetica* BOL I 145:28–146:6

331 *Epistola apologetica* BOL I 146:11–15

332 The 'evangelicals'

333 *Epistola apologetica* BOL I 146:27–8

so many pamphlets about abolishing the mass? Or what sort of a mass is it which lacks the body and blood of Christ? And when they take these away, they have the audacity to say that they have only taken away the vices – the greed of the priests and their other crimes – and not the thing itself. So, are we to believe that the apostles celebrated the mass without the body of Christ? For vestments and rites are not 'tares,' as he calls them, but instruments that can be discarded or used or changed to suit the time.[334]

They are pained by my hyperbole when I wrote they could not abide any of the traditions.[335] Let them show, then, the sum total of what Luther and Zwingli find good in the traditions; they will find nothing. Further, as to what he says has been written by me that 'they replace good or at least tolerable things by introducing what is worst,'[336] I do not think this can be read anywhere in my epistle, and if I had written it, I would have done so with the approval of many. Nevertheless, that exaggeration[337] gave them a convenient excuse to excite hostility against me. They insist I should reveal the names of those whom I say have deteriorated after joining the sect[338] (they mention a prince as a counter-example but he is unknown to me);[339] as if they are nowhere to be seen or as if those whom they want to be pointed out by name are not obvious to the public. Let them allow me to remain civil in this matter! But if they press me, I will direct them to Saxony, where there are people who have need of ecclesiastical visitors – the same people who refused the emperor subsidies against the Turk,[340] and who have confounded all the marriage laws.[341] Let them learn from the visitors[342] which cases they should hear. But what need is there to mention

* * * * *

334 *Epistola apologetica* BOL I 147:7–10, in which Bucer writes *Nam solas blasphemias precum nomine venditas, solum fucum, solum quaestum ex demurmuratis sine mente sacris hymnis factum et reliquum imposturarum instrumentum removimus; quae si non zizania sunt, haud scio quid zizania vocari debeat.* Cf Matt 13:24–30.
335 *Epistola apologetica* BOL I 147:13–14
336 *Epistola apologetica* BOL I 147:16
337 For the Greek term Erasmus uses, δείνωσις, see *Spongia* above n238.
338 *Epistola apologetica* BOL I 147:26–7
339 Philip of Hesse: see above n305; cf *Epistola apologetica* BOL I 140:23–141:10.
340 Cf above nn57, 258.
341 Cf Allen Ep 2267:124–8. S. Ozment *When Fathers Ruled: Family Life in Reformation Europe* (Cambridge, MA 1983) 46–7 describes the confusion that occurred throughout the 1520s at the first introduction of Lutheran challenges to Catholic marriage laws.
342 On the visitations, see above n57.

anyone by name, since they themselves admit that many rush into crimes more licentiously on the advent of the 'gospel'?[343] Let them name them themselves instead of asking me to do so.

Again he gathers together some manifest mendacities: I 'permit myself,' so he says, 'to condemn their whole confession of faith because of some evil individuals mixed up in it.'[344] This cannot be found anywhere in the epistle or in my other writings; rather the opposite can be read. I only say that the impure life of some harms their cause. They themselves do not deny this. The same goes for these words: 'as if nothing but crimes were advocated amongst us';[345] since nothing like that is in my writings I am astounded at the shamelessness of the writer. This too is a patent falsehood: as if 'no one has become a follower of our teaching who has not become worse as a result'; all I do is to say that I have known such people.[346] I have known only a very small number of these people well, and none in Strasbourg. And after such a shameless lie comes a rhetorical flourish: 'Oh what a grave insult to Christ,' etc. Not yet satisfied, he goes on to speak of those whom 'this great vindicator of the Catholic church' exposes and 'denounces as real monsters and the most nefarious of two-legged creatures and hands over to the hatred of all and the extreme cruelty of princes.'[347] Who will not admire an exaggeration[348] confected of utter lies? And here is that teacher of 'evangelical' gentleness, who without any justification and in order to whip up sedition sounds forth in this way on the trumpet of Alecto.[349] I have always urged people to moderation and tranquillity, and still do. This war-cry deserved to be directed at others. Perhaps it escaped this heedless man that he calls my church Catholic. Because if ours is Catholic, it must mean he is calling their church heretical. Someone else might well conclude: whoever moved from being orthodox to heretical surely becomes worse than he was. But this is not my belief and I will not defend it.

* * * * *

343 *Epistola apologetica* BOL 1 147:29–32: *Venit enim istis Christus 'ut videntes non videant'* [Mark 4:12] *et personam detrahit hypocritis, quo fit ut hi insanius contra veritatem furant, illi licentius in scelera ruant.*
344 *Epistola apologetica* BOL 1 148:29
345 Ibidem
346 *Epistola apologetica* BOL 1 149:1–2; the passage Bucer refers to is in *Epistola contra pseudevangelicos* above 231: *Ego tibi multos ostendam qui facti sunt seipsis deteriores,* after asking Geldenhouwer whom he knows who has improved as a result of joining the reform; see also Allen Ep 2134:74–5, 2205:135.
347 *Epistola apologetica* BOL 1 149:3–7
348 See *Spongia* above 79 n238.
349 Alecto is one of the Furies; cf Virgil *Aeneid* 7.513–14.

I have always disapproved of removing images the way they do.[350]
Whoever removes the pictorial from life, removes one of life's special joys
and also something that has various good uses. We often see more in pictures than we grasp from words. It is, therefore, false when he says that
images are of no benefit.[351] Once upon a time, after all, there were images
even in the Jewish temple, the cherubim representing the face of a man and
the likeness of lions.[352] Nor is it likely that God intended that there should
be no image of any kind, but that there should be no idols in the pagan
manner. Many images are displayed not to be adored but in order to ornament a building or to point those who are present to some good thing. Is it
useless to depict on the porticoes of the churches the whole life of Christ,
so that those who walk there at leisure may have some edifying material
to talk and think about? But among Christians no image is displayed for
adoration. For the honour directed towards them is directed to what they
represent.

Now, if every image were to be removed without exception, the figures of Atlas and the flautists which the craftsmen add to the supporting
pillars[353] would have to be removed too, not to mention the cock generally
placed at the top of the sacred spire. It is probable, therefore, that God did
not mean any kind of image, but pagan likenesses to which they used to
sacrifice as if they were alive; if God meant his prohibition of images in the
strictest sense, it was commanded for those particular times, just as many
other things were. Now there is no danger from idolatry. Nor am I hinting
(as they interpret) that idols of vices remain in their hearts; I am talking
about the main issue. Luther exhorts them in the same way.[354] But if they
assert that they are free of all carnal inclinations of the heart, it would be
idle for me to exhort them to remove the idols from their hearts. But they
themselves admit that they still have to struggle with the flesh, so I wonder
why they take offence.

* * * * *

350 *Explanatio symboli* CWE 70 365–6 / ASD V-1 303–4; cf *Epistola contra pseudevan-*
    gelicos above 231.
351 Cf *Epistola apologetica* BOL I 149:18–21.
352 Cf Ezek 41:17–20
353 Homer describes the Titan Atlas as the guardian of the pillars of heaven
    (*Odyssey* 1.53); later mythology has Atlas himself holding the heavens on his
    shoulders (Hesiod *Theogony* 517).
354 Perhaps in Luther's *Against the Heavenly Prophets in the Matter of Images and
    Sacraments* (WA 18 37–125 / LW 40 79–223) or in his *Ein Brief an die Fürsten von
    Sachsen von dem aufrührerischen Geist* (WA 15 210–21, especially 219:19–34).

What I wrote about the destruction of images (that I could not see its point if not as a symbol of conspiracy) he grossly exaggerates, as if I were accusing them of a seditious conspiracy against the princes, which they consider to be a nefarious crime;[355] what I had in mind was the treaty some cities made with one another, into which the Strasbourgers were not admitted until they had cast away their images.[356] Since Vulturius even celebrated this treaty with a poem,[357] why do they fly into such a fury at me because I mentioned it? Besides, I was talking there in a general way, not about the Strasbourgers in particular. Against whom this treaty is directed does not interest me; what many of the 'evangelicals' brag about the common folk know as well. The word *conspiratio* can be taken two ways: positively, as well as pejoratively. Not every conspiracy is against the princes, and a conspiracy against the princes can be legitimate. Let them spare me, therefore, these tragic exaggerations!

Their treaty I neither approve nor disapprove. To the bishop of Toledo, as he says, I wrote that 'I predicted that they' were endeavouring to initiate a 'new democracy.'[358] 'What has this to do with the Strasbourg ministers? I am speaking about the common folk in general. And yet he always has that pronoun: us, us, on his lips. Whether this prediction is an empty one, the final outcome will tell – his pronouncement is premature. There are cities that acknowledge no prince, and I was writing about them. 'Here,' he says, 'we have an aristocracy.'[359] How ridiculous! Cannot an aristocracy be turned into a democracy? And if already many cities have come to the point of deposing their bishops, cannot others proceed to the point of expelling their princes? Is it inadmissible when writing to a friend to indicate what I divined to be the

* * * * *

355 Cf *Epistola contra pseudevangelicos* above 231: 'I do not see with what purpose they have destroyed some images so zealously unless to provide a rallying point for their conspiracy.' As Erasmus indicates below, the Latin word *conspiratio* need not have the negative connotations its English cognate has; see above 231 n77. In *Epistola apologetica* BOL 1 151:9–18 Bucer takes issue with this contention.

356 The treaty in question was concluded between Basel, Bern, Strasbourg, and Zürich, signed on 5 January, 1530. Called the 'Christian League,' it represented a defensive move prior to the Diet of Augsburg, in anticipation of being attacked by the emperor.

357 Cf Allen Ep 2261:29–31; see Prinsen *Collectanea* 92.

358 *Epistola apologetica* BOL 1 151:24, referring to Allen Ep 2134:218

359 *Epistola apologetica* BOL 1 170:33–171:3. It should be noted that the concept of democracy was not in good odour in the sixteenth century.

feelings of some people? And do we not see that what I predict has already been attempted by the peasants?[360] What I added about their crafty councils, I learned from men belonging to their sect. I did write that to me some seemed to have discarded their humanity, but I wrote only of those whose conduct was known to me.[361] Does not a man appear to have discarded his humanity who has suffered no injury and been showered with kindness, but who forgets friendship, loyalty, or politeness, just as an enemy to an enemy?

And this most silly man imputes to me in tragic words 'manifest mendacities,' with which I not only injure them but 'reveal my contumely towards Christ.'[362] Hear his 'evangelical' clemency! His apostolic sincerity! Although he frequently repeats: 'manifest mendacities,' he has not yet proved a single one. He depicts for us the holy deeds done in Strasbourg.[363] Whether what he says is true I do not know; certainly I would hope that it is completely true. But they cannot deny that this whole business (which he decks out with so many verbal trappings) has been undertaken without Christ, although he boasts that they do only the things instituted by Christ.

I saw with my own eyes people who were coming home from church, and there was not so great a throng that one was not perfectly able to see individuals. I never went into their churches,[364] lest I might seem to be of their persuasion; and if I had gone, I would not have been welcome, since they knew I had very different views. But I often carefully questioned those who professed to belong to that sect about what happened in church, specifically, whether they had seen anyone weeping or groaning over their sins when Oecolampadius was preaching.[365] This they denied, but said they saw many yawning, no one sighing or weeping. It was about these people I spoke, being in a position to know them close to home, not at all about Strasbourg. And they want this to appear as one great lie whereby I reveal my 'contumely towards Christ.' Even those who gave the sect its name tell a very different story. Let them say that those people are no 'evangelicals'! What is to be said of that? Whoever thinks badly of them is not an 'evangelical.'

* * * * *

360 Allen Ep 2134:218–20; Bucer complains about this passage in *Epistola apologetica* BOL I 151:25–6.
361 *Epistola apologetica* BOL I 151:29–31
362 *Epistola apologetica* BOL I 154:10–15
363 *Epistola apologetica* BOL I 153:16–154:5
364 Cf *Epistola contra pseudevangelicos* above 231.
365 Cf *Epistola contra pseudevangelicos* above 232; *Epistola apologetica* BOL I 154:15–18. As to Oecolampadius' preaching, Gordon Rupp in *Patterns of Reformation* mentions complaints in his early years that he had no humour in his sermons (12), and concerns about his soft voice (15).

I wrote that 'paganism will follow Pharisaism'; since they do not understand my words they accuse me falsely.[366] By Pharisaism I was referring to the superstition of some of our people, which these people have shaken off in such a way that I feared that many who were now free from the trammels that had hitherto restrained them would rush into pagan licence. What has this to do with the ministers or ceremonies at Basel?[367] Undoubtedly, under this cloak of the gospel are hidden many who bear the title of Christians but at heart are pagans. And we often see it happen that while we avoid some evil eagerly but none too carefully, we fall into a worse evil and are swept, as the saying goes, from the lime-kiln to the charcoal-burner's fire.[368] What I fear is already common knowledge. For recently at Basel they burned such a monster of depravity.[369]

Of such trifles our most modest author repeatedly makes great, terrible, and poisonous lies, poured out against the members of Christ in published books. He will not have anything put in writing unless we have seen it with our eyes and heard it with our ears,[370] although he himself is continually repeating so many stories to us: what has been done in Hesse, Zürich, Basel, Bern. Where has he drawn them if not from the reports of others? And where is this heap of lies, which I rake together in the epistle? Before the priests left Basel, it was not opponents but supporters who reported that some of the ministers never preached a sermon without their hurling abuse at the canons.[371] If the canons had wished to fight back, would we not have witnessed a sorry state of affairs in that city?

I said that confession had been abolished in such a way that 'many do not even confess their sins to God,' and that 'the distinction of foods,

* * * * *

366 *Epistola apologetica* BOL I 154:27–9, referring to Allen Ep 2134:208–9
367 *Epistola apologetica* BOL I 154:29–33; cf above n119. Erasmus, writing to the archbishop of Toledo from Basel, in the sentence prior to this one (*Ego misere metuo ne pharaismo succedat paganismus* [Allen Ep 2134:205–8]) had been complaining about the manner in which psalms were sung in German rhyme, mixing women and boys together, although as he claimed in the *Epistola contra pseudevangelicos* (above 231) he did not frequent the evangelicals' ceremonies.
368 *Adagia* II iv 96: *De calcaria in carbonariam* CWE 33:236: 'When the moment comes that we swerve off our intended course into something entirely different ....'
369 Williams *Radical Reformation* 309 reports executions in Basel in January and August of 1530; the latter was Conrad in der Gassen, who was beheaded August 11 1530; ie after the *Epistola ad fratres Inferioris Germaniae* was published. C. Augustijn (ASD IX-1 379 116–7n) believes that this was the person Erasmus has in mind, and that this reference was a later interpolation.
370 *Epistola apologetica* BOL I 155:19–33
371 Cf *Epistola contra pseudevangelicos* above 232; *Epistola apologetica* BOL I 155:24–6.

along with fasting' had been abolished in such a way that 'all the same, they eagerly indulge in drunkenness.'[372] Was this not a public complaint of the common people, not only of the butchers? On this account too, I believe, many were displeased by Oecolampadius.[373] Do they require examples also of this? But I am astonished that they number this among my lies, when they themselves admit that so many have used the pretext of the gospel as an unlimited licence for their crimes. But they do not recognize these people as their own. Let them cease, then, to be angry at me and upbraid me for empty accusations, since I spoke about them in generalities, and specified neither city nor city council! And so often we hear this chirping: 'us, us.' They tell us what they teach at Strasbourg,[374] even though I was speaking about the behaviour of some of their fellow countrymen, not about doctrine, not knowing what it is like in Strasbourg. But see the carelessness of this writer! A little earlier he deplores the sort of people I refer to, and soon goes on to add: 'why does Erasmus falsely attribute these things to us?' If the pronoun 'us' refers to the ministers at Strasbourg, I am not talking about them; if to the whole mass of those who share the name 'evangelicals,' there are indeed among them such as I have mentioned, as they themselves admit. And yet, although we both are saying the same things, Erasmus is a liar, while he says nothing but the gospel truth.

I wrote, so he says, 'the yoke of human constitutions has been abolished' by them 'to such effect that no one now submitted his neck to the gentle yoke of the Lord.'[375] No, I did not say anything of the kind, oh 'evangelical' man. What I said was this: 'where are those who have submitted their neck,' etc.![376] I do not deny that there are such people but I do wish to see them. They give thanks for my valuable testimony in saying that the apostles did not know of prescribed days for fasting or dietary regulations.[377] 'No one, he says, 'can be forced to do what the apostles did not institute.' If secular princes have the right to determine a matter in the external commonwealth, why should the leaders of the church have any less

* * * * *

372 *Epistola contra pseudevangelicos* above 232; *Epistola apologetica* BOL I 155:26–8
373 In June of 1530, Oecolampadius delivered the oration *'De reducenda excommunicatione'* to the reformed clergy at Basel, outlining his plan for church and civic discipline; see Staehelin *Briefe und Akten* 2 no 750.
374 *Epistola apologetica* BOL I 156:8–22
375 *Epistola apologetica* BOL I 157:17–19
376 *Epistola contra pseudevangelicos* above 233: 'have they submitted their neck to the sweet yoke of the Lord?'
377 *Epistola apologetica* BOL I 157:4–9, referring to *Epistola contra pseudevangelicos* above 232

right to make decisions in the ecclesiastical realm? But these statements are made shamelessly by the very people who demand of their followers many things not instituted by the apostles. Besides, how does this testimony of mine support their cause, when they have such contempt for the rules about fasting that they never fast at all?

They demand of me to specify what human constitutions they have laid upon those over whom they have jurisdiction.[378] Let them ask those who have long since left their cities, and continue to do so daily! What use is it, though, to cite these constitutions, since whatever is done by them or is instituted at their urging has proceeded from the Spirit of God for the public good! I have certainly not known any bishop to whom I would not dare to entrust myself, and I have always been assisted thus far by the emperor's favour, and by the court in Brabant as well.[379] The main reason for my departure from Brabant was to avoid the blame being laid on my shoulders for any unpleasant measures then being taken against the Lutheran business. Although I was in no danger from the government, these people (though they have no knowledge of it) declare that I was. If I had strongly defended the cause of the Catholic church, perhaps I would have been closer to grave peril.

But what do I hear: has even the odour of my libation bowls reached their nostrils? For they make a distorted passing reference to that.[380] The archbishop of Canterbury gave me a goblet, and that was before Luther became known.[381] After that Albert, the cardinal of Mainz gave me another,[382] before Luther was toiling under such hostility, indeed when

* * * * *

378 *Epistola apologetica* BOL I 158:8–11
379 Cf *Epistola contra pseudevangelicos* 233; Bucer responded to this passage in *Epistola apologetica* BOL I 162:11–21, accusing Erasmus of having received gifts from powerful bishops for writing against Luther; see also *Spongia* above 115 nn453, 455.
380 *Epistola apologetica* BOL I 162:17–21
381 William Warham (c 1456–1532) was made archbishop of Canterbury in 1503. He was an especially loyal friend and patron to Erasmus, who dedicated both his 1516 edition of Jerome (cf Ep 396) and the 1524 vol 2 of Jerome to him (CWE 61 99–103). The preface to Chevallon's 1533 edition of Jerome includes a laudatory portrait of Warham (cf CWE 61 xxx).
382 Albert of Brandenburg (1490–1545), archbishop of Mainz from 1514 onward, was a beneficiary of Johann Tetzel's papal indulgence sale, the trigger for Luther's *Ninety-Five Theses* in 1517. Ironically, he was also an early patron of Hutten. See Ep 745, Erasmus' 22 December 1517 dedication to him of the first separate edition of the *Ratio* . Cf *Spongia* 47 above n51.

he was hardly known at all. A third bishop gave me one recently,[383] followed by a fourth.[384] None of these ever as much as hinted that I should write against the sects. Nor am I the least ashamed of gifts of that kind, spontaneously given by these men of supreme authority. For I consider this kind of gift a real distinction – a tribute of which I may not be worthy, yet a reliable indication that such leading men are favourable towards letters and piety, considering me to be endowed with these qualities. In fact, I was so far from being the πρόμαχος 'champion' of the bishops that I am said to be napping in this great church crisis.

How many things he brings falsely together out of his fantasies, he who will not have anything said unless experienced at first hand. I do not know whether his hint that some here in Freiburg are becoming rich pertains to me.[385] From Froben I received very little (scarcely enough to maintain one amanuensis), and what he actually tried to give me (such as the house where I lived) I consistently refused to accept.[386] At present, I have not received a cent of the imperial pension because of my absence,[387] but in Germany, where everything is very costly, I have already spent some thousands of florins of my money and owe no one a cent. From where would these riches come? The demands of this poor body are not few, nor is it cheap to keep my amanuenses, and finally I do not keep a mean household and cannot be a penny pincher.

Then he just about goes mad because I wrote: 'I have a greater fear that many will carry, instead of the yoke of men, the heavier yoke of the devil.'[388] Since even they admit there are such people among those who bear the name of 'evangelicals,' why do they rage so much against me? Since I too know some are like this, what wonder if I said I feared worse things to come? He concludes in this way: 'whatever false charges Erasmus permits himself to

* * * * *

383 Christopher of Stadion (1478–1543), bishop of Augsburg, was an enthusiastic proponent of an Erasmian approach to church reform. He made the indicated present to Erasmus in a 1530 visit to Freiburg; see Allen Ep 2029:446–9 and introduction.

384 Konrad von Thüngen (d 1540), prince bishop of Würzburg, made a gift of a goblet to Erasmus in May of 1530; see Allen Ep 2314:36–40.

385 *Epistola apologetica* BOL I 160:9–13

386 Cf Allen Ep 1900:52–67.

387 See *Epistola contra pseudevangelicos* above 220 n14; cf *Spongia* above 115 n453.

388 *Epistola apologetica* BOL I 163:6–7, referring to *Epistola contra pseudevangelicos* above 233

spew out upon us have been fed him by the very devils themselves, that is, by calumniators.'[389] Such bitterness against me is spewed out by these most long-suffering 'evangelicals,' although up to now they are unable to prove even one charge or a single lie. All I hear is: 'us, us,' as if I only wrote against the Strasbourg preachers. But the courteous man helps me: I did not devise these lies myself but (stirred up by a headlong rage induced in me by devils) spewed them out against the members of Christ. Since I reported what I have ascertained myself (or had reported to me by those of his own confession), where are these devils?

'We,' he says, 'give honour to whom we owe honour and pursue tranquillity in every way possible.'[390] If the pronoun 'we' denotes the Strasbourgers specifically, I contest nothing. It may well be that he tells the truth. But if he means that among the whole body of those who profess the 'gospel' there are none who fail to give honour to those to whom it is due, or who disturb the public tranquillity, then it must be an empty rumour that at Augsburg the magistrates were forced for some time to maintain soldiers because of popular riots.[391] In the city where I was then staying,[392] how often an edict warned against men of different parties provoking one another by insults! How seldom was that observed by some of the 'evangelicals'! I do not speak about all of them. How often the magistrates ordained that no clandestine gatherings be held by the 'evangelicals,' how often they gathered contrary to the edict of the city council and against the oath they had taken.

A witness to this was at that time a guildmaster, now a burgomaster, who at the instance of the city council dispersed the crowd of almost three hundred who had gathered in the Augustinian monastery, and denounced their oath-breaking with great indignation.[393] Again, when so many armed

* * * * *

389 *Epistola apologetica* BOL I 163:10–12

390 Cf *Epistola apologetica* BOL I 163:14–16

391 These are the 'Schilling riots' of 1524, sparked by the dismissal of the popular preacher Johann Schilling, who assailed from the pulpit the greed of the Fuggers; see T.A. Brady *Turning Swiss: Cities and Empire, 1450–1550* (Cambridge 1985) 170–1.

392 Basel

393 This incident occurred on 22 October 1527; see R. Wackernagel *Geschichte der Stadt Basel* 3 (Basel 1968) 495. Wackernagel's history describes the progress of the Reformation in that city, as does the less detailed Guggisberg *Basel in the Sixteenth Century* chapter 2. Erasmus seems to refer to Jakob Meyer zum Hirzen (cf Ep 2158: 65), who was a burgomaster of Basel in 1530.

men besieged the marketplace and demolished the images, it is no secret what answer they gave to the city council.[394] And in this gathering, against the long-standing edict of the city council, there are said to have been many armed mercenaries. When at another meeting the city council proposed terms for a negotiation with the Catholics, someone from the crowd shouted with a tumultuous voice: 'We do not want this, we do not want this, good lords!'[395] Some one who was present told me.

Was this not the period when that distinguished man, Jakob Sturm, burgomaster of his own city and an envoy to Basel, reproached the people from a public platform (and this with the approval of all the really sensible men) because they had committed several acts of violence?[396] Although the city council had so often ordained that no one should give occasion to sedition, a certain notable zealot for the 'gospel' went (in a noble state of inebriation) from a wedding banquet into the cathedral. He found Marius[397] preaching. While Marius was not saying anything concerning any sect – for he was just finishing the sermon – with a seditious voice our zealot shouted: 'You are lying, monk, may the black plague strike you!'[398] Now, if any Catholic had done this in a church of another confession, what reward would he have had gained? What punishment was exacted of our zealot? He withdrew to some village for three days and then returned. Do you hear this 'evangelical' clemency? If it had been committed by a Catholic,

* * * * *

394 L. Wandel *Voracious Idols and Violent Hands* (Cambridge 1995) chapter 4 describes and examines the iconoclasm in Basel of 9 February 1529.

395 See R. Wackernagel *Geschichte* (above n393) III 506–7; the incident in question took place on 3 January 1529.

396 Jakob Sturm (1489–1553) was a supporter of the Reformation and member of the magistracy in Strasbourg. Of an old aristocratic family, he worked closely with Bucer to reform the city and to negotiate between the reformed church and the emperor; see Brady *Protestant Politics*, also Chrisman *Strasbourg and the Reform* 94–5. For Erasmus' early impressions of Sturm, see his 1514 letter to Jacob Wimpfeling (Ep 305:132–7); cf CEBR III 293–4. For his speech in Basel in 1529, see ASD I-ix 383:215–17n.

397 Augustinus Marius (1485–1543), a member of the Augustinian canons regular, was cathedral preacher in Basel from 1527 and auxiliary bishop from 1527. He was a vehement opponent of the evangelicals, frequently preaching against them; cf CEBR II 391–2; see Wackernagel *Geschichte* (above n393) 3 469, Rupp *Patterns of Reformation* 30, and Allen's introduction to Ep 2321, in which Erasmus complains to Marius about Geldenhouwer's unauthorized annotations to Erasmus' *Epistola contra pseudevangelicos* and about Bucer's *Epistola apologetica*.

398 There is no independent verification of this incident.

there would have been fears for his head. There is an endless number of examples such as this.

Although there was a fear of sedition in those days, and many citizens were thrown into prison, one inflexible follower of the 'gospel' – I wish he would do some good to correspond with his name – was ordered into exile.[399] Afterwards Farel, if he had not absconded, was also to have been taken into custody.[400] These matters are hidden from no one, and not reported for the infamy of the magistrates but rather for their praise, because by their vigilance they tempered the violence of the uncouth multitude. It is the nature of the mob to incite disorder. What has this to do with the cities? With the magistrates? With the ministers? Unless one claims that whatever was done even by wicked people, was done at the instigation of the magistrates. The magistracy is held in honour, but only if it prescribes agreeable things. What honour was rendered to the burgomaster who fled in secret? And he was the chief magistrate.[401] What honour was rendered to the magistracy of Strasbourg by those who in defiance of its edict so often printed stupid pamphlets? The printer of Vulturius' glosses was thrown into prison on account of the honour he rendered to the magistracy.[402]

I could list numerous examples, but I will desist. Yet let them also desist who say that I was being more false than falsehood itself when I wrote that some have thrown off the bishops' yoke in such a way that they will not even submit to the secular magistracy.[403] I speak in general, but if this advocate were wishing to refute me, he would have to prove that nowhere in their churches were the edicts of the magistrates disregarded. He denies

* * * * *

399 Bonifacius Wolfhart was expelled from Basel on 7 May 1525; see above n253. Erasmus' comment on his name is a pun on *'boni facere.'*
400 Guillaume Farel (1489–1565) was expelled from Basel in July 1524; see *Guillaume Farel 1489–1565: Biographie nouvelle* (Neuchâtel and Paris 1930) 124–30, the introduction to Ep 1477A, and Farel's account of his expulsion in Herminjard *Correspondance* I 151; cf CEBR II 11–13. For the mutual enmity between Erasmus and Farel, see the General Introduction above xvii–xviii nn51–2.
401 See below 329 and n412.
402 Cf Allen Ep 2321:27–8. Erasmus has in mind the printer Johann Schott, who published Hutten's *Expostulatio* in 1523. In late March 1530 Erasmus wrote a letter of complaint to the magistrates of Strasbourg (Allen Ep 2293) and in a 1532 letter to Bucer, which is a follow-up to *Epistola ad fratres Inferiores Germaniae*, he lists objectionable publications from Schott's press including forged documents (Allen Ep 2615, especially lines 357–80). On Johann Schott see CEBR III 230–1.
403 *Epistola apologetica* BOL I 163:12–14; *Epistola contra pseudevangelicos* above 233

that the 'evangelicals' have ever caused disturbance or rushed to arms.[404]
When there was recently a rush to arms from all sides by twenty thousand
armed men prepared for a brawl, was it not over a paltry amount of money?
And was it not the 'evangelicals' who first took up arms?[405] For they had
mobilized. That it was a cherry-picking expedition is their term, not mine.[406]
And the shameless fellow challenges me about what disturbances and what
arms I am speaking about, and he adds: 'who stirred you up so against so
many harmless churches of Christ?'[407] If he had asked this of someone less
civil than me – someone who could call a fig nothing else but a fig[408] – that
man would immediately have countered 'Who stirred all of you up against
the harmless churches of Christ scattered throughout the Christian world
so that you disrupt them with your teachings and defections, so that you
draw so many lambs away from them and send them to hell?' I am not so
uncivil as to reply in this way, I only complain that some falsely boast that
they are evangelicals, when they neither care for peace nor pay heed to the
commands of the magistracy.

Here he tells us a totally vacuous story, which not even the 'evangelicals' in the city where this took place can read without laughing: the
Catholics obtained arms, the unarmed 'evangelicals' presented a petition
to the city council, a crumbling statue was accidentally touched by a spear
and collapsed, and those who had heatedly opposed the 'gospel' were removed from the city council.[409] In fact, when the city council issued an
edict that there must be no public gatherings, and all had sworn more than
once to abide by that edict, yet the 'evangelicals' would not stop assem-
bling together, now here, now there; at length the Catholics approached the
city council seeking that it enforce its edict, declaring that, if fear stood in
the way of its doing so, they would risk their lives in defence of munici-
pal authority. The city council thanked them for this consideration promising to be mindful of their concern. The Catholics added that, unless it did,
they would not put up with seditious assemblies of this kind. Then, since

* * * * *

404 *Epistola apologetica* BOL I 163:14–22, 170:12–13
405 Erasmus is referring to the so-called First Kappel War 1529: Switzerland's
    Protestant and Catholic cantons each formed alliances and mobilized for war,
    but fighting was averted when the two sides accepted terms of peace; cf Allen
    Epp 2173, 2180. For the Second Kappel War of 1531, in which Zwingli was
    killed, see General Introduction ix n2.
406 Cf *Epistola apologetica* BOL I 168:16–18.
407 *Epistola apologetica* BOL I 164:1–2
408 Cf above n281.
409 Cf *Epistola apologetica* BOL I 164:3–166:18 on the 1528–29 disturbances in Basel.

the 'evangelicals' were gathering in still greater numbers, the Catholics on one occasion armed and gathered together. Nor were the 'evangelicals' exactly unarmed. Whenever they met, they had swords and daggers. When they realized that the Catholics were armed, they also took up arms themselves. Thereupon the Catholic burgomaster Meltinger (as he had often done on other occasions) rendered distinguished service to the city. For in a stern address he checked his own people and forced them to abandon their arms.[410]

He[411] denies that it was boasted that the burgomaster would have been nailed to a cross unless he fled in secret.[412] So, this writer assumes the right both to lie and to impute the falsehood to me. In fact, the boast was made openly by the armed 'evangelicals' in the marketplace. Those who heard it have related the story. And even the city council was at that time in their power. They had cannon set up in the marketplace and there, with a fire lit, they passed the night until they had obtained what they wanted by force. Whether the burgomaster was called back I do not know.[413] I hear that he has died. And what else is it to tear a man of declining years and infirm health from wife and home but to kill him?[414] Who would be not be scared away by that proviso: 'unless he had committed some wrong against the city'?[415] Yet to have attacked the 'gospel,' having said something against this or that minister, would have been regarded as against the city.[416] But those who are said to have attacked the 'gospel' are convinced that they attacked a wicked and ungodly heresy harmful to that city, and that on that account they are owed considerable gratitude. I do not act in this way, but I think it fair that if they [the 'evangelicals'] allow themselves to protect a doctrine condemned by leaders the world over, they ought to show clemency to those

* * * * *

410 Heinrich Meltinger (d 1529) was a member of the Basel city council from 1512, *Oberzunftmeister* since 1516, and burgomaster since 1522; cf CEBR II 430–1, and the account in Staehelin *Briefe und Akten* 2 no 636 280–2.

411 Bucer

412 *Epistola apologetica* BOL I 166:9–12, citing Allen Ep 2201:38–42, where Erasmus writes of Heinrich Meltinger's flight from Basel. In the night from 8–9 February 1529 he escaped to Colmar where shortly afterwards he died.

413 Bucer (*Epistola apologetica* BOL I 166:13–16) claims that Meltinger had been recalled and was offered an amnesty.

414 See Allen Ep 2112:57n, describing him as having died of grief; cf *Basler Chroniken* ed Historische und Antiquarische Gesellschaft zu Basel (Leipzig 1915) VII 434:6.

415 Cf *Epistola apologetica* BOL I 166:15–16.

416 Cf *Epistola apologetica* BOL I 166:16–18, referring to Augustinus Marius (see above n397).

who cannot immediately abandon that teaching which they are convinced is truly Christian.

They[417] will say: 'the majority of the populace was on our side.'[418] The greatest part of the populace called out against Christ: 'crucify him!'[419] The majority of the bishops condemned Athanasius.[420] The greater part is not necessarily the better. But who has given a motley crowd the right to pronounce on articles of faith? 'It was following,' they will say, 'the judgment of the ministers.' Another might reply: 'but they were those whom the emperor and the leaders of the church have condemned as heretics.' 'But undeservedly,' they say. What heretics ever vaunted that they were condemned deservedly? Did not the Montanists, the Arians, and the Manichees complain of being wrongfully condemned?[421] 'What can this be,' says someone, 'but an inspiration from the Spirit?'[422] As if Muhammed might not well say the same with greater probability. I mention these things, not out of any desire to draw disgrace upon them by these reproaches but to show that for those unskilled in letters it ought not to be a capital offence to decline to abandon the religion handed down by their forebears and to refuse to join with sects which they see condemned by the highest rulers in church and state, and by the most trustworthy theologians of our time.

Now, as to his accounts of the disturbances at Bern, at Zürich, at Rottweil, in Hesse, I will leave it to others to reply because only the light and fickle breeze of rumour about those events trickles down to us.[423] However, I have little doubt that he has dressed up the story with many embellishments. What else would you expect from someone who maintains that the 'gospel' should be spread with tricks and deceits? Here he rants and raves against me, just as if he had pleaded his case elegantly. Indeed, I do not think it dishonourable to be attacked by such people, whom by far the greatest part of the Christian world regards as under condemnation.

* * * * *

417 The 'evangelicals'
418 *Epistola apologetica* BOL I 164:11
419 Matt 27:22–23, Mark 15:13–14
420 Athanasius, the great foe of Arianism, was condemned at the synod of Arles 353 and Milan 355; cf. W.H.C. Frend *The Early Church* (Philadelphia and New York 1966) 164–6.
421 The Montanists were second century schismatic followers of the prophet Montanus; Arians: see above n45; Manichees, see above n76.
422 See above n78.
423 Bern: *Epistola apologetica* BOL I 166:19–167:34; Zürich: 167:35–168:27, 177:13–24; Rottweil: 169:1–5; Hesse: 169:16–18

They praise themselves and as the saying goes: one mule scratches another.[424] However, a minister must 'have a good report,' even 'from those who are outsiders.'[425] Who can be more saintly than Luther if we were to believe what he proclaims about himself? Paul says: 'I think also that I have the Spirit of God.'[426] These people insolently lay claim to the Spirit for themselves, while they contemptuously deny it to others. Paul says he is the first among sinners.[427] This man[428] says: 'If you consider the conduct of my life from childhood on, could any good person doubt that I should be ranked among the good?'[429] 'Which of you will convict me of sin?':[430] Christ alone was able to say that. This one says: 'as we have earned our keep for many a year now, both in theological and humane scholarship, it cannot be that we teach rashly.'[431] How much more fitting if it were another's mouth that praised them! The case is easily won if you give the defendant the right to deliver the verdict both on himself and on the attorneys and the judges.

Whenever Catholics attempt anything in defence of their own faith, it is a mutinous disturbance. Whenever these people do the same in defence of what they have established, it is most holy zeal for the 'gospel.' And he glosses over what is too clear to be excused[432] but so shamelessly that he seems to be writing for people of the Indies, who are otherwise unable to know anything about the facts. Nor does this advocate ever retreat from his plea: what is said in a general way he twists to apply to all churches, each church, all churches collectively and entirely, as if I wish so many cities, so many churches, and so many princes utterly destroyed. How is this so? Because I have not given my approval to the behaviour of some of those who put themselves forward deceptively under the banner of the 'gospel.' Let

* * * * *

424 *Adagia* I vii 96: *Mutuum muli scabunt* CWE 32 125–6: 'when rascals and men of no reputation admire and cry up one another.'
425 Cf 1 Tim 3:7.
426 1 Cor 7:40.
427 1 Tim 1:15.
428 Bucer
429 No such statement occurs in the *Epistola apologetica*. Erasmus may be thinking of a passage in which Bucer imagines readers wondering how Erasmus could so vehemently attack such 'learned and not at all bad men' as the Strasbourg preachers (BOL I 127:24–28:2).
430 John 8:46
431 Bucer extols the education offered by the evangelicals in *Epistola apologetica* BOL I 175:20–177:3.
432 ὑποκορίζει, literally, speaks like a child.

them count up their cities and ours, their churches and ours, their princes and ours, and they will acknowledge how many more are those they wish utterly destroyed, for they keep calling them blasphemers against Christ, enemies of the evangelical truth, vessels of wrath, slayers of the innocent! They will never find anything so savage written in my books.

Does not he who detests so much the crime of sedition declare by his book that he was born to stir up sedition?[433] Why does he not launch his hyperboles against those who in so many published books denounce these people[434] as manifest heretics and deadly schismatics, who call their churches conventicles of Satan, and depict their ministers as slayers of souls if not worse? These are the people who urge that all of their churches be completely eliminated. Let my opponents cry out against those who so stir up the emperor to vent his rage on them, with every kind of punishment.[435] I continue to do what I have always done, trying to turn the minds of the princes away from cruelty. If only they[436] would show equal enthusiasm in turning away from their contentious doctrine! I said: 'in some communities ultimate authority is in the hands of the common people.'[437] When people of the lowest character sit on the city council, when those who displease the people are removed from the council, when the people do not obey its edicts unless it suits them, when the people are taught to occupy the marketplace with arms and to threaten the city with their cannons drawn up, might it not be said that ultimate authority in the hands of the people?[438]

They cast another splendid lie at me: I wrote that Otto went forth from Capito's house to publish the pamphlet he had written against me.[439] In fact,

* * * * *

433 No such declaration occurs in the *Epistola apologetica*; Bucer defends Zwingli against the imputation of sedition in BOL I 177:7–24.
434 The 'evangelicals'
435 On the basis of Allen Ep 1688:9–11, C. Augustijn infers that Erasmus means Fisher and Cochlaeus: ASD I-ix 389:334–7n
436 The 'evangelicals'
437 Cf *Epistola apologetica* BOL I 170:19–28, citing Allen Ep 2188:262–9.
438 Erasmus is referring to the events in Basel of 8–9 February 1529. The upshot was that Catholic worship was banned altogether, and that the craft guilds gained (for a time) greater representation on the city council. See Guggisberg *Basel in the Sixteenth Century* 29–31.
439 The following section concerns Bucer's response in *Epistola apologetica* BOL I 172:13–175:15 to Ep 1496, a letter Erasmus wrote to Philip Melanchthon in September of 1524, outlining his complaints against numerous reformers whom he identifies by name, including Otto Brunfels (382:120–2) and Wolfgang Capito (see above nn31, 59). The pamphlet was Brunfels' *Responsio* (see General Introduction above xvii), a defence of Hutten and a pointed attack on

Capito himself told me in a letter written in his own hand that Otto had returned from Basel and was at his house two days before he published the pamphlet.[440] How little shame has this 'evangelical' tub-thumper! Now I say nothing about Thraso,[441] even though I understood sufficiently from Capito's letters how estranged he was from him, and my servant (whom I sent to Strasbourg) reported that every now and then they frequented the same public bath. Nevertheless, I can tell of other super-'evangelicals' who eagerly courted Thraso. But what are they complaining about here? Was it not Hutten that so many 'evangelicals' regarded as their darling? All know the man's life. My *Spongia* offended Luther,[442] although I had kept quiet about so many things, some of which he [Hutten] had done against me and some of which were commonly bruited about. If Hedio did not show [Capito] the letter of which I spoke, how did Thraso hear about it?[443]

At first I had not the least suspicion that Capito was an accomplice of Otto, and I was surprised at his painstaking apology. He was particularly careful to apologize on this point, although no one had demanded it from him, and I had suspected nothing. He wrote to me twice, and (not content with this) he wrote on the same matter twice to Oecolampadius, to Beatus Rhenanus and, if I am not mistaken, to Froben.[444] When, on the basis of the first letter he received, Oecolampadius wrote me to exculpate Capito, he asked whether I still had any doubts about him. 'Far be it from me,' I said, 'to keep in my heart such a doubt about such a friend.' When, having received a second letter, he spoke with me again, he asked the same thing. I replied that I had suspected nothing before, but that this kind of anxious self-justification made me a little suspicious. Oecolampadius laughed as if he

* * * * *

Erasmus that cut him deeply. In Ep 1485 Erasmus accuses Capito directly of having instigated Brunfels' attack.

440 This letter has been lost.

441 Thraso, a character from Terence's play *Eunuchus,* was Erasmus' nickname for Heinrich Eppendorf (c 1490 to after 1551). Originally a member of Erasmus' circle of friends in Basel, Eppendorf fell under suspicion of having urged Hutten to publish the *Expostulatio,* and of having supplied him with much of his libellous material. He migrated to Strasbourg in 1523. See *Spongia* above 51 n70, 132 n569; Epp 1371, 1376, 1377, and 1383; and the intructory note to the *Admonitio adversus mendacium* below 370–1.

442 See above n314; cf Ep 1443:27–32.

443 In a letter to Philip Melanchthon, Erasmus speaks of a letter Melanchthon had written to a third party that had been forwarded to him, in which Melanchthon had been critical of Eppendorf. Erasmus sent a copy to Hedio, who showed it to Capito, who then showed it to Eppendorf himself; see Ep 1496:126–132.

444 Cf CWE 10, 382–3, Ep 1496:120–32.

agreed with me. But when writing to Hedio I denied I had any unfriendly suspicions concerning Capito.[445]

What is the inconsistency here if (though I had not done so earlier) I began to have suspicions, or if (as I did) I concealed them for reasons of courtesy? What crime is it if I attribute cunning to Capito? I do the same for the apostle Paul.[446] Otto is now a god-fearing and learned man of value to the community,[447] although, as I said before, a certain minister (I wonder if it is not the author of the book to which I am responding) in a letter to me[448] called him a scoundrel and one whom his church could scarcely endure. With regard to Hedio, I did not accuse him of suppressing or concealing that letter [of mine to Strasbourg], I merely say he gave sympathetic encouragement to those who undertook a most holy business contrary to the city council's edict.[449] However, he regretted his sympathy afterwards. For (as he himself told me in a letter)[450] after he had twice given aid to those who otherwise would have been punished severely, he said that he wished to assist them no longer since he realized that they had returned to the same game a third time. Instead he gave me permission to act against them as I might wish, because I had suffered injury three times. But those were 'evangelical' brethren; and they certainly were to be helped by my misfortune. Such are the men who fear God, and love all that is honourable, and obey the magistrate. They devote themselves to benefiting all and harming no one. And these, these are the manifest and frightful lies of Erasmus!

I pass on to what he goes on to write concerning the teachings they condemn.[451] Does not Luther call the whole philosophy of Aristotle diabolical?[452] Has he not written that every discipline, both practical and

* * * * *

445 Ep 1477B:74–7. Erasmus goes on to say that not everyone thinks Capito wholly innocent; cf *Epistola apologetica* BOL 1 173:18–22.
446 Cf Erasmus' annotations on Acts 17:23 / LB VI 501E, and above 291. Erasmus' argument here is disingenuous, as he exonerates Paul while condemning the evangelicals for their cunning.
447 *Epistola apologetica* BOL 1 172:19–20
448 Cf Allen Ep 1901, VII 229–33. P.S. Allen identified Martin Bucer as the addressee of this letter, and C. Augustijn suggests that Erasmus is referring here to a now-lost letter from Bucer to which Ep 1901 was his response: ASD 1-ix 391:372–4n.
449 Epp 1429, 1496:77–79, also 1477B; the 'holy business' in question was the publication of Hutten's *Expostulatio* by the Strasbourg printer Johann Schott.
450 Not extant
451 *Epistola apologetica* BOL 1 175:16–177:6
452 Cf *Disputatio contra scholasticam theologiam* (1517) theses 42–50 (WA 1 22), concluding with thesis 50: 'Briefly, all of Aristotle is to theology as darkness is to

speculative, has been condemned, and that all speculative knowledge is sinful and erroneous?[453] Did not Melanchthon at one time condemn the public universities?[454] Now he says: 'let the universities which are good remain and let their faults be reformed!' Why does he not say the same of the church practices they tear down indiscriminately? Did not Farel say in public, everywhere, that all human disciplines were inventions of the Devil?[455] Later, when the sects saw that ideas of this sort would cause inconveniences, they changed their tune and began to hire professors (to what end and with how much benefit I know not).[456] In regard to the Strasbourg minister who in a sermon had condemned all disciplines except Hebrew and a smattering of Greek, he himself admits that this story has been spread throughout the world.[457] How he manages to explain that, I do not know, but I certainly lack faith in anyone who approves the use of deceits by an 'evangelical.'

In defence of Zwingli he begins his discourse with a splendid lie. 'He[458] always represents Zwingli as seditious,'[459] he says, and offers no evidence except two passages, each limited to a few words and hidden in long letters.[460] However, I do not call Zwingli seditious but express my disapproval of the seditious way in which he handles the 'evangelical' cause. Did I not say upon my first taste of Luther's pamphlets that the business would come to sedition?[461] Let Capito, if he will, be witness to this. Doesn't

* * * * *

light.' See also Luther's *Ad Johannem Eccium epistola super expurgatione Ecciana 1519* (WA 2 708:3).
453 Cf *De votis monasticis* (WA 8 608:2–4); see Eck *Articuli 404* articles 397 and 398.
454 Cf Eck *Articuli 404* article 396.
455 See *Epistola contra pseudevangelicos* above 251, and Bucer's response in *Epistola apologetica* BOL I 215:26–9. Erasmus' source for the assertion he attributes to Farel is unknown.
456 Cf above nn139, 141.
457 Cf *Epistola apologetica* BOL I 176:7–177:3 (the reference is to sermons preached in 1524 by Johannes Lonicerius [d 1569] and by Bucer himself). Bucer here complains about Erasmus' remark to Melanchthon in Ep 1523:162–3. Erasmus also repeated the story in *Hyperaspistes 1* CWE 76 143. Bucer admits that the story has been spread about, but insists that he had not been attempting to discourage study of Latin, only to encourage Hebrew and Greek studies as well.
458 Erasmus
459 *Epistola apologetica* BOL I 177:9–10
460 Bucer cites three passages, all from letters of Erasmus to Philip Melanchthon: Ep 1496:83–4, 88–9, and 1523:159–60.
461 Erasmus urged Capito to warn Luther, in a letter of 4 September 1518, to bridle his vehement temper; cf WA Br 1 no 91:1–54, no 147:18–19.

he[462] manage things in a seditious way when he rages so impudently against the emperor, kings, the most powerful princes, the pope, cardinals, and bishops? It has always displeased me that from the beginning Zwingli wrote so hatefully to his bishop.[463] Then, is not the removal of the images in itself a seditious act?[464] A bloody one, too, if the canons and the Catholics had wished to protect what they think should be protected. Surely an excellent proof that I never represent Zwingli as anything but seditious! But why do they bridle so much at the term sedition when Luther has written that it is characteristic of the 'gospel' to incite sedition,[465] and Zwingli's saying is well known: 'the gospel demands blood'?[466] Finally, when even those who are most closely committed to Luther condemn the violence of his writings,[467] when Karlstadt has acknowledged the charge of petulance, and when my opponent admits that Farel conducted himself with rather ill-considered zeal,[468] on what grounds are they indignant at me when I say the same thing? Was faith going to perish if the images were left unharmed? Again, was it not seditious to melt down holy vessels into coin, to drive abbots from power, to remove from the magistracy those who would not abandon the ancient discipline of the church? Nor can anyone fail to see that whatever a city council does, it does at the instigation of the preachers.

I will pass over some of the trivial matters he quibbles about. He goes on to say that I censure the preachers at Basel because they stirred up Luther against me.[469] Perhaps this is true, but nowhere did I write it, nor did I even think of it. I wrote to Michael, bishop of Langres,[470] referring, in a general

* * * * *

462 Zwingli
463 Erasmus is referring to Zwingli's *Apologeticus Archeteles* (1522), his defence of the Zürich Reformation in response to complaints from Hugo von Hohenlandenberg, the bishop of Constance (*Zwinglis Werke* I 249–327); see the introduction to Ep 1314, and Ep 1315, in which Erasmus expresses his concern to Zwingli about the *Apologeticus*.
464 This is in direct response to *Epistola apologetica* BOL I 177:15–16: *Quas turbas, quem tumultum concitavit propter imagines?* 'What crowds, what tumult did he stir up over images?' Bucer explains that images were removed by order of the town council; see L. Wandel *Voracious Idols and Violent Hands* 53–101 for a description of the process by which images were removed in Zürich.
465 Cf *De servo arbitrio* WA 18 626:8–627:2.
466 Cf Eck *Articuli* 404 article 403.
467 See Melanchthon's comments to Erasmus in Allen Ep 1981:22–5.
468 *Epistola apologetica* BOL I 179:14–16
469 *Epistola apologetica* BOL I 179:3–9, referring to Allen Ep 1678:37–9
470 Michael Boudet (1469–1529), bishop of Langres, was a friend of Guillaume Budé and sympathetic to humanist scholarship. Erasmus presented several of

way, to 'these new preachers,' having in mind someone in Augsburg who (as I was told by an eminently trustworthy man) had energetically goaded Luther to finish a book he had begun but had, I think, set aside on the advice of certain people.[471] So, how does that vehement polemicist know that there was no one at Basel who stirred up Luther?[472] If some advised him against it, does that mean there was no one who advised in favour of it?

Elsewhere he calls me an 'ungrateful guest' because I did not approve of the behaviour of certain people in Basel.[473] Should the city council of Basel wish to declare war on all those who disapprove of some of its citizens, it will have its work cut out. Every aspect of the behaviour of all the 'evangelicals' does not please that same city council either, as is demonstrated by the fact that they took punitive action against many of them.[474] I admit that I enjoyed the hospitality of that city for many years, but (unless I am mistaken) I in turn showed myself such a guest that the city could congratulate itself if a more troublesome guest never befalls it. For if I may be permitted to say something boastfully about myself, I think the city of Basel owes me no less than I owe it. Its treasury I reduced by not a cent, and I spent there some thousands of florins from my own resources. From Froben I received very little, not even a penny from his estate, for his death was sudden.[475] Moreover, I lived there in a way that no one can have any reason to complain of me, except that I did not give my name to a sect. Finally, Oecolampadius in the preface to his *Isaiah* reckoned me among the ornaments of that community[476] – in case they reject my own evidence.

There remains Farel. Oh good Lord, what a devout, what an innocent man![477] They do not report what I wrote against him. If he has now mended his ways, I congratulate the fellow. What he once was greatly offended me: seditious, foul-mouthed, and utterly conceited. He behaved at Montbéliard in such a way that he had to flee from there twice.[478] When the city council of

* * * * *

his books to him, including the *Lingua* (see Ep 1612); cf Allen Ep 1678:36–7.
471 Allen Ep 1678:36n suggests that the Augsburg preacher may have been Urbanus Rhegius (1489–1528).
472 In response to Bucer's assertion in *Epistola apologetica* BOL 1 179:8–9
473 *Epistola apologetica* BOL 1 186:9–12
474 For example, Guillaume Farel was expelled in July of 1524; see Ep 1477A introduction.
475 See Allen Ep 1900:75–83.
476 See Staehelin *Briefe und Akten* 1 no 241 350–1.
477 *Epistola apologetica* BOL 1 179:10–11; cf the following with Ep 1510:11–81.
478 Farel's ministry at Montbéliard, controversial because of his stinging attacks from the pulpit on the Catholic priests and monks, was cut off first in March

Basel desired the city to be protected against sedition, it ordered Farel to go into exile.[479] Oecolampadius, whose hospitality he then enjoyed, reproached the fellow more than once because he would not put an end to his verbal attacks, and he declared that he could not support such bitter slanders in his company.[480] One who sat at the same table told me this – a man of quite uncommon honesty.[481] He had called me Balaam and gave no satisfactory reply when upbraided for it but evaded the question, saying that it was a certain businessman, Antoine du Blet, who had said this.[482] That man had since departed; and it could have been as Farel alleged, but if so the man was put up to it by Farel.

He wrote to the brethren in Constance a letter about our conversation, in which there was often not one true word in ten lines.[483] I will not mention less important matters. Having experienced him as he was, it is no wonder if I have portrayed him as he was. What he is like now, I do not know. What some Carthusian said and alleged against him matters nothing to me.[484] But in a letter I criticize him under a pseudonym.[485] My unassuming opponent prefers to set aside the truth so that he is freer to increase the hatred, and again he has recourse to that remarkable lie that I besmirch all those preachers and all their churches with innumerable lies.[486] Meanwhile he calls all those who fight for the Catholic church 'professed enemies of innocence'[487] and sees himself as never telling lies. Although he constantly repeats and emphasizes 'innumerable lies,' he has yet to prove a single one.

* * * * *

of 1525; see *Biographie nouvelle* (above n400) 145–52. He returned briefly in 1526 but was forced to flee the city again. Cf above n400.

479 See above n474.

480 In several letters, Oecolampadius urged Farel to moderate his approach; see Staehelin *Briefe und Akten* I no 208 299; no 212 307–8; Herminjard *Correspondance* I no 111 255–6, no 115 265–7.

481 Herminjard *Correspondance* I no 126 299 n4–5 suggests this is Pierre Toussain, who in 1524 lived in Oecolampadius' house; see also Ep 1510 n5.

482 Erasmus describes this incident in more detail in Ep 1341A:1192–1215. The prophet Balaam (Num 22–24) was exhorted by the Moabite King Balak to curse the Israelites; God induced him to bless them instead. Antoine du Blet of Lyon accompanied Farel when he came to Zürich in 1524; cf CEBR I 407–8.

483 Cf Ep 1496:145–8, Ep 1510:46–8; see also Herminjard *Correspondance* I no 121 286 and no 123 n4, suggesting Ambrosius Blarer.

484 Erasmus' allusion here cannot be traced in Bucer.

485 In Epp 1496:145–56, Ep 1510:11–81, Erasmus calls him 'Phallicus.'

486 *Epistola apologetica* BOL I 179:25–180:1

487 *Epistola apologetica* BOL I 179:18

I won't mention the priest of Basel who was flogged and then thrown out of the city.[488] What does it matter when he had stopped preaching? He was of the same persuasion. As common rumour has it, he assented in public, both in prison and outside the gate (after he was released by the torturer) that, after he had become involved in that sect, he had flung himself into every kind of disgraceful conduct. What he said about the whole sect I will not relate, because I am reporting hearsay (though about something close at hand).

Of the peasant at Altdorff, who suddenly died after having taken that bread which people call the host, I have written nothing except what the common report (and that a persistent one) recounted.[489] Nor does his version of the story differ so much from mine.[490] He took the host and having broken it he ate it in the way priests do, then he drank and perished. I have no doubt that in all other things he gives a full account of this event. 'Falling softly against the sacristan,' he says, 'he expired.'[491] Why did he not say instead: 'he fell asleep in the Lord'? If he had committed no sin, why was his corpse buried in an unconsecrated grave?[492] But he gives a sympathetic account of the fellow because he mocked the Eucharist, and that crime found favour.

There is still one lie left, but a splendid one (for a civil man overlooks much). I wrote somewhere, that wherever Lutheranism rises to ascendancy, there the study of letters comes to a standstill.[493] If this was not true, why was Luther constrained to recall people to the love of letters?[494] Why was Melanchthon forced to do the same, who did not pretend that what I say is untrue?[495] How the University at Wittenberg is prospering I don't know.[496] If there is any literary study left there, it is due to Melanchthon. I don't

* * * * *

488 *Epistola apologetica* BOL I 180:1–4, 184:3–5, referring to Peter Frauenberger, who was expelled twice from Basel, once in 1525 and again in 1528, this time for adultery; cf Allen Ep 2054:30–33. On Frauenberger see CEBR II 54–5.

489 Erasmus relates this incident in Allen Ep 2054:37–50.

490 Bucer's account is in *Epistola apologetica* BOL I 180:9–181:11.

491 *Epistola apologetica* BOL I 181:2

492 *Epistola apologetica* BOL I 181:7–11

493 Cf *Epistola apologetica* BOL I 181:22–3, repeating a remark from Allen Ep 1977:40–1. For the following section, cf above 286–7.

494 Cf *Hyperaspistes* 1 CWE 76 131. In 1524, Luther wrote *An die Ratsherren aller Städte deutsches Lands: dass sie christliche Schulen aufrichten und halten sollen* (WA 15 27–53), a defence of liberal learning against attacks by Karlstadt.

495 See above n454 and Ep 1500:6–9.

496 For Bucer's praise of the University at Wittenberg see *Epistola apologetica* BOL I 181:25–8.

know what is happening in the countryside.[497] Granted, some cities recently began to hire professors, but they will also have to hire students.[498] This is the degree to which the love of learning is burning! I won't examine now the reason why this has come about. Let him compare the University of Wittenberg with that of Louvain and Paris, even though these experienced no small amount of damage through Lutheranism!

The printers say that prior to this 'gospel' they were able to sell three thousand volumes more quickly than they now sell six hundred.[499] This perhaps suggests how literary studies are prospering! Just what do they teach there except languages?[500] They may cite the examples of even a handful who have advanced successfully in the study of letters under Lutheranism. Here he blames the scarcity of those dedicating themselves to letters on the priests (for he expands readily on this subject),[501] whereas in England so many colleges for students have been splendidly founded at the bishops' expense with generous provision extended to them, so many young men are supported through the liberality of these same priests.[502] And this is not just in England, but in Brabant,[503] and in France[504] as well.

As to what I wrote somewhere else – for they do not let anything pass – namely that some 'evangelicals' take richly dowered wives, that they are after nothing but wealth and a wife, and that some seem to have married for no other reason than because it was forbidden,[505] the first two points are well known in themselves. It was said of some and not of all (and the somewhat more sensible of their fellow ministers are admitting this). I am amazed that they deny the third point, since they themselves maintain that the ungodly laws of the pontiffs are to be resolutely broken and the very fact that some things are forbidden in the edicts of the pontiffs is reason enough to do them.[506] If Luther

* * * * *

497 See above n141.
498 See above n140.
499 Cf Epp 1531:33–6 and 1397:3–5.
500 Cf above n142.
501 *Epistola apologetica* BOL 1 182:6–9
502 Cf H. Rashdall *The Universities of Europe in the Middle Ages* (3 vols, London 1936) III 169–235, 293–324.
503 Cf H. de Jongh *L'ancienne faculté de théologie de Louvain au premier siècle de son existence (1435–1640)* (Louvain 1911) 40–51.
504 Cf H. Rashdall (above n502) I 497–539.
505 Bucer in *Epistola apologetica* BOL 1 182:15–22 cites *Epistola contra pseudevangelicos* above 234; see Allen Ep 1977:42–3, Ep 1477B:102–4.
506 Bucer in *Epistola apologetica* BOL 1 183:18–23 cites 1 Tim 4:1–3 in support of clerical marriage, claiming that one ought to put aside human regulations against it.

and Zwingli teach this in their published books, why are they irritated with me?

But their defence is like a fig tree,[507] if they really think that they are permitted to contract a marriage because many, contrary to divine law, keep concubines.[508] They make an assumption because, while praising the apostles' voluntary continence, I said that the apostles, though they were permitted to marry wives, abstained from marital relations, and if they married regarded their wives as sisters.[509] Christ says in the gospel: 'he who is able to receive this, let him receive it,'[510] and we do not read anywhere that he annulled the right to marriage for the apostles. So, he says, 'no one can compel us to celibacy.'[511] Certainly, the apostles did not forswear marriage. Who compelled them to give up the right to contract marriage? In this at least they differ from the apostles. They praise honourable marriages and spotless marriage beds,[512] but I hinted that some of the 'evangelicals' – for I spoke in general terms – live in marriages in a no more chaste fashion than the Catholics.[513]

He bids me offer some examples.[514] What is the point, since they are all recounted in public? He denies that these cases are common knowledge, since they are false,[515] and yet himself concedes two cases.[516] I know of a monk who has married three wives rather than one. I know of a priest, a man who is otherwise honest, who took a wife and found out afterwards that she was married to another. Very many similar stories are told about the marriages of monks and nuns, who divorced their spouses by the same right by which they had married them.

Now, is licentiousness among the 'evangelicals' less indulged in, are there fewer adulteries? I don't know what is happening at Strasbourg. The people know as well as I do what has been revealed elsewhere. Now, supposing we grant that it is permissible for these heralds of the 'gospel' to

* * * * *

507 *Adagia* I vii 85: *Ficulnus* CWE 32 118–19: 'The wood of the fig-tree, breakable as it is and useless ...'
508 Cf *Epistola apologetica* BOL 1 183:7–18.
509 Cf *Epistola apologetica* BOL 1 182:23–4, citing *Epistola contra pseudevangelicos* above 234 n98.
510 Matt 19:12
511 Cf *Epistola apologetica* BOL 1 183:2–4.
512 *Epistola apologetica* BOL 1 183:13–14; cf Heb 13:4.
513 Cf *Epistola contra pseudevangelicos* above 234 n98.
514 *Epistola apologetica* BOL 1 183:1–2
515 *Epistola apologetica* BOL 1 183:32–4
516 *Epistola apologetica* BOL 1 184:3–6, giving the cases of Peter Frauenberger (see above n488) and Gerhard Entringer, vicar at Old St Peter in Strasbourg.

take wives, who would not rightly be amazed that these lambs appointed for slaughter,[517] seeking nothing in this world except Christ's glory, bothered by so many worries, exposed to so many afflictions (to which poverty is added, and a wretched and heavy burden at that), cannot live without the wives whom so many men for more trivial reasons either do not marry or do not wish to marry. But for them every tragedy has a comedic ending. When a wife has come on the scene, they cry: 'Goodbye, and give your applause!'[518] Alas, what is this great lustfulness which the many evils cannot drive out? Whence this great rebellion of the flesh in those who claim that they are moved by the spirit of Christ?

In a letter to Stromer of Auerbach I wrote that this new 'gospel' had produced for us a new race of men which pleased me not at all.[519] This logic-chopper reckons that I committed a grave offence by failing to add that the gospel provided the occasion for their birth, since their 'gospel' was undoubtedly the gospel of Christ.[520] But isn't what is born on a specific occasion born all the same? Didn't Luther write triumphantly that it was in the nature of the gospel to tear apart those who had been joined together?[521]

God eternal, how great a lust for defamation this man possesses who hunts in my words for something at which he can quibble! This is the sort of thing: I had written in the letter that the apostles had not destroyed idols, even those of the pagans.[522] He wonders what has happened to me that I should write these things (as if Christians had idols at that time).[523] But if you read closely, there is no difficulty. The apostles were so far from doing away with things which were not evil that they did not remove the idols even of the gentiles. And here again, what was said in a general sense is interpreted by him as if it applied to every single instance. And here no

* * * * *

517 Cf Luke 10:3.
518 These are the concluding words to the *Moria* CWE 27 153.
519 In Ep 1522:95–100 (10 December 1524) Erasmus writes 'In these parts our new gospel provides us with a new sort of men: headstrong, impudent, deceitful, foul-mouthed, liars, scandalmongers, quarrelsome among themselves, no good to anyone, and a nuisance to all – subversive, crazy, noisy rascals; I dislike them so much that if I knew any city that was free of these gentry, I would move there.' Melanchthon, writing to Camerarius, remarked on the extreme bitterness of this letter (CR I 722). Heinrich Stromer von Auerbach (1482–1542) was the dean of the medical faculty at the University of Leipzig; cf CEBR III 291–2.
520 Cf *Epistola apologetica* BOL I 186:1–11.
521 *De servo arbitrio* WA 18 626:8–627:2
522 Cf *Epistola contra pseudevangelicos* above 242.
523 *Epistola apologetica* BOL I 193:7–9

doubt was the cause of his cry: 'Oh ill-advised and rash anger, ὦ φιλαυτία "oh self-love"!'[524] How much more fitting if someone were to shout back at him: 'Hurrah, Bacchus!'[525]

I have reproached several who call themselves Lutherans because they neglect the thing he chiefly values: faith. This again is interpreted as if it were said against all 'evangelicals.'[526] If there are none like this in their flock, then let him cry out against me! If there are several mixed in among them, then what is the reason for him to wail the inflammatory: 'us, us, us'? Yet, all the same, he doesn't wish us to know who this 'us' is. Lo and behold another crime for you: I compared Luther to Ate, and Melanchthon to Lite![527] This he twists as if I said Ate because he[528] greatly praised faith.[529] From where did this dream enter his mind? In fact, that passage shows that I am speaking of the violence of his writing which threw the world into confusion and troubled the minds of many. For a long time it has vexed me to have to respond to this kind of trifling stuff. Again, my saying I feared that under the cover of the 'gospel' people would emerge who believed in nothing at all, he interprets as if it were said of them all.[530] In fact, some like this are already appearing, to the great distress of God-fearing people. And such people have no safer shade to hide under than that 'gospel' of theirs. And then the large number of the weak in faith begins to doubt the whole Catholic faith, when they see the ancient decrees of the church overthrown and these people differing among themselves in their teaching. What is the matter with him that he cries: 'us, us, us'?

He scolds me because I said: 'Turn your gaze to good people,'[531] when he does not understand what I meant by these words. This is what my words were: 'You will say, "Nothing in human affairs is so fortunate that it is not corrupted with some admixture of evil. Direct your attention to the virtuous among us!"'[532] For these words are fashioned for the 'evangelical'

* * * * *

524 BOL I 186:24: Bucer aims at Erasmus a word often used in his *Praise of Folly*.
525 Cf Vergil *Aeneid* 4.302. In hailing the Roman god of wine, Erasmus is indirectly calling Bucer a drunkard.
526 See *Epistola apologetica* BOL I 186:31–187:15, in response to *Epistola contra pseudevangelicos* above 235.
527 See *Epistola contra pseudevangelicos* above 240 n126.
528 Luther
529 Cf *Epistola apologetica* BOL I 187:16–25.
530 *Epistola apologetica* BOL I 188:5–8, referring to *Epistola contra pseudevangelicos* above 236
531 *Epistola apologetica* BOL I 190:23–7
532 *Epistola contra pseudevangelicos* above 241

who advises that, ignoring those who live wickedly under the cover of the
'gospel,' we should turn our gaze to those who live a pious life. He interprets it as if I meant that even the best among them was under the sway
of the vices which I have mentioned; and he wrote in the margin: 'egregious insults to Christ.'[533] How he would prattle on about me if something
like that happened! That apostolic man will never be ashamed of such a
stupid deed, though I have spoken in good clear Latin. With similar inac-
curacy they charge me with lying when I said they teach that the miracles
of the saints are the magic tricks of demons, and they refute me by referring to the example of the apostles and the other saints who became famous through their miracles, though I am speaking about miracles which
come to pass through the invocation of the saints.[534] Do not Zwingli and
Oecolampadius teach these things, who also attribute ghostly visitations to
the deceptions of the demons?[535] What is there more shameless than this
slanderer?

Again he twists what I mentioned as perhaps my 'bad luck' that I
had 'known not one who has not become worse than his former self'[536]
as if it were said of all of them. He throws in my face the examples of
Oecolampadius, Capito, Zwingli, and many others, asking in what way
they have become worse.[537] I had no dealings with Pellicanus after he gave
himself over to the 'gospel.' In his published letters he certainly presented
himself very differently from what I had hoped or what he once seemed to
be.[538] With Oecolampadius, whose ability and learning, I admit, I loved, I
have had no intimacy for some years now.[539] With Zwingli I had dinner a
few times.[540] I conversed with him on several occasions eight years ago. At
that time I warned the fellow frankly to keep away from novel teachings;
he either heeded the advice or made a good pretence of doing so at that

* * * * *

533 See *Epistola apologetica* BOL 1 190 n575.
534 See *Epistola apologetica* BOL 1 87:11–12, referring to *Epistola contra pseudevangelicos* above 242.
535 C. Augustijn notes that many of Erasmus' accusations against the evangelicals
were culled from his reading of Eck's *Articuli 404*; see his introduction to the
Epistola ad fratres Inferioris Germaniae ASD IX-1 324 and above 293. This particular
claim might be based on article 130.
536 *Epistola apologetica* BOL 1 191:1–2, referring to *Epistola contra pseudevangelicos*
above 241.
537 *Epistola apologetica* BOL 1 191:14–17
538 See above n185.
539 See above n60.
540 See Epp 401, 404.

time.[541] With Hedio I had dinner on only one occasion that I know of and nothing significant was said.[542] Capito, I admit, I loved like a friend. He seemed to me then a pious and humane man.[543] I have revoked my polite friendship with none of them. I broke off close friendship with them lest the common people think we agreed in matters of doctrine. I never saw Pellicanus from the time he moved away to Zürich, nor Capito either, after he left for Strasbourg.

So, I had the opportunity to know, to some extent, what they used to be like; what they are like now I scarcely know except what I can gauge from their pamphlets (and I have kept away from those for three years, feeling that there is no way I can benefit from reading them). If the common people say something against them, I am not so capricious as to put it into writing, and if I knew of any secret fault, I would scarcely make it public, however much this contriver of sedition may provoke me. At least Vulturius once evinced a different kind of sincerity and dependability from what he now displays. In short, from what I have been able to gauge from their writings and other indications, I would not want to entrust the salvation of my little soul to any of them. Moreover, I know that many will not read without a smile that they liken themselves to the apostles also because of their abstention from violence.[544] Perhaps they will not refrain from smiling also when they compare their martyrs with the martyrs of the ancient church, who bore witness to Christ with their blood. If they are right in comparing them with Stephen[545] and Lawrence,[546] then the emperor deserves to be compared with Nero,[547] Diocletian,[548] and Maxentius.[549]

* * * * *

541 See Epp 1315, 1327.
542 For Erasmus' relationship with Hedio see Ep 1477B; cf above n31.
543 See above n31.
544 See *Epistola apologetica* BOL I 191:27–193:21.
545 St Stephen (Acts 6–7) is designated as the first Christian martyr, stoned to death by a mob when he spoke before the council.
546 St Lawrence (d 258), a deacon of the Roman church, was put to death by order of the Emperor Valerian, who issued an edict condemning all Christian clergy in August of 258.
547 Nero Claudius Caesar, Roman emperor AD 54–68, persecuted Christians as a means of combating the suspicion that he set the fire that devastated Rome in AD 64.
548 Diocletian, emperor from 284 until his abdication in 305, was responsible for the last sustained persecution of Christians, beginning in 303.
549 Maxentius was defeated by Constantine in 312 at the battle of the Mulvian Bridge. Constantine's conversion to Christianity occurred as a result of this victory.

He calls it a slanderous lie when I said that according to them the bride of Christ was blind for so many years while her Bridegroom was snoring.[550] He denies that her Bridegroom ever snored, as though I had not been saying this εἰρωνικῶς 'ironically.' But in fact, from the point of view of those who regard as idolatry and abomination what the church reverently practised for so many years, wasn't she blind while her Bridegroom was snoring? They who teach that baptism is not necessary for salvation, who teach that in the Eucharist there is nothing but bread and wine, and many other similar things, who say that the ancient Doctors of the church wrote sheer nonsense, and that there is danger that they are all in hell,[551] how do they represent the church if not as blind?

It was also a great lie when I wrote that Luther, whom they previously very nearly regarded as god, now is crazy in their view.[552] They are unable to recognize a not altogether shameless hyperbole. They received his doctrines as oracles, so much so that they are prepared to go to the stake for them. They preferred him to popes, general councils, and all the Doctors of the church. They claimed that he had nowhere erred. How far short is that of regarding him as god? Now they say: 'For us he is not at all crazy.'[553] 'Us, us,' who you are I don't know. I spoke in general. Every day we heard people at Basel saying: 'Luther is crazy, a human spirit directs his writing.'[554] If they always want to respond with 'us,' then all that Erasmus said is lies. For they can make up anything they like about persons unknown to me. What impertinence many will attribute to the following I do not know. For he writes: 'Show us just one person from whom we took a penny because he followed a different religion,'[555] when it is well known that here and there that many have been fined because they received the Eucharist in the neighbouring villages.[556] I will keep quiet about plundered churches and the many people whose assets have been depleted.

He also scolds me that I wrote that the most light-minded people join these sects, speaking, of course, of the common people and of persons

* * * * *

550 Cf *Epistola apologetica* BOL 1 193:30–5, referring to *Epistola contra pseudevangelicos* above 242.
551 See above n276.
552 Cf *Epistola apologetica* BOL 1 171:20–8, referring to *Epistola contra pseudevangelicos* above 233.
553 Cf *Epistola apologetica* BOL 1 171:25.
554 Cf Allen Ep 2059:67–71, *Hyperaspistes* 1 CWE 76 98.
555 *Epistola apologetica* BOL 1 194:25–6
556 See above n156.

I know.[557] For there are among their number many who are trifling, bankrupts, fugitives, deserters from their institution, those attracted by riots and licence, youths, silly wenches, hirelings, those of scant judgment, vagabonds, soldiers, and even those notorious for their crimes. It was by people of that ilk that a large part of the drama was initially acted out in some places. I assert again that I speak of people I know. What they are like at Strasbourg I don't know. 'God chose,' he says, 'what is foolish in the world';[558] but among them are those distinguished with quite other titles which I won't mention here. In order to show that not all who embrace the 'gospel' are light-minded, he presents the prince of Hesse, whom he calls an exceptional 'ornament of Germany,' and the elector of Saxony,[559] neither of whom I even know by face, and both of whose territories are located a great distance from me so that scarcely a hint of their reputation has wafted this way. I do not know what they[560] approve or disapprove. It does not seem to me probable that they give blanket approval to what they[561] do or write, especially with regard to the Eucharist. Therefore, when I wrote those things, nothing was less in my mind than the princes, though there is nothing to prevent a prince from being light-minded.

I don't know to what extent the preachers despise wealth or how much they have in their coffers.[562] The rumour about some is hardly favourable. Here, of course, he artificially stirs up the emotions of pity, crying out that they alone have both poverty or riches held against them.[563] Who wouldn't weep? But what wonder is it if among the many needy there are some who are rich? Poverty, if it is by necessity, should not be cast in anyone's face, but those who market themselves under the name of the 'gospel' deserve derision when they have nothing 'evangelical' about them save poverty. And anyone has the right to condemn people for accumulating wealth under the

* * * * *

557 *Epistola apologetica* BOL I 195:25–8, referring to *Epistola contra pseudevangelicos* above 243 n139

558 Cf 1 Cor 1:27; *Epistola apologetica* BOL I 195:33–5.

559 Cf *Epistola apologetica* BOL I 196:3–9. On Landgrave Philip of Hesse see above n305. Frederick III (the Wise), Elector of Saxony (1463–1525), protected Luther without embracing Lutheranism. His brother and successor, Elector John (d 1532), to whom Bucer refers, was an ardent Lutheran. Cf CEBR III 203–5, 208–9.

560 The two princes

561 The 'evangelicals'

562 The following two paragraphs are a response to *Epistola apologetica* BOL I 196:16–198:9, Bucer's refutation of *Epistola contra pseudevangelicos* above 243 n139.

563 Cf *Epistola apologetica* BOL I 145:19–20.

cover of the 'gospel.' Time, which uncovers all things,[564] will make it clear if there were none who did this.

As to what I wrote about their reign: that they control the people by their tongues; that the magistracy does nothing unless it accords with their opinion; that they expel from the city council those who dissent from their teaching; that they throw in prison those who have criticized them; that they defend themselves with treaties – doesn't this mean to reign? That outstanding man, Lefèvre, censured them on this account at the time when he had left France in fear and withdrew into Germany.[565] A much lengthier reply would be required to counter his[566] prolixity, his tragic exaggeration of single words of mine.

I said the injudicious writings and seditious preaching of some of them had ensured that their cause went in the opposite direction and instead of gaining freedom slavery was redoubled and the tyranny of those whom they were trying to cast down from their tyranny strengthened.[567] If there are (or were) none who fit that description, Erasmus has lied. However, if there are many such, then these people, who never fail to exaggerate the ferocious, savage, and brutal lies I concocted against them and with which I roused the princes and the whole world to destroy them, are quite shameless. But, I imagine, they will not dare deny that by the violence of his writing, by his mockery and his invective, Luther has either estranged the hearts of many or indeed provoked them against his doctrine. They themselves admit as much in that very

* * * * *

564 *Adagia* II iv 17: *Tempus omnia revelat* 'Time reveals all things' CWE 33 198.
565 Lefèvre d'Étaples (1460–1536) was a humanist reformer and biblical scholar in France. In later life he joined Bishop Briçonnet at Meaux to take part in a reform movement there that was strongly evangelical, at which time he translated the New Testament and the Psalms into French. In 1525 he left France to go to Strasbourg, as a result of persecution by the Parlement in Paris at the behest of the faculty of theology at the Sorbonne. King Francis I, under normal circumstances sympathetic to the reformers at Meaux, was during that time imprisoned in Spain, and thus the more conservative forces had the opportunity to move aggressively against their enemies. While there is no record of Lefèvre making such a remark about the German evangelicals as Erasmus records here, he did stop in Basel to visit Erasmus on his way back to France in 1526, and may have said something along these lines in conversation. For Erasmus' friendly relations with Lefèvre, and their disagreements, see *Spongia* above 130 n558.
566 Bucer's
567 See *Epistola apologetica* BOL I 198:22–203:14, in response to *Epistola contra pseude-vangelicos* above 243–4.

book.[568] They admit the same thing of Farel.[569] What? Does Luther appear to have done everything he could to attract to his 'gospel' the pope, Duke George, the king of England, and the emperor, whom he also rebuked in an offensive manner?[570] Does Zwingli seem to have left nothing untried to win over the bishop of Constance?[571] I will pass over the others.

'The apostles,' he says, 'censured the shortcomings of the Jews and the gentiles.'[572] But their reprimand was spread with an abundant honey of charity and bore absolutely no resemblance to this. Sometimes Christ was angry at the Pharisees,[573] but he knew the hearts of all. Paul called the false apostles 'dogs' and 'evil workmen,'[574] refraining, though, from naming them. All these may seem mere blandishments compared to what the 'evangelicals' have written against the pope, all the bishops, against the priests, and the Christian princes. What was appropriate for Paul is not automatically appropriate for anybody. It is unbecoming for them to cry out against others, when much more terrible accusations can be levelled against them. 'Which?' they will say. To mention nothing else: schism and heresy! When someone states in offensive language what might have been well received if presented pleasantly, is he really doing all he could to win everyone over? Doctor Wessel[575] has many things in common with Luther, but how much more Christian, how much more modest is the manner in which he states his teachings than that of many of those men.

This Bucephalus would not deny that some distinguished men existed among the monks. Why does he not admit that there are also some such today? Yet how could they have been pious when they employed rituals, offered mass, said the prayers, fasted according to rule, observed dietary regulations – all things which they[576] consistently affirm as contrary to the 'gospel'? Has the desire to abuse me so overwhelmed the man that in the same work he contradicts himself? 'They have,' as he says, 'overthrown

*　*　*　*　*

568 Cf *Epistola apologetica* BOL I 189:21–3.
569 *Epistola apologetica* BOL I 179:14–16
570 *Epistola apologetica* BOL I 204:15–205:21, referring to *Epistola contra pseudevangelicos* above 241.
571 See above n463.
572 Cf *Epistola apologetica* BOL I 101:24–5.
573 As, for example, in Matt 15:1–14, 23; Luke 11:37–54
574 Phil 3:2
575 Wessel Gansfort (1419–89) studied and taught at the Zwolle school of the Brethren of the Common Life before moving to Paris, where he became an outspoken critic of ecclesiastical abuses; cf CEBR II 74.
576 The 'evangelicals'

the sway of pope over the consciences of many,'[577] but countless people had already done so in their own conscience without giving it any thought. However, I did not speak of consciences but of an external tyranny (for this is what they call ecclesiastical power). Meanwhile, what I said about the rage of certain theologians and monks is interpreted as if I said it of each and all of them. He seems to regard every unspecified statement as if it applied to all!

He approves of my wish 'that obstacles to piety might be cured by suitable, prudent attention. As for the things that are pious, let us agree about them in a Christian spirit. In things that are indifferent,[578] let us allow each person to content himself as he sees fit; let each, testing all things, hold to what he supposes good. Difficult matters, and those that seem not yet fully discussed, let us put off until another time, so that, in the meantime, a benevolent harmony may prevail among people disharmonious in their opinions; until God may deign to reveal these things to some one. If any wrong creeps in through human failing, let our action be that of a worthy physician: let the faults in things be removed, not the things themselves.' [579] He approves this advice of mine, doubtless on condition that they determine for us which things hinder piety, which are neutral, and which are difficult. And among the difficult things he places the doctrine of the Eucharist.[580] I marvel at their nerve in making this concession when they boldly affirm that it is the most wicked idolatry to adore the bread as Christ, when they will in no way tolerate sacred vestments and images, the saying of the office, and the prescribed fasts. If the doctrine of the Eucharist is so difficult that the human intellect has not yet been able to follow it, why do they assert what they do not understand? Why do they burden us with so much invective, when all we do is simply embrace what has been handed down to us by the church? So, they offer us peace on these terms: that all of us, whether popes, bishops, princes, or commoners, together should come to our senses and admit that whatever they have done or will do is the pure 'gospel.' Unless this happens they threaten dreadful things.

They request that we content ourselves with one Holy Communion, but without Christ, contrary to what the church has believed over so many

* * * * *

577 Cf *Epistola apologetica* BOL I 201:30–202:11.
578 See above n93.
579 *Epistola apologetica* BOL I 207:7–16, referring to *Epistola contra pseudevangelicos* above 245.
580 Cf *Epistola apologetica* BOL I 209:25–8.

centuries.[581] But Erasmus has written: 'no passage can be found in Holy Scripture which clearly demonstrates that the apostles consecrated bread and wine into the Lord's body and blood.'[582] So what follows? Did they therefore not consecrate? In fact, there is no passage showing that they did not consecrate. But suppose the apostles never consecrated – this is absurd since they heard from the Lord: 'as often as you do this, do it in memory of me,'[583] and Paul: 'I received this from the Lord and I have handed it on to you.'[584] Nor should there be any doubt that they themselves did it and handed it on to others to do – does this mean that what Christ instituted, what the church has held, is void? But they cannot be persuaded that this is the true sense of Scripture. From where is it evident to them that the body of Christ is not there? They deny that the Fathers understood things as we interpret them.[585] What response can I make except that it is a manifest lie since there are so many passages in the books of the Fathers where they express quite clearly what they mean?

But Erasmus said he could take sides with Oecolampadius, unless the universal consensus were not so great as to hinder him.[586] I admit that I said this, but what else is this than to confess that I agree with the Catholic church (which I call 'the interpreter of the Scriptures')[587] and that what they teach seems heretical? Someone had added that Oecolampadius' opinion seemed better to me, if the consensus of the church did not stand in the way. This is completely false.[588] I said in a private conversation only that it was simpler and clearer, that is, complicated by fewer difficulties and questions. If I judged it better, I would have said so. 'The consensus of the majority,' he says, 'is sometimes the greatest error.'[589] But the consensus of a minority is more often the greatest error. If he does not believe the church, he does what heretics are accustomed to do. If he is looking for a new church, he does what schismatics are used to do. He admits that Christ

* * * * *

581 Cf *Epistola apologetica* BOL I 209:9–13. Bucer does not say that Holy Communion is 'without Christ,' only that Christ's presence is not physical.
582 *Epistola apologetica* BOL I 209:14–16, quoting from Allen Ep 2175:24–6
583 Cf 1 Cor 11:25.
584 1 Cor 11:23
585 Cf *Epistola apologetica* BOL I 209:22–3.
586 *Epistola apologetica* BOL I 209:16–18, quoting from Allen Ep 2175:21–2; see above n207. See also Allen Epp 1717:52–61, 1729:25–7.
587 Bucer in fact cites this point; cf *Epistola apologetica* BOL I 190:18–19, quoting from Allen Ep 2175:23–4.
588 Cf Allen Ep 1893:56.
589 Cf *Epistola apologetica* BOL I 219:5–6; *De libero arbitrio* CWE 76 16.

is received and eaten by the faithful, but he does not wish to add anything, even though they themselves add: 'not in substance but spiritually.'[590] If they cry: 'the body of the Lord is in the Eucharist, but under a sign only and not in substance,' and if we profess: 'the body of the Lord' adding nothing more, what else will our silence achieve except that we seem to agree with them?

Nor, again, is he ashamed to compare Christianity as it has so far existed in the church with the impious superstition of the pagans,[591] the image of the crucified with an image of Venus, our saints with the demons, the Platonists' dreams of the first cause and the *logos* with the Christians' most firmly fixed faith in the Father, the Son, and the Holy Spirit.[592] He says the gentiles did not worship the idols as gods.[593] Not to speak of the common folk, Plato himself teaches that statues skilfully wrought are brought to life by demons.[594] If the gentiles did not worship images as gods, then Paul lies when he writes that the gentiles worshipped a creature in the place of the creator,[595] and Isaiah in chapter 44 is quite deranged.[596] If I had written anything of this kind, how fiercely he would bring against me the accusation

* * * * *

590 Cf *Epistola apologetica* BOL I 209:11–13: *Sic cum fateamur caenae christianorum adesse Christum ipsum eosque vero suo corpore et sanguine pascere, non requiratur a nobis addere 'corporaliter' et 'sub pane' sive 'panis speciebus.'* 'Thus when we profess that Christ is present in the supper of Christians, and that they feed on his true body and blood, we do not have to add "bodily," or "under the bread" or "the appearances of bread."'

591 Cf *Epistola apologetica* BOL I 208:13–19.

592 In *Epistola apologetica* BOL I 205:25–31 and 207:25–208:8, Bucer draws upon Macrobius' *Commentary on the Dream of Scipio* 1.2.14–15: 'But when the discussion aspires to treat of the Highest and Supreme of all gods, called by the Greeks the Good (*agathon*) and the First Cause (*protoaition*), or to treat of Mind or Intellect, which the Greeks call *nous*, born from and originating in the Supreme God and embracing the original concept of things, which are called Ideas (*ideai*), when, I repeat, philosophers speak about these, the Supreme God and Mind, they shun the use of fabulous narratives ...' Bucer does not make a comparison between the image of the crucified and Venus, or between the demons and the saints.

593 Cf *Epistola apologetica* BOL I 149:33–150:1.

594 Plato's writings do not contain such a claim; however, see Augustine *De civitate dei* 8.14–27 (CSEL 40 76:19–407:11), which includes a dialogue between the god Hermes and Asclepius, taken from the *Asclepius* of the Pseudo-Apuleius, describing the gods or demons as taking up their abode in idols created by human artistry.

595 Rom 1:25

596 Isa 44:9–20

of blasphemy. He emphasizes these things so often in order to argue that what they do requires no greater licence than what the apostles did, and that the gentiles and Jews could have protected their religion against the gospel they scorned with no less probability than we protect the rites and doctrines of the Catholic church.

To grant them this no less impious than absurd idea, and to admit as parallel things that have nothing in common – since they themselves admit that miracles were necessary at the beginning[597] – we will rightly require miracles from them too. If they set before us as miracles the multitude of their churches, one can reply that once the Arians had more churches than the orthodox[598] and that the Muhammedan sect has spread more widely than the Christian religion. And yet if they are comparing themselves with the orthodox, how large a portion of the Christian world is theirs? If they set before us their martyrs, those of the Jewish persuasion are more steadfast. Moreover, nothing is easier than to fool people with a feigned witness of the Spirit. If many of them lead a blameless life, we have certainly not yet seen such extraordinary holiness from any of them that apostolic conduct could take the place of miracles. He is angry at me because I strike at what he calls their 'harmless churches which seek nothing but Christ,'[599] although in all their writings they have the temerity to charge the churches of the whole world, the leaders of the church, and the universal flock of Christ with idolatry and blasphemy.

But I am already sick and tired of the brash prolixity of this writer. They 'have not innovated at all,' he says, 'except where something stood in the way of piety.' They wish to give no occasion to sedition, but to be 'all things to all men,'[600] providing their doctrine can remain unharmed (which they know with absolute certainty is endorsed by Christ). They are prepared to lose all for the sake of the 'gospel,' if only Christ be not taken from them.[601] They are eager to be of benefit to all and to hurt no one. They are moved by, and cannot withdraw from, the Spirit of God. To cut a long story short, there awaits them, after their struggle for the 'gospel,' the

* * * * *

597 *Epistola apologetica* BOL I 90:7–15
598 See above n45. During the fourth century, Arian Christianity made substantial inroads, particularly in the East where it became established in the imperial court. The Nicene Creed was finally enforced by the Council of Constantinople in 381.
599 Cf *Epistola apologetica* BOL I 164:1–2, 222:24–5.
600 1 Cor 9:22; *Epistola apologetica* BOL I 151:21–2, 217:31–2
601 Cf *Epistola apologetica* BOL I 217:30–218:1; in the following section, Erasmus loosely summarizes his interpretation of Bucer's main points.

reward of eternal life, while for us, unless we come to our senses, an end
more frightful than the punishment of the people of Sodom[602] – for us, I
say, who kill the innocent ministers of the word, who with all our might
fight against the 'evangelical' truth, who stubbornly resist the Holy Spirit,
who worship idols, who blaspheme against Christ, who wrongly interpret
the canonical Scripture, who being quite ignorant of Christ, worship Satan.
For in this way they regard all those who dissent from their doctrines.

He rages against me like this, chattering away non-stop about the
splendid lies of Erasmus and his insults and injuries against Christ, because
I dared to open my mouth about the behaviour of some of the 'evangelicals.'
Don't they see that these horrendous charges fall back on the emperor, on
so many of the Christian princes, so many cities devoutly professing Christ,
so many churches, the flock of Christ spread so far and wide? Yet someone
harsher than I might say that in the conventicles of the heretics there is
neither Christ, nor the Spirit of Christ, nor Holy Writ, nor piety, nor the hope
of forgiveness. There are those who think and write such things of them
and pressure the princes to do away with such a breed of men altogether.
Why don't they hurl at them what they have been raging against me – I
who have until now held my pen back, although urged by powerful men
day in, day out; I who – more carefully than it is expedient for them to
know – act to ensure that division be healed before it come to bloodshed,
so much so that I thought it preferable that the sects be left in their present
position until either time or God himself should provide a cure than that
all of Germany be embroiled in slaughter.[603]

Against Eck, against the bishop of Rochester,[604] against Josse Clichtove,[605] and against Johannes Cochlaeus[606] they are mute. Against Erasmus
they pour out all their bile so that it appears to be a private feud and one
started by some drunkard. But if they conceived this resentment from the

* * * * *

602 Gen 19:24–5; Matt 10:15; cf *Epistola apologetica* BOL I 203:34–204:2.
603 Cf *Epistola contra pseudevangelicos* above 246; Allen Ep 2328:73–82.
604 See above nn307, 308.
605 Josse Clichtove of Nieuwpoort (1472/73–1534): a Paris-educated theologian
who in his early years was a collaborator of Lefèvre d'Étaples. Clichtove broke
with Lefèvre in early 1521 and wrote against Luther, and became increasingly
critical of Erasmus at the same time that he gravitated towards Noël Béda in
the mid-1520s. See CEBR I 317–20.
606 Johannes Cochlaeus (Dobnek, 1479–1552) of Nuremberg wrote a series of pamphlets severely rebuking Luther; see D.V.N. Bagchi *Luther's Earliest Opponents:
Catholic Controversialists 1518–1525* (Minneapolis 1989); cf *Spongia* above 94
n326.

writings in which I make it clear that I do not approve the sects, why did they hide this for so long? Perhaps it was because this marvellous expert in the art of stirring up mutiny and in the art of fleeing elsewhere (once disturbances had begun) had not yet moved to Strasbourg.[607] He was the sort of fellow to note all the passages in my letters fit for misrepresentation[608] and soon would pretend that the book had been stolen in secret from him by his brethren. He was so on fire with uncontrollable hatred that he could not wait for this book (pieced together out of lies and insults no differently than a patchwork out of rags) but secretly dispatched the most absurd glosses[609] – and meanwhile wrote me nice letters: I was the master and the teacher from whom he would gladly take advice. He could not live without a picture of me. In his next letters he even comforted me, urging me to be of good cheer and disparaging the clamorous agitators and scribblers.[610] Then (long after I published my epistle, something I had written I was going to do),[611] in his letters to my secretary he wished to be commended to me.

Meanwhile, they[612] were preparing these pages with such stinging skill that their praise does me more harm than their insults affect me. And these people compare themselves with the holiness of the apostles, although what Vulturius did comes closer to the example of the traitor Judas than that of Christ. What else are those grand words but pure hypocrisy when combined with the conduct we have found in many of them? But what else could we expect from those who declare that it is right to spread their 'gospel' by deceits and tricks;[613] that is, their sect which has been certainly condemned by the judgment of the external church at large?

Why doesn't this trickster affix his name? Ministers of the word at Strasbourg! All of them? What cheek they have then to shower so much praise on themselves. Whoever he was, he secured wondrous praise for the people of Strasbourg for supporting such preachers, and then for the ministers aiding and abetting that silly, slanderous, and seditious pamphlet.[614]

* * * * *

607 Geldenhouwer arrived in Strasbourg in 1525.
608 See above n28; see also C. Augustijn's introduction to *Epistola ad fratres Inferiores Germaniae* ASD IX-1 320.
609 See introductory note above n1.
610 This seems to be a reference to a lost letter from Geldenhouwer. See *Epistola contra pseudevangelicos* above 219 n8; see also ASD IX-1 273:75n
611 See ASD IX-1 314:18n
612 Geldenhouwer and his collaborator; see above nn28, 34.
613 See above n35.
614 The *Epistola apologetica*

Indeed, I would have wished more auspicious things for that community than to have ministers no wiser than the one who wrote this book.

One lie slipped out: They say I am easier on Luther than on them; Melanchthon has even been praised by me.[615] I praised Melanchthon for the sincerity of his character and his diligence in promoting good letters, but I always excluded his doctrines.[616] Although he owes a great deal to Luther, he was not so offended either by the *Diatribe* or the two books of *Hyperaspistes* as to renounce his friendship with me or write anything ill-natured against me, whereas these people insanely rage against me for attacking (or rather admonishing) Vulturius. The two books in response to Luther show just how restrained I was against him.[617]

But if the pronoun 'us,' again, points to the people of Strasbourg, I have not yet written anything harsh against any of their ministers; I have never uttered a word against the people of Strasbourg since I knew no one there. What invective have I poured out against the ministers? I only suggested that I had some suspicion about Capito's sly ways.[618] I complained mildly to Hedio that he neither delivered my letter to the city council nor kept it a secret.[619] I never replied to Otto. Johann that well-known printer[620] told my secretary that he was not an 'evangelical.' And these are the weighty reasons why they publish such a querulous book against me. They have no doubt persuaded the magistracy that I have done serious injury to the reputation of its city, although I never unsheathed the point of my pen against the ministers, the people, or the magistracy.

They say it is incumbent on them to be 'all things to all people' and that they are prepared to give a calm and modest account of their life and teaching to anyone seeking it.[621] Someone could have believed this, had not

* * * * *

615 *Epistola apologetica* BOL 1 86:8–13
616 See Ep 1496:37–51. T.J. Wengert's *Human Freedom, Christian Righteousness: Philip Melanchthon's Exegetical Dispute with Erasmus of Rotterdam* (New York and Oxford 1998) emphasizes the doctrinal chasm underlying Erasmus' and Melanchthon's outwardly cordial relationship. On their early rhetorical differences cf M. Hoffmann 'Rhetoric and Dialectic in Erasmus' and Melanchthon's Interpretation of John's Gospel' in *Philip Melanchthon (1497–1560) and the Commentary* ed T.J. Wengert and P. Graham (Sheffield 1997) 48–78.
617 Erasmus is referring to his *Hyperaspistes* 1 and 2 CWE 76 and 77.
618 In Erasmus' 6 September 1524 letter to Melanchthon he wrote that Capito 'always smelled like a rascal' (Ep 1496:77).
619 Cf Ep 1477B.
620 Johann Schott; see above n402.
621 1 Cor 9:22; see *Epistola apologetica* BOL 1 217:30–218:1.

this scurrilous book, so cleverly drafted for sedition, declared the opposite. It is a piece of barefaced nonsense, too, when he says many have striven with all their might to wipe them out completely,[622] although they have been tolerated with great mildness so far by the emperor, princes, and bishops. It wouldn't have been difficult to deal with them just as the insurrectionary peasants were treated.[623] But some exploit the mildness of the princes, all the time boasting that, 'having forsaken all fleshly protection' and relying on the word and protection of Christ alone, they preach the truth.[624]

If, as he claims, Vulturius is in the fold of Christ,[625] I am glad. We are certainly not in the same church, nor has he any reason in the future to fear Erasmus' encouragement. I have given up being anxious on his account. As far as I am concerned, he can amuse himself as often as he likes with glosses and pamphlets parading my name on the front page. Nor will he persuade me or any mortal who has a nose for these things that he does them from a pure and simple heart. If he is so high-minded that he now endures 'evangelical' poverty, it is fine, although he complained of his indigence in more than one of his earlier letters to me from exile.[626] And if the bishops so greatly displease him, let him betake himself to his prince, Charles, duke of Guelders, to whom he is known and to whom he writes in such friendly terms.[627]

At last the epilogue to this most holy work has been reached.[628] They deny, he says, that they 'introduce new doctrines, but are restoring the ancient ones'[629] – as if those which the church has taught and preserved with the great consensus of the world for fourteen hundred years until this date were not ancient, or as if they are certain of what the apostles handed on to their churches. If the ministers of the word are supposed to add

* * * * *

622 See *Epistola apologetica* BOL I 218:1–4.
623 The defeat of the peasants was accomplished with great severity and loss of life; however, in the aftermath of the struggle the Imperial Diet at Speier (1526) did attempt to address their grievances. See Peter Blickle *The Revolution of 1525: The German Peasants' War from a New Perspective* tr Thomas A. Brady and H.C. Erik Midelfort (Baltimore 1981) 165–85.
624 *Epistola apologetica* BOL I 219:25
625 *Epistola apologetica* BOL I 219:29–31
626 Cf *Epistola contra pseudevangelicos* above 219 n8.
627 Karel van Egmond, duke of Gelderland (1467–1538), was an ally of France and adversary of the Hapsburgs, who undertook to incorporate Gelderland into the empire's dominions. See Tracy *Politics of Erasmus* chapter 4; CEBR I 422.
628 The epilogue begins at 220:14 of BOL I.
629 *Epistola apologetica* BOL I 220:15–16

nothing to the Scriptures, why did Paul dare to institute in his churches things which the Lord did not teach?[630] Is this not a new doctrine: This consecrated bread is the body of the Lord, this wine is the blood of the Lord;[631] the body under the bread is without blood, the blood under the wine is without body, there is life in neither?[632] Is this not a new doctrine: In the Eucharist there is nothing except bread and wine?[633] And this new: Baptism is necessary for no one?[634]

They teach the gospel pure and unadulterated. And which 'gospel' is that? 'That through faith all justification and salvation is obtained from the one God through one Saviour and our reconciler Jesus Christ.'[635] What could be more religious than these words? But what a great deal of poison lurks in them! It is impious to invoke the saints or to venerate them, since they have no influence with God. It is impious for people to beseech the priests to pray to God on their behalf in the sacrament. Faith alone justifies, nor does it matter what kind of works a person does. There is no need for works of satisfaction, for this means to mistrust Christ who has ransomed us. In purgatory there is no satisfaction through suffering. Confession is useless, for this is to seek justification from a human being. All these things lurk under that most religious language.

Moreover, I am not completely sure on what grounds he so often has left out the Holy Spirit in this discourse. I fear also under this stone there sleeps a scorpion, which they are later going to throw at us.[636] For they also declare that in the beginning they hid certain things which at the appropriate time they bring forth in keeping with people's capacity.[637] They

* * * * *

630 Erasmus may have had in mind Paul's specifications regarding marriage in 1 Cor 7 or regarding food in 1 Cor 8 and Rom 14.

631 Erasmus probably got his information from Eck *Articuli 404* article 326; see above n535. Eck refers, as his own source, to Luther's *De captivitate babylonica* WA 6 511:20–21: 'I will firmly believe not only that the body of Christ is *in* the bread but that the bread *is* the body of Christ.'

632 Eck's source would have been Luther's *Bericht an einen guten Freund*; cf WA 26 607:35–608:2: 'I only know, that I take Christ's body and blood in the Sacrament, as his Word proclaims, but how the body, without the blood or with the blood, or on the other hand how the blood, without the body or with the body, is present, that I ought not to know nor do I seek to know.'

633 See above n17.

634 See above n105.

635 *Epistola apologetica* BOL I 220:17–19

636 *Adagia* I iv 34: *Sub omni lapide scorpius dormit* CWE 31 344:1–17: 'a man should beware of speaking heedlessly in the presence of fault-finders and slanderers.'

637 *Epistola apologetica* BOL I 138:3–4

deny that they have in mind anything except to be of benefit to everyone. If all the Strasbourg ministers are writing this in their own name, I shall hold off my attack, but if it is in the name of all who are included under the label of the 'gospel,' it is an utterly shameless lie. I, at any rate, spoke in general terms.

They deny they have left the church, since they were thrown out and banned from it by those whose life is such that it proves they are anything but members of the church.[638] I leave the defence against this to the emperor and Ferdinand who do consider themselves members of the church. But since they[639] teach that God alone knows who belongs to the church (except in so far as one is aware of it oneself), since they also teach that the nature of our works has no bearing on justification, how do they judge that those they oppose are estranged from the church? Is it from a disposition of their minds? This God alone knows. From their deeds? What they are matters nothing as long as faith is present.

They say that they are engaged in the same business as the apostles.[640] If that is true, then as often as we differ from them we must be Jews or idolatrous pagans. I do not know to what extent they have furthered the study of letters. They certainly burden them with no mean ill will. They humour all princes, bishops, and magistrates as far as they can without harming piety, but whatever does not come from them or is not approved by them harms piety. They shy away from all disturbance and sedition more than anyone, though only as long as no one opposes their design. They do not acknowledge that under the label of the 'gospel' there are those who serve their own belly. I could mention many such people whom they not only accept but look up to as leaders. And what wonder if among their number are those who embrace spendthrifts, profligates, and gamblers, since there are those who do the same themselves? I shall leave it to others to judge whether, trained in none of the liberal arts, putting no trust in evil people, they rely solely on their trust in Christ.

Hear now the dreadful exaggeration and weep! 'Erasmus raged,' he said, against such gentle lambs at whom a world in arms roars 'with dreadful lies, with persistent slanders, and like a battle trumpet sounding out to all the earth. Who is so mild,' he says, 'who so gentle in disposition and goodness that he would not think that arms should immediately be taken up

* * * * *

638 *Epistola apologetica* BOL I 220:20–4
639 The 'evangelicals'
640 *Epistola apologetica* BOL I 220:27–9; in this paragraph Erasmus responds line by line to BOL I 220:27–221:7.

against those who, confessing the saving gospel of Jesus Christ, live most wickedly, confound, overthrow, and destroy everything treacherously, replace the best with the worst, weaken the power of the princes, arm the masses against all the best people, whip up disturbances repeatedly, rush to battle without reason again and again, encourage all the worst people, are unmitigated tyrants towards the good, eradicate all religion so that paganism is the inevitable outcome. Can anyone count how many monstrous, savage, and entirely false accusations he hurls at us with such fierceness?'[641] This is what he says. Is this the voice of the gentlest lamb desiring to please all or rather that of a wolf summoning with his howling other wolves to the slaughter?

You may say that he, whoever he is, had learned rhetoric. But some allow orators to lie only when appropriate to place and with skill. Yet in an evangelical man it is utterly disgraceful. They themselves also admit that some live in an abandoned manner under the label of the 'gospel.' That they destroy everything by rebellion and replace the best with the worst is the verdict of many. I myself have only written that when they departed from the old ways they did not introduce anything better.[642] Although I wrote nothing about how they weakened the power of the princes, it will nevertheless seem to many that they have said so themselves and that this description fits those who revile the monarchs of the world with great insolence, who recognize neither pope nor their bishops and at the moment do not acknowledge the emperor as emperor. All I wrote is that it seemed to me that some of them were building a democracy.[643] That they were arming the people against the dignitaries did not come from my writings but from their own conscience. He nicely exaggerates the accusation that they rush to arms 'for no reason,' since I said, 'for trivial reasons.'[644]

That they support some people who live impure lives is evident, and they do not deny it. That they are nothing but tyrants[645] towards good people was nowhere written by me, but produced by him as a rhetorical exaggeration. Many say they wish to eradicate all religion; nowhere did I say so. He will most certainly nowhere read in my writing that I think paganism

* * * * *

641 *Epistola apologetica* BOL I 221:8–21, partly paraphrased
642 Cf *Epistola contra pseudevangelicos* above 230.
643 Allen Ep 2134:218
644 *Epistola contra pseudevangelicos* above 233
645 Cf *Adagia* I x 86: *Phalaridis imperium* CWE 32 273–4: 'used of those who make a cruel use of absolute power or of some authority entrusted to them.' See above n267.

is inevitable; I only said I feared that paganism will follow such dissolute
manners and casting doubt on everything.[646] What a dreadful exaggeration
of lies, how much ferocity, how much zeal to whip up sedition! And so
often he cries out at us: 'us, us' as though we wrote any of these remarks
against the Strasbourgers. Where in my writings is this ferocity? I treat my
own side almost more harshly and, while they are silent, he shouts.

They are wondrously aggrieved by my popularity and influence, although they make a sport of spitting on Erasmus. It annoys him that my
epistle about abandoning the sects should have been published at this
time.[647] It would not have appeared, had they left me alone. If my vin-
dication was untimely, it should be blamed on him who twice slung the
mud.[648] He calls those who undertook to translate my epistle into German
'enemies' not only of 'letters,' but even 'of all better judgment.'[649] However,
the magistrates who undertook that task against my advice consider themselves undeserving of those appellations.[650] They nicely excuse me alleging
that I did not invent such dreadful and splendid lies myself, but that I 'accepted' them 'with' foolish 'credulity from utterly untruthful and reckless
informants';[651] this despite the fact that everything I reported was either
general knowledge or based on specific information, much of it passed on
by fellow members in that sect. Let them adduce just one 'evangelical' endangered because of me; on the other hand, some I looked out for, and some
I helped from my own small assets. Yet he never stops repeating: 'dreadful, fierce, bloody, lies invented with unbelievable cruelty.'[652] Against his
person I shall say nothing, for I do not know for certain who he is, but certainly this book is utterly untruthful, and slanderous and treacherous, as
stupid as it is uninformed.

Please listen to this raving trickster: Erasmus 'assails those things
which have been conformed to the very word of God in so many regions
and communities, not through' those 'wicked deceits about the gospel, but
through its honest followers the most pious princes, the most worthy councillors, and with the consent and the desire of the better part of the common

* * * * *

646 Allen Ep 2134:208–9
647 *Epistola apologetica* BOL I 221:31–3, referring to the *Epistola contra pseudevangelicos*
648 Geldenhouwer
649 *Epistola apologetica* BOL I 221:29–31
650 The Freiburg magistrates got the *Epistola contra pseudevangelicos* translated into
     German; see C. Augustijn's introduction ASD IX-1 278.
651 *Epistola apologetica* BOL I 221:23–4
652 Cf *Epistola apologetica* BOL I 222:7–13.

people. Zürich, Basel, and Strasbourg are censured by name, and he calls their ministers patriarchs of the new church and bishops of the new gospel. And' we wish, he says, 'to defend here only those who' of course 'devote themselves wholeheartedly to the glory of Christ,' etc.[653] Oh rebellious spirit, let me reply briefly: if I were persuaded that you all followed the integrity of the gospel, I should be in your camp by now. Your discord among yourselves makes it quite clear that this is not the case. And if I were persuaded that whatever is changed is renewed according to the very word of God, I could not disapprove of it. Yet, since they never cease to assail the things which we have received for so many centuries, how many most pious princes, how many distinguished councillors, how many regions, how many cities, how many thousands of people are they holding up to abuse? They hold before us the gospel, Christ, the Spirit of Christ, and Scripture. I consider none of these lacking in the Catholic church.

But where did I censure Zürich? Is it because I wrote to a friend: 'As for Zwingli, how subversive his methods are' in Zürich?[654] Where do I censure Basel? Is naming a place enough to have censured it? Never have I hit out at a community, Strasbourg least of all, and yet the names of cities are repeated to create hostility. Those who 'shy away from sedition more than anyone' write these things. I call the ministers 'patriarchs of the new church' and 'bishops of the new gospel'[655] with, I think, somewhat more civility than those who call them heresiarchs. For they themselves lay claim to the appellation of bishop.[656] Don't they introduce a 'new gospel' when they interpret it differently from the way the church has interpreted it until now? The soul of Scripture is its meaning; agreement on words is vain if one disagrees about its sense. Nor can anything new exist unless the old is overturned.

Finally, where do I find the ministers guilty of lèse-majesté? I wrote in this way, they say, to Botzheim: 'Those who market themselves under the label of the gospel behave almost as if they have their sights set on wickedness, wealth, anarchy, or the right to embark on anything with impunity.'[657] Who could fail to see that this was not directed at the ministers, who are

* * * * *

653 *Epistola apologetica* BOL I 222:16–24
654 Ep 1496:83–4 to Melanchthon
655 Erasmus sarcastically refers to Capito as a bishop (Ep 1477B:18–19).
656 In *Epistola apologetica* BOL I 197:6–7 Bucer, in an effort to defend the evangelical clergy against Erasmus' accusations of greed, cites Paul's admonition in 1 Tim 3:2 that a bishop should be hospitable.
657 Cf *Epistola apologetica* BOL I 223:17–20, citing Allen Ep 2205:132–5.

more likely to come under the suspicion of desiring dominion rather than anarchy? This was said against the 'evangelical' people and not against all of them, since I add 'almost,' and finally against the pseudo-evangelicals whom they themselves despise. My words run like this: 'those who market themselves under the label of the gospel.' Why do the authentic heralds of the gospel – for so they wish to appear – take offence at something directed at those deceptively named 'evangelicals'? So, what prompted the complaint about 'the fierce and deadly slanders against us,' and 'aimed' against us?[658]

So often I am forced to hear 'us, us,' when it is not yet clear what kind of creature lurks beneath that syllable. And where is that 'rash anger which has driven out' of me 'any feeling of humanity'?[659] Those who repeatedly provoke the princes against themselves seem to be their own worst enemy. He who turns anything to slander, who leaves nothing untried to foster sedition, who so often and without justification chants: 'splendid lies, fierce slanders, insults against Christ,' now says: 'although we acted in such an artless and candid way.'[660] And lest that artless and candid fellow overlook anything, he produces for the public what I wrote to Oecolampadius: 'It would be best in the present state of things to receive from you neither praise nor blame; but if that is too much to ask, then I would prefer a lambasting to a eulogy and especially a eulogy addressed to "our friend."' 'Now,' he[661] says, 'since' we know for sure that 'we belong to Christ, we can' not 'wholeheartedly praise anyone unless we also regard that person as our own.'[662] Who they belong to I do not know, but I know what has been made publicly known about them. Under this condition I do not seek their wholehearted praise. What they declare as certain to them, to me is exceedingly ambiguous.

Finally, he himself admits that he criticizes me throughout the book. 'We are often compelled,' he says, 'not so much to marvel as to lament that so far so little evangelical vitality shines forth in his life, although he has been fortunate in being graced with such knowledge.'[663] But this is the very thing of which I complain, that few live up to the name of the gospel. This is the way he honours the city where he lives and writes. What the

* * * * *

658 *Epistola apologetica* BOL I 223:22–5
659 *Epistola apologetica* BOL I 223:30–1
660 *Epistola apologetica* BOL I 223:25–6
661 Bucer
662 *Epistola apologetica* BOL I 224:12–16
663 *Epistola apologetica* BOL I 224:20–2

intentions of the magistrates are, the Lord knows; about them I have never uttered anything.

He finds it extremely humorous to beg my forgiveness for conferring no magnificent titles on me but just calling me Erasmus (often in capital letters), repeatedly, however, using the name theologian to abuse me. But why does he leave out those illustrious titles? 'It was unsuitable,' he says, 'to confer titles of honour on one to whom we attribute such splendid lies and so many insults against Christ.'[664] How much leisure this buffoon had to chatter about such trifles! Later he apologizes for his want of eloquence and praises my matchless eloquence.[665] What eloquence did an extempore epistle have? Nevertheless, although in fact no rhetorical artifice was overlooked there, he yet declares about himself: 'It seemed good to the Lord for our cause to be like that of a remnant, that our side should be of no account and reveal the cross,'[666] and 'our cause relies on the truth alone and the inspiration of the spirit.'[667] If they really want that to be believed, they ought to publish different pamphlets.

Apologizing for his rather long-winded book he says: 'we had not quite realized how teeming with accusations Erasmus' epistle is.'[668] In fact, that spider[669] had not yet supplied the poison gathered everywhere from my published letters, and I recognize some of his turns of style. Moreover, unless I am mistaken, as to where he acquired the volume of letters, he bought it with my money. If such a great diligence in apologizing for things, however trifling, has seized him, why doesn't he apologize for the fact that (having confessed that he would answer the letter written to Vulturius) he spent a good bit of the book enlarging on what Vulturius had plucked from the volumes of my letters; that he diligently explained and emphasized the names which either lay hidden or were disguised, in order to spur everyone's pens against Erasmus; that he wrote a book in response to me to the East Frisians and the brethren of Lower Germany; and that the epistle in which he claims he will answer for his teaching and way of life abounds in so many tricks, so much abuse, and so many lies? Let him go now and count up the list of these points, and he will discover that the splendid lies of which he falsely accuses me really belong to him! They would do well if

* * * * *

664 *Epistola apologetica* BOL I 224:3–11
665 *Epistola apologetica* BOL I 224:29–33
666 *Epistola apologetica* BOL I 224:33–4
667 *Epistola apologetica* BOL I 225:1–2
668 *Epistola apologetica* BOL I 225:10–11
669 Geldenhouwer; see above n608.

they had proven what they promise, if they had kept their innocence in the face of good and ill report so that those who now disparage them would be shamed into silence.

I had come to the end of that very verbose book and thought that was also the end of his deceptions. But just as he began with deceit so he ended with deceit. The title-page left the authorship uncertain, the colophon indicated neither the printer nor the place of the volume's publication, and this makes it liable to the charge of being a clandestine edition, contrary to the edicts of the magistrates, by people who always obey the orders of the magistrates.[670] Appended was: 'Strasbourg, the twenty-first day before the calends of May, 1530,' so the reader who was paying little attention would think it published there, since it is the title of the volume written. Nevertheless, here too the imposture reveals itself, for there is no twenty-first day before the calends of May.[671] They have given us an excellent example for prejudging the book which they themselves admit was not going to please the magistracy! If this had not been the case, surely they would have included the name of the city. Moreover, it is clear from this that they acted with a bad conscience because they distrusted their own magistrates whom they regarded as favourable to their cause. They boast that they produced the book to further the 'gospel,' but several of the magistrates are wise enough to see that what they want facilitated is hindered by such writing and estranges those they wish to attract. So much for the infantile ditties of the *Epistola apologetica*!

For the rest, dearest friends, I entreat you, that no kind of false religion deceive your simplicity, that no one bewitch you to abandon the fellowship of the church, but (standing in the fear of God) look for the divine oracle from those whom the Lord wished to be at the helm of the church. It has not escaped their notice that many things which should be pruned away altogether and many things which should be corrected have crept into the church's usage, and the rulers are devoting their attention to this so that disturbances can be calmed down, corruption rectified, impiety curtailed. Countless things could be put right without disturbance by the personal

* * * * *

670 Cf *Epistola apologetica* BOL I 117:36–40; see C. Augustijn's introduction to *Epistola apologetica* BOL I 67–8.
671 According to the Roman style of dating, one would not count back twenty-one days from the calends, or first, of May, but rather would begin the count at the ides, or thirteenth, of April. Erasmus appears to be claiming that the author has been intentionally deceptive in the dating, and that the same can be surmised about the place of publication as well.

zeal of each individual. There are things which it is permissible to remedy through special ordinances of the people, just as bishops or magistrates can reduce the host of feast days, and they, too, can abolish the sordid type of mass-priests, the disgraceful wealth of priests can be restrained, lawless life curbed, and tyranny (if there is any) put down.

If anyone does not approve of the whole mob of monks, let him choose the best of the lot! If the whole class is displeasing, let each keep his children and wife away from their company! No one is compelled to make any donations or bequests to them. If each would ensure that in his parish there are suitable stewards of the divine word, the orders of the mendicants would be shut out without any tumult. If the chapters of canons turned to the study of sacred letters and to purity of life, they would cast great discredit on the monks who live impurely. Indeed, even the monks themselves can rehabilitate themselves if they strive to be what they are called to be.

Already the leaders of the church may easily relax certain things for the sake of public tranquillity, such as the obligation to fast and the prohibition of foods, even though I do not see how these things are burdensome. The eating of fish doesn't harm anyone, nor is one burdened by it, indeed the variety offers no little pleasure.[672] The pontifical law does not bind anyone for whom fasting is inconvenient because of age, poverty, health, or some other reason. If fasting benefits soul and body, why complain of a burden, especially when the church makes fasting more bearable by moving dinner to lunchtime. If someone is feeble-minded or demented, he should on both counts go to the doctor; if someone in his right mind has a good conscience, on both counts he can be a doctor for himself.

No one who does not need pontifical indulgences is compelled to give a penny; if the need is there, what ground is there for complaint? If someone finds he is ensnared by vows which he cannot fulfil without neglecting matters essential to his salvation, let him seek a release (obtained by many and obtained for very little). If one is not so ensnared, let him abstain from such vows; the only proviso is that fleshly licence should not be sought. How each can lighten the burden of confession is something we have shown in the *Exomologesis* (which has now seen two editions).[673] And before innovations

* * * * *

672 Readers of the 1526 colloquy 'A Fish Diet,' or Ἰχθυοφαγία CWE 40 675–762, might be surprised by this statement; there is in addition Erasmus' claim 'For fish he had such a loathing as a youth that at the mere smell of it he felt a severe headache and a touch of fever' (Ep 447:444–5). See also *De esu carnium* ASD IX-1 1–50.

673 The *Exomologesis sive modus confitendi* (LB V 145–70) was published by Froben in February of 1524 and again in March of 1530; cf Ep 1426.

are introduced, let the voice of the church be heard. Finally, if anyone is stronger in conscience (provided it is not an erroneous conscience), and his soul is not vexed, let him relish his strength, but not disturb the weaker conscience of others. Cleansing the state of the church as a whole will be a matter for the princes' care, through whom it can be done without tumult.

Meanwhile, see to it that you stay in the unity of the body, deviating neither to the right nor the left, keeping a careful watch against those whose seductive but pestilential 'talk eats away like canker.'[674] They bring up the evil life of the priests, they exaggerate the tyranny of the popes, they make much of the monks' absolute power, and they promise freedom of the spirit. This is the bait, but watch that beneath it doesn't lurk the death-bringing hook. Now, what is more stupid than to have hated wicked priests or monks so much that you make yourself worse than them and fail to make them any better? For there is no vice worse than heresy or schism. Even should luxury, lust, ambition, avarice, and whatever other crime there is besides be all united in one priest, one heresy outweighs this accumulation of vices. The state of affairs in human life has never been so happy that complaints did not abound, not only about the morals of priests and princes but also about those of the people. In different times, different vices prevailed, at no time were there none. Let our indignation at the priests be tempered by remembering that both they and all of us are human beings.

What cannot be endured any longer will be much more effectively cut away by the authority of the princes than by heaven knows what unskilled doctors, whose inappropriate medication does nothing but exacerbate the evil. Christ will do this more properly through Emperor Charles, endowed as he is with supreme power and supreme clemency, matched by his religion. The German princes will come to his assistance, and there are very many hopeful signs that the supreme pontiff will set his mind on the same aim. He has indicated his intention to do this. The improvement of the church will not succeed unless it begins from the top. Only the pope and emperor can achieve that, and Christ has inspired them with this intention, unless we are completely deceived.

Meanwhile, let us do penance for our earlier life and prepare ourselves for the coming kingdom of God. Let no one's rash arrogance incite you, nor should the chaotic state of affairs perturb you and make you lose heart. The church has not only weathered but also overcome worse storms in the past. What irremediable controversies troubled the world under Emperors Arcadius and Theodosius, when no place was free of Arians,

* * * * *

674 2 Tim 2:17

Origenists, Donatists, Circumcellions, Marcionists, Manichees, Anthropo-
morphists, Pelagians! These plagues were not, as now, restricted to ordinary people but embroiled the very leaders of the churches in implacable
ill will, and even the imperial courts were not left unscathed. Within the
same enclosure or, rather, within the palace walls the emperor had pagans,
Arians, Manichees, and orthodox, and yet by his authority and prudence
was able to preserve the public peace in the midst of such an unsettled state
of affairs. Without bloody battles step by step he cleansed the world of so
many monstrosities, first depriving the pagan and heretical temples of their
privileges, next removing the temples from the city when they incited rebellion, and in the end completely destroying all the sects. Moreover, the
invasions of the Huns, the Vandals, and the Goths exacerbated these evils.

How much more easily will Emperor Charles put an end to these evils,
since he has the agreement of all the kings, the compliance of the princes
(with a few exceptions), the consent of all the bishops and by far the greatest
part of the world, and also – in view of his exceptional piety of life there
can be no doubt – the favour of Christ. In the meantime, let nothing move
you from a right state of mind, but pray the Lord that he will deign to
restore tranquillity to us through his servants and representatives.

Freiburg im Breisgau, on the calends of August 1530.

AN ADMONITION AGAINST
LYING AND SLANDER

Admonitio adversus mendacium et obtrectationem

translated by
PETER MATHESON

annotated by
MANFRED HOFFMANN

Heinrich Eppendorf[1] hailed from the small village of Eppendorf near Freiberg in Meissen, Saxony, where his father, Nikolaus, most likely was a local judge and a hereditary reeve (*Erbschulze*), probably also a brewer and innkeeper.[2] After Latin school at Freiberg in Saxony, young Eppendorf earned his BA at the University of Leipzig in 1508. His prince, Duke George of Saxony, was persuaded to support the young man's studies.[3] In 1520 it was Eppendorf that Duke George sent to deliver a gift to Erasmus in Louvain, 'three lumps of native silver.'[4]

Having matriculated at Freiburg im Breisgau later in 1520, Eppendorf led a chequered life, and was eventually thrown out of town.[5] In 1522 he set out for Basel, where he joined the humanist circle and lived for a time in the household of Erasmus. Erasmus later said that Eppendorf 'forced himself on my acquaintance ... forced himself into my house when visitors came to see me,' and 'forced himself on me unasked as a travelling-companion' to visit Botzheim at Constance.[6] Nevertheless, he had admitted Eppendorf into his inner circle and considered him his close friend.

Heinrich Eppendorf pretended to be a nobleman, and most of his acquaintances took his word for it. Because, as he still maintained in early 1531, he 'was born in the region that received its name from my family,'[7] he wished to be called 'Heinrich von Eppendorf.'[8] No wonder, then, that

* * * * *

1 Secondary literature: introductions to Allen Epp 1122 and 1934, and Kaegi 'Hutten und Erasmus' 469–79 are still basic; C. Augustijn (ASD IX-1 97–101) enlarged the picture significantly, and B. Koennecker's biography (CEBR I 438–41) is a helpful addition; see also P.G. Bietenholz's annotation to Ep 1122 n5. Eppendorf was born c 1490 and died probably after 1551. B. Koennecker lists 1496 as his birth-year which is probably an error.
2 For this and the following, see Kaegi 'Hutten und Erasmus' 469–71.
3 On George of Saxony (1471–1539), the duke of the Albertine line of Saxony as distinct from the Ernestine line of Saxony (Elector Frederick III and Elector John), see CEBR III 205–8. Erasmus later states that, according to Petrus Mosellanus, 'it was on recommendation from me that Duke George first gave him 100 florins to complete his studies' (Ep 1437:13–15).
4 Epp 1122:12–18, 1125:57–9
5 H. Schreiber *Geschichte der Albert-Ludwigs-Universität zu Freiburg im Breisgau* (Freiburg 1857–66) II 100.
6 Ep 1437:18–21
7 *Iusta querela* EB 2 451:22–3; in the beginning of February 1528 Erasmus reported, ironically, that Eppendorf feared the seizure of his 'paternal castles' by an angry Duke George (Allen Ep 1934:146).
8 Erasmus called him 'ab Eppendorf' in the revision of his 1521 *Epistolae ad diversos* but in the 1529 *Opus epistolarum* the 'ab' was deleted (Ep 1122 n5).

Erasmus at first considered him a nobleman, a knight, and 'a kinsman of Hutten.'[9] After the publication of the *Spongia*, however, friends in Saxony made it clear that the man Erasmus now distrusted was in fact 'of humble origin.'[10]

Before the controversy with Hutten in 1523, Erasmus had nothing but praise for his friend Eppendorf. On 25 May 1522 he wrote from Basel to Duke George, 'My one comfort in these great troubles is Heinrich Eppendorf, a young man both scholarly and civilized, whose character attests his noble birth.'[11] On 5 December 1522 Erasmus worried that letters to Duke George were being intercepted, but there was as yet no indication that he suspected Eppendorf.[12] In the letter to Laurinus on 1 February 1523 – the one that triggered Hutten's *Expostulatio* – Erasmus continued to praise Eppendorf, '. . . besides his lineage and his learning [he] is a most charming person.'[13]

Meanwhile Hutten, in Basel since late November, was openly critical of Erasmus. He then departed for Mulhouse, where he vented his anger in the *Expostulatio*. It was Eppendorf who took the manuscript to Strasbourg, where Johann Schott published it in late June (or early July) 1523.[14] But with Erasmus in Basel and Hutten in Mulhouse, Eppendorf, ostensibly a friend of both, was a natural go-between. Erasmus did not realize at the time that Eppendorf was taking an active, if not leading, part in shaping the course of events.

Eppendorf increasingly sided with Hutten, and seems to have found a way to help him in his battle with Erasmus. While studying at Freiburg, Eppendorf had bought in March 1522 a copy of Erasmus' *Epistolae ad diversos* (August 1521). As he read them he made marginal notes that disclose what he was thinking. Instead of claiming Erasmus as a German hero, as

* * * * *

9 See *Spongia* above 47 n53 and Ep 1437:88 where Erasmus called Eppendorf *generosus* (of noble birth) and *cognatus* (kinsman). Erasmus continued to identify him, more or less ironically, as a 'knight'; see Ep 1371:1; Allen Epp 1901:6, 1933:1, 1934:351.

10 Mosellanus: 'How can he be a kinsmen, when it is well known that he is a man of humble origin?' (Ep 1437:89–90); Emser: 'he was born in a peasant hut in our part of the world' (Ep 1551:27–31).

11 Ep 1283:16–18

12 Later in April 1524, Erasmus suspected Eppendorf of intercepting George's letter and gift 'worthy of a king' (Ep 1437:95–100); cf introduction to Ep 1313, and Ep 1325:8–9.

13 Ep 1342:370–1

14 See above 24 (introductory note to *Spongia*), and *Spongia* 41–5.

he formerly did, he now reproached him bitterly. One sees too his rancour against Egmond, Hoogstraten, and Johann Faber, stalwarts of Catholic orthodoxy with whom Erasmus kept up a civil correspondence. By contrast, there are his frequent positive references to Hutten, and words of passionate admiration for Luther. According to P.S. Allen, who discovered these notes, Eppendorf wrote them, 'for the most part during the period of [his] close association with Erasmus in 1522–3.'[15]

Though still unaware of what Eppendorf was up to, Erasmus was suspicious. His comments in the *Spongia* (written in the second half of July 1523) and in the letters of that period show a growing distrust. In fact, during the Hutten controversy, Eppendorf kept Erasmus in the dark, or deceived him. He played down Hutten's anger about Erasmus' refusing to see him,[16] and he most likely failed to deliver the message that Erasmus would, after all, accept a visit from Hutten.[17] All that Hutten knew was that Erasmus had initially refused to receive him.[18] As to the extortion, there is first of all no doubt that both Hutten and Eppendorf were hard pressed for money: 'they were both at their last gasp'[19] and needed funds. They evidently extracted money from friends of Erasmus (Froben, Bentius, and Botzheim) and from Erasmus himself in exchange for the promise to suppress the publication of the *Expostulatio*.[20]

By 19 July 1523, shortly before writing the *Spongia*, Erasmus had decided that 'Heinrich Eppendorf is the skilled hand behind this story.'[21] While Eppendorf denied any connection with the *Expostulatio*,[22] Erasmus

* * * * *

15 See Allen 4 615–19 app 14; *Spongia* 108 n408. Cf ASD IX-1 104:71n for C. Augustijn's thorough list of parallels between Eppendorf's marginal notes and the *Expostulatio*.
16 See *Spongia* above 34, 41, 51; cf Allen Ep 1934:252–8.
17 There is no indication from the *Expostulatio* that Eppendorf relayed the point that Hutten would be welcome, if he could tolerate a cold room, since Erasmus could not abide a room-stove. See *Spongia* above 39–40; cf Allen Ep 1934:275–83.
18 See *Spongia* above 45; cf Kaegi 'Hutten und Erasmus' 465–8, 474–5; *Spongia* above nn9 and 38.
19 Ep 1383:4, 1437:54–5
20 See *Spongia* above 44; Epp 1383:5, 1437:45–55; Allen Ep 1934:297–338; cf *Spongia* above nn29, 36, 606, 629; C. Augustijn ASD IX-1 102:58n.
21 To Pirckheimer Ep 1376:27–9 (Allen Ep 1376:26). Erasmus describes this controversy as a 'drama' (*fabula*) with Eppendorf as the 'master,' 'choreographer,' 'author,' or 'trickster' behind the story; cf for instance *Spongia* above nn70, 89, 264; Ep 1437:36; Allen Epp 1934:12–13, 1992:301.
22 Ep 1377:2–3

suspected him of having instigated Hutten to write the book, and of having supplied quotations from his works that Hutten could attack.[23] In the second preface to the *Spongia* (c October 1523, after Hutten's death) Erasmus asserted, without naming names, but obviously having Eppendorf in mind, that 'certain persons ... deliberately [have] seen to it' that he and Hutten 'should never meet and talk.'[24] Thus by the time he wrote the *Spongia* Erasmus was willing to believe that Eppendorf had deliberately engineered the breach between himself and Hutten.[25]

Despite the annotations in Eppendorf's copy of the *Epistolae ad diversos*, it is possible that he at first tried to mediate between the two and only afterwards fell increasingly under Hutten's spell. Perhaps because Erasmus was slow in discovering Eppendorf's duplicity, he then became so suspicious that he antedated its beginnings to the end of November 1522, or even earlier.[26] Moreover, because of Eppendorf's spurious claim to nobility and his habit of extracting money from friends and patrons, Erasmus now considered him deceitful by nature. To put it mildly, he seemed to dislike Eppendorf more than Hutten. As if to burnish the reputation of Hutten, dead by now, it may have been convenient for Erasmus to believe that both he and Hutten were duped by Eppendorf.[27] In the ensuing flow of incrimination and recrimination back and forth, Erasmus' jibes and lampoons seem to have outweighed in number and intensity the reproaches of Eppendorf. He mercilessly taunted Eppendorf, even after the arbitration of 1528 was supposed to have settled the matter. After Hutten's death (August 1523) Eppendorf withdrew to Strasbourg, where he made a living over the years by translating classical and other texts into German; he produced no controversial writing,[28] save for the *Iusta querela* 1531 in response to Erasmus'

* * * * *

23 Ep 1437:28–9; cf Kaegi 'Hutten und Erasmus' 473:4n and C. Augustijn ASD IX-1 103:67n. Erasmus reports in the *Spongia*, above 137 n606, that Hutten admits that Eppendorf advised him not to publish the *Expostulatio*. See also Ep 1383: 2–4.

24 Ep 1389:24–5 (above 34).

25 Epp 1376:27–9, 1384:2–4, 1389:29–30 (above 34), 1437:45–9; cf *Spongia* above 98.

26 Ep 1437:20–6; Allen Ep 1934:246–9

27 See Kaegi 'Hutten und Erasmus' 509.

28 *Kurtzweise und höffliche Sprüch* (Plutarch's *Apophthegmata*) 1534; *Römischer Historien Bekürtzung* 1536; *Türckischer Kayser Ankunfft, Kryeg und Handlung gegen und wider die Christen* 1540; translation of Pliny's *Naturalis historia* 1543; translation of Albert Krantz's Latin chronicle of Sweden and Denmark 1545–6; etc.

Admonitio adversus mendacium. The fact that he lived in Strasbourg, a centre of South German Protestantism,[29] did not sit well with Erasmus. For his part, even though Eppendorf kept the respect of close friends of Erasmus like Beatus Rhenanus, Boniface Amerbach, and Paul Volz,[30] he found ways to pursue the quarrel – he charged Erasmus with defamation of character and went so far as to challenge him to a duel and threaten him with a noose.[31] According to Erasmus, he also suborned his friends to send 'forged letters under false names,' and he managed to intercept mail to and from Duke George.[32]

Following the publication of the *Spongia*, Erasmus gave free rein to his animus against Eppendorf. A confidential letter to Conradus Goclenius (April 1524) that contained a lengthy attack on Eppendorf, denouncing him as 'a rascal born for every sort of chicanery and virulence ... all the time plotting trouble ... a rogue ... a half-witted hero ... the greatest rascal.'[33] In May 1524, replying to a letter in which Erasmus apparently sought to incriminate Eppendorf, Duke George was cautious but 'rather indignant' about Eppendorf's behaviour.[34] George was reluctant to recall or punish his subject, but Eppendorf himself was said to be convinced 'that Erasmus has set the prince's mind against him.'[35]

Erasmus also thought that his erstwhile friend in Strasbourg, Wolfgang Capito, had been 'taken in by Eppendorf's tricks.'[36] By August 1524 he believed that Strasbourg's whole company of 'gospellers' were plotting against him, but specifically Capito, 'the bishop of your new gospel,' since he was the one who kept company with 'this wholly disreputable bankrupt [Eppendorf].' Addressing Capito directly on 2 September 1524, Erasmus blamed him for collusion with Eppendorf and Brunfels: 'So much points to it that I know rather than suspect it is you who stirs up Eppendorf to

* * * * *

29 See the introductory note to *Epistola ad fratres Inferioris Germaniae* above.
30 BRE Epp 275, 295, 343, 348
31 Epp 1377:3–5, 1496:132, 1551:29–31
32 Epp 1437:82–4, 1429:10–26, 1437:95–101, 1543:10–13
33 Ep 1437:10–1, 22, 67, 91, 100–1. Conrad Goclenius (c 1489–1539), a native of Westphalia who seems to have studied in Deventer before matriculating at Louvain, was from 1579 professor of Latin at the Collegium Trilingue and an intimate friend of Erasmus. See CEBR II 109–111.
34 Ep 1448, 1521:3. Erasmus' letter is not extant. This content of this letter later on became the bone of contention in the Eppendorf-Erasmus quarrel of 1528–31.
35 Ep 1449:51–2; cf Allen Ep 2124:25–34.
36 Ep 1437:106–7

attack me as you did Otto before.'[37] Erasmus wrote in a similar vein to Melanchthon on 6 September 1524: He has 'ugly suspicions' about Capito; and refers to Eppendorf under the caustic nickname 'Thraso from Planodorp' or 'the braggart' – a mockery that was frequently repeated.[38]

Mutual recrimination between the two men continued for several years. Then in 1528 the controversy came to second head when Eppendorf decided to bring a court action against Erasmus. He had managed to get hold of a letter from the spring of 1524 in which Erasmus complained to Duke George, and suggested that he call the 'young man, endowed as he otherwise is with good gifts of nature, back from years of idle and extravagant living to some respectable function.'[39] Duke George's reply indicates that he took Erasmus' message to heart: 'When I recall the virtues which you once described him as possessing, it seems to me impossible to imagine a more exquisite example of an abandoned man whose conscience and sense of shame have gone to rack and ruin.'[40]

For Eppendorf, however, Erasmus' denunciations amounted to character assassination, the more so as Duke George's favour was vital for his livelihood. He acknowledged having sent three letters threatening Erasmus with 'duel and noose,' or 'sword and gallows,' and a reopening of the 'Hutten tragedy.'[41] But he was angered by a letter from his sovereign ordering him to stop harassing Erasmus.[42] Hence Eppendorf resolved to travel to

* * * * *

37 Ep 1485:2–3; on Capito see *Spongia* 42 n19.

38 Ep 1496:120–32. On Thraso see *Spongia* above 132 n569 and *Epistola ad fratres Inferioris Germaniae* 333 n441. Planodorp is a derisive construction of Erasmus turning Eppendorf into Evendorf (level or plains village). Erasmus uses Thraso of Planodorp increasingly and at the end almost exclusively; cf Allen Epp 1934:80–1, 2111:28, 2188:10, 2191:106.

39 Erasmus' letter to George from the spring 1524 is lost; only George's reply is extant (Ep 1448); but Erasmus mentioned this sentence in his letter to Pirckheimer on 1 May 1528 (Allen Ep 1992:36–8). This statement is the only part of the letter that Erasmus ever acknowledged to Eppendorf; cf Allen Ep 1934:23–43.

40 Ep 1448:30–7; George's letter also urges Erasmus in no uncertain terms 'to prove to the world by an open confrontation with Luther what your opinions really are and at the same time defend the church from a most abominable heresy' (Ep 1448:57–60).

41 All three are not extant, but cf Allen Ep 1934:48, 101, 174; see also Epp 1377:3–5, 1449:67–8.

42 Allen Epp 1929:11–12, 1934:35, 203–4, and 489, 1940:1, 1943:6, 1992:106, 191, and 215

Basel and talk with Erasmus; if he could not impose silence on him, he would go to law.[43]

Arriving in Basel at the end of January 1528, he met on the first evening with Beatus Rhenanus, and unburdened himself.[44] In the morning he saw one of the burgomasters (who informed him that the town council was too busy to hear a law suit); afterwards he visited Erasmus, who was joined by Beatus and others. A bitter altercation between Eppendorf and Erasmus ensued. As Eppendorf left, he promised to send his terms; they in fact arrived on 1 February 1528.[45] Beatus Rhenanus was able to preclude a formal trial by convincing the two antagonists that an arbitration by Boniface Amerbach and himself was the better course of action. Both sides agreed. Erasmus immediately invited Boniface Amerbach and Beatus Rhenanus to meet with him in Ludwig Baer's house, but the actual arbitration took place the next day, 3 February 1528, in Erasmus' own rooms,[46] with Boniface Amerbach and Beatus Rhenanus present as arbitrators and Ludwig Baer and Henricus Glareanus as witnesses.

Eppendorf demanded that Erasmus 1/ write a letter to Duke George retracting the (alleged) charges against him and restoring him to the prince's favour; 2/ write a book to exonerate him and dedicate it to him; and 3/ hand out 100 ducats compensation to the poor in Basel plus 200 ducats to be distributed among the poor in Strasbourg at Eppendorf's discretion. If these terms were met, Eppendorf promised to suppress publication of what he had written against Erasmus. Erasmus, for his part, agreed to write a mitigating letter to the prince and to compose a book with a dedication to Eppendorf, provided they could be friends again. But he refused to acknowledge the letter Eppendorf had produced and rejected compensating the plaintiff with such an enormous sum of money – a demand that certainly smacked of another extortion.[47]

Eppendorf agreed with everything but Erasmus' refusal to pay. As Erasmus probably had expected, the whole matter came down to haggling over money, so they turned to the arbitrators. Their decision was that

* * * * *

43 Erasmus gives a detailed account in his letter to Botzheim from Basel, 1 February 1528 (Allen Ep 1934); nicely paraphrased in Allen Ep 1934 introduction.
44 Allen Ep 1934:6–8, 19; on Beatus Rhenanus see *Spongia* above 41 n15.
45 Allen Epp 1934:19–22, 157–62, and 463–86, 1992:169–207; *Admonitio adversus mendacium* below 382–3.
46 Cf Allen Epp 1933, 1992:279–86; and *Admonitio adversus mendacium* below 384; on Ludwig Baer see *Spongia* above n66.
47 Allen Ep 1934:180–99, 463–85; *Admonitio adversus mendacium* below 376–7.

Erasmus pay twenty florins to be dispensed among the poor at their discretion.[48] Erasmus and Eppendorf signed the agreement. To show his good will Erasmus threw a dinner party on the next day, 4 February 1528. When Eppendorf was about to leave at 9:00 pm he insisted that Erasmus write the promised letter to Duke George and the dedication to the promised book. Erasmus, already in bed, reluctantly agreed and dashed off the pieces.[49]

This was not the end of things. Erasmus' letter to Duke George resulted in Eppendorf's again being commanded not to bother Erasmus. Yet Eppendorf, as if oblivious to his prince's wishes, escalated his demands, requiring financial reparations beyond the agreement of 3 February.[50] He also insisted that Erasmus meet his obligation to write a book and dedicate it to him.[51] But Erasmus declared that he never received Eppendorf's letter of June 1528. On 1 October 1528 Boniface Amerbach sought to excuse Erasmus: He had no time to write something for Eppendorf because he was busy with editing Augustine and Seneca – an excuse that Erasmus himself amplified and repeated to Eppendorf in January 1529.[52]

To his friends Erasmus told a different story. In a letter to Pirckheimer (1 May 1528), he not only gave an account of the whole affair but also revealed his true reasons for not living up to his part of the bargain: Eppendorf had failed to comply with the stipulation that friendship be restored. He also did not cease causing trouble, for he and the evangelicals spread the rumour that he had confronted Erasmus so forcefully that Erasmus had to submit to degrading conditions. Erasmus had been defeated and Eppendorf had won the day.[53]

In the beginning of 1529 Erasmus still had not dedicated a book to Eppendorf.[54] In fact, he never did. Instead, he marshalled his skills in sarcasm and ridicule. In September 1528 he lampooned Eppendorf in his *Adagia* as a German *Junker* living beyond his means: Ornithoplutus von

* * * * *

48 Allen Epp 1937, 1992:279–89. Both Spanish ducats and Venetian ducats have a higher gold content than the Rhenish florin or Rhine gulden: see John Munroe's essay on coinage to be published with CWE 14. But in common parlance the terms florin and ducat were sometimes used interchangeably.
49 Allen Epp 1940, 1941; see Allen Ep 1992:287–90, 378–80.
50 Allen Ep 1950
51 Allen Ep 2086 is perhaps a reply to Eppendorf's letter of June 1528, which Erasmus declared he had never received; see also Allen Ep 2099, Eppendorf's response to 2086.
52 Allen Ep 2086:27–40
53 Allen Epp 1992:13–14, 222–6, and 335–7, 1991:22–7, 2086:14–16
54 Allen Ep 2086:28

Isocômum.[55] Some months later, in March 1529, Eppendorf was recognizable as the target of a colloquy entitled Ἱππεὺς ἄνιππος *sive Ementita nobilitas*
'The Knight without a Horse, or, Feigned Nobility.'[56]

To set the record straight about who had bested whom in this controversy, Erasmus published towards the end of 1530 an expanded version of his 1 May 1528 letter to Pirckheimer,[57] entitled *Admonitio adversus
mendacium et obtrectationem.*[58] The *Admonitio adversus mendacium* gave an account of the whole negotiation interspersed with self-serving remarks and
self-justifying arguments about the reasons for Erasmus' behaviour, especially his non-compliance with the requirement to dedicate a book to Eppendorf. Eppendorf's reply, *Iusta querela*, came out surprisingly fast in February
1531.[59] Reporting the conflict from different perspectives, the two accounts,
Admonitio adversus mendacium and *Iusta querela*, do not altogether agree.

Eventually, Duke George charged Julius Pflug, his irenic counsellor,
with settling the Eppendorf affair. While Erasmus suspected for a while that
Pflug might fall for Eppendorf,[60] Pflug accomplished the nearly impossible;
he was able to bring the two enemies to agree on a truce and to pledge
to keep silence.[61] The public dispute between Erasmus and Eppendorf was
over.

MH

* * * * *

55 *Adagia* I ix 44: *Proterviam fecit* 'He has made a clean sweep' CWE 32 204–5. Ornithoplutus (Fowl-rich, Hühnreich, = Heinrich) of Isocômus (Equal- or Even-
village, = Eppendorf); see CWE 32 358 n5; Allen Ep 2129:28–9.
56 ASD I-3 612–19; see C.R. Thompson CWE 40 880–90.
57 Allen Ep 1992
58 Freiburg: Johann Faber Emmeus (?) 1530; LB X 1683–92.
59 Haguenau: Johann Setzer 1530; EB II 447–54; cf BRE Ep 275.
60 Allen Ep 2400:11–15, 2406:38–42; cf 2395.
61 Allen Ep 2450:3–7; cf 2451

AN ADMONITION AGAINST
LYING AND SLANDER

Rumour, as Virgil wrote, is 'the swiftest of monsters, as persistent in pretence and perversion as in conveying the truth.'[1] I doubt whether this has ever been truer of a century than of our most garrulous one, in which some boast that the gospel has been reborn.[2] Who, I beg you, are those evil, idle chatterers, who spread the news rapidly through virtually all Germany that Erasmus was treated by Heinrich Eppendorf harshly and was reconciled with him only on horrible conditions?[3] Even if this were partly true, what is there that makes those who market themselves under the banner of the gospel[4] jump for joy, exult, and triumph – those who begin everything with a prayer for grace and peace? Let them imagine that Eppendorf was injured by me, let them imagine that I was injured by him, let them imagine that each was injured by the other, and finally let them imagine that none of the offences took place at all but that our harmony was disrupted by human suspicion and by the tittle-tattle of sycophants. Is it right for me to be polemical in this matter, or should I rather offer congratulations that harmony has been mended on both sides? Where is that spirit of the gospel that is always swimming on their lips? Where the peace that is portrayed in the Epistles? Where the Christian charity that does not rejoice in anyone's wrongdoing but delights in everyone's well-being?[5]

* * * * *

1 *Aeneid* 4.174–88
2 Cf *Epistola contra pseudevangelicos* above 229.
3 Allen Epp 1991:22–36, 1992:1–7. Erasmus targets here not only the upper-Rhenish 'evangelicals,' but also the German 'Lutherans' in general. He mocks the 'evangelicals' by calling them 'pseudo-evangelicals,' even 'diabolicals' (Ep 1437:111–13).
4 Cf *Epistola ad fratres Inferioris Germaniae* above 331.
5 Allen Ep 1992:1–13

They applaud the victory of Eppendorf. Why? There was some reason for them to applaud Hutten's audacity, and it would have been deserved had his temerity been successful. For he professed himself a champion of the gospel truth, though in fact no one harmed their gospel more. But, leaving that aside, why are they so concerned about Eppendorf? Have they convinced themselves that he has taken Hutten's place, believing that just as he was so close to him when he was alive, so now he vigorously protects his reputation when dead? Since I have never detected this desire in him, I do not think he expresses it. But let us suppose it is so, what has it to do with the evangelical cause? Unless, perchance, whatever makes trouble for Erasmus gives them pleasure. But to delight in the misfortunes of others, even though you gain nothing from it, indicates truly diabolical malice and could not be further from the spirit of the gospel.[6] I shall now show how futile it was for them to tickle their fancy in that manner. I had in fact decided to swallow these inanities in silence,[7] especially since so much else had to be done.[8] However, because I can see no end to their lying, I shall now summarize in good faith what actually happened; I do not think it is more in my interest than Eppendorf's.

Almost three years ago Eppendorf arrived in Basel.[9] Somehow or other a rumour spread at once through the city that he intended to take Erasmus to court and that he was uttering terrible threats. Knowing that he had no reason to go to law with me, I decided to ignore the fellow's threats. Friends, however, agreed on a way to settle whatever was disputed between us privately.[10] They pointed out, too, that the leaders in the council were fervently attached to teachings of Oecolampadius that I openly opposed.[11]

* * * * *

6 Allen Ep 1992:13–22
7 Allen Epp 1992:23–6, 1937:7–9
8 Erasmus worked primarily on his edition of Augustine and Seneca. Cf Allen Epp 1934 introduction, 1991:65–7, 2086:27–40.
9 For the following account, see Allen Ep 1934:4–165.
10 Earlier, Erasmus also attempted to settle the dispute with Hutten privately rather than publicly; cf Ep 1356. In a private settlement the laws of friendship would prevail instead of the laws of the court.
11 Cf Epp 1620:97–100, 1636; see introductory note to *Detectio praestigiarum* above 151 n21. While Erasmus found Oecolampadius' Eucharistic theology generally appealing, he rejected it because it was 'at variance with the general opinion of the church.' Oecolampadius' book was banned in Basel, but his influence in the city became so strong that he was eventually able to bring it over to the Reformation. Erasmus left Basel in 1529 and took up residence in Freiburg.

So they feared that, however good my case, I might not have altogether
impartial judges. For my part, I was not too worried, but it did strike me
that I would be ill-prepared for such a battle, being an outsider, an old man,
an invalid, unfamiliar with the [legal] language, and unpractised in public
affairs. For up to that time I had never brought charges against anyone,
nor had I been accused by anyone. A final consideration was that I was
overwhelmed at the time by so much work that it almost killed me. I felt
sorry, too, for the friends on whose patronage I would have had to rely. I
would have had to run to and fro[12] but I have always been anxious to be
as little trouble to my friends as possible.

On their advice, therefore, an initiative was taken to settle the quarrel.
Eppendorf came to my chamber.[13] Beatus Rhenanus and Ludwig Baer were
also present.[14] He produced a letter – the cause of all the animosity – that
he thought I had written to the most illustrious Duke George of Saxony.[15]
As far as I remember, the gist of that letter was that the duke should call the
young man back from his idle and extravagant living to his native country
and entrust him with a position in which he could put his distinguished
talents to work.[16] However, it contained certain remarks that seemed gravely
to offend him, especially where it said that he had passed himself off as
a noble though he was a commoner,[17] and that he presented himself as the
leader and protagonist of a most wretched band of evangelicals.[18] When
he had read out the letter I replied that I did not recognize it as mine,
and that there was no need for me to answer for another. It was written
in an unknown hand, it did not bear my signature or the imprint of the
ring with which I am accustomed to seal letters and finally there was no
date or year on it. What I could remember having written to the duke
I acknowledged.[19] But since I did not remember all that was written in
the letter, I was under no obligation to acknowledge it unless he would

* * * * *

12 *Adagia* I iii 84: *Ultro citroque* CWE 31 302:1–11
13 Amerbach invited Erasmus to Baer's house (Allen Ep 1933), but the actual
    confrontation between Erasmus and Eppendorf took place in Erasmus' house
    (Allen Ep 1992:279–86). The two antagonists evidently met first at Baer's house
    (2 Feb 1528) and the next day at Erasmus' house.
14 Beatus Rhenanus and Boniface Amerbach were the two arbitrators; Ludwig
    Baer and Henricus Amerbach were witnesses.
15 Not extant; George's reply is Ep 1448.
16 See introductory note above n39.
17 Allen Ep 1934:94–135
18 Allen Epp 1934:66–77, 1940:9–10, 1992:15–17
19 See above n16.

convince me by producing my handwriting and my seal[20] – even though handwriting can sometimes be forged and a seal, stolen from somewhere, affixed.

When the disagreement appeared to become rancorous, those present urged us to set aside our mutual accusations so that steps could be taken to end our grievances. I confessed to being much more inclined to this than to litigation. There began some discussion about terms. Eppendorf replied that he was rather upset at the moment but that he would hand these over to Beatus Rhenanus in written form the next day. Beatus passed on to me the charges of Eppendorf in his own hand, and I append a verbatim copy of it here.[21]

THE CHARGES OF HEINRICH EPPENDORF

1/ He betrayed me not only to the prince, who lawfully seems to have jurisdiction over my life and death, but also to a number of private citizens. For that reason our good name is in peril and it is incumbent upon him to make amends for this, something that will hardly be achieved by a letter or two but will require the dedication to me of a pamphlet of his, wherein he prudently takes the heat out of this affair so that it is beyond his scandalmongering and the reader is left with no suspicion about me. I have otherwise no great desire for dedications of this kind.

2/ Let him write to the prince or the court, where I know his letter circulated, and restore their former esteem for me. However, the letter first must pass through my hands, lest his innuendos and ambiguities do more to aggrieve me than to rehabilitate me.

3/ He really tried to ruin me, an innocent man, and fabricated the story about me that I was forced to leave Freiburg after causing a riot – though the city knows otherwise and all the citizens can testify to my upright conduct. For the injury done to my good name in that place let him donate one hundred ducats, and do the same in this city, and certainly two hundred ducats in Strasbourg, which I shall carry off and distribute to the needy as I see fit. All

* * * * *

20 Allen Epp 1934:39–41, 1992:59–60. Erasmus' ring and seal were engraved with the image of Terminus, the Roman god of boundaries and property limits. He received the ring in 1509 from young Alexander Stewart, archbishop of St Andrews, and added the motto *Concedi nulli* which he understood as a reminder of the finality of death rather than as an expression of personal intransigence. Cf CWE 2 150; Epp 604 n4, 1558:24–32; Allen Ep 2018; and J.K. McConica 'The Riddle of "Terminus"' *Erasmus in English* 2 (1971) 2–7.
21 Allen Ep 1934:463–86; cf Allen Ep 1992:169–207.

these things are to be done for the sake of my integrity and innocence. Even if the damage my reputation has suffered is immeasurable, I willingly forgive, as much because of his former goodness towards me as out of piety, if he agrees to the above. But if Erasmus objects, let him know that I would rather put my life in peril than my reputation.

I replied to this in my own hand, and append an exact copy:[22]

THE RESPONSE OF ERASMUS OF ROTTERDAM

1/ I do not recognize the letter that he read out, nor do I think that I wrote in this way, nor can I find a copy of it in my papers. And if the letter of the duke were brought to light, it would confirm that I did not write in this way. I only urged the duke to recall him from his idleness to an honourable position, or at least to ensure that he leaves me in peace. As to the dedication of a pamphlet, I will not begrudge it if I see evidence of a friendlier disposition on his part, and I will do more than that in the name of friendship.

2/ How angry his prince is I do not know, nor am I aware of the reasons for his anger. Eppendorf treated Emser as his mortal enemy in the presence of the prince.[23] If my complaint made the prince more antagonistic towards him I shall not begrudge writing courteously and playing this down so far as this is permissible with such great princes.

3/ As to the alms, I shall see to them myself as God prompts me to do so. It is no business of mine how he lived here or at Freiburg. The holier his life the happier I am. As to the gold ducats that he demands be given him, he would do well to keep silent lest it seems that it is on this account that he is threatening court action. Let him behave in a friendly manner and stop stirring up people against me, and I will vie with him in courtesy. I can be of much more benefit to him through my good services than if I gave him two hundred ducats.

He found my response to the first two articles acceptable but about the third there was considerable dispute until we agreed on Doctor Boniface Amerbach and Beatus Rhenanus as arbiters,[24] and more learned and principled men could scarcely have been found in the city, as Eppendorf does not deny. As witnesses to his good character Doctor Ludwig Baer and Henricus

* * * * *

22 Allen Ep 1934:487–505; cf Allen Ep 1992:208–41.
23 Cf Allen Ep 1934:151–3.
24 Cf Allen Ep 1934:163–5; on Beatus Rhenanus see (*Spongia* above 41 n15) and CEBR I 104–9; on Bonifacius Amerbach see CEBR I 42–6.

Glareanus were summoned.[25] The meeting was in my chamber. Before giving his finding Amerbach asked whether or not we would abide by the arbiters' judgment. We both replied that we would. The written judgment was read out. A word for word copy of it is appended.[26]

THE DECISION OF THE ARBITERS

Inasmuch as you have both agreed to give us the right to settle the dispute between you amicably, it is our view that to avoid annoyance and to foster Christian concord Desiderius Erasmus should implement the first two articles as he has pledged in his writing. As to the third article, in the same spirit he will not begrudge giving about twenty florins to be dispensed for the assistance of the poor at our discretion. And we consider these things should be done without blaming one side or the other, so that once the offences, complaints, and suspicions on both sides have been dispelled, the only rivalry between you will be one of good will, all that is past being forgotten, as if nothing had ever been said or done. Let D. Heinrich Eppendorf suppress anything he wrote, and we leave it open to both parties whether they wish to exchange some sign of good will or simply indicate their agreement. Basel, the day after the Purification, in the year of the Lord 1528.

                                        B. RHENANUS AND B. AMERBACH

Afterwards we were asked once again whether the decision was acceptable. Both replied that it was. And to confirm what had been done, we both added our signatures to the arbitration and both received a copy of the arbitration from the arbiters. After this, having broken bread, we both drank from the same cup, offered one another the right hand, and took our leave. The next day I put on dinner for everyone so that there was no lack of proof of our restored good relations.[27] This was how the affair was settled.

I have no idea at all who was responsible (though it is established that it was before Eppendorf left Basel) but a rumour spread among the entire populace that Erasmus was forced by Eppendorf to terms he was unwilling to accept involving many thousands of ducats. And soon the horrible rumour coursed throughout Germany that Erasmus had been treated by Eppendorf in a dreadful manner. The world soon resounded with these quite

* * * * *

25 Cf Allen Ep 1934:279–83; on Ludwig Baer see CEBR I 84–6; on Henricus Glareanus see CEBR II 105–8.
26 Allen Ep 1937
27 Allen Ep 1992:280–8

baseless stories, spread with such a speed that it rivalled that of the imperial couriers. While my ill-wishers gloated, my friends lamented my fate, and quite a few thought I needed a letter to console me. I do not know who started this rumour, but whoever they were, they must be completely shameless. The world is full of such people at the moment.

What, I beg you, is harsh or disgraceful for me in this agreement? I acknowledge no guilt. The arbitration is prefaced with, 'in order to avoid annoyance and to foster Christian concord.' And it adds, 'and we consider that these things should be done without blaming one side or the other.' This is the spirit in which I promise to implement the terms. When the arbitration goes on 'so that once the offences, complaints, and suspicions on either side have been dispelled,' it surely puts us on an equal footing in the matter. Indeed, if peace had not been far sweeter to me than revenge, I would have had far more serious reasons for complaint. But, they say, he dictated the terms, I bowed to them.[28] To what do discriminating people attribute this but to my modesty and desire for peace? I accepted the conditions, but I acknowledged no guilt. I was superior in my love of peace, not inferior in the issue.

Does not the holy gospel urge us to put an end to a controversy before it reaches the judges,[29] even if the terms are inequitable? Why cannot these evangelicals at least recognize an evangelical action? Whoever accepts the law is not at once the loser, since honest and prudent people often prefer ceding a case to a dishonest litigant than going to law and often pay the disgraceful sycophant, buying their peace with money and considering it a bargain if they have procured quite cheaply what they dearly love. The most precious asset of all is peace of mind. Whoever buys it with money acquires it at little cost. Sometimes a traveller is happy to accept the terms of pirates, robbers, and brigands. Wise people secure peace for themselves from a pimp, from a comedian, from a drunkard, from a mad person, and from a gabby woman. They speak quite pleasantly and moderately. Indeed we obtain peace from an annoying dog by throwing it bread.

And they turn this into my fault when I bought peace – which is indispensable for so many reasons – on the easiest terms from someone of some eloquence and with considerable free time, especially since there had been considerable familiarity between us so that it would have been both troublesome and even disgraceful, after having lived with him on familiar terms, to take legal action against him. They pretend that

* * * * *

28 Allen Ep 1992:119–31
29 Matt 5:25; Luke 12:58

I was forced to accept considerably harder terms. They imagine that a goodly sum of money was extorted from me. No sensible person who knew us both would doubt that I had purchased something very precious rather cheaply. By nature I am a lover of peace and, as he says, 'I have always bought my independence by selling all my possessions.'[30] For if that companion of wealth and of dignities, dependency, had not deterred me, I would have had a considerably more sumptuous and splendid fortune. Indeed the leisure that some hidden instinct in my nature has always made so precious and sweet to me was (in addition to the burden of old age and the continual vexation of my impaired health) more imperative than ever, distracted as I was with a host of different things. Where would a person who cannot find leisure to look after the health of his old body have obtained leisure for a public lawsuit? Moreover, studies demand that one be in good spirits as well as having sufficient time and a mind free from annoyances.

The considerable labours I carry out to assist public education would have had to be interrupted[31] and I, more unskilled in legal matters than almost anyone else, would have had to go to law, assisted by lawyers and agents, confronting a litigant who is known for his loquacity, and in front of lay judges several of whom supported teachings with which I disagree.[32] And which of my friends could I have dared to burden with such a case?[33] Consequently I chose what was more beneficial for my studies, advantageous to myself and my friends, fitting for a Christian and, finally, more expedient also for the plaintiff, who had been warned by his most illustrious prince's letter not to disturb my studies.[34] For since this was the crux of the whole dispute – that the duke became estranged from him as a result of my letter – he was going to alienate him still more if he showed contempt for his authority by continuing to stir up trouble for someone whom the prince had treated with signal favour.[35]

* * * * *

30 On extortion, Allen Ep 1992:134–8; for the quotation, Martial *Epigrammata* 2.68.4
31 Allen Ep 1992:140–1
32 See above n11.
33 Allen Ep 1992:142–3
34 Allen Ep 1992:145–7
35 Duke George of Saxony was a patron of humanists and especially well disposed towards Erasmus, with whom he had maintained a regular correspondence since 1517 (21 letters by Erasmus and 10 by George are preserved). In his effort to make his provincial university at Leipzig famous, especially as compared with Wittenberg, George added humane studies to the traditional curriculum and appointed several humanists; he also extended an invitation to Erasmus (Epp 527, 553, 809). The duke showed Erasmus his favour by sending

This counsel directed at all Christians ought to meet with particular approval among evangelical people. But they lay great store on being
feared. And whoever accepts the written law shows fear. Yet no one is
feared more than a dishonest man, and the best people are feared by no
one at all. Is it such a great thing to be feared when lunging bulls are feared
by everyone, scorpions and vipers are feared, and in the comedies Chremes
and Demipho fear Phormio?[36] I did not recognize the letter of which Eppendorf accused me. What then? Ought I to have recognized what I did in
fact not recognize, and, lying against myself, hand a weapon to my adversary? I did not, as I said, find a copy of that letter among my papers. The
duke had written to Eppendorf that in my letters to him there was none
of the kind of invective that the letter contained.[37] I had only urged him
to recall a young man endowed by nature with distinguished talents from
his extravagant living and idleness to some honourable position.[38] I do not
deny that I did that – but it was a number of years ago. Do they imagine
that I keep in my memory whatever I write; sometimes in one day, in addition to my books, I may write or dictate forty letters, few of which I read
again?[39] It could be that someone forged that letter. It could be that someone interpolated into it what suited him. If I knew it was not mine, I would
have been mad to lie to my own detriment. If I was in doubt, it would have
been utter stupidity to go against my own interests and to declare certain
what was doubtful.

I insisted that he produce the letter (which he claimed he had) with
my signature [and] with the seal of Terminus,[40] and I would then give him
my reply. However much I insisted, he did not do it – as if he could have!
Even if he had actually produced the letter with the signature and the seal,
unless it were clear that it had been written by me, it would be stupid to
admit forthwith that my case was fatally flawed.[41] For there are people so

* * * * *

occasional gifts (Epp 1126:57–60, 1326:8–13; Allen Ep 1691:26–7), but did not
fail to admonish him seriously to write still more against Luther (which he
finally did: *De libero arbitrio*; *Hyperaspistes* 1 and 2). See CEBR III 205–8.
36 In Terence's comedy *Phormio*, the leading character is a clever manipulator
who in an underhanded way influences his two cousins' love affairs. In Allen
Ep 1934:5 Erasmus noted that Eppendorf had changed from 'a Thraso to a
Phormio.'
37 Cf Allen Epp 1934:34–6, 202–4, and 489–90, 1940:1–3, 1943:4–7, 1992:106–8,
189–91, and 214–16.
38 Allen Ep 1992:36–8; see introductory note above n39.
39 Allen Ep 1992:63–5
40 See above n20.
41 Allen Ep 1992:76–88

skilled at forging another's handwriting that not even the person imitated discovers the trick. Once in Siena Alexander, archbishop in the see of Saint Andrew, son of King James of Scotland, the brother of the reigning king, played that trick on me.[42] He showed me a printed book which I knew for certain I had never read. In it he had made many annotations in the margins. I immediately recognized my handwriting. I asked where he had obtained the book. 'I recognize my figures of speech,' I said, 'but I have never read or owned this book.' But he challenged me, 'You did read it once, otherwise where did these notes in your hand come from?' Though I could not deny that it was my writing, I knew for certain that such a volume had never been mine. Finally he confessed his trick with a laugh, and I said, 'You could make a splendid forgery indeed if you wished.'

Did not the man who was executed in Strasbourg long ago stir up a dreadful scandal with counterfeit letters?[43] Almost ten years ago a certain man in Brussels was put to death because, having by deceit taken away the prince's seal, he had affixed it to another's diplomatic documents. This is the familiar ploy of those who commit a crime. If people can forge whole letters, what a minor matter to counterfeit three words in the signature? Need I mention here the fabricated treaty, a matter of common knowledge, to which some forger or another tried to commit the princes of Germany?[44] For these reasons, in troublesome court cases, the handwriting of some person or other is not regarded as indicating the guilt of the defendant unless more reliable evidence has been brought to bear. I need hardly add that, if the letter had really been written by me as he claimed and I knew this, I still would not have lied at all if I had denied that it was written by me, because it was written out in another's hand.[45] It will be objected that this

* * * * *

42 Alexander Stewart (c 1493–1513), illegitimate son of James IV, received the archbishopric of St Andrews in 1504 as a minor. In 1507 he left Scotland on a diplomatic mission to the continent and afterwards continued his travels as part of his education. In 1508 he came to Padua, where he and his brother became private students of Erasmus, who taught them rhetoric. Erasmus was very fond of Alexander and mentioned him in several of his publications. Threat of war drove the tutor and his two protégés to Ferrara and then to Siena. Erasmus went on but then returned to take Alexander Stewart to Rome for Holy Week 1509, and afterwards to Naples. After his Italian sojourn, Alexander returned to Scotland. On Alexander Stewart see Allen Epp 604:2n, 216 introduction, 604:4n; CEBR III 286.

43 Johann Jacob Schutz was killed in Strasbourg for stirring up a conspiracy against the town council of Sélestat by forged letters; see Allen 1992:89n.

44 The Pack affair of 1528; see 'Pack Affair' OER III 194.

45 Allen Ep 1992:99–102

is wilful deception. On the contrary, it is a well-meant deception whenever someone is misled for his own good, or when someone who deserves to be is deceived.[46] Thus David deceived King Achish,[47] thus Michal tricked the scouts of Saul,[48] not without praise for her piety. Such deception is usually highly praised in battle. In this way a physician sometimes deceives an ill person. And finally, Christ tricked the Jews on several occasions in a similar way;[49] so let no odium be attached to the expression. Now just as in war so in a court case no one is compelled to incriminate himself. However, the fact that I am saying these things outside the court indicates that I am unwilling to cause harm to myself or be moved to insult anybody. The letter I acknowledge as mine sought no personal vengeance, but his betterment. Its aim was that he be called away, through the offices of the prince, from what was, according to common report, a blameworthy life to an honourable station, and through this to wealth and esteem.[50] What intention could be friendlier? Is it not what a father would write for his son, a brother for a brother? If there was any slight bitterness in this letter, it was that of healing medicines. To sum up, if there was anything offensive in it (I shall not say here whether or not it was deserved, for I am not inclined to open an old wound) yet since I wrote it to one person, and a friend and well-wisher to boot, one should be angrier with those who spread the letter about than with its writer. So much for the letter which I do not acknowledge.

I return to 'the horrible terms'[51] concerning which attention should be focused on what I agreed to, not on his demands. Usually satisfaction is sought so justice can be done, but there is nothing to stop anyone from seeking anything from anyone. Therefore, let those who keep bringing up his demands look at what I promised and what the arbitrators prescribed. For a good part of the arbitration depends on my response. I promise to write either to the duke or to some official at his court, provided the prince was indeed alienated as a result of my letters. I say, 'courteously,' and not content with this I add, 'so far as this is permissible with such great princes.'[52] And the arbitration excluded either party being censured. So where are the 'horrible conditions'?

* * * * *

46 Allen Ep 1992:102–3
47 1 Sam 21:10–15
48 1 Sam 19:11–17
49 Allen Ep 1992:104–5
50 See introductory note above n39.
51 Cf above 379.
52 Cf above 383; Allen Ep 1992:173.

Secondly, I promise to dedicate a pamphlet but without being held to a timetable or a particular content; and not even that without reserve, for there is the condition, 'if I see evidence of a friendlier disposition on his part.' And I also added 'in the name of friendship,' just as the arbitration also puts it,[53] so that it is seen as an obligation, not a punishment.

Thirdly, what burdensome conditions do the arbitrators prescribe: that I should do what I would do voluntarily? There is no time set, nor are the poor defined, and it says explicitly, 'in order to foster concord.'[54] Moreover, I knew that the arbiters were fairer than to prescribe something burdensome here, as they knew nothing else was at stake than buying the leisure for my studies. Every hint of disgrace was ruled out; my wallet suffered no injury. I am accustomed to give liberally and unbidden to the poor. So what is this boast about dreadful terms being exacted from Erasmus? So much for the grievances.

Sometime after these stories, another rumour emerged about Erasmus' enormous treachery in not observing the agreement.[55] This is fabricated in six hundred letters; it is repeated at every banquet. What if I inform people that I have done a good deal beyond the agreement so that there is absolutely no ground for accusing me of treachery? It was left open whether I write to the duke or to some other official at his court.[56] Eppendorf insisted that I write to the duke himself. This was granted in addition to the agreement. He wanted certain statements in my letter to the duke that pleased him more than me. Though this was not stipulated in the arbitration, it was nonetheless conceded, lest the good will dissolve before it had consolidated.

In the evening, before his departure early next morning, he demanded the letter.[57] And so that night I wrote it – not without danger to my health. Since the arbitrators had not prescribed this and equity did not demand it, it was granted out of fondness for him. He insisted that he see and read the letter before it was signed and sealed. This was so discourteous as to indicate a distrustful mind – but it was pointless, for had I wished to deceive him, I could have written through someone else what I wanted to say to the duke. I stomached this as well. He demanded that the letter should be entrusted to him for delivery to the prince. This also was granted in addition to the agreement.

* * * * *

53 Cf above 383 and 384.
54 Cf above 384.
55 See Allen Ep 1992:335–7.
56 See Allen Ep 1992:372–4.
57 See Allen Ep 1992:378–87.

Apart from all this he demanded, then and there, to see the preface of the pamphlet as yet unborn. Because that demand seemed to the arbitrators not only unfair but inappropriate and silly as well (what after all is more stupid than to show the preface without its book: that is, the head without the body) they did not dare propose it to me, especially since this demand suggested a mind with little sincere friendliness. In the end, however, Boniface did suggest it, not without embarrassment. It was granted, lest what had been begun should grind to a halt. He had also sought ten ducats for the journey. I would perhaps have done this too, had I been asked in time. But I only heard of it when he was already setting out.

You see how much was at once conceded beyond what was prescribed. Yet the promised book did not appear.[58] Firstly there was no deadline set for it, and if I had seemed rather dilatory it should have been prescribed by the arbitrators according to justice and equity. The compact was made just before the spring fairs, and shortly after Easter he was already blustering about treachery[59] as if we blew books from our nostrils like snot. Let us admit that once a year had passed, a friendly complaint was in order. He still had no right to pin on me the crime of treachery.

Now let us suppose there was a deadline.[60] Is someone who does not fulfil a promise on the appointed day at once guilty? And is someone who does not repay money to a creditor at a given time, or the one who keeps a loan beyond the day set, to be arrested for treachery? Is the blacksmith or the tailor arraigned for not completing a task by the target date? One can possibly complain to them but there is no case for treachery. And here they shout about treachery when neither the day nor the year was fixed in advance! If in civil contracts there is a place for a plea of leniency (in case it is impossible or hard to keep a promise), how much more should there be in this negotiation conducted between friends by the laws of friendship, in which the strict letter of the law does not obtain, but rather, the consideration of what equity and humanity prescribe.

Let me again suppose that the arbitrators had determined a day [for publication] and the matter was to be dealt with under the severity of the law rather than the auspices of good will.[61] The promise to produce a book was not unqualified but with two conditions, 'in the name of friendship'

* * * * *

58 See Allen Ep 1992:335–44.
59 Agreement on 3 February 1528 (Allen Ep 1992:339); Easter fell on 12 April 1528 (see Allen Ep 1992:340).
60 See Allen Ep 1992:344–52
61 Cf Allen Ep 1992:352–63.

and 'if I find for certain that he had become friendly towards me from his heart.'[62] If someone insists on a book as compensation for an injury, I owe him nothing. If a book is insisted upon as a prize in a conflict and insisted upon contrary to agreement, I owe him nothing unless I consider him a friend. But as that wise Hebrew warns us: we ought not to take reconciliation with a friend for granted nor right away believe any proof whatever until sincere good will has replaced hatred.[63] If this is not certain, the book is not due.

Whether Eppendorf showed such an attitude, his companions and correspondents may know better than I. For I should not now wish to move this Camarina.[64] But although everything the rumour has reported is false, by taking any opportunity to deliver tirades against my name at every meal, by pouring out scandal and bitterness about the pamphlet to his hosts on every possible occasion, by sending no less hostile letters to his friends, has he given me any clear evidence that he has become a genuine friend of mine? Who ever heard him speaking honourably of me? Whom did he ask to greet me? What letters has he sent either to me or to others that show good will towards me? Was he ever silent when people slander me? And there is nothing more basic than such good offices, though to excel in them is a matter of courtesy, not friendship.

Now if we look at it from the perspective of equity, the arbiters did not decide that he should exact a pamphlet from me in the way an incendiarist would squeeze out every clause of a deal from peasants by threatening to set fire to the granary unless he is paid immediately. Rather, it should be a testimony, as it were, to an already restored and growing friendship against the false accusations of people. It should have been solicited in a respectful way rather than demanded so abusively.[65] Besides, someone who demands in this manner, by the very act of demanding forgoes the right to demand, and someone who makes demands contrary to an agreement is nearer to treachery than the one who is tardy carrying out a promise, especially when the delay costs nothing. That is more than enough about treachery. I wonder if these people may think it is a fine thing to stir up trouble for someone by extorting what is not due and complaining where there is no blame. If they imagine it will reflect credit on Eppendorf, they

* * * * *

62 See above 383; cf Allen Ep 1934:492–4.
63 Cf Allen Ep 1992:361–3.
64 *Adagia* i i 64: *Movere Camarinam* CWE 31 107:1–108:21: 'To move Camarina, is to bring trouble upon oneself.'
65 Allen Ep 1998:364–9

are either vain or stupid. It is vain to spread abroad what doesn't exist. It is stupid to praise what deserves contempt.

There was never any particular covenant of friendship between Eppendorf and myself, beyond what is common to all Christians. He himself initiated an intimate acquaintance with me, and he was a cheerful companion for a while in the afternoon hours I normally reserve for studies or devote to conversations with friends. In his accusation he acknowledges several of my favours to him. I do not solicit his company, nor do I seek his good offices. He would have done more than enough by desisting from injuring me. As to the pamphlet, I am prepared this very day to fulfil our agreement, even though I have done so much beyond, not against, the agreement. Let him fulfil half the terms and I am prepared to fulfil all I promised. He will fulfil all conditions if he not only desists from hurting me but also demonstrates his good will by kindness. He will have fulfilled half if he stops hurting me. This is enough for me.

Meanwhile my complaint is not against Eppendorf[66] but against those who spread baseless rumours and thereby injure him whom they mean to support more than me whom they malign. The saying 'wherever two have gathered he who is truth and loves truth is in the midst'[67] should apply to those who profess the gospel truth. Slander is a godless thing, even when it is free of vanity. Yet when they broadcast rumours no less vain than slanderous, who then is supposed to be in the midst? Who but he who takes his name from slandering and is the father of lies, and who lies as often as he opens his mouth?[68] Why do those who prattle on endlessly about the Sacred Scriptures not listen to the apostle Paul when he urges all of us to 'put away falsehood and speak the truth to our neighbours'?[69] Now the invention of stories that can easily be proven false has as much stupidity about it as malice. Recently at the much celebrated gathering at Augsburg[70] some spread about, among many other things, that at Basel Erasmus begged forgiveness on his knees from Eppendorf, though there were a great many people present who would know for certain that this is a remarkably barefaced lie, since I saw no magistrate at all, did not admit the accusation before the

* * * * *

66 Cf Allen Ep 1992:401, 413–14.
67 Matt 18:20
68 John 8:44
69 Eph 4:25
70 At the Diet of Augsburg 1530 Eppendorf told Duke George of Saxony about his struggle with Erasmus; cf Allen Epp 2333:47, 2344:21–3, 2384:80–9, 2392:1–22, 2400, 2406:22–60.

arbitrators, and never made an abject statement. Is their appetite for mendacity so great that they will buy the enjoyment of the briefest pleasure at the cost of lasting shame? Nevertheless, I reckon there is more impudence than brains in those who are in the grip of this disease. Can we find such plagues of mind among men confessing the name of Christ? Divine wisdom cries out: 'Beware then of useless grumbling, and keep your tongue from slander; because no secret word is without result, and a lying mouth destroys the soul.'[71] Those who rob a traveller of money are called bandits and they are put to death with fearsome punishments. Yet what a detractor steals is more valuable and therefore deserves more painful punishment. To injure someone's reputation is a kind of murder. A brigand kills the body, the mouth of a detractor destroys the soul; first his own, and then, as the evil infection spreads to many others, the souls of those whom he corrupts with his baneful words; and frequently he also destroys the soul of the person against whom he wagged his lying tongue. Thus the mouth of Ulysses destroyed Palamedes.[72] Moreover those who have not yet learned to follow Christ, like St Paul, bravely through ill and good repute,[73] are often consumed with grief.

Some people in our days, you may say, are much the same. They conspire to attack me with their pens and their tongues, thinking: He is a little old fellow, he is an invalid, he lacks courage and is unable to bear insult. In this way he will perish from the wound, and we shall not be the murderers. In the eyes of men this may be true, but before God they will have no better case than assassins or poisoners. Clearly they will now achieve their wishes, unless God strengthens our weakness. May they at least come to their senses now that they have been warned, and cease murdering themselves and others.

The End

* * * * *

71 Wisd of Sol 1:11 (NRSV)
72 Palamedes was a clever hero of the post-Homeric Trojan legends. Resorting to cunning stratagems while serving with Agamemnon, he became an enemy of Ulysses. After Palamedes detected Ulysses' feigned madness to avoid going to Troy, Ulysses revenged himself by outwitting his rival Palamedes. Ulysses forged a letter from Priam to Palamedes and hid it, together with a sum of gold, in Palamedes' tent. After the discovery of the ruse, Palamedes was accused of treason and executed by the army.
73 2 Cor 6:8

DESIDERIUS ERASMUS OF ROTTERDAM AGAINST A MOST SLANDEROUS LETTER OF MARTIN LUTHER

Purgatio adversus epistolam non sobriam Martini Lutheri

translated by
PETER MACARDLE

introduced and annotated by
JAMES D. TRACY

Luther's violent denunciation of Erasmus was published as a letter on 11 March 1534, addressed to Nikolaus von Amsdorf, superintendent of the Lutheran church in Magdeburg.[1] Luther had been promising to 'confess Christ against Erasmus.' The theology students boarding at the former Augustinian friars' cloister in Wittenberg, now home to Luther and his wife, knew his mind best: 'By divine authority, I enjoin hatred of Erasmus upon all of you ... I have decided to slay him by the pen.'[2] To Luther, Erasmus was 'the worst enemy of Christ, such as there has not been for a thousand years.'[3] Erasmus' books were full of pious exhortations, but these good words Luther found 'most frigid.' 'Only in giving vent to his mordant wit does he show spirit, only then, as in his *Praise of Folly* or *Julius exclusus*, do his words have real warmth.'[4] As for the *Colloquies*, 'On my deathbed I will prohibit my sons from reading them.'[5] This manifest disparity between the professed intent of Erasmus' writings and their insidious effect must disclose a conscious design. In his *Epistola* to Amsdorf, Luther says that he called Erasmus an Epicurean and a Sceptic in his *De servo arbitrio* of 1525 merely to provoke 'that cold and sluggish debater' to respond vigorously.[6] But Luther's settled belief that Erasmus had no religion whatever is clear from his *Table Talk*.[7] The two men were alike in one sense, for Luther attributed to Erasmus the same utter cynicism that Erasmus attributed to the 'mendicant tyrants' whom he saw as the worst enemies of true Christianity.[8] But if Erasmus was characteristically guarded in voicing his gravest

* * * * *

1 Amsdorf's letter to Luther of 28 January 1534 and Luther's reply of 11 March were published under the title *Epistolae Domini Nicolai Amsdorfii et D. Martini Lutheri de Erasmo Roterodamo* (Wittenberg: Lufft 1534); modern edition: WA Br 7 2093:27–40.

2 WA Tr 1 446 (early in 1533).

3 WA Tr 1 837

4 WA Tr 2 1319

5 WA Tr 1 817

6 WA Br 7 2093:55–60

7 WA Tr 2 1597: 'Father, Son, and Holy Spirit are a laughing matter for Erasmus'; 2 2170: 'Erasmus thinks the Christian religion is a comedy or a tragedy, containing no true events (*factas*), but only stories (*fictas*) made up for he purpose of forming human morals.'

8 WA Tr 1 37: 'This is the opinion of the pope and all of the cardinals, and of Erasmus: religion is altogether a fable, but must be observed nonetheless, for the preservation of the pope's monarchy and kingdom'; Erasmus to Johann von Botzheim, 13 August 1529 (Allen Ep 2205:258–63): 'Why should anyone worry lest the church fall into ruin, when there are those who defend her by such tactics? All their hope is in the foolishness of the people. They say

suspicions about Luther,[9] the Wittenberg Reformer, with breathtaking arrogance, claimed to see into the depth of his adversary's soul: 'If I cut open the heart of Erasmus, I will find jokes about the Trinity and the sacraments: this I know for certain.'[10]

Luther had many things to occupy him, and if his idea of 'slaying' Erasmus by the pen came to fruition, it was because of other pressures within the Wittenberg movement. In 1532, Georg Witzel, a one-time Lutheran pastor, launched a literary salvo in defence of Catholic teaching on good works. He was opposed by Justus Jonas, a Wittenberg theology professor. Having once supported Witzel's temporary incarceration on suspicion of anti-Trinitarian leanings, Jonas now defended justification by faith and accused Witzel of harbouring other heresies even worse than the doctrine of free will.[11] There was talk in Wittenberg of Luther himself joining in the attack on Witzel, as Amsdorf notes in a letter to Luther of 28 January 1534.[12] Amsdorf's point was that since Witzel 'stole' his ideas from Erasmus, Luther should ignore Witzel and attack the source of the problem,

* * * * *

they mean to make the world aware, but in my view it would be better to be aware of what they are about. If the authority of the princes has thus far accomplished nothing against the new religious factions, or very little, what can the scurrility of the mendicants do?'

9 *Spongia* above 112: 'Nor have I been able to persuade myself that the spirit of Christ – than whom no one is more gentle – dwells within a heart from which such bitterness gushes forth. Would that I am deceived in what I suspect! Yet the spirit of the gospel can also wax wrathful. Yes, but this is a wrath that never lacks the honey of charity to sweeten the bitterness of reproach.' The chilling implication of these words was not lost on Protestant readers; cf Ep 1510:73–4: '[Guillaume Farel] developed this anger at my expense because in my *Spongia* I threw doubt on Luther's spirit.' See also *Spongia* above 90 nn300, 301 and *Purgatio adversus epistolam Lutheri* below 462 n300.

10 WA Tr 1 484; cf 2 1597: 'Erasmus is as certain that there is no God, no eternal life, as I am certain that I see.'

11 O. Clemen 'Georg Witzel und Justus Jonas' ARG *Texte und Forschungen* 66 17th Jahrgang (1920) 132–52; W. Trusen *Um die Reform und Einheit der Kirche: Zum Leben und Werk Georg Witzels* Katholisches Leben im Kampf 14 (Münster 1957); G. Richter *Die Schriften Georg Witzels bibliographisch bearbeitet* (Nieuwkoop 1963). While studying the church Fathers in the library of a local nobleman, Witzel fell under suspicion because Johannes Campanus, who was expressing doubts about the Trinity, used the same library (see CEBR III 458–9). This was in 1531, the same year in which Michael Servetus published his *De Trinitatis erroribus libri septem*.

12 Amsdorf to Luther on 28 January 1534 (WA Br 7 2086:11). Cf Brecht *Martin Luther* III 80.

'so that Erasmus might finally be shown in his true colours, that is, ignorance and malice.'[13] Witzel was not in fact the issue, for Luther's *Epistola* of 11 March denounces him and moves on, while Erasmus in his *Purgatio adversus epistolam Lutheri* claims he never responded to Witzel's letters.[14] But the charge of anti-Trinitarianism lodged against this 'Erasmian' may have seemed to support Luther's charge that Erasmus himself only pretended to believe in those fundamental doctrines 'that we hold in common with the church under the papacy.'[15]

Labouring at Luther's side, Philip Melanchthon saw Erasmus quite differently.[16] For his part, Erasmus appreciated Melanchthon's efforts for a Catholic-Lutheran compromise at the 1530 Diet of Augsburg; in one of the letters that he published with his *Epistolae floridae* of September 1531, he endorsed the praise of Melanchthon by Julius Pflug, a Catholic moderate and adviser to Duke George of Saxony.[17] A year later, Melanchthon sent a copy of his *Commentary on the Epistle to the Romans*, with a letter urging Erasmus, as Pflug had done, to 'exert your authority' on behalf of religious peace.[18] Erasmus had mixed reactions to Melanchthon's

* * * * *

13 WA Br 7 2086:14–16. The editors give Witzel's response to the charge of plagiarism, in a letter of 28 March to Johann Haner: 'Show me a page of Erasmus that expounds fully the things I discuss. Indeed show me a single phrase from Erasmus that I have copied as my own. Unless you can do these things I will call you a Cretan [cf Titus 1:12]; for you say that I have stolen from Erasmus, not imitated him. Even boys know the difference between stealing and imitation.' For the importance of Erasmus' ideas in Witzel's subsequent career as a Catholic reformer, see J.P. Dolan *The Influence of Erasmus: Witzel and Cassander in the Church Ordinances and Reform Proposals of the United Duchies of Cleve* Reformationsgeschichtliche Studien und Texte 83 (Münster 1957) 37–8.

14 See WA 7 2093:19–38; ASD IX-1 443:15–4:21, and below 413. The index of Allen XII lists correspondence from Witzel in 1532 and 1533 (Epp 2715 and 2786) but no reply from Erasmus. On the other hand, Erasmus also says: 'I warned the man not to give free rein to his wrath against Luther' (Allen Ep 2918:7–9, a letter to Georg Agricola [c April init] 1534.

15 WA Br 7 2093:67–74

16 Cf his relatively favourable evaluation of Erasmus' *De libero arbitrio* (CWE 76 lxxi–lxxii).

17 Pflug to Erasmus on 12 May 1531 (Allen Ep 2492:44–9). Erasmus' reply to Pflug on 20 August 1531 is found in Allen Ep 2522:148–55; cf 152–5: 'At Augsburg, he [Melanchthon] worked sedulously for what you propose; had my health permitted me to be there, I would gladly have joined my efforts with his.' On Julius Pflug see CEBR III 77–8.

18 Melanchthon to Erasmus on 25 October 1532 (Allen Ep 2732:13–16, 26–9).

Commentary.[19] But when Pflug repeated his request, Erasmus responded with his *Liber de sarcienda ecclesiae concordia* (July 1533).[20] His proposals for advancing theological negotiations between Catholics and Lutherans require separate discussion;[21] what matters here is that some of Luther's followers reacted favourably. With encouragement from Melanchthon, the Hessian pastor Antonius Corvinus discussed Erasmus' proposals in an imaginary dialogue between himself and Julius Pflug, entitled: *Dissertatio quatenus expediat Erasmi de sarcienda ecclesiae concordia rationem sequi*, which appeared in Wittenberg prior to November 1534, possibly early in that year, or even late 1533. To make the book sell, the printer 'extorted' a preface from Luther, albeit one that set clear limits to any compromise: 'We cannot condone what manifestly conflicts with Scripture, or that scarcely admits of what they call a middle ground.' Moreover, though some might be casual about their own salvation, 'a soul fearing God, and desiring eternal life rather than eternal death, cannot find peace in doubtful and uncertain doctrines.' Nonetheless, Luther praised Corvinus for his elegant style, and acknowledged that 'Erasmus' disciples and perhaps Erasmus himself' acted in good faith when they proposed mutual concessions as a path to religious peace.[22] Luther was not in a position to condemn out of hand the theological negotiations that Melanchthon and others favoured. But he could in effect discredit the very idea of compromise by demonstrating the duplicity of its chief proponent,[23]

* * * * *

19 Erasmus to Melanchthon on 6 October 1534 (Allen Ep 2970:26–9). Erasmus says he has bought three copies of the *Commentary* and sent one to Jacopo Sadoleto, bishop of Carpentras, who had also published *Commentaries on Romans*. But cf Erasmus' letter to Boniface Amerbach on 12 June 1533 (Allen Ep 2818:63–70), telling him to send a copy of Melanchthon's work to Sadoleto, but with the advice that he should 'pick out the gold from the shit.'

20 Pflug to Erasmus on 5 May 1533 (Allen Ep 2806:11–40); cf his previous request along the same lines on 12 May 1531 (Allen Ep 2492:37–44). Erasmus sent the preface of *De concordia* to Pflug on 31 July 1533 (Allen Ep 2852). Both Pflug (May 1531) and Melanchthon (October 1532) ask Erasmus to exert his 'authority' in this way. Melanchthon could have seen Pflug's letter to Erasmus in the latter's *Epistolae floridae* of September 1531.

21 A translation of *De concordia* is planned for CWE.

22 WA 38 276–9 (Luther's preface); the passages quoted are 277:7–9, 278:3–6, and 276:5, 12–14: *Facile et ipse credo, Erasmum forte et suos discipulos bono animo velle rebus, seu turbis potius, consultum per istam mediocritatem et mutuam partium condonationem.* For the dating, WA 38 274 and Allen Ep 2993:80n.

23 Erasmus had been promoting the idea of a dialogue between reasonable men on both sides since the anonymously published *Consilium cuiusdam* of 1520, co-authored with the Dominican friar Johannes Faber: CWE 71 108–12.

that 'king of double meaning secure on his throne of ambiguity,'[24] who was always claiming that his own statements should be 'taken in the best light' rather than at face value.[25] Luther's *Epistola* to Amsdorf should thus be seen as a counter-stroke to the tepid endorsement he was obliged to produce for Corvinus' dialogue.

To expose Erasmus as duplicitous Luther needed proof texts. How well did he know Erasmus' writings? The *Explanatio symboli apostolorum sive catechismus* (1533)[26] was a subject of current discussion in the Wittenberg circle.[27] Luther gives an extensive critique of the *Explanatio*,[28] with particular reference to a passage referring to salvation history as a 'drama.'[29] And he did make a careful study of the fourth edition of Erasmus' *New Testament* which appeared in 1527.[30] Thus to show that Erasmus encouraged doubts about the doctrine of the Trinity, he cites a preface to the 1527 *Annotations on Romans*, saying that Peter in preaching to the rude multitude calls Christ a man, not God.[31] He remembered how Christ was 'robbed of his glory as the Redeemer' in a 1522 preface to the *New Testament*, where Erasmus says that the Lord came down from heaven to accomplish 'more perfectly and completely' all that the saints had done: 'this was the first passage that turned me against Erasmus.'[32] Given Luther's keen interest in the Epistle

* * * * *

24 WA Br 7 2093:305
25 WA Br 7 2093:169–83
26 CWE 70 231–388. Erasmus referred to the *Explanatio* as his *Catechism*.
27 WA Tr 1 837; 3 3795
28 WA Br 7 2093:80–124
29 WA Br 7 2093:109–11; CWE 70 251: 'You now have the introduction, the body, and the conclusion of this salvific drama; you have all the acts and the celestial scenes of this heavenly *choragus* "director" set forth in an arrangement beyond powers of description.'
30 Brecht *Martin Luther* III 78; WA 60 192–228.
31 WA Br 7 2093:122–4; as the Weimar editor notes, the reference is to the *Argumentum in Epistolam ad Romanos* in the 4th ed of the *Annotationes* (Basel: Froben 1527) 318 (LB VI 552).
32 WA Br 7 2093:142–62. C. Augustijn points out (ASD IX-1 471:785n) that Luther refers to the following passage in Erasmus' *Epistola de philosophia evangelica* (LB VI *5): *Siquidem hic erat vere sermo ille contractus et in compendium redactus, quem tandem fecit Dominus super terram, in quo recapitularetur omnia, quae in caelis et quae in terris, ut quecunque e tot libris, e tot sanctis viris ante petebantur, nunc compendio ab uno Christo longe tum expressiora, tum absolutiora, compendio sumi possent.* 'For here truly was the divine Word, concentrated down to its essential form, which the Lord has at last sent out over the earth, in whom he has recapitulated all

to the Romans,[33] he may also have recalled from earlier reading the preface to the first edition of the *Paraphrase on Romans*, where Erasmus (Luther thought) so stresses the difficulty of the text as to discourage people from reading it.[34] But Erasmus' chiding of the sacred author for using the word 'world' too often – from a preface to the First Epistle of John, only in the 1519 *Paraphrase*[35] – is not something one would remember for fifteen years. Moreover, one doubts that Luther perused the books in which Erasmus replies to Catholic critics; yet he uses the *Apologia adversus rhapsodias Alberti Pii* in charging Erasmus with Arianism for saying that 'we dare to call the Holy Spirit God, but the ancients did not.'[36] Similarly, denouncing Erasmus for using the word 'intercourse' when describing the angel's promise of how the power of God would overshadow the Virgin Mary, he cites not the *Paraphrases*, where this locution occurs, but Erasmus' defence of himself in a published letter to an eminent Carthusian.[37] In other words, someone was helping Luther gather material. In fact, Amsdorf had been compiling 'annotations on Erasmus,' a copy of which he sent to Luther some time

* * * * *

things on heaven and earth, so that whatever might previously have been sought from all the books of wisdom and all the lives of holy men can now be taken from Christ alone, in a far more pure and concentrated form.'

33 See the letter from Georg Spalatin (Ep 501 11 December 1516), conveying to Erasmus the concerns of an unnamed friend (Luther) about how Romans was interpreted in his 1516 New Testament.

34 WA Br 7 2093:116–22; cf Erasmus' letter to Domenico Grimani on 13 November 1517 (Ep 710:14–19, 27–49).

35 WA Br 7 2093:129–37; Cf ASD IX-1 475:884n and below 452 n241

36 WA Br 7 2093:224–36. The reference is to Erasmus' letter to Jean Carondelet (Ep 1334:475–9, the preface to his edition of the works of Hilary of Poitiers) on 5 January 1523. For Erasmus' response on this point to the criticism of Pio, see *Apologia adversus rhapsodias Alberti Pii* (CWE 84 277–80); see also *Apologia adversus monachos* (LB IX 1050C–2B).

37 WA Br 7 2093:244–7, 335–8. C. Augustijn's notes (ASD IX-1 465:588n, 467:688n) show that Luther had Ep 1687 in mind when he says that Erasmus speaks of *coitum dei cum virgine* in *quadam epistola* (Allen Ep 1687:100–12); cf paraphrase on Luke 1:35 LB VII 290B: *Sanctus hic divinae naturae cum humana coitus, non violabit pudicitiam tuam sed consecrabit* 'This holy intercourse (*coitus*) between the divine nature with a human nature will not violate but will rather consecrate [your] chastity'; also paraphrase on Luke 1:26 LB VII 288F: God *misit Angelum Gabrielum veluti paranymphum, ac divini cum virginis congressus conciliatorem* 'sent the angel Gabriel like a groomsman and promoter of the congress between the divine and the virgin.'

prior to 31 March.[38] Amsdorf will thus have provided Luther not merely with an occasion for his *Epistola* of 11 March, but also with some of his ammunition.

For Erasmus, this latest blast from Wittenberg, of which he had a copy by the beginning of April 1534, was completely unexpected.[39] Since the appearance of the second part of his *Hyperaspistes* in 1527,[40] he had, by his own account, refrained from attacking Luther,[41] to the point that some Catholics accused Erasmus of making excuses for him.[42] Thus he could not imagine giving any provocation for what has been described as 'the most severe attack that ever touched the person and works of Erasmus.'[43] What was he to do? He apparently sought the advice of Johann Koler, canon of St Moritz church, a trusted friend and a leader among Augsburg's embattled Catholic minority.[44] He also contacted Erasmus Schets, Antwerp's greatest banker, and other friends close to the court of Mary of Hungary in Brussels, who had been trying to persuade Erasmus to return to Brabant and resume his position as an honorary councillor to Emperor

* * * * *

38 Luther to Amsdorf on 31 March 1534 (WA Br 7 2103:1–10). Luther expresses his surprise at a passage Amsdorf had found in the *Paraphrase on Romans*, showing that Erasmus, 'before Luther,' asserted that no man could be justified before God by observance of the law of Moses. At Luther's suggestion, Amsdorf published his treatise (or some of it) in Magdeburg under the title of *Consilium et ratio epistolae de Erasmo ad Lutherum* (Magdeburg: Michael Lotther 1534). From the excerpts from Amsdorf's preface given by the Weimar editors, it seems the purpose of the published version was to justify Amsdorf's role in an attack on Erasmus that some of Luther's followers (see below nn64, 65) found unwarranted or excessive.

39 The earliest extant reference to Luther's *Epistola* in Erasmus' correspondence comes in a letter to Georg Agricola dated by Allen at the beginning of April (Allen Ep 2918:1–20); for its being 'completely unexpected' *praeter expectationem*, see below 412.

40 CWE 77

41 See below 412. In the correspondence for these years, Erasmus' more critical comments about Luther are found in texts that he passed over in choosing which of his letters to send to the printer for publication. See eg Erasmus to Willibald Pirckheimer on 20 March 1528 (Allen Ep 1977:37–44).

42 Agostino Steuco to Erasmus on 25 July 1531 (Allen Ep 2513:329–61)

43 The opinion of J.N. Bakhuizen van den Brink; see introduction ASD V-1 182.

44 Johann Koler to Erasmus on 22 May 1534 (Allen Ep 2936:7n); Koler had been ill when he received Erasmus' letter of April 4 (no longer extant) to which he responded here. Erasmus followed events in Augsburg closely; see his correspondence with Koler, Bishop Christoph von Stadion, bankers Anton Fugger and Johann Paumgartner, and the latter's son, Johann Georg.

Charles v.[45] The earliest such letter to have survived was to a protégé of another patron, Duke George: the Catholic humanist physician and metallurgist Georg Agricola. In this letter Erasmus takes it for granted that Luther slandered him deliberately: 'Does it not shame the man to lie so impudently?'[46]

Judging from Koler's response, Erasmus' Catholic friends reacted the same way:

> I do not believe you can ignore such an egregious calumny. Believe me, Erasmus, this is a great matter, more important than you realize. For it is not enough that he heaps every kind of abuse on you, without any justification; this great man, this heroic restorer of the Christian religion, adds his own judgment of Erasmus, and promises to make the whole world believe it ... I know how much your friends expect of you, especially here in Augsburg: they come to me often, asking again and again what I have heard from you, and whether you will answer Luther, instead of swallowing this awful contumely, or responding to these vile insults with flattery.[47]

In other words, Erasmus' admirers feared his timidity might get the better of him, but longed to see him repay Luther in the same coin. As Koler said, 'if you do not defend your honour and reputation against Luther, and give your judgment of him (as is only fair), I fear lest you suffer a great loss to your name and reputation.'[48]

Yet if Erasmus indeed had reason to respond in kind, his first instinct was not to do anything. The letter to Agricola expresses hesitations that may also have been contained in the now lost letter to Koler:

> I have no spirit for engaging with Luther. Each day I prepare for my last day, an old man afflicted in health, broken by labours, and overwhelmed with rabid

* * * * *

45 Erasmus to Nicolaus Olahus (Mary of Hungary's court preacher) on 22 April 1534, and to Erasmus Schets (who often served as Mary's loan-broker on the Antwerp exchange) on 23 April 1534 (Allen Epp 2922 and 2924). For invitations to return to Brabant, see Schets to Erasmus on 12 July 1531 (Allen Ep 2511:34–46), Jean Carondelet (archbishop of Palermo and president of Mary's Council of State) to Erasmus on 19 July 1532 and 27 March 1533 (Allen Epp 2689 and 2784), Olahus to Erasmus on 26 July 1532 and 29 March 1533 (Allen Ep 2693:100–25 and 2785:51–77).
46 Erasmus to Agricola (Allen Ep 2918:2)
47 Koler to Erasmus on 22 May 1534 (Allen Ep 2936:31–45)
48 Koler to Erasmus on 22 May 1534 (Allen Ep 2936:49–52)

and furious pamphlets. I do not see what fruit there might be in provoking Luther with another pamphlet. The rope of contention is drawn tighter on all sides: no one has been able to compose the quarrel, not even crowned heads. Now the Franciscans are leading the charge. I think I have declared my zeal for the church with sufficient clarity. Let others do what they can; my only concern now is to save this soul of mine. There is nothing of which I am prouder than that I have never given my allegiance to any sect.[49]

Nonetheless, within a few weeks, he had completed his *Purgatio adversus epistolam Lutheri* and sent it off to Basel, for it was issued by the Froben press before the end of April 1534.[50] By 11 May, when Erasmus wrote again to Schets, he expected that copies of the *Purgatio* would already be on sale in Antwerp, because Froben had sent 'several hundred copies' to Brabant by wagon.[51] The next day he sent a copy to Cardinal Bernhard von Cles, prince-bishop of Trent and chancellor of Archduke Ferdinand's government in Vienna.[52]

The few letters that have survived from this period give no hint as to why Erasmus overcame his reluctance to do battle with Luther once more. Koler's impassioned call to arms might have done the trick, save that, owing to Koler's illness during the month of April, the *Purgatio* had already appeared by the time he sent off the letter quoted above. But Koler's reaction offers an indirect clue as to Erasmus' aims in writing the *Purgatio adversus epistolam Lutheri*:

> You have done more than I urged you to do in the letter I wrote a few days ago, but you have treated Luther more mildly than his petulance deserves; I wish that you had sharpened your pen. I particularly dislike the fact that you say you have never ceased to regard Luther with Christian love. How can you love a man who has charged you with such atrocious crimes, and

* * * * *

49 Ep 2918:12–20
50 The title-page reads *mense Aprili*; on 7 May Boniface Amerbach sent a copy to Alciato (see C. Augustijn ASD IX-1 434:57n).
51 Erasmus to Schets on 11 May 1534 (Allen Ep 2933:9–10)
52 Cles to Erasmus on 4 June 1534 (Allen Ep 2941:1–2), referring to a now lost letter of May 12 that Erasmus had sent along with a copy of his *Purgatio adversus epistolam Lutheria*. Cf Cles to Erasmus on 2 April 1534 (Allen Ep 2921:1–8): Cles sends Erasmus a copy of Luther's *Epistola* given him by Pier Paolo Vergerio (then Pope Clement VII's nuncio to Archduke Ferdinand) 'not because we think it detracts in any way from your honour, any more than gnats can trouble an elephant, but because it seems to us disgraceful that you are treated in this shameful and impudent way.'

heaped upon you so many outrageous calumnies? Moreover, a man struck by
so many censures and thunderbolts of pope and emperor, and consigned to
all the Furies? A man who has never in his life written anything that was not
crammed full of raging insults, prodigious lies, and seditious outbursts? Tell
me, Erasmus, have you really never ceased to love this man, rather, this plague
of mankind? ... I am not such a Christian; in your patience you surpass me
by far.[53]

In his disappointment, Koler exaggerated Erasmus' mildness. In the
Purgatio Erasmus refrains, as usual, from calling Luther's doctrine a
'heresy'; but he charges that Luther's 'unrestrained abusive language' produces 'nothing but schism.'[54] He does not impute conscious malice to his
adversary, as he did in the letter to Agricola, but he does suggest, repeatedly, that Luther's vicious outbursts are indicative of dementia.[55] Yet Koler
was not entirely wrong either. In contrast to the counter-blast that his Augsburg friends hoped for, giving the world Erasmus' 'judgment' of Luther,
the *Purgatio* reflects a 'conscious decision' to defend himself rather than to
attack in return.[56]

This strategy fitted Erasmus' image of himself. On the one hand, as
he said in justifying the pugnaciousness of his replies to Catholic critics: 'It
is impious to put up with accusations of impiety.'[57] On the other hand, he

* * * * *

53 Koler to Erasmus on 25 August 1534 (Allen Ep 2937:12–35). Erasmus does
not say in the *Purgatio adversus epistolam Lutheri* that he regards Luther with
Christian love. Koler is probably reacting to the following remark: 'How much
more humane Erasmus is. He has never turned his feelings against Luther'
(see below 451). He may also be thinking of a passage near the beginning:
'Therefore, I will not throw back his insults, but as far as ever I can I will
imitate my Lord and teacher, who, when asked, "Are you not a Samaritan,
possessed by a demon, and casting out demons with the help of Beelzebub?"
did not reply to the accusation of being a Samaritan (for it is absurd to reproach
someone for his country of birth, which no one chooses for himself, or for
anything else not under human control). Nor did he throw back the other two
accusations on those who slandered him, but dismissed them with arguments,
for this was the way expedient to the gospel.' See below 414–15.
54 See below 414. In his *De libero arbitrio* and *Hyperaspistes*, Erasmus speaks of
heresy and heretics, but never in reference to Luther's teaching; see the combined index for CWE 76 and 77 in CWE 77 773–810.
55 See below 416, 423, 432, 437, 451.
56 So C. Augustijn in his introduction to the *Purgatio adversus epistolam Lutheri*
(ASD IX-1 434).
57 Erasmus to Cuthbert Tunstall on 31 January 1530 (Allen Ep 2263:16–17, tr E.
Rummel in Rummel *Catholic Critics* II 154).

liked to believe that he exemplified in his own conduct the civility that, for humanists, was supposed to be formed by the study of *bonae literae*: 'I have written numerous *apologiae* but, I am pleased to say, no invectives. I have ignored many spiteful pamphlets, and those I answered I surpassed by far in modesty and civility.'[58]

Moreover, in responding to attacks from the Protestant side, Erasmus never forgot his own belief that 'the tyranny of the monks' was the real enemy of true religion, worse by far than Luther.[59] In 1523, he was pressured to write against Luther in order to preserve his credibility among Catholics. But just as he was about to begin his *De libero arbitrio* he wrote to Huldrych Zwingli of his resolve 'either not to write, or to write in such a strain that my writing will not please the pharisees.'[60] Now, eleven years later, had he produced the spirited invective Koler and his friends wanted, he would also have given aid and comfort to the Observant Franciscan heresy-hunters who were his worst enemies.[61]

Finally, he had not abandoned the idea that serious theological discussions might yet produce accord between Catholics and Lutherans. While composing the *Purgatio adversus epistolam Lutheri* in April 1534, he may or may not have known of preparations for continuing the conversations begun at Augsburg at the Leipzig Colloquy of that year, sponsored by Duke

* * * * *

58 Erasmus to Jacopo Sadoleto [c 14 May 1530] (Allen Ep 2315:225–8, slightly modifying the translation by Rummel *Catholic Critics* II 154). One might well class the *Julius exclusus* as an invective (CWE 27 155–97), as vicious as any penned by Erasmus' critics, but Erasmus never acknowledged responsibility for it; see eg Erasmus to Martin Bucer on 2 March 1532 (Allen Ep 2615:182–5).

59 Erasmus to Krysztof Szydłowiecki on 27 August 1528 (Allen Ep 2032:20–3): 'If the new sects be brought to ruin in such a way that the tyranny of wicked monks be revived, or that of those who until now have used the name of the Roman pontiff to do whatever pleases them, we will simply exchange one plague for another.' Erasmus to Pierre de Mornieu [c 14 May] 1529 (Allen Ep 2162:34–7): 'I do not dislike France at all, but you have there lots of magpies and grackles, not to mention certain Beddaites [the reference is to Noël Béda, syndic of the theology faculty at Paris], whose wickedness injures the church of Christ far more seriously than any Lutherans.'

60 Erasmus to Zwingli on 31 August 1523 (Ep 1384:50–3)

61 Erasmus to Alonso Virués [c 15 March] 1529 (Allen Ep 1968:38–50); Erasmus to Nicolas Maillard on 28 March 1531 (Allen Ep 2466:30–6). Cf Erasmus to Johann Koler on 9 September 1533 (Allen Ep 2868:28–30): 'My books are handed over to the Franciscans to be examined, they find a thousand heresies. What is more insane than these Furies? I plainly foresee that if the Lutheran cause goes down, there will arise such a tyranny of monks that we will miss Luther.'

George, in which Julius Pflug was one of the Catholic interlocutors.[62] In any case he died years before these discussions of a possible compromise brought real progress at the Regensburg Colloquy (1541), even if no agreement could be reached.[63] But he surely understood that his part in the 'drama' was to clear his name in such a way that men of good will on the Lutheran side would not take offence. In fact, Luther's *Epistola* 'displeased' Melanchthon.[64] By the fall Erasmus had got wind of the fact that there were 'loyal Lutherans' who did not like it.[65] Taking an occasion that presented itself, he wrote Melanchthon to make sure the point was not lost on those he had meant to impress:

> About Luther I will say nothing, save that I am surprised that he raved against me in such a way at the urging of Amsdorf, who, so I hear, is a foolish and ignorant man; and that he brings against me charges that a reading of my books would show to be completely baseless, even if I had not responded to him. The sting of his words would have given me reason to respond more sharply, and there were those who wanted me to do so. But I wanted to respond in a way that might be approved by good and learned men.[66]

One may plausibly identify the 'good and learned men' of this letter – that is, Lutherans of good will – with those 'unprejudiced' or fair-minded readers to whom the *Purgatio adversus epistolam Lutheri* often appeals.[67] In sum, if one of Luther's aims in attacking Erasmus was to close the door on any compromise of essential doctrine, Erasmus tried to write his *Purgatio* in such a way as to keep the door open.

* * * * *

62 For the Leipzig Colloquies of 1534 and 1539, in which Pflug and Melanchthon (among others) participated, Robert Stupperich, 'Julius Pflug and Melanchthon,' in *Pflugiana: Studien über Julius Pflug (1499–1564)* ed Elmar Neuss and J.V. Pollot (Münster 1990) 43–59, here 50–3.

63 Matheson *Cardinal Contarini* is the most recent book-length study. It may be noted that at the Leipzig Colloquy of 1539, the Protestant interlocutors included Melanchthon and Bucer, while their Catholic counterparts included Pflug and Witzel.

64 WA Tr 4 4899: *Ergo in mea epistola, quae displicuit Philippo, provocavi [Erasmum]* ...

65 Erasmus to Jean de Pins on 13 November 1534 (Allen Ep 2976:3–5)

66 Erasmus to Melanchthon on 6 October 1534 (Allen Ep 2970:16–21). This letter was written as an introduction to the *Poemata* of Georg Sabinus, but not published until the 1558 edition.

67 See below 416, 430, 432, 446, 451.

To persuade the fair-minded reader, Erasmus takes up the charges against him more or less in the order in which they occur in Luther's *Epistola*, deploying defensive strategies appropriate to each case. In a few places, Luther's well-known preoccupation with the devil provides an opportunity for *ad hominem* arguments. If Luther waxes indignant because Erasmus mentions the opinions of heretics in his *Explanatio symboli* why does he himself make the devil such a persuasive sower of doubt in his *Von der Winkelmesse*?[68] If Luther thinks that only the devil would ask such questions about the Apostles' Creed as Erasmus poses in his *Explanatio*, perhaps 'he means that devil who previously attacked his soul concerning the mass.'[69] Sometimes he draws on the knowledge of usage that was his own stock in trade. If Luther attacks him for speaking of salvation history as a 'drama' or a *fabula*, Erasmus is ready with a definition of terms – *fabula* can mean not just a 'fictional narrative' but also 'the recounting of true and familiar things' – and also with a long list of similarly 'profane' metaphors for sacred subjects used in the New Testament and in the liturgy of the church.[70] As to the charge that he had spoken of 'intercourse' between God and the Virgin Mary, on which he evinces some embarrassment, he tries to muddy the waters a bit by showing that the word he supposedly used (*coitus*) is at least not 'obscene' in and of itself, as Luther contended.[71] On a point lacking in doctrinal implications, he judged that his best defence would be to admit to a mistake: He had indeed made fun of the author of the First Epistle of John for using the word 'world' too often, but 'these words slipped out in the first edition'; in other words, he was more respectful in the second edition.[72]

The standard defence in a controversy of this kind is of course to show that the opponent has taken one's own words out of context. To be sure, this approach has its pitfalls. When Luther charges him with saying that Christ had come merely to perfect the work of the saints, Erasmus asks: 'Where have the saints (*sancti*) come from all of a sudden?' since Luther had been talking about a comparison between Christ and the pagan philosophers; Erasmus fails to notice that in the passage Luther cites he had referred to

* * * * *

68 See below 420; *The Private Mass and the Consecration of Priests* tr M. Lehmann LW 38 139–214. On Luther and the devil, see H.A. Oberman *Luther: Man between God and the Devil* tr E. Walliser Schwarzbart (New Haven 1989).
69 See below 422. The reference is to *The Private Mass* LW 38 155–8.
70 See below 423–5.
71 See below 439–43.
72 See below 452–3; cf above n35.

Christ as perfecting 'all that had previously been sought from so many books, and so many holy men (*sanctis viribus*).'[73] As to the passage about 'intercourse' between God and the Virgin Mary, said by Luther to be found 'in a certain letter,' Erasmus cannot remember any such letter, and dares to take an oath 'that those words are nowhere to be found in my letters, nor anywhere in my works.' Then, apparently deciding that he had better check likely places in his works, he finds and quotes in full the appropriate passage, from the *Paraphrase on Luke*, stressing the qualifying words Luther had omitted.[74]

On another sensitive point, if Erasmus had indeed written that 'Peter calls Christ a man, but avoids the word God,' the bare citation has a different meaning in the text from which it comes, where he distinguishes between the teachings the apostles conveyed to the initiate, and what they said before a promiscuous crowd.[75] The teachings of ancient heretics were indeed discussed in the *Explanatio symboli*, but not 'right at the beginning' or without giving catechumens 'solid foundations,' as Luther asserted, for the passage in question occurs in the second of five lessons, after Erasmus' catechist and catechumen have gone over the basic teachings of the Christian faith in lesson one.[76] Erasmus had indeed said in the preface to his edition of the works of Hilary of Poitiers that ancient Christian writers did not 'dare' call the Holy Spirit God, but this passage was wrenched from its context by the Spanish friars who first brought it up, then by Alberto Pio, who (Erasmus thought) borrowed from them, then by Luther, who borrowed from Pio.[77]

Finally, Erasmus marshals the Fathers of the church as witnesses to his orthodoxy. Does Luther censure Erasmus for citing the opinions of heretics in his *Explanation of the Creed*? Then he also would censure Augustine, Ambrose, Cyprian, and Jerome among the Latins, and, among the Greeks, Athanasius, Cyril of Alexandria, Epiphanius, John Chrysostom, John Damascene, and Philastrius.[78] If Luther objects to the fact that Erasmus discusses differences of wording among the creeds recited by the church, he must

* * * * *

73 See below 449; cf above n32.
74 See below 439, 444; cf above n37; Erasmus to Erasmus Schets on 11 May 1534 (Allen Ep 2933:6): 'Nowhere have I written that God had intercourse with the Virgin' (he uses the verbal form *coisse*).
75 See below 427–8.
76 See below 416–18 and CWE 70 236–77 (lessons 1 and 2).
77 See below 431–3. Cf above n36. On the Valladolid Articles of 1527, see Rummel *Catholic Critics* II 89–93.
78 See below 417–18.

object also to Jerome.[79] If Erasmus talks about how difficult it is to understand the Epistles of St Paul, so do Origen and Jerome.[80] When he comments on the passage in Acts where Peter calls Christ a man, but not God, he follows the example of Chrysostom, Ambrose, and Bede.[81] Even in regard to his use of sexual imagery for Mary's conception of Jesus by the power of the Holy Spirit, he can cite analogues, if not parallels to his own usage, in Damascene, and in a hymn by Prudentius used in the liturgy of the church.[82] And if Luther is scandalized when Erasmus points out that Hilary of Poitiers did not call the Holy Spirit God, let him think again. For if Luther professes to rely only on 'bare, naked Scriptures,' 'from what scriptural source' does he elicit those doctrines now considered essential that were overlooked or ignored by early Christian writers like Papias, Ignatius of Antioch, Origen, and Irenaeus, 'seeing that the Scripture has always been the same?'[83]

It is clear that, despite being 'an old man afflicted in health,' as he complained to Koler, Erasmus continued his ongoing study of the church Fathers, as is reflected in his reference here to otherwise obscure authors like Papias, Philastrius, and Ignatius of Antioch.[84] In so doing, he developed an appreciation, rare in his age, for the intricacies of dogmatic controversy in the early Christian centuries. In *De libero arbitrio* Erasmus described himself as one who loved dogmatic assertion so little that he would 'seek refuge in scepticism wherever this is allowed by the inviolable authority of Scripture and the church's decrees'; in the *Explanatio symboli* he has shrewd (if not always correct) guesses about how specific credal assertions were needed to rule out this or that false belief.[85] As late as 1526 Erasmus believed that Arius was a learned man driven from the church by the envy of the clergy, and that he and his followers were willing to confess that Christ was 'of the same nature' as God the Father; in other words, he confused the two parties that more recent church historians have called Arian and Semi-Arian. In the *Explanatio symboli* and the *Purgatio adversus epistolam Lutheri*, he says

* * * * *

79 See below 421–2.
80 See below 426–7.
81 See below 427–9.
82 See below 442–3.
83 See below 433–4.
84 Papias and Philastrius are not mentioned in the index of Allen XII. In the only reference to Ignatius [24 June 1530], Erasmus tells Koler that although 'I cannot understand what pleases you so about the *Letters* of Ignatius,' he would gladly send him a copy if he had one (Allen Ep 2331:8–9).
85 CWE 76 7; CWE 70 eg 265 n93.

that Arius, in his 'ungodliness,' acknowledges the Son as son by will and resemblance, but not by nature; he and his followers 'might have appeared reverential save for the fact that they disagreed with the Catholics concerning the reality' conveyed by the disputed term, *homoousios*, or 'consubstantial.'[86] Although he does not wish to argue matters of doctrine in the *Purgatio*, he does assert his belief that 'bare, naked Scriptures' will not provide unambiguous support for many fundamental doctrines that are indeed held in common by Lutherans and Catholics.[87] Thus while Erasmus retreated not at all from his conviction that 'mendicant tyrants' were the worst threat to true Christianity, he also found more and more reason to acquiesce in the authority of the church, and of the Catholic tradition it represented. If not a master of ambiguity, as Luther thought, he was at the very least a master of complexity.

JDT

* * * * *

86 Tracy 'Erasmus and the Arians' 1–10; CWE 70 273–4; below 436–7.
87 See below 433.

DESIDERIUS ERASMUS OF ROTTERDAM AGAINST A MOST SLANDEROUS LETTER OF MARTIN LUTHER

Lo and behold, Martin Luther's θυμὸς ἀγήνωρ 'proud spirit'[1] is inflamed against me again. He has sent out a letter, completely unexpected, every line of which breathes a murderous hatred, though for my part, after the conflict brought upon me on account of my *On the Freedom of the Will* against his *On the Bondage of the Will*,[2] I have never attacked either him or his doctrine in a hateful way.[3] Truly, I have always been working and hoping for what all Christian-minded folk hope (unless I am mistaken): that the supreme moderator of human affairs might some day direct these tumults in the church to a favourable conclusion. So far am I from attacking Luther with my pen that I am rebuked by some in private letters, and reprimanded by others in published books,[4] for having supported and made excuses for the Lutherans in some matters. I have always disapproved of defamatory dialogues,[5] the picture of the seven-headed Luther, and similar

* * * * *

1 Description of the lion to which Sarpedon is compared as he rushes against the Achaeans (Iliad 12.300). Achilles is called ἀγήνωρ (9.699), but the epithet for his θυμός is μέγας 'great' (9.496); see G.S. Kirk, R. Janko, et al *The Iliad: A Commentary* 6 vols (Cambridge 1985–93); on θυμός cf N. Blössner 'Thymos' *Historisches Wörterbuch der Philosophie* x 1187–92.

2 For Erasmus' *De libero arbitrio diatribe sive collatio* (1524) see *A Discussion of Free Will* CWE 76:1–90; for Luther's *De servo arbitrio* (1525) see Watson and Drewery *Bondage of the Will*; and for Erasmus' response to Luther's response see *Hyperaspistes* I and II (CWE 76 and 77).

3 This was true, even for letters Erasmus chose not to publish; eg to Martin Bucer (March 1532) he cites scurrilous rumours about Luther, but without giving credence to them; cf Allen Ep 2615:477–83.

4 Eg Augustino Steucho to Erasmus on 27 March 1531 (Allen Ep 2513:329–61), a letter that was later published.

5 Eg Ep 1519:432–3 n26. In 1524 Erasmus prevented republication of the *Dialogus bilinguium ac trilinguium*, a savage lampoon of the Louvain theologians (for the

provocations; I even tried to dissuade Johannes Cochlaeus from such fierce controversy.[6]

The matter which has poured so much oil on this fire,[7] or rather has added sulphur and stirred up the glow covered by ashes, seems to be of little moment. One Georg Witzel, previously a prominent follower of Luther's, later fell away from him for some reason or other. He wrote to me again and again, making no secret of his disapproval of Luther. However, I did not reply to his letters, partly through lack of time, partly because he wrote from distant, obscure places;[8] then, too, he himself was utterly unknown to me. Had I had the opportunity to write to this man, I would have warned him not to attack Luther, or certainly not to indulge his anger, which his letters demonstrated was easily sparked off. This Witzel, it appears, has now published some book[9] or other against certain of Luther's opinions. Since I have not seen these books, I can pronounce no opinion on them.

Then one Nikolaus von Amsdorf came along and took it on himself well and truly to give the cart a good shove downhill,[10] urging that Witzel should be disregarded, and that Erasmus should be attacked, and be 'painted at last in his true colours, which are,' he says, 'ignorance and malice; for the sum of my teaching,' to use his words, 'is this: Luther's teaching is heresy, since it has been condemned by the emperor and the pope, but his own is in fact orthodox, since bishops and cardinals, princes and kings

* * * * *

text see CWE 7 329–47). Yet he was, despite his denials, the anonymous author of a scurrilous satire on the late Pope Julius II (1503–13), *Julius exclusus e coelis*; see the preface to Ep 502.

6 The seven-headed Luther was a satirical wood-cut printed as title-page of Cochlaeus' *Septiceps Lutherus* (1529), one of the author's many polemics against the Saxon reformer. For Johann Cochlaeus von Wendelstein, see M. Spahn *Johannes Cochlaeus: Ein Lebensbild aus der Zeit der Kirchenspaltung* (Berlin 1898, repr 1964) 145–8 and CEBR I 321–2. Cf Allen Ep 1863:18–21, where Erasmus suggests to Cochlaeus that polemics are not the best use of his time.

7 Cf Adagia I ii 9 and 10: *Oleum camino addere* and *Oleo incendium restinguere* CWE 31 151–2.

8 In the two surviving letters, Witzel wrote from Frankfurt and from his home town, Vacha an der Werra (Allen Epp 2715, 2786). That Erasmus had not heard of the latter is not surprising; cf Allen Ep 2918:6–10. On Georg Witzel see CEBR III 458–9.

9 Witzel's only published work to date was his *Pro defensione bonorum operum adversus novas evangelistas* (Leipzig 1532).

10 *Plaustrum perculit*. Cf Plautus *Epidicus* 4.2.22; *Adagia* I vi 13 CWE 32 11–12; Ep 1389:29–30 above 34.

send him presents of golden cups and the like; if there is anything else in his books, I will die.'[11] And Luther not only approves this man's judgment on me, he actually admires it,[12] even though it is absurd and patently false. For it is incorrect to attribute ignorance and malice to the same man, since when he sins through ignorance it is a mistake, not malicious. Then, I never call Luther's teaching heresy anywhere in my writings[13] (if I did, I would hardly be the first or the only person to do so). Nor do I ever reason thus: my teaching is sound because princes send me presents.[14] I use this argument to encourage my friends, who are grieved that everywhere I am being torn to shreds in speech and in furious books. Against my detractors' hatred I set the favour of good men, amongst whom are many exalted in rank, admirable for their piety, and renowned for their learning. I also sometimes adduce their judgment against those who complain of my unauthorized boldness in laying hands on the New Testament. Nothing of this relates to Luther's teaching. Nor has any of the princes sent me golden cups; some have honoured me with gifts, but I myself have never solicited or expected them. What Luther may receive is no concern of mine. And so, although what Amsdorf has asserted is nowhere to be found in my writings, yet he swears his life away if anything else can be found in them: 'I will die,' he says. I will not wish him so great a misfortune; rather I wish that in him falsehood may die and truth live.

Such is the beginning of the drama,[15] and Luther's letter fits with it perfectly. It teems with excessive, even demented, rebukes and malicious untruths throughout. I am not particularly offended by the abusive language. Is it surprising, after all, that he should vent his spleen on me, given that he revels in the same kind of impudence towards kings and princes as often as it pleases him? Therefore, I will not throw back his insults, but as far as ever I can I will imitate my Lord and Teacher, who, when asked: 'Are you not a Samaritan, possessed by a demon, and casting out demons with the help of Beelzebub?'[16] did not reply to the accusation of being a Samaritan (for it is absurd to reproach someone for his country of birth,

* * * * *

11 Amsdorf to Luther (WA Br 7 2086:15–20); on Nikolaus von Amsdorf see CEBR I 51–2.

12 WA Br 7 2093:39

13 This is correct. Erasmus saw theological differences between Lutherans and Roman Catholics as matters of opinion, not as doctrines binding on the faithful; cf the colloquy *Inquisitio de fide* (CWE 39 419–47).

14 Many such presents are listed in *Catalogus lucubrationum*, Allen 1 42:34–44:29.

15 See Ep 1389 above 35 n21; *Spongia* above 38 n5.

16 A collation of John 8:48–52 and Matt 12:25–30

which no one chooses for himself,[17] or for anything else not under human control). Nor did he throw back the other two accusations on those who slandered him, but dismissed them with arguments, for this was the way expedient to the gospel.[18] To be ignorant, forgetful, slow, mistaken, or deceived, are faults of human nature; and being mindful that we are nothing but human,[19] we readily ask pardon for them and pardon them in one another. But what Luther reproaches me with is so far from human as to be more than diabolical. For he is trying to convince the world that Erasmus not only is an unbeliever as regards divine matters, but that for a long time now he has been using tricks, stratagems, and everything in his power to unsettle the whole Christian religion, then dash it down entirely and in its place bring paganism back into the world.

And yet, I have no fear that such wild, uncontrolled abuse (for it is nothing else) will attach itself to me in the minds of those who have read my works or have closely examined my conduct and my character in private dealings with me. I must try to satisfy those who do not know me and have not read my books, yet are such dedicated followers of Luther that they think anything he says is an oracle. I wish that in my life I had shown obedience to the divine commandments to the same degree that I feel clear and quiet in conscience before God with regard to the things pertaining to faith. As far as my behaviour is concerned, I beg God's mercy every day with sighs and a heavy heart. Yet I would not wish him ever to be gracious to me if the most tenuous thought of diabolical villainy has ever impelled my mind even so much as to desert the Catholic faith myself,[20] let alone to obscure the whole glory of Christ. And oh, if by sacrificing this little body of mine I could quell this discord in the church, how pleased, how joyful I would be to take that death on myself! Meanwhile, in my prayers night and day I ask the Lord's forgiveness for the sins I have committed. It is not to give me faith that I beg him, but to strengthen and increase the faith he has already given me. I say this sincerely, with God as my witness; may he punish me immediately if any of it is a lie.

* * * * *

17 For Erasmus on his own Low Countries 'fatherland,' see M.E.H.N. Mout '"Het Bataafse Oor": De Lotgevallen van Erasmus' Adagium "Auris Batava"' in *Nederlandse Geschiedenisschrijving, Mededeling van de Koninklijke Nederlandse Akademie van Wetenschappen, Afdeling Letterkunde* ns 5 vol 56 no 2 (Amsterdam 1993); cf *Spongia* above n486.
18 See also John 7:21–4.
19 An allusion to Cicero *Epistulae familiares* 5.16.2
20 Erasmus often makes this point, eg Allen Ep 2136:147–66.

Moreover, I will never be brought to believe that Luther supposes of me what he is trying to persuade others. Rather, the man is driven off course[21] by uncontrolled hatred, the wish to domineer, and the promptings of those who incite him. This will become clear if I quote some of the words from which he claims he has reached his opinion of me.

To begin with, he is displeased by my *Catechism*. Since I mention various of the ancient heretics' errors in it, he accuses me of 'making the doctrines of faith seem suspect' to the catechumens, 'since I omit the solid foundations' at the start, 'and mention only the heresies and scandalous opinions by which the church was troubled in the beginning; so that I practically define that there has never been anything certain in the Christian religion.' And he adds: 'If an inexperienced soul is overwhelmed by these examples and dangerous questions at the very beginning, what else will he think or do but shrink secretly from Christianity as if from the plague, or, if he dares, abhor it openly?' This is precisely how he begins.[22]

First of all, I am not entirely clear what these 'solid foundations' are that he accuses me of having omitted. The foundations that I lay at the very beginning are like this:[23] that it pleased God in his mercy to restore the world, which had fallen from its original state as a result of Adam's and Eve's sin, through his Son Jesus Christ; that the way to this grace is equally open to all through a sincere faith in Christ; that faith is a gift of God, which no one gives himself but must be sought of God. I make the canonical Scripture of the Old and New Testament the subject matter of faith, and using many arguments I teach that its [Scripture's] authority, as proceeding from God, is absolutely certain and inviolable, independently of the philosophy of this world and human reasonings and proofs from experience. This is more or less the gist of the first catechesis, in which there is never an ambiguous word, but firm, forceful assertion. And though this is constant throughout the whole book, yet the catechist says at one point: 'But here, where God is all things to all people, there can be no error, no darkness, no ambiguity. He himself is the beginning, he is the movement forward, he is the consummation.'[24] Unprejudiced reader, I beg

* * * * *

21 Cf *Adagia* II viii 92: *Transversum agere* CWE 34 86: 'A man is said to be driven off course who is deflected by some violent force from his intended path.'

22 WA Br 7 2093:90–107

23 For what follows, see the work Erasmus here refers to as his *Catechism*, *Explanatio symboli* CWE 70 236–47.

24 *Explanatio symboli* CWE 70 246; cf 1 Cor 15:28; on *initium-progressus-consummatio* see Hoffmann *Rhetoric and Theology* 250 n96, 260 n90, 268 n52.

you, are these not the solid foundations of the Christian faith which Paul
and all the orthodox Fathers used? If Luther has any sounder ones, no one is
preventing him from bringing them forward for the benefit of the church.
And I do not know whether he has published any version of the Creed
in German;[25] I was quite ignorant concerning this, and took on that work
simply at the request of a highly esteemed man.[26]

In the second catechesis,[27] the Creed is recited, and for greater clarity the whole of it is divided into three parts after the fashion of the three
divine persons, whose unity of nature and difference of properties are explained in passing. Immediately after this, in a second section, the individual articles are set forth in what might be called brief commentaries so
that, when the catechumen has taken in and learned the gist of the whole
argument, he may the more easily understand the remaining details and the
more faithfully remember them as well. Then, when these points [loci] have
been established, the discourse goes back over the same tracks, discussing
individual aspects in greater length and detail. This kind of teaching, as
being that most suited to making progress in learning, has been followed
by Aristotle,[28] and by many other learned men besides – and not only by
pagans, but by the most distinguished of the orthodox writers as well.

And so, I ask you, in handing on the truth, do I really give the
example of recording opinions which have departed from the truth, and
the 'heresies by which the church was troubled in the beginning'? Is this
to smother the truth, and not rather to clarify and confirm it, and to
fortify the minds of my audience? If I now cite the example of Aristotle, whose constant practice it is to propound and refute various opinions,[29] or Quintilian, who emphatically believes that it is conducive to
eloquence for the teacher to point out not only the things that are correctly said in the orator's writings, but also those which are falsely

* * * * *

25 There is nothing in Erasmus' writings to indicate that he had seen Luther's
   Grosser Katechismus or *Kleiner Katechismus*, both published in 1529; for the ecclesiastical visitations in Saxony that made the need for such manuals clear,
   cf *Epistola ad fratres Inferioris Germaniae* above 273 n57.
26 Thomas Boleyn, the father of Anne Boleyn, to whom the *Explanatio symboli* was
   dedicated; see Allen Ep 2772:165–6.
27 *Explanatio symboli* CWE 70 247–51
28 Erasmus contributed a preface for the 1531 Froben edition of Aristotle's works
   (Allen Ep 2432), but he often criticized the Philosopher whom the medieval
   scholastics so admired (eg Allen Ep 2463:60–3), and critics wondered whether
   he had even read Aristotle (Allen Ep 2682:36–8).
29 Eg Aristotle *De anima* 403b20–405b30.

said,[30] Luther will cry: 'Pagans, pagans!' But what will he say of the Doctors of the Holy Church, not one of whom works differently, whether one
considers the ancient writers or those more recent? Does St Augustine keep
silent about the heretics' various blasphemies when instructing catechumens? Does the blessed Thomas Aquinas, or Jean Gerson in his writings on
the Creed, not do the same?[31] For if there is the danger that someone may
fall away from the Christian religion if it becomes known that the church
has been troubled by various heretics' errors, then St Epiphanius and Philastrius among the Greeks,[32] and Augustine among the Latins, undertook a
ruinous task in displaying the catalogue of all heresies to the world's view.

   And yet, who is there, among either the ancient or the recent Doctors, whose books are not everywhere replete with allusions to heresies
and heretics? I would cite Athanasius, Basil, John Chrysostom, Cyril, John
Damascene, and of the Latin Doctors, Cyprian, Ambrose, Jerome, and Augustine. Young people ought to be kept away from these writers' books,
lest they shrink offended from Christianity as from the plague. Still, men
of great holiness as well as great learning have judged that it would contribute pre-eminently to the glory of Christ and the stability of the church
for the world to know in what storms and tempests the truth has stood
invincible till this day – undoubtedly because Christ has protected it. Ad-
mittedly, I make the proponent of these [heretical] ideas an ignorant catechumen, for I invent persons, so that the discussion is clearer and the matter made visible, so to speak. But there is a precedent for this: The blessed
Athanasius, Cyril, Jerome, and Augustine did the same.[33]

   I wrote this work, though, less for catechumens than for catechists. If
I had written for the unlearned, I would have written in German, not Latin.

* * * * *

30 Quintilian *Declamationes* 2.5.10–13
31 The works of Augustine, Aquinas, and Gerson to which Erasmus alludes are
   discussed in the introduction to *Explanatio symboli* ASD V-1 186–92.
32 Epiphanius Πανάριον (*Adversus Haereses*) PG 41 173–42 832; Filastrius *Diver-
   sarum haereseon liber* CCSL 9 207–324. Erasmus mistakes Filastrius, bishop of
   Brescia (d before 397), for a Greek, though there had been an edition of his
   Latin treatise in Basel in 1528.
33 For Athanasius, Erasmus perhaps has in mind *De trinitate libri septem*, a work
   attributed to Athanasius in a 1528 edition, but now thought to have been written at least in part by Eusebius of Vercelli CCSL 9 1–118; Cyril of Alexandria
   De adoratione et cultu in spiritu et veritate PG 68 133–210, and *De sancta et consub-
   stantiali trinitate* PG 75 657–1124 (both works were included in a 1528 collection
   of Cyril's works by Johann Oecolampadius); and Jerome *Altercatio luciferiani
   cum orthodoxo* CCSL 79 and *Dialogi contra Pelagianos libri* III CCSL 80. Many of
   Augustine's works would fit this description.

For nowadays there are no ignorant catechumens, provided that parents, teachers, and pastors do their duty. A number of scruples are presented which might affect the ignorant reader. Sectarian delusions are mentioned. But they are refuted most diligently by the catechists, and rejected using true, valid arguments, and this not in a lifeless way, or using ambiguous words (so that anyone could reasonably expect trickery) but in clear words and in a vigorous spirit, which can be recognized as coming from the heart, not from mockery.

Consequently, it is patently false for Luther to argue that I have omitted the solid foundations, given that I begin from the most utterly solid foundations of Christian doctrine. It is also wrong (or hyperbolic,[34] if he prefers) for him to say that all I do is bombard catechumens with heresies and scandalous opinions, since I include these only in passing. But it is the highest of falsehood for him to add that I practically state that there has never been anything certain in the Christian religion. For throughout the entire dialogue I work constantly and eagerly at persuading the reader that the Christian philosophy is the one and only faith which is unassailably certain.

On this foundation, built not with rubble but with downright lies, Luther constructs an edifice of abuse, and does it in his own way: He is constantly feeding his soul in these pleasant places. In doing so, he fails to notice that whatever abuse he heaps on me falls also on the most outstanding Doctors of the church. He says: 'And he thinks that this sly advice cannot be understood by any man, as though we did not have countless examples of the devil's disguises like this in the Scriptures.'[35] Oh, the apostolic eloquence! It would be more to be wondered at that this diabolical notion should have entered any man's mind. And to this end he quotes the serpent from Genesis,[36] who first brought Eve into the state of uncertainty, then cast her into destruction. How did he call her into doubt? By querying: 'Why did God command you not to eat of any tree of Paradise?' So, if anyone who queries is imitating the serpent, all the Doctors of the church, ancient as well as modern, are among the devil's disguises, and so are all the theological schools. For here not only are questions concerning matters

* * * * *

34 On Luther's conscious use of *hyperbole*, see Boyle *Rhetoric and Reform* 7, 90, 92; Hoffmann *Rhetoric and Theology* sv *hyperbole*; on Erasmus' rhetoric in *De libero arbitrio* cf M. Hoffmann 'Reformation Ways of Speaking: Erasmus' Rhetorical Theology in *De libero arbitrio*' ERSY 24 (2004) 1–22.
35 WA Br 7 2093:98–100
36 WA Br 7 2093:100–3; cf Gen 3:1.

of faith propounded, but in addition the doctrines of Christianity are subjected to attack by the strongest arguments possible. And the ignorant are not kept away from these discussions; all who want to can look on.

Luther will say that it is not my subject matter that distinguishes me from other teachers, but my spirit. They ask questions not in order to weaken the truth, but to corroborate it against the insult of the irreligious. What does Erasmus do? He creeps about with snake-like cunning,[37] tempting the souls of simple folk in order to hurl them headlong into paganism. If I had been of this mind, the very first thing I would have done would have been to betake myself to the fellowship of the sects. For there is nothing more ideally suited to the destruction of the Christian religion than the licence of the sects,[38] who allow themselves to change their doctrine as often as they please, when they can get away with doing so. But what makes it apparent that I raise the question with the intention of bringing the reader into doubt? Is it because I imitate the serpent by denying the truth of what the church has handed down in the Creed, just as the serpent said: 'You will not die'?[39] If the catechist answers the question I put, not ambiguously or lifelessly, but rigorously, firmly, and assertively, stating what is the Catholic doctrine, whom do I most resemble – a serpent, or the most approved Doctor of the church? What would Luther say if I had introduced the devil disputing with a man, as he does in his *Von der Winkelmesse*,[40] giving the devil such strong arguments that he admits he cannot refute them? But I will not cast any of Luther's arguments back on him, though I would be justified in doing so with all of them. Then in the same way, as though he had by now convinced his readers that I believe none of the articles of the Creed, he has interwoven the witty remark: 'unless

* * * * *

37 WA Br 7 2093:103ff; cf Matt 10:16. Erasmus sometimes spoke of combining 'the simplicity of the dove' with 'the prudence of the serpent,' eg paraphrase on Matthew 10:16 CWE 45 170–1, *Ecclesiastes* ASD V-4 64:579–84, 76:897–8; cf Augustine *De doctrina christiana* 1.14.13.

38 Erasmus uses the term *sectae* to refer to the 'evangelical' or Swiss and South German branch of the reformation, for which he had no sympathy whatever. Cf his denunciation of the evangelicals, in terms similar to this passage, in a nearly contemporary letter to one of their leaders, Martin Bucer: Allen Ep 2615:328–38.

39 Gen 3:4

40 Luther's treatise against private masses was published in German in December 1533 (WA 38 197–205). Two of Erasmus' Catholic friends called his attention to the Latin version of April 1534 (Allen Ep 2906:10–14 and Ep 2921:8–14). Cf Allen Ep 3000:32–5: The duke of Württemberg has banned the mass altogether, even though Luther 'in a recent book full of imprecation only condemns private masses.'

Erasmus may think this is a fable too'[41] so that no part of his text should be without its sting.

But what, I ask you, are these snake-like questions in my Catechism? Luther asks: 'Why have there been so many sects and errors in this one religion of truth, as it is believed to be? And why are there so many different creeds?'[42] Luther has made up these questions by himself, by the authority he enjoys, for the catechumen asks no such question. Rather, the catechist does what has been done by all the Doctors of the church and is done today: he puts forward an unbending rule of faith, and in passing shows in how many ways the philosophers' and heretics' ways of thinking have diverged from it. But he shows this divergence in such a way that it is made hateful. Luther's own addition of 'as it is believed to be' is humorous indeed, as though I doubted whether this rule of faith was true! This indeed is no serpent's wile, it is the oracle of the Holy Spirit speaking through Luther's mouth. It shows the same degree of honesty that he makes up these questions in such a way that it looks as if the catechumen were amazed that the religion in which there have been so many errors and which has so many creeds could be true. I never speak of there having been heresies in the Christian religion. I say that it has been plagued by various philosophers' errors, but has persisted till the present in its incontrovertible integrity.[43] Augustine and other orthodox theologians mention the very same fact[44] as proof that only the truth of faith, given by God, is unassailable. Yet when Erasmus mentions the same fact, he is calling the church's universal teaching into doubt and trying to show that it is nothing but a fable.

If it is dangerous to know that there are many creeds, why are the Athanasian and the Nicene Creeds said and sung publicly in churches[45] in addition to the Apostles' Creed? Why are so many creeds with different titles mentioned in Jerome's work?[46] If I had said that the creeds, especially

* * * * *

41 WA Br 7 2093:102ff. Luther used the indicative form *putat* 'thinks,' but Erasmus quotes him in the subjunctive *putet* 'may think.'

42 WA Br 7 2093:104ff

43 *Explanatio symboli* CWE 70 293–8

44 Eg in Augustine *Sermo de symbolo ad catechumenos* 6.14 (CCSL 46 197:377–83).

45 For the Creed long attributed to St Athanasius, recited (until 1955) as part of the Office of Prime on Sundays, see *New Catholic Encyclopedia* 1 995–6. *Explanatio symboli* CWE 70 253: Erasmus distinguishes between the 'Nicene' and 'Constantinopolitan' Creeds; he understood that the Creed commonly called Nicene represents not the text approved by the Council of Nicaea (325), but a revision approved by the Council of Constantinople (381).

46 In his 2nd edition of the *Lucubrationes omnes* of St Jerome (Basel 1525) LB IV 123B, Erasmus notes that though Jerome wrote no creed, many such texts are

those which have been handed down to us by the authority of the councils, contradict one another, I could indeed have been accused of having given the weak cause for scruple. But I show that there is nothing lacking in the very short so-called Apostles' Creed, and nothing superfluous in the other Creeds, but what is condensed summarily in the former is set out at greater length and more explicitly in the latter, and that this was done to counter the continual spread of heresies.[47] So what have I done, I ask, that is new? Do not all those who have discussed this argument compare the creeds with one another, pointing out what has been said more explicitly in others? Just as it is a very praiseworthy way of teaching to examine the meaning of Scripture by comparing different passages, so those who explicate the concise first Creed by comparison with other Creeds are worthy of praise.

But Luther brings up another dreadful question: Why, in the Apostles' Creed, the Father is called God, the Son Lord, and the Spirit Holy. He adds the tragic exclamation: 'Who, I ask, bothers ignorant souls, whose instruction he has undertaken, with these questions, apart from the devil himself?'[48] I believe he means that devil who previously attacked his soul concerning the mass[49] using such effective stratagems. For indeed he does not take into consideration the fact that the catechist has beforehand diligently instructed the catechumen that the Father, Son, and Spirit are one God, and that there is no difference in their nature, which is rather one and numerically identical in the three Persons.[50] He has also pointed out the fact that in the original Creed the words 'I believe in the Holy Spirit' are not repeated, so that the name of God might the more equally apply to all the Persons;[51] as we say, 'I believe in God,' and then, after a brief pause for breath, there follows: 'the Father Almighty, and in Jesus Christ, and in the Holy Spirit.' And so the distinction of Persons subjoined in effect explicates the name 'God,' which includes all the Persons. The catechumen, therefore, being instructed on the mystery of the Trinity, only asks about scriptural usage for the sake of those

* * * * *

attributed to him, including 'The Creed of Damasus' (actually, of Gregory of Elvira CCSL 69 272); ' Explanation of the Creed to Damasus' (by Pelagius PL 30 182–7); an 'Explanation of the Creed' (by Pelagius PL 48 488–91); an 'Explanation of the faith to Cyril' (PL 30 182–7); and a 'Creed of Rufinus' (cf his *Commentarius in symbolum apostolorum* PL 21 335–86).

47 *Explanatio symboli* CWE 70 253–4
48 WA Br 7 2903:105–9; *Explanatio symboli* CWE 70 258–9
49 See introductory note above n69.
50 *Explanatio symboli* CWE 70 215
51 *Explanatio symboli* CWE 70 256

who may not have grasped the distinction of speech which I had pointed out.[52] In the same way, to prevent those who think 'I believe in God the Father' should be read as one phrase from supposing that the name 'God' applies to the Father alone, as the Jews and Arians do, I remove that scruple by demonstrating scriptural usage. There will be an opportunity to speak on this later. Does the devil teach like this? And is the person who has been taught the whole mystery of the Trinity, and has believed it, 'ignorant'?

Then the plot of the tragedy really thickens. Luther asks, 'Who, apart from the very mouthpiece and instrument of Satan, has dared to speak of the Creed in this way: "Here you have the exposition, complication, and denouement of this *drama* of salvation"?'[53] He prates on here about nothing except Satan, devils, spectres, Furies, and other tragic terms.[54] Perhaps 'the mouth is speaking from the abundance of the heart';[55] certainly language like this usually presages the onset of madness. After the catechist has explained the persons mentioned in the Creed, the Father and Creator, the Son and Redeemer, the Holy Spirit and Reconciler, and the church as the mystical body of Christ, and then has fully expounded the beginning, continuation, and consummation of the church in their order,[56] he adds: 'Here you have the exposition, complication, and denouement of this drama of salvation; all the acts and scenes, disposed under the heavenly director's ineffable dispensation.'[57] Luther has related these words in a mangled form, and in those he has related he has added some things, taken some away, changed others. He has added 'look,' plainly in irritation; he has removed the pronoun 'this,' which shows which drama I am talking about; and instead of *fabula salutifera* 'drama of salvation' he has written *fabula salubria* 'wholesome drama.'[58] Yet when explaining the chief point of redemption, I added

* * * * *

52 *Explanatio symboli* CWE 70 258
53 WA Br 7 2093:109–11. In quoting Erasmus, Luther had substituted an ambiguous word for 'of health' or 'of salvation' (*salubris*) for the uneqivocal term used by Erasmus (*salutiferae*). Erasmus here gives his own original wording, but Luther's self-serving change of nuance is noted below n58. On *fabula* and *protasis-epistasis-catastrophe* see above Spongia 38 n5.
54 WA Br 7 2093:81, 83ff, 99, 109–11, 195, 196, 229, 240, 261ff, 303, 372, 381. For Erasmus, a 'tragedy' was not just a type of drama, but a situation in which differences of opinion were falsely elevated to the status of an ultimate choice between good and evil; eg Ep 447:478
55 Matt 12:34
56 *Explanatio symboli* CWE 70 248–51
57 *Explanatio symboli* CWE 70 251
58 See above n53.

'this' precisely so that it could not be understood simply of any kind of drama; and I added 'of salvation' so that no one could imagine that it was anything similar to the poet's fables; finally, so that it would not be unclear that my language was metaphorical, I added 'here you have all the acts and scenes' etc, the words which Luther in his cunning has left out.

But Luther objects that profane words adapted to divine things are offensive – as though the biblical writings, and those of the orthodox theologians, did not abound with similar figures of speech. God is compared to a money-lender;[59] Christ's second coming is compared to a thief in the night;[60] the heralds of the gospel are compared to an unfaithful steward;[61] the indescribable union of the divine nature with human nature in Christ, and the union of Christ with the church, are compared to the marriage of a bride and bridegroom.[62] The reward of eternal life is called *brabeum* 'prize,' a word drawn from the circus, and *stipendium*, a military term for wages.[63] Paul describes wrestling against the flesh using the language of prize-fighters and compares the quest for perfect piety with runners in the stadium. But what subject matter is so profane that Paul does not borrow metaphors from it in order to express his thought more significantly: the public games, theatres, soldiering, pagan triumphs.[64] Yet I am 'a mouthpiece of Satan' because I have adapted a single metaphor to describe something sacred – a metaphor that seemed highly suitable to express my thought. *Fabula* 'drama,' in Greek δρᾶμα, means a coherent argument involving various persons, each of whom plays his part, the whole action being arranged in such a way that from a reasonably calm beginning it increases in intensity, but finally reaches a happy ending.[65] The metaphor implicitly com-

* * * * *

59 Luke 7:41–3
60 Matt 24:43; Mark 13:33; Luke 12:39–46
61 Luke 16:1–12
62 Scripture nowhere compares the union of Christ's human and divine natures to a marriage. Erasmus was perhaps thinking of Hilary of Poitiers' interpretation of the parable of the ten virgins in Matt 25:1–13; cf his *Annotationes* on Matt 25:1 ASD VI-5 316–18; Eph 5:21–33.
63 Robert Young *Young's Analytical Concordance to the Bible* (Nashville 1982) gives two such uses of βραβεῖον: 1 Cor 9:24 and Eph 3:14, and three uses of ὀψώνια (*stipendium*): Luke 3:14, Rom 6:23, and 2 Cor 11:8, but none refer to eternal life.
64 1 Cor 9:25, Phil 1:30, 1 Tim 4:7–10 (public games); 1 Cor 4:9, Heb 10:32–3 (theatres); 2 Cor 10:3–4, Eph 6:11–17, 2 Tim 2:3–4 (soldiering); and 2 Cor 2:14, Col 2:15 (pagan triumphs).
65 For Erasmus' conception of the *drama* or *fabula* of redemption, and its place in the theological tradition, see Chantraine *Mystère* 274–95 and Hoffmann *Rhetoric*

pares God the Father to the director, who is the author of the entire dispensation. The Son takes on the weaknesses of the flesh, concealing his divine nature,[66] rather as an actor assumes a role (no slight is intended in the comparison). The Holy Spirit moderates the church until, at the resurrection of the just, God wipes away every tear from the eyes of the saints.[67] Man being created good is like the exposition [of the drama], the cross is like the complication, the resurrection is like the denouement. Luther will say that the unlearned do not understand that. But I do not write for the unlearned, as the whole form of the argument sufficiently shows, and no one could translate these terms into German or French.

The word *fabula* is two-headed indeed; certainly if nothing is added to it. For sometimes it means a fictional narrative, sometimes the recounting of true and familiar things, as when we say *liter[at]ae fabulae* 'learned conversations,'[68] and sometimes, as I said above, it means a coherent argument acted by different persons. Yet I have taken care so that it cannot be ambiguous to anyone. But Luther will object that it is a profane word. Πυκτεύω 'I box' is a more profane word, yet Paul uses it to express something that is not profane.[69] Do we not hear the words 'Before this virgin's couch repeat the drama's sweet strains to us' sung publicly in churches in praise of the Virgin Mother?[70] Yet we read the same word 'drama' at the beginning of Aristophanes' plays, which are not merely profane but to a large extent obscene. Does this fail to give offence because fewer people understand the Greek word 'drama' than the Latin word 'fabula'? And what is more, in this hymn there are no additional words which might remove the ambiguity or explain the metaphor, both of which I have carefully done.

* * * * *

and Theology 250 n96. For Erasmus' defence of this metaphor against Catholic critics, see *Supputatio* LB IX 563–5D and *Responsio ad epistolam Pii* CWE 84:57–8.

66 The idea of Christ concealing (*dissimulans*) his divinity, the better to accommodate himself to all, was grist for the mills of Erasmus' critics; cf *Spongia* above 115–16 and *Apologia adversus Petrum Sutorem* LB IX 806A–D. On the theme of Christ's *accommodatio* in Erasmus see Chantraine *Mystère* 295–316, and Hoffmann *Rhetoric and Theology* 263 n122, 281 n84.

67 Rev 7:17, 21:4

68 On *litteratae fabulae* cf *Spongia* above 76 n222 and Ep 1342:122. *Literas fabulas* (ASD I-ix 452:295) is perhaps a misprint for *literatas fabulas*.

69 1 Cor 9:26

70 This antiphon, mentioned elsewhere by Erasmus (*Supputatio* LB IX 564D), was sung as part of the Office of Compline for certain Marian feasts; see the references in S.J.P. van Dijk *Sources of the Modern Roman Liturgy: The Ordinals by Haymo of Faversham and Related Documents (1243–1307)* (Leiden 1963) II 127:8, 132:6, 160:7ff, 182:10, 188:14.

Here I pass over the garden of insults[71] in which Luther delights to feed his soul, which cannot be sated by any amount of abuse. He brings up another passage from the Introduction to the *Paraphrase on the Epistle to the Romans*, 'in which,' as he says, 'I praise and extol Paul in such a manner that no rhetoric could be more effective in deterring and restraining the simple, unsuspecting reader from reading and becoming acquainted with Paul, so confused, intricate, self-contradictory, changeable, and uncouth does he depict him as being that he forces one to believe that this Epistle was the work of some madman, so far from helpful does it seem.'[72] These are his words. When he writes this, he seems to himself marvellously δεινός 'forceful.' But to reasonable people this δείνωσις 'forcefulness, exaggeration' seems out-and-out insanity.[73] He will call this hyperbole.[74] But these hyperboles are downright lies, since in that Introduction, having discoursed at length on the usefulness of the Epistle, which was given pride of place by the consensus of the church, not without reason, I also point out its difficulty, partly to stimulate the reader's attentiveness, and partly to demonstrate that this Introduction, which might well appear to have involved small exertion, cost me no little labour.

I cite three reasons for the Epistle's difficulty. There are problems of the language, owing to instances of *hyperbaton, anantapodosis*,[75] and Hebraism. The second is the sublimity of the matters Paul deals with, which can hardly be explained in any human words. The third is the frequent change of person,[76] because in the course of his discussion the Apostle turns his attention now to some people, now to others, and himself takes on different roles in order to instruct. I say nothing here that I have not taken from the ancient Doctors, above all from Origen.[77] And indeed the words 'confused,'

* * * * *

71 WA Br 7 2093:112–15
72 WA Br 7 2093:118–22. For Erasmus' *Argumentum* to Romans, published with his *Paraphrase on Romans* in 1517 see CWE 42 6–14; for Luther's reaction cf WA Tr I 500:224: 'Praefatio Erasmi in epistolam ad Romanos geht eim christen durch leyb und leben.'
73 On δείνωσις see *Spongia* above 79 n238.
74 See above n34.
75 For *hyperbaton* (artificial word order) see *Medieval Rhetoric* ed J.J. Murphy (Berkeley 1978) 153–9; for *anantapodosis* (the omission of the second part of a periodic sentence) see H. Lausberg *Handbuch der literarischen Rhetorik* 3rd ed (Stuttgart 1990) 459.
76 The idea that Paul can suddenly shift from his own *persona* to that of a sinner was for Erasmus a 'special key' to understanding his theology of sin and grace; see eg his annotations on Romans 7:24 CWE 56 195.
77 Erasmus believed he had learned 'more of Christian philosophy from a single page of Origen than from ten of Augustine' (Ep 844:272–4). For how

'intricate,' 'self-contradictory,' 'changeable,' 'uncouth' and 'like a madman' appear nowhere in what I write. These monstrous words are spawned by Luther's noble wrath,[78] which was aroused by my having dared to point out difficulties, whereas his doctrine is that there are no difficulties in Scripture, but that everything is lucid and obvious, at least to anyone with grammatical knowledge and common sense.[79] Yet it would have been proper for him to have behaved more fairly towards me, for I wrote this Introduction before he made his oracles known to the world.

If I have erred, I have done so honestly, following authors of great repute: Origen, whom I cite here expressly;[80] Jerome, whose *Preface to Ephesians* shows that Epistle to be a tangle of great difficulties and profound questions.[81] Why is this? To deter readers? Not at all, but to stimulate the reader's attention and to enjoin him to apply himself. And who is there, or who has there ever been, who has written on Paul's Epistles without immediately grappling with difficult passages? If all of them were as blind as moles,[82] then my mistake indeed deserved forgiveness. It was Peter, the divinely inspired Prince of the Apostles, who gave me the handle: He admits that 'some things' written by Paul are 'hard to understand.'[83] Who is more to be trusted – Peter, who acknowledges the difficulty, or Luther, who denies that there is any obscurity at all?

Luther continues: 'And among other wholly slanderous attacks,' he says, 'Erasmus could not bear to keep back the one that Peter calls Christ a man, but avoids the word God.'[84] What, are those who acknowledge that there are some difficulties in Paul's writings slanderers attacking him? Indeed, how many accomplices I have in this crime, among them the Apostle Peter! It is rather Luther who is slanderous in reporting my words, making them appear to say that Peter had never called Christ God, that is, had never preached in such a way that Christ's divinity should be understood from his words. At this point in my text I am praising Paul's careful management, because like a wise steward of the mysteries

* * * * *

he read Origen over the years see A. Godin *Érasme, lecteur d'Origène* (Paris 1982).

78 In Latin *generosus stomachus*, a fair translation of θυμὸς ἀγήνωρ; cf above n1.

79 For Luther on the 'clarity of Scripture' see Watson and Drewery *Bondage of the Will* 109–12.

80 *Argumentum* to *Paraphrase on Romans* CWE 42 13

81 Jerome *Commentarii in epistolam ad Ephesios* PL 26 470B–C.

82 Cf *Adagia* I iii 55: *Talpa caecior* CWE 31 281–2: 'referring to people . . . who have no judgment.'

83 2 Pet 3:16

84 WA Br 7 2093:122–4

of God[85] he does not disclose everything everywhere: Among the perfect he imparts wisdom in secret,[86] among others he knows nothing except Jesus Christ, and him crucified.[87] He feeds the weak on milk, those grown up on solid food.[88] And immediately after, I add: 'On the basis of this counsel the Apostle Peter, when he was going to speak about Christ before an assembly of untaught people, calls him a man, and avoids the word God.'[89] By saying 'on the basis of this counsel' I show that Peter's prudence is like Paul's; by saying 'before an assembly of untaught people' I indicate that he did not fail to mention Christ's divinity when addressing those initiated into the mysteries of the Christian faith. And this is the only passage in Acts where Peter calls Christ a man.

Returning to this false accusation shortly afterwards, Luther becomes so heated that he declares that Erasmus should be condemned for heresy for having written: 'Peter calls Christ a man, but avoids the word God.'[90] In that case a great many distinguished luminaries of the church, who have also carefully commented on this and other scriptural passages, should be condemned along with me, among them St John Chrysostom in his *Homilies on the Acts of the Apostles* chapter 2.[91] Bede also mentions it, apparently following Ambrose;[92] he is quoted thus in the *Glossa Ordinaria*: 'Nor does Peter authoritatively call' him 'the Son of God before, but a man approved' by God, 'a righteous man, a man raised from the dead.'[93] Bede points out that the beginning of the Apostle Peter's talk, when he preached Christ in the centurion Cornelius' house in Acts 10 (34–43), is similar. And again, in chapter 17 of the same work, he comments that before the Athenians Paul calls Christ a man rather than God.[94] John Chrysostom also comments on the fact that he does not expound the mysteries of the divine nature, but only speaks of God in general, with no mention of the Son of God or the

* * * * *

85 1 Cor 4:1
86 1 Cor 2:6
87 1 Cor 1:23
88 Heb 5:11–14
89 *Argumentum* to *Paraphrase on Romans* CWE 42 13
90 WA Br 7 2093:206–8
91 Chrysostom *Homiliae in Acta apostolorum* PG 60 49–50, 55–6
92 Bede *Super Acta apostolorum expositio* CCSL 12 20 (on Acts 2:20–2); Ambrose *Expositio evangelii Lucae* 6 106 CSEL 32 279:14ff.
93 *Biblia latina cum glossa ordinaria* (fac repr of the *editio princeps* [A. Rusch: Strasbourg 1480–81]) 4 vols (Turnhout 1992) IV 457 (on Acts 2:22). See *Detectio praestigiarum* above 190 n159.
94 Bede *Super Acta apostolorum expositio* CCSL 20 22 (on Acts 2:34)

Holy Spirit.[95] Why did Peter prefer to call Christ a man rather than God in that first speech? So that the Jews, who only knew the Father and had heard nothing of the Son and the Holy Spirit, and who had been taught by the Law that there was only one God, would not be repelled if they heard a man called God, especially a man who was dead, crucified, and buried. He preferred to lead them little by little from those events to reflect on them in such a way that they would realize there was something greater than human in that man. Since the gentiles, however, believed that there were many gods, they might have been confirmed in their error if Paul had preached Christ as God to them when they were ignorant and as yet unable to grasp the mystery. Seeing that this has been carefully commented on by the most approved Doctors of the church, and that in praise of the apostles, whose mouths and tongues were governed by the Holy Spirit, how do I all of a sudden come to be an Arian[96] for commenting the same way they do?

But, says Luther, these words 'offend Christian' ears, 'as they are put: Peter calls Christ a man, and avoids the word God.'[97] They are put like this by Luther, not by me! He adds: 'especially' in 'a suspect author.' Here I can hardly stop myself laughing. Martin, condemned in so many judgments, censured in so many books, struck by so many thunderbolts, is calling me 'a suspect author'! But to whom have I appeared suspect? To a few monks,[98] who do not merely suspect Luther, but condemn him as the most noxious heresiarch of all since the world was made. He now calls them Christians[99] and uses their authority to disparage me! But how have they equalled his accusations except in so far as they have made themselves a laughing-stock to all men of learning and virtue? As for what he adds, that these words, as they are placed and as they sound, strongly intimate to the Arians that I do not approve of Christ being called God, but prefer him to be called a man:[100] If it is a question of his words, he must look to their sound and significance; if it is a question of my words as they were arranged by me, it is a thundering great lie! I pass over other abuse which falls rather on the holy Doctors of the church than on me. I prefer to reply to saner accusations.

* * * * *

95 Chrysostom *Homiliae in Acta apostolorum* Migne PG 60 269
96 For Erasmus' view of the Arian controversy, and how he was read by contemporaries, see Tracy 'Erasmus and the Arians' 1–10.
97 WA Br 7 2093: 206ff, 212ff. For Erasmus' words, see below n104.
98 Cf *Apologia ad annotationes Stunicae* ASD IX-2 124:319–130:425, and *Apologia adversus monachos* LB IX 1040A–50C.
99 Cf introductory note above nn36–7.
100 WA Br 7 2093:209–11

Luther says that these words could have been left out or expressed in a more reverential manner.[101] I would certainly have done one or the other of these if I had the slightest suspicion that there would prove to be any people who would find this small detail a stumbling-block.[102] I feared nothing from the Jews. I thought that the Arian heresy had been so utterly weeded out that it would have no chance of sprouting forth again. Then the very fact that I speak following the ancient Fathers' example seemed sufficient to exclude the Arian heresy. For when that plague was still raging in the church, the orthodox writers often mentioned the fact that Christ is rarely called God in the Scriptures precisely in order to deprive the partisans of Arianism of that handle.[103] But, Luther objects, they give reasons why the title of God is not used, whereas I do not. That is so – in Luther's words; in my own words, I do. Whoever likes may reread the passage[104] and will find this to be the case. Yet Martin pretends that this reason, which I learned from the most approved Doctors of the church, is a fabrication of mine. 'It is not satisfactory,' he says, 'to pretend that Peter called' Christ 'a man on account of the masses.'[105] Once again he is distorting my words. Today, in front of the Christian people, Christ is openly called God and man, but here I am pointing out the single passage in the Acts of the Apostles where Peter is preaching Christ to an ignorant, mixed crowd. 'Someone' who calls 'Christ a man,' Luther says, 'has not avoided saying that he is God, except in so far as he has not used the' three 'letters G-O-D in that place.'[106] Since he thinks this is a subtle thing to say, he repeats it; and at the end he writes: 'In my judgment Peter did not avoid

* * * * *

101 WA Br 7 2093:208ff

102 Erasmus knew of Michael Servetus' *De trinitatis erroribus libri septem* published in 1531 (Allen Ep 2615:335–6; cf Allen Ep 2961:113–16).

103 Cf *Adagia* I iv 4: *Ansam quaerere* 'To look for a handle' CWE 31 321–2: 'that is, on watch for an opportunity to go back on an agreement and invalidate it.'

104 *Argumentum* to *Paraphrase on Romans* CWE 42 13: 'And furthermore, as a prudent man, [Paul] so touches upon certain mysteries as to display them as through a window only, accommodating his speech to the situation of the times and to the capacity of those to whom he writes. Paul knew and saw certain things which it was unlawful for one to say, and he knew to what extent milk and to what extent solid food were needed. He knew the stages of growth in Christ, and what had to be applied to each one. On the basis of a similar judgment, the apostle Peter, when he was going to speak about Christ before an assembly of untaught people, calls him a man and avoids the word God.'

105 WA Br 7 2093:218ff

106 WA Br 7 2093:119–121

calling Christ God.'[107] For love of Christ this apostolic man suffers so much, and for love of him, I believe, he writes these false accusations. But what use are these verbal sophistries? When I say: 'He calls him a man, but avoids the word God,' what else does the sensible reader understand other than that he uses the title of man, but not that of God? In the same way Christ avoided calling himself God, and forbade the preaching of the Messiah for the time being.[108] For Christ nowhere calls himself God, and it was a more effective means of persuasion for him to show himself as God in his deeds rather than by taking the name to himself.

Now, whoever hands on those things about Christ which show that God was hidden in the man is not failing to say that Christ was God. But I never said that this amounted to not mentioning his divinity. I only point out that the three letters (G-O-D) which Martin scoffs at were not mentioned for the time being. And it was an effective means of assuring persuasion for us first to come to know the man, and then to be led by stages to a recognition of his divine nature. The way of persuasion was shown to us by the Lord himself, imitated by the apostles, and praised by the Doctors of the church. Where, indeed, do I strictly demand those three letters G-O-D?[109] Does he demand them who, writing against the Arians, mentions the fact that in the apostles' writings Christ is more often called Lord than God, and points out why this is the case, saying frankly that the name Lord is appropriate for the Father and the name God for the Son, since both are the same God and Lord?[110] Because the ancients mention this so often, they win renown for their reverence. Erasmus, according to Luther, is 'setting a snare for the ignorant, and' making the Christian 'religion suspect.'[111] I would be surprised if Martin was free of the fever when he scrawled these ravings on those fateful sheets of paper!

The paroxysm continues, and Luther praises Pio of Carpi in order to discredit me.[112] Yet, though some Spanish monks had cited that passage against me in a botched, shamefully mistaken manner, Pio fell foul of it

* * * * *

107 WA Br 7 2093:418
108 Matt 16:20
109 WA Br 7 2093:221
110 For arguments of this kind in Erasmus' *Annotationes in Novum Testamentum* see CWE 56 31–2 (on Romans 1:7), CWE 56 249–52 (on Romans 9:5), and LB VI 930E–F; on 1 Tim 1:17 see CWE 44 11, and Reeve *Galatians to the Apocalypse* 667.
111 WA Br 7 2093:222ff
112 WA Br 7 2093:224–6. For the controversy between Pio and Erasmus see Rummel *Catholic Critics* II 115–23 and N.H. Minnich 'Some Underlying Factors in the Erasmus-Pio Debate' ERSY 13 (1993) 1–43.

too.[113] He had not read my writings. He composed his malicious accusations on the basis of notes taken down by some hired youths. And now Martin is stumbling over the same passage. In it I show that the early Christians were more reticent and cautious in speaking about divine things than we are, whereas they honoured them in their minds and in their way of life more religiously than we do. I cite an example to support this opinion: 'We dare to call the Holy Spirit true God, which the ancients did not dare to do, but we have no scruples about driving him repeatedly out of the temple of our soul by our evil deeds, just as if it were our belief that the Holy Spirit is nothing more than a meaningless name,'[114] and so on. I do not condemn the fact that we dare to call the Holy Spirit God, but the fact that the godliness of our lives has not increased along with our knowledge and the confidence with which we profess it. Yet this is the passage where Luther bids the reader to notice the 'devil incarnate'![115] However, so as not to delay the reader with unnecessary detail, he should read the passages where I refute the accusations of the Spanish monks and Pio concerning the Trinity,[116] then he will admit that Luther is, not the devil incarnate (these are madmen's words), but a man crazed by hatred.

Luther continues: 'Nonetheless, Erasmus confesses belief in the Trinity most earnestly, and he wants it to seem that he has not in the least denied the Trinitarian nature of God.'[117] Most impudent of men, what are you saying? Has Erasmus ever denied the Trinitarian nature of God? I profess and defend it in a great many places in my writings! I will quote the passage, albeit loathsome, which follows, so that the reader can see that an unreasonable man is speaking: 'Except that he relates how the curiosity of recent scholars (which he later demands must be charitably understood as diligence) has dared to infer many things from the Scriptures which the ancients would not have dared. As though the Christian religion depended on human authority (this he tries to demonstrate) and this is nothing other than for all religions to be considered fictions.'[118] So he παραφρονεῖ 'raves on.' In

* * * * *

113 In the preface to his edition of the *Opera* of Hilary of Poitiers (1523), Erasmus noted that the 4th century church Father 'has scarcely anything to say about the Holy Spirit' (Ep 1334:430–487). For Erasmus' defence of this passage see *Apologia adversus monachos* LB IX 1050C–1054A.

114 Ep 1334:475–9

115 WA Br 7 2093:239ff

116 *Apologia adversus monachos* LB IX 1029E–33F, and *Apologia adversus rhapsodias Alberti Pii* CWE 84 275–90.

117 WA Br 7 2093:230–2

118 WA Br 7 2093:232–6

my preface to the edition of Hilary I do call a more demanding diligence concerning the Scriptures 'curiosity,' but I add the word 'pious.' The passage reads: 'Although the devout probing (*pia curiositas*) of the orthodox later ascertained with sufficient proof from Holy Scripture that whatever was attributed to the Son was appropriate to the Holy Spirit, except for the individuality of the person.'[119] And shortly afterwards I write: 'what has been handed down to us from Holy Scripture by the authority of the orthodox Fathers.'[120] Is it to talk nonsense to interpret the pious curiosity of the orthodox Fathers as a more demanding diligence? Moreover, instead of 'with sufficient proof,' Luther distorts it into 'bold inference.'[121]

Straight after that, based on his distorted version, he declares that my aim is to demonstrate that the Christian religion depends on human authority, which is nothing other than to aim at all religions being considered fictions. I do not know what he is referring to as 'all religions,' unless perhaps he is thinking of the law of Moses and the gospel. For indeed, until now I have always thought that there is only one religion. Is what those with trained minds bring together from Holy Scripture and teach to the ignorant no more than a fiction? But Martin admits nothing except the bare, naked Scriptures. Yet from what scriptural source did he elicit so many things of which the church has been ignorant for so many centuries, seeing that the Scripture has always been the same? Will he deny that Papias, Ignatius, Irenaeus, Origen, and their like failed to examine the Scripture carefully enough and so were ignorant of certain things that we know, or absorbed some errors which we condemn,[122] or doubted certain things which may not now be doubted? For how many centuries did the church, particularly the Greek church, profess that the Holy Spirit proceeds from the Father, and did not dare to add 'and from the Son' (*filioque*)? Yet we openly confess that the Spirit proceeds from them both,[123] and that in this procession the Father and the Son are not two origins of the Spirit, but one. The ancient theologians thought that there were two resurrections, one of bodies and one of souls.[124] We believe

* * * * *

119 Ep 1334:452–5
120 Ep 1334:469–71
121 Compare WA Br 7 2093:232–6 with Allen Ep 1334:424–7 / CWE 9 259:452–5.
122 For heresies taught by the Fathers see *In psalmum 38* ASD V-3 192:795–196:948 / CWE 65 42–51.
123 For the *filioque* controversy – one of the reasons for the schism of 1056 between the Latin and Greek churches – see Pelikan *Christian Tradition* III 183–98. For Erasmus' view cf *Explanatio symboli* CWE 70 321.
124 Erasmus may have in mind the belief of some early Christian writers that

that once souls have sprung free from bodies they are either in glory or in torment.

There are countless other examples of this kind, as all the theological schools admit. And to whom do we owe the fact that the church began to know for certain things about which it had been in doubt before, if not to men of particularly fertile minds who were especially diligent in investigating the obscurities of the Scripture? But does this necessarily mean that 'all religions are considered to be fictions'?[125] Whose gorge does not rise at these utterly crazy ideas? 'To argue with a drunken man' is to talk to someone who is not there, says Publilius Syrus.[126] But to be intoxicated by self-love and hatred is vastly more destructive than to be drunk on wine. And, so help me God, I would say nothing in reply to these demented ideas, if I were not moved by the scandal they give to ignorant souls.

When Pio accuses Luther of heresy so many times and calls him insane,[127] this is nothing. But when the same person has my words reported to him in a mangled, erroneous form, and for that reason fails to understand them, and accuses me of the Arian error, he judges correctly, and is a rational, intelligent man.[128] But I do not simply shout: Malice, malice! Slanderer, slanderer![129] I refute the false accusations with solid, clear arguments. Luther calls it 'unexampled pride'[130] that I rebut the savage, flagrantly false accusation against me. Nor do I call everyone idiots and blockheads; I prefer to call them people making wild, groundless accusations. Luther says: 'I will not believe Erasmus even if he professes clearly that Christ is God. I will call that Chrysippus' sophism: If you are lying, even when you say something

* * * * *

the souls of both the just and the wicked dwell in Hades until the time of the final resurrection; cf B. Altaner *Patrology* (New York 1960) 125, 158. This opinion was defended by Jacques d'Euse, a Dominican theologian elevated to the papacy as John xxii (1316–34), but condemned as heretical by his successor, Benedict xii (1335–42).

125 WA Br 7 2093:232–6; Luther used the word *fabula* for what is translated here as 'fiction'; see above nn54, 65, and Ep 1389 above 35 n21.

126 Publilius Syrus *Sententiae* letter A:12; Erasmus had edited this text in 1502 and again in 1514 (see Ep 298), with short commentaries of his own, and the quotation as he gives it here blends commentary and text.

127 For the life and works of Alberto Pio, prince of Carpi (1475–1531), see C. Vasoli *Alberto iii Pio da Carpi* (Carpi 1978) and CWE 84 xvii–xxxix.

128 WA Br 7 2093:234, 237ff does say that Pio judges 'correctly' about Erasmus, but not that he is rational or intelligent.

129 Again, the first expression occurs in WA Br 7 2093:228ff, but not the second.

130 WA Br 7 2093:238ff

that is true, you are lying.' If Chrysippus expounded such a sophism,[131] then he certainly was completely out of his senses. Perhaps Martin is vaguely thinking of the syllogism which the Greeks call ψευδόμενος 'the liar': 'Cretans are always liars, said Epimenides the Cretan ...'[132] And yet Martin speaks exactly as though I had never called Christ or the Holy Spirit God anywhere in my books, though all my works profess this distinctly, openly, and forcefully. Do I say this emphatically so often in order to deceive everyone, lying when I say things that are true, imitating Davus in Terence's *Andria*?[133] The goddess Fever[134] herself could not talk more deliriously.

Then, since Luther cannot stop once he has begun, he gnaws at the term 'we dare,'[135] which he claims I have used in a favourable sense to suit myself, though he can read it very frequently in Paul referring to confidence, as in Romans 10: 'Then Isaiah is so bold as to say'[136] or in Ephesians 6: 'That I may declare it boldly, as I ought to speak.'[137] And then, for many centuries the church has sung in the mass, in the presence of people and on their behalf: 'Schooled by the divine ordinance, we make bold to say: Our Father ...'[138] And so, Erasmus does not distort the word, but Luther does not fail to distort anything to make a false accusation.

The paroxysm has still not abated. 'It is a palpable lie,' Luther says, 'to say that the ancients did not dare to call the Holy Spirit God, unless Erasmus, after his excellent fashion, understands the ancients to mean Democritus' or 'Epicurus, or else understands God materially, that is, as the three

* * * * *

131 Cf *Epistola ad fratres Inferioris Germaniae* above 304 n273.
132 WA Br 7 2093:241–3. The writings of Chrysippus, head of the Stoic school in Athens (3rd c BC), are known only from quotations by later philosophers. In the colloquy 'A Profane Feast' CWE 39 136–7), Erasmus made fun of his concentration on 'logical subtleties.' For what is called the paradox of Epimenides the Cretan see H. Diels *Fragmente der Vorsokratiker* 6th ed 3 vols (repr Zürich 1989) I 31–2. Luther may have been thinking of Cicero *Academics* 1.2.96, where this paradox is described as a 'Chrysippean' puzzle, not to be solved even by Chrysippus himself.
133 In the play, the slave Davus invents the story that a female character is an Athenian, as she in fact turns out to be.
134 According to the *Oxford Classical Dictionary* 2nd ed (Oxford 1970) 433, the goddess Febris had three places of cult in Rome.
135 WA Br 7 2093:246–7, referring to the passage cited above 432.
136 Rom 10:20
137 Eph 6:20
138 Erasmus quotes the preface to the 'Our Father' from the canon of the Latin mass.

letters G-O-D.'[139] Appropriate indeed that he mentions Democritus and Epicurus here, when the divinity of the Holy Spirit is the subject! If Martin is
saying that there were some ancient theologians who did not dare attribute
these three letters to the Holy Spirit on account of a certain reverential anxiety, he is agreeing with me. For I have said nothing other than that certain
ancient theologians were so scrupulous in their pronouncements on divine
matters that they avoided words which were not expressly used in the Holy
Scriptures, until the authority of the church should persuade them on the
basis of the divine Scriptures that this was a pious way of speaking.[140] If
Luther maintains that this is wrong, he should show us the reason why, in
the ancient Creed[141] sung in the mass, the Son is called 'God from God,
true God from true God,' whereas the title 'God' is not explicitly attributed
to the Spirit, though much is ascribed to the Spirit, from which divinity can
plainly be inferred. Or he should explain to us why, in all the many books
in which he deals with the Trinity, the blessed Hilary gives Christ the name
of God in a great many passages, and devoutly professes his belief in the
Holy Spirit, yet never explicitly concedes to the Spirit the name of God,[142]
those three letters, that is, which Martin makes fun of. Why is this? Was Hilary's view of the Holy Spirit not especially elevated? I doubt it. Rather, he
was waiting, with a kind of reverence, for a clear judgment of the church
about the words in which it was proper to speak about the Spirit. For long
ago, those who did not dare to call Christ 'true God' were even less bold
in speaking of the Holy Spirit.

Here Luther mentions *homoousios* 'of the same substance' and *ingeni-
tus* 'unbegotten.'[143] It was not only the Arians who thought that the word
homoousios should be avoided, but some of the orthodox theologians too,
and precisely for the reason that this word (that is, these five syllables)
was found nowhere in Holy Scripture, nor even in the earliest theologians'
writings, though their doctrine of the identical nature of the Father and the
Son was Catholic.[144] But these men's devout fear yielded to the authority

* * * * *

139 WA Br 7 2093:248–51
140 In his original preface to Hilary's *Opera*, Erasmus said that ancient Christian
    writers 'thought it was wrong in theology to use words other than the words
    Holy Scripture used.' For the 1535 edition, he added the words: 'and the
    general authority of the church handed down'; see Ep 1334:457–9; cf Allen Ep
    1334:430.
141 The Nicene-Constantinopolitan Creed; see above n45.
142 Hilary's major work *De trinitate libri* 12 (CCSL 62 and 62A) does not attribute
    the name of God to the Holy Spirit.
143 WA Br 7 2093:155-257
144 For Arius (d 336) and his followers, Christ was a creature of God, see Pe-

of the councils. And yet, who, subsequently, dared to say that the Holy Spirit is *homoousios* with the Father, though the nature of all three Persons is equally the same?[145] For my part, I think nothing was involved beyond the reverential fear of speaking about divine matters, for the Son is no more ὁμοούσιος 'of the same substance' with the Father than the Holy Spirit is with both. The Arians might have appeared reverential but for the fact that they disagreed with the Catholics about the matter.

Ἀγένητος 'unbegotten,' a dangerously ambiguous word, was rightly held in suspicion, and finally rejected. Who nowadays ascribes the epithet 'innascible' to the Father as a proper title? If ἀγένητος means the same as 'not begotten,' the Spirit is not begotten either but 'proceeds.' If ἀγένητος describes someone who has never begun to exist, the designation is common to all the Persons alike.[146] I pass over the fact that at this point Luther calls the Arians 'my forefathers,'[147] as though with his abusive rantings he had shown I was of one opinion with the Arians. And how sane it is for him to say that I intimate, with malicious subtlety, that this is of absolutely no account, unless the three letters G-O-D are not written in every place where I might leave them out?[148] I think Orestes of old spoke more rationally, even outside his lucid periods![149] However (so as not to follow up every detail), just as though Luther had clearly shown me to be an out-and-out Arian, refusing to let Christ be called true God unless the two words 'true God' are found in the Holy Scripture, and on no account ready to allow the Holy Spirit to be called God unless it is described in those three letters in the canonical Scriptures, he attempts to embellish his argument

* * * * *

likan *The Christian Tradition* I 191–200. Those who accepted Christ's divinity but rejected the term ὁμοούσιος are called by modern scholars Semi-Arians; on this see Pelikan I 208–10. For a fuller treatment see R.P.C. Hanson *The Search for the Christian Doctrine of God: The Arian Controversy 318–381* (Edinburgh 1988).

145 Erasmus had said this before (annotations on 1 Cor 7:39 LB VI 696D; Reeve-Screech 472), but he was not correct; see Pelikan *Christian Tradition* I 214.

146 The Council of Nicea asserted that Christ was ἀγέννητος 'having no beginning' and yet γεννήτος 'begotten' from God the Father; see Pelikan *Christian Tradition* I 202.

147 WA Br 7 2093:255

148 WA Br 7 2093:253–5, slightly distorted in Erasmus' version. Luther had said that for Erasmus 'the Christian religion' was of no account unless the name of God were found; Erasmus has him saying that 'this' (referent unclear) was of no account.

149 In the third play of Aeschylus' *Oresteia*, after Orestes avenges the murder of his father, Agamemnon, by killing his mother, Clytemnestra, he is pursued by the three *Erinyes* 'Furies' and driven insane.

using fictitious comparisons. 'The devil,' he says, 'might speak to Christ himself like this: Although what you say is true, because you do not say it using words of the kind I would wish, you are saying nothing. But I do not wish it to be said in any words, just as Marcolf wanted to be hanged from a tree of his own choosing, but refused to choose any tree.'[150] With pleasantries like this he defends the glory of Christ, who alone was able to speak of matters of faith in appropriate language. Do these ravings really seem to be the product of a reasonable mind? It is genuinely amazing how readily he brings in the devil in person. And yet he claims that he will say more about these matters 'if God will grant me leisure and length of life.' For he has resolved to 'leave behind him a sure, reliable testimony about Erasmus,' of which he intended this to be an example and foretaste.[151] A frightful judgment indeed from a man who professes to judge both angels and the world! But if he wants his testimony to carry any weight, he should drink some hellebore[152] first, so as to write sounder things than these. Moreover, he appears to have forgotten himself in the meantime, for his doctrine is that nothing should be asserted which is not explicitly stated in the canonical Scriptures[153] (whereas I declare that in many matters I acquiesce in the judgment of the church).[154] And so here he contradicts his own doctrine.

Luther could have stopped at this point, but he takes on the task of inveighing against ambiguous words, ambiguities he regards not just as a rock to be avoided, as Caesar said,[155] but as something τραγικώτερον 'more tragic,' like the devil.[156] As if Holy Scripture and the orthodox Fathers' writings as well were not full of ambiguous words! For anything metaphorical

* * * * *

150 WA Br 7 2093:262–6. In the folk-tale referred to, Marcolf is to be hung by the servants of Salomon. But Marcolf is allowed to choose his own tree, and, finding no tree acceptable, he is in the end let off by Salomon; see *Salomon et Marcolfus* Kritischer Text mit Einleitung ed W. Benary (Heidelberg 1914).

151 WA Br 7 2093:266–8, 402ff

152 Hellebore was deemed a remedy for insanity, see *Adagia* I viii 51: *Bibe elleborum* CWE 32 152–3; cf Ep 1400 n43, and Luther's statement in Watson and Drewery *Bondage of the Will* 106 n4.

153 This was why Erasmus proposed at the outset of his *De libero arbitrio* to conduct their debate solely on the basis of Scripture; see CWE 76 14.

154 Erasmus gave particular stress to the consensus of the church, eg 'I do not condemn the Roman church, least of all when it has all the other churches on its side,' Ep 1637:64–6; cf below n298.

155 Quoted by Aulus Gellius *Noctes Atticae* 1.10.4; in WA Br 7 2093:164–6 Luther ascribes the saying to Quintilian.

156 WA Br 7 2093:302–4; for Erasmus on 'tragedy' see above n54.

is ambiguous, and there are no plain human words in which we can speak adequately of divine things. Here I am not thinking of types, through which all sorts of things are attributed to God (when he is called a lion, a stone, a lamb, a vine, and so on)[157] but when hatred, love, anger, rage, regret, and mercy are attributed to him.[158] Indeed, that is a ghastly blasphemy that, as Luther says, 'in a certain letter I speak of the intercourse (*coitus*) of God with the Virgin.'[159] He does not specify which letter it is, though I have sent countless numbers of them. Yet I would dare to take my oath that those words are nowhere to be found in my letters, nor anywhere in my works; or if they are, that they are put very differently from the way in which Luther quotes them.[160] For why should he quote honestly, having once determined to accuse me falsely? Here, in the most remarkable way, he exaggeratedly states that *coitus* is a word of abominable obscenity.[161] *Stuprum* 'fornication' means illicit intercourse, and yet it is a decent word, as is *incestus* 'unchastity.' *Cognoscere mulierem* 'know a woman' is a decent phrase, but *futuere* 'screw' – if you will excuse the word – is obscene. Just so, *cacare* 'shit' is an indecent word, and *exonerare alvum* 'empty the bowels' is decent; *meiere* 'urinate' is not indecent. Therefore, since not every word denoting a disgraceful action is obscene (like *incestus*), nor every word signifying a matter or action which may not really be disgraceful but should be concealed out of a certain human modesty, one must conclude that it is human usage which distinguishes obscene from decent words. Just as in Brabant if anyone were to say 'wedding' or 'be loved' in the vernacular, he would be speaking obscenely.[162]

* * * * *

157 On tropes and allegories in Scripture, see eg *Ratio,* Holborn 259:32–63:28 / LB V 117A–19B; cf Hoffmann *Rhetoric and Theology* sv *allegoria* p 299.
158 Cf *Ecclesiastes* LB V 1043C–5B.
159 WA Br 7 2093:274–7
160 In his paraphrase on Luke 1:35, Erasmus has Gabriel explain to Mary that there will be a 'holy intercourse between divine and human nature that will not violate but rather consecrate' her virgin modesty (*sanctus hic divinae naturae cum humana coitus, non violabit pudicitiam tuam sed consecrabit* LB VII 290B); cf LB VII 288F and the paraphrase on Matthew 1:18 CWE 45 41. Pierre Cousturier (Sutor), a Carthusian professor of theology at the University of Paris, accused Erasmus of 'blasphemy' on this point. In 1526 Erasmus wrote a letter to the prior of La Grande Chartreuse (printed with the *Opus epistolarum* of 1529) defending himself against this charge; see Ep 1687. As C. Augustijn notes in ASD IX-1 465:588–90n, Luther had this letter in mind; cf WA Br 7 2093:335–8.
161 WA Br 7 2093:275, 281ff
162 In contemporary Netherlandish, *bruiloft* 'wedding' and *gemind zijn* 'be loved' could also mean 'sleeping together outside of marriage,' see *Woordenboek der*

Popular usage is diverse, though I say that anyone speaking to ordinary people should have a care for it. Yet someone writing for the educated is not restricted by this consideration. One may use any words that are found either in the canonical Scriptures or in approved authors whose style is pure, provided they are suitable to express what we wish to be understood. To many foolish people *vulva* 'womb' is an obscene word, and yet it is heard in churches. And St Ambrose was not afraid to speak about Christ and his mother in these terms: 'This is the' only 'one to open his mother's womb and go out unstained.'[163] And today, the learned are not deterred by the foolish people's custom of avoiding such words. *Coire* 'come together' is not the proper term for the intercourse of man and woman; it has been used figuratively in this sense for the sake of decency, like *congredi* and *convenire*; Matthew uses συνελθεῖν 'come together.'[164] *Concubitus* 'lying together' more exactly expresses the sexual union of man and woman, and yet the Catholic church uses this word reporting Paul speaking about Isaac and Rebecca: Rebecca 'having children by "lying with one man ..."'[165] But *coitus* is more decent in two respects: First, because it has been used as a metaphor in a decent way – for metaphorical words are sometimes more indecent than literal terms; second, because it is very often employed for pure purposes.[166] It can mean 'the joining together of the two sides of a wound' as we say: 'Does your friendship, like a poorly stitched wound, refuse to close?'; or it can mean 'the clash of armies' as in: 'The first clash is the hardest';[167] or it can refer to two sides entering into agreements. But *concubitus* is employed only to speak of the congress of male and female. Συνεῖναι 'come together' and συνουσία 'intercourse' in Greek are words such as *coire* and *coitus* are in Latin. But the Greek βινεῖν and οἰφεῖν 'copulate' are of the same kind as *futuere*, which I am forced reluctantly to mention.

Those words which are indecent *per se* should be avoided completely;

* * * * *

Nederlandsche Taal 3 1656, and 9 782. Erasmus gives both examples on another occasion: *Ecclesiastes* LB V 855D–E.

163 St Ambrose *Expositio evangelii Lucae* 2 57 (CSEL 32 73:7ff)
164 Matt 1:18; for Erasmus' comment see *Annotationes* ASD VI-5 76:247–72.
165 For Erasmus' discussion of Romans 9:10 in his *Annotationes* see CWE 56 255–60.
166 Erasmus made the same point against Pierre Cousturier (*Appendix respondens ad Sutorem* LB IX 806E). But in his *Annotationes* (on Matt 1:18 ASD VI-5 76:250–2) he recognizes that the meaning of *coitus* has been affected by 'usage that is not very chaste.'
167 The first quotation is from Horace *Epistles* 1.3.31–4, the second from Terence *Phormio* 346.

and such words are not found in Holy Scripture. But *coitus* and *concubitus* are not of this kind; they are frequently encountered both in the divine Scriptures[168] and in the Fathers. Others must deal with *concubitus*, but I certainly believe that it is permissible to use words such as *coitus* and *coire* metaphorically. If someone, speaking in this way, says that intercourse never took place between Mary and Joseph, I believe that he would be speaking with propriety, whereas a word that is indecent in itself is indecent even when it is negated. If the word *coire* was as indecent as Luther wants it to appear, it would not be found so often in the Old Testament.[169] And even if some word is somewhat profane or lacking in propriety, other words are generally used along with it to tone it down. Although I invariably do this, Luther the brawler conceals this fact and merely repeats, hammers home, and dins in those few words: 'God has intercourse with the Virgin,' which are his, not mine.[170] And having laid this foundation, he moves off into the realm of slander. To speak of God having had intercourse with the Virgin in the same way as Jupiter lay with Semele or Mars with Rhea[171] is clearly impious and blasphemous. But this is Luther's wording, not Erasmus'. And if purity of language when dealing with sacred matters were so dear to him, he would never have pronounced those words in any circumstances. It is a wonder he did not add something about *incubi*,[172] who are said to copulate with women.

The orthodox Fathers spoke piously and modestly[173] in saying that God the Father begot his own Son a second time from the Virgin Mary, whom he loved as a bride; that the angel Gabriel was an intermediary between God and the Virgin, and a kind of groomsman, a representative of the bridegroom who received the Virgin's assent, without which there is no legitimate marriage; that, once her assent had been received, the power of the Most High overshadowed the Virgin as if in a mystic embrace, and, by

* * * * *

168 F.P. Dutripon *Concordantiae Bibliorum Sacrorum Vulgatae Editionis* (Paris 1938) lists ten usages of *coitus* in the Vulgate Bible, and four of *concubitus*.

169 F.P. Dutripon gives no instance of the use of the verb *coire* in the Vulgate, but the verb 'to know' (*cognoscere*) is used in a sexual sense thirteen times.

170 WA Br 7 2093:267ff, 336, 347

171 WA Br 7 2093:347ff

172 For beliefs of contemporary demonologists about devils assuming male or female form, see H. Institoris and J. Sprenger *Malleus Maleficarum* tr M. Summers (New York 1928) I 4.

173 In his *Appendix respondens ad Sutorem* LB IX 806E–7E, Erasmus says that he 'drew this image partly from the words of Hilary, and partly from John Damascene.'

the action of the Holy Spirit in the place of a seed, made her pregnant with the heavenly issue, who would take the nature of both parents: the divine nature of the Father, the human nature of his mother.[174] These things, I stress, cannot only be said piously about the Incarnation of Christ, they are also in agreement with what St Luke relates.[175] Now, to Luther the Christian man, all words like 'bridegroom, bride, groomsman, seed, the sexual act' are indecent.[176] But when Paul speaks of Christ and the church, what words does he use more readily than 'bridegroom' and 'bride'?[177] And John the Baptist says: 'He who has the bride is the bridegroom,' and the Lord himself says: 'The bridegroom's guests cannot fast etc.'[178] Nor do the pious Doctors fear to interpret the wedding at which Christ turned water into wine as the wedding of Christ and the church.[179] Now, if the Greeks are modest and pious in calling Gabriel a *paranymphus* 'bridegroom's attendant,'[180] why do I appear indecent when I call him a *pronubus* 'groomsman' in Latin? Does not a Greek author, whose words are quoted in the *Catena*

* * * * *

174 Apropos Luke 1:35, where Mary wonders 'what manner of greeting this might be,' Erasmus wrote of the Virgin in his 1516 and 1519 *Annotationes*: *audiret salutationem amatoriam et nescio quid procorum prae se ferentem* ASD VI-5 461:452–5. The attack on this passage in Edward Lee's *Annotationes in annotationes* (1519) was answered in 1520 by Erasmus' *Responsio ad annotationes Lei* LB IX 151A–3D. On the advice of Maarten Dorp Erasmus changed the passage in the third edition (1522) of his *Annotationes* (not the second edition, as Erasmus says in his reply to Pierre Cousturier LB IX 807C). Nonetheless, Cousturier's *Antapologia* (1526) attacked the original wording as well as similar phrasing in Erasmus' paraphrase on Luke 1:35 LB VII 290A–E. As the *Antapologia* was being set in Paris, a friend 'wheedled' from the printer a copy of the first four *quaternions* and sent it to Erasmus (Ep 1687). Hence Erasmus sent off Ep 1687 immediately, then published an *Appendix* (above n166) when Cousturier's book appeared.
175 Luke 1:26–38
176 WA Br 7 2093:335–43, 678–9
177 Paul nowhere speaks of Christ and the church as bridegroom and bride, but cf 2 Cor 11:2 and Eph 5:22–33.
178 John 3:29, Mark 2:19
179 Erasmus gives no examples of this in his *Annotationes*, but C. Augustijn (ASD IX-1 467 n652–4) suggests he may have been thinking of Augustine's *In Ioannis evangelium tractatus* 8 4 (PL 35 1452).
180 F.W. Danker *A Greek-English Lexicon of New Testament and Early Christian Literature* 2nd ed (Chicago 1979) gives no such usage. In his *Responsio ad annotationes Lei* LB IX 152B–E Erasmus cites a passage from John Damascene, as quoted in the *Sentences* of Peter Lombard, only to acknowledge that it does not 'exactly' support his calling Gabriel a groomsman.

aurea, mention a 'betrothal'?[181]

Is *pronubus* 'groomsman' an indecent word too? Does John Damascene, whose words are related in the *Sentences* book 5 dist 3 not teach that the Holy Spirit 'covered' the Virgin to give her the power to conceive that holy birth?[182] Does Ambrose not say the same thing more explicitly? 'For no male congress uncovered the hidden recesses of the virginal womb, but the Holy Spirit infused unstained seed into an inviolable womb.'[183] Does the church choir not chastely sing: 'Not from male seed, / But by mystic breath etc' from Prudentius' hymn?[184] Then too Thomas Aquinas, interpreting Romans 5, speaks like this: 'In the begetting of Christ there was the bodily substance which he took from the Virgin, but in place of the seed as cause there was the active power of the Holy Spirit.'[185] I could collect countless examples of this kind from the authorities.

All these authors have spoken in a Christian way. It is only Erasmus, the Epicurean,[186] who speaks intolerable blasphemies because he wrote that in the Incarnation of Christ there was a certain mystical union and holy embrace between God the Father and the Virgin, which Luther distorts into the fictitious, adulterous copulation of Jupiter and Semele, or Mars and Rhea. He admits that I interpret what I have written in a Christian way, yet asks: 'But why did he not speak according to the Christian form?'[187] Why, rather, does he distort what I say into an obscene form, occasionally lying openly, an example being the accusation (which we shall mention shortly) that I wrote that John the Evangelist 'prates about nothing but worlds'?[188] We Christians find this offensive, he says.[189] But we hear the phrase 'we Christians' so often, as if Erasmus was a pagan Epicurus, and his sympathizers too. Luther thinks he himself is to be forgiven if any word

* * * * *

181 Thomas Aquinas *Catena aurea in quattuor evangelia* on Luke 1:28, 30 in *Opera omnia* (New York 1948, repr of the Parma edition of 1852–73) 12 12; the Greek author cited by Aquinas from *In catena Graecorum* is Geometer.

182 John Damascene *Expositio fidei orthodoxae* 3 2 (PG 94 985) cited in Peter Lombard *Sententiae* 3 dist iii 1 (PL 192 761).

183 Ambrose *Expositio evangelii Lucae* 2 56 (CSEL 32 72:12–14)

184 Not from Prudentius, but from the third strophe of Ambrose's hymn *Intende, qui regis Israel*; see *Analecta hymni medii aevi* ed C. Blume and G.M. Dreves (Leipzig 1907) 50 13.

185 Thomas Aquinas *In omnes S. Pauli apostoli epistolas commentaria* cap 5 lectio 3 on Romans 5:12, *Opera omnia* 13 53.

186 WA Br 2093:58, 155, 202, 250, 319ff; cf WA 60 203 n2.

187 WA Br 2093:277–9

188 See below n239.

189 WA Br 2093:306, 324, 356

escapes him inadvertently, but he assumes a kind of divinity to himself and judges my intentions firmly and audaciously: I knew that Luther's Christian ears would be offended, and wrote this phrase in this way precisely in order to offend them.[190] At one point in the *Paraphrase on Luke* I call the union of the divine with the human nature in the one person of Christ a *coitus*, because the two natures come together into one hypostasis. The Greeks call it ἕνωσις 'union.' Since the word *unio* is not good Latin in that sense, and even if it were, is ambiguous (because we call a pearl a *unio*), the word *coitus* pleased me more, and I even tone it down by adding the word 'holy.' The sentence reads thus: 'This holy intercourse of the divine with the human nature will not violate, but will consecrate your chastity.'[191] Shortly afterwards, I follow the ancient orthodox writers in explaining the image of the mystical union of God the Father and the Virgin in these words: 'The heavenly Father has resolved to bring his own Son to birth a second time, in a different manner, from you. For this divine conception there will be no need of any mortal man's seed; the Holy Spirit from heaven will enter into you, and in your womb, as though in a heavenly workshop, he will work at forming the holy offspring. In the place of your husband's physical embrace, the Most High will overshadow you, so tempering his boundless power to the limits of human nature that it can endure the union. Where lust is involved in intercourse, what is born is born impure and subject to sin. Yet what will be born from you will be conceived by the holy embrace of the Most High, from the workmanship of the Holy Spirit who sanctifies all things, from the purest Virgin alone chosen by God to be free from any taint of sin; and so it will be holy as it was conceived' and so on. Where in this passage are the words: 'God had intercourse with the Virgin,' with which Luther charges me?

Now this new world νομοθέτης 'legislator' is dictating laws to us: that an ambiguous word must be shunned like the devil or death,[192] and, if one slips out, it should be understood in the worst sense.[193] If we accept this decree, we must interpret St Gregory's words: 'Christ is always acting so as to instruct us'[194] as meaning that Christ performed as a stage-player,

* * * * *

190 WA Br 2093:279–85
191 On Luke 1:35 see LB VII 290B–C. The wording Erasmus quotes here varies slightly from the original, quoted above in n160.
192 WA Br 2093:302–4
193 WA Br 2093:174ff, 284ff
194 A phrase used not by St Gregory, but by Nicholas of Lyra, Thomas Aquinas, and others; see G.A. Benrath *Wyclifs Bibelkommentar* (Berlin 1966) 185 n389.

since acting is what actors do, and actor means player. And every time we read 'beloved' in the Holy Scriptures, we will interpret it as 'whore'; every time we read 'lover,' we will interpret it as someone in sexual thrall to a whore! Yet how often do we find the word 'beloved' in the Song of Solomon?[195] In Proverbs 7, Solomon calls wisdom his 'beloved.'[196] Likewise, we will interpret Wisdom of Solomon 8: I 'was a lover of her beauty'[197] in the worst sense. As often as we read 'kiss,' we will interpret it as 'erotic kiss.' But I will stop going over things which are innumerable. Luther boastfully claims that if ambiguities are permitted, everything can be interpreted favourably, 'everything that all the heretics have ever said, even anything the devil himself has said, or may do or say throughout eternity.'[198] The evangelical doctor delights in these tragic hyperboles, which certainly seem very much like madness. In one respect, however, we believe him: even if there are no ambiguities he claims the right to mangle quotations and distort things that in context are correct, and to make whatever false additions he pleases.

At length, Luther even adduces the laws of the pagan emperors to support his malicious accusation.[199] These laws decree that an ambiguous statement is to be interpreted against the person who says obscurely what he could have said more clearly. I believe Luther is thinking of the passage in the *Pandects*, in the section 'Obligations Expressed in Words,' where this judgment of Ulpian's is quoted: 'In demands for payment of debt, when what has taken place is being investigated, the words are to be interpreted against the party making the demand. Someone who says: "Ten for myself and ten for Titius," is to be taken as having spoken of the same ten, not two tens.'[200] Yet, I believe, this passage is not free from error. For in the words: I demand 'ten for myself and ten for Titius,' there is no ambiguity about the fact that the speaker means two tens. It would be different if he had made the demand: 'Ten for Titius and myself,' or 'Titius and I demand ten.' But why did Martin not quote the passage, also from Ulpian, under the heading 'Legal Proceedings': 'If in intention or speech anyone is ambiguous,

* * * * *

195 *Young's Analytical Concordance* (above n63) lists for the Song of Solomon 27 usages of the Hebrew word for 'beloved.'
196 Prov 7:4
197 Wisd of Sol 8:2
198 WA Br 2093:193–5
199 WA Br 2093:184–6
200 *Digesta* 45 1 38; cf *Adagia* I x 77: *Idem Accii quod Titii* CWE 32 269–70, 384 n77.

that which is more advantageous to him is to be understood'?[201] There is also the passage, again from Ulpian, that demands made by the praetor for repayment take their conditions from the praetor's intention;[202] and the statement saying that if someone is granting prerogatives to a lender and there are any ambiguities in the document, he interprets them himself.[203] And does not Ulpian decree that if someone mistakes the name of a slave whom he has demanded to be given to him, but has the right body in mind, the contract is valid?[204] Luther conceals these and many other details in the laws of princes and quotes only this one judgment about private contracts, in which it is not unjust for the person who speaks in his own case in such a way that his meaning is unclear to suffer some penalty.

What relevance has this to the person who publishes books for the purpose of teaching? Will Luther subject him to the rule that, if any ambiguous word escapes him, he is constantly confusing Babylon and Chaos, and everything sacred and profane, and that we should interpret that word in the worst sense we can, condemning everything the author has written on the same subject clearly and unambiguously in a host of other places? How much more worthy of Christian equity[205] it is that, as with the Holy Scripture, if we come across anything ambiguously or obscurely phrased, we explain it by comparing other passages, so with books dealing with Sacred Scripture, if we meet anything ambiguous in meaning, we should either interpret it in the more favourable sense, or else elicit the meaning of what is written from other passages. And what if we turn the law which Luther applies to us back on him? To avoid hunting elsewhere for something to quote, what does he mean when he says again and again in his letter that I have a horror of all religions, especially Christianity?[206] Is this not a dark, even scandalous, thing to say? For what else is the reader to understand but that Erasmus, following Lucian's example,[207] condemns the religions of the Spartans, the Scythians, the Thracians, the Athenians, and

* * * * *

201 *Digesta* 45 1 66
202 *Digesta* 45 1 52
203 Not found
204 *Digesta* 45 1 52
205 For Erasmus on *aequitas* see G. Kisch *Erasmus und die Jurisprudenz seiner Zeit* (Basel 1960); on *aequitas naturae* see P. Walter *Theologie aus dem Geist der Rhetorik* (Mainz 1991) 72–8 and Hoffmann *Rhetoric and Theology* 261 n104, 262 n107.
206 Luther says this directly (WA Br 2093:175–7; cf 169–73, 236).
207 With Thomas More, Erasmus had translated a selection of the satiric dialogues of Lucian of Samosata (117–67), some of which mock superstition; see ASD I -1 379–628.

so on, and that the Christian religion is one of them? But there is only one religion which teaches the true worship of the true God.

Indeed, though Luther babbles, even clowns, so much about 'King Ambiguous' and 'Queen Ambiguity,'[208] he has not yet produced any obscure or ambiguous passage from my writings. It may be ambiguous to say: 'We dare to call the Holy Spirit God,'[209] but in my *Preface* it is not ambiguous. For what follows shows that 'dare' is a term expressing confidence, not temerity. And even if it were temerity, it would be so not in the actual profession, but in the fact that we profess God with our lips, but drive him out of his temple with our impious behaviour. If the person demanding payment had said: 'I demand ten for Stichus and Titius,' and in the same contract had added: 'so that the total of twenty sesterces may be divided equally between them,' no one would argue that the contract was ambiguous. I believe that the same would apply if the intention of the party demanding payment were clear from other contracts.

But Luther, the tyrant of hyperbole,[210] refuses to credit me with the fact that I state what I mean in the course of the same argument; or with the fact that I explain my intention as clearly as can be in scores of other passages. The phrase: 'Peter calls Christ a man, but avoids the word God' is admittedly ambiguous – but these are Luther's words, not mine. And if anyone sees that I praise Paul's prudence in knowing how to dispense the mysteries of the gospel teaching to the strong and the weak, to each according to his capacity, and that I point out that Peter, in Acts, speaking with the same prudence to a crowd not yet capable of grasping that mystery, called Christ a man, not God, then that person cannot find my meaning unclear.[211] Although I am convinced that *coitus* is not an intrinsically indecent word, being used very often in the divine Scripture, I would still not wish to speak of God and the Holy Virgin in the way that Luther misrepresents me as doing: 'God the Father had intercourse with the Virgin.'[212] But if someone, explaining the similitude, says that a certain mystical intercourse, so to speak, between God and the Virgin was involved, it is malicious to interpret this as meaning at once that God had intercourse with the Virgin in the same way as Jupiter copulated adulterously with Semele, or Mars with Rhea. In speech of such a kind

* * * * *

208 WA Br 2093:230, 283ff, 301–6, 315–19, 324–7
209 Ep 1334:475 (cited above n113).
210 For Luther and *hyperbole*, see above n34.
211 See above nn97, 104.
212 See above nn160, 191.

there is no ambiguity. And if there should be any, the dignity of the persons involved dispels any adverse suspicion. I will deal with this subject shortly.

There is one further passage, the very harshest of all, but also the most untruthful of all. In an Appendix which I added to my translation of the New Testament as the occasion offered,[213] when I happened to have time to write a page or two, Luther says that I have 'posed the question of why such a great master as Christ should have come down from heaven, given that there are many similar stories amongst the pagans, perhaps even more polished ones.'[214] Reader, just look at what falsehood and effrontery the man shows in making this statement! Speaking about Christ's teaching, I ask what is new or special about it that is not in Old Testament writings, since there is hardly anything to be found in the gospels which is not found many centuries before in the Law and the prophets. And this doctor free from all falsehood, whose every word is utterly prophetic, distorts my words as though I were comparing the gospel teaching with the pagans' writings! Not content with this, he adds 'so great a master' of his own inspiration, to make the phrase smack of disdain and irony. Yet this animus is Luther's, not mine, for there is nothing of the kind in that Appendix. Not content even with this, he adds on his own initiative: 'perhaps even more polished ones,' even though there I do not compare the philosophy of Christ with the wisdom of the pagans. I only add in passing that some sparks of the gospel truth are found in the pagan philosopher's writings.[215] What truthfulness can one expect from someone who has woven so many lies into his statements from the beginning, and who, in passing, works in the

* * * * *

213 In 1519, Dirk Martens in Louvain published a separate edition of Erasmus' Latin translation of the New Testament, with a preface (Ep 1010). For the edition by Andreas Cratander (Basel 1520) Erasmus wrote a new preface, and for the Froben edition of August 1522 he added a new preface at the beginning plus a longer statement at the end, cited by Luther as an 'Appendix' (WA Br 2093:142ff). None of the later prefaces are given in Allen or CWE, but for the one Luther has in mind, see *Epistola de philosophia evangelica* LB VI f 4v–5.
214 WA Br 2093:144–6
215 LB VI f 5: *Quumque evangelica doctrina sit instauratio simul et perfectio naturae, ut erat primum condita sincere, mirum videri non debet, si Philosophis quibusdam ethnicis datum est, naturae ut quaedam animadvertere quae cum doctrina Christi consentiant.* 'Although evangelical doctrine is both a new beginning and a perfection of nature, nature itself was originally created good, and it need not be surprising if it has been given to certain pagan philosophers to discern things in nature that comport with the teaching of Christ.'

wild insult: 'I think he believes this in a most Erasmian way,'[216] meaning that I do not even believe that Christ took on human flesh?

Yet surely it is not impious to ask whether Christ taught anything that went beyond the Law and prophets, or whether, just as he did nothing while on earth that was not foreshadowed by the types of the Law and foretold by the prophets' oracles, he also taught nothing which had not been handed down, albeit less clearly, in the books of the Old Testament.[217] Is the question which I propound here not asked by the most Christian Doctors, and even disputed in the theological schools? Is Tertullian not pious in writing that all the doctrines of the evangelical perfection have been expressed in the writings of the prophets?[218] As well as others, does not Eusebius, in his *Preparation for the Gospel*, strive to demonstrate that many things are found in the pagans' writings which agree with the canonical Scriptures?[219] So what is there that dims Christ's glory or calls his teachings into doubt?[220] My opinion emphatically confirms Christ's teaching, since it accords with the prophets and is not inconsistent with the natural order. For thus it could more easily be accepted by Jews as well as gentiles. And so it is a shameless misrepresentation for Luther to say that I attribute no more to Christ than that as one of the saints he performed what they all performed, in a more perfect and complete degree.[221]

But where have the saints come from all of a sudden,[222] given that in stating his arguments Luther has mentioned only pagans? Do I compare Christ with these saints? 'Christ,' says Luther, 'came down from heaven to redeem the human race from sin and death.'[223] Did Erasmus deny this? All I did was pose a question about how new his teaching was. And it is true that one of the reasons that Christ was sent to earth was to teach us the Father's will more fully, and to give us an example of virtue complete in every respect. The subject of the passage in question was not a comparison of the whole Christ with the prophets; it was only Christ's teaching and example of living. Why I posed this question is explained by the conclusion of the

* * * * *

216 WA Br 2093:147
217 Cf *Ratio* Holborn 209:1–11:27 / LB V 91C–92D; *Explanatio symboli* CWE 70 351.
218 Tertullian *Adversus Marcionem* 4 6–43 (CCSL I 552–663)
219 Eusebius *Praeparatio evangelica* 11–13 (*Eusebius Werke* ed K. Mras [Berlin 1956] 8.2.5–256)
220 WA Br 2093:88–91, 148–150
221 WA Br 2093:146–150
222 See introductory note above n73.
223 WA Br 2093:151–3

question: so that we might embrace the gospel teaching more eagerly and enthusiastically.[224]

Perhaps Luther wanted Christ to be placed above the saints because he was God and man, because he redeemed the human race by his death. Though this was not the subject of the passage, it was mentioned in passing by me, at the beginning of the inquiry, when I said: 'Yet no mystery is more relevant to us than the ineffable counsel by which God restored the human race through his own Son' etc.[225] When I mention 'God's Son,' do I not profess belief in God? When I say, 'restores the human race,' do I not profess belief in the Redeemer? And when I say a little later: 'so that the very Son of God made man might show us the way of salvation by his teaching,'[226] do I not profess belief in Christ as God and man, even as I explain that here I am examining his teaching and example of life, to see what he had in this respect that was exceptional compared with others? And I propound this precisely in order to teach that, even as regards his human nature, Christ is superior in many respects to all the saints, and so superior that there is no comparison. Then, when I add: 'Although this virtue that shone forth in the saints is itself a gift of Christ,'[227] do I not attribute to Christ what is worthy of his exalted status? Anyone who will take the trouble to read the Appendix in question will learn that the facts are thus.

And so, what was Luther's intention in raving for a whole page, quite as though he had absolutely confirmed his point, beginning: 'Christ, this wretched renewer of all things – for thus Erasmus impugns the glory of the Lord – has lost the glory of the Redeemer,' etc?[228] I call Christ the 'renewer of all,' suggesting that there must have been something new and exceptional in his life and teaching as well. Is this impugning the Lord's glory? In that case he impugns it himself when he says in Revelation: 'Behold, I make all things new.'[229] Paul impugns it when he says that all are a new creation in

* * * * *

224 *Epistola de philosophia evangelica* LB VI f 5: *Amplectamur et nos doctoris ac principis nostri monumenta, demusque operam vt illius philosophia quam latissime propagetur. Id fiet, si eam omnibus innocentia vitae mutuaque caritate commendemus.* 'We too embrace the principles of our teacher and prince, and work to spread his philosophy as widely as possible. This will come to pass, if we commend it to all by mutual love and a blameless life.'

225 *Epistola de philosophia evangelica* LB VI f 4v

226 *Epistola de philosophia evangelica* LB VI f 4v

227 *Epistola de philosophia evangelica* LB VI f 5: *Quanquam hoc ipsum, quod virtutis emicuit in sanctis, Christi munus est.*

228 WA Br 2093:148ff

229 Rev 21:5

Christ.[230] Besides, how has Christ lost the glory of the Redeemer, seeing that in this passage I say he has restored the world? And if I had not said that – while I was dealing with Christ's teaching, not with his death – would he have lost the glory of the Redeemer for that reason?

Indeed, how devoutly Martin is able to speak of divine matters: Here he calls Christ 'wretched'![231] I know this is irony, but Luther rejects figures of speech;[232] and although he makes me into Epicurus, I would not dare to joke about Christ using words like that. Note that this is the passage which first estranged Luther's sympathies from Erasmus.[233] How much more humane Erasmus is: he has never turned his feelings against Luther.[234] From this passage he first started to suspect that I was another Democritus or Epicurus, a clever mocker of Christ.[235] Yet this Appendix as a whole expresses Christ's glory. Similarly absurd and deranged are Luther's accusations concerning my hatred towards Christ, my fellowship with Epicureans, the deceptive figurative language in which I furiously rave against Christians, my odious, double-tongued mode of expression, my aim of doing away with the Christian faith altogether.[236] It would be tiresome to list the rest of these. One would think it was passion itself speaking, not a human being. I am glad that my works are published. They, I trust, will convince the reader that I am as far removed from this attitude that Luther thrusts on me as he is removed from mental balance and Christian moderation.

Then he is displeased by my *Methodus* with its circles.[237] I do not claim

* * * * *

230 2 Cor 5:17
231 WA Br 2093:209
232 WA Br 2093:154
233 WA Br 2093:154
234 See introductory note above nn41–2.
235 WA Br 2093:155ff
236 WA Br 2093:156, 158, 169, 172
237 Erasmus' description of the church in its relation to Christ in terms of concentric circles comes not in his *Methodus*, published as a preface to his 1516 *Novum Instrumentum*, but in the expanded version published separately as *Ratio verae theologiae* Holborn 202:1–4:33 / LB V 88C–9F. Luther's language (WA Br 2093:125, 128) indicates he was thinking of a later passage in the *Ratio* (Holborn 210:4–6 / LB V 91F–92A): *Totus doctrinae [Christi] circulus, ut secum consentit, ita cum ipsius vita consentit.* 'The whole circle of Christ's teaching is as consistent with itself as it is with the life he lived.' See M. Hoffmann *Erkenntnis und Verwirklichung der wahren Theologie nach Erasmus von Rotterdam* Beiträge zur Historischen Theologie 44 (Tübingen 1972) 96–101; and G.B. Winkler *Erasmus von Rotterdam und die Einleitungsschriften zum Neuen Testament* Reformationsgeschichtliche Studien und Texte 108 (Münster 1974) 160–8.

that it seems particularly learned, and so it is absolutely false for Luther to say that it is nothing but a mockery of Christ and all his deeds, and that the reader can absorb nothing from it but loathing and hatred towards learning about a religion so confused, baffling, and possibly fictitious. But if the *Methodus* had hammered home Luther's doctrine throughout, Lord, how learned, how Christian, it would be! Not, indeed, that it is surprising that Luther finds it a mockery of Christ, given that he finds it an impugning of the Lord's glory to call him the 'renewer of all things.' What the Scriptures ascribe to Christ as the highest praise Luther interprets as dishonour: a real καρδιογνώστης 'man who knows the hearts of all,'[238] as he wants to be reckoned, yet all the while wildly mistaken about obvious matters.

We are not finished yet. Luther asks: 'Who has dared to speak with such loathing and hatred, not to say hostility, about John the Apostle and Evangelist, who after Christ has supreme authority among Christians, saying that he "prates about nothing but worlds"? Who but someone who thinks that John is an absolute blockhead?'[239] And so on. Luther does not indicate the place where this can be found in my writings, and I would take it on myself to swear that it is not to be found anywhere. Nor can I conjecture in what sense the words 'prates about nothing but worlds' could have been said by me. I suspect, rather, that this falsehood was suggested to Luther by a combination of two passages, as monstrous visions in dreams are combined from various images shifting at random. In the *Argumentum* asserting that the First Epistle of John was the genuine product of John, from its characteristic style of speech (because he repeatedly uses certain particular words like 'world,' 'light,' 'love,' etc; and also because he arranges the elements of his discourse so that he takes the beginning of the next phrase from that immediately preceding it), I cite the example: 'Do not love the world, or the things in the world. If anyone loves the world' etc[240] and I add, 'How many worlds there are here'![241]

These words slipped out in the first edition. And although I meant nothing by them other than that the word 'world' was frequently repeated,

* * * * *

238 An attribute of God: Acts 1:24, 15:8.
239 WA Br 2093:129–32
240 1 John 2:15
241 Erasmus' *Argumentum* to 1 John appeared for the first time in the 2nd ed (1519) of his *Novum Instrumentum*, not the 1st; the phrase: 'How many worlds there are here!' was changed in the 3rd ed (1522) to read: 'How often the word 'world' is repeated here!' For the revised text, see LB VI 1069–70.

nevertheless on a friend's advice I changed the wording in the very next edition, keeping the sense, and wrote: 'How often the word 'world' is repeated!' The reader will find this version in the 1533 edition of the *Paraphrases*,[242] and the same in the later editions of the *New Testament*. Then, in the Appendix added to the *Paraphrase on the Gospel According to John*, I speak of him in this way: 'Just as he was especially loved by the one who is eternal love, likewise speaks nothing else, breathes nothing else, than pure love' etc.[243] I suspect that from these two passages Luther, not properly remembering what he had heard or read, fabricated 'prates about nothing but worlds.' Yet under this delusion, how impudently he spits on me, lashes, and stones me, constantly flinging the words 'prates about nothing but worlds' in my face! But since he rages so fiercely at 'nothing but worlds,' which is found nowhere in my writings, he may well seem to the observer not so very different in appearance from Ajax raging against the pigs, one of which he thought was Ulysses and the other Agamemnon.[244] And he cries out that there are countless examples of this kind in my writings,[245] and that in theology I am always exactly the same, though the very detail which he cites by way of example is found nowhere in my writings, and never has been in my mind.

Here he also exaggerates John's dignity and authority, which he claims is foremost among Christians after that of Christ. Yet the apostles' dignity is known only to Christ, and the authority of all the apostles is equal.[246] And if there is any difference, the chief authority is ascribed to Peter, the prince of the apostolic order, who in Acts plays the part of the chief herald of Christ while the other apostles stand by; and the next highest authority is ascribed to Matthew and Paul. And here I am called 'a mouthpiece and instrument of Satan,'[247] even deserving of capital punishment if I were to speak thus when of sound mind and judgment. But if the Remmian Law were in force, capital punishment would fall on anyone who falsely asserted

* * * * *

242 Erasmus is perhaps thinking of the 1532 edition of his New Testament *Paraphrases* (there was none in 1533).

243 CWE 46 226 / LB VII 649–50

244 In the *Ajax* of Sophocles (332), Ajax rages in this way not against swine, but against sheep and cattle.

245 WA Br 2093:138ff

246 In his *Annotationes* on Matt 10:2 ASD VI-5 185:23–6:30 Erasmus makes the same point, citing Jerome's *Commentaria in evangelium Matthaei* PL 26 61B.

247 WA Br 2093:112ff, 205ff

that a capital crime had been committed.[248] Yet I am excused by madness, to which I should be very grateful. Indeed, the more Luther exaggerates and repeats these charges, the more ridiculous he shows himself to be, fighting a ghost.[249]

These are the dreadful words 'indirect, ambiguous, insidious, inde-cent, Satanic'[250] with which Erasmus, utterly ignorant and foolish and in-deed truly crazed[251] (yet still amazingly cunning) has long been striving to overthrow the whole of Christianity.[252] And (something I have never heard of before) Luther even attaches a sect to me: not, indeed, sophists or pa-pists or Sacramentarians, but followers of Epicurus and Democritus,[253] who so utterly disbelieve in divine things that they deride them completely. Ad-mittedly, I am quite prepared to believe that there are some people of this kind concealing themselves under the name of Christians, but I do know that there is no one who has derived this attitude from my writings. And if I did know someone prone to this impiety, I would refuse to eat with him[254] unless there was a great hope of his repenting. On the other hand, I feel a natural inclination towards those who genuinely love the Lord Jesus, and I sincerely regret that I am not like such people in all ways, though I am doing my very utmost to improve myself.

And if because of imprudence something slipped out in my writings that could present the least stumbling-block to any weak person, it will be little trouble to correct it, just as I have already changed many things[255] which in my simplicity I had not expected would offend anyone at all. As soon as I have become aware of a difficulty, I have willingly removed it. And I wish that Martin had been either as able or as readily willing to correct the things in his books which have embroiled the Christian church in such uproar. Reconciliation is easy where only the words are in dispute, but there is agreement about the actual matter. I do not deny that before Luther there were some who were offended by certain words of mine, but their offence was usually caused by the fact that they knew neither Latin nor Greek. Some thought that the word *coelebs* 'bachelor' meant 'celibate,'

* * * * *

248 Cicero *Pro Roscio Amerino* 19.55; the *lex Remmia* called not for execution but branding on the forehead; cf *Digesta* 20 5 13 and 48 16 1.
249 *Adagia* IV vi 48: Σκιαμαχεῖν 'Shadow-boxing' CWE 36 246–7
250 WA Br 2093:154–83
251 WA Br 2093:54, 63, 66, 316ff
252 WA Br 2093:171–3
253 WA Br 2093:58, 155, 202, 250, 319ff
254 Cf 1 Cor 5:11.
255 For examples see above nn140, 174, 241.

but learned readers were pleased by the elegance of the word.[256] Some were offended by the word *fabula*, but amends were made to the learned. The proof is that the *Censures* of the Paris theological faculty left out this detail, though it had been noted by Béda.[257] But Martin accepts no excuses. He thinks that anyone who corrects offensive details deserves condemnation twice over.[258] Yet he, who is skilled in so many languages, ought not to have been offended. The others are excused by their ignorance of languages and of antiquity. Yet none of them has declared Erasmus ἄθεος 'atheist,' an Epicurus, a Democritus, a mouthpiece of Satan, a mocker and hater of Christ and his whole religion. If their hasty judgments are to be counted against me, Luther ought to remember that they are the very people who detest him for a pestilential heresiarch, but are hostile towards me solely because they say that there are many things in my writings which seem at first sight to be related to Martin's doctrines.[259] These people are now out of their minds in all other respects; they are sane solely in so far as they

* * * * *

256 In an academic address of February 1519, theologian Jean Briart of Ath, vice-chancellor of the University of Louvain, attacked Erasmus for how he used the term *coelebs* in a 'declamation' in praise of matrimony that had been published the previous year (*Encomium matrimonii* ASD I-5 333:416). For this contretemps Erasmus blamed not so much Briart himself, with whom he was normally on good terms (eg Ep 675), but his real enemy among the Louvain theologians, Jacques Masson (Latomus); see *Catalogus lucubrationum* Allen 1 22:23–3:6; on Masson see Rummel *Catholic Critics* I chapter 4. Erasmus defended his declamation, and in particular his usage of *coelebs*, in an *Apologia de laude matrimonii* LB IX 105–12, esp 109A–B; see also H. de Vocht *History of the Foundation and the Rise of the Collegium Trilingue Lovaniense 1517–1555* 4 vols (Louvain 1951–55) I 313ff, and *Apologia adversus monachos* LB IX 1089E–F. On Briart cf CEBR I 195–6; on Latomus cf CEBR II 304–6.

257 In his *Annotationes* of 1525 (see introduction to Ep 1664) Noël Béda, syndic of the theology faculty at the University of Paris, attacked Erasmus' use of the term *fabula* in the preface to his *Paraphrase on Matthew*, and in the paraphrase itself, at 11:7 (LB VII 3V, 66 / CWE 45 20, 184). For Erasmus' response, see *Supputatio* LB IX 563C–5D, 654D–C. For the *Determinatio facultatis theologiae in schola Parisiensi super quam plurimis assertionibus D. Erasmi Roterodami* (1531), see introduction to Allen Ep 1902:233–4, and Rummel *Catholic Critics* II 46–55. On Noël Béda see CEBR I 116–18.

258 WA Br 2093:331–4

259 See below n262; cf J.B. Payne 'The Significance of Lutheranizing Changes in Erasmus' Interpretation of Paul's Letters to the Romans and the Galatians in his Annotations (1527) and Paraphrases (1532)' *Histoire de l'exégèse du XVI siècle* ed P. Fraenkel and Oliver Fatio (Geneva 1978) 312–30.

are offended by a few of Erasmus' words.[260] And note how inconsistent human judgments are. Martin proclaims that I know nothing, that I do not in the least understand the subtleties which he writes against the papists, and not even my own more simple ideas, for I teach nothing at all.[261] But the papists reproach me with the fact that Luther has derived those very subtleties to a great extent from my books.[262] I confess that I have derived much of what I write from the books of the ancient orthodox authors. Yet, if you remove the hyperbole, the abuse, the facetiousness, the tautologies, the exaggerations, and the assertions from Luther's books, as well as the details in which he agrees with Jan Hus and John Wyclif,[263] and some others, there will probably not be much left which he can boast of as his own. I prefer to occupy my leisure time with these 'simple ideas' than to trouble the peace of the whole church with Luther's subtleties, setting city against city, people against princes and bishops, and princes against one another. I am not so dull, though, that I cannot understand those paradoxes of Martin's which weavers and shoemakers chant to us from memory.[264] I am speaking of his Latin publications.

Even assuming there was nothing false or erroneous in Luther's books, his quite unrestrained abusive language directed at everyone infects the minds of his readers, especially the uneducated ones, and produces nothing but schism. He wants to force me into line, so that I speak of sacred

* * * * *

260 WA Br 2093:224ff, 237ff
261 WA Br 2093:63–79
262 Eg in his *Supputatio* (cf above n257) Erasmus has to defend himself for using Lutheran-sounding terms like *fiducia* 'trust' or *sola fide* 'by faith alone' when referring to faith, eg in his paraphrase on John: LB IX 476C, 597B–C, 630F–1A. For the passages from the paraphrase on John noted by Béda see LB VII 629E, 630B, 630F, 633C, 631E (CWE 46:198–201); cf CWE 46 367 where J.E. Phillips assembled references to Béda's objections sv Béda, Noël.
263 Erasmus associated Luther's doctrine that 'whatever we do happens not by free will but by absolute necessity' with two theologians condemned by the Catholic church, Jan Hus (born c 1372, burned at the stake at the Council of Constance 1415) and John Wyclif (c 1330–87); see *De libero arbitrio* CWE 76 12 and *Hyperaspistes* 1 CWE 76 250, 252.
264 Cf *De libero arbitrio* CWE 76 12–13: 'Supposing that what Wyclif taught and Luther defended is in some sense true – that whatever we do happens not by free will but by absolute necessity – what could be more useless than to spread this paradox abroad,' with the comment by C. Trinkaus (CWE 76 introduction lxix): 'He feared these doctrines would make it too easy for the masses of simple Christians ... to find justification for any behaviour, however heinous.'

things in the prescribed manner.[265] But where did he come by this new kind of teaching? From Christ, or from the apostles, or the approved Doctors of the church? Not at all! Where then? I leave others to judge. Note also that staunch adherents of his doctrine disapprove of his lack of moderation, because it hinders this drama from having a propitious outcome.[266] If I, the Epicurean, had been around in the apostles' time and had heard them preach the gospel with abuse so great and so constant, I am afraid I would have stayed an Epicurean. Nevertheless, Luther makes me into a king exercising an unbearable tyranny over all people.[267] But I am a king without a guard, without so much as a captain under whose shield I could hide in safety, hurling spears dipped in poison at everyone; without a city, or a school, or pupils to draw their pens for me![268] If Luther's conscience is clear, and he is persuaded in his mind that his teaching is holy and pious, he should take his example from Paul, who wants the evangelist to be διδακτικός 'an apt teacher,' not πλήκτης 'violent' or λογομάχος 'fighting over words,'[269] and take care not to put the slightest stumbling-block in the way of the gospel which he wants to spread around the world. At present he does not consider how many people shrink or distance themselves from his teaching, because they are offended by the constant, insolent invective, especially if frenzied abuse is accompanied by shameless falsehood and malicious distortion.

Luther makes the accusation that 'in these troubled times,' as he calls them – it would have been more accurate to say: these mad times – I sport and, in his words, play the fool.[270] I wrote the *Praise of Folly* in a light-hearted way when times were quiet. I will gladly deliver it up for punishment if it seems right to do so.[271] The *Colloquies* appeared without my

* * * * *

265 WA Br 2093:80ff, 288, 300
266 See introductory note above nn64, 66.
267 WA Br 2093:177, 180, 270–2, 305, 327
268 For a similar assertion of his independence from courts and factions, see *Hyperaspistes* 1 CWE 76 116.
269 1 Tim 3:2–3, slightly misquoted by Erasmus (Paul says that a bishop should be ἄμαχος 'not quarrelsome').
270 WA Br 2093:53. Luther coins a Latin word, *morioner*, alluding to the fact that Erasmus had given his *Praise of Folly* a Greek title in Latin letters (*Moriae encomium*).
271 This was Erasmus' common response to the criticisms of Catholic critics concerning the sharpness of his denunciations of traditional beliefs and practices, whether directly (as in his New Testament *Annotationes*) or in the form of a lampoon (*Moriae encomium*); see eg Ep 1581:153–5 to Noël Béda: 'I saw much evidence of a decline, and it was a time of peace. Could anyone have foreseen that the whole world would soon be engulfed in this fateful storm [ie

consent,[272] indeed to my annoyance. I had added several colloquies to them to please the printer, in a very careless way, sometimes finishing three in a single day.[273] However, I do not jest everywhere in the *Colloquies*, and, if I do jest, I do not jest to no purpose.[274] But Martin plays with words and figures of speech even in the most dreadful matters, seeming to take pleasure insatiably in delights of this kind. I confess that I am by natural inclination rather given to jesting, both in my writings and in my conversations with friends.[275] This has not always worked for me, since I judge other people's character by my own innocent disposition. But since no single person is free of every fault, I prefer to seem slightly foolish to some than a

* * * * *

the Reformation]?' But nothing he said in the last ten years of his life could take away the sting of these earlier attacks. For how Erasmus was read in Italy by Protestants and Catholics alike (whether he wanted to be read this way or not) cf Seidel Menchi *Erasmo in Italia*.

272 The Froben edition of the *Familiarium colloquiorum formulae* (Basel November 1518) was based on a manuscript Erasmus had not seen since he prepared it for his pupils twenty years earlier; see Ep 909, his preface to an emended edition (Louvain March 1519), and the introduction to *Colloquia* CWE 39 xxii–xxiv. In addition to the title-piece 'Patterns of Informal Conversations' *Familiarium colloquiorum formulae* and 'A Short Rule For Copiousness' *Brevis de copia praeceptio*, the text featured a colloquy or dialogue on 'The Profane Feast' *Convivium profanum* CWE 39 134–63.

273 For the Froben edition of the *Familiarium colloquiorum formulae* of March 1522 (see Ep 1262), Erasmus added ten new colloquies: 'Rash Vows' *De votis temere susceptis*, 'In Pursuit of Benefices' *De captandis sacerdotiis*, 'Military Affairs' *Militaria*, 'The Master's Bidding' *Herilia*, 'A Lesson in Manners' *Monitoria paedagogica*, 'Sport' *De lusu*, 'The Whole Duty of Youth' *Confabulatio pia*, 'Hunting' *Venatio*, 'Off to School' *Euntes in ludum litterarium*, and 'The Godly Feast' *Convivium religiosum*; see CWE 39 35–243. A few of these are quite brief (eg 'Hunting,' 'Off to School') and could have been dashed off in a day, but Erasmus' claims to speak his mind freely with no second thoughts, eg *Spongia* above 60 n128, are best taken with a grain of salt. For example, 'whatever I publish is better termed a miscarriage than a birth. This vice is deeply ingrained in me. I cannot endure the tedium of revision' *Responsio ad epistolam Pii* CWE 84 19; 'By nature I am extemporaneous, and wondrously lazy about revising' Allen Ep 3043:36–7.

274 See his 'On the Usefulness of the Colloquies' *De utilitate colloquiorum*, first published with the 1526 edition (CWE 40 1095–1119); cf Bierlaire *Colloques* 85–111.

275 An old refrain in Erasmus' letters; see eg Ep 114:8–10: Erasmus has no fear 'that my plain-speaking may have upset you [Thomas More], for you are quite well aware of my Spartan habit of sparring until I draw blood.'

kind of harsh, πλήκτης 'violent,'[276] Procrustean character, constantly puff-
ing tragic words. Rhetoricians must first of all teach using arguments, then,
if the matter demands, stimulate the emotions, but must not rashly excite
the violent feelings known as πάθη 'passions.'[277] But never to stop being
δεινός 'forceful,' never to cease thundering truly tragic words, this is lunacy
rather than fluency.[278]

Luther asks where so many sorts of sects in the church spring from.
Among them he mentions the Sacramentarians (as though his own teaching about the sacraments was the same as the Catholic church hands
down);[279] he mentions the Donatists, the Arians, the Anabaptists, the Epicureans, and so on.[280] He should have added those enthusiasts the sabbatarians,[281] who actually have the effrontery to get circumcised; and I do
indeed mean 'front,' because there are those who scratch their face with
a knife until they draw blood, then anoint the spot with oil, and this is
how they are initiated in Christ.[282] 'Where have these tares in the Lord's
field come from?' Luther asks.[283] Where but from four ambiguous words
of Erasmus (although the reality described by them is certainly not ambiguous); that he pointed out that the apostles did not immediately call

* * * * *

276 1 Tim 3:3, Titus 1:7
277 This idea comes not from classical rhetoric but from Erasmus himself; see
James D. Tracy *Erasmus: the Growth of a Mind* (Geneva 1972) 72–7. Cicero prided
himself on his ability to stir up an audience's vehement emotions – this was
the best way of winning cases; cf J.M. May 'Ciceronian Oratory in Context'
Brill's Companion to Cicero: Oratory and Rhetoric ed J.M. May (Leiden 2002) 61–5.
278 On δεινός see above 426 and *Spongia* above 79 n238.
279 When his friend Willibald Pirckheimer published a treatise endorsing Luther's
understanding of the Eucharist (asserting the real presence of Christ in the
sacrament, but rejecting the Catholic doctrine of transubstantiation), Erasmus
expressed mild disapproval; see Ep 1717. He knew that Luther also rejected the
Catholic understanding of the mass as a sacrifice; cf *Apologia adversus monachos*
LB IX 1064F.
280 WA Br 2093:359–61
281 The rejection of Sunday in favour of the Jewish sabbath was preached by
Andreas Fischer (1480–1540) in Silesia and Moravia; see D. Liechty *Andreas
Fischer and the Sabbatarian Anabaptists* (Scottdale PA, 1988). Erasmus mentions
a group of this kind *apud Bohemos* in *De concordia* LB V 505D–6A; cf *Ecclesiastes*
ASD V-5 228:643–4. Here in the *Purgatio*, Erasmus uses the Latin transliteration
(*Suermeri*) of Luther's German *Schwärmer* to characterize the sabbatarians.
282 There is no reference to this practice in Williams *Radical Reformation*. Someone
with a lot of nerve was said in Latin to *perfricere frontem* 'to rub or scratch the
forehead.'
283 WA Br 2093:361; cf Matt 13:24–9.

Christ God in front of all and sundry;[284] that he pointed out that the words of the gospel are indirect, owing to tropes and figures of speech;[285] that he said that Paul becomes all things to all men so as to win all men, and compared him to a chameleon;[286] that he wrote that the Epistle to the Romans is a tangle of many difficulties, and mentioned labyrinths in this respect;[287] that he wrote that John the Evangelist 'prates about nothing but worlds,'[288] though these words never entered my mind even in my dream; that when speaking of the Incarnation of the Lord he used an image drawn from sexual intercourse.[289] Undoubtedly, this is the source of this great crop of heresies! Yet up till now, no one, with the sole exception of Luther, has accused Erasmus of this. Rather, some have accused me of having sown the seeds of Luther himself.[290] But he will cry straight away that they are lying shamelessly, that Erasmus is not a Lutheran, but entirely Erasmus. Granted, this lie does come closer to the truth than for someone to say that Anabaptists, Donatists, Arians, and Epicureans (that is, pagans) had sprung forth from my three ambiguous statements. If this is true, human ingratitude amazes me. To this day, none of these people has ever acknowledged or thanked me, though there are countless disciples by whom Luther is addressed as 'reverend father' and 'restorer of the gospel truth.' On the other hand there are not a few orthodox Christians who profess they owe it to me that they were able to know and love Christ.[291]

Luther thinks that my books should be banned from his followers' schools[292] – as if I had ever sought to be taken into their schools. Perhaps he has schools for theologians in mind, and he seems somehow to have an inkling that this may come to pass. I am well aware that some monks have been clamouring for this for some time now.[293] But their assumption

* * * * *

284 See above n84.
285 See eg Watson and Drewery *Bondage of the Will* 220, 229, 237.
286 Erasmus says this in the preface to his *Paraphrase on 1 and 2 Corinthians* (1519); see Ep 916; cf 1 Cor 9:19–23; on Erasmus' principle of accommodation see above n66.
287 See above n72.
288 See above n239.
289 See above n160.
290 See above n262.
291 Eg Erasmus Schets to Erasmus, relaying opinions from Spain as well as his own; see addEp 1541. On other Catholic admirers of Erasmus cf B. Mansfield *Phoenix of his Age: Interpretations of Erasmus c 1550–1750* (Toronto 1979) 7–20.
292 WA Br 2093:409. For the influence of the *Colloquies* in particular, also in Protestant Germany (despite Luther's wishes), see Bierlaire *Colloques* 123–47.
293 This debate was especially acute in Spain, where many of Erasmus' works

is that Luther's doctrine cannot be suppressed unless Erasmus' works have been got rid of first. I imagine he will now applaud them and side with them for all he is worth out of antipathy to me. If only this could have the effect of making him reconcile himself to the pope, the papists, and all the theologians and monks, and restore Christ's church to its peace once again! I would readily pay for the loss of my books with such a gain for the world, since no one can or will be able to separate me myself from Christ unless I forsake him voluntarily.

Yet after having been breathed on by the prophetic spirit, Luther foresees that my judgment is coming speedily, and that it will not be long before I betray and destroy myself with my own noises, like a shrew.[294] He observes paganism and hatred of Christianity, which I, being a cunning man, have concealed till now, as he thinks (or rather does not think but pretends to think). Until now, my opinion regarding Christ and the Christian religion has been what is worthy of one who has fixed all his hope on Christ, and I am making an effort to believe more fully, and certainly to be more loving, day by day. If I am in error along with the papists in some respect, I trust that I will be among those whose error God has excused in his mercy, as Luther says, because they were misled and erred honestly. It is enough for me if I am received into the bosom of the divine mercy along with Jerome, Chrysostom, and Bernard. Yet Luther says that there is no hope of pardon after the light of truth has been revealed by him – as if Hus and Wyclif had not taught the same before him.[295] If God has brought him into such wonderful light after he has dwelt for so long in such deep darkness,[296] it would be fitting for him to employ the same gentleness towards us wretched men still groping in the gloom of the primitive church.[297] But to speak seriously. If it is a question of behaviour and

* * * * *

were published in vernacular translations, until conservative theologians launched a counter-attack, starting with a formal debate in Valladolid (1527); see vol I of M. Bataillon *Érasme et l'Espagne* 3 vols rev ed (Geneva 1991).

294 WA Br 2093:141; cf *Adagia* I iii 6: *Suo ipsius indicio periit sorex* 'The shrew-mouse gave itself away' CWE 31 289:1–15: 'the proverb is directed against people who give themselves away by their own talk.'

295 WA Br 2093:1–18. On Wyclif and Hus see above n263.

296 An allusion to Luther's argument that 'The true church, which does not err, is hidden from sight': Watson and Drewery *Bondage of the Will* 154–8 (WA 18 649–52).

297 The primitive church was not, for Erasmus, the touchstone of truth; see István Bejczy *Erasmus and the Middle Ages: The Historical Consciousness of a Christian Humanist* (Leiden 2001) 18–24.

ceremonies, I would like much to be corrected, but by the authority of a council. If it is a question of doctrines, I too could assent to certain teachings if I heard the public voice of the church.[298] My mind is not put at rest by Luther's assertions, however strong, as long as in my reading I come across much that could refute what he asserts. Anyone acting against his conscience is building hell.[299] In such a global conflagration each must look out for himself. My concern will be to hand over this poor soul to Christ who saved it. If Martin has indeed made it his aim to persuade the world that Erasmus is employing his cunning wiles and insidious devices to bring all Christians to hate true religion, his efforts are in vain. He is more likely to persuade everyone that he is either crazed with hatred, or in the grip of mental illness, or driven by some evil spirit.[300] Let him rather persuade people of what he had sworn in the Jewish manner[301] to be true: 'As' the Lord 'lives,' he says, 'they do Erasmus great wrong and I must defend him against his enemies, who call him a Lutheran, though as I can only too truly and faithfully witness, he is in no sense a Lutheran, but merely Erasmus. He should be abandoned to the papists, who are worthy of such an apostle.'[302] I do not know who he is calling papists; I am glad to stay with the

* * * * *

298 In *De libero arbitrio* Erasmus defended the doctrine of free will 'since all true believers have handed it down with an overwhelming consensus and the church has clearly defined it as something not to be disputed but to be believed' (CWE 76 121; cf 139). In another context, it is the 'consensus of the church' that holds him back from a certain sympathy for Johann Oecolampadius' view of the Eucharist; see *Detectio praestigiarum* above 180. Cf Ep 1729:29–30: 'By the church I mean the consensus of Christ's people throughout the world.'

299 Identifying this expression as 'clearly proverbial in character' (ASD IX-1 481), C. Augustijn locates a possible source in Jean Gerson's *Regulae mandatorum* 7 (*Oeuvres complètes* ed Msgr Glorieux 10 vols [Paris 1960–73]) IX 96: *Omnis agens contra conscientiam aedificat ad gehennam.* Cf a usage nearly contemporary with Erasmus': *Die politische Korrespondenz der Stadt Strassburg im Zeitalter der Reformation* ed H. Gerber 4 2 (Heidelberg 1933) 1014, a statement by Strasbourg's deputies: 'dan Paulus spricht: wer wider sin gewissen handelt, bauet zu der hollen.'

300 In his *Spongia* above 112 Erasmus says: 'Nor have I been able to persuade myself that the spirit of Christ – there is nothing more gentle – dwells within a heart [Luther's] from which so much bitterness gushes forth. Would that I am deceived in what I suspect!' Cf Ep 1510:72–3: 'Phallicus [Erasmus' name for the Geneva reformer, Guillaume Farel] developed this anger at my expense because in my *Spongia* I throw doubt on Luther's spirit.'

301 For oaths of this kind, see 1 and 2 Sam and 1 and 2 Kings, eg 1 Sam 1:26.

302 WA Br 2093:405–8

orthodox,[303] whether he abandons me or not.

Nor will what he threatens be unpleasant: that he will hand over the contemptible Erasmus to everlasting darkness and perpetual oblivion, along with others whom he has not deigned to answer.[304] Along with whom? With Eck, Emser, Johannes Cochlaeus, and others, who might, he says, perhaps have become famous if he had deigned to give them a reply.[305] He might have added: with Josse Clichtove, Jacobus Latomus, John Fisher the bishop of Rochester, and many others whose names are now buried and given over to the waters of Lethe. Yet he did indeed deem me worthy of this honour some time ago, in *On the Bondage of the Will.* He will say: I did not reply, I only stung the man a little to stir up his sluggishness[306] for the whole of his book speaks of nothing but Erasmus the Epicurus, the Democritus, the Sceptic, the Christ-hater, the mocker of Christian piety,[307] the corrupter of the Scriptures, the babbler, the drunkard. Because I did not thank him for these charming remarks but dared to refute his accusations,[308] I have suddenly become a viper, bringing 'viper-asps' to birth.[309] But which one is the viper – the one who breathes venom like this, or the one who wards it off? The one who inflicts fatal bites, or the one who cures them? Then, when he had raved against his fellow man in this way, he had 'only stung' me. And after this work was published he wrote a letter to me trying to persuade me that he was still fair-minded and friendly to me, whether I believed it or not.[310] If he pinches a sluggish friend like this, what wounds would he inflict if he wanted to kill an enemy? But in this way the αὐτοκόλαξ 'self-flatterer' deludes himself, and convinces himself that people do not understand his

* * * * *

303 For the implied distinction between 'papist' and 'orthodox,' see Ep 1195: 'I am not impious enough to dissent from the Catholic church, I am not ungrateful enough to dissent from [Pope] Leo [X], of whose support and exceptional kindness to me I have personal experience.'

304 WA Br 2093:46–9

305 WA Br 2093:27–32, slightly misquoted by Erasmus. In *Hyperaspistes* 1 CWE 76 97–8 Erasmus complained that Luther had answered his *De libero arbitrio* while not responding to the works of other Catholic critics, some of whom are named here as well.

306 Cf WA Br 2093:55–60.

307 Erasmus was particularly offended by the places in *De servo arbitrio* where Luther calls him an Epicurean and an atheist, a mocker of Christian belief; see eg Epp 1670, 1690.

308 Ie in *Hyperaspistes* 1 and 2 (CWE 76 and 77).

309 WA Br 2093:60–2, 114, 268; *viperaspistes* is a derogatory wordplay on *hyperaspistes*; cf CWE 76 96 n1.

310 This letter is lost, but Erasmus' reply survives: Ep 1688.

deceitfulness in boasting that he refuses to reply to certain critics.

And yet, if he believes in his own teaching, and judges it worthy of being embraced by everyone, it would help if he were to make a serious reply to some, relying not on taunts and abuse, but on Scripture and argument.[311] There are books flying through the world now, which, I hear, cast up a good many passages at him where he contradicts himself, or where he has manifestly distorted the Holy Scriptures, using a false interpretation to twist them to fit his doctrine; or which confute his opinions with incontrovertible arguments. And he thinks it a splendid victory not to honour them with a reply! Yet it would have been more fitting, it would even have been more useful, to honour them with a reply than to attack them with mockery and invective. Will he say: I have no time? Well, he would have saved himself a great deal of time if he had left out the insults and worked only with Scripture and necessary arguments. If he does envy them their celebrity, what difference does it make whether he brings them renown by arguing with them or by insulting them? Now, because all he does is insult them, he is giving them honour and acclaim in the sight of many, and is attaching no small discredit to his own reputation as well, especially in the eyes of wise, unbiased people, who favour moderation, uprightness, and civility in all circumstances. This would have been worthier of the herald of the gospel, as Luther wishes to appear, than to incite the minds of men to sedition and war in these irascible times. The gospel trumpet plays a very different tune from Pan's conch or Allecto's horn.[312] But the Lord lives, and does not desert those who hope in him.[313]

En of the purgation of Desiderius Erasmus of Rotterdam
against the letter of Martin Luther

* * * * *

311 The basis for debate proposed by Erasmus in his *De libero arbitrio* CWE 76 15.
312 The rural divinity Pan, half-man and half-goat, is usually associated with the Pan-pipe. I have not found a reference to his 'conch,' but Erasmus may have in mind the story of how, when Pan fell into the sea, his hind-quarters were transformed into the sea-goat Capricorn (literally, 'goat-horn'). Allecto was one of the Furies (see above n149). In Book 7 of the *Aeneid* she rouses the Latins to war against Aeneas and his Trojans; for her horn cf 7.511–15.
313 Jth 13:17

WORKS FREQUENTLY CITED

SHORT-TITLE FORMS
FOR ERASMUS' WORKS

INDEX OF
BIBLICAL AND APOCRYPHAL REFERENCES

GENERAL INDEX

WORKS FREQUENTLY CITED

This list provides bibliographical information for works referred to in short-title form in this volume. For Erasmus' writings see the short-title list following.

Allen	*Opus epistolarum Des. Erasmi Roterodami* ed P.S. Allen, H.M. Allen, and H.W. Garrod (Oxford 1906–1958) 11 vols and index
Aquinas *Summa theologiae*	Thomas Aquinas *Summa theologiae* trans and ed Thomas Gilby OP (Blackfriars edition, New York 1964)
ARG	*Archiv für Reformationsgeschichte*
ASD	*Opera omnia Desiderii Erasmi Roterodami* (Amsterdam 1969–)
Augustijn 'Gelden-houwer'	Cornelis Augustijn 'Gerard Geldenhouwer und die religiöse Toleranz' ARG 69 (1978)
Bernstein *German Humanism*	Eckhard Bernstein *German Humanism* (Boston 1983)
Bierlaire *Colloques*	F. Bierlaire *Les Colloques d'Érasme: réforme des études, réforme des moeurs et réforme de l'Église au XVIe siècle* (Liège 1978)
Bierlaire Familia	Franz Bierlaire *La Familia d'Érasme* (Paris 1968)*
BOL I	C. Augustijn, P. Fraenkel, M. Lienhard *Martini Buceri Opera Latina* 1. Studies in Medieval and Reformation Thought 30 (Leiden 1982)
Boyle *Rhetoric and Reform*	M.O. Boyle *Rhetoric and Reform: Erasmus' Civil Dispute with Luther* (Cambridge and London 1983)
Brady *Protestant Politics*	T.A. Brady *Protestant Politics: Jacob Sturm (1489–1553) and the German Reformation* (Atlantic Highlands, NJ 1995)
BRE	*Briefwechsel des Beatus Rhenanus* ed A. Horawitz and K. Hartfelder (Leipzig 1886; repr Hildesheim 1966)
Brecht *Martin Luther*	Martin Brecht *Martin Luther* 3 vols, 1: *His Road to Reformation 1483–1521* tr J. Schaaf (Philadelphia 1985); 3: *The Preservation of the Church 1532–1546* tr J. Schaaf (Philadelphia 1993)
Brunfels *Responsio*	Otto Brunfels *Pro Ulrico Hutteno vita defuncto ad Erasmi Roterodami Spongiam responsio* (Strasbourg 1524); see EB.

CCSL — *Corpus christianorum, series Latina* (Turnhout 1954–   )

CEBR — *Contemporaries of Erasmus: A Biographical Register of the Renaissance and Reformation* ed P.G. Bietenholz and T.B. Deutscher (Toronto 1985–7) 3 vols

Chantraine *Mystère* — Georges Chantraine SJ *'Mystère' et 'Philosophie du Christ' selon Érasme* (Namur and Gembloux 1971)

Chrisman *Strasbourg and the Reform* — M.U. Chrisman *Strasbourg and the Reform: A Study in the Process of Change* (New Haven 1967)

CR — *Corpus Reformatorum*

CSEL — *Corpus scriptorum ecclesiasticorum latinorum* (Vienna 1866–   )

CWE — Collected Works of Erasmus (Toronto 1974–   )

Denzinger-Schönmetzer — *Enchiridion symbolorum, definitionum et declarationum de rebus fidei et morum* ed H. Denzinger and A. Schönmetzer 32nd ed (1963)

EB — Eduardus Böcking *Ulrichi Hutteni Equitis Germani Opera Quae Reperi Possunt Omnia* (Leipzig 1859–61) 5 vols. Vol II contains Hutten *Expostulatio cum Erasmo*, followed by a German translation; vol III contains Otto Brunfels *Pro Ulrico Hutteno vita defuncto ad Erasmi Roterodami Spongiam responsio*

ERSY — *Erasmus of Rotterdam Society Yearbook*

Ferguson *Opuscula* — Ferguson, Wallace K. *Erasmi Opuscula, A Supplement to the Opera Omnia* (The Hague 1933)

Gebhardt *Stellung* — Georg Gebhardt *Die Stellung des Erasmus von Rotterdam zur Römischen Kirche* (Marburg 1966)

Glossa Ordinaria — *Biblia Latina cum Glossa Ordinaria* Facsimile reprint of the *editio princeps* by Adolph Rusch of Strasbourg 1480/1 with and introduction by Karlfried Forelich and Margaret Gibson (Turnhout 1992) 4 vols

Guggisberg *Basel* — Hans R. Guggisberg *Basel in the Sixteenth Century. Aspects of the City Republic before, during, and after the Reformation* (St Louis 1982)

Herminjard *Correspondance* — *Correspondance des Réformateurs dans les pays de langue française* ed A.-L. Herminjard, vol I (Geneva and Paris 1866–97, repr 1965–6)

Hoffmann *Rhetoric and Theology*   Manfred Hoffmann *Rhetoric and Theology: The Hermeneutic of Erasmus* (Toronto 1994)

Holborn   *Desiderius Erasmus Roterodamus Ausgewählte Werke* ed Hajo and Annemarie Holborn (Munich 1933)

Holborn *Ulrich von Hutten*   Hajo Holborn *Ulrich von Hutten and the German Reformation* (New Haven, CT 1937)

Holeczek *Novum Instrumentum*   Erasmus von Rotterdam *Novum Instrumentum Basel 1516* ed H. Holeczek (Stuttgart-Bad Cannstatt 1986)

Holeczek *Erasmus Deutsch*   Holeczek *Erasmus Deutsch* 1 (Stuttgart-Bad Cannstatt 1983)

K   German translation of Hutten *Expostulatio*; see EB.

Kaegi 'Erasmus und Hutten'   Werner 'Kaegi Hutten und Erasmus. Ihre Freundschaft und ihr Streit' *Historische Vierteljahrschrift* 22 (Diss. Dresden 1924)

Kaufmann   T. Kaufmann *Die Abendmahlstheologie der Strassburger Reformatoren bis 1528* Beiträge zur historischen Theologie 81 (Tübingen 1992)

Kittelson *Wolfgang Capito*   James M. Kittelson *Wolfgang Capito: From Humanist to Reformer* Studies in Medieval and Reformation Thought 17 (Leiden 1975)

LB   Erasmus *Opera omnia* ed Jean Leclerc (Leiden 1703–6; repr Hildesheim 1961–2) 10 vols

LW   *Luther's works* ed Jaroslav Pelikan and Helmut T. Lehman (St Louis, MO and Philadelphia 1955–1976) 54 vols

Matheson *Cardinal Contarini*   Peter Matheson *Cardinal Contarini at Regensburg* (Oxford 1972)

Maynung   'Lodovicus Leopoldi' [Leo Jud] *Des hochgelerten Erasmi von Roterdam unnd Doctor Martin Luthers maynung vom Nachtmal unnsers herren Jhesu Christi* ([Zürich: Froschauer] 1526)

McConica 'Grammar of Consent'   James K. McConica 'Erasmus and the Grammar of Consent' *Scrinium Erasmianum* ed J. Coppens 2nd ed (Leiden 1969) 2 vols II 78–99

McConica 'Erasmus and the "Julius"'   James K. McConica 'Erasmus and the "Julius": a Humanist Reflects on the Church' in *The Pursuit of Holiness in Late*

Medieval and Renaissance Religion ed Charles Trinkaus and Heiko A. Oberman (Leiden 1974) 444–82

NAK · *Nederlands Archief voor Kerkgeschiedenis* (now *Church History and Religious Culture*

Nicholas of Lyra · Nicholas de Lyra *Postilla super totam Bibliam* (Strasbourg 1492; facsimile ed Frankfurt am Main 1971) 4 vols

NRSV · *The Holy Bible ... New Revised Standard Version* (New York 1989)

OER · *The Oxford Encyclopedia of the Reformation* ed H.J. Hillerbrand (New York and Oxford 1996) 4 vols

Payne *Sacraments* · J.B. Payne *Erasmus: His Theology of the Sacraments* (Richmond, VA 1970)

Pelikan *Christian Tradition* · Jaroslav Pelikan *The Christian Tradition: A History of the Development of Doctrine* (Chicago 1971–1991) 5 vols

Peremans *Correspondance* · N. Peremans *Erasme et Bucer d'apreès leur correspondance* (Paris 1970)

Prinsen *Collectanea* · Prinsen, J. *Collectanea van Gerardus Geldenhauer Noviomagus* (Amsterdam 1901)

Reeve *Gospels* · *Erasmus' Annotations on the New Testament: The Gospels. Facsimile of the Final Latin Text with All Earlier Variants* ed Anne Reeve, intro Michael A. Screech (London 1986)

Reeve *Galatians to the Apocalypse* · *Erasmus' Annotations on the New Testament: Galatians to the Apocalypse. Facsimile of the Final Latin Text with All Earlier Variants* ed Anne Reeve, Studies in the History of Christian Thought 52 (Leiden 1993)

Reeve-Screech · *Erasmus' Annotations on the New Testament: Acts – Romans – I and II Corinthians. Facsimile of the Final Latin Text with All Earlier Variants* ed Anne Reeve and Michael A. Screech, Studies in the History of Christian Thought 42 (Leiden 1990)

Rummel *Catholic Critics* · Erika Rummel *Erasmus and his Catholic Critics* (Nieuwkoop 1989) 2 vols

Rupp *Patterns of Reformation* · Rupp, Gordon *Patterns of Reformation* (Philadelphia 1969)

Seidel Menchi *Erasmo in Italia* — Sylvana Seidel Menchi *Erasmo in Italia: 1520-1580* Nuova cultura 1 (Turin 1987)

Spitz *Religious Renaissance* — L. Spitz *The Religious Renaissance of the German Humanists* (Cambridge, MA 1963)

Stadtwald *Roman Popes and German Patriots* — Kurt Stadtwald *Roman Popes and German Patriots. Antipapalism in the Politics of the German Humanist Movement from Gregor Heimburg to Martin Luther* (Geneva 1996)

Staehelin *Lebenswerk* — E. Staehelin *Das theologische Lebenswerk Oecolampads* Quellen und Forschungen zur Reformationsgeschichte 21 (Leipzig 1939)

Staehelin *Briefe und Akten* — E. Staehelin *Briefe und Akten zum Leben Oekolampads* (Leipzig 1927, repr New York 1971)

Stephens *Theology of Huldrych Zwingli* — W.P. Stephens *The Theology of Huldrych Zwingli* (Oxford 1986)

Stokes — Francis Griffin Stokes *Epistolae Obscurorum Virorum: The Latin text with an English Rendering, Notes, and an Historical Introduction* (London 1925)

Thompson *Fide* — Thompson, C.R. *Inquisitio de fide* Yale Studies in Religion 15 (New Haven 1950)

Thompson *Colloquies* — Craig R. Thompson *The Colloquies of Erasmus* (Chicago 1965)

Tracy *Politics of Erasmus* — James Tracy *The Politics of Erasmus. A Pacifist Intellectual and his Political Milieu* (Toronto 1978)

Tracy *Low Countries* — James D. Tracy *Erasmus of the Low Countries* (Berkeley 1996)

Tracy 'Erasmus and the Arians' — J.D. Tracy 'Erasmus and the Arians: Remarks on the *Consensus Ecclesiae* ' *Catholic Historical Review* 67 (1981) 1–10

TRE — *Theologische Realenzyclopädie* ed H.R. Balz et al. (Berlin and New York 1977-   )

WA — *D. Martin Luthers Werke, Kritische Gesamtausgabe* (Weimar 1883-   ) 73 vols to date (with indexes)

WA Br — *D. Martin Luthers Werke: Briefwechsel* (Weimar 1930–78) 12 vols

WA Tr — *D. Martin Luthers Werke: Tischreden* (Weimar 1912–21) 6 vols

Watson and Drewery *Bondage of the Will*	Luther *On The Bondage of the Will* tr P.S. Watson and B. Drewery in *Luther and Erasmus: Free Will and Salvation* ed E.G. Rupp and P.S. Watson, Library of Christian Classics 17 (Philadelphia 1969)
Williams *Radical Reformation*	G.H. Williams *The Radical Reformation* 3rd ed (Kirksville, MO 1992)
Zwinglis Werke	*Huldreich Zwinglis Sämtliche Werke* ed Emil Egli et al (Leipzig 1905) 8 vols
Zwinglis Briefwechsel	*Zwinglis Werke* 8 ed E. Egli, G. Finsler, and W. Köhler (Leipzig 1914)

Titles following colons are longer versions of the same, or are alternative titles. Items entirely enclosed in square brackets are of doubtful authorship. For abbreviations, see Works Frequently Cited.

Acta: Acta Academiae Lovaniensis contra Lutherum *Opuscula* / CWE 71

Adagia: Adagiorum chiliades 1508, etc (Adagiorum collectanea for the primitive form, when required) LB II / ASD II-1–8 / CWE 30–6

Admonitio adversus mendacium: Admonitio adversus mendacium et obtrectationem LB X / CWE 78

Annotationes in Novum Testamentum LB VI / ASD VI-5, 6, 8, 9 / CWE 51–60

Antibarbari LB X / ASD I-1 / CWE 23

Apologia ad annotationes Stunicae: Apologia respondens ad ea quae Iacobus Lopis Stunica taxaverat in prima duntaxat Novi Testamenti aeditione LB IX / ASD IX-2

Apologia ad Caranzam: Apologia ad Sanctium Caranzam, or Apologia de tribus locis, or Responsio ad annotationem Stunicae ... a Sanctio Caranza defensam LB IX

Apologia ad Fabrum: Apologia ad Iacobum Fabrum Stapulensem LB IX / ASD IX-3 / CWE 83

Apologia ad prodromon Stunicae LB IX

Apologia ad Stunicae conclusiones LB IX

Apologia adversus monachos: Apologia adversus monachos quosdam Hispanos LB IX

Apologia adversus Petrum Sutorem: Apologia adversus debacchationes Petri Sutoris LB IX

Apologia adversus rhapsodias Alberti Pii: Apologia ad viginti et quattuor libros A. Pii LB IX / CWE 84

Apologia adversus Stunicae Blasphemiae: Apologia adversus libellum Stunicae cui titulum fecit Blasphemiae et impietates Erasmi LB IX

Apologia contra Latomi dialogum: Apologia contra Iacobi Latomi dialogum de tribus linguis LB IX / CWE 71

Apologia de 'In principio erat sermo' LB IX

Apologia de laude matrimonii: Apologia pro declamatione de laude matrimonii LB IX / CWE 71

Apologia de loco 'Omnes quidem': Apologia de loco 'Omnes quidem resurgemus' LB IX

Apologia qua respondet invectivis Lei: Apologia qua respondet duabus invectivis Eduardi Lei *Opuscula* / ASD IX-4 / CWE 72

Apophthegmata LB IV

Appendix de scriptis Clithovei LB IX / CWE 83

Appendix respondens ad Sutorem LB IX

Argumenta: Argumenta in omnes epistolas apostolicas nova (with Paraphrases)

Axiomata pro causa Lutheri: Axiomata pro causa Martini Lutheri *Opuscula* CWE 71

Brevissima scholia: In Elenchum Alberti Pii brevissima scholia per eundem Erasmum Roterodamum CWE 84

Carmina LB I, IV, V, VIII / ASD I-7 / CWE 85–6

Catalogus lucubrationum LB I / CWE 9 (Ep 1341A)

Ciceronianus: Dialogus Ciceronianus LB I / ASD I-2 / CWE 28

Colloquia LB I / ASD I-3 / CWE 39–40

Compendium vitae Allen I / CWE 4

Conflictus: Conflictus Thaliae et Barbariei LB I

[Consilium: Consilium cuiusdam ex animo cupientis esse consultum] *Opuscula* / CWE 71

De bello Turcico: Utilissima consultatio de bello Turcis inferendo, et obiter enarratus psalmus 28 LB V / ASD V-3 / CWE 64

De civilitate: De civilitate morum puerilium LB I / CWE 25

Declamatio de morte LB IV

Declamatiuncula LB IV

Declarationes ad censuras Lutetiae vulgatas: Declarationes ad censuras Lutetiae vulgatas sub nomine facultatis theologiae Parisiensis LB IX

De concordia: De sarcienda ecclesiae concordia, or De amabili ecclesiae concordia [on Psalm 83] LB V / ASD V-3 / CWE 65

De conscribendis epistolis LB I / ASD I-2 / CWE 25

De constructione: De constructione octo partium orationis, or Syntaxis LB I / ASD I-4

De contemptu mundi: Epistola de contemptu mundi LB V / ASD V-1 / CWE 66

De copia: De duplici copia verborum ac rerum LB I / ASD I-6 / CWE 24

De esu carnium: Epistola apologetica ad Christophorum episcopum Basiliensem de interdicto esu carnium LB IX / ASD IX-1

De immensa Dei misericordia: Concio de immensa Dei misericordia LB V / CWE 70

De libero arbitrio: De libero arbitrio diatribe LB IX / CWE 76

De praeparatione: De praeparatione ad mortem LB V / ASD V-1 / CWE 70

De pueris instituendis: De pueris statim ac liberaliter instituendis LB I / ASD I-2 / CWE 26

De puero Iesu: Concio de puero Iesu LB V / CWE 29

De puritate tabernaculi: Enarratio psalmi 14 qui est de puritate tabernaculi sive ecclesiae christianae LB V / ASD V-2 / CWE 65

De ratione studii LB I / ASD I-2 / CWE 24

De recta pronuntiatione: De recta latini graecique sermonis pronuntiatione LB I / ASD I-4 / CWE 26

De taedio Iesu: Disputatiuncula de taedio, pavore, tristicia Iesu LB V CWE 70

Detectio praestigiarum: Detectio praestigiarum cuiusdam libelli Germanice scripti LB X / ASD IX-1 / CWE 78

De vidua christiana LB V / CWE 66

De virtute amplectenda: Oratio de virtute amplectenda LB V / CWE 29

[Dialogus bilinguium ac trilinguium: Chonradi Nastadiensis dialogus bilinguium ac trilinguium] *Opuscula* / CWE 7

Dilutio: Dilutio eorum quae Iodocus Clithoveus scripsit adversus declamationem suasoriam matrimonii / *Dilutio eorum quae Iodocus Clithoveus scripsit* ed Émile V. Telle (Paris 1968) / CWE 83

Divinationes ad notata Bedae: Divinationes ad notata per Bedam de Paraphrasi
Erasmi in Matthaeum, et primo de duabus praemissis epistolis LB IX

Ecclesiastes: Ecclesiastes sive de ratione concionandi LB V / ASD V-4, 5
Elenchus in censuras Bedae: In N. Bedae censuras erroneas elenchus LB IX
Enchiridion: Enchiridion militis christiani LB V / CWE 66
Encomium matrimonii (in De conscribendis epistolis)
Encomium medicinae: Declamatio in laudem artis medicae LB I / ASD I-4 /
CWE 29
Epistola ad Dorpium LB IX / CWE 3 / CWE 71
Epistola ad fratres Inferioris Germaniae: Responsio ad fratres Germaniae Inferioris
ad epistolam apologeticam incerto autore proditam LB X / ASD IX-1 / CWE 78
Epistola ad graculos: Epistola ad quosdam imprudentissimos graculos LB X
Epistola apologetica adversus Stunicam LB IX / Ep 2172
Epistola apologetica de Termino LB X
Epistola consolatoria: Epistola consolatoria virginibus sacris, or Epistola consolatoria
in adversis LB V / CWE 69
Epistola contra pseudevangelicos: Epistola contra quosdam qui se falso iactant
evangelicos LB X / ASD IX-1 / CWE 78
Euripidis Hecuba LB I / ASD I-1
Euripidis Iphigenia in Aulide LB I / ASD I-1
Exomologesis: Exomologesis sive modus confitendi LB V
Explanatio symboli: Explanatio symboli apostolorum sive catechismus LB V /
ASD V-1 / CWE 70
Ex Plutarcho versa LB IV / ASD IV-2

Formula: Conficiendarum epistolarum formula (see De conscribendis epistolis)

Hyperaspistes LB X / CWE 76–7

In Nucem Ovidii commentarius LB I / ASD I-1 / CWE 29
In Prudentium: Commentarius in duos hymnos Prudentii LB V / CWE 29
In psalmum 1: Enarratio primi psalmi, 'Beatus vir,' iuxta tropologiam potissimum
LB V / ASD V-2 / CWE 63
In psalmum 2: Commentarius in psalmum 2, 'Quare fremuerunt gentes?' LB V /
ASD V-2 / CWE 63
In psalmum 3: Paraphrasis in tertium psalmum, 'Domine quid multiplicate' LB V /
ASD V-2 / CWE 63
In psalmum 4: In psalmum quartum concio LB V / ASD V-2 / CWE 63
In psalmum 22: In psalmum 22 enarratio triplex LB V / ASD V-2 / CWE 64
In psalmum 33: Enarratio psalmi 33 LB V / ASD V-3 / CWE 64
In psalmum 38: Enarratio psalmi 38 LB V / ASD V-3 / CWE 65
In psalmum 85: Concionalis interpretatio, plena pietatis, in psalmum 85 LB V / ASD
V-3 / CWE 64
Institutio christiani matrimonii LB V / CWE 69
Institutio principis christiani LB IV / ASD IV-1 / CWE 27

[Julius exclusus: Dialogus Julius exclusus e coelis] Opuscula / CWE 27

Lingua LB IV / ASD IV-1A / CWE 29

Liturgia Virginis Matris: Virginis Matris apud Lauretum cultae liturgia LB V / ASD V-1 / CWE 69

Luciani dialogi LB I / ASD I-1

Manifesta mendacia ASD IX-4 / CWE 71

Methodus (see Ratio)

Modus orandi Deum LB V / ASD V-1 / CWE 70

Moria: Moriae encomium LB IV / ASD IV-3 / CWE 27

Notatiunculae: Notatiunculae quaedam extemporales ad naenias Bedaicas

Novum Testamentum: Novum Testamentum 1519 and later (Novum instrumentum for the first edition, 1516, when required) LB VI / ASD VI-2, 3

Obsecratio ad Virginem Mariam: Obsecratio sive oratio ad Virginem Mariam in rebus adversis, or Obsecratio ad Virginem Matrem Mariam in rebus adversis LB V / CWE 69

Oratio de pace: Oratio de pace et discordia LB VIII

Oratio funebris: Oratio funebris in funere Bertae de Heyen LB VIII / CWE 29

Paean Virgini Matri: Paean Virgini Matri dicendus LB V / CWE 69

Panegyricus: Panegyricus ad Philippum Austriae ducem LB IV / ASD IV-1 / CWE 27

Parabolae: Parabolae sive similia LB I / ASD I-5 / CWE 23

Paraclesis LB V, VI

Paraphrasis in Elegantias Vallae: Paraphrasis in Elegantias Laurentii Vallae LB I / ASD I-4

Paraphrasis in Matthaeum, etc LB VII / ASD VII-6 / CWE 42–50

Peregrinatio apostolorum: Peregrinatio apostolorum Petri et Pauli LB VI, VII

Precatio ad Virginis filium Iesum LB V / CWE 69

Precatio dominica LB V / CWE 69

Precationes: Precationes aliquot novae LB V / CWE 69

Precatio pro pace ecclesiae: Precatio ad Dominum Iesum pro pace ecclesiae LB IV, V / CWE 69

Prologus supputationis: Prologus in supputationem calumniarum Natalis Bedae, or Prologus supputationis errorum in censuris Bedae LB IX

Purgatio adversus epistolam Lutheri: Purgatio adversus epistolam non sobriam Lutheri LB X / ASD IX-1 / CWE 78

Querela pacis LB IV / ASD IV-2 / CWE 27

Ratio: Ratio seu Methodus compendio perveniendi ad veram theologiam (Methodus for the shorter version originally published in the Novum instrumentum of 1516) LB V, VI

Responsio ad annotationes Lei: Responsio ad annotationes Eduardi Lei LB IX / ASD IX-4 / CWE 72

Responsio ad collationes: Responsio ad collationes cuiusdam iuvenis geronto-didascali LB IX

Responsio ad disputationem de divortio: Responsio ad disputationem cuiusdam
Phimostomi de divortio LB IX / ASD IX-4 / CWE 83
Responsio ad epistolam Alberti Pii: Responsio ad epistolam paraeneticam Alberti
Pii, or Responsio ad exhortationem Pii LB IX / CWE 84
Responsio ad notulas Bedaicas (*see* Notatiunculae)
Responsio ad Petri Cursii defensionem: Epistola de apologia Cursii LB X /
Ep 3032
Responsio adversus febricitantis libellum: Apologia monasticae religionis LB X

Spongia: Spongia adversus aspergines Hutteni LB X / ASD IX-1 / CWE 78
Supputatio: Supputatio errorum in censuris Bedae LB IX

Tyrannicida: Tyrannicida, declamatio Lucianicae respondens LB I / ASD I-1 / CWE 29

Virginis et martyris comparatio LB V / CWE 69
Vita Hieronymi: Vita divi Hieronymi Stridonensis *Opuscula* / CWE 61

Index of Biblical
and Apocryphal References

General Index